Intimacies *of* Global Sufism

Neʿmatullahi Shrines and Material Culture Between Iran and India

Peyvand Firouzeh

INDIANA UNIVERSITY PRESS

This book is a publication of

Indiana University Press
Herman B Wells Library
1320 East 10th Street
Bloomington, Indiana 47405 USA

iupress.org

Manufactured in China

First Printing 2025

Cataloging information is available from the Library of Congress.

ISBN 978-0-253-07413-3 (hardback)
ISBN 978-0-253-07414-0 (paperback)
ISBN 978-0-253-07416-4 (ebook)
ISBN 978-0-253-07415-7 (web PDF)

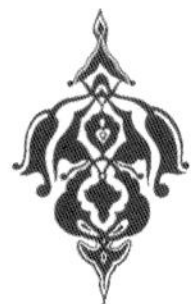

Publication of this book has been supported by a grant from the Persian Heritage Foundation (persianheritagefoundation.org).

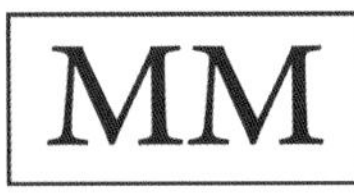

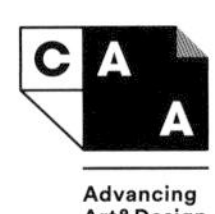

Publication of this book has been aided by a grant from the Millard Meiss Publication Fund of CAA.

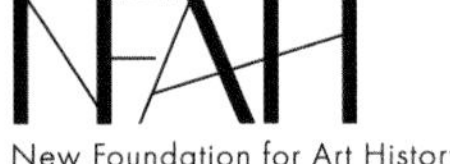

Publication of this book has been supported by a grant from the New Foundation for Art History (nfah.org).

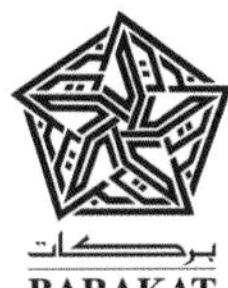

Publication of this book has been supported by an Iradj Bagherzade Publication Grant from the Barakat Trust.

Intimacies *of* Global Sufism

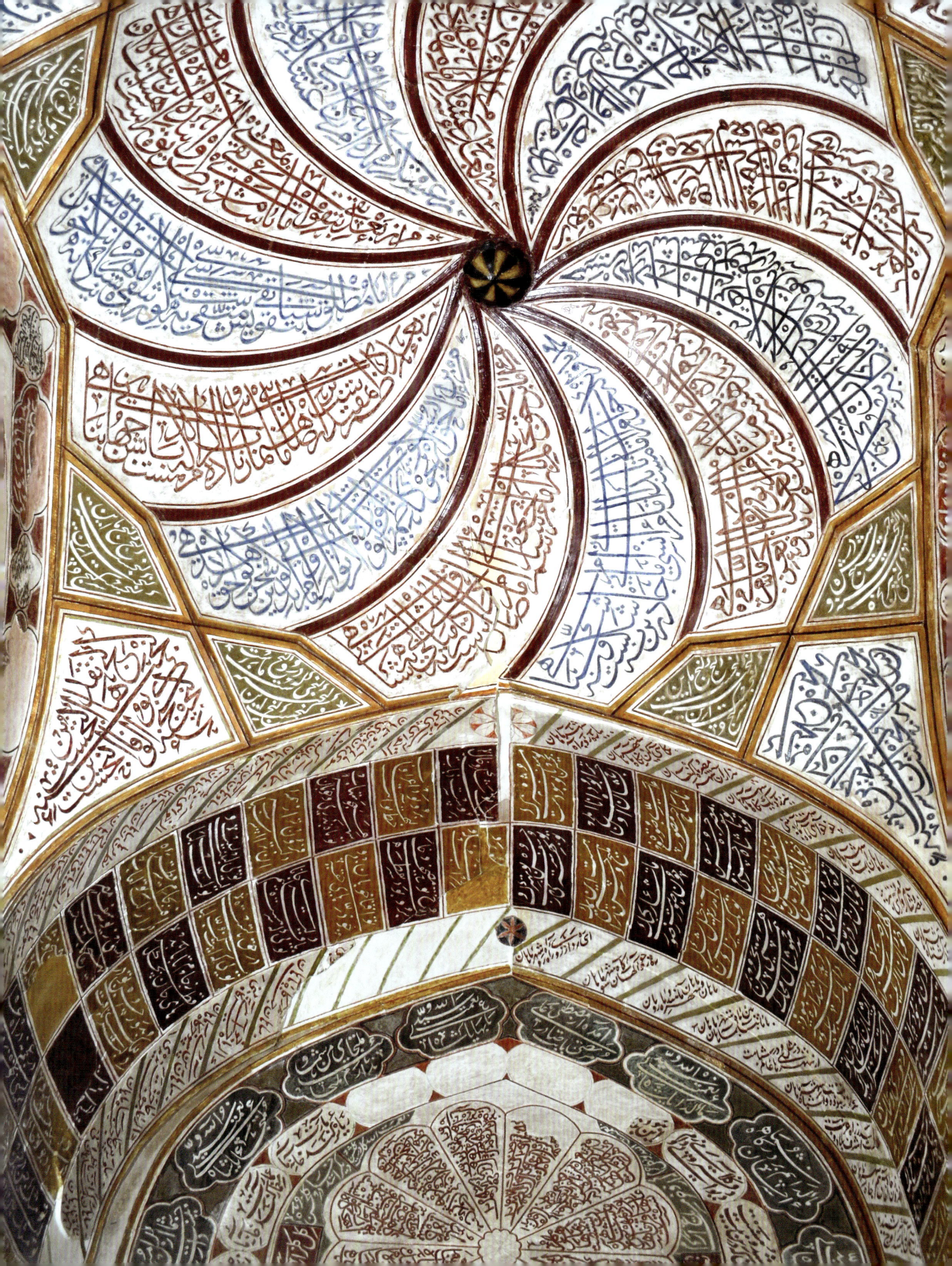

تقدیم به پدر و مادرم

To my parents

CONTENTS

ACKNOWLEDGMENTS

I have collected many debts to friends, colleagues, and mentors who inspired, challenged and encouraged me along the journey that has resulted in the completion of this book. I am grateful to mentors and teachers Charles Melville, Sussan Babaie, Bernard O'Kane, Hannah Baader, Gerhard Wolf, Deborah Howard, Ladan Akbarnia, Christine Van Ruymbeke, and Nadieh Imani for insightful advice and formative conversations that helped me shape this project at various stages.

For their generous readings of drafts and thoughtful suggestions, I am thankful to Mary Roberts, Dipti Khera, Rachel Parikh, Keelan Overton, Alya Karame, Naciem Nikkhah, and Charles Li. I owe a great deal to scholars who helped me push my research in new directions through generative conversations and incisive questions at conferences, workshops, and public lectures, especially Gülru Necipoğlu, Robert Hillenbrand, Lorenz Korn, Francis Robinson, the late Robert Skelton, George Michell, Ebba Koch, Vesta Curtis Sarkhosh, Fabrizio Speziale, Denis Hermann, Melanie Gibson, Lloyd Ridgeon, Ali Anooshahr, Blain Auer, Barry Flood, Gül Kale, Rakhee Balaram, Çiğdem Kafescioğlu, Megan Boomer, Ashley Dimmig, the late Rick Asher, Roy Fischel, Derek Mancini-Lander, Alain George, Zeynep Yürekli, Teresa Fitzherbert, Eleanor Sims, Evrim Binbaş, Elaine Wright, Barbara Brend, Priscilla Soucek, Mark Ledbury, Roger Benjamin, and John Gagné. Similarly, I am grateful to numerous colleagues and experts in the field who generously shared not only their knowledge but also their field research notes, archival material, images, and unpublished and forthcoming works: in particular, Helen Philon, the late Bruce Wannell, Jeff Spurr, the late John Thompson, Steven Cohen, Omid Reza'i, Hamidreza Ghelichkhani, and Margaret Squires. A special word of thanks is due to Michelle Quay and Adam Benkato for looking over some of my translations. I would like to thank Miranda Luo for her work on the bibliography and Jennifer Yang for proofreading the manuscript. For drawings and 3D reconstructions, I thank Farah Michel for her many hours of hard work. I also wish to thank the anonymous reviewers of this book for their thoughtful suggestions as well as Bethany Mowry and Sophia Hebert at Indiana University Press for their enthusiastic support of this book and their patience.

This book would not have come to fruition without the generous financial support from institutions that provided research fellowships and travel grants toward the completion of this project: the Getty Foundation and the American Council of Learned Societies; the University of Sydney's School of Art, Communication and English; the Willison Foundation Trust; Kunsthistorisches Institut in Florenz; Forum Transregionale Studien; the Association for the Study of Persianate Societies; the H. K. Sherwani Centre for Deccan Studies at Maulana Azad National Urdu University in Hyderabad; the Gibb Memorial Trust; the British Institute of Persian Studies; the Iran Society in London; Pembroke College and the Faculty of Asian and Middle Eastern Studies at the University of Cambridge; the Kettle's Yard in Cambridge; and the Rajiv Gandhi Traveling Scholarship. I would like to offer special thanks to Salma Ahmed Farooqui and Abdul Majid for kindly hosting me at the H. K. Sherwani Centre for Deccan Studies and facilitating my research and travel in and around Hyderabad with much care and generosity.

Several individuals provided access to data, collections, and sites under their care at cultural institutions in Iran, India, the United Kingdom, and Bosnia and Herzegovina. I wish to thank Mr. Yazdi Nezhad at the Astan-e Qods Museum in Mashhad; Ms. Mahnaz Gorji, Dr. Jebrael Nokandeh, and Mr. Shahiri at the National Museum of Iran; the staff of the Iran Cultural Heritage Organization in Kerman, Yazd, and Taft, especially Elahe Khakbaz Alvandian in Yazd; Mr. Shojaee, the keeper of the Shah Vali Mosque in Taft; Mr. Mahani at the shrine in Mahan; the staff of the Henry Martyn Institute in Hyderabad, especially Dr. Packiam T. Samuel and Mr. Javeed Khan; the staff of the Asafiya library and the Salar Jung Museum in Hyderabad; Ursula Sims-Williams at the British Library; and Marica Filipovic and Azra Becevic at the National Museum of Bosnia and Herzegovina.

I am equally grateful to all friends, family, and colleagues who, at some point, shared the joys and hardships of accompanying me during fieldwork: my sister, Pegah, and my parents, Arman and Ali; Fereshteh Alikhani; Reihaneh Sajjad; Mahdieh Mirahmadi; Reyhaneh Ghamsarian; Ali Aslani; Mona Valikjazi; and Daniele Cuneo. I am also indebted to the family of Mr. Mehdi Kermani-Irani for their hospitality in Kerman; Mahdi and Negar for the catch-up breakfasts during my visits to Tehran; and Pegah Roodgarmi, Farshad Mahmoodi Kashani, Marjan Afsharian, and Mehrdad Gilak for always keeping their house open to me during work trips to London.

It is a pleasure to thank my wonderful colleagues at the University of Sydney and the British Museum for their patience, humor, and encouragement. Special thanks to Hélène Sirantoine in Sydney for helping me carve out research and writing time during our many writing sessions and shared breakfasts. I am grateful to the friendship and moral support of Kathrin Göransson, Ünver Rüstem, Adam Benkato, Dipti Khera, Gül Kale, Rakhee Balaram, Megan Boomer, Maggie Bell, and Sria Chatterjee in Cambridge, Berlin, and Florence.

Without the unconditional love and support that I have received from my family, I would never have been able to start this project. Through the many

Skype calls and our long-awaited reunions, their wisdom and humor have made this journey all the more enjoyable. I wish to thank my sister, Pegah, for her unwavering emotional support. My heartfelt thanks to Jackie, Bill, Kiki, Katie, Ellis, Oli, and Emmy for cheering for me along the way. I thank my dear grandmother, Iran, who continues to be a source of courage and persistence for me, even after her passing. It is hard for me to find the right words to thank Bobby for all that he has brought to my life and to this project, both emotionally and intellectually.

I am indebted to my parents, Ali and Arman, for their love and strength and for always helping me keep things in perspective. I dedicate this book to them.

NOTE TO THE READER

This book follows a simplified transliteration system where diacritical marks have been limited to ʿayn (ʿ) and hamza (ʾ) for a glottal stop. For place names and names of individuals, the common pronunciation in the relevant language or geographical region has been preferred. Frequently used transliterated terms are italicized on their first occurrence but not thereafter.

Dates are provided in the Common Era. *Hijri* calendar dates are given when mentioned specifically in an inscription or document or when significant in the discussion, in which case the hijri date is followed by the Common Era date.

Family trees of the Neʿmatullahis in the fifteenth and sixteenth centuries are provided as charts in the appendixes and should be consulted when names of the Neʿmatullahi family members appear in the text. These charts are referenced in the introduction but not thereafter.

Given that the sites discussed in this book are revisited in multiple chapters, a map-diagram of the distribution of architectural sites vis-à-vis the chapters has been provided in the introduction (fig. 0.5). In case of interest in a specific site, readers should use this diagram, alongside the table of contents and index, to follow the discussion of individual sites.

Intimacies *of* Global Sufism

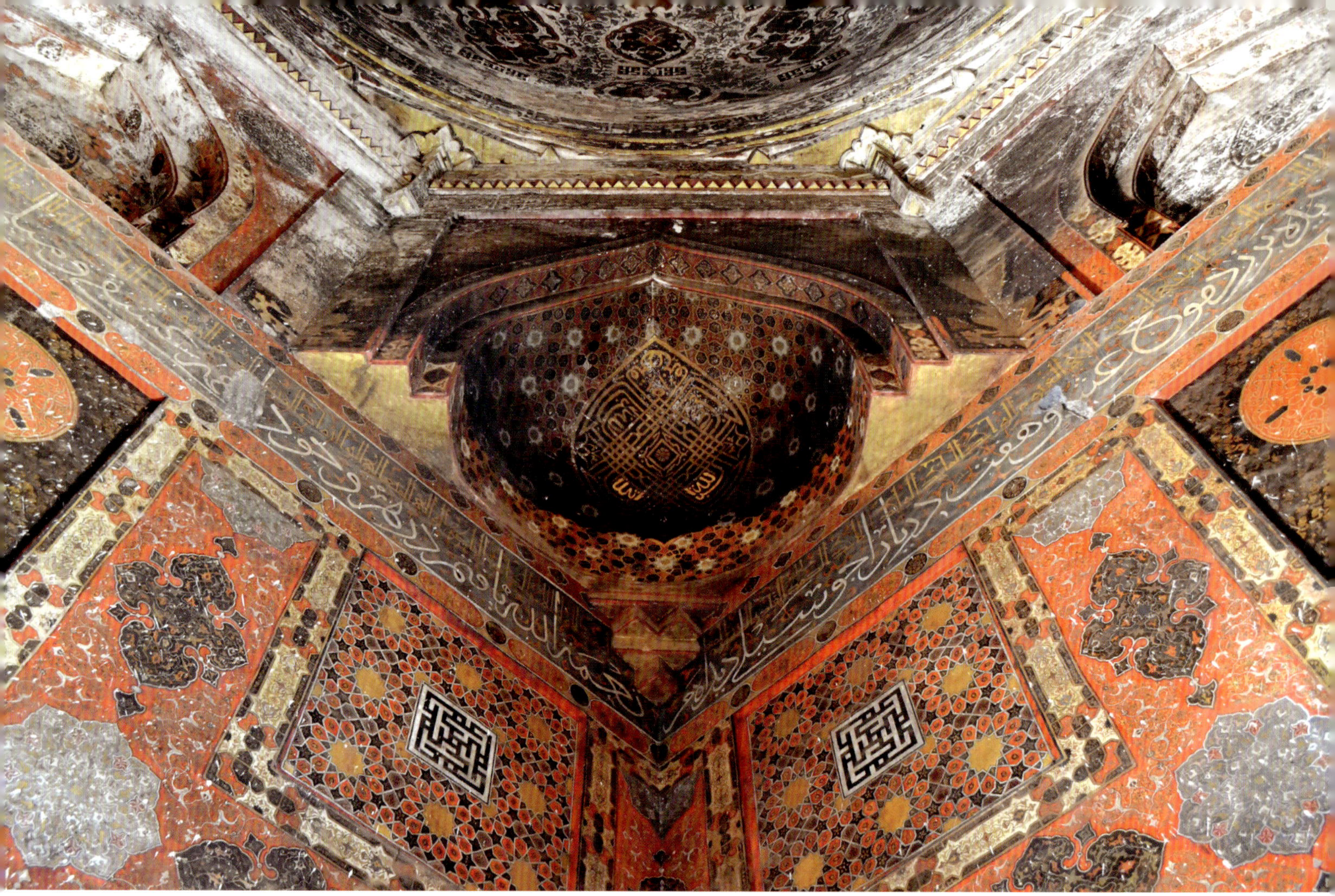

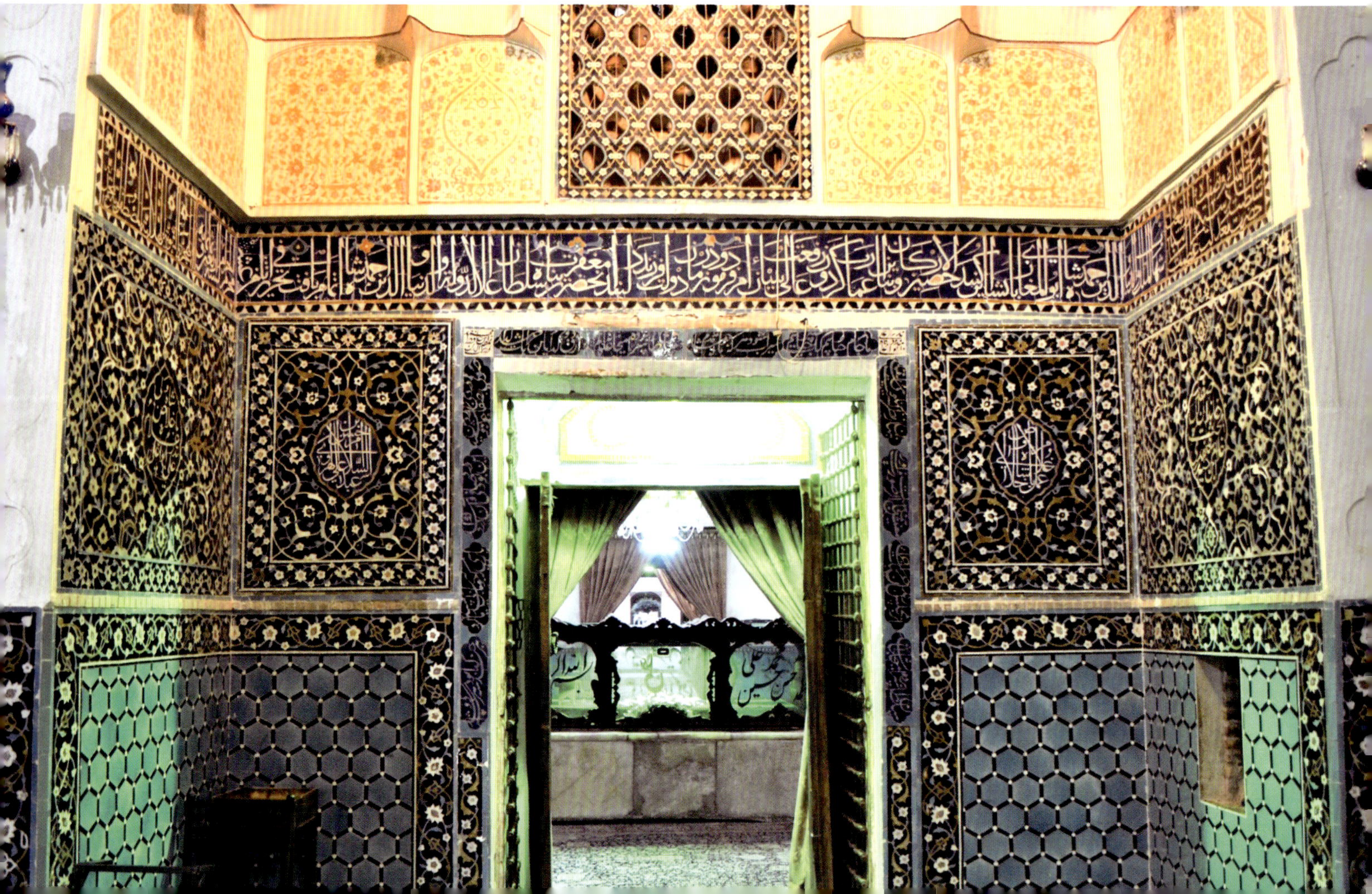

Introduction

FACING TOP, FIGURE 0.1. Interior of the tomb of Ahmad Shah Bahmani, outside Bidar (India), view from a corner, looking up toward the dome. *Photograph by author, 2013.*

FACING BOTTOM, FIGURE 0.2. Shrine of Shah Neʿmatullah Vali, Mahan (Iran), view of the western portal. *Photograph by author, 2013.*

Outside Bidar in Karnataka, India, once the capital of the Bahmanid sultanate, an extensively painted royal tomb completed in the 1430s is inscribed with the poetry of the Iranian Sufi Shah Neʿmatullah Vali (d. 1431) in monumental calligraphy (fig. 0.1). Around the same time, a response to this invocation was materialized in mosaic tilework across the ocean in the small town of Mahan in Iran, on the portal of Shah Neʿmatullah's tomb, blessing the Indian king Ahmad Shah Bahmani (r. 1422–36) as the Sufi's long-distance disciple (fig. 0.2). The epigraphical dialogue between the two buildings mimics a conversation between a Sufi (generally defined as an "Islamic mystic") and a disciple—a conversation that, in the case of Shah Neʿmatullah and Ahmad Shah, never took place outside the realm of dreams and visions.

The materiality and affective appeal of the two inscriptions connected them beyond the realm of texts and visions. Both inscriptions were part of extensive epigraphic programs of funerary structures that were initially constructed as stand-alone dome chambers but expanded considerably over time into a royal necropolis in the case of Bidar and a multilayered shrine complex in the case of Mahan. Both inscriptions are written in the *thuluth* calligraphic script in Persian, in white against a blue background, painted on plaster in the tomb in Bidar and executed in polychrome tiles in Mahan. Both also hold a proportionally dominant position in relation to the inscription panels surrounding them, legible to readers and shaping the experience of pilgrimage to the two sites by foregrounding transregional connections across the ocean.

The two buildings in Bidar and Mahan were part of a network of shrines and related funerary structures associated with Shah Neʿmatullah Vali and his followers that emerged in the fifteenth century across southern Iran and the central-south region of India known as the Deccan, mobilized by the sea routes and monsoon winds that facilitated connectivity between the southern ports of Iran and ports of western India. These sacred spaces were meeting points for itinerant Sufis, local and peripatetic artists, merchants, courtiers, and kings. Their collaborations and competitions developed the shrines into rich palimpsests of artistic innovation, devotion, and transoceanic dialogue. Encompassing monumental shrine complexes, small retreat cells, devotional wall paintings, and ritual carpets, these artifacts demand to be examined as part of a transregionally connected story.

The visual conversation between the tombs in Bidar and Mahan did not merely reflect the inherent mobilities of the Islamic and Indian Ocean worlds—it also actively *forged* a physical and sensorial mode of connection between sacred landscapes that were increasingly felt to be, as one contemporary letter described, "united by the sea in between."[1] Such dialogues invite us to reconsider the power of devotional art and visual culture to redefine the global, the transregional, and the early modern beyond the scope of European voyages of exploration.

Roughly two hundred years later, a small retreat cell tucked into the corner of the same shrine at Mahan was turned into a colorful canvas of abstract paintings and self-referential poems by another Neʿmatullahi disciple (fig. 0.3). While some of these poems place this room and the shrine into the broader Islamic sacred landscape, connecting with distant locales such as Mecca and Najaf, most verses are intimately tied to the microgeography of the room. Poems that were written for specific corners of the cell pull us into the smallness of the space. Talismanic swords painted on the walls engage the body of the viewer through somatic metaphors, conflating the hilt of the painted sword with the hand of the viewer and the hand of the Sufi teacher.

The embodied sensory aesthetics of the room's epigraphic program revolve around what can be called *spatial poetry*: poetry that is written or adapted for a specific space, inscribed on its walls and textiles, and understood in terms of the reader's passage through that space.[2] This close entanglement between the poetry and the spatial configuration of the room amount to a visual program that is deeply local, site specific, and intimate. The room's program invites us to think about the hand of the Sufi artist who time and again inscribed reminders of his authorship into this devotional artistic endeavor. Spatial poetry is also deeply bound up with concerns over politics and materiality, often establishing a measured separation between spaces reserved for Sufi bodies and those used to promote ruling patrons. It was a crucial means of crafting intimacy, even as it situated devotees within distant networks of sacred spaces.

What did it mean for Sufis and artists to construct shrines that engaged local audiences, invoked distant places, and simultaneously appealed to transregional pilgrims and merchants? How did they navigate tensions between place-making and spirituality vis-à-vis their expanding transregional network? The two examples offered here, the retreat room and the transoceanic dialogue between the tombs in Bidar and Mahan, stand for two of the perennial problems of art history's approach to Sufi material culture—problems that lie at the heart of this book. First, despite visual and textual evidence,

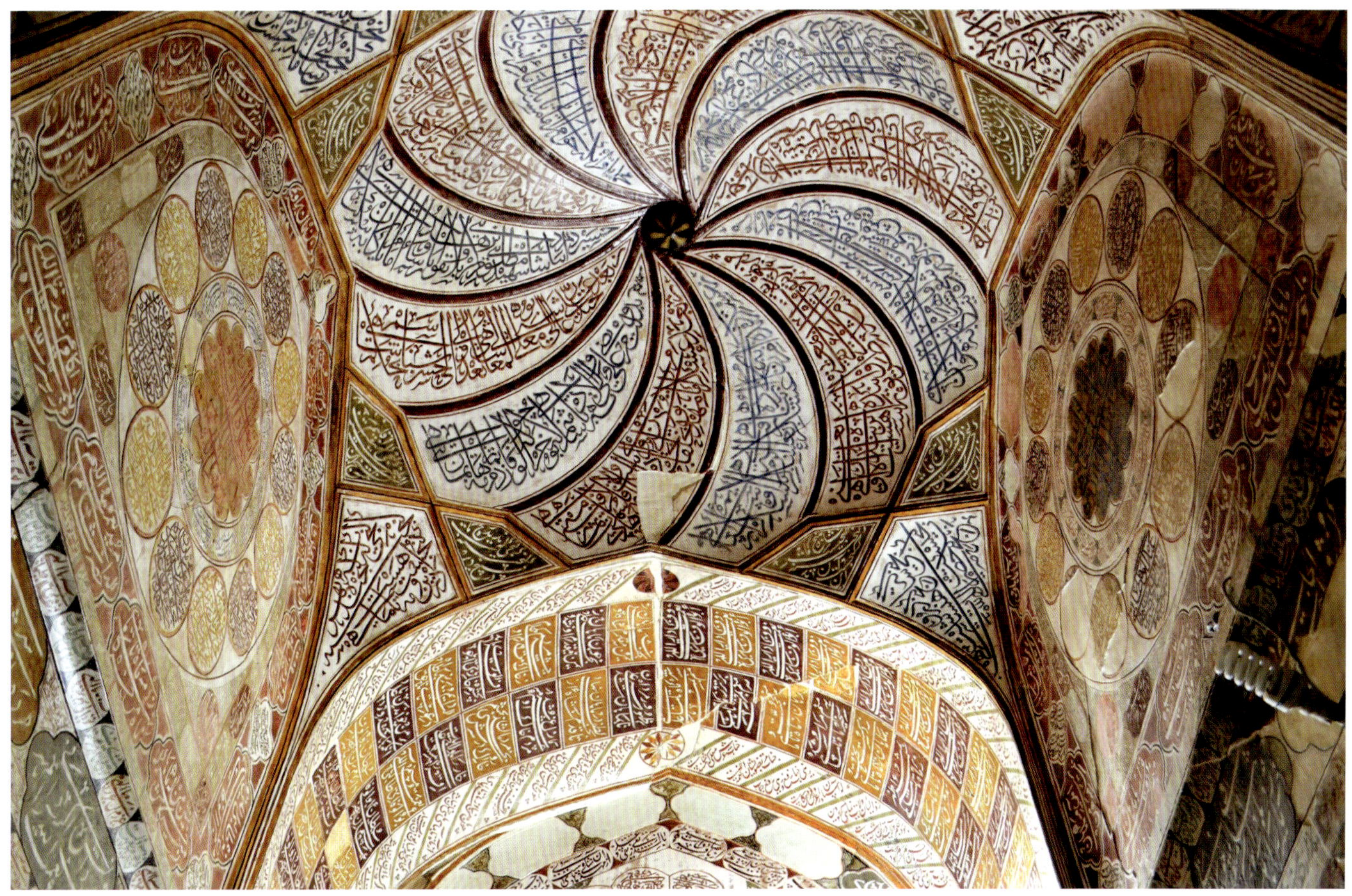

FIGURE 0.3. Interior view of the chelleh khaneh (retreat cell) at the shrine of Shah Neʿmatullah Vali in Mahan (Iran), looking up standing against the south wall. *Photograph by author, 2013.*

Sufi artists and Sufi patrons have been assigned a peripheral place in shrine studies and global art histories. Second, despite the inherent mobility of Sufi networks and their recognition as a global phenomenon by historians such as Nile Green, Sufism's potential for global art histories has not been adequately explored even as questions of global connectivity have become central, if contentious, themes in the field.[3] The unifying aim of *Intimacies of Global Sufism* is to make sense of two seemingly contradictory sides of Sufi material culture: its tendency toward asceticism and its investment in monuments of global expansion.

Intimacies of Global Sufism combines methods of sensorial and global art histories to recover the sensory richness of art making in Sufism and the efficacy of Sufi material culture in shaping the politics of global connectedness. The book is structured around the shrines and devotional objects of Neʿmatullahi Sufis: a politically influential Sufi network made up of followers of the Sufi poet Shah Neʿmatullah Vali, who crisscrossed sea and land routes that connected central Asia, Iran, and India.[4] I consider some of their major extant shrines in this study: the Shah Vali *khanaqah* (Sufi lodge) in Taft, the shrine complex of Shah Neʿmatullah Vali in Mahan, the funerary complex of the Sufi's son outside the city of Bidar, and the neighboring tomb of Shah

Neʿmatullah's disciple, the Bahmanid king, Ahmad Shah I. The former two are in Southern Iran, the latter two in Deccan India. These sites will also be studied alongside a number of projects patronized by the Sufi family outside their shrine networks.[5]

Despite the canonical status of some of these surviving monuments in Persian and South Asian art history, the sites and the objects they contained have only ever been discussed in survey books and single articles; some have never been published before. While the religious history of the Neʿmatullahi network has been the subject of a number of studies, no art historical monograph has ever been dedicated to their sacred spaces. Nor have their sites in Iran and India ever been studied together from a transregional perspective.

In many ways, the Neʿmatullahi shrines offer an ideal case for addressing the problems of Sufi material culture outlined above. Shah Neʿmatullah himself was an avid traveler whose journeys took him from Cairo and Mecca to Samarqand and Herat as well as areas around Kerman and Yazd—travels undertaken for pilgrimage, in search of well-known teachers, to disseminate his own teachings, and at times at the request of ruling authorities, as was common among Sufis (map 0.1). Shah Neʿmatullah was not a renunciatory Sufi. The Neʿmatullahi doctrine was shaped around the principle of *khalwat dar anjuman* (solitude within society), which encouraged integration into the society while practicing Sufism. The Neʿmatullahis' interpretation of such principles, which led to their intermingling with powerful political and social factions of the society, combined with their remarkable transregional mobility, has resulted in an abundance of material traces across the regions concerned in this book.

Shah Neʿmatullah's followers, organized as a network of sedentary and mobile Sufi communities, flourished in several parts of what is today Iran and Uzbekistan from the late fourteenth century, spreading into Deccan India from the first half of the fifteenth century. After the disintegration of the Bahmanids and the return of some members of the family to Iran during the Safavid period, another wave of transregional movement took a number of family members to the Mughal courts in Lahore and Delhi and subsequently, alongside Mughal campaigns in the seventeenth century, to the Deccan once again (map 0.2). As they expanded their transregional network, acting as agents of mobility and cross-cultural exchange between Iran and India, they grappled with debates about materiality and transcendence—challenges that were brought about in part by their constant land and sea crossings. The large number of family members and disciples, their presence in multiple centers in Iran and India, and their constant travels between these nodes make the task of mapping their histories difficult (app. 0.1). But this multiplicity of centers is exactly what makes it possible to break away from the dynastic models that have pervaded Sufi shrine studies in the past.

This book charts out a field of inquiry that has fallen between the cracks of global art history and area studies. While pushing against eurocentrism in global art histories, the book also builds on the work of scholars who question

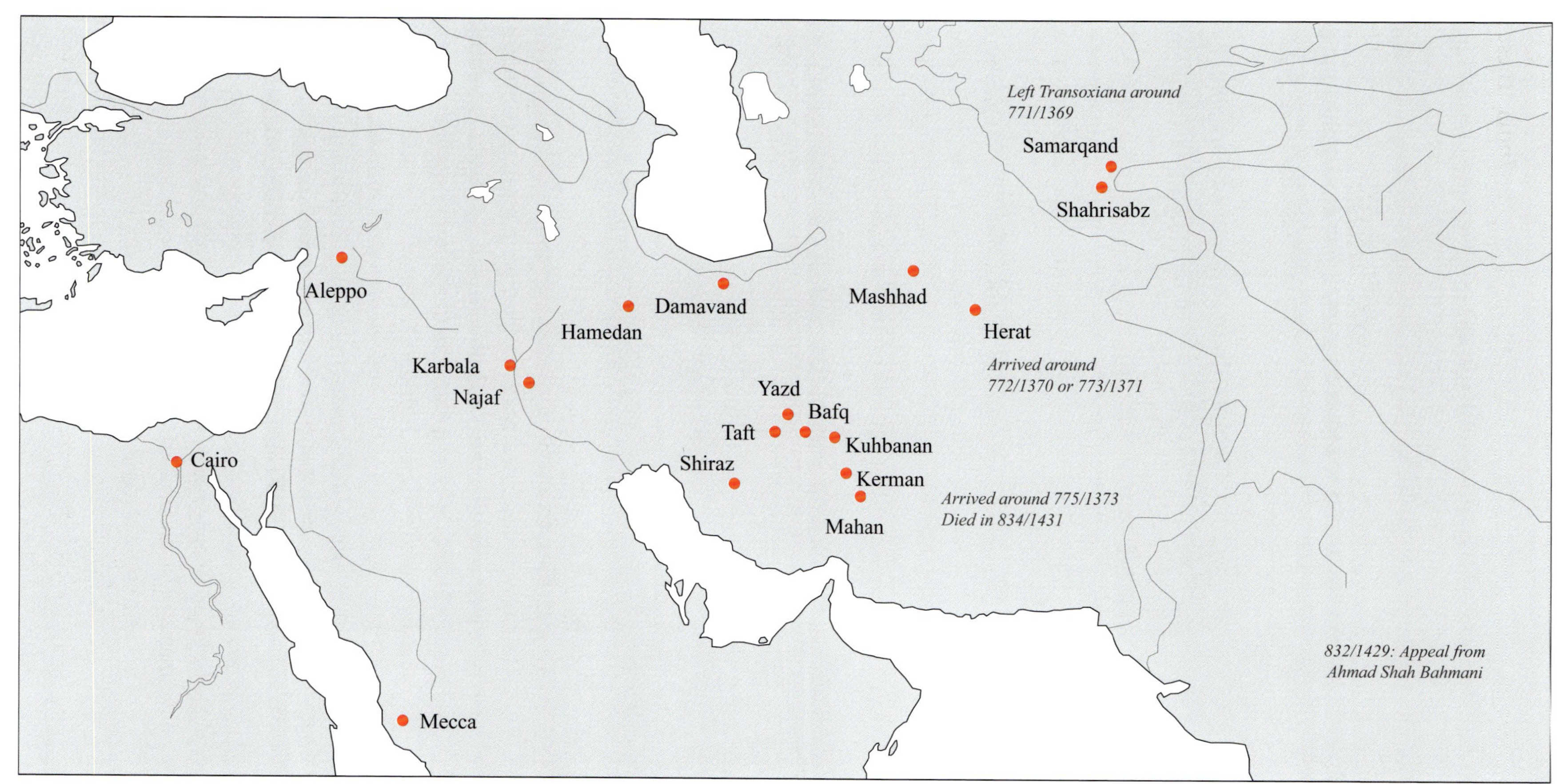

MAP 0.1. Map of Shah Neʿmatullah's travels in the fourteenth and fifteenth centuries. *Drawing by Farah Michel.*

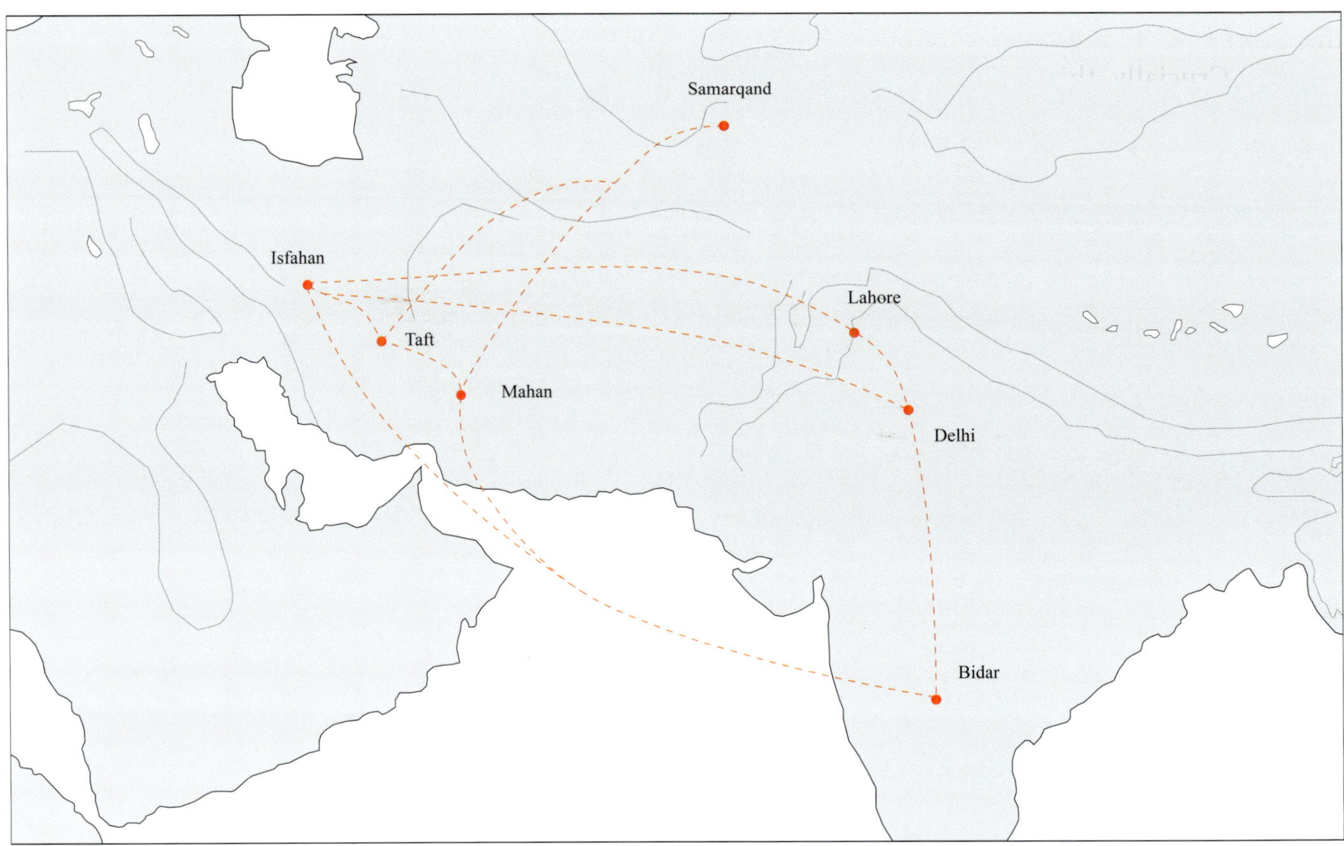

MAP 0.2. Schematic map of the mobility of the Neʿmatullahi network between the fourteenth and seventeenth centuries. *Drawing by Farah Michel.*

the geographical distribution of the canon of Islamic art history. The field of Islamic art in South Asia has historically been dominated by the study of the Mughal Empire, traditionally held up as the epitome of high-art production.[6] The current book shares an interest with recent art historical scholarship in sultanate and Deccan subfields, which, although growing rapidly, remain understudied. Richard Eaton and Philip Wagoner's *Power, Memory, Architecture*, Finbarr Barry Flood's *Objects of Translation*, and exhibition catalogs like Navina Najat Haidar and Marika Sardar's *Sultans of Deccan India* focus on the hybridity and cosmopolitanism of visual material from India to challenge text-based perspectives that privilege Hindu-Muslim binaries in cultural production. Like Keelan Overton's recent edited volume, *Iran and the Deccan*, this book explores cross-cultural connections between Iran and Deccan India but also brings a new emphasis to the period prior to the sixteenth century and to the local conditions on the ground that shaped these transregional artistic connections.

The time frame of the book spans from ca. 1400 to the 1650s, beginning with the foundation of the Neʿmatullahis' first complex in Taft and ending with a number of smaller-scale projects in Mahan and the refurbishment of the Nizamuddin *dargah* (lit. threshold; shrine) in Delhi in the seventeenth century. Crucially, this time frame corresponds with the development of Neʿmatullahi material culture rather than dynastic periodization. My goal in setting the historical framework of this book is to show that the Sufi network's material history was not defined simply by patterns of dynastic patronage or power, despite close political entanglements between courts and the shrines. On the contrary, multiple projects that fall toward the end of the book's time frame were led by the Neʿmatullahis themselves as artistic patrons; some were even shaped by the aftermath of an unsuccessful political revolt that pitted the Neʿmatullahi Sufis against the Safavid dynasty. Ending the book at this moment in the 1650s should by no means imply a value judgment on the network's material culture in the following centuries. The art of the Neʿmatullahis in the nineteenth century, for instance, is an area that merits more attention from art historians, building on Reza Tabandeh's detailed historical study of the Neʿmatullahis in that period and Maryam Ekhtiar's exploration of their artistic endeavors.[7]

FIGURE 0.4. Shrine of Shah Neʿmatullah Vali in Mahan during the Norouz (Persian New Year) holidays in 2012. *Photograph by author.*

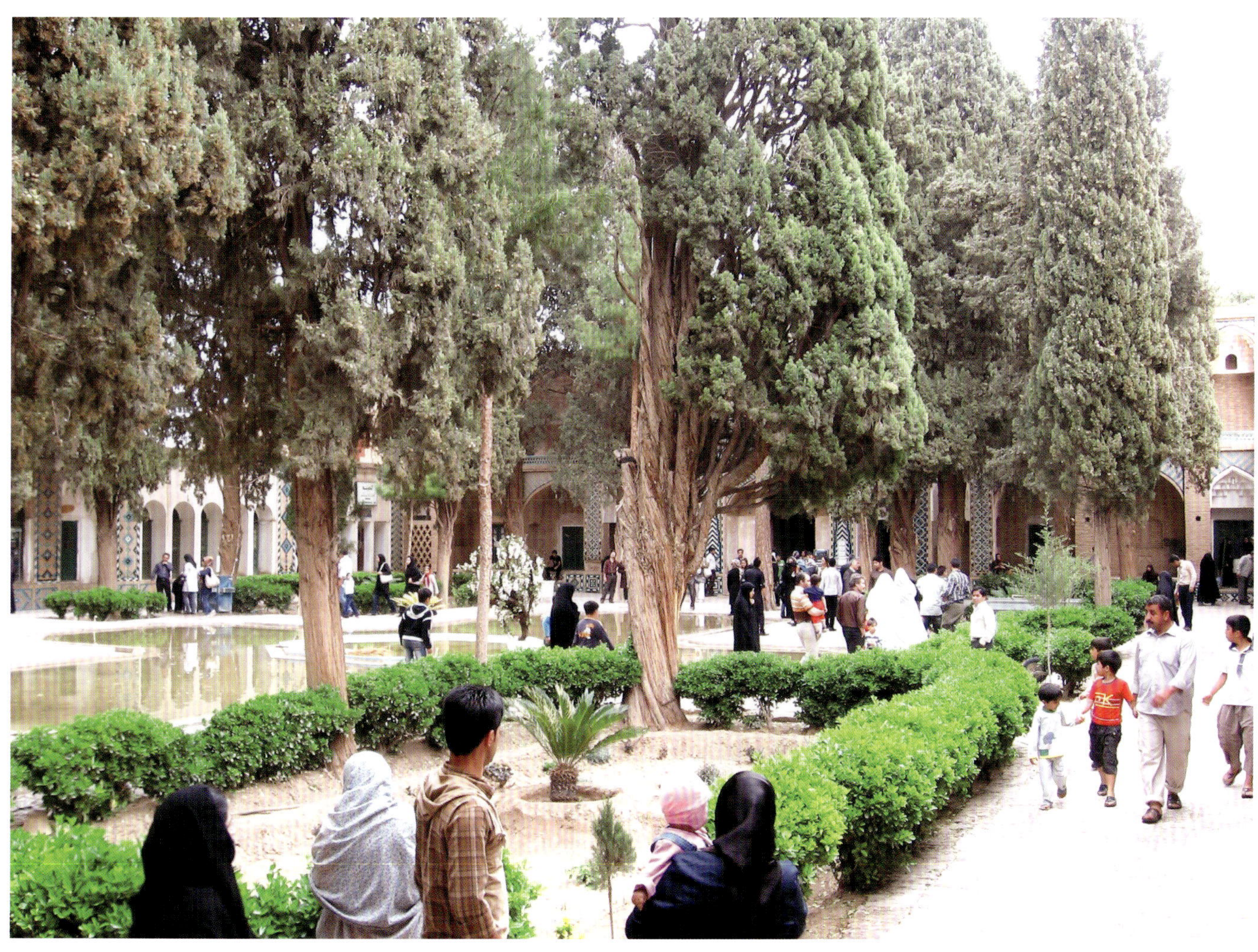

The Neʿmatullahi Sufi shrines have been threatened by loss and forced musealization, driven variously by political pressure, religious or sectarian nationalism, or lack of funding for preservation. The urgency of documentation and in-depth historical analysis of Neʿmatullahi material culture stems from multiple factors such as prohibitions against the use of shrines for rituals—part of a broader pattern of restrictions that are enforced in several modern-day states across the Islamic world.[8] Within the framework of this book, the process is especially acute in Iran, where such restrictions work in tandem with the transformation of Sufi shrines into museums as well as the redefinition of their significance in terms of pan-Shiʿa nationalist rhetoric. In India, Muslim or shared Hindu-Muslim spaces of pilgrimage, such as those discussed in this book, are threatened by processes of Hinduization, promoted by Hindu nationalists. While the Mausoleum of Ahmad Shah Bahmani is a site of pilgrimage for both Muslims and Hindus, various subsidiary shrines dedicated to his veneration around Bidar and Gulbarga have undergone forced Hinduization.[9]

The lives of the network's shrines, like their physical structures, have changed a great deal over the centuries, whether as a result of their expansion through patronage campaigns, their destruction due to urban modernization, the removal of their objects due to colonial patterns of collecting, or the banning of Sufi rituals as a result of political persecution. Yet such threats stand in tension with the ongoing popular appeal of these spaces in Iran and India. The site in Mahan, for example, remains a living shrine despite suffering various losses. It is heavily frequented not only by local pilgrims who arrive even on the frozen mornings of desert winters but also by crowds of pilgrims and tourists from across the country who visit during the Norouz holidays (Persian New Year) (fig. 0.4). However, as a result of the changes outlined above, many layers of the sites' meanings and histories are inaccessible to the contemporary visitor. The current book sets these spaces back into a transregionally interconnected landscape of devotion, recovering their rituals and their intimate human and spatial connections to counterbalance the current tendency toward musealization and reinterpretation in light of various nationalisms.

I. The Global and the Intimate

The field of global art history is beset by many gaps. One is that the focus has fallen predominantly on east-west connections that remain partially or fully grounded in Europe. Against this background, my use of the term *global* in the title of this book is intended as a provocation. I am not using the term in a geographically exhaustive sense—an interpretation that, arguably, would always be riddled by blind spots. My aim, rather, is to continue the work of scholars who have carved out a space for transregional art histories that take place outside of a eurocentric or euro-proximate framework.

Nancy Um reminds us of the dangers of the global framework, such as its propensity toward elite, top-down histories that prioritize "acts of sovereigns and states, trading partners, diplomacy, wars and treaties."[10] Acknowledging these dangers, and drawing on recent conversations around scale, empire, and global encounters by scholars such as Swati Chattopadhyay, Lisa Lowe, and Francesca Trivellato, I use the concept of intimacy as a methodological intervention within debates around the polarity of the global and local in the arts and humanities.[11] Intimacy resists the grand view from above that the global framework gravitates toward. On the other hand, defined against the intimate and affective, the global becomes more a matter of scale than a strict geographic notion. I also argue that the global is a matter of perception and self-representation: as I show in this book, whether in poetic metaphors or explicit engagements with transregional politics, the Neʿmatullahis described and presented themselves as sociopolitical actors on an expansive scale that, to them, encompassed the "whole world."[12] Through such push-and-pull effects, the book probes how the categories of *intimate*, *global*, and *Sufism* mutually transform one another when viewed through an art historical lens, reshaping interdisciplinary debates about mobility and belonging.

I use *intimacy* in a variety of ways in this book to navigate between the micro and the macro, the proximate and the distant, the devotional and the political. First, the intermingling of the intimate, local, and global in the politics of shrine projects presents an unprecedented urgency in the historical context considered in this book in general, and specifically for the Neʿmatullahi network. The fifteenth- and sixteenth-century Islamic world was marked by the formation of empires, messianic hopes, and ideals of divine kingship forged out of collaboration and competition between Sufis and courts of varying size and ambition. Sufis' participation in politics was not new; however, with the intensity of cultures of travel in the long fifteenth century, which has been linked with early modernity, Sufi networks took on new transregional dimensions.[13] The Neʿmatullahi Sufis and their shrine networks, due to their geographical and political *in-betweenness*, are uniquely positioned to expand our understanding of early modern global networks.

Moving between small towns and dynastic capitals, the Neʿmatullahis came to be entangled with local governments and revolutionaries as well as many influential dynasties of the Islamic world: the Timurids (1370–1507), the Aq Qoyunlus (lit. White Sheep; 1378–1501) and Qara Qoyunlus (lit. Black Sheep; 1375–1468), the Safavids (1501–1722), the Bahmanids (1347–1528), and the Mughals (1526–1857). Such transregional interdynastic mobilities furnish a vantage point that unravels histories written from the perspective of ruling authorities without conflating their specificities. This is also a vantage point that, depending on the position of the Neʿmatullahis in relation to these various courts, moves between sociopolitical centrality and marginality several times throughout the history of the Sufi network. By investigating such mobilities, we are able to trace the contours of the place that Neʿmatullahi Sufis carved out for themselves in this global interdynastic picture as well as the broader implications that the mobility of people, objects, and financial resources around Sufi networks had for transregional politics between ca.

1400 and 1650. This is a dynamic that patronage-based narratives typically occlude due to their focus on a single region or dynasty.

Such a multifocal view, grounded in small, local nodes of power and piety while encompassing vast geographical areas and politics of grand empires, makes it possible to explore both the opportunities and the challenges that Sufis encountered in developing a transregional network of material culture. This relates to another problem that Nancy Um has cautioned against: a "new global art history should resist applauding the triumphs of cross-cultural interaction."[14] The issue is not only that mobility was at times driven by persecution and desperation. In addition, there is the methodological problem that, while mobility is relatively easy to detect, the forces that impose immobility can be much harder to chart prior to the formation of modern nation-states. I try to tease out the nebulous traces of such impediments, especially with regard to shrine maintenance, taxation, and modes of self-representation. As I argue, the making of material networks around Sufis was at once facilitated, stymied, and politicized by their increasingly transregional reach.

I use the concept of intimacy in a second sense to map the affective dimension of the interconnections between people as well as objects and ideas that were mobilized alongside the transregional expansion of Neʿmatullahi networks. The infusion of transregional encounters into the shrine provoked a need for intimate connections: visual citations, poetic invocations, and epistolary exchanges that grounded the devotional and multisensorial engagement of individuals within the vast spatial distances opened up by the expansion of the Sufi network. Intimacy, in this sense, helps us to navigate the transregional map through imagining how the Sufi family and their affiliates inhabited and journeyed in these expansive spaces and the distances between them. From this perspective, the book emphasizes the value of family history for global history. While this is not necessarily a ground-up history, given the elite status of the Neʿmatullahi Sufi network, it is a story told through movements between centers and margins of political power. In effect, this is the material history of a family and their friends, disciples, and political collaborators—a network that expands far and wide in multiple and sometimes circular directions, in and out of regional and imperial courts, capitals, and rural areas.

Finally, I use the notion of intimacy to rethink the significance of small places and their multisensorial innerworkings for writing global histories of art. In dialogue with the works of scholars such as Christiane Gruber and Nina Ergin, *Intimacies of Global Sufism* builds on the sensorial turn in the arts and humanities to reinvigorate studies of Sufism.[15] Taking up a point of view from within the shrines, I explore small retreat cells, extensively refurbished corners of shrine complexes, and ritual objects such as carpets, all of which served as sites of devotional, multisensorial, and intimate engagement for Sufi bodies. The poetics of lived experience and the intimacy of material practices that engaged humans with the space and its objects thus come to stand at the center of shrine studies.

The vantage afforded by these small places and objects, considered alongside expansive monuments, balances architectural history's traditional preference for monumentality and grand narratives of patronage, to which Chattopadhyay alerts us.[16] The intimate, in this sense, redraws the boundaries of the regional and local by locating the affective appeal of sacred space at the heart of global stories.

II. The Problem of Sufi Material Culture

Practicing spirituality while living a day-to-day life embedded in the material world has posed contradictions in a range of belief systems. These contradictions have given rise to recurrent debates in the study of Sufism and its relation to material culture. Traditionally, orientalist approaches characterized Sufism as an inward-looking dimension of Islam, its rituals centered around seclusion and detachment from worldly matters. This detachment certainly has a historical basis, most evident in the figure of the lone wandering Sufi. Yet the orientalist emphasis on this particular image of Sufi life needs also to be understood as a historiographical phenomenon in itself, emerging especially out of travel writing in the nineteenth century.

From as early as the medieval period, Sufis were recognized as belonging to two classes: wandering and sedentary Sufis. But as Nile Green has pointed out, whether in urban or rural contexts, "Sufi traditions for the most part remained connected with wider community life."[17] Shahzad Bashir similarly notes that only a small "minority rejected all material comforts," but because these Sufis "wore their asceticism and rejection of society on their bodies," they were "highly visible."[18] They were also a subject of criticism by the medieval and early modern elite for their rejection of social norms.[19] The other side of this story manifests itself in scattered critiques of materialism among Sufi networks, epitomized perhaps most forcefully in Wahhabi movements, which, as Scott Kugle has noted, have criticized Sufis precisely for their engagement with material bodies and images.[20]

The gravitation toward renunciatory Sufis in historiography is rooted in perceptions of Sufism as mysticism.[21] This denomination, as Bashir has argued, creates a separation between Islam and Sufism, presenting Sufism as a "worthy form of Islam" that favors "spiritual universalism" over "religious particularity."[22] This romanticized notion of Sufism has important implications for art history and studies of material culture. The historiographical leanings discussed here are akin to approaches that, in broad brushstrokes, consider Islamic art esoteric and its processes of making art mysterious and inexplicable. Barry Flood has explained such approaches in the study of Islamic art as "a disaggregation of meaning from medium" and the privileging of the immaterial over the material.[23]

Jules David Prown notes a related tension in the concept of material culture in that *material* "is a word we associate with base and pragmatic things; *culture* is a word we associate with lofty, intellectual, abstract things."[24] Such tensions resonate with those we recognize between the material and spiritual. Like intimacies of the global, the constant push-and-pull effect in Sufi material culture is a useful mechanism in balancing the narratives around art making in Sufism. Pairing the notion of material culture with the lens of intimacy, this book confronts the complexities of the relationship between asceticism and materiality in Sufism. The heavily refurbished corners, meditative wall paintings, and sumptuous textiles of the shrines both conceal and reveal the fault lines of Sufi debates around materiality, which were fueled by the expansion of sacred networks across the Arabian Sea and the Indian Ocean.

Several historians have pushed against romanticized perceptions of Sufism as detached from the material world.[25] The project of undoing the myth of Sufism is more complicated in art history. To start with, while the study of Sufism has been established as a strong subfield in history and religious studies, its material aspects, which demand art historical modes of analysis, have not been adequately explored. The problem of Sufi material culture especially comes to the fore in modes of scholarship that treat the study of objects as a study of symbols. This kind of discourse usually hovers above the object without fully engaging with it, using objects as means to demonstrate theological convictions.[26] At the heart of this approach is an orientalizing impulse that further mystifies the object and its processes of making.

On this front, my book is in dialogue with recent works in shrine studies by Kishwar Rizvi, Zeynep Yürekli, Stephennie Mulder, and Ethel Sara Wolper, who have pushed against the immaterial treatment of the arts of Sufism by turning their attention to the shrine and its patrons.[27] The lens of architectural patronage in this body of work has brought about a more nuanced image of Sufism and of the Sufi shrine as a physical site where piety was entangled with state politics and social change. Their focus on the monument and its patronage has been a useful corrective in dismantling myths about materiality in Sufism.

As I contend, patronage studies can also underplay the inner dynamics of Sufi shrines—in particular, the tensions and reconciliations between place-making and spirituality that such shrines brought about. What remains underexplored is exactly how Sufis' yearning for transcendence, their innermost spaces of retreat, and their intimate devotional writings went hand in hand with the construction of the monumental architecture that materialized their outward-looking global and political aspirations. This gap in scholarship not only downplays the significance of materiality in shaping Sufism but also runs the risk of locating the agency of *making* with patrons rather than Sufis—in other words, obscuring Sufis' own agency in the making of their global networks of material culture.[28]

Building on the recent studies of Sufi shrines, this book aims to rethink the role of patronage in writing about the arts of Sufism. I study the politics of the shrine from a resolutely devotional and multisensorial angle, aiming to highlight Sufi voices and artistic agency. Delving into the small space foregrounds the agency of Sufis in shaping their material environments. I approach the making of these shrines as an artistic and intellectual process through which Sufis, at times working as artists and patrons, sought to resolve tensions between materiality and transcendence provisionally through art and architecture. Here, the intimate draws Sufis and artists into the center of global stories of material culture.

By carving out a locally informed Sufi vantage point within the politics of early modern globalism, this book seeks to establish a nuanced account of the forces that continuously defined and redefined boundaries between material and spiritual worlds. Distance from worldly matters was in fact valued—though by no means absolutely—by the leaders of the Neʿmatullahi community. In the face of the transregional nature of the Sufi network and the diversity of their sources of patronage, the proper degree of distance at times became a source of conflict. The Sufi shrine, in this view, becomes not just a stage for the intermingling of piety with political power but also a space where distances between them are set. The profound implications of these tensions for Sufi material culture manifested themselves in visual and textual strategies that both installed and collapsed such boundaries. By reconstructing the opportunities, negotiations, and justifications wrapped into these anxieties, *Intimacies of Global Sufism* offers a fluid image of the relationship between Sufism and material culture as it developed through and surfaced in concrete acts of building, writing, painting, and weaving.

III. Overview of the Book

Sufi networks are held together by relationships between disciples and teachers, veneration of shrines, shared rituals, and ideologies. But alongside these bonds, there is also a great deal of flexibility: Sufi networks can be transregional and transterritorial, and affiliations with one Sufi network do not exclude the possibility of affiliation with another. As a result, Sufi networks are ever changing and ever moving, just as their shrines remained in flux or, in Stephennie Mulder's words, in a state of "perpetual renovation."[29]

Writing about networks, by its nature, can never be exhaustive. It also involves a certain degree of disorderliness. To reflect these exigencies, I have refrained from writing about the spaces and objects in this book in a linear fashion. The four main sites considered in the book are not treated in single chapters but are revisited multiple times to address specific themes. To some extent, the structure of the book also replicates the movements—sometimes dizzying—of the individuals involved. We start in Mahan in chapter 1 and follow a gradual movement between central Iran and the Deccan in the next two chapters. After that, most chapters involve back-and-forth movements between these and other places (fig. 0.5). In structuring the book, my goal has been to foreground the dynamics of an inherently mobile network that has both shaped and been shaped by material culture.

The book is divided into eight chapters, laid out in three parts, that unfold both thematically and in large part chronologically, leading the reader through a spatial and methodological journey that shuffles among rural, urban, and

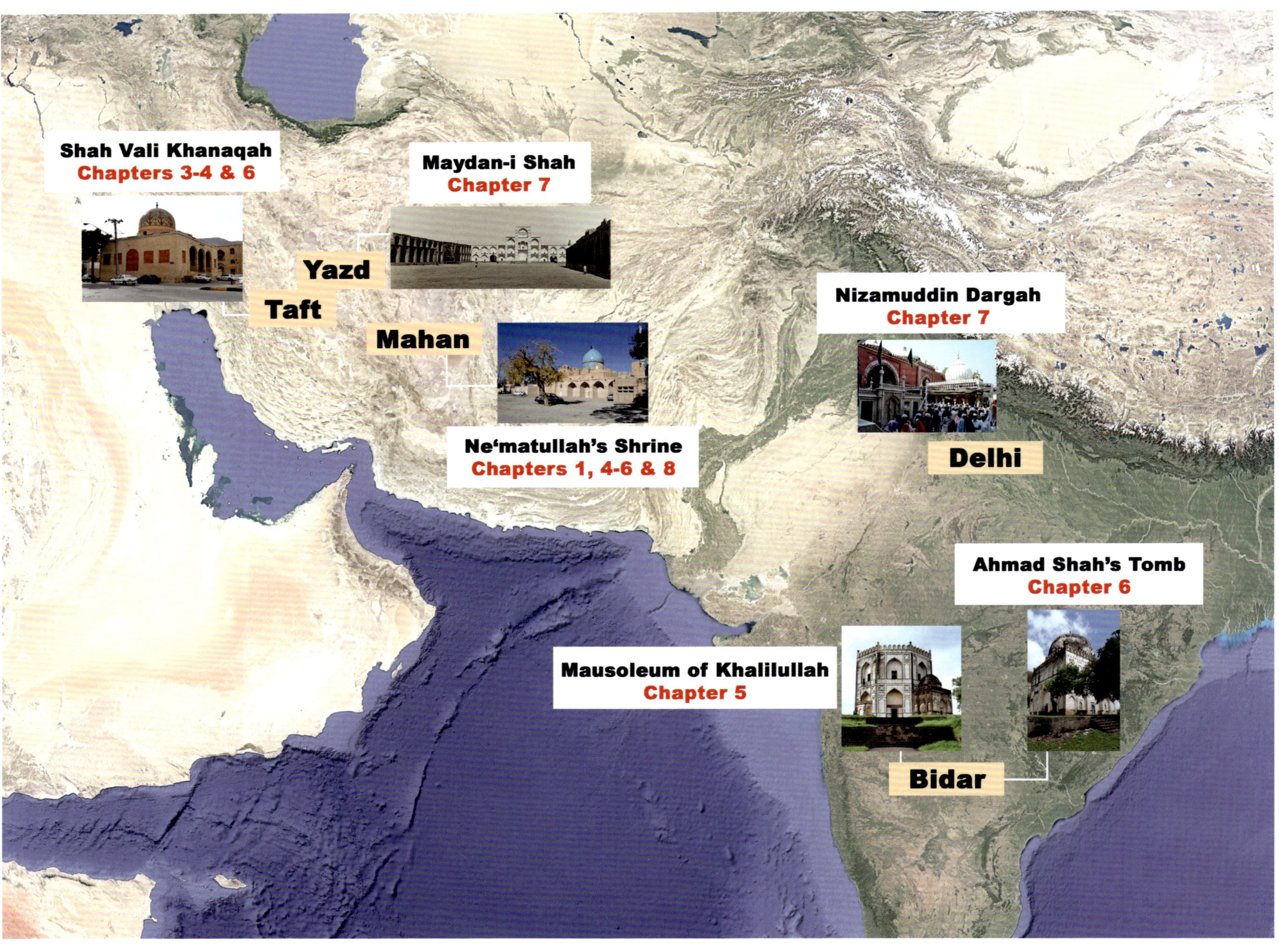

FIGURE 0.5. Map of the distribution of sites discussed in various chapters. © *Google Earth Pro; with additions by author.*

transregional domains. In part 1, three chapters establish methodological and historical parameters. Chapter 1 takes a portal in the shrine at Mahan as its point of entry into questions of patronage and politics that have shaped the historiography of Sufi shrines and material culture in art history. The intricacy of architectural genealogies and the appearance of artist signatures, as well as Sufi poetry, alert us to the agency of Sufi makers that is sometimes overshadowed by patronage-based perspectives. The chapter thus sets the scene for the following two chapters' analysis of the role of Sufi material culture in global connectedness and the pitfalls of a top-down approach to the transregional patronage of Sufism.

Chapters 2 and 3 excavate literary and architectural sources to trace how spatial and artistic imaginaries of Neʿmatullahi material culture engaged the shifting yet connected politics of fifteenth-century Iran and India. Here, through a shift from shrine *patronage* to shrine *diplomacy*, I also pay attention to what happens before a monument is built—not just the act of patronage but also the formation of social networks that make patronage possible. In addition to architectural remains, textual accounts of lost objects and the ephemeral theatrics of gift exchange are crucial here.

Building on the transregional dimensions of the Mahan portal in the first chapter, chapter 2 takes us to Deccan India around the 1420s and 1430s in order to examine transregional shrine diplomacy. Textual sources give us a glimpse into the motivations behind the Deccani gifts that were sent to the shrine in Iran as well as the reception of these gifts by Sufis and the ruling authorities. Synthesizing the local and dynastic perspective with the view from within the network, chapter 3 takes up the task of reconstructing the Neʿmatullahis' earliest, largely lost architectural complex, the Shah Vali khanaqah in Taft, based on surviving architectural elements. The picture that emerges suggests how an anthropocentric idea of the universe and its crystallization in the space of the khanaqah came together with dynastic interests in a sacral model of kingship, materializing relations between the complex and its Timurid patronage in the first half of the fifteenth century. The first part of the book ends with a reflection on the opportunities as well as the tensions that the geographic expansion of the network posed for the maintenance, development, and perception of the Neʿmatullahis' sacred sites at both the local and the transregional levels.

In these and other chapters of the book, I depend on a combination of sources from Iran and India such as hagiographies, local and dynastic histories, documents related to diplomatic exchanges between these regions, poetry written by the Sufi Shah Neʿmatullah and his disciples—especially those dedicated to spaces and objects—endowment documents, and intimate letters exchanged between members of the Neʿmatullahi family in Iran and the Deccan. Four surviving hagiographies of Shah Neʿmatullah Vali serve as key sources throughout the book. Three of these were gathered by Jean Aubin in *Matériaux pour la biographie de Shāh Niʿmatullah Walī Kermani*. The earliest was written by ʿAbd al-ʿAziz b. Shir Malik Waʿizi in the Deccan around the mid-fifteenth century. The second, written by ʿAbd al-Razzaq Kermani (completed in 1506), was commissioned by a descendant of Shah Neᶜmatullah in Iran to cover the stories that Waᶜizi had not included. The third, and last of Aubin's sources, was completed in the seventeenth century by Sunᶜullah Neᶜmatullahi and incorporated in the *Jamiᶜ-i Mufidi* (*Mufid's Compendium*, or *The Useful Compendium*), a history of Yazd by Muhammad Mufid Mustawfi Yazdi completed in 1679 in Multan.[30] A fourth hagiographical treatise by Sadid al-din Nasrullah Abarquyi survives as an appendix to a manuscript of the *divan* (collection of poems) of Shah Neᶜmatullah that is dated 909/1503 and held in the Yahuda collection at Princeton University.[31] Alongside these, the *Munshaʾat* (*Compositions*) of Sharaf al-din ᶜAli Yazdi (d. 1454) is a valuable source containing records of fifteenth-century petitions and personal letters involving the Neᶜmatullahi family. Together, the hagiographies and the compilation of writings in the *Munshaʾat* offer a view of the Neᶜmatullahi network from the inside out.[32] Local and dynastic histories balance these hagiographies by providing a view of the Sufi network from outside as well as clarifying period perceptions of center-periphery dynamics. In this regard, some of my principal sources are the *Burhan-i maʾasir* by ᶜAli ᶜAziz Allah Tabataba and *Tarikh-i Fereshteh* by Muhammad Qasim Hendu Shah Astarabadi (known as Fereshteh), written in the Deccan in the late sixteenth century and early seventeenth century, respectively, as well as local histories of Yazd, the *Tarikh-i jadid-i Yazd* (*The New History of Yazd*) by Ahmad b. Husayn b. ᶜAli Katib and the aforementioned *Jamiᶜ-i Mufidi*.

The second part of the book consists of two chapters that address the visual and spatial means by which Neᶜmatullahi Sufis fashioned themselves as transoceanic auratic mystics. Moving between Taft and Mahan, chapter 4 conceptualizes the role of physical distance in navigating tensions between asceticism and monumentality. Chapter 5 turns to the role of *spatial poetry* in architectural epigraphy, textiles, and rituals of the innermost sacred spaces of the shrines. I demonstrate how in Bidar and Mahan, in the most intimate parts of the shrines, inscriptions regarding relations of kinship were prioritized over those dedicated to their ruling patrons. I use methods of digital humanities to reconstruct one such intimate space within the shrine in Mahan: the mausoleum that housed the cenotaph of Shah Neᶜmatullah Vali, for which a group of inscribed carpets were commissioned in the seventeenth century. Since the carpets were removed from the shrine in the nineteenth century, these 3D reconstructions shed light on the intimate relationship between the space and its textiles, between architecture and ritual, and the close ties between the family and the building. The digital, in this sense, seeks to simulate a spatial and corporeal experience of the sacred space.

The final part of the book develops over three chapters that turn the notion of patronage and authorship inside out, shifting to case studies where Neᶜmatullahi Sufis took on the roles of patron and artist. Chapter 6 draws on examples from Bidar, Mahan, and Taft in the fifteenth and sixteenth centuries to probe how shrines lent their visual authority to early modern uprisings and ambitions of sacral kingship. The intimate alliances that made such projects possible, whether bonds of discipleship or marriage, blur the lines between court patronage and Sufi patronage. They also shed light on the role of women as interlocuters between the court and the shrine. Chapter 7 focuses on instances when Neʿmatullahi Sufis took on the role of art collectors and patrons of urban projects outside of their own shrines—from Yazd to Delhi and beyond. The final chapter returns to Mahan and a small retreat room in the corner of the shrine to examine the work of disciple-artists active in the design of devotional spaces where art making converged with rituals of meditation.

Existing literature in Sufi shrine studies has, to a large extent, resolved the problem of assumed dichotomies between the shrine and the court, or the figure of the Sufi and the king, who, as Azfar Moin points out, were "portrayed in opposing spheres of cultures, one sacred and the other profane."[33] These two realms were regularly intertwined with or gave birth to one another, as in the case of the Safavid Empire, which originated from the Safavid Sufi network. However, while such crossovers have brought more nuance to the image of Sufis, we know less about the visual implications of what falls between the two sides of the Sufi-king spectrum. Sufis occupied a variety of sociopolitical roles: not only as spiritual and political leaders but also as urban elites, cultural patrons, artists, connoisseurs, collectors, merchants, warriors, and martyrs. The last part of the book plays a key role in charting some of these social roles and their implications for the making of material culture.

My examination of the vibrant design of these shrines and their material culture is committed to a transregional microhistory of the arts of devotion. This is an art history that acknowledges the global itineraries of mobile people, objects, and ideas but is equally invested in the local, intimate, and material histories that they reflect. The art and architecture of Sufi networks offer a flexible vantage point onto early modernity, one that not only spans a wide geographical area but also shifts between politically marginal and central positions in relation to a diverse range of political regimes. Within these expansive horizons, an interplay of intimate and monumental spaces serves to challenge historiographically entrenched narratives of Sufism's approach to materiality. Taking off from the palimpsest-like portal that opens the first chapter, the book unpacks what it means to pass through the shrine's sedimented layers of patronage and artistry and, in doing so, enter into the intimate inner workings of a connected early modern world.

Notes

1. Letter from the Timurid governor of Shiraz to the ruler of the Deccan: Yazdi, *Munshaʾat*, 125.

2. The term *spatial poetry* has been used recently to refer to "an aesthetic space created by the juxtaposition of poetry and a rich visual context that is tailored to and responds to the literary text": Gupta, "Interpreting the Eye," 190. Contrary to the primacy given to text over space in the above definition, and building on Paul

Losensky's work, what I am specifically interested in is how the space and its rituals and dynamics *shaped* the text in the case of commissioned poetry or created new layers of meaning for reused poetry. See Losensky, "The Palace of Praise," 1–29.

3. Green, *Sufism: A Global History.*

4. I follow Binbaş and Bashir in their use of *Sufi network* as opposed to *Sufi order.* Bashir argues that *Sufi order* creates an impression of "internal cohesion and discipline" that is a result of the comparison between Sufi communities and Christian monastic institutions. Bashir, *Sufi Bodies*, 11–3, 78–104.

5. References to other lost spaces of the network such as those in Abarqu and Kuhbanan in central Iran appear only in passing, based on textual sources.

6. Flood, *Objects of Translation*, 2.

7. Tabandeh, *The Rise of the Niʿmatullāhī Order.* For art historical scholarship on the Neʿmatullahis, see Ekhtiar, "Ahl al-Bayt Imagery Revisited," 80–93; Ekhtiar, "Exploring Ahl al-bayt imagery," 146–54.

8. Lewisohn, "Sufis and Their Opponents," in Tabandeh and Lewisohn, *Sufis and Their Opponents*, xxviii.

9. Sikand, "Shared Hindu-Muslim Shrines," 178–79. For the case of Hinduization of Ayodhya, see also Jacobsen, "Pilgrimage Space, Hinduization of Space," 95–112.

10. Um, "A New Agenda," in Collins et al., "Reflections on HECAA at 25."

11. Lowe, *The Intimacies of Four Continents*; Chattopadhyay, "Architectural History or a Geography of Small Spaces," 5–20; Trivellato, "Microstoria," 122–34, especially 127.

12. See Subrahmanyam's discussion of the different categories of the global, including its subjective interpretation that is emphasized here: Subrahmanyam, "Global Intellectual History," 126–37. See also Dunlop, *The Mongol Empire*, 27–28, n.41.

13. Subrahmanyam, "Connected Histories," 736–39.

14. Um, "A New Agenda." See also Juneja, *Can Art History be Made Global?*, 18–23.

15. See, for instance, Gruber, "The Rose of the Prophet," 223–49; Ergin, "The Fragrance of the Divine," 65–105, among others.

16. Chattopadhyay, "Architectural History or a Geography of Small Spaces," 5–20.

17. Green, "Migrant Sufis and Sacred Space," 493–94.

18. Bashir, *Sufi Bodies*, 58.

19. Karamustafa, *God's Unruly Friends*, 4–6.

20. Kugle, *Sufis & Saints' Bodies*, 265–94.

21. See, for instance, Palmer, *Oriental Mysticism*, especially pp. x–xi, and his characterization of Sufism as the "Primaeval Religion of the Aryan Race." For a criticism of Palmer, see Ernst, "Situating Sufism and Yoga."

22. Bashir, *Sufi Bodies*, 10–11. See also Flood, "The Kaʿba Orientations," 152.

23. Flood, "Bodies, Books, and Buildings," 49.

24. Prown, "Mind in Matter," 2.

25. Adding to those already cited in this introduction, see, for example, Paul, "Forming a Faction," 533–48; Gross, "The Economic Status of a Timurid Sufi Shaykh," 84–104; DeWeese, "Yasavī Šayhs in the Timurid Era," 173–88; Safi, *Religion and Politics in Saljuq Iran*; Moin, *The Millennial Sovereign.*

26. See, for instance, Ardalan and Bakhtiar, *The Sense of Unity*. See also Flood's reflection on this point with regard to recent scholarship: Flood, "The Kaʿba Orientations," 151.

27. Rizvi, *The Safavid Dynastic Shrine*; Yürekli, *Architecture and Hagiography in the Ottoman Empire*; Mulder, *The Shrines of the ʿAlids in Medieval Syria*; Wolper, *Cities and Saints*.

28. For a similar critique of patronage vis-à-vis the role of intellectuals, see Binbaş, *Intellectual Networks*, 5–6.

29. Mulder, *The Shrines of the ʿAlids in Medieval Syria*, 186.

30. For a detailed study of local and transregional connections in history writing focused on the *Jamiʿ-i Mufidi*, see Mancini-Lander, "Tales Bent Backward," 23–54.

31. Connell draws heavily on this manuscript: Connell, "The Nimatullahi Sayyids of Taft."

32. See also Yürekli, *Architecture and Hagiography*, 3. On historiographical problems of the genre of hagiography, see Paul, "Hagiographische Texte als historische Quelle"; Ernst, *Eternal Garden*, 85–93; Manz, *Power, Politics and Religion*, 72–73.

33. Moin, *The Millennial Sovereign*, 5.

PART ONE

Shrine Diplomacy Between Kerman, Yazd, *and the* Deccan

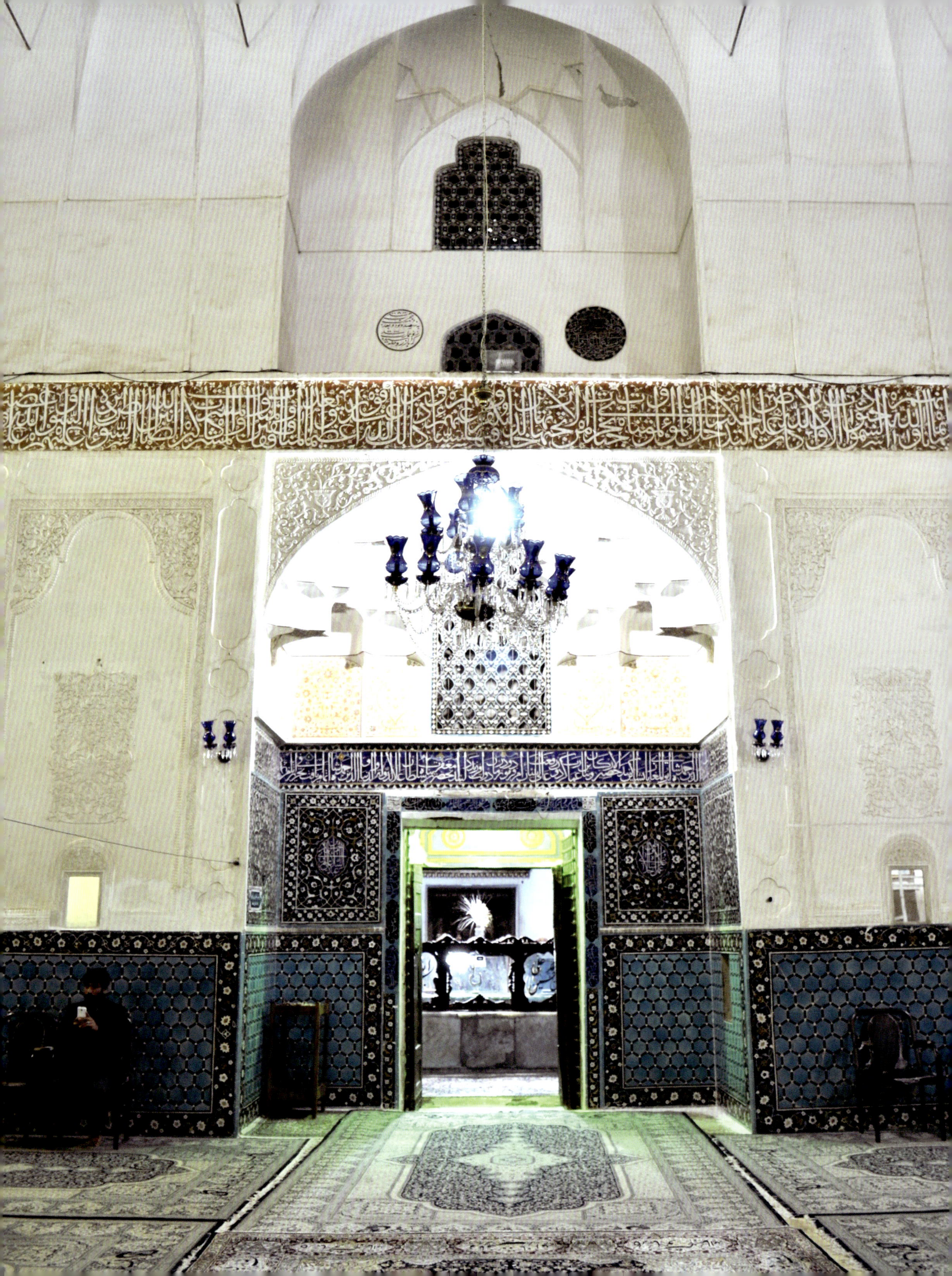

1

Shrines, Thresholds, Palimpsests

The Portal at Mahan

His essence is here, [even] with his appearance gone,
He has not passed into annihilation, he is [just] hidden from sight.

Shah Neʿmatullah Vali, *Divan*, *ghazal* 551.

This epigraph and its accompanying verses adorn a portal at the tomb of the Sufi poet Shah Neʿmatullah Vali (d. 1431) in the small southern Iranian town of Mahan, about twenty-six kilometers to the southeast of Kerman (fig. 1.1). The poem, written in the fifteenth century by Shah Neʿmatullah himself, laments the passage of the beloved, "the sultan of Sufis," from this world to the next. Shah Neʿmatullah's verses originally amounted to a devotional poem likely dedicated to the Prophet Muhammad or his son-in-law and successor, ʿAli, whom Shiʿa Sufis consider the first Sufi masters. In six lines, the arc of the poem takes us from an expression of the pain of separation toward a reassurance of the everlasting presence of the beloved and a promise of salvation in both worlds for those who devote themselves to his service (app. 1.1.a).

FACING, FIGURE 1.1. Portal leading to the domed mausoleum of Shah Neʿmatullah at the Mahan shrine, Iran. *Photograph by author, 2018.*

The subject of these verses shifted when they were transformed into polychrome mosaic tiles at the shrine of Mahan in the sixteenth century. The verses were repurposed as an architectural inscription to reflect on both the loss of Shah Neʿmatullah and his eternal presence, installed in proximity to his cenotaph. The architectural rendition of the poem at the Sufi's tomb puts Shah Neʿmatullah himself in the place of the holy figures that he had alluded to in the verses. The poem's themes of lamentation and consolation are in turn projected onto the Sufi's own followers, who are called to reflect on both the inevitability of death and the eternal presence of the Sufi's essence "here" in this world and in its microcosm, the shrine. This essence was bound up with the corporeal presence of the Sufi's body in the tomb, but it also relied on how intimately his body, aura, and words were tied into the stone, mortar, and glazed tiles that made up the surrounding architecture. This interplay between poetic meaning and architectural space cuts to the heart of broader tensions between spirit and matter in the study of Sufi material culture.

In a general sense, the Sufi's essence lives on through his writings, his teachings, and his poetry, which enjoyed wide circulation throughout the centuries that followed his death. But there is a much more specific sense in which this essence has been materialized "here," at the portal, not just by the inscription of Shah Neᶜmatullah's words in stone but also by the resulting self-reflexivity of the inscription, which now identifies the tomb's threshold as the place where his essence becomes manifest. It is as if the aura of the Sufi's body were affixed to the threshold through the force of his own words, just as the tiles bearing those inscriptions were attached to the walls. The word *here* in the poem thus turns the preexisting verses into a site-specific inscription and, indeed, into what this book defines as *spatial poetry*.[1] By extension, the architecture itself is drawn into the play of concealment and monumentalization that follows in the verses. The Sufi's "appearance" is gone, "hidden from sight," which in context now doubles as an allusion to the material body hidden in the crypt. It is the materiality of the architecture that accounts for both the absence of the Sufi body and the aura of his presence at this place.

The subject of this chapter is the portal into which this poem is inscribed. The portal serves as an entrance to what was originally a stand-alone domed chamber housing the tomb of Shah Neᶜmatullah Vali, surrounded by the Sufi's garden, in Mahan. Due to its prominent location and function as the threshold of the venerated mausoleum, the portal has accumulated interwoven layers of political and architectural genealogies over the centuries. In the juxtaposition of layers, created through multiple alterations and additions, a history unfolds not only of the patronage of the Neᶜmatullahi Sufis—a who's who of the ruling elite throughout the region and beyond—but also of early modern architecture itself.

This chapter disentangles the layers, names, and human relations that mark this portal, shedding light on each intervention one by one before considering them together as a whole. The goal is to understand why this portal was claimed, remade, and reframed so many times throughout the centuries by local and transregional rulers who did not always wield political authority over the shrine and its territory. In other words, my aim is to understand the forces that turned this portal into a *restless* object, an unstable architectural element, constantly changing as it was reshaped by different political agents and artists. As I contend in this and other chapters, it was the dialectic of "essence" and "absence" itself—encapsulated so pithily in the epigraph of the present chapter—that transformed this stationary architectural element into a restless object. When read carefully, the portal articulates the dynamics that convert architectural spaces into palimpsests.

The portal serves also as a point of entry for discussing the multilayered fabric of the shrines that will be examined in this book, epitomizing the range and intensity of patronage campaigns at Neᶜmatullahi shrines. In particular, the portal's complex stratigraphy concentrates some of the fundamental questions dealt with in the first part of my study: intersections between art and power, religious and dynastic modes of representation, and what have come to be regarded as centers and peripheries of the Islamic world's early modern political milieu. On another level, however, the portal also points to the agency of Sufis and their artistic networks, intimating the material and sensorial inner workings of the shrines that the second and third parts of the book will explore. In what follows, I will first offer an introduction to the shrine at Mahan and then proceed to focus on the portal, parsing out the art historical and methodological questions that a highly charged architectural element of this kind poses for the study of Sufism and its material culture.

I. The Mahan Shrine and Its Development

Upon the death of Shah Neʿmatullah Vali in 1431, the garden that housed his humble khanaqah in Mahan became the site of a mausoleum. Over a period of more than five hundred years, the mausoleum has expanded into what is today one of the largest shrines in Iran (fig. 1.2), exceeded only by the shrine of Imam Reza in Mashhad and that of Maʿsumeh in Qum.[2] Unlike many Sufi shrines in the Islamic world that have developed in an accumulative organic manner, the gradual enlargement of the Mahan shrine followed a strong axial layout, with four courtyards aligning along the east–west axis, oriented roughly toward the Kaʿba (fig. 1.3).[3] Lisa Golombek and Donald Wilber once described the complex as standing "within its own grounds in an area removed from village and commercial life," but urban development in recent decades has drawn it into the heart of Mahan.[4]

The oldest part of this expanded shrine complex is the sepulchre of Shah Neʿmatullah, which lies near the center of the east–west axis (figs. 1.3 and 1.4). This is the dome chamber that was built over Shah Neʿmatullah's grave in the years proceeding his death in 1431 and whose portal is the main focus of this chapter. According to one of Shah Neʿmatullah's biographers, Sunʿullah, the Sufi's death in Kerman was followed by a prayer service at the city's *Jamiʿ* (congregational) mosque, after which his body was carried to Mahan and buried in his khanaqah and garden.[5] It remains unknown exactly when the old khanaqah was lost or whether its destruction coincided with the erection of the mausoleum.

Several terms have been used to refer to the shrine throughout its physical evolution. While the earlier structures used by Shah Neʿmatullah during his lifetime were usually referred to as a khanaqah, the mausoleum and its expansions have been called a *mazar* (tomb, grave), *rawza* (tomb or garden), or *astana* (doorway or threshold), among other terms found in textual sources.[6] Etymologically, astana denotes the intermediary role of the sacred space as a threshold connecting the material and spiritual realms. In Ottoman Turkey, Iran, and central Asia, the term astana usually refers to major shrine complexes. More broadly, however, it can also be applied to the space created around the Sufi or to places that came into contact with the Sufi's body: indeed, any place where the Sufi *shaykh* stepped, resided, or lay buried.[7] It is in relation

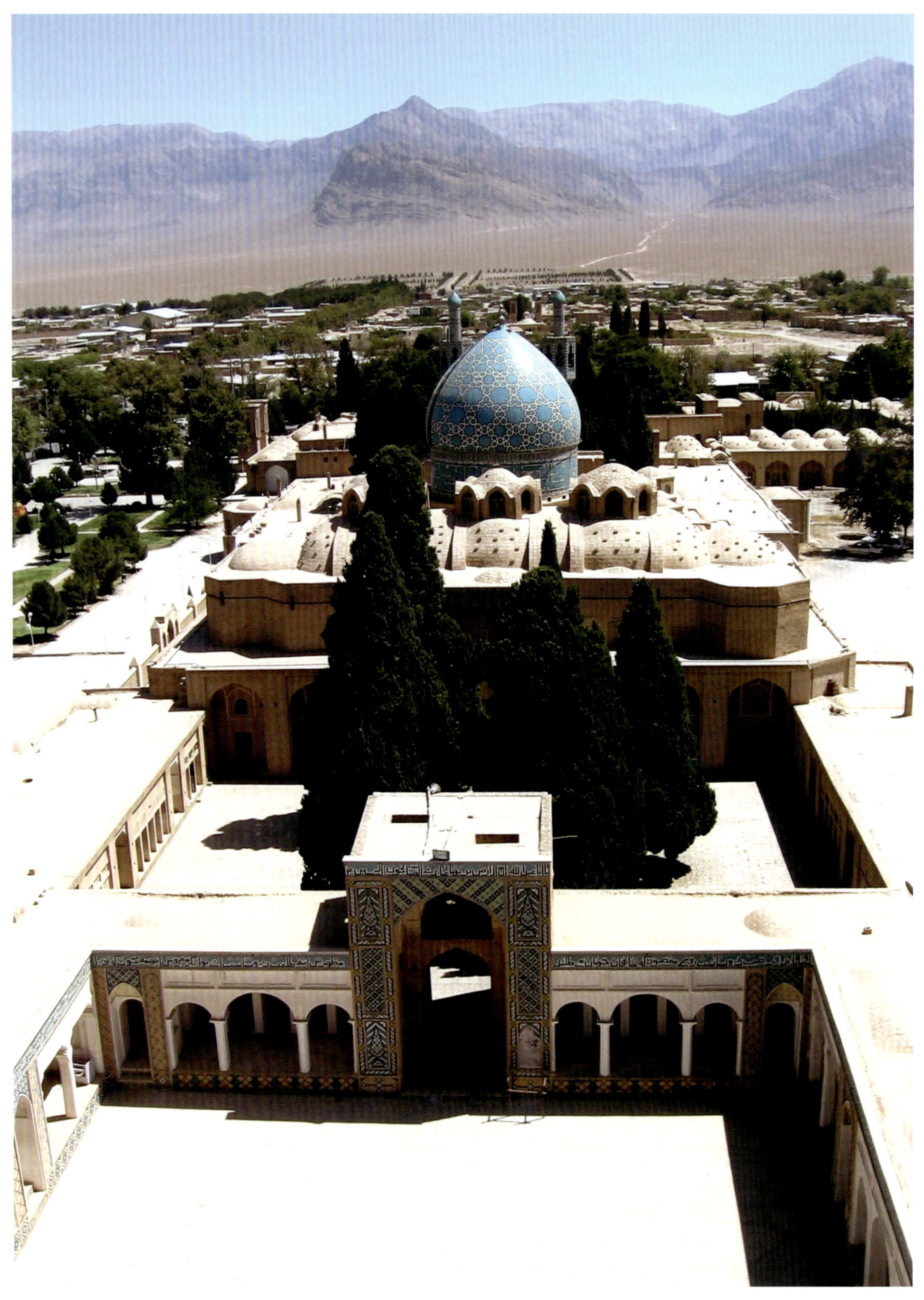

FIGURE 1.2. The shrine of Shah Neʿmatullah Vali at Mahan, view from western minarets. *Photograph by author, 2012.*

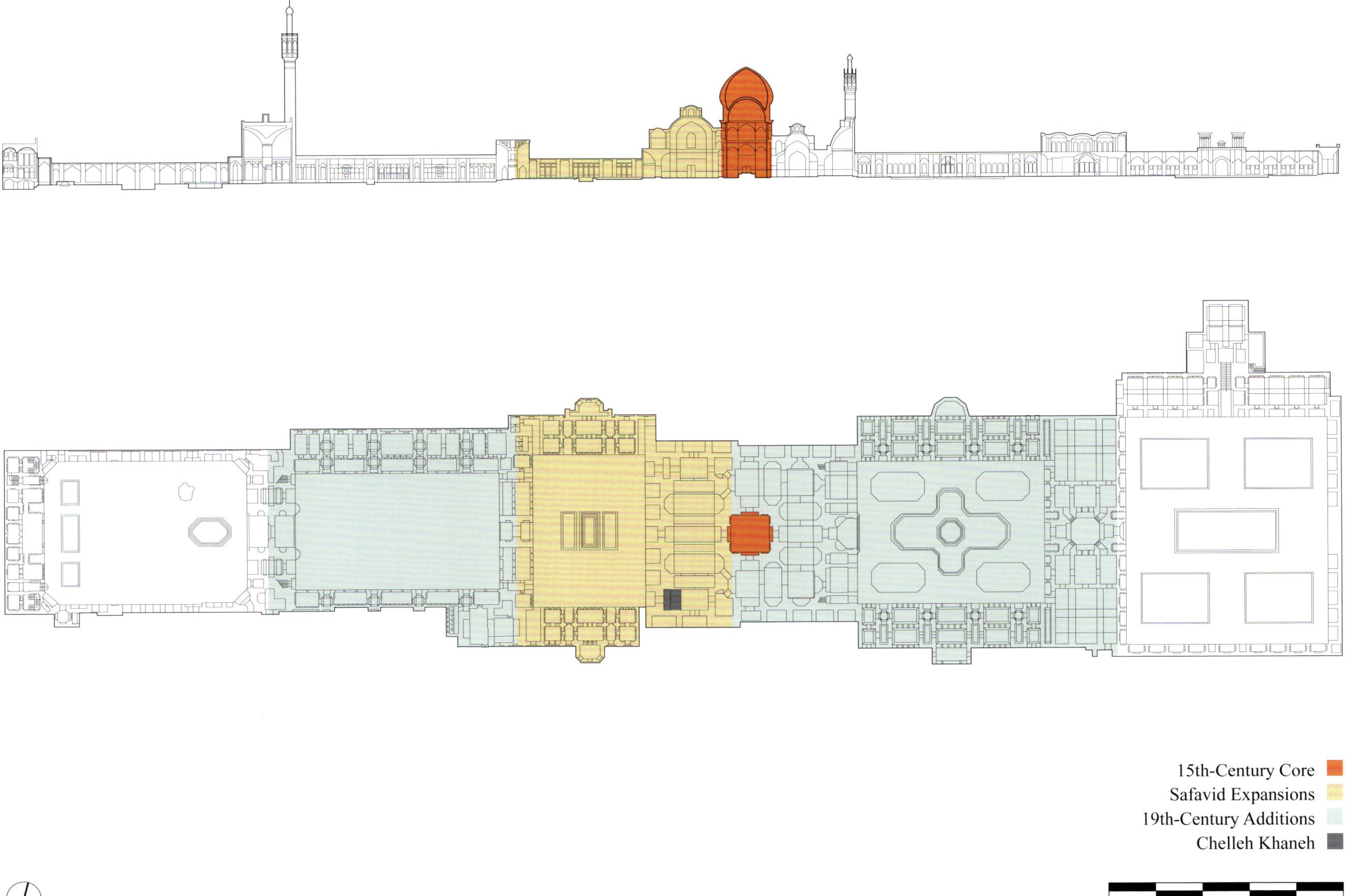

FIGURE 1.3. Plan and section of the shrine complex in Mahan. *Drawings by Farah Michel, after plans by Iran's Cultural Heritage Organization in Kerman.*

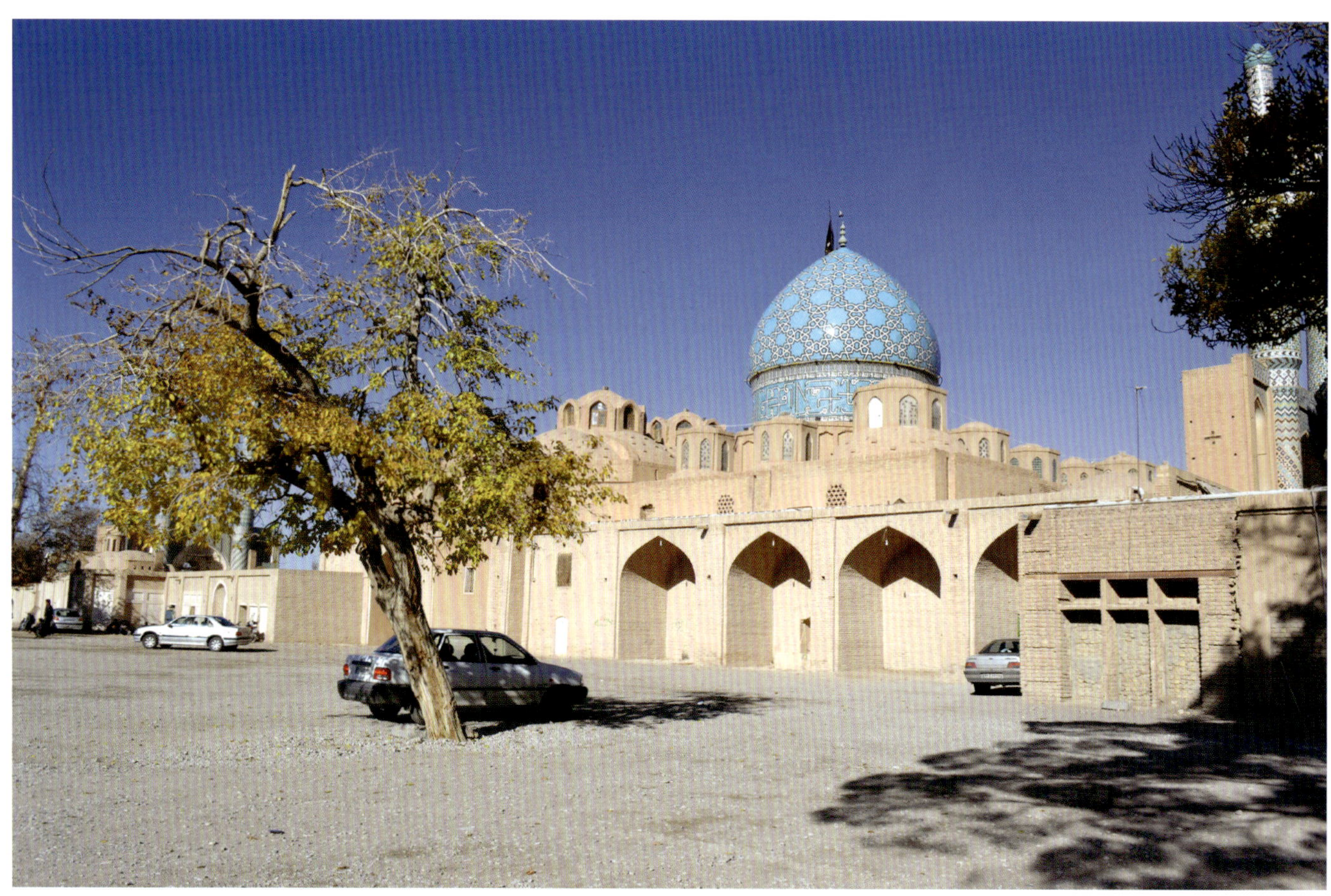

FIGURE 1.4. View from the south of the dome covering the mausoleum of Shah Neʿmatullah Vali at Mahan. *Photograph by author, 2014.*

to this larger doorway that the portal under study in this chapter should be understood: a threshold to the most sacred part of a shrine that itself functions as a doorway to the invisible realm.

As mentioned earlier, the mausoleum was originally a single building located in the middle of a garden (fig. 1.3). Apart from this fifteenth-century core, the rest of the complex gradually expanded from the late sixteenth to the twentieth century, with the majority of additions dating from the nineteenth and twentieth centuries (fig. 1.3).[8] The overall form of the sepulchral chamber at Mahan remained unaltered until the late sixteenth century, when the complex was expanded westward by the addition of a vaulted hall known as the *dar al-huffaz* (Qurʾan recitation hall) (fig. 1.5). This expansion most likely coincided with the addition of the courtyard (*sahn*) beside it, which is known as the Old Courtyard (Sahn-i kuhan) or the Shah ʿAbbasi courtyard after the Safavid monarch with whose reign the patronage of the courtyard is associated (figs. 1.2 and 1.6).[9]

The westward orientation of the complex corresponded with the old Kerman-Mahan road, located to the west, from which pilgrims would reach the mausoleum.[10] This is especially important in light of the political and economic roles that Kerman assumed during the reign of Shah ʿAbbas I (r. 1588–1629) and under the governorship of Ganj ʿAli Khan (d. 1624–25), when the

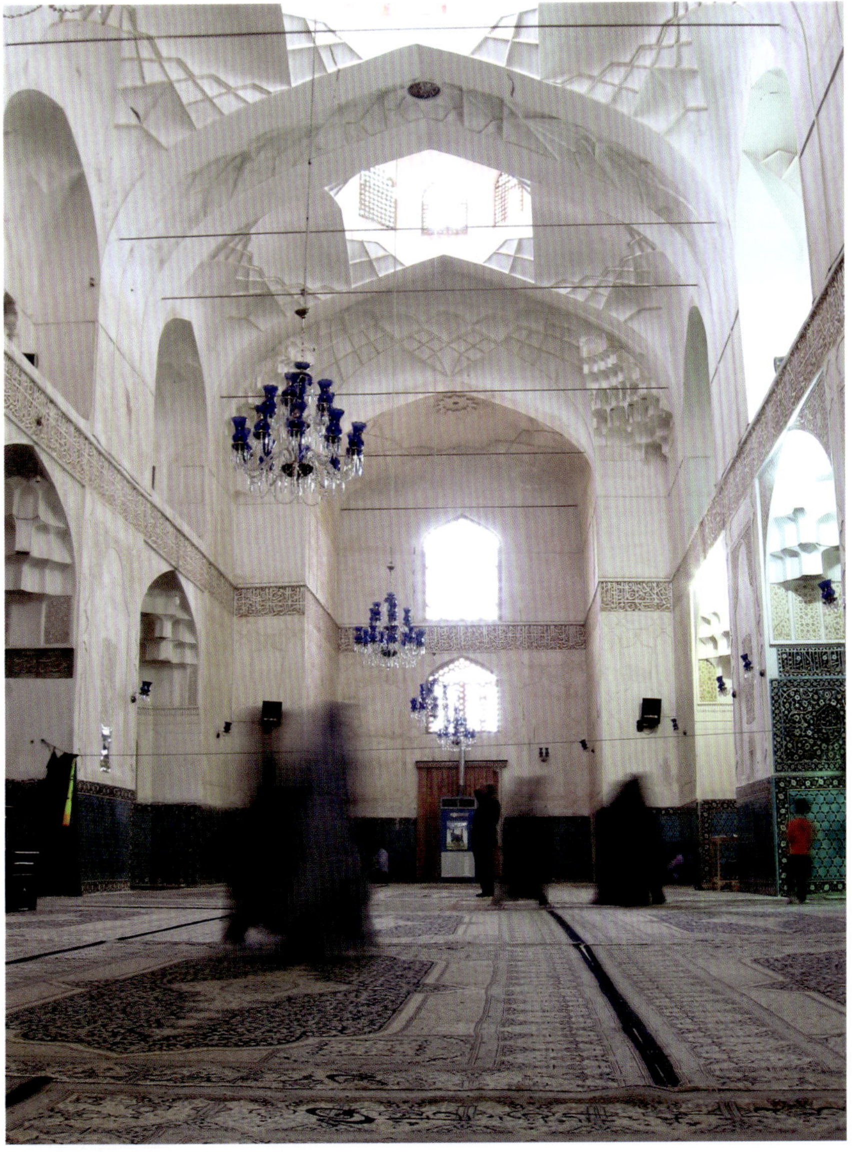

FIGURE 1.5. The dar al-huffaz (recitation hall) at the shrine complex in Mahan, view facing north. *Photograph by author, 2013.*

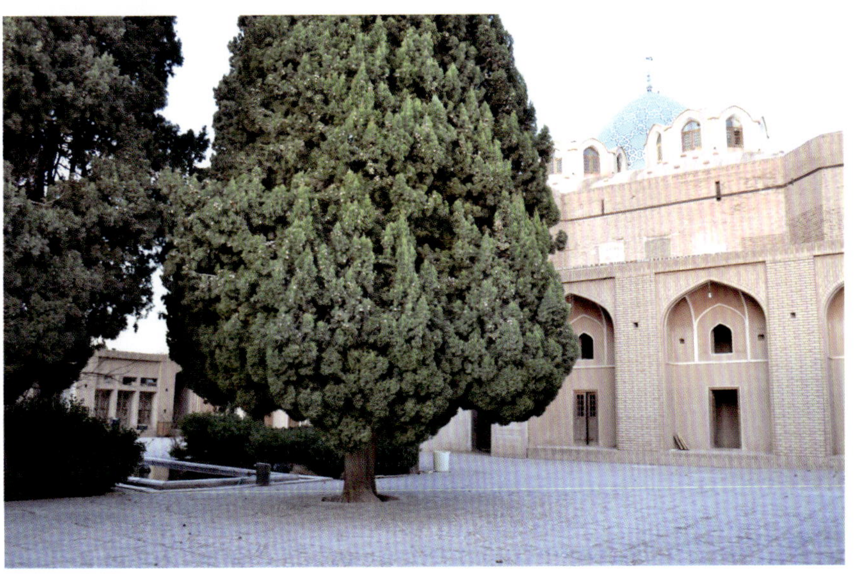

FIGURE 1.6. View of the Shah ʿAbbasi courtyard at the shrine at Mahan showing cells around the courtyard. *Photograph by author, 2018.*

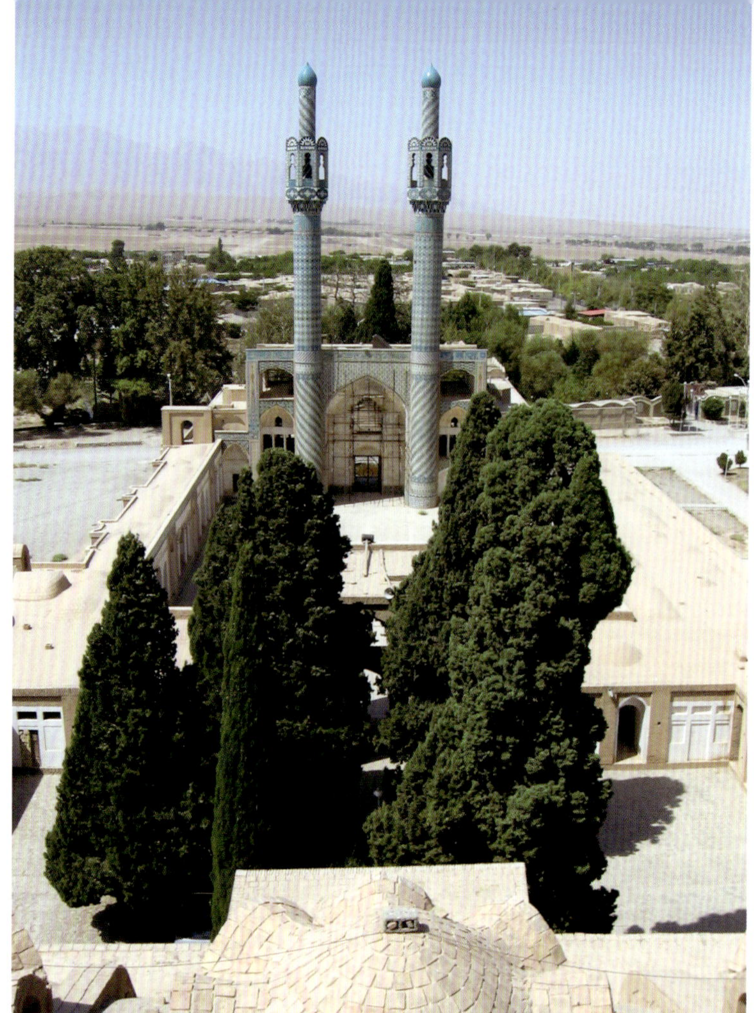

FIGURE 1.7. View of the Muhammad Shahi and Shah ʿAbbasi courtyard from the mausoleum's dome with the portal indicating the former orientation of the complex. *Photograph by author, 2012.*

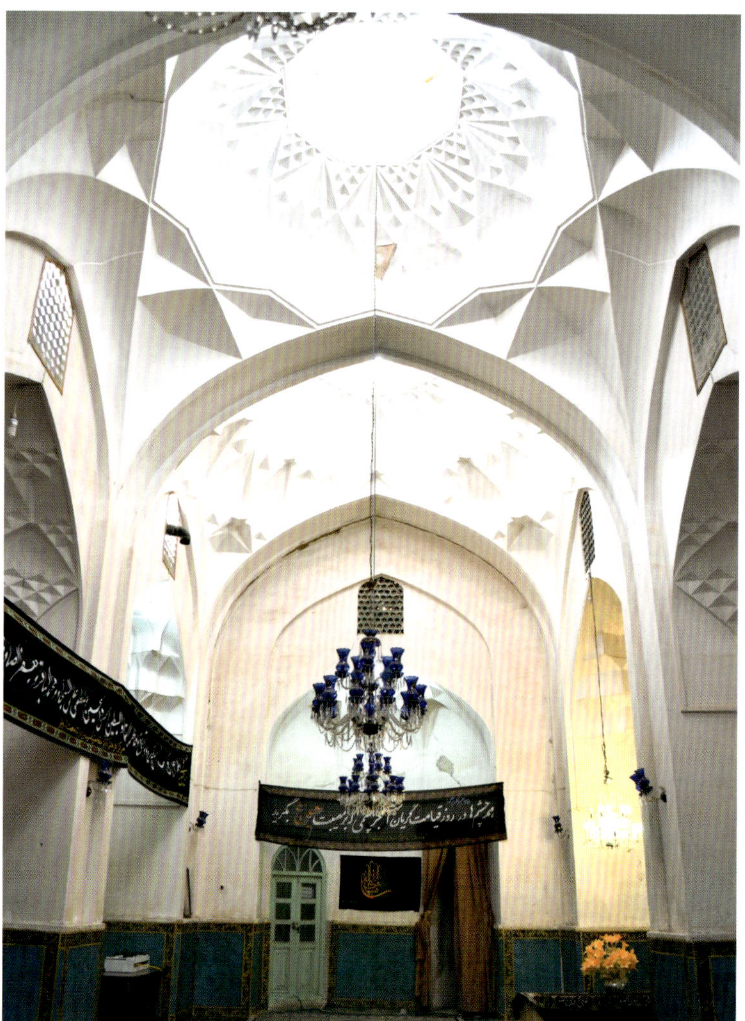

FIGURE 1.8. Qajar-era halls surrounding the fifteenth-century dome chamber at the shrine at Mahan. *Photograph by author, 2014.*

FACING, FIGURE 1.9. Qajar-era courtyard (Wakil al-Mulk) with the entrance leading to the fifteenth-century mausoleum in the background. *Photograph by author, 2018.*

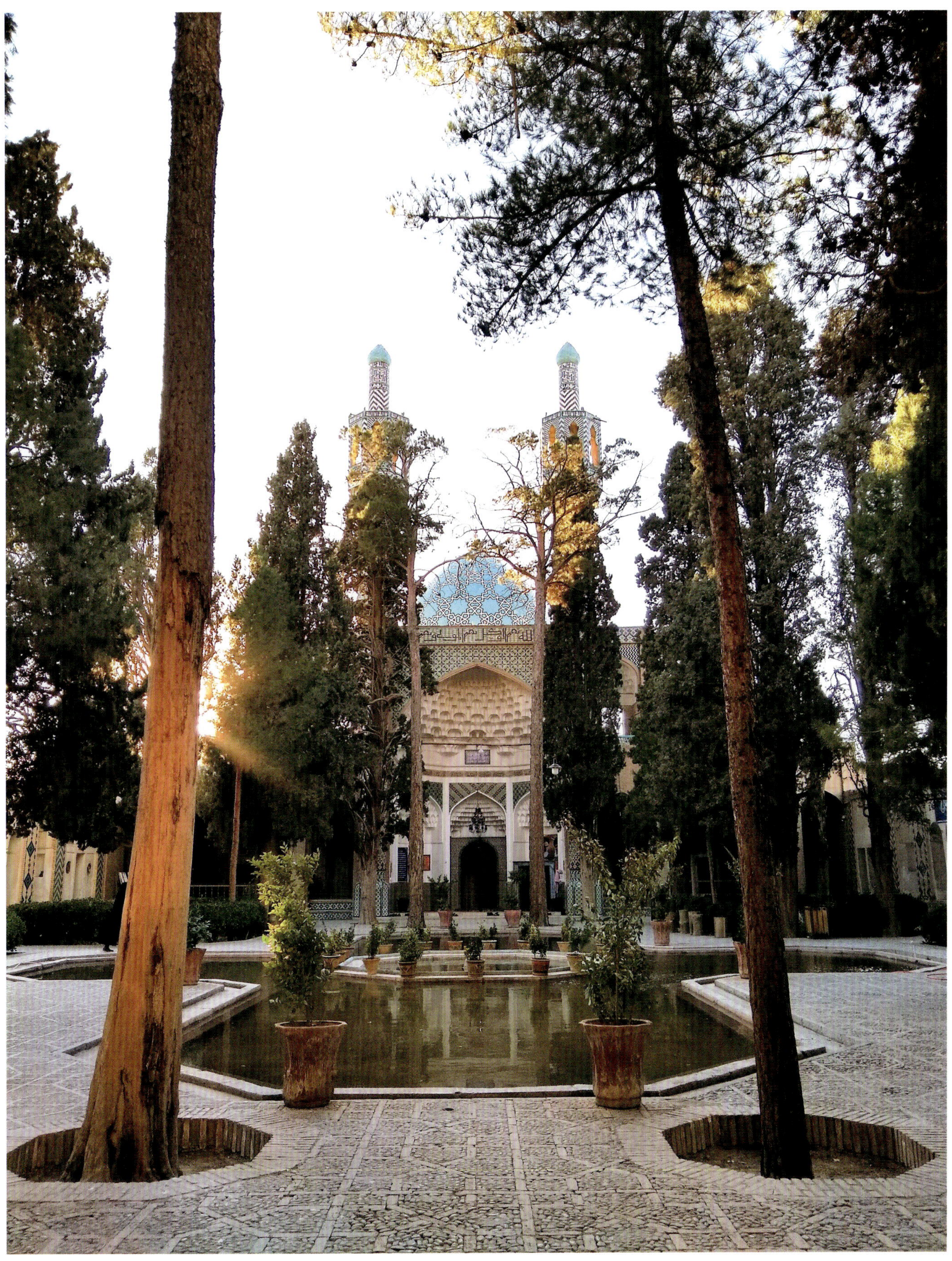

shrine at Mahan began to expand westward.[11] Expansions along this same axis continued under the Qajars (r. 1789–1925) with the Sahn-i Muhammad Shahi (also known as the Husayniya) and a grand portal built during the reign of Muhammad Shah Qajar (r. 1834–48) (figs. 1.7–1.9).[12] Shifting direction, further expansions in the nineteenth century extended eastward from the fifteenth-century dome chamber, corresponding with a new Kerman-Mahan road built to the east of the complex.[13] The nineteenth- and twentieth-century additions include vaulted galleries wrapping around the north, east, and south sides of the dome chamber; two courtyards with a two-story residence separating them; a cistern; a caravansary to the southeast of the complex; and an entrance portal, which is currently the main one in use (fig. 1.3).[14]

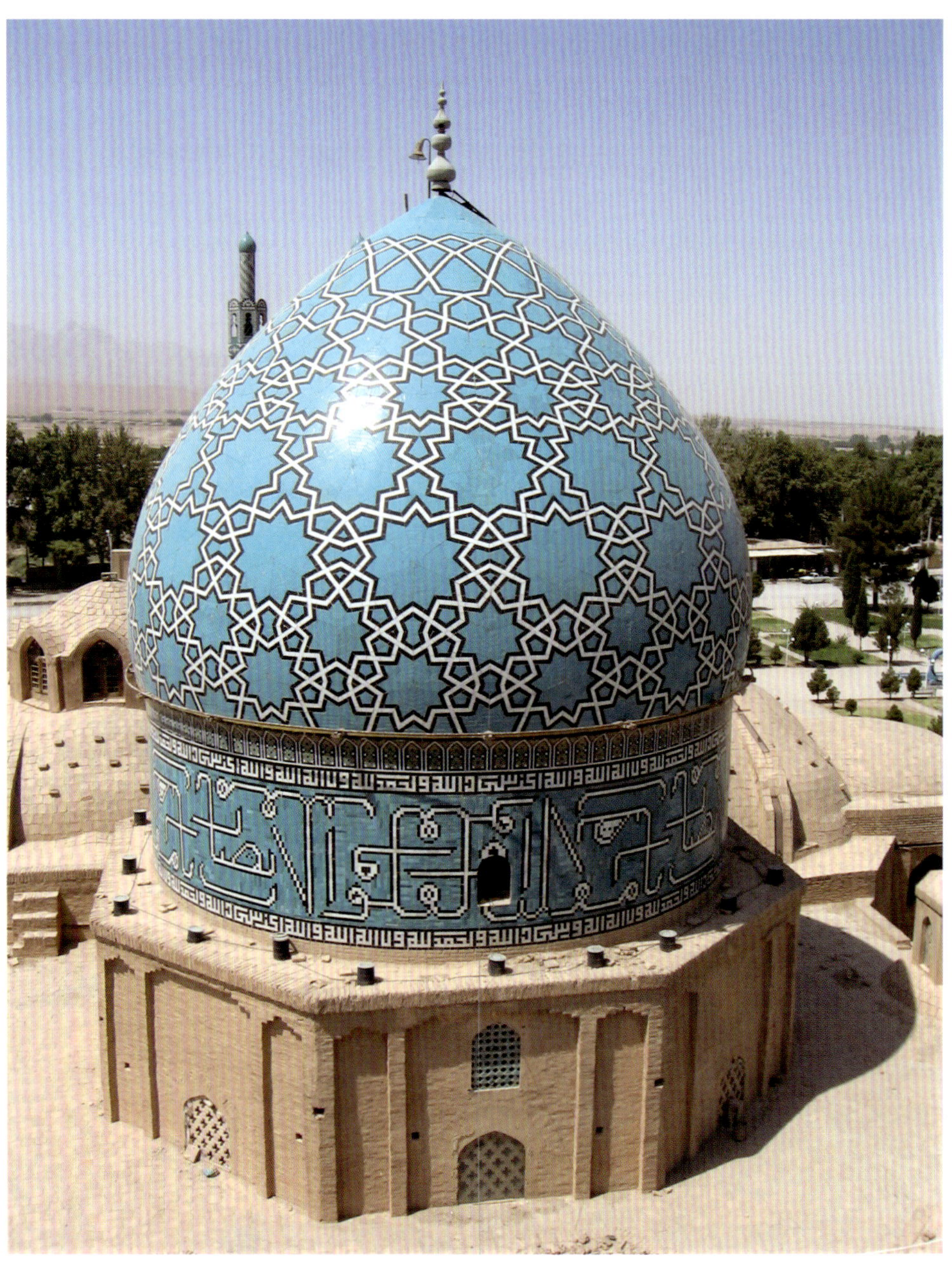

FIGURE 1.10. The transition zone, drum, and dome of the Mahan mausoleum, view from the east. *Photograph by author, 2012.*

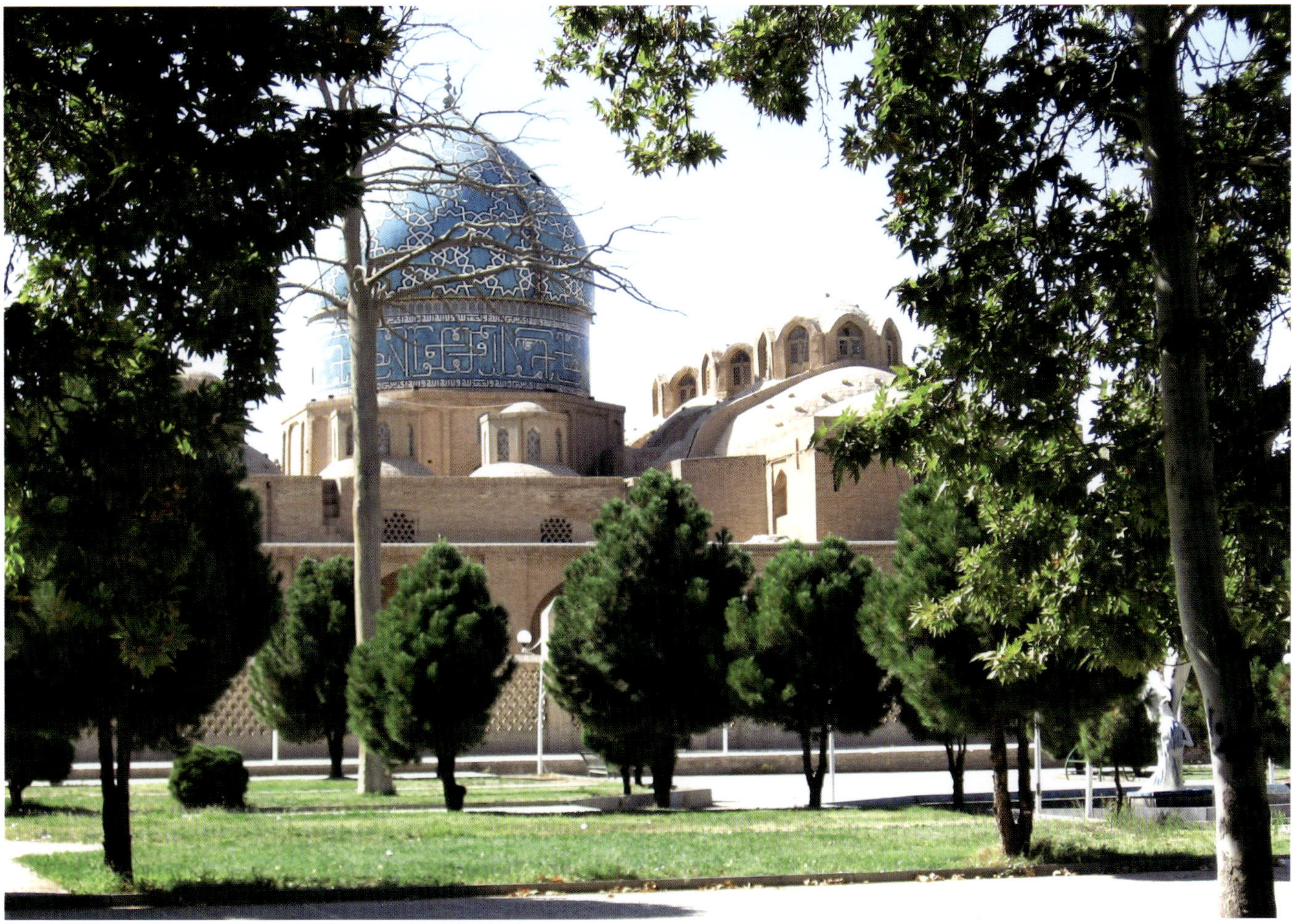

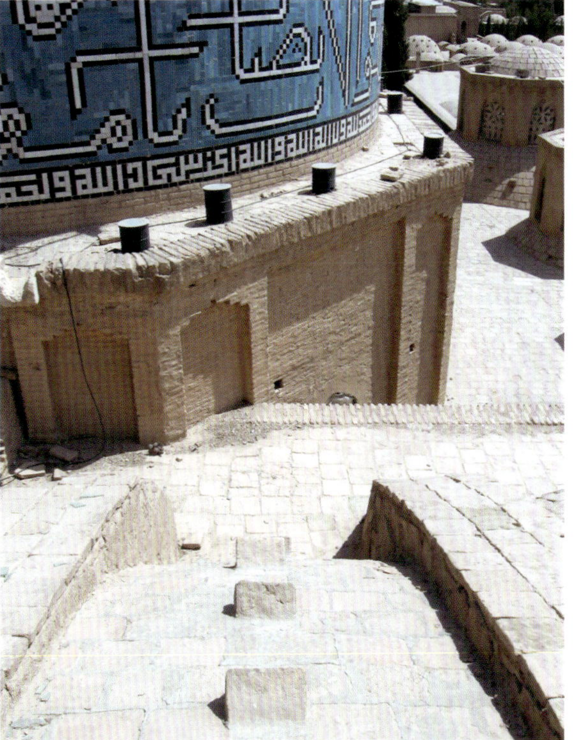

ABOVE, FIGURE 1.11.
View of the recitation hall to the west (right) of the dome chamber at the Shrine at Mahan. *Photograph by author, 2012.*

LEFT, FIGURE 1.12.
View from the roof of the recitation hall at the Mahan shrine, looking onto the area where the hall joins the dome chamber. Due to the height of the recitation hall, more of this side of the octagon was covered by the expansion. *Photograph by author, 2012.*

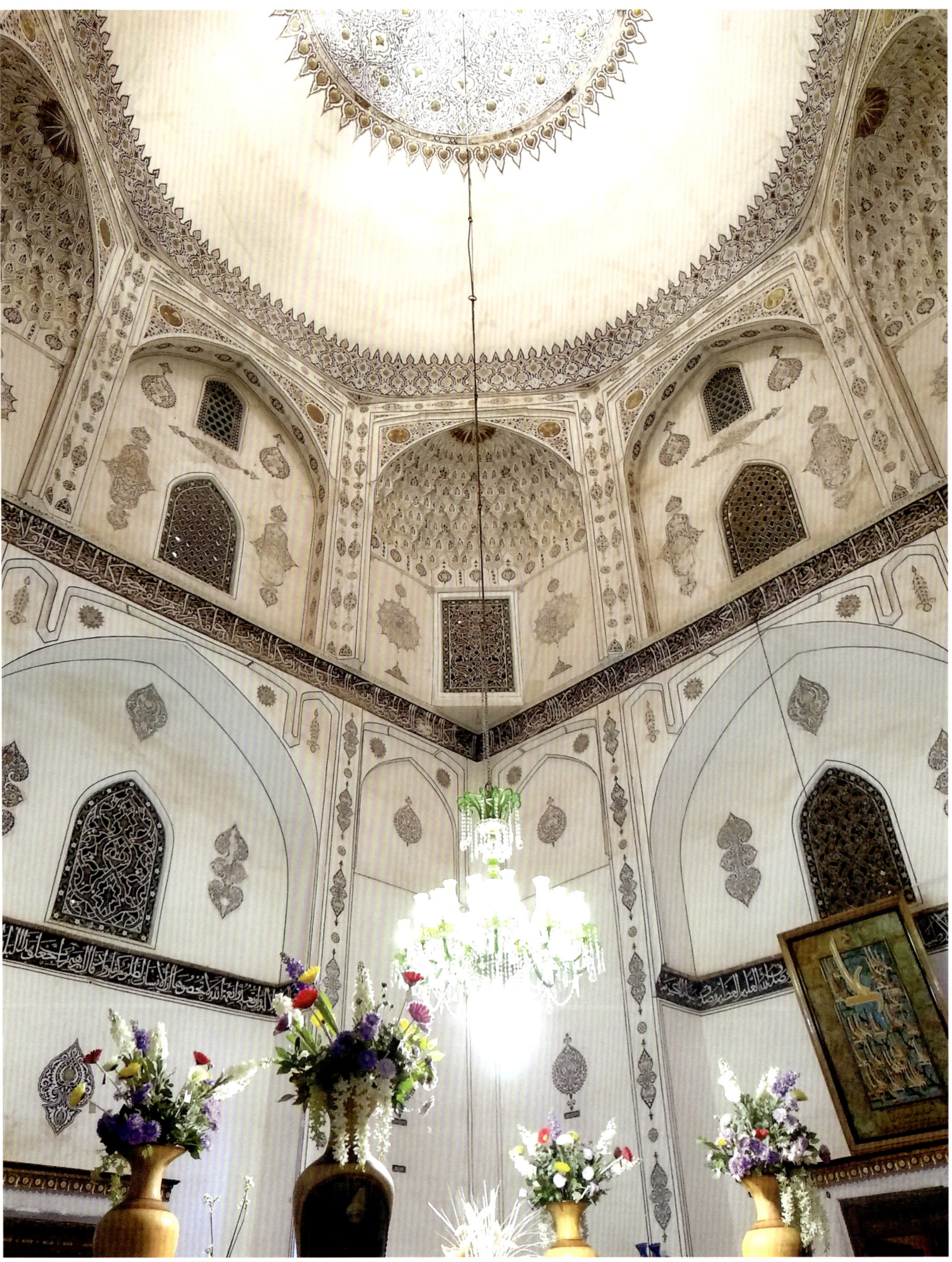

The fifteenth-century mausoleum at the heart of the complex is a square-shaped chamber that rises into an octagon at the zone of transition, topped with a double-shell dome sitting on a tall drum (fig. 1.10). While the later expansions of the shrine wrap around the lower parts of this dome chamber, its octagonal zone is still partially visible on the exterior—less on the west side, where the sixteenth-century double-story dar al-huffaz was added, and more on the east, south, and north, where the nineteenth-century vaulted halls rise just one story (figs. 1.11 and 1.12). The surface of the outer dome is covered with a radial-based pattern of white and black glazed bricks arranged in stars against a blue background. The glazed tiles on the exterior of the dome have been restored several times, but their design likely originated in the Safavid period (fig. 1.10).[15]

FACING, FIGURE 1.13. Interior view of the fifteenth-century mausoleum at the shrine at Mahan. *Photograph by author, 2018.*

The interior surfaces of the dome chamber are largely covered with white plaster, aside from light-blue glazed hexagonal tiles that cover the dadoes (fig. 1.13). Set against these light surfaces are perforated windows, inscription panels, and modern as well as possibly Timurid wall paintings of floral and geometrical patterns, all of which belong to shared idioms of art making and architecture in the fifteenth century. I will return to this interior in chapter 5.

The dome chamber has four entrances, one on each side, which originally connected the interior with the exterior garden setting. The western facade constituted the main entrance, as indicated by a foundation inscription and the presence of more elaborate decorations compared to the other facades.[16] This orientation matches the direction that pilgrims would have approached from the Kerman-Mahan road at the time (fig. 1.7).[17]

The western portal is covered in several registers of tilework from different time periods. Most of these surfaces are inscribed with epigraphic content featuring dates, the names of patrons, and artist signatures as well as poetry by Shah Neʿmatullah (fig. 1.1). Analyzing the portal, four different layers can be identified, each of which corresponds to a distinct moment in the expansion of the building and the political circumstances of the Neʿmatullahi Sufi network. At once concealing and revealing one another, these dense layers span the period between 1436 and 1590, grounding a narrative that unfolds diachronically and transregionally from the Bahmanid rulers of India to the Turkmen tribes controlling western Iran and local governors acting on behalf of Safavid kings. The remainder of this chapter works through each of these four moments in the history of the portal and, by extension, in the architectural history of the Neʿmatullahi shrines. In doing so, it sets the scene for the first part of this book, which scrutinizes the relationship between the Neʿmatullahis and their patrons.

II. Between Global and Local: Transregional Implications of an Inscription

The earliest layer on the portal coincides with the completion of the funerary dome chamber in 1436, five years after the Sufi's death. Among the elements surviving from this period is a foundation inscription above the doorway (fig. 0.2). Executed in mosaic faience, the tile panel has a dark-blue background

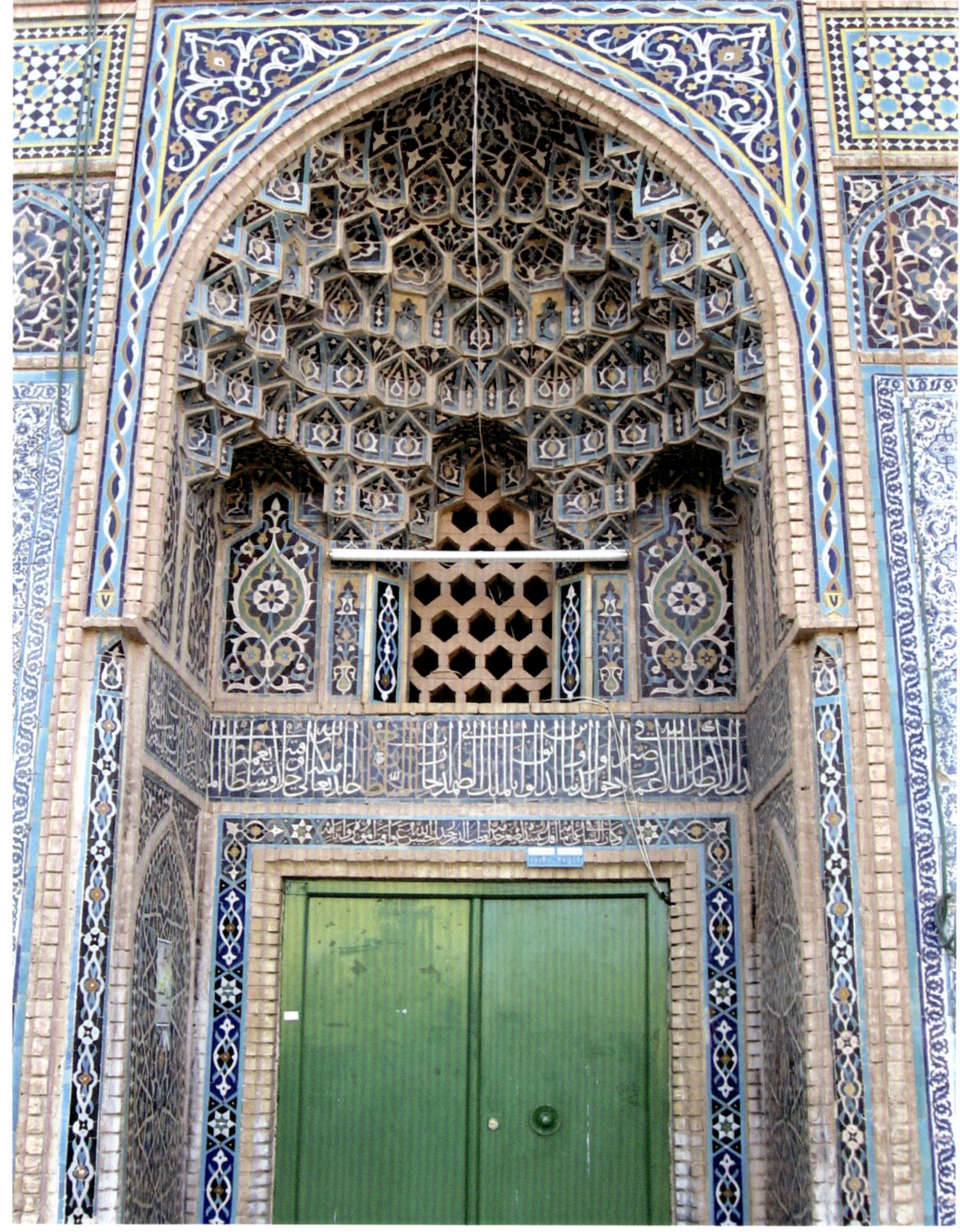

FIGURE 1.14. Portal and foundation inscription of the Pa-Minar mosque in Kerman, Iran. *Photograph by author, 2012.*

decorated with minimal foliage and is inscribed in thuluth script—a common combination of forms and techniques for foundation inscriptions in the first half of the fifteenth century.[18] It is here that we find one of the earliest material representations of the wide geographical reach of the Neʿmatullahi network. According to this Persian foundation inscription, the patron of the stand-alone mausoleum was the reigning Bahmanid sultan of Deccan India, Ahmad Shah I (r. 1422–36), who had sent generous donations to Mahan (app. 1.2.b): "Ahmad Shah Abu'l-Maghazi (the father of conquests) ordered the construction of this stable dome and lofty well-founded structure, which was finished during the reign of his beloved son Sultan ʿAla al-dawla wa al-din wa al-dunya Ahmad Shah. Written in Muharram of 840 [July–August 1436]."[19]

As I will discuss in detail in chapter 2, the Bahmanids' patronage of the mausoleum transpired in the context of long-standing, widespread contacts between the Deccan and Iran, mediated by sea routes and monsoon winds. For reasons that I will explore there, the Bahmanid ruler invited the Sufi to travel to the Deccan, prompting recurring journeys and resettlements from some of his most prominent descendants. Here, my aim is to think through the implications of this inscription panel in light of its function within the program of the portal.

Since the late sixteenth century, when the recitation hall was added, this foundation inscription has been seen by visitors standing within the hall. With the modern orientation of the complex and entrance from the east, the portal becomes visible only after one has passed through layer after layer of courtyards and interior spaces as well as through, or around, the dome chamber itself. To understand the visual and political effect of this foundation inscription, however, it is crucial to think of its position on the once primary facade of the mausoleum, one that defined the threshold between the exterior and the Sufi's sepulchre, engaging visitors upon their arrival at the tomb and the surrounding garden. It was this facade, in other words, that initiated the beholder's spatial encounter with the funerary structure.[20] For local visitors who read it, the epigraphy embedded the experience in a geographical framework that extended beyond the range of a typical regional pilgrimage itinerary—one that situated the shrine in an expanded network across the Indian Ocean. For pilgrims coming from the Deccan, it affirmed the spiritual and political bonds established between their region and the Sufi saint, materializing their connected histories in stone.

And yet, despite this transregional message, the visual language of the epigraphy belongs to an aesthetic familiar within the region. In this period,

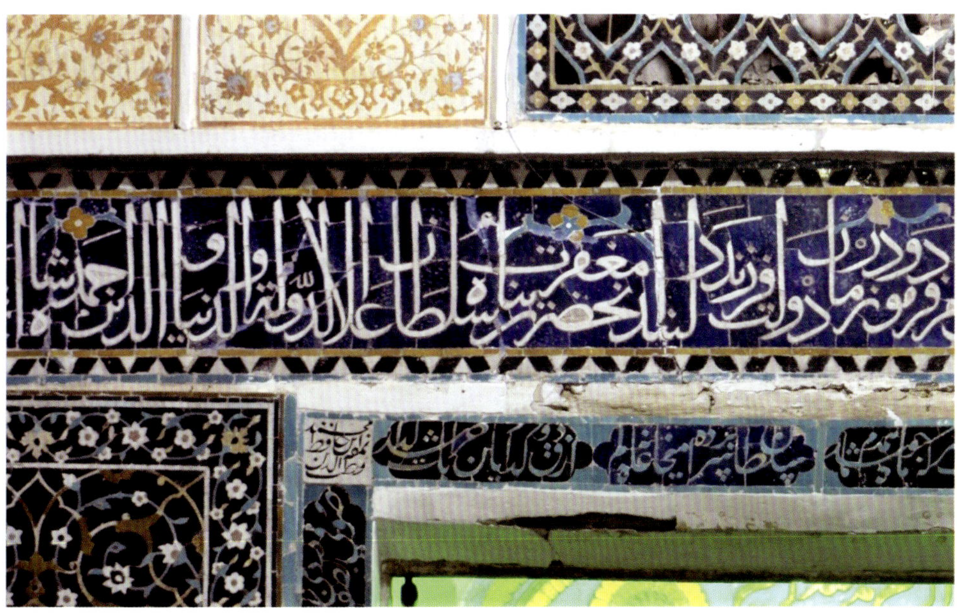

FIGURE 1.15. Detail of the fifteenth-century foundation inscription on the western portal of the mausoleum in Mahan. *Photograph by author, 2018.*

foundation inscriptions in the region were commonly rendered in mosaic faience technique, with two lines of inscriptions: one usually in white and thuluth script containing dates and patronage information and another in amber and *kufic* script, containing verses of the Qurʾan in Arabic. One-line foundation inscriptions like the one at Mahan, however, were also known. For instance, our portal bears a resemblance to such local examples as the Pa-Minar Mosque in Kerman, dating back to the late fourteenth century (fig. 1.14).[21]

In both single- and double-line foundation inscriptions, such as the ones mentioned above, it was customary to inscribe the name of the patron or reigning king in a different color, such as amber, to distinguish it from the rest of the line written in white.[22] This is not the case in Mahan's foundation inscription, as the name of both Bahmanid kings, Ahmad I and his son Ahmad II (r. 1436–58), are written in white, undistinguished from the rest of the foundation formula (figs. 0.2 and 1.15). The choice of color palette does not reflect a simple preference for monochrome. Small flowers with foliage in amber and turquoise are sprinkled across the panel, and it is likely that a color other than white, perhaps turquoise or green, was used to fill several looped letters in the inscription, which are now missing their central tile pieces. Indeed, the decision not to use amber for the patrons' names proves quite deliberate—although not without exceptions—on comparison with other epigraphic evidence in Neʿmatullahi sites, especially the inscriptions at the Mahan shrine.[23]

Across the hall from the portal under study here, a doorway leads to the adjacent courtyard. This entrance bears another foundation inscription, documenting the construction of the late sixteenth-century recitation hall by the governor of the region, Bektash Khan (d. 1589), under the Safavid ruler Shah ʿAbbas I (fig. 1.16 and app. 1.3.a). Like the fifteenth-century foundation inscription that records the patronage of the Bahmanids, this Safavid-era panel is inscribed in uninterrupted white, leaving the names of both the Safavid ruler and Kerman's governor undistinguished. By contrast, in a contemporary roundel under the hall's ceiling, which contains the signature of an artist who held the title Neʿmatullahi, the word *Neʿmatullahi* is set off in amber, distinguished from the rest of the signature formula in white (app. 1.4.a and fig. 1.17).

While the contrast of amber and white is not an unwavering universal rule for foundation epigraphy, the disparity suggests a conscious decision to privilege the commemoration of the Sufi and not the ruling authorities among the Neʿmatullahi network. At least two other mosaic tile panels made in the fifteenth century and belonging to the Sufi network's complex in Taft affirm this visual strategy, reserving the amber to project a sacred aura onto the names of the Prophet, his descendants, and members of the Neʿmatullahi family.[24] In the Mahan shrine, this gesture of reverence toward the Sufi is augmented by the orientation of writing within the sixteenth-century signature roundels on the ceiling, which can be read while facing the mausoleum's portal.

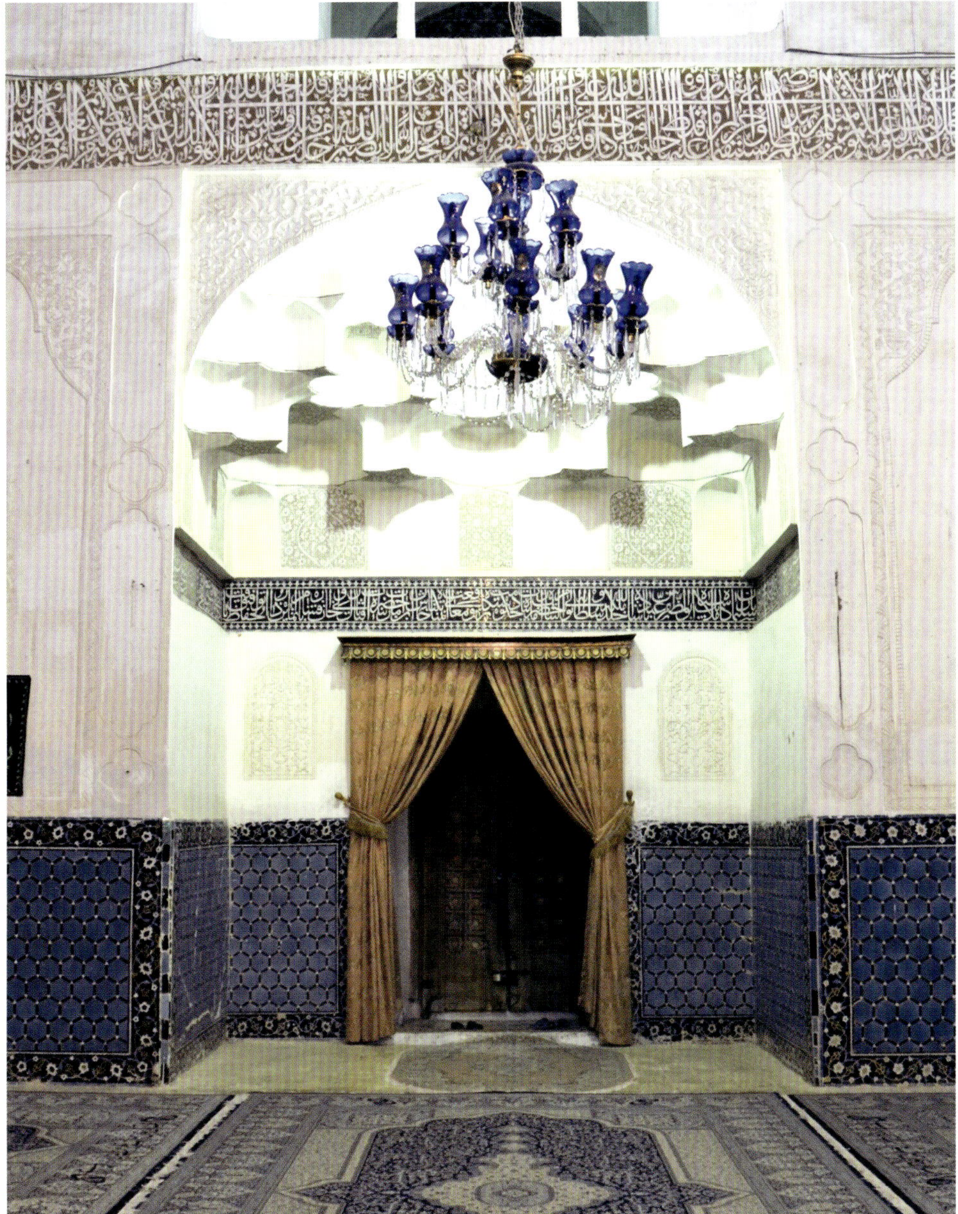

FIGURE 1.16. Safavid-era foundation inscription above the door opposite the western portal of the mausoleum at the shrine in Mahan. *Photograph by author, 2013.*

As is the case for other structures associated with Sufi networks in the Islamic world, the architectural inception of the sacred site reflects power dynamics between the Sufis and their patrons at a critical moment in the consolidation of their relationship. The inscription panel discussed in this section raises two interesting points in this regard. First, the portal points to a conspicuous absence. At this time in the fifteenth century, the Mahan mausoleum did not receive patronage from the Timurid courts that ruled the surrounding territory, as will be discussed further in chapter 3. The second point concerns the extent of donations arriving from the Deccan. These enabled the Neʿmatullahis to monumentalize this most sacred site associated with the

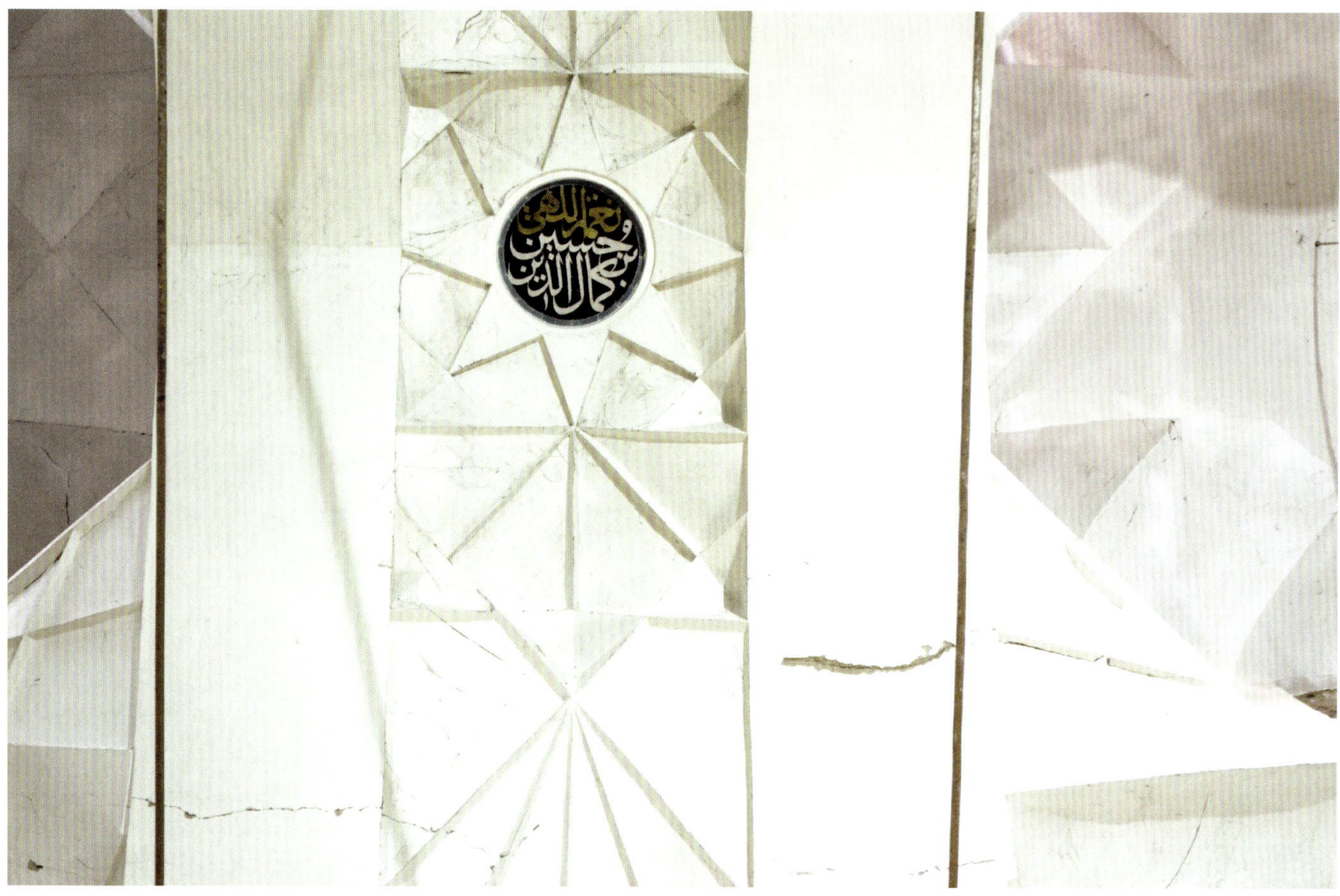

FIGURE 1.17. Inscribed roundel in Mahan with the signature of craftsman Kamal al-din Husayn-i Neᶜmatullahi, the latter word written in amber. *Photograph by author, 2013.*

family around the very same moment that the tomb of the Bahmanid king and patron of the Mahan shrine was erected in Bidar with elaborate references to Shah Neᶜmatullah and Mahan.[25] In Mahan, the quality of surviving original tilework on the monument, some of which has been lost due to expansion campaigns (see below), manifests the generous financial resources offered by the Deccani rulers for the construction of the building and the hiring of skilled craftspeople. Against this rather unusual background to patronage of the mausoleum, the decision to render the name of the Deccani patrons in white rather than amber is even more significant. This subtle detail diverts the attention that would have gone to the patrons toward the Sufi shaykh and his devotees.

The portal projects an authority that rests on the containment of the body and the words of Shah Neᶜmatullah embedded within the architecture. As such, it establishes a canvas, as it were, on which subsequent rulers and artists would leave their marks.[26] The collage-like picture drawn on this canvas consists of various colors, styles, and names of people who paused before it, had a hand in making it, or sought to claim it. The more we scrutinize the segments, joints, and gaps of this composite picture, the more the dynamics of its power start to emerge.

III. Inscribing the Reach of a Dynasty

A second key moment in the life of the portal is registered by an inscribed roundel located on the facade of the mausoleum, datable to the second half of the fifteenth century (figs. 1.1 and 1.18). Like the foundation inscription, the roundel's tilework is executed in mosaic faience with the text in Persian and thuluth script, except that here the epigraphy is composed in verse. The roundel has a rosary-shaped frame, with circles and diamonds alternating in white and turquoise. The inscription is written in white against a dark-blue background while turquoise fills the diamonds and looped letters of the epigraph dotting the surface of the roundel. The style, color palette, and execution all point to a fifteenth-century date of production. The content of the verses inscribed in the roundel confirms this as it contains, written in amber, the name of Yaʿqub Sultan (r. 1478–90), the ruler of the Aq Qoyunlu (lit. White Sheep) dynasty, a powerful confederation of Turkman tribes who ruled in Eastern Anatolia and western Iran until the Safavid conquest at the beginning of the sixteenth century (app. 1.5.a).

> During the time of Yaʿqub Sultan, this grave
> was constructed for a second time, may it last.

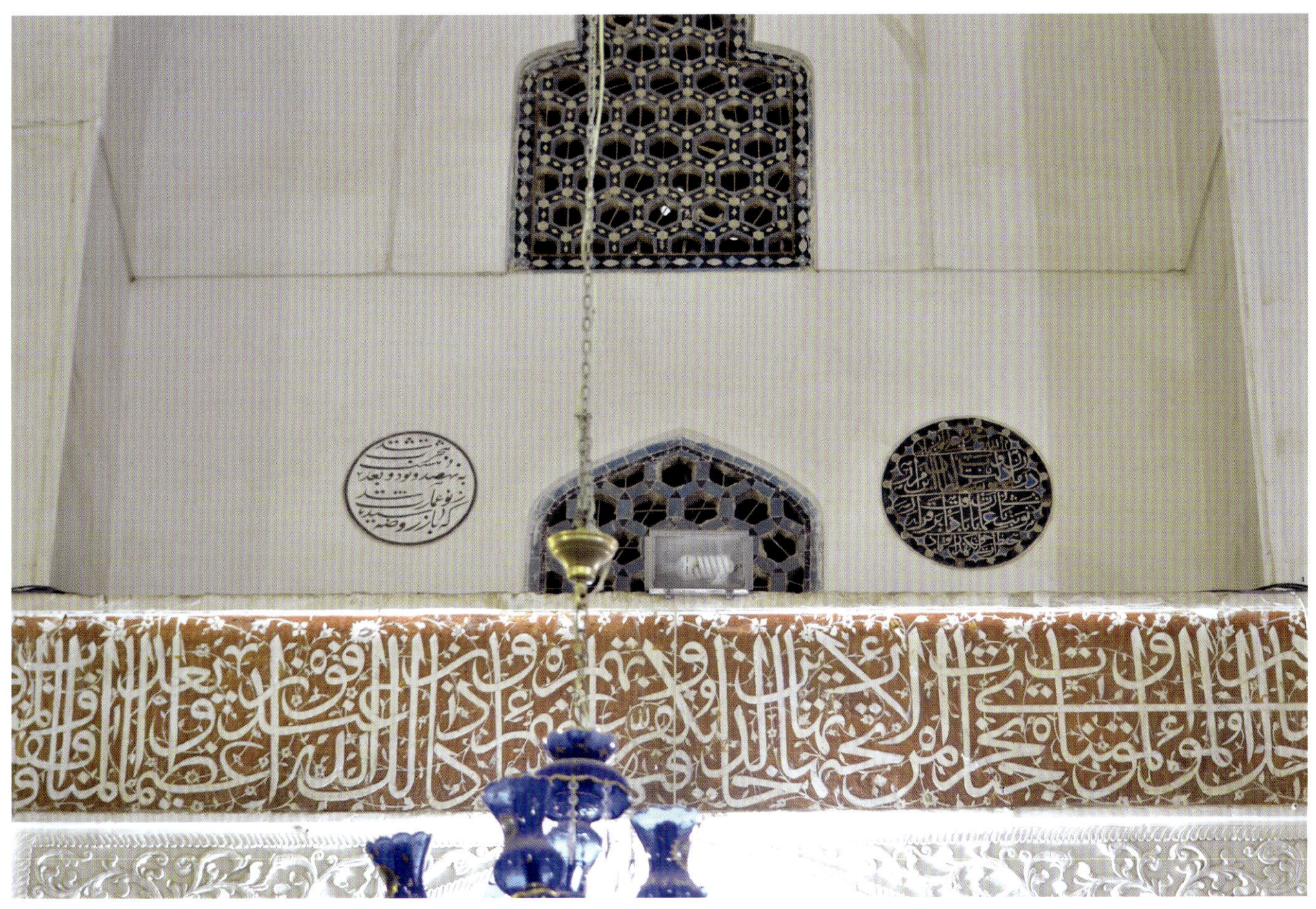

FIGURE 1.18. Inscribed roundels recording the restoration of the mausoleum at Mahan under Yaʿqub Sultan (*right*) and Safavid-era annexations (*left*). *Photograph by author, 2018.*

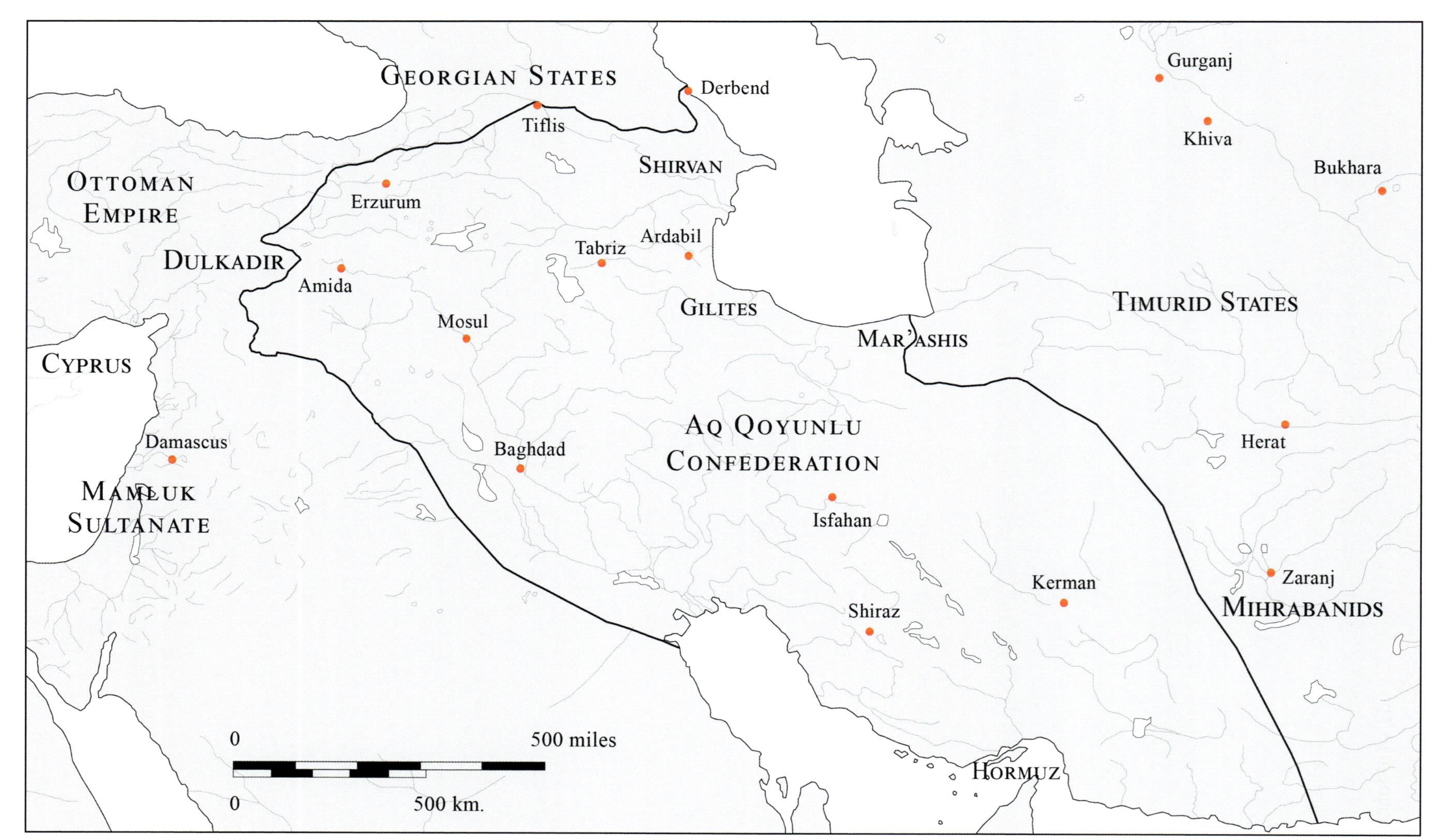

MAP 1.1. Map of Aq Qoyunlu territories at their greatest extent in the fifteenth century. *Drawing by Farah Michel.*

The extent of the Aq Qoyunlus' contributions to the building is not clear. The verses inscribed in the roundel speak of a second construction, which could commonly refer to the restoration of a building. It is possible, however, that some of the fifteenth-century tilework once covering the exterior of the dome chamber derived from this phase of the building. The location of the roundel on what was originally the facade of the dome chamber also raises questions. As it stands, the roundel is high up on the wall, hardly legible from the ground (fig. 1.1). It is not uncommon to find messages of patronage, power, or protection inscribed in locations that would render them illegible.[27] But given the later history of constructions at the Mahan shrine, it is also possible that this roundel was moved to its current position from a more accessible spot on the facade.

This short, formerly unpublished and unidentified roundel inscription has significant implications for our understanding of the religious alliances of the Aq Qoyunlu dynasty. Throughout their history, the Aq Qoyunlus were key players in the configuration of regional and transregional politics, maneuvering between alliances and clashes with the Timurids, Mamluks, and Ottomans as well as their own direct competitors, the Qara Qoyunlus (lit. Black Sheep). They also allied with Venetians against the Ottomans over control of Mediterranean maritime trade.[28] Under Uzun Hasan (r. 1453–78), Yaʿqub Sultan's father, the Aq Qoyunlus saw themselves as an empire on par with the Mamluks of Egypt.[29] Uzun Hasan was the first Aq Qoyunlu ruler to declare himself a sultan, a title also adopted by his son, as attested by the roundel inscription on the facade of the Mahan mausoleum. Most importantly, under Uzun Hasan, the Aq Qoyunlus expanded their territories from Eastern Anatolia and the area known as ʿIraq-i ʿArab (Mesopotamia) eastward into ʿIraq-i ʿAjam (western Iran)—mainly Fars and Kerman, which were under Timurid and Qara Qoyunlu control (map 1.1).[30] In this light, the Aq Qoyunlu's presence in Mahan represents more than the routine patronage of a local ruler, for the Mahan shrine was located close to the easternmost boundary of these newly acquired territories, which Yaʿqub maintained in the face of revolts. As such, the portal marks not only the threshold of a sacred space but also the contour of the Aq Qoyunlu dynasty's holdings in the Iranian plateau.

While a restoration campaign might have been needed by the second half of the fifteenth century, another factor behind the Aq Qoyunlus' intervention in the Mahan shrine could relate to their rival Turkmen confederation, the Qara Qoyunlus. The latter are known to have had an established relationship with the Neʿmatullahis, strengthened through intermarriages with the Sufi family and possibly the patronage of another Neʿmatullahi khanaqah complex in Taft, as will be discussed in chapter 3.[31] After their defeat by the Aq Qoyunlus, a faction of the Qara Qoyunlu tribe migrated to the Deccan, where they eventually established the Qutb Shahi Sultanate (r. 1518–1678) after the disintegration of the Bahmanids. Their connections with the Neʿmatullahis, who by then had a strong presence in the Deccan, must have helped their cause.[32] In fact, in Neʿmatullahi hagiographic traditions, one of Shah Neʿmatullah's descendants, Naʿim al-din Neʿmatullah II, is said to have predicted their rule in the Deccan.[33] While we do not have any hard evidence that this intricate network of relationships played a role in the Aq Qoyunlus' patronage at Mahan, it is plausible to see a subtle statement of rivalry between the two dynasties, the Aq Qoyunlus and the Qara Qoyunlus, projected onto the two different Neʿmatullahi centers in Mahan and Taft, which themselves had a convoluted relationship with one another.[34]

The significance of the Aq Qoyunlu roundel also lies in the new paths of research that it opens into the history of the dynasty and its religious alignments or beliefs at the time. Uzun Hasan is known for his maintenance of relations with a range of Sufi networks such as the Khalwatis, Kubravis, Naqshbandis, and Safavis, evident in the marriage of his daughter to his nephew Haydar, the head of the Safaviyya Sufis in Ardabil from which the Safavid dynasty in the sixteenth century originated.[35] While the Aq Qoyunlus' relationship with the Neʿmatullahis has been acknowledged briefly in past literature, the roundel at Mahan offers a unique piece of material evidence for their investment in this relationship—one that is accessible to us only through the study of architecture.[36] This epigraphic source is even more significant for its association with Yaʿqub, who, compared to his father, Uzun Hasan, is usually characterized as having less interest in popular religion and Sufism.[37] As such, the inscription roundel in Mahan highlights how visual sources can facilitate a more nuanced rethinking of histories of religious sentiments and their entanglements with politics.

IV. Growth and Concealment

The next major phase in the evolution of the portal was the addition of the recitation hall to the dome chamber in the late sixteenth century. This moment left several traces on the portal and necessitated a great deal of rearrangement. Like a palimpsest, the portal took on new life within its transformed surroundings while some of its older layers were hidden. In this section, I briefly attend to what was concealed before turning to the new segments added in the sixteenth century.

The recitation hall covered most of the western side of the dome chamber's exterior wall up to the point that matches the chamber's zone of transition on the inside (figs. 1.11 and 1.12). This means that the exterior decorations of the dome chamber on most of these sections are no longer visible to visitors of the shrine. Based on the remaining traces—which to my knowledge can be found in two places at the shrine—it is evident that these decorations included exquisite mosaic tiles in a style familiar from the exterior of other significant monuments in the fourteenth and fifteenth centuries.

The first place where traces of this hidden fifteenth-century tilework can be found is at the portal itself. Remnants of extensive tilework that likely covered large borders around the entrance are revealed through a hole opened in the gap between the walls of the recitation hall and the dome chamber during a

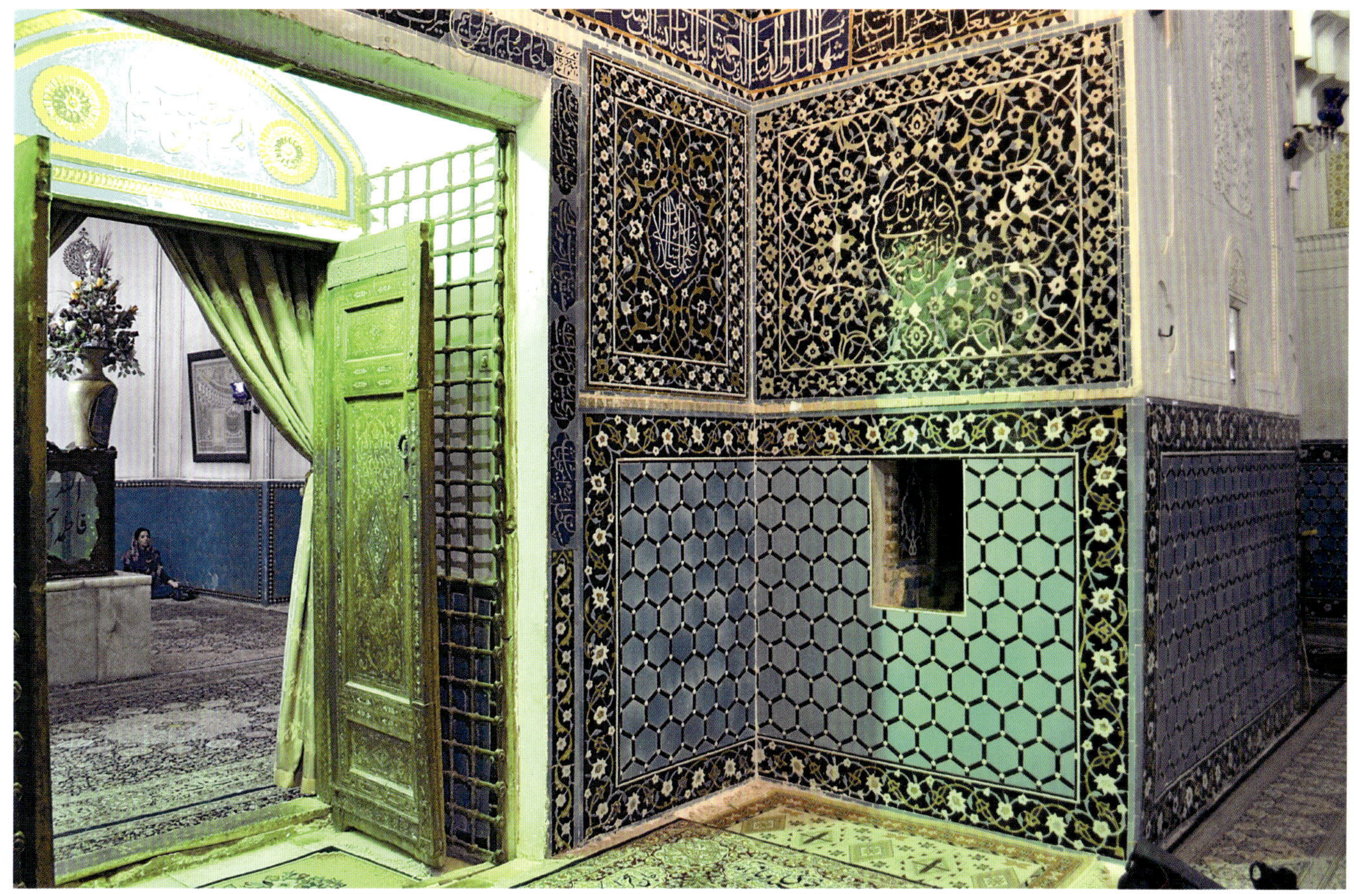

FIGURE 1.19. The hole opened into the wall of the mausoleum at Mahan with remnants of fifteenth-century tilework. *Photograph by author, 2013.*

restoration campaign at the shrine (fig. 1.19). The reasons for concealing the original outer wall of the dome chamber seem to have been structural. The annexed monumental recitation hall consists of five vaults (fig. 1.5). For these vaults to fulfill their load-bearing function without threatening the stability of the dome itself, the walls had to be reinforced at the meeting point of the facade of the dome chamber and the vaults. This is how the distance between the original facade of the dome chamber and the current wall of the recitation hall was created (fig. 1.20).

Looking through the hole gives us a glimpse of an earlier state of the building. In what remains, three different sections of mosaic faience can be recognized (fig. 1.21). The lowest section is the former dado of the facade, made up of white and turquoise glazed bricks. Above the dado, the segment farther from the portal includes mosaic tiles in light blue, white, black, and amber, arranged in a design comprising six- and twelve-pointed stars and hexagons, a versatile arrangement adaptable to any architectural surface on both the exterior and the interior. Another vertical segment hidden within this same compartment features stylized floral designs, including a lotus that adds green to the color palette mentioned above. Comparative examples, which indicate the stature of the Mahan dome chamber, include elements of such significant, roughly

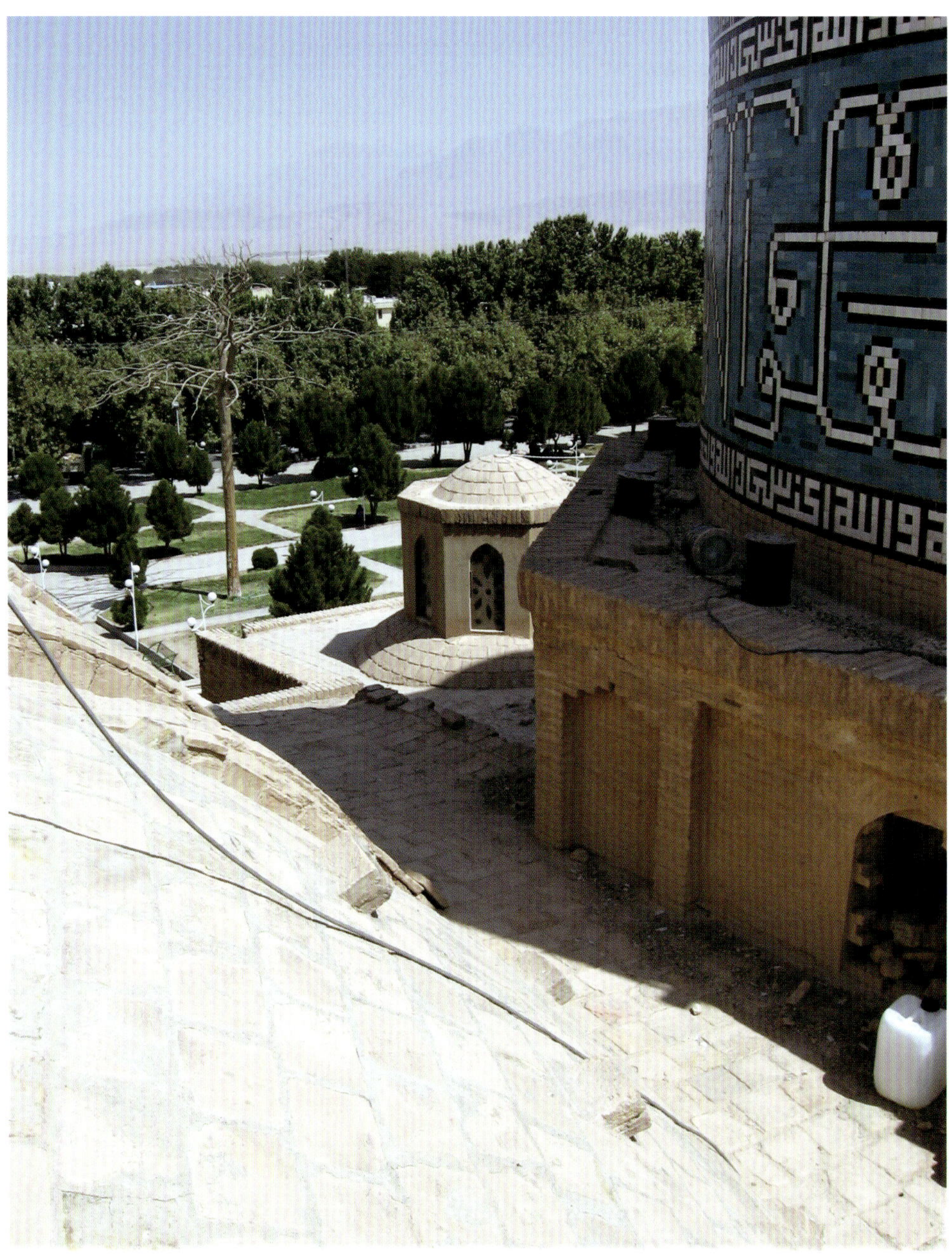

FIGURE 1.20. View from the roof of the recitation hall showing the distance between the former facade of the dome chamber and the beginning of the hall's vaults. *Photograph by author, 2012.*

contemporary monuments as the Jamiᶜ mosque of Yazd, the *mihrab* (prayer niche) of the Mir Chaqmaq Mosque also in Yazd, and the design and colors on the star-shaped fragments from the complex of Gowharshad in Herat, to name just a few (figs. 1.22–1.24).[38]

While this level of decoration is to be expected in a prominent segment alongside the portal of a mausoleum, hidden surviving tilework elsewhere on the original facade of the Mahan dome chamber gives a sense of the sheer extent of decoration and the prestige of the building. The second area where segments of hidden tiles can be seen is accessed through the roof of

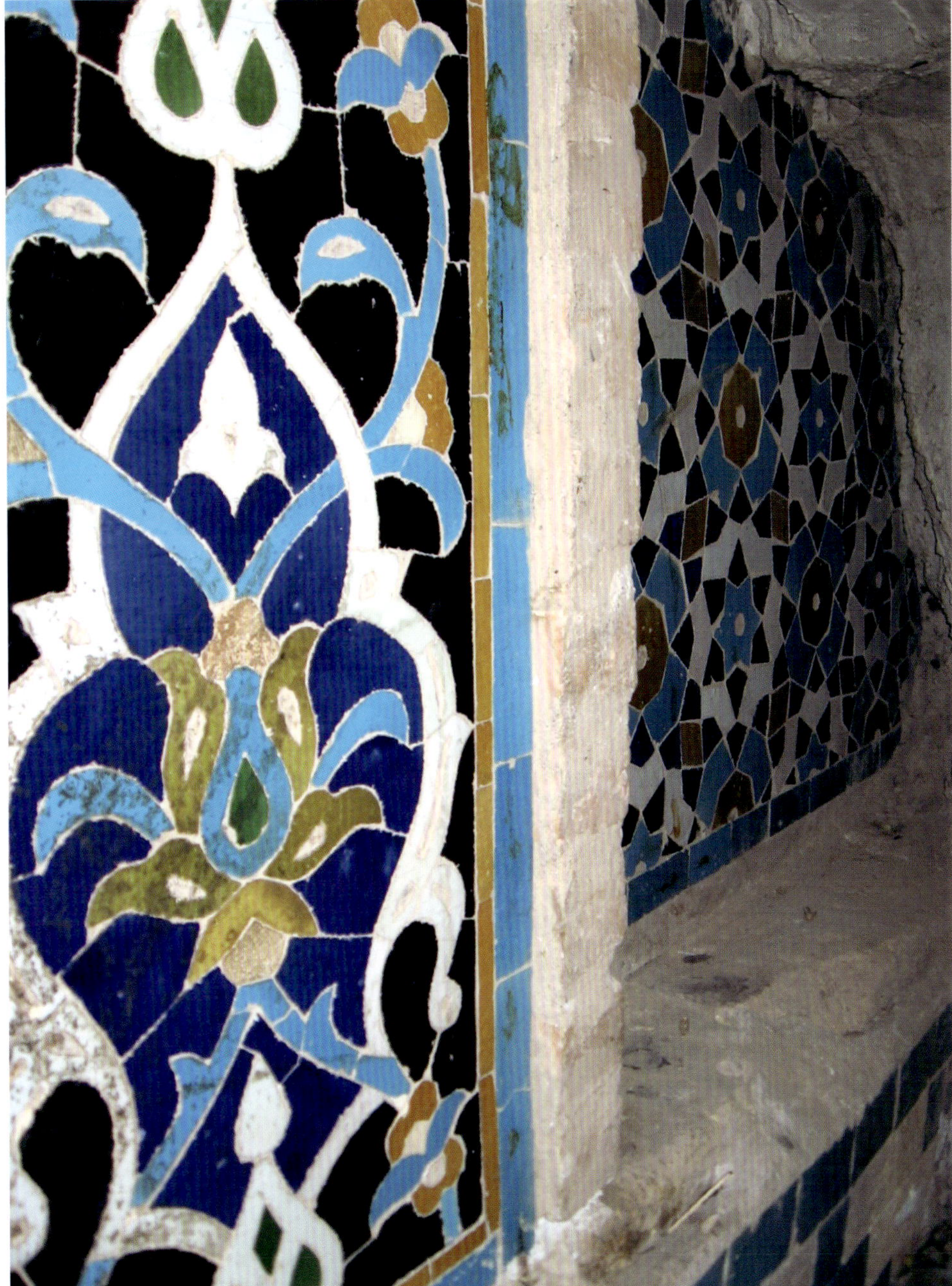

FIGURE 1.21. Remnants of fifteenth-century tilework seen through the hole opened into the portal's side wall at the shrine at Mahan. *Photograph by author, 2012.*

the post-Safavid one-story vaulted halls (*riwaq*s) that wrap around the dome chamber.[39] On the spot where these one-story riwaqs meet the two-story recitation hall at the corner of the chamber, a small patch of tilework is still attached to what was once the outer surface of the domed mausoleum (fig. 1.25). It consists of small pieces of white, amber, and dark and light-blue tiles arranged in a pattern of six-pointed stars, a common configuration covering the exterior of transition zones in architecture from the Timurid period and beyond. We do not know exactly how much of the facade of the mausoleum was covered in tiles. Yet these small traces indicate that the exterior decoration

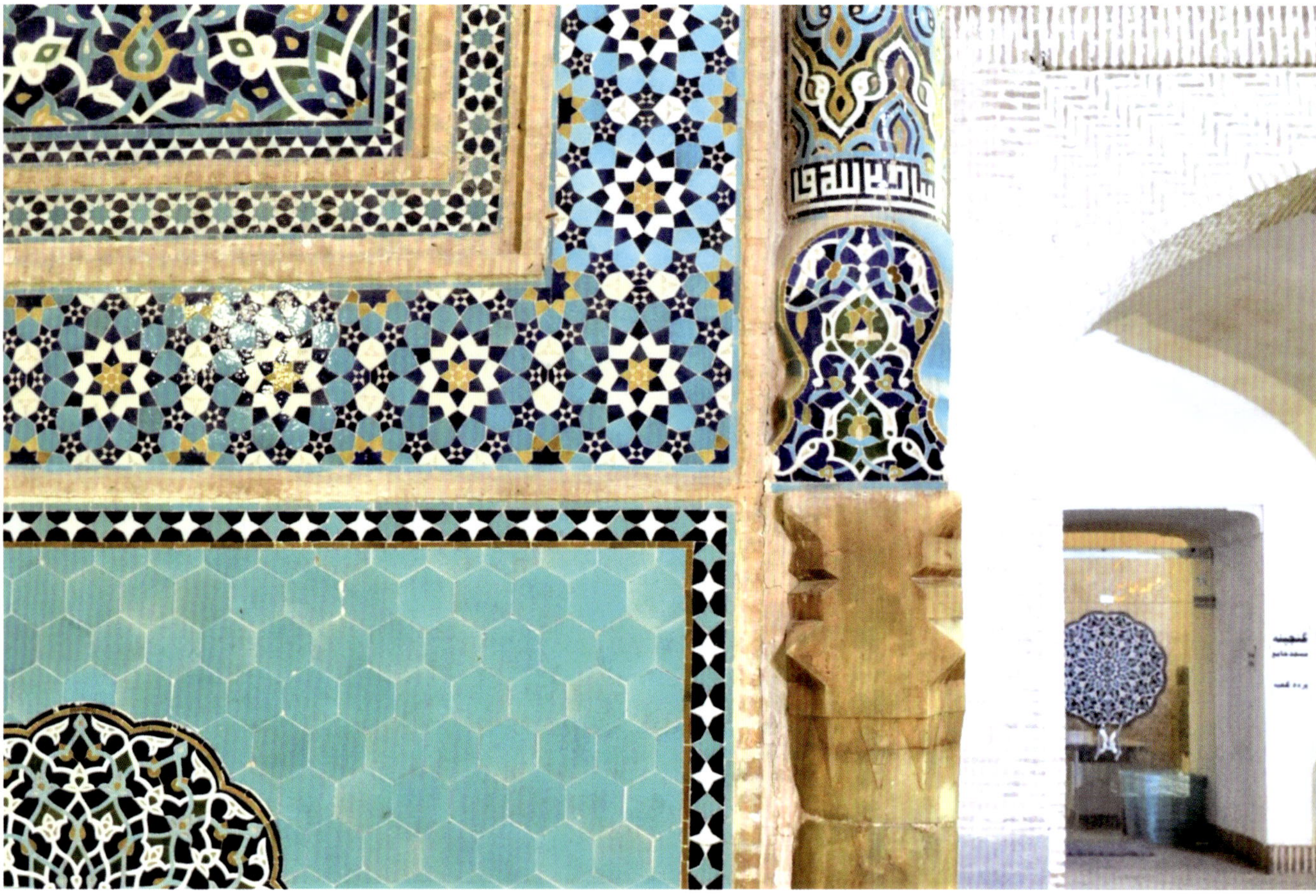

ABOVE, FIGURE 1.22.
Detail of tilework at the Friday mosque of Yazd, similar to configurations of original tiles above the dadoes at the Mahan portal. *Photograph by author, 2014.*

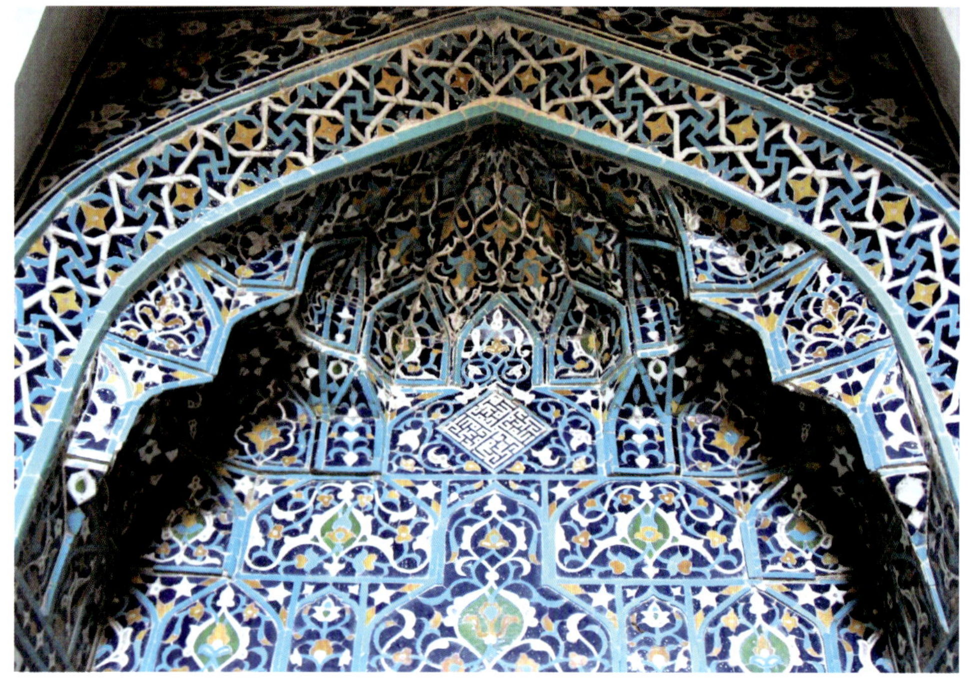

RIGHT, FIGURE 1.23.
Detail of tilework at the mihrab of Mir Chaqmaq Mosque in Yazd, completed 1436–37. *Photograph by author, 2012.*

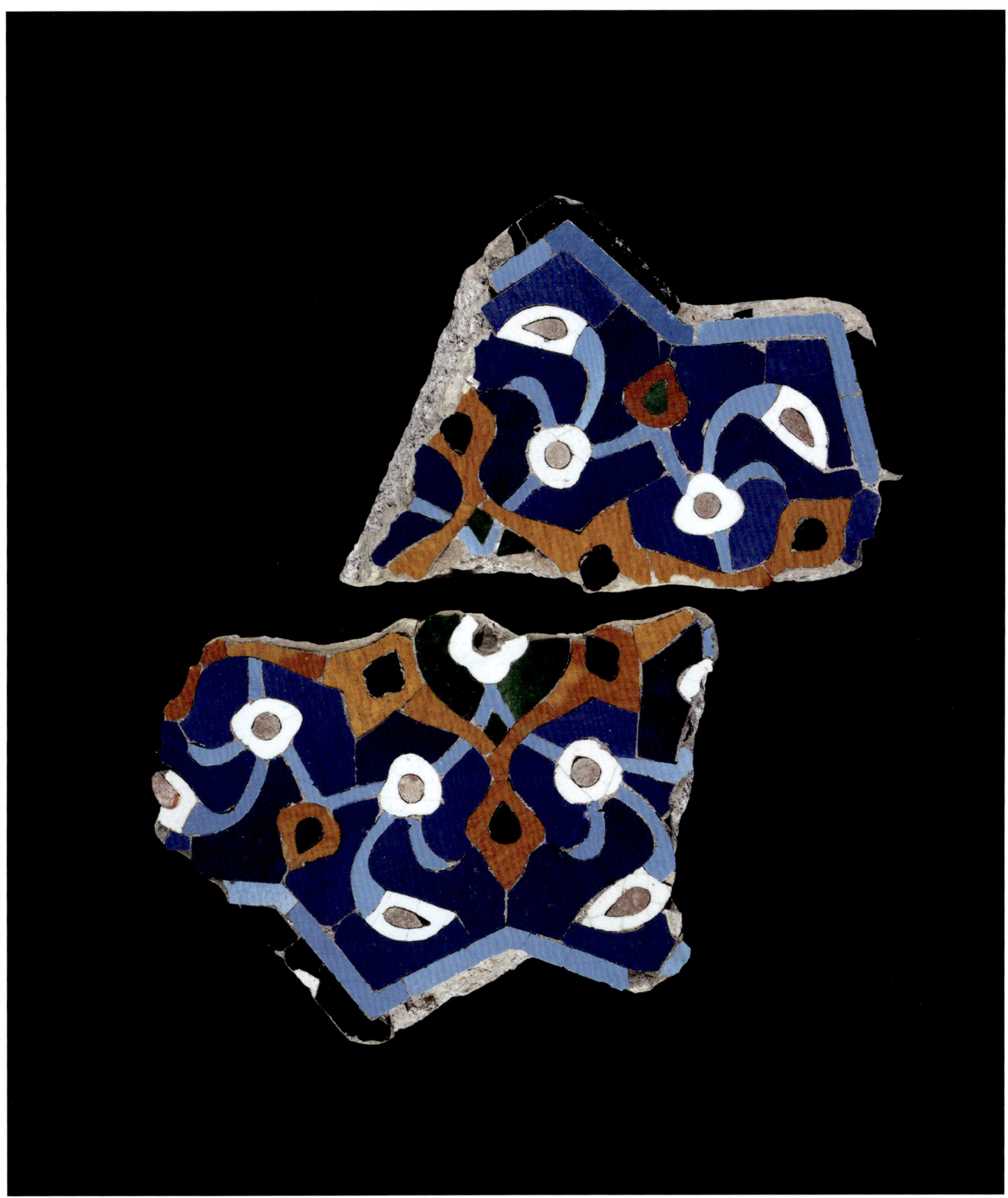

FIGURE 1.24. Fragments of a twelve-pointed star tile from the Gowharshad complex, Herat, early fifteenth century. *Collected by Colonel Charles Edward Yate after the destruction of the complex's minarets in in 1885 and transferred to the British Museum from the Quetta Museum in 1907. © The Trustees of the British Museum, 1907, 1011.1.*

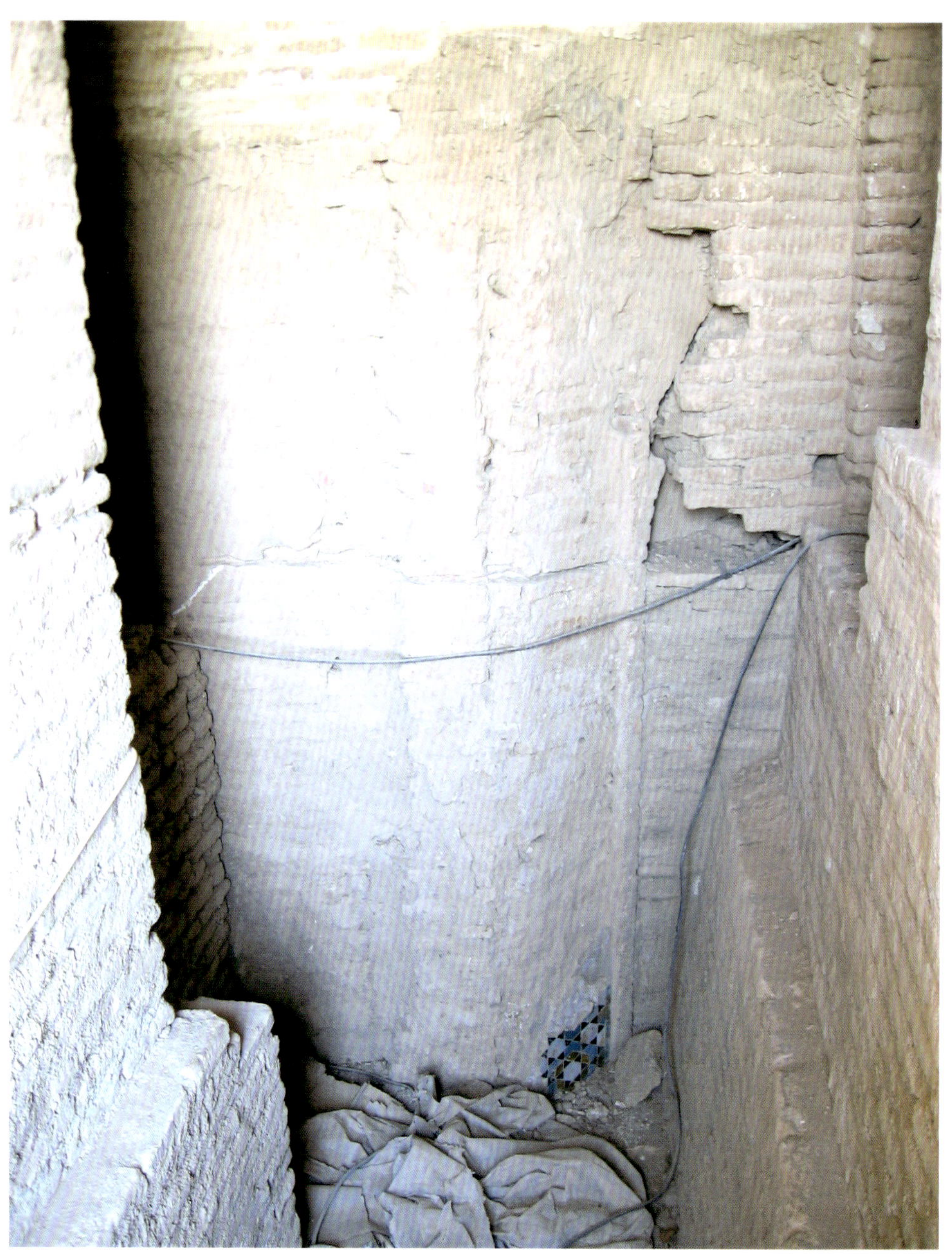

FIGURE 1.25. Fragments of fifteenth-century mosaic tilework on the original facade of the dome chamber in Mahan accessed through the roof. *Photograph by author, 2012.*

program extended far beyond the portal itself.[40] Given the height of this spot on the exterior vis-à-vis the minute intricacy of the tiles, the extant fragment suggests a high level of investment from either Bahmanid or Aq Qoyunlu patronage.

V. Exhibiting Architectural Genealogies

The enlargement of the Mahan shrine during the Safavid period was a moment of institutional transformation for the Neʿmatullahis. The expansion turned the single funerary chamber into a grand monumental building and brought a stronger sense of orientation to the whole complex, comparable to other

Safavid expansions of existing sites such as the shrine of Shaykh Safi al-din at Ardabil.[41] This meant that the shrine at Mahan could accommodate travelers, pilgrims, and assemblies on a far greater scale than before. These changes reflect the prominent social and political roles that the Neᶜmatullahis played in Safavid Iran: their intermarriages with the royal family and their appointments to powerful positions in government administration.

While concealing some earlier layers of the portal, the annexation of the recitation hall involved a great deal of new additions as well as several rearrangements necessitated by the conversion of the exterior of the dome chamber into an interior surface. In many ways, these changes simultaneously speak to and distinguish themselves from the earlier layers of the portal, turning it into a stage where an architectural genealogy spanning over a century and a half unravels before our eyes.

One such dialogue can be seen in the relation of an inscribed roundel above the doorway, located to the left of the Aq Qoyunlu roundel discussed earlier (fig. 1.18). The line of poetry inscribed on this new roundel contains the date of the Safavid expansion as 998/1590 (app. 1.5.b).

> [It was] nine hundred and ninety-eight [years] after *hijra*
> (journey of the Prophet),
> that this rawza of the Sayyid was constructed anew.

In its overall shape, location, and content, the new roundel roughly mirrors the Aq Qoyunlu precedent, which similarly documents the date of a restoration campaign in verse. Yet the designers of the hall make it clear to us that the two do not belong to the same construction phase. The inscription in the Safavid-era roundel is in the cursive *nastaᶜliq*, a script that had not come into full use in architecture when the Aq Qoyunlu roundel was executed. More obvious is the use of different materials: in contrast to the polychrome mosaic tiles in the Aq Qoyunlu roundel, the Safavid inscription is painted in black against the white plaster covering the walls.[42] The white plaster here, which was added to turn the exterior surface of the mausoleum into the interior of the recitation hall, becomes an important agent: while the new inscription is written over it, the plaster refrains from covering the Aq Qoyunlu roundel, intentionally revealing a glimpse of what lies beneath.

Similar patterns of intentional distinction and mirroring can be observed around the fifteenth-century foundation inscription documenting the Bahmanids' patronage. I mentioned in the previous section that, as a result of the addition of the hall, the side walls of the portal had to be doubled. This created additional spaces at both the beginning and the end of the foundation inscription, which followed the U shape of the recessed entrance niche within the portal (fig. 1.19). To cover this added length, two small panels in a slightly different style were added to the two ends of the fifteenth-century inscription band (figs. 1.26 and 1.27). The content of these two new sections accords with the hypothesis that they were added at a later date. They do not contain any essential information about the patrons or the date of the construction but

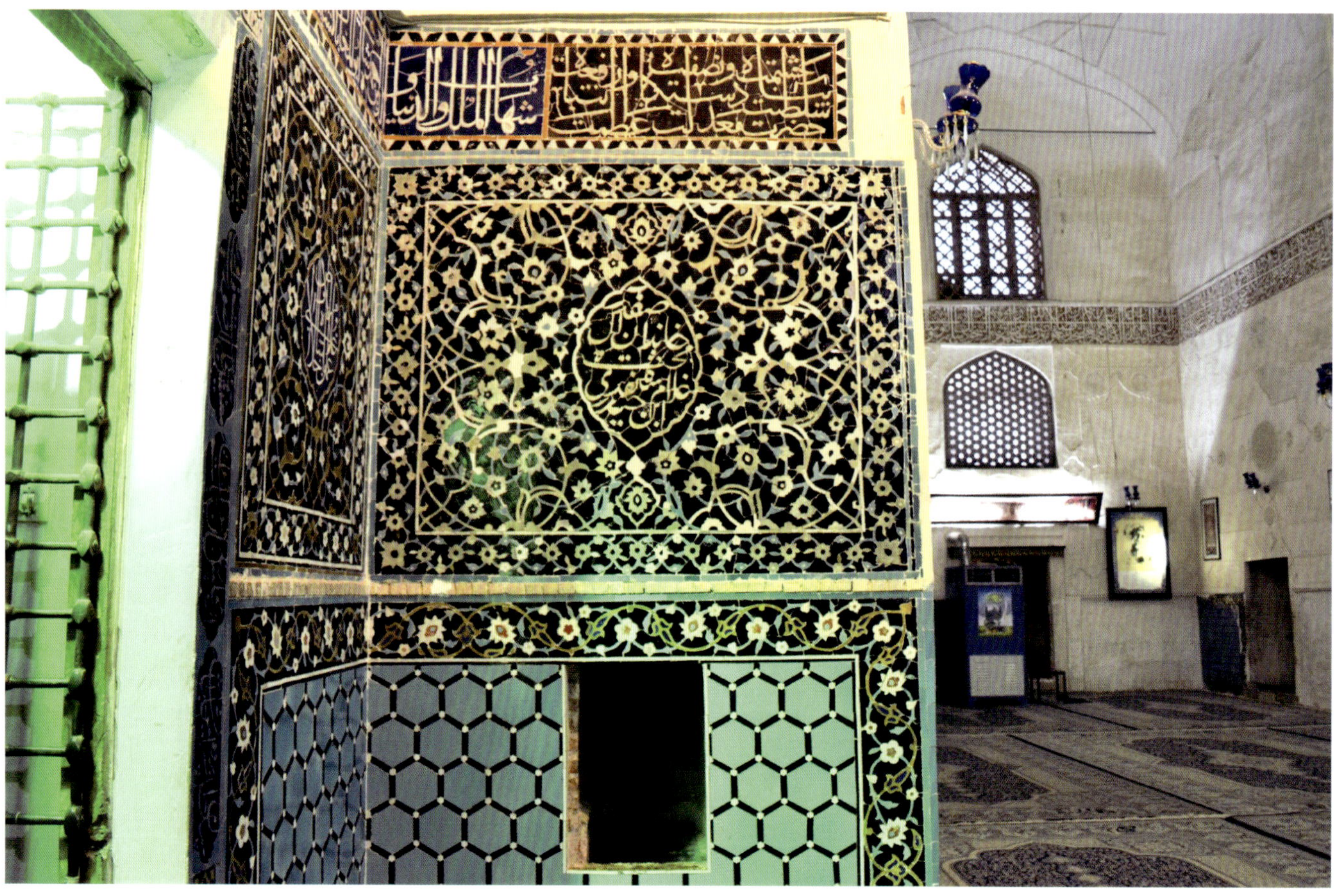

FIGURE 1.26. Safavid-era inscribed tiles added to the beginning of the foundation inscription on the western portal of the dome chamber in Mahan (upper register of photo). *Photograph by author, 2013.*

simply add eulogizing titles for Ahmad Shah, the Prophet Muhammad, and the auspiciousness of the hijra year that marked the completion of the foundation inscription (app. 1.2.a–c).

The words on these newer panels are written in a thuluth script that is close to the style and proportions of the fifteenth-century panels, although they are executed in a relatively smaller size and the elongations are more exaggerated. The color palette and design of the background remind us that despite these similarities, we are looking at two works executed by different people at different times: the inscriptions are in pastel yellow instead of white, the background is black instead of dark blue, and the floral ornaments dotting the black background at the end—which match those in the Safavid-era panels below them—manifest a change of style from the fifteenth-century panel. A narrow string of amber tiles that once marked the outer frame of the fifteenth-century panel now stands as a subtle yet decisive marker that defines a boundary between the old and the new.

A similar strategy toward the framing of the old within the new can also be seen across the hall, in the other foundation inscription related to the Safavid-era additions (fig. 1.16). Repeating the date 998/1590 recorded on the plaster

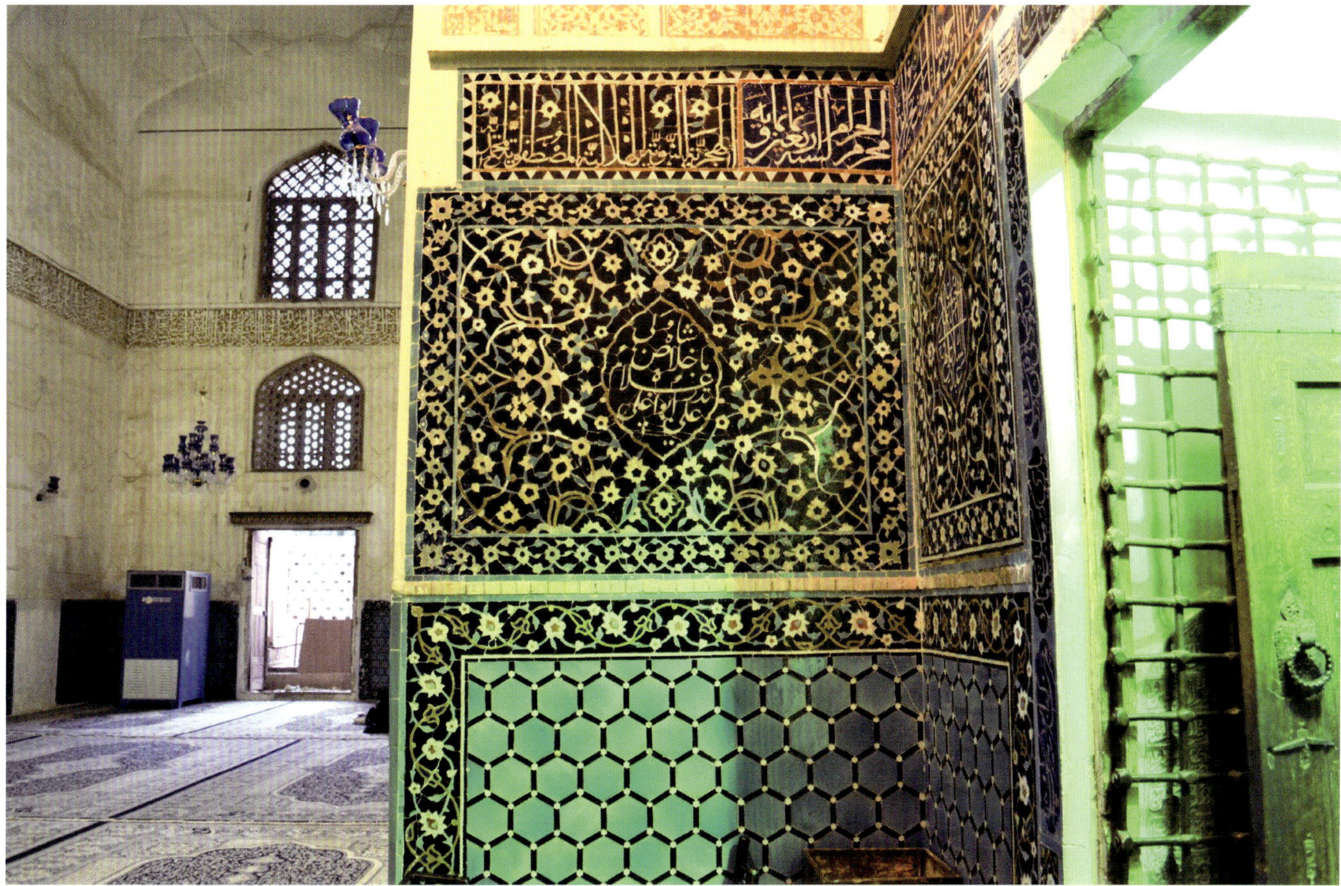

FIGURE 1.27. Safavid-era inscribed tiles added to the end of the foundation inscription on the western portal of the dome chamber in Mahan (upper register of photo). *Photograph by author, 2013.*

roundel above the fifteenth-century portal, this inscription band contains the name of the governor of Kerman and Baluchistan, Bektash Khan, who patronized the new construction, as well as the Safavid ruler Shah ʿAbbas I, under whom these expansions materialized (app. 1.3.a).

This inscription panel, which runs across the recessed arched entrance to the adjacent courtyard, also contains two different segments from two historical periods and building campaigns. The larger central part that evokes the length as well as the technique and overall color palette of the fifteenth-century panel across the hall contains the date and names of patrons of the Safavid-era construction. Added to each end of it are sections in a visibly different style that were added in the Qajar period in relation to another restoration campaign and document the date 1300/1882–83 and the name of the ruler, Nasir al-din Shah (r. 1848–69) (fig. 1.28 and app. 1.3.b). The Qajar sections of the panel bear inscriptions in nastaʿliq of two different sizes, written in white against an elaborate background of vegetal motifs, with scrolls in a sharp yellow and pink. The two sections of the panel engage in dialogue not only with one another but also with the corresponding sections of the foundation inscription across the hall. Beyond juxtaposing the old and the

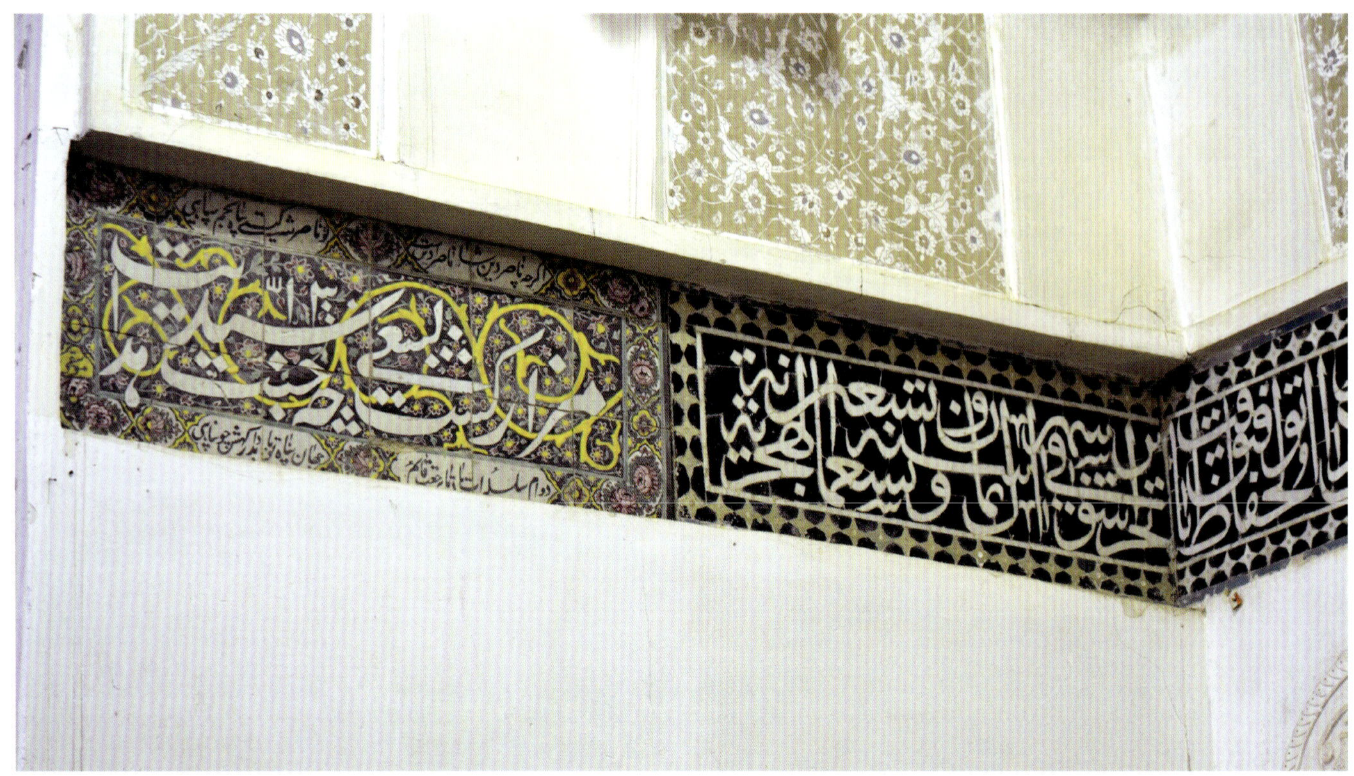

FIGURE 1.28. Qajar-era inscribed tiles (*left*) juxtaposed with the Safavid-era foundation inscription (*right*) opposite the western portal of the dome chamber in Mahan. *Photograph by author, 2018.*

new, these panels show how the makers of these segments decided to use the new to preserve, alter, and showcase their architectural predecessor in distinctive ways.

Returning to the portal of the fifteenth-century mausoleum, right below the foundation inscription, four square panels with vegetal motifs and signatures tie the different segments of the portal together (fig. 1.1). All four panels were added during or after the construction of the recitation hall and feature scrolling vegetal motifs in the same style and colors as the Safavid-era segments added to the foundation inscription above them. In the middle of each, there is a lobed cartouche bearing the signature of craftspeople and possibly also patrons responsible for the (re)construction of the portal and the recitation hall. The medallions in the middle of the panels immediately to the right and left of the doorway are inscribed in thuluth and contain the name ʿAbd al-Salam Hasan b. ʿAli Herawi, his title denoting an association with the city of Herat, an important center of art making under the Timurids and Safavids (fig. 0.2 and app. 1.6.a). His name also appears inside a roundel under the ceiling at the far north of the recitation hall (fig. 1.29). There, his titles include the words *ustad* (master) and *kashi-tarash* (tile-maker), telling us a bit more about his primary skills and status (app. 1.4.b).

The two similar square panels on the side walls of the recessed section of the portal include lobed cartouches that provide us with two more names: Shah Naqdi b. Haydar (right side), probably a patron for a restoration campaign, and a certain ʿAli Abu Ughli (left side) (figs. 1.26 and 1.27 and app. 1.6.b).[43] The

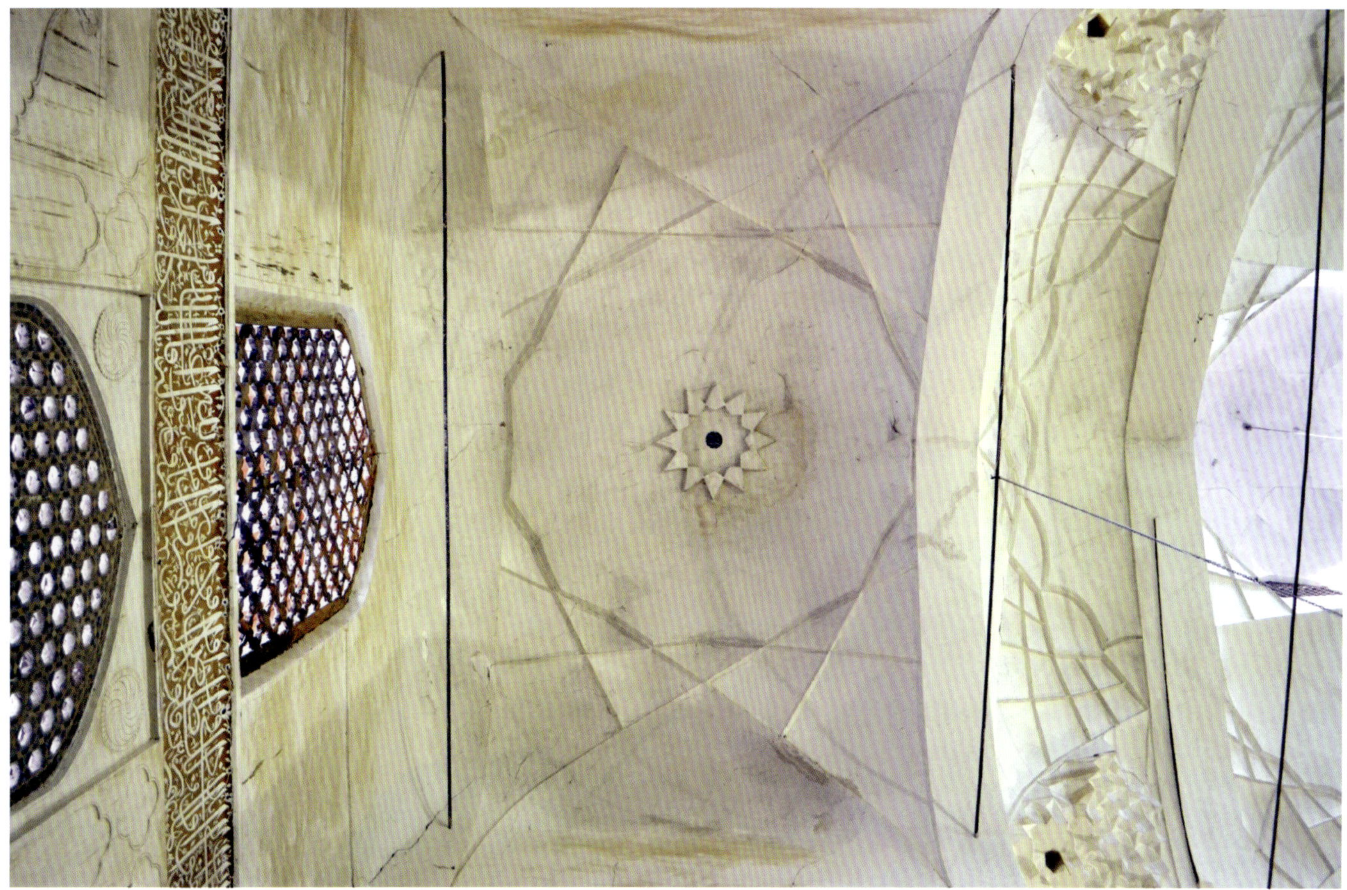

FIGURE 1.29. View toward the ceiling under the northernmost vault of the recitation hall at the shrine at Mahan. The signature of tile worker ʿAbd al-Salam is located in the center of the twelve-pointed star. *Photograph by author, 2014.*

latter is likely the same Abu Ughli whose name appears as a patron, written in small script on the corner of another narrow band of inscription that frames the mausoleum's door and contains the epigraph of this chapter, the poem by Shah Neʿmatullah Vali (fig. 1.30 and app. 1.6.c). The density of identities exhibited through this multiplicity of signatures reminds us of the significance of portals as crucial markers of sacred space, signaled by an amalgamation of styles and human skills.

Executed in cursive nastaʿliq script and mosaic faience technique, the poetic inscription band that borders the door is inscribed in light blue and arranged in cartouches of alternating dark-blue and black background, interrupted in the corners by two white squares bearing the signature.[44] While it has been suggested that this poetic inscription was part of the original portal and thus dates back to 1436, the earliest appearance of the nastaʿliq script on architecture dates only to the last decades of the fifteenth century. The style of the nastaʿliq at the portal exhibits cursivity and proportions that are usually associated with a mature nastaʿliq and could not date earlier than the late fifteenth or early sixteenth century.[45] In all likelihood, the poetic inscription band was added to the portal with the other Safavid-era segments—especially likely given the possibility that Abu Ughli, whose name appears on the

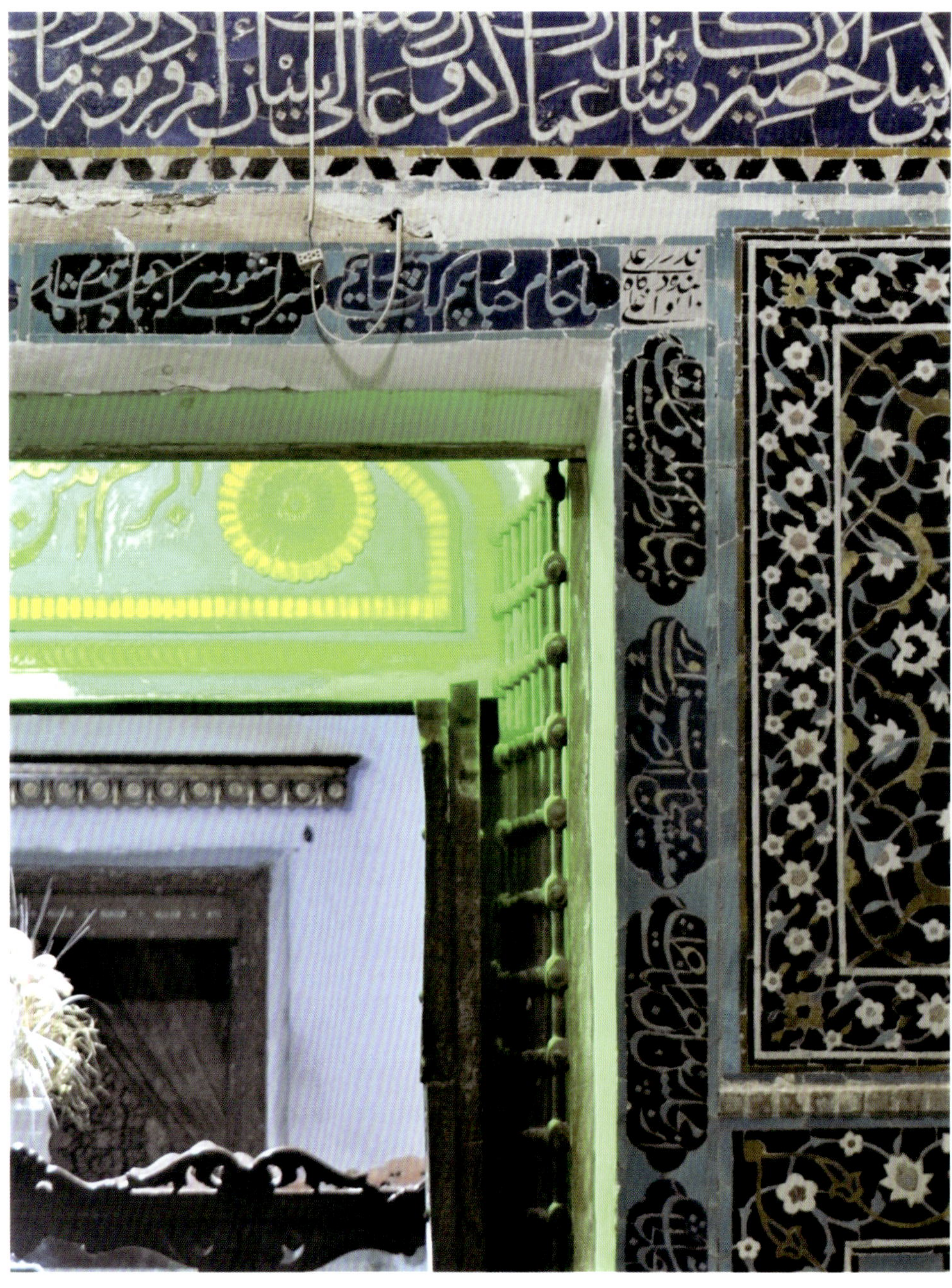

FIGURE 1.30. Detail of the front view of the western portal at Mahan, showing part of the narrow band of inscription containing poetry by Shah Neʿmatullah. *Photograph by author, 2018.*

Safavid-era panel, is the same as the ʿAli Abu Ughli inscribed in the nastaʿliq band of poetry.

The location of this band corresponds to a similar inscription at the northern entrance of the dome chamber, the only other side with a surviving inscription (fig. 1.31). Like its counterpart on the western entrance, the northern band has the same width, frames the door above the dadoes, and contains verses from Shah Neʿmatullah's poetry, with the difference that the north entrance is inscribed in the thuluth script (compare figs. 1.30 and 1.32). The thuluth script here bears enough similarities to the main part of the foundation inscription on the western portal—notwithstanding differences in size and width—to

FACING, FIGURE 1.31. Northern entrance of the fifteenth-century dome chamber in Mahan. *Photograph by author, 2018.*

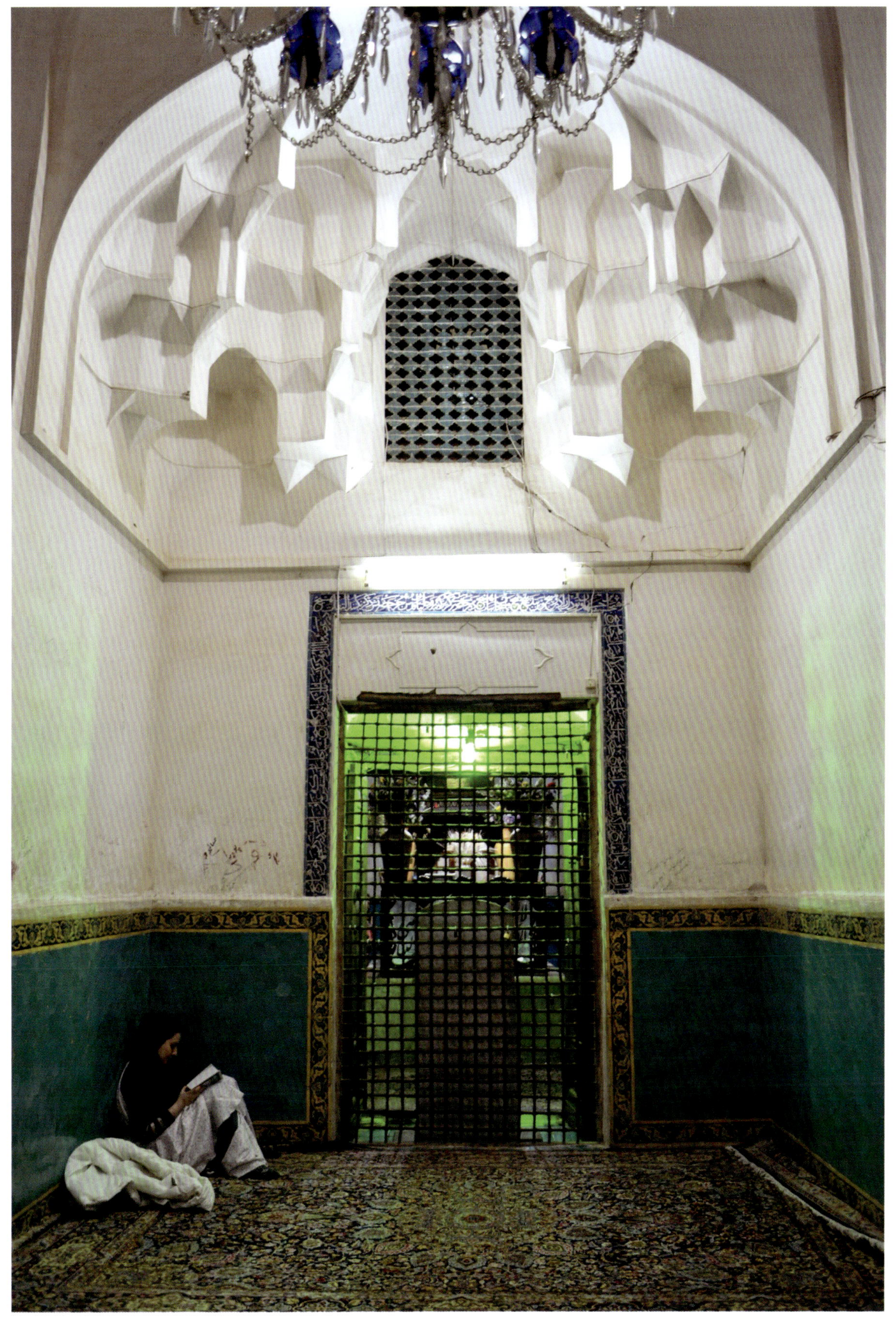

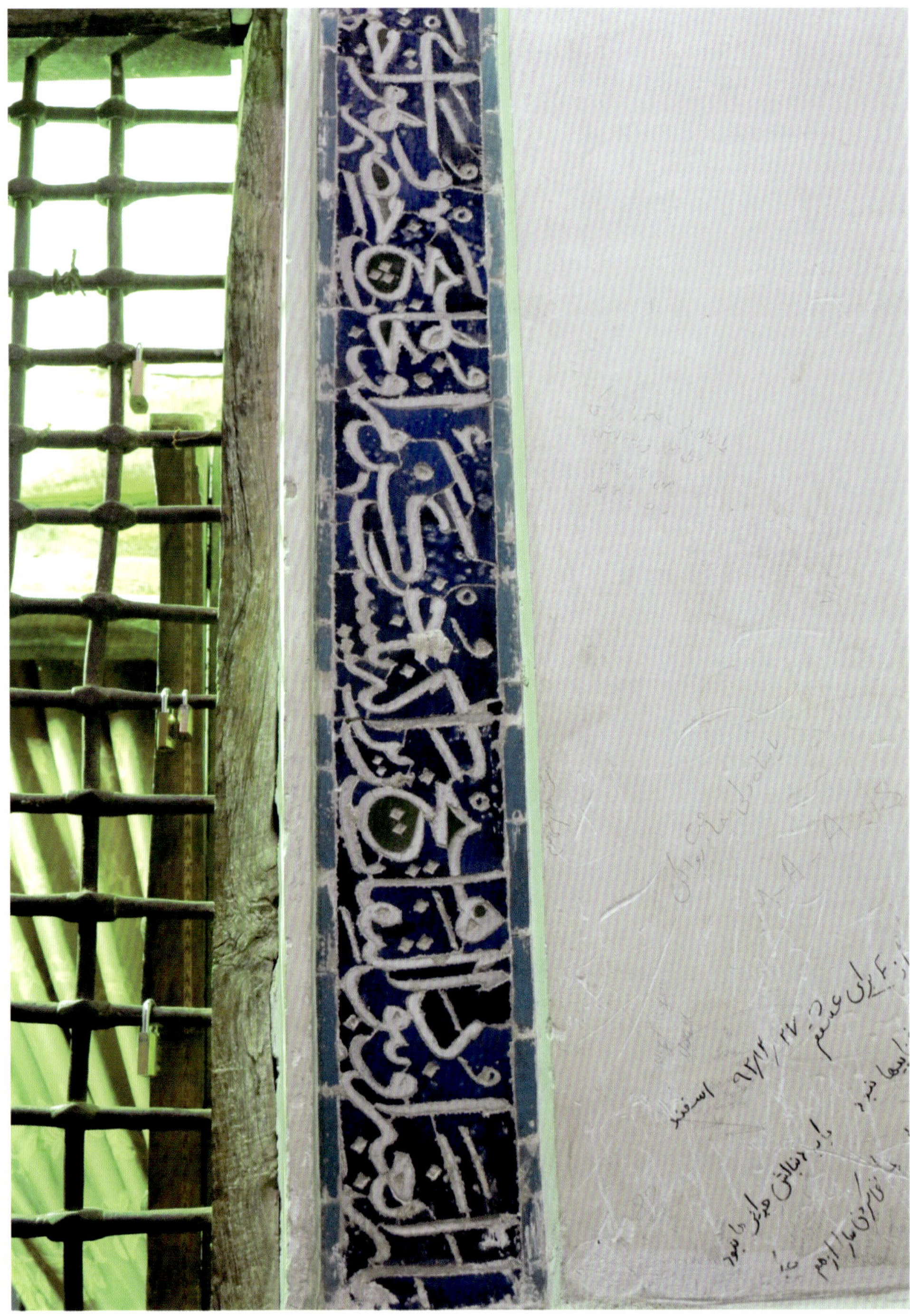

FIGURE 1.32. Detail of the inscription band around the northern entrance of the dome chamber in Mahan. *Photograph by author, 2014.*

assume that they both originated from the same workshop and building campaign (compare figs. 1.32 and 1.15). As in the foundation inscription, the maker has playfully filled the looped letters of the poem in a different color—here in green—with an emphasis on the rhyming word *heech*, meaning "nothing" or "annihilation" in Persian.[46]

It is possible that all four sides of the dome chamber originally had similar inscription bands containing poems by Shah Neʿmatullah and that the western poetic inscription was replaced by a new one in nastaʿliq during the Safavid-era expansion. Another possibility is that the western portal, which was originally the main entrance, contained the poetic inscription in thuluth, and the latter was moved to the northern side with the addition of the new nastaʿliq band in the late sixteenth century. The reasons for the present arrangement are uncertain based on extant evidence. However, it is important to note that the two poems, both *ghazal*s (lyric poems) by Shah Neʿmatullah, while overlapping around themes of divine love and annihilation (common tropes in Sufi poetry), bear significant differences with regard to their relevance for a funerary context.

The poem on the northern facade of the dome chamber deals with themes of divine love, salvation, and the annihilation of the self (app. 1.1.b).[47] The verses emphasize that God is the only refuge, the only object worthy of attention, and that divine union is the ultimate goal of the Sufi. By comparison, this world amounts to nothing (heech).

The poem on the western portal, on the other hand, starts as follows (app. 1.1.a):

> Where has the sultan of the veiled quarters of [our] tavern gone?
> Why did he leave the assembly of the drunken [Sufis] (*rindan*)?
> His essence is here, [even] with his appearance (*surat*) gone,
> He has not passed into annihilation (*fana*), he is [just] hidden from sight.[48]

Compared to the verses on the northern entrance, these lines grapple with more overtly eschatological themes of death, lamentation, and eternal presence. All of these themes are introduced immediately in the first two couplets of the poem, thus engaging directly with the funerary purpose of the structure for which the portal acts as a threshold. While the word *heech*, which marks the end of each couplet in the northern portal, is an apt choice of terminology for a Sufi shrine and a funerary context, the concept of annihilation is treated differently on the western panel. There, annihilation (fana) has a kind of redemptive quality: the absence is negated in favor of the beloved's eternal, albeit invisible, presence.

A sense of collective lamentation for the departure of the Sufi is also conveyed in verses on the western portal, as if giving voice to the disciples left behind. The collective sentiment could also be responding to the enlargement of the shrine in the sixteenth century, complementing the expanded ritual usage of the site with the addition of the vaulted hall. If the western poetic inscription in fact replaced the one now at the north entrance, one reason for the change could be the sharpening of this commemorative message. But the contrasts between the two poems also speak to broader tensions and entanglements between materiality and transcendence. If the northern portal inscriptions reduce everything in this world to nothingness, the western portal poem morphs the transcendence of death into presence. In opting for these verses, the sixteenth-century makers of the portal brought more specificity to the relationship between poetry and architecture. By acknowledging the power inherent "here" at the threshold of the sepulchre, they in effect justify the remaking and redefining of the space through their poetic choices.

VI. Beyond the Portal

Untangling the architectural genealogies embedded in the portal, we arrive at the meeting point of a whole network of relationships—synchronic and diachronic, micro and macro, local and transregional—that will be explored in the following chapters. On one level, we see how a combination of local, regional, and transregional artistic skills and financial resources established an architectural canvas on which later Sufis and dynasties left their marks in a process of periodic rearrangement and renewal. On another level, the lineages that the portal displays and conceals alert us not only to the practice of preserving genealogies but also to subtle strategies of tweaking the architectural history of the site and bending it toward contemporary needs. Detail after detail, the portal's layers show us how artists working under various dynasties placed themselves, and by extension their patrons, at the end of a line of artistic succession rather than attempting to set themselves up as the sole or even principal proprietors.

On a broader level, these minute architectural details tell a history of empires and political transition. The reordering of the portal stands as an emblem of the new order that each government brought into place. Each of these transitions was stamped by a local or dynastic ruler: the Bahmanids of the Deccan, the Aq Qoyunlus, Kerman's governor Bektash Khan, and the Safavid ruler Shah ʿAbbas. The portal was a space where entanglements between the court and the Sufi network took shape—where the politics of sacred patronage were constructed, inscribed, and depicted yet also subordinated to popular piety and veneration. Such dynamics continue into the contemporary life of the portal as a restless object, pulled in different religiopolitical directions. An annual tradition at the portal is the installment of temporary banners that commemorate the martyrdom of the third Shiʿa Imam (fig. 1.33). These are by no means uncommon in shrines around Iran, but they are particularly pointed in Mahan due to the strained relationship between the shrine and the state. At a time when the activities of the Neʿmatullahis are banned by the government, the official narrative promotes the shrine through Shah Neʿmatullah's genealogy as a descendant of the seventh Shiʿa Imam—in other words, as a Twelver Shiʿa site of pilgrimage rather than the shrine of a Sufi saint with a robust following in Iran and across the world.

By telling these stories, the layers of the portal also unwind some aspects of the politics of center and periphery in the early modern period. Kerman and Yazd, in the central-south regions of modern-day Iran, were centers of the Sufi network's activity but were ruled indirectly by local governors or princes appointed by the Timurids, Turkmen dynasties, and Safavids. As a result of this arrangement, local rulers constantly needed to define and redefine themselves with or against the centers of power—a process in which Sufis' religiopolitical authority had an important intermediary role to play. Small towns

FACING, FIGURE 1.33.
Western portal of the mausoleum at Mahan.
Photograph by author, 2014.

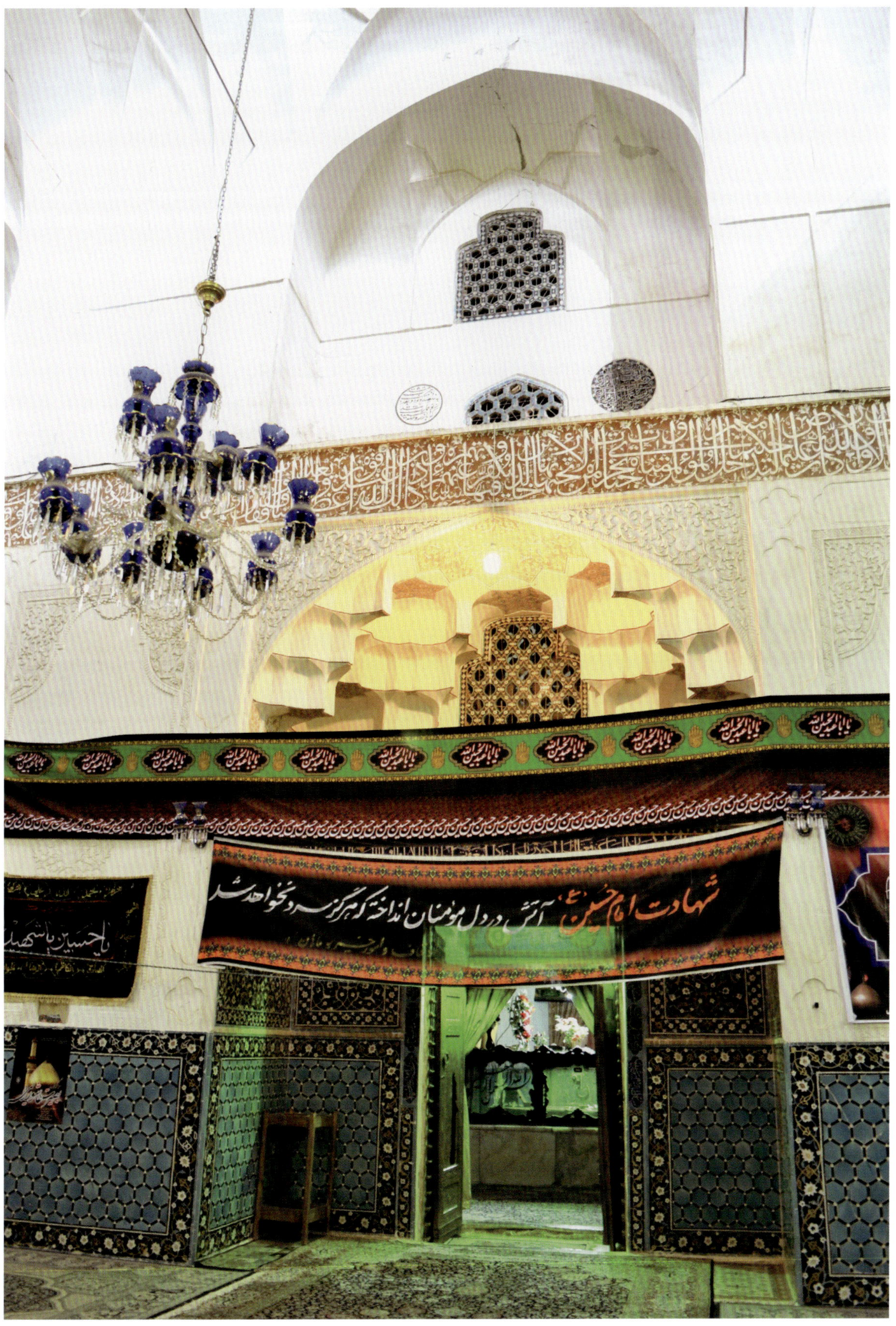
شهادت امام حسین ع آتش در دل مومنان انداخته که هرگز سرد نخواهد شد

such as Mahan and Taft, where the Neʿmatullahis' most important khanaqahs in Iran were located, thus offer crucial vantages on broader dynastic histories of the early modern western Iran to the Deccan.

The oldest layer of the Mahan portal points to yet another aspect of center-periphery dynamics that converge in Deccan India. While carving out a place for themselves in Bidar, the Deccani capital of the Bahmanids, the Neʿmatullahis open up invaluable perspectives on the cultural histories of this understudied dynasty, not to mention the history of diverse migrant communities in the region. In Bidar, a whole new pattern of geographical relations emerges: relations between north and south India as well as between the Deccan and the rest of the Islamic world. As a scholarly problematic, these dynamics owe their existence in large part to the Mughal-centric and Persian-centric historiography of South Asian art and history. How the Bahmanids and Timurids viewed one another, and how the Neʿmatullahis came to serve as mediators between them, is a question I return to in chapters 2 and 3.

In its function as the public-facing threshold of a sacred space, the portal in Mahan attracted a dense amalgamation of markers of political power and ambition, which raises a number of questions: Why and under what circumstances did these factions of the ruling elite patronize the shrine? Likewise, what potential patrons opted not to patronize the shrine and why? How did internal conflicts and imperial ambitions in fifteenth- and sixteenth-century Iran inform these choices? And what role did the transregional politics of early modern Iran and India play? The staging ground of the Mahan portal, facilitated by a Bahmanid patron, is but one manifestation of a more general dynamic by which the local and global intertwined with one another.

For all the pathways that the portal opens into the history of the Sufi network and their patrons, we must also consider what it might conceal—not just materially, as I have shown in this chapter, but also methodologically. All of the questions posed above concern the politics of patronage. They hardly speak to the agency of Sufis or even to their presence at their own shrines. Much of what I have laid out in this chapter deals with the ripple effects of spaces that are laden with spiritual meaning, offering us a top-down view of state politics entangled with the stone and mortar of the portal. Viewed from another perspective, however, these elite patrons were merely drawing on the authority and popularity that the Sufis had established for themselves. This underlying authority is clearly acknowledged and, indeed, manifested architecturally in the use of Shah Neʿmatullah's poetry on the portal. We have already seen how artist signatures and Sufi poetry creep into the story of the portal, demanding that we consider their side of the story as interdependent and inextricable from that of their patrons. In the chapters that follow, I will gradually move from the patron to the Sufi perspective, not in an attempt to disregard the politics of shrine patronage or the religious motivations of their patrons but rather to balance these against the role that Sufis played in attracting patronage and, in the second and third parts of the book, to explore how they crafted these intimate yet transregionally connected spaces.

Notes

1. See the introduction in this book.
2. Qayyumi Bidhendi, "Majmu[c]ih Mazar," in Pazuki, *Majmu[c]ih maqalat*, 175. The shrine was recorded as a national monument in 1932.
3. For an example of nonaxial shrine development, see Dadlani, "The City Built," in Rizvi, *Affect, Emotion, and Subjectivity*, 152. For an axially formed shrine in Fahraj (near Yazd, Iran), with ties to the Ne[c]matullahi family, see Katib, *Tarikh-i jadid-i Yazd*, 48–49, 189, 273; Afshar, *Yadgarha-yi Yazd*, I:215.
4. Golombek and Wilber, *The Timurid Architecture*, 394.
5. Aubin, *Matériaux*, 193.
6. See the following for references to the Mahan shrine as a mazar: Nafisi, "Maqamat," 112, and Katib, *Tarikh-i jadid-i Yazd*, 217; as *qubbih, bargah, gunbad,* and *khabgah*: Samarqandi, *Matla[c]-i sa[c]dayn*, II:416–17; as rawza: Khan, *Faramin wa Asnad-i Salatin-i Deccan*, 3–4; and as astana: Aubin, *Matériaux*, 146–47. Throughout the book, I use the *shrine at Mahan* versus the *khanaqah at Mahan* to distinguish the latter from the structures that were built after 1431 on the site at Mahan.
7. On astana, see Lifchez, "The Lodges of Istanbul," 75–76; McChesney, *Waqf in Central Asia*, 68; Green, "Migrant Sufis," 498.
8. Contrary to Golombek and Wilber, *The Timurid Architecture*, 395.
9. Hillenbrand, *Studies in Medieval Islamic Architecture*, II:496; Qayyumi Bidhendi, "Majmu[c]ih Mazar," 179.
10. Qayyumi Bidhendi, "Majmu[c]ih Mazar," 185–86.
11. Babaie, "Sacred Sites of Kingship," 175–215.
12. Qayyumi Bidhendi, "Mururi bar barkhi az asar-i mi[c]mari-yi tariqa-yi Ne[c]matullahiyya," in Pazuki, *Majmu[c]ih maqalat*, 200–202.
13. Qayyumi Bidhendi, "Majmu[c]ih Mazar," 194; Eisazadeh, "Tak-negari," 95.
14. Eisazadeh, "Tak-negari," 130–78; Qayyumi Bidhendi, "Majmu[c]ih Mazar," 184, 187–94; Parizi, *Rahnama-yi asar-i tarikhi-yi Kerman*, 74–81; Qazvini, *Sharh-i hal*, 149–50.
15. Golombek and Wilber, *The Timurid Architecture*, 394–95; Qayyumi Bidhendi, "Majmu[c]ih Mazar," 181; Eisazadeh, "Tak-negari," 124.
16. Qayyumi Bidhendi, "Majmu[c]ih Mazar," 180.
17. Ibid., 185–86; [c]Uqabi, *Dayirat al-ma[c]arif*, 68.
18. O'Kane, *Timurid Architecture*, 69.
19. See Bastani Parizi's reading of the inscription in Waziri, *Tarikh-i Kerman*, 580, fn.43; Nurbakhsh Kermani, *Zendegi va athar-i qutb al-muwahhidin*, 128. On the rarity of Persian foundation inscriptions in religious building in this period, see O'Kane, *The Appearance of Persian*, 127, 156 n 110; Blair, "Epigraphy iii. Arabic inscriptions in Persia."
20. On thresholds as mediators, see Bush, *Reframing the Alhambra*, 86.
21. Wilber, *The Architecture of Islamic Iran*, 188–89; Golombek and Wilber, *The Timurid Architecture*, 393.
22. O'Kane, *Timurid Architecture*, 73. On the use of colored inks for sacred names and patrons in manuscripts, see Gruber, *The Praiseworthy One*, 9.
23. An exception is the fifteenth-century roundel above the portal, discussed in the next section of this chapter.
24. See chapter 4, section VII, "The Khanaqah at Taft: Architecture and Familial Legacy," and chapter 5, section V, "Weaving an Epigraphic Network."
25. See chapter 6, section I, "Ahmad Shah's Tomb in Bidar: Architecture as Transoceanic Dialogue."

26. On architect signatures on facades of early modern buildings, see Babaie, "Chasing After the Muhandis," in Rizvi, *Affect, Emotion, and Subjectivity*, 42.

27. Blair, *Text and Image*, 125.

28. Woods, *The Aqquyunlu*, 50–54, 68–70, 90, 114, 136–37.

29. On Uzun Hasan, see ibid., 78–120.

30. Ibid., 100; Quiring-Zoche, "Aq Qoyunlu."

31. For intermarriages, see Aubin, *Matériaux*, 213–15.

32. Minorsky, "The Qara-qoyunlu and the Qutb-shāhs," 50–73; Mancini-Lander, "Tales Bent Backward," 32–39.

33. Aubin, *Matériaux*, 213–14; Minorsky, "The Qara-qoyunlu and the Qutb-shāhs," 73.

34. See chapter 4 for further information on this relationship.

35. Woods, *The Aqquyunlu*, 83–84, 89; Newman, *Safavid Iran*, 10.

36. On the Aq Qoyunlu-Neʿmatullah relationship, see Abouʾi Mehrizi, *Sadat-i Neʿmatullahi*, 94–95; Mancini-Lander, "Memory on the Boundaries of Empire," 456.

37. Quiring-Zoche, "Aq Qoyunlu."

38. Golombek and Wilber, *The Timurid Architecture*, 414–18, 421–23, 305–307; Wilber, *The Architecture of Islamic Iran*, 159–60; Hillenbrand, *Islamic Architecture*, 110; Holod-Tretiak, "The Monuments of Yazd," 102–22; Shayesteh Far, *Shîʿah Artistic Elements*, 275–77; Aube, Lorain, and Bendezu-Sarmiento, "The Complex of Gawhar Shad," 62–83; Knobloch, *The Architecture and Archaeology of Afghanistan*, 134–37; Allen, *A Catalogue of the Toponyms and Monuments of Timurid Herat*, 92–93, 113–15, 122–29; Blair and Bloom, *The Art and Architecture of Islam*, 45–46.

39. I am grateful to Mr. Mahani, who was in charge of restoring the tilework at the Mahan shrine during my 2012 visit, for his knowledge and guidance in navigating these areas in the shrine complex.

40. On the commonality of limiting the tilework program of monuments to the entrance portal and mihrab under Shahrukh and Timur, see Golombek, "Discourses of an Imaginary Arts Council," 6–10.

41. Rizvi, *The Safavid Dynastic Shrine*, 14, 75; Morton, "The Ardabil Shrine," 51.

42. On whitewashed surfaces and antiquarianism in Safavid interiors, see Hillenbrand, *Studies in Medieval Islamic Architecture*, II:523–24.

43. On the possibility of Naqdi b. Haydar being a grandson of Ganj ʿAli Khan (d. 1626), governor of Kerman, Sistan, and Qandahar, see Bastani Parizi, "Haram-i Shah Vali," in Pazuki, *Majmuʿih maqalat*, 150; Mashizi, *Tazkira-yi Safaviyya-yi Kerman*, 295, 247–48.

44. On the increasing use of Persian poetry on architecture in the fourteenth and fifteenth centuries and its relationship with the political rise of Sufism, see O'Kane, *The Appearance of Persian*, 113–58.

45. For the counterargument on the dating of this inscription, see Hasheminezhad, "Muʿarrifi-yi yiki az qadimitarin katibeh-ha bi khatt-i nastaʿliq," 247–51. On the lag in the appearance of nastaʿliq in Persian architectural inscriptions, see O'Kane, *The Appearance of Persian*, 144; Ghelichkhani, *Daramadi bar khushnivisi-yi Irani*, 112, 115.

46. O'Kane, *The Appearance of Persian*, 128.

47. Neʿmatullah Vali, *Divan*, 150. English translation in: O'Kane, *The Appearance of Persian Art*, 128–29.

48. Neʿmatullah Vali, *Divan*, 182.

2

Across the Arabian Sea

Gift Diplomacy in an Expanding Shrine Network

In chapter 1, we encountered a foundation inscription at the shrine in Mahan that points across the Indian Ocean (figs. 0.2 and 1.1). This chapter traces the background story of this inscription, opening up connections between Iran and the Deccan that encompass both spiritual and financial exchanges. At the outset, the chapter deals with the history of the Bahmanid dynasty in the Deccan from the perspective of their transregional connections and their attitudes toward Sufism and itinerant Sufis. I then show how the Neʿmatullahi Sufis both integrated themselves within and facilitated the mobility of the commercial and intellectual networks of the Indian Ocean world, building on long-standing connections.[1] Sea travels, real and dreamed encounters, and accounts of gift exchange converge around the foundation inscription at the shrine in Mahan, an immobile architectural fragment that unravels several interconnected stories of mobility.

In this and the next chapter, I gradually shift from more conventional views of patronage toward an emphasis on the agency of Sufis in shaping their transregional and transoceanic networks and in negotiating the fate of their physical spaces. This chapter outlines the possible reasons for both the Bahmanids' interest in the Neʿmatullahis and the Neʿmatullahis' interest in expanding their network to the Deccan. Several real or imaginary objects, some only from the realm of dreams, some never materialized, that traveled or were intended to travel across the Indian Ocean unfold the history of exchanges between Iran and the Deccan. I use these objects—Sufi initiation hats, a golden throne, and mundane and prestigious textiles—to draw a picture of how the Neʿmatullahis styled a politically engaged cross-regional image for themselves.

I. The Iconography of Encounter: Sufis in the Sacred Landscape of the Bahmanid Deccan

The fifteenth-century Deccan was a flourishing landscape for a variety of regional and transregional Sufi networks. The rise in the arrival of Sufis in the Deccan from the fourteenth century has been associated with the conquests of the Turkic sultanates of Delhi, which precipitated a short-lived relocation of the sultanate's capital from Delhi to Daulatabad in 1329 and, with it, the increased movement of people from northern India to the Deccan.[2]

As in other Islamicate societies of this period, relations between spiritual and temporal powers in the Deccan varied from utter antagonism to political allegiance and financial support. Both rulers and opponents of reigning regimes actively sought the support of Sufi shaykhs in order to strengthen their claims to the throne. Whether based on actual or imaginary meetings, accounts of Sufis bestowing kingship appeared frequently in Deccani textual sources and played a significant role in legitimizing the rule of specific sultans or constructing historical memories of their political agency in courtly circles.[3] In contrast to their Timurid counterparts, as I will discuss in the next chapter, the Bahmanids repeatedly patronized living Sufis. In particular, the Bahmanids actively engaged the Neʿmatullahis in courtly life and festivities, patronized architecture for them, and organized their own funerary sites in relation to theirs.

By the time of the Bahmanid dynasty's foundation, Sufis already had a considerable presence in the Deccan, especially members of the Chishti Sufi network. Early examples include the relationship between the founder of the Bahmanid dynasty, Hasan (r. 1347–58) and two Sufi shaykhs who predicted his rule: Nizamuddin Awliya (d. 1325), the Chishti Sufi in Delhi, and Siraj al-din Junaydi (d. 1380). Upon his enthronement, Hasan made a large donation of gold and silver to Shaykh Burhan al-din Gharib, a student of Nizamuddin Awliya, who was in Daulatabad (the first capital of the Bahmanids).[4] Shaykh Muhammad Siraj al-din Junaydi was characterized as the axis mundi (*qutb-i duran*) during the reign of the Bahmanid founder's successor, Muhammad Shah I (r. 1358–75), who sought the Sufi's blessings before several significant military campaigns.[5]

In the next transitional moment in Bahmanid politics, another Chishti shaykh known as Gisu Daraz (d. 1422) played an instrumental role. He arrived in Gulbarga in 1407–8 during the reign of Firuz Shah (r. 1397–1422).[6] Although textual sources record Firuz's welcoming attitude toward Gisu Daraz, his brother and successor, Ahmad Shah I (r. 1422–36), patron of the Neʿmatullahis in Mahan, is presented as the more enthusiastic supporter of the Chishti Sufi. Ahmad built a khanaqah for Gisu Daraz, attended his *majalis* (teaching sessions) to benefit from his lectures, and, in the event of a *samaʿ* (musical performance) at the khanaqah, treated the disciples with gifts.[7] The memory of Gisu Daraz's significance in the shaping of the sacred landscape of the Deccan lives on today through his shrine in Gulbarga and was recognized by successor states such as the Adil Shahis (1490–1689), as well as the Mughals (1526–1857), through their refurbishments and expansion of the site.[8] The Mughals' recognition of his significance is also evident from pilgrimages to his shrine performed by Aurangzeb (r. 1658–1707) and Nizam al-Mulk (r. 1724–48), who was assigned as Mughal viceroy in the Deccan, among others.[9]

Given the retrospective nature of the sixteenth- and seventeenth-century chronicles that supply the information on Bahmanid-Chishti relations, it is possible that the interactions between Ahmad Shah, Gisu Daraz, and Firuz Shah were devised anachronistically to grant Ahmad Shah more authority and legitimacy. Due to circumstances surrounding the end of Firuz Shah's reign, Ahmad *needed* to emerge as the legitimate ruler in the eyes of such writers and their audiences. In fact, one way these textual sources distinguished the fate of each brother lies in their treatment of the Chishti Sufi shaykh. Ahmad Shah is said to have embraced the Sufi as his spiritual adviser and offered him financial support. Firuz Shah welcomed him warmly at first, but as someone "interested in exoteric sciences" (such as mathematics and geometry), Firuz eventually grew ambivalent toward Gisu Daraz, who was no expert in the field.[10] Firuz's defeat at the hands of his brother Ahmad Shah in the events that followed, as will be discussed below, seem to find an almost cosmic justification in these textual accounts' emphasis on his interest in nonesoteric knowledge instead of esoteric branches of knowledge that were associated with sacral kingship.

Gisu Daraz took on an even more prominent role in the histories of the Bahmanid dynasty in 1415–16, when Firuz Shah nominated his elder son, Hasan Khan, as the crown prince and asked Gisu Daraz for his blessing.[11] The shaykh denied Firuz's request and, in response, suggested that the crown had been promised to the Sufi's supporter and advisee, Firuz's brother, Ahmad Khan, insisting that any attempt to usurp his succession would be in vain. The confrontation gave way to outright clashes between the two factions. First, Firuz Shah asked the Sufi shaykh to leave the capital city of Gulbarga because his "khanaqah was too close to the fort."[12] The second clash was between Firuz Shah and his brother Ahmad Khan.[13]

Convinced that his brother posed a threat to his reign and that of his son, Firuz Shah decided to blind Ahmad. Having learned of his brother's plot, on the night when he was planning his escape from Gulbarga, Ahmad took his son, ʿAla al-din, to visit Gisu Daraz in order to request his advice and blessings. Gisu Daraz tore his turban in two and wrapped each piece on the head of father and son with his own hands, predicting that they both would rule the Deccan, and proceeded to share food with them on a common plate.[14]

Exchanges of these materials, textiles, and food are of broader significance in narratives of Sufi-sultan encounters. Often set before a conquest or the foundation of a political dynasty, such multisensorial encounters involved the exchange of objects endowed with talismanic power, capable of transmitting the Sufi's blessings.[15] These objects typically included edibles shared on a plate with the Sufi as well as amulets, rings, or textiles worn in close contact with the skin, or objects such as bows and arrows that bore connotations of power and kingship.[16] The choice of a turban as the item of exchange between Gisu Daraz and Ahmad Shah alludes to the crown of kingship that Ahmad would win in the battle against his brother.

This was not the only instance in which Ahmad would receive an initiation hat in a legitimacy encounter of this kind. As chronicler Muhammad Qasim Fereshteh (fl. 1609) recounts, Ahmad Shah grew disheartened by the possibility of defeat in the middle of the battle with his brother Firuz and decided to rest under the shadow of a tree. He dreamed of a man dressed like a dervish who approached and offered him a green twelve-segmented devotional hat, placing it on Ahmad Shah's head and congratulating him on his reign.[17] He told Ahmad that this gift was sent to him from an ascetic. Later, when a disciple of Shah Neᶜmatullah, named Mulla Qutb al-din Kermani, arrived in the Deccan with gifts from Shah Neᶜmatullah, including the aforementioned hat, Ahmad Shah recognized him from the dream.[18] This account presents an instance of the commonly shared idioms between the temporal and spiritual realms: the word for the Sufi initiation hat in Persian, *taj*, is the same as the word for a king's crown. In Fereshteh's account, when meeting the aforementioned disciple Mulla Qutb al-din, Ahmad Shah is said to have recited a poem that played with the ambiguities of the word *taj* and the idea of kingship.

> The king in India and the Shaykh in Mahan,
> This is how the kings bestow a crown (taj).[19]

Imagined or dreamed encounters between Sufis and ruling elite were a common way of securing legitimacy and blessing for a political act and became a recurring topos in early modern historiography, including Neᶜmatullahi literature.[20] In addition to its practical advantages, such as affording rulers a pathway to initiation and the desired blessings without having to negotiate a physical meeting, the capacity for such visions was considered a mystical, prophetic quality befitting a sovereign.[21] While Ahmad Shah's dream of Shah Neᶜmatullah's disciple performs these ideological functions, several additional points should be taken into account regarding the way it is historicized in Fereshteh's chronicle and in comparison to other sources. First, that Shah Neᶜmatullah himself did not appear in Ahmad Shah's dream reflects the fact that their relationship was always mediated by a disciple or descendant—the two never actually met. Although they were contemporaries, the geographical distance between Shah Neᶜmatullah and Ahmad Shah renders the function of the dream akin to that of visions of saints and prophets from the historical past—that is, the vision (almost) collapses distance, be it geographical or temporal.

This marks a key difference between Fereshteh's account and other versions of the story that appear in Shah Neᶜmatullah's biographies: in the latter, Shah Neᶜmatullah himself is the one who appears in Ahmad Shah's dream. In a section on notable successors of Shah Neᶜmatullah, biographer Sunᶜullah introduces Ahmad Shah as one of the outstanding (*makhsusan*) disciples of the Sufi, having experienced "the Dream of the Righteous," in which Shah Neʿmatullah personally placed one of his Sufi hats on the king's head and predicted his success. Sunʿullah indicates that as a result of this dream encounter, Ahmad achieved military victories and brought new parts of India under his control.[22]

Shir Malik Waʿizi's fifteenth-century biography of Shah Neʿmatullah contains the earliest record of the dream account. Interestingly, he discusses Ahmad Shah's dream as one of Shah Neʿmatullah's miracles, attributing agency to the Sufi for making an appearance in the future king's dream. Waʿizi also draws a distinction between the initiation hat that Shah Neʿmatullah places on Ahmad Shah's head in the dream and the crown that he earns later as a Bahmanid ruler. The latter is called the "crown of kingship" (*taj-i shahi*) while the former is referred to as the "crown of the caliphate" (*taj-i khilafat*, with *khalifa* denoting a spiritual heir).[23] This distinction intertwines the realms of spiritual and political power in the figure of Ahmad Shah, who embodies both temporal kingship and spiritual inheritance.

The fact that not one but two Sufi shaykhs from influential Sufi networks of Chishtis and Neʿmatullahis—albeit with different degrees of influence in the Deccan at the time—were involved in clashes between Ahmad Shah and his brother indicates the sensitivity of this moment in Bahmanid history, which Richard Eaton has characterized as a "dynastic revolution."[24] It is not uncommon to find a multiplicity of legitimacy narratives lending support to a ruler, involving either different Sufis or different versions of the same encounter.[25] A relationship with one Sufi did not exclude relations with another, at least not in the fifteenth century.[26] Sultans could affiliate themselves with no small number of Sufi shaykhs and *ʿulama* (religious scholars) and might also change allegiance, as indicated by narratives of competition among and within Sufi networks.

With all the benefits that this "king-making" role would bring to Sufis, support for the ruling powers could also prove a dangerous game to play. As Robert McChesney notes, transitional moments, when political power passed from one group to another, were delicate times for shrine administrations. Unforeseen consequences could follow from active support for the political fortunes of an unsuccessful faction or failure to declare allegiance to a political victor at the right moment, resulting in a loss of formerly granted fiscal privileges.[27] Likewise, for the court, the choice of Sufi networks and the extent of support granted to them could have significant political implications. A multiplicity of affiliations was one way to lower the risk on both sides. Indeed, Ahmad Shah's dream should be read in light of the privileges it offered to both. In addition to officially buttressing the Bahmanid lineage with that of the Neʿmatullahis, it also justified the introduction and integration of Neʿmatullahi networks into the Deccani landscape in the years to follow—a function suggested by the investment of both hagiographies and dynastic chronicles in the anecdote.

Ahmad Khan was crowned as Ahmad Shah Bahmani in 1422.[28] After his enthronement, Ahmad endowed lands around Gulbarga to Gisu Daraz and built him a grand residence connected to the town. Fereshteh states that during the time of ʿAdil Shahis of the Deccan in Gulbarga, these endowments still belonged to the descendants of Gisu Daraz.[29] It is also known, based on a *farman* (decree) dated 957/1550 in Muhammadabad (Bidar), now kept at the Metropolitan Museum of Art (no.1998.260), that the descendants of Gisu Daraz were exempt from paying *zakat* (alms tax) on the produce of their *waqfi* (endowed) lands.[30] The veneration of Gisu Daraz continued after his death in 1422, the same year as Ahmad's enthronement, but at that point Ahmad also turned to Shah Neʿmatullah in southern Iran in search of a new spiritual leader. Given this chronology, the historicization of Ahmad Shah's dream may be read as an imagined account that seamlessly connected the past and future spiritual landscape of the Bahmanid Deccan into a coherent whole.

II. Why the Neʿmatullahis: The Bahmanid Perspective

Why would Ahmad Shah look so geographically far in search of a spiritual adviser when he could have invited one of the numerous Sufi leaders active in India? A range of factors, some immediate and practical, some far-reaching and visionary, may have played a role. Starting with Ahmad Shah's immediate circumstances, it is possible that after Gisu Daraz's death, Ahmad sought to distance himself from the Chishtis, who had been so deeply involved in the Bahmanid clashes. Eaton points out the advantage of "importing shaykhs from a distant land" to achieve this goal, since the Neʿmatullahis "had no prior record of involvement in Gulbarga's deadly politics."[31] In the long run, the Neʿmatullahis would ultimately engage in such political conflicts.[32] Nevertheless, the intent is not far-fetched considering Ahmad's relocation of the capital to Bidar in 1423, which, as Eaton and Helen Philon suggest, likewise represents an attempt to disassociate himself from the early line of Bahmanid rulers.[33]

It is also possible to read Ahmad Shah's invitation to Shah Neʿmatullah in light of the Chishtis' strong connection with North India. The Bahmanids claimed independence from the Delhi Sultanates in the fourteenth century—an experience they shared with their powerful southern neighbors the Vijayanagara state.[34] Insofar as the dynasty's association with and continued reverence toward the Chishtis represented a link with their northern neighbors and predecessors in the Deccan, their connection with the Neʿmatullahis could be read as an attempt to craft a regionally independent dynastic self-image.

The invitation to Shah Neʿmatullah took place in the already established, already lively context of relations between the Deccan and the western Islamic lands, especially Iran. The sea routes to the ports that yielded access to south and central India, such as Chaul, Dahbol, Goa, and Masulipatnam, made the Deccan a convenient destination from regions with access to the Persian Gulf, the Arabian Sea, and the Indian Ocean more broadly.[35] At least since the fourteenth century, Sufis, artists, scholars, merchants, and soldiers from Khurasan and ʿIraqayn,[36] alongside peers from elsewhere throughout the

Islamic world, had been attracted by generous salaries and gifts offered by the Deccani courts, financed by the diamond fields of the eastern Deccan, the export of Deccani textiles and cotton, and Bidar's involvement in the horse trade.[37]

Shah Neʿmatullah was not the Bahmanid ruler's only choice of invited spiritual teachers, and there must have been further negotiations in play—a point I will return to later in this chapter. But one factor that might have played a role in Ahmad Shah's choice of Shah Neʿmatullah is that several of the latter's disciples were already migrants with close ties to the Bahmanid court. While the exact number and status of these disciples remains unknown, textual sources offer glimpses into their social life in the Deccan. One of them, for instance, Habib Junaydi, accompanied the first group of envoys from the Bahmanid court who traveled to Mahan in order to invite Shah Neʿmatullah to the Deccan.[38] Before Ahmad Shah turned to Shah Neʿmatullah Vali, another Iranian Sufi and poet, Shaykh Azari Isfarayini (d. 1461–62), resided temporarily at the Bahmanid court and held an important place there, comparable to that of Gisu Daraz, though it lasted only briefly. As Dowlatshah Samarqandi recorded, Azari, too, was a student of Shah Neʿmatullah, having received his *ijaza* (permission to teach) and *khirqa* (patched frock; cloak of initiation) from him.[39] Under the patronage of Ahmad Shah, Azari was authoring the now-lost *Bahman-nama* (*Book of Bahman*), a dynastic history of the Bahmanids in verse. According to the chronicler Fereshteh, after completing the last section of the book about Ahmad Shah, Azari requested a return to his homeland, but Ahmad Shah asked him to stay since "the death of Gisu Daraz had caused him so much grief and sorrow that he was not willing to bear the Shaykh's departure as well."[40] Ahmad Shah's connection with Azari must have been a motivating factor to pursue his teacher, Shah Neʿmatullah. Shaykh Azari left the Deccan later on during the reign of Ahmad Shah but maintained a connection with and received gifts from the Bahmanid court at least until the time of ʿAla al-din Ahmad Shah II (r. 1436–58).[41]

Given this background, the Bahmanids must have had near insider knowledge of the Neʿmatullahi networks and their political affiliations. It is therefore reasonable to speculate that one factor in Ahmad Shah's invitation to Shah Neʿmatullah lay in the Sufi's amenability to models of sacral kingship. In chapter 3, I will discuss the king-philosopher-saint model that the Timurid prince Iskandar b. ʿUmar Shaykh (r. 1409–15), a patron of the Neʿmatullahis, pursued through his connections with Sufis, among other pathways. Iskandar was well known for his pursuit of sacral kingship in the intellectual circles in Yazd and Shiraz, which were connected to those in the Deccan by several links.[42] One reason Ahmad Shah chose Shah Neʿmatullah as the appropriate spiritual leader could have been Ahmad's interest in establishing a similar model of kingship in Bidar. However brief, Fereshteh's comment in presenting Ahmad as the king interested in esoteric knowledge and Sufism—as opposed to his brother Firuz—attests to this inclination. This inclination is further implied by the attempt to officially historicize Ahmad Shah as a successor of Shah

Ne‘matullah Vali in the Sufi's early hagiography as well as the existence of a *Risala-yi khirqa* (*Treatise on the Cloak*), for Ahmad Shah I, among the works written by Shah Ne‘matullah.[43] This treatise—now lost, to my knowledge—must have been on Ahmad Shah I's chain of initiation (*silsila*), integrating his line of descent with that of the Ne‘matullahi. As will be seen in chapter 6, this Deccani aspiration for models of sacral kingship also finds a visual and spatial manifestation in Ahmad Shah's tomb in Bidar.

III. Reorienting the Gaze: Economic Intermediaries

Having considered why the Bahmanids would have invited the Ne‘matullahis to the Deccan, in this and the following sections of the chapter I want to take up the Ne‘matullahis' point of view: how they envisioned the prospect of migration, the kind of network they intended to build, and the agency they saw themselves exerting in their relationship with the Bahmanid court. The challenges they faced in securing patronage from the Timurid court in the early decades of the fifteenth century must have been an important factor, coinciding with the offer of patronage from the Bahmanid rulers. But what other factors lay beyond this patronage-based view? Given the challenges it entailed, the decision to relocate across the Arabian Sea—or, rather, to initiate a phase of constant mobility—could not have been taken lightly.

Mercantile opportunities seem to have been an important though elusive factor, due to the scarcity of direct evidence in the sources. Jean Aubin has argued for the centrality of trade in the organization of the Ne‘matullahi network and their shrines.[44] On the Iranian side, Aubin's argument is based on the proximity of Ne‘matullahi centers to major trade routes: Kuhbanan, an early residence of Shah Ne‘matullah and his family, was a caravan stop on the route from Khurasan to the south; Taft was close to silk workshops in Yazd and lay on the route to Shiraz, which itself connected to Hormuz and from there to India and Mecca; Mahan was near Kerman, which especially rose to economic prominence under the Safavids.[45] Among these three sites, the Shah Vali khanaqah at Taft seems to have had the greatest potential as a caravan stop and mercantile center due to its spatial arrangement—a point I will return to in chapter 4.

While the significance of the mercantile aspect of these shrines remains speculative, more solid evidence exists on the Deccani side, especially in later periods. As Emma Flatt has pointed out, when in the sixteenth century Rafi al-din Shirazi, a merchant, a courtier at the court of Bijapur, and author of the chronicle *Tazkirat al-muluk* (*Biographies of Kings*), arrived in Saghar in the Deccan to trade textiles, he stayed at a khanaqah in Gogi that belonged to the Ne‘matullahis.[46] Another oblique indicator is the Ne‘matullahi family's seemingly constant travel between Kerman, Yazd, and the Deccan. Letters exchanged between members of the family point to the maintenance of shrines and their fiscal privileges as the primary purpose of these travels, but it is not hard to imagine that they involved mercantile activities as well. Given that the prominent position of *malik al-tujjar* (prince of merchants) was held by the Iranian merchant and Bahmanid vizier Mahmud Gavan, and given his possible connections with the Neʿmatullahi family, the likelihood of entangled relationships between mobility, socioeconomic networks, and religious circles in the Deccan is impossible to ignore.[47]

However, the role played by Sufi networks in facilitating movement across regions must be balanced against other factors in order to avoid mystification.[48] In all likelihood, the presence of the Neʿmatullahi family in the Deccan contributed to some extent to the increase of these mobilities, but as mentioned earlier, there was already a context, a base of human networks, for the Neʿmatullahis' interest in the Deccan. That being said, links between the Neʿmatullahi family and many Iranian immigrants in the Deccan could have been established after the latter's arrival in the region. For artists, scholars, or merchants from Iran arriving in the Deccan for the first time, the strong political and religious status of the Neʿmatullahi network at court could have offered a mediating ground on the path to mobility and resettlement.

IV. The Making of a Transregional Sufi Network

In building a transoceanic network between Iran and the Deccan, economic factors played a part for the Neʿmatullahis, but textual sources are significantly silent on this point. On the other hand, there are idealistic reasons that the Sufi network foregrounded in their own story. How could our view of the network's transregional movement change if we looked beyond what forced or allowed the Neʿmatullahis to make this move and instead imagine them as active agents engaged in a process of decision-making?

The dominant narrative of the Neʿmatullahis' mobility revolves around the Bahmanids' invitation of the family to the Deccan, as presented in dynastic histories. However, it is still possible to glimpse how the family took part in setting the scene for this invitation. One such occasion can be found in descriptions of another Sufi initiation hat (*taqiya*) that traveled from Iran to the Deccan. Shah Neʿmatullah's fifteenth-century biographer, Waʿizi, notes the Sufi's relationship with a potential disciple in the Deccan, just after establishing a settlement in Mahan and likely before any official contacts from the Bahmanids. Waʿizi recounts how Shah Neʿmatullah sent a hat of initiation to Gulbarga (Hasanabad), the Bahmanids' capital before Bidar. The recipient was a shaykh named Nizam al-din Ahmad, also known as Shaykh Khujan-i Faruqi. In Waʿizi's text, Nizam al-din Ahmad is immediately positioned at the intersection of two of the most important lineages in the temporal-spiritual landscape of the Deccan. On one side, his lineage was traced back to Shaykh Farid al-din Ganj-i Shakar (d. 1265), a major Sufi shaykh of the Chishtis. On the other side, he was a descendant of Hasan, the founder of the Bahmanid dynasty.[49] The convergence of these two interdependent genealogies—the Bahmanids on the one side and the Chishtis on the other—points to the Neʿmatullahis' active pursuit of prominently positioned disciples in the Deccan. Other sources confirm that Nizam al-din Ahmad accepted Shah Neʿmatullah's initiation hat and subsequently became one of his leading disciples and successors. Another of Shah Neʿmatullah's biographers, Kermani, lists Nizam al-din Ahmad's name among the notable successors of Shah Neʿmatullah, and Waʿizi himself ranks Nizam al-din Ahmad right after a small group of Shah Neʿmatullah's most righteous successors: the Sufi's only son, four grandsons, and the Bahmanid ruler Ahmad Shah I.[50]

Beyond this individual episode, Neʿmatullahi interest in the Deccan can also be discerned in the broader structure and function of Waʿizi's biography. As noted above, Waʿizi's text is the earliest surviving hagiography of Shah Neʿmatullah and was written in the Deccan during the reign of Ahmad Shah II—that is, sometime between 1422 and 1458. This time frame corresponds with Ahmad Shah II's offering of financial support for the construction of the Mahan shrine, following his father's earlier contribution, as recorded in the Mahan foundation inscription. Given this conjunction, it is plausible that one of the purposes behind dedicating this hagiography of Shah Neʿmatullah to the Bahmanid king was to secure the Bahmanids' patronage for the shrine at Mahan.

In comparison to later biographies of Shah Neʿmatullah, Waʿizi's text is considerably more didactic in character.[51] It contains extensive instructions on samaʿ (musical session) in the Neʿmatullahi network, postures of the body during samaʿ and khalwat (seclusion), restrictions on the types of music to be played, and information about Shah Neʿmatullah's clothes and manners, all of which either are absent from other biographies or, if present, lack such pedagogic framing.[52] It is thus possible that apart from courting patronage, the text could also have served as a handbook for new initiates in the Deccan, particularly in Bahmanid courtly circles, allowing initiates to familiarize themselves with the doctrine of the Sufi network and its rituals and, as a result, facilitate the spread of the Neʿmatullahi Sufi network in the region.

Textual descriptions of rituals and festivities, such as coronations and wedding ceremonies, testify to the growing agency of the Neʿmatullahis in the Deccan as well. ʿAla al-din Ahmad Shah II's coronation in 1436 is the earliest of these grand spectacles. As Tabataba reports, the ceremony was officiated in the presence of the grand *sadat*s (descendants of the Prophet Muhammad) and Sufi shaykhs of the Deccan, among whom the highest in status (*malik al-mashayikh*) was Burhan al-din Khalilullah (d. before 1454), the son of Shah Neʿmatullah Vali who had traveled to the Deccan after the death of his father in 1431. The text suggests a bold assertion of the Neʿmatullahis' position at court: Khalilullah held the king's right hand while Sayyid Hanif (whose affiliations are unclear) held his left hand and sat him on the throne. On either side of the throne was a seat for each shaykh while other sadats and religious scholars sat at the bottom of the throne, emphasizing the Neʿmatullahis' status and proximity to power.[53] The fact that this coronation likely took place in the midst of further patronage for the shrine at Mahan by the newly enthroned king adds to its significance. Shah Muhibbullah (d. ca. 1505), who succeeded his father, Khalilullah, as the *qutb* (leader) of the Neʿmatullahi network, later took part in the coronation of two Bahmanid kings: Nizam Shah or Ahmad Shah III (r. 1461–63) and Muhammad Shah III (r. 1463–82).[54]

Like Nizam al-din Ahmad, the aforementioned disciple who expanded his Sufi affiliations from the Chishtis to the Neᶜmatullahis and fused royal and spiritual lineages, the first generation of the Neᶜmatullahi family born in the Deccan was the product of Neᶜmatullahi-Bahmanid intermarriages. As Tabataba writes, "At the occasion of each coronation, one of the women of the Bahmanids had the honor to marry one of the descendants of Shah Neᶜmatullah."[55] Two of Shah Neᶜmatullah's grandsons married into the Bahmanid family and became the sons-in-law of Ahmad Shah I and II: Shah Muhibb al-din Habibullah married Ahmad I's daughter, and Habib al-din Muhibbullah married Ahmad II's daughter.[56] Why should we see these marriage bonds in light of the agency of the Sufi network? After all, both sides played parts in the marriage. The key to understanding the power dynamic between the court and the Sufi network lies in the fact that these intermarriages were believed to have brought blessings and spiritual legitimacy to the side of the Bahmanids and were recorded as such in Tabataba's dynastic history.[57]

The Neᶜmatullahi family took on military positions at the Bahmanid court and, at times, played a central role in political uprisings. As Flatt points out, there seems to have been a considerable overlap between the elite of the Bahmanid sultanate and military officials.[58] In addition, the presence of Sufis on the battlefield, to offer blessings and to serve as spiritual guides for the soldiers, was taking shape as a common trope.[59] We see the Neᶜmatullahis taking on similar roles later in the Safavid period in Iran too.

However, one instance in the history of the Neᶜmatullahis' presence in the Deccan reminds us that their involvement in politics was not a given and that, in fact, despite the family's deep entanglements with the court, some members could take issue with the intertwinement of politics and spirituality. After Shah Khalilullah's death, Shah Habibullah, his elder son who is referred to as a *pir* (Sufi master), is said to have refused to follow the path of his father as he (i.e., Habibullah) was more inclined toward a lonesome manner of *tariqa* (the path of Sufism).[60] Instead, Shah Muhibbullah, the younger son, accepted his father's *sajjada* (prayer mat), a metaphor of his official religious responsibilities.

It is clear that by this time the leadership (*sajjada neshini*, i.e., the inheritance of the prayer mat) of the Neᶜmatullahis in the Deccan involved more than initiating disciples, teaching students, performing rituals, and undertaking retreats: it was a position deeply entangled with the politics of the court. As Andrew Peacock has shown in his study of a previously neglected manuscript of ᶜIyani, a Shirazi poet and historian active at the Bahmanid court, this merging of the spiritual and material realms was deeply engrained in the figure of the qutb and the literature dedicated to Muhibbullah himself in Bahmanid Deccan.[61] The distance that Shah Neᶜmatullah himself kept from political and financial matters a few decades earlier no longer seems to have been vital for the image of the qutb in the Deccan. By the time Shah Neᶜmatullah's grandsons were active, the leadership of the Sufi network had evolved in ways that placed it in opposition to "a lonesome manner of Sufism." Shah Muhibbullah's activity as a warlord during the reign of Nizam Shah and Sultan Muhammad, while he was the qutb of the Neᶜmatullahis, is a case in point.[62] Shah Habibullah's decision to forgo his official responsibilities might have been a personal choice. But the necessities of the political and social landscapes of the Bahmanid Deccan, similar to those of the Safavids, must have had an impact on this structural change in the sociopolitical image of the network.

V. Shrine Diplomacy and Gift Exchange: Behind the Mahan Inscription

Textual references to gifts sent to the Neᶜmatullahis from the Deccan during the lifetime of Shah Neᶜmatullah vary in different sources.[63] They all take us back to the shrine at Mahan and offer a behind-the-scenes story for its portal's foundation inscription. To reconstruct the gift exchanges at the Mahan shrine, I will focus on the *Tarikh-i Fereshteh*, the dynastic history that seems to have given priority to the number of trips from the Deccan and their chronology, although its descriptions are less detailed than in the hagiographies (ᶜAbd al-Razzaq Kermani's and the *Jamiᶜ-i Mufidi*). Later in the chapter, I will return to the hagiographies to sketch the politics of receiving these gifts in the Neᶜmatullahi network.

According to Fereshteh, the first person to arrive in Kerman with such donations was one of the disciples of Shah Neᶜmatullah, Shaykh Habib Junaydi, who resided in the Deccan. The result of this journey was that a disciple of Shah Neᶜmatullah in Kerman, named Mulla Qutb al-din Kermani, returned with the Deccan-based disciple to Bidar, taking along a green devotional hat and a letter from Shah Neᶜmatullah.[64] This is when Ahmad Shah Bahmani recognized the disciple from his dream amid the battle with his brother and predecessor Firuz Shah, as recounted earlier.

Fereshteh adds that in the same year two other envoys, Khwaja ᶜImad al-din Semnani and Sayfullah Hasanabadi, were sent from the Deccan to Kerman with more gifts and a request for Shah Neᶜmatullah to send one of his sons to the Bahmanid court.[65] In response, Shah Neᶜmatullah sent his grandson, Mir Nurullah b. Khalilullah (d. 1431), who, as Fereshteh notes, was received warmly. His arrival was celebrated by the construction of a mosque and other structures in a village near Bidar, which was named Neᶜmatabad after the family.[66]

The last mention of gifts from Ahmad Shah in the *Tarikh-i Fereshteh* corresponds with the exchange in 1431, when the king learned of Shah Neᶜmatullah's death. ᶜAbd al-Razzaq Kermani specifies that a large sum was sent to Mahan for the building of a lofty dome over the grave of Shah Neᶜmatullah.[67] Tabataba did not record this donation but noted the king's grief upon the death of his spiritual leader by recounting the *ᶜurs* (lit. wedding; celebration commemorating the death of a Sufi) organized in the Deccan for Shah Neᶜmatullah. Ahmad invited all the sadats and shaykhs and grandees of the city and served them himself, signaling his humility toward the deceased. Shah Nurullah, the Sufi's grandson, was given a higher status than everyone else at the ᶜurs.[68]

There must have been another round of donations to the mausoleum at Mahan, as implied in the shrine's foundation inscription, but here the textual sources grow blurrier. Fereshteh notes that Shah Khalilullah, along with his sons Habibullah and Muhibbullah, arrived in the Deccan at some point after Shah Neᶜmatullah's death in 834/1431, although the exact dates of the trip are unclear.[69] As mentioned above, Shah Khalilullah's presence is also recorded at the coronation of ᶜAla al-din Ahmad Shah II in 838/1435.[70] After two of Khalilullah's sons were married to the sister and daughter of the reigning sultan, he was offered abundant gifts and returned home.[71] Although Fereshteh also reports rumors that Shah Khalilullah "was not able to return and died in the Deccan," an account by ᶜAbd al-Razzaq Samarqandi, an envoy to India of the Timurid ruler Shahrukh (r. 1405–47), confirms Shah Khalilullah's presence in Iran a few years later.[72] On 18 Ramadan 845 (January 30, 1442), Samarqandi reached Kerman on the way to India and stayed there, noting that "his holiness Amir Burhan al-din Sayyid Khalilullah b. Amir Naᶜim al-din Sayyid Neᶜmatullah who was deputed [by God] in the city of Kerman, and even the whole world, had then returned from India."[73]

Amid this extensive series of travels back and forth between India and Iran, at least one trip seems to have been undertaken for the purpose of securing more funding for the completion of the mausoleum at Mahan. Shah Neᶜmatullah died in 1431, and the mausoleum was not completed until the second half of 1436, following the death of the building's first patron, Ahmad Shah I, in 1436. If the first round of donations from Ahmad Shah did not suffice to complete the mausoleum, the problem of funding would have fallen to the two sons, Shah Khalilullah and Ahmad Shah II. In this light, Shah Khalilullah's trip to the Deccan, where he blessed the coronation of Ahmad Shah II and married off his sons, takes on another layer of significance as a crux of the shrine's patronage campaigns and a possible occasion to finalize such a deal. This is how prophetic dreams, the sea travels of a Sufi family, and the coronation ceremony of the Bahmanid king all coalesce in the tile inscription over the portal at the Mahan shrine: a modest object with vast transregional implications.

VI. The Power of Transregional Gifts

What exactly were the gifts the Deccani king Ahmad Shah sent to Mahan? There is no list to give us a comprehensive image, only glimpses. Among the known exchanged gifts, one object stands out: a throne (or seat, *takht* or *kursi*) sent to Shah Neᶜmatullah. A takht is first recorded by one of his disciples in Iran, Darwish Muhammad Tabasi, in his treatise *Jam-i Jahan-nama-yi Shahi* (*The Royal World-Revealing Cup*), completed in 1436.[74] No details about the material qualities of the takht are given there, but a later hagiography of Shah Neᶜmatullah has a more detailed description of a kursi—likely made of wood and probably the same as the one recorded by Tabasi—that had been sent as a gift from the sultans of Hindustan and belonged to Shah Khalilullah, the Sufi's son.[75] The four legs of the seat were made of gold alloy (possibly combined with copper), and the body was inlaid with precious jewels.[76] In both accounts, the seat was then regifted by Shah Neᶜmatullah to the Timurid ruler Shahrukh in Herat.

Before delving into the account of the throne, it is important to note that despite the rather cold and conflict-ridden relationship between the Timurid ruler and Shah Neᶜmatullah, as I will discuss further in chapters 3 and 4, gifts from him to Shahrukh were not uncommon. These gifts can be seen in light of Neᶜmatullahi ambitions to forge a deeper relationship with the Timurid central government and, in the process, project an image of the Sufi network as a strong contender in shaping regional and transregional politics. Such aspirations are crystalized in ᶜIyani's *Jangnama-yi Shahrukh* (*The Conquests of Shahrukh*), written in Bahmanid Deccan, in which—as Peacock has shown—the author elaborates on Shah Neᶜmatullah's appearance to Shahrukh in a vision during battle, securing his victory.[77] The clear parallels that connect this account to that of Shah Neᶜmatullah's appearance in Ahmad Shah Bahmani's dream point to the similarity of the Sufi network's ambitions in the Deccan and Iran as well as the Bahmanid fascination with the Timurids and their relation with the Neᶜmatullahis.

Shah Neᶜmatullah's shipment of the Bahmanid throne to Herat had significant implications for these multilateral relations. From the central Timurid perspective, the Deccan occupied an ambiguous position, having never been conquered by Timur (r. 1370–1405) during his Indian campaigns. After Timur's conquest of Delhi in 1398–99, the Bahmanid ruler Firuz Shah sent the son of his Shirazi vizier, Mir Fazlullah Inju, to the Timurid court with diplomatic gifts and a letter in Persian verse expressing his loyalty to Timur.[78] The Bahmanids' northern counterpart, the Sayyid dynasty ruler Khizr Khan, had the *khutba* (Friday sermon) read in the name of Shahrukh during the first half of the fifteenth century, but the Bahmanids never took up a similar position.[79] Ali Anooshahr has argued that in the fifteenth century, the Timurids did not necessarily have an interest in controlling India and were "happy to claim imperial prerogative there" without necessarily getting their hands dirty.[80] Shah Neᶜmatullah's decision to send a throne from Hindustan to Shahrukh might well have satisfied such sentiments, implying a reiteration of the loyalty that Firuz Shah had expressed to Timur, albeit without the Bahmanids' consent.

The story of the bejeweled seat is entangled with another object: the *kiswa*—the textile covering the Kaᶜba. Shah Neᶜmatullah's hagiographies present him as eager to engage with Shahrukh and the politics of Timurid governance in the wider Islamic world, and one such example is Shah Neᶜmatullah's initiative in Timurid-Mamluk clashes over the kiswa. For almost two decades in the first half of the fifteenth century, the Timurids were in conflict with the Mamluks over the preparation of an inner cover for the Kaᶜba—a prestigious act of textile making with direct implications for access to and control over the most significant site of Muslim pilgrimage. The norm was that the dynasty ruling Egypt had the honor of fulfilling the task. Shahrukh's insistence on partaking in the preparation of the cover, as İlker Evrim Binbaş has pointed out, was probably intended to challenge the legitimacy of Mamluk rulers, asserting himself and the Timurids as legitimate rulers beyond the geographical boundaries of their realm.[81] These conflicts took place from around 1424 for about two decades until the Mamluk sultan, al-Malik al-Zahir Jaqmaq (r. 1438–53), accepted Shahrukh's request in 1444. Shah Neᶜmatullah's involvement in this conflict is recorded by the aforementioned disciple Tabasi. It is significant, but not surprising, that Shahrukh ordered the inner kiswa to be made in Yazd rather than in his capital, given the prominence of the silk and weaving industries in the city.[82] Shah Neᶜmatullah's status in the region, and his circle's possible involvement with the silk industry, may have played a role in his claim to act as a representative.

Tabasi notes that Shah Neᶜmatullah sent Shahrukh a message with a Haji Khusraw-yi Turk who was traveling to Herat. In the message, Neᶜmatullah suggested he would be willing to take the cover that the Timurid court had prepared to Mecca: "If he [Shahrukh] wishes so, he should write to me, and I will prepare for the journey to the Kaᶜba, and take [the cover] and bring back the kings of the Mamluks before Shahrukh, carrying them by their collars." The author, Tabasi, adds that he himself traveled to Herat a year and two months later, only to find that the messenger was dead, and the message may never have reached Shahrukh.[83] Beatrice Manz and Binbaş both refer to this account: Manz in terms of an unsuccessful attempt by Shah Neᶜmatullah to connect with Shahrukh's court and Binbaş in relation to the Timurids' internal and external politics.[84] The episode also has important implications for the self-image of Shah Neᶜmatullah and his followers, demonstrating that the Neᶜmatullahis saw themselves as key actors in transregional politics. Shah Neᶜmatullah is imagined as no less than an authority who could bring the Mamluk kings under Shahrukh's command and shape narratives of Timurid legitimacy in the wider Islamic world.

These implications are amplified by the episode's placement in the text immediately before the account of the bejeweled seat from the Deccan. Tabasi writes that Shah Neᶜmatullah decided to send the Hindustani takht to Herat for Shahrukh after thoughts of the ruler came to him several times over the course of a day.[85] He then moves directly into the account of Shah Neᶜmatullah's involvement in the controversy over the cover of the Kaᶜba. Through the juxtaposition of these two notes, then, Tabasi allows the political and religious dimensions of the two objects to link distant nodes in the realms of the Islamic world, from Deccan India to Herat, Kerman, Hijaz, and Egypt. And Shah Neᶜmatullah is, of course, presented as the man who could tie all the various threads together: the recipient of the throne from Hindustan, the sender of the gift to the Timurid King, the bearer of the textile to Mecca, and the subjugator of the Mamluks.

The reception histories of the gifts discussed above shed light on how the players in this transregional trio—the Bahmanids, the Timurids, and above all the Neʿmatullahis—envisioned themselves as actors on a transregional and interconnected stage. The Neʿmatullahis, whether Shah Neʿmatullah himself or the hagiographers, regarded the gifts from India as symbolic capital that could multiply authority through regifting and transportation. The geographical association of these gifts—where they came from and where they were (intended to be) taken—presents an interplay of their poetics and politics. The fact that one of these objects was a throne lends even further political significance to such acts of transregional regifting and is reminiscent of Ahmad Shah's wordplay on kingship and crowns in his poem discussed earlier in the chapter. Receiving these potent gifts was by no means free of sociopolitical complications. In the next chapter, after a detailed overview of the Neʿmatullahis' relationship with the Timurids around the making of the khanaqah complex in Taft, I will return to these gifts to reflect on the challenges that they, and the transregional expansion of the Sufi network, brought about.

Notes

1. Sivasundaram, "The Indian Ocean," 31–61.
2. Green, "Migrant Sufis," 498–99.
3. Digby, "The Sufi Shaykh and the Sultan," 75; Ahmad, "The Sufi and Sultan," 142–47. For comparative examples, see Auer, *Symbols of Authority in Medieval Islam*; Moin, *The Millennial Sovereign*; Yürekli, *Architecture and Hagiography*; Safi, *Religion and Politics in Saljuq Iran*.
4. Astarabadi, *Tarikh-i Fereshteh*, 239.
5. Ibid., 263–66, 272–73.
6. Tabataba, *Burhan-i maʾasir*, 43–44.
7. Astarabadi, *Tarikh-i Fereshteh*, 348–49.
8. Allan, *The Art and Architecture of Twelver Shiʿism*, 65.
9. Green, "Auspicious Foundations," 72.
10. Astarabadi, *Tarikh-i Fereshteh*, 348.
11. Tabataba, *Burhan-i maʾasir*, 46.
12. Astarabadi, *Tarikh-i Fereshteh*, 348–49.
13. Ibid., 351–56.
14. Ibid., 351–52; Tabataba, *Burhan-i maʾasir*, 48.
15. For a variety of examples, see ʿIsami, *Futuh al-Salatin*, 123–24, 225–26; Melville, "History and Myth," 137; Digby, "The Sufi Shaykh and the Sultan," 76; Safi, "Bargaining with Baraka," 271. On the timing of physical or dream encounters, see Moin, *The Millennial Sovereign*, 62. On the sensorial elements of encounters, see Bashir, *Sufi Bodies*, 13.
16. Flood, "Bodies and Becoming," 482; Jowzjani, *Tabaqat-i Nasiri*, 160–67.
17. On the Neʿmatullahi headgear, see chapter 8, section V, "A Vaulted Initiation Hat."
18. Astarabadi, *Tarikh-i Fereshteh*, 382–83.
19. Ibid., 383.
20. Quinn, *Persian Historiography*, 62–63; Bashir, *Sufi Bodies*, 88, 92–96; Bashir, "The World as a Hat," in Mir-Kasimov, *Unity in Diversity*, 348; Manz, *Power,*

Politics and Religion, 193; Moin, *The Millennial Sovereign*, 72; Samarqandi, *Matlaᶜ-i saᶜdayn*, 518; Peacock, "ᶜIyani," 176–77.

21. Green, *Sufism*, 3; Moin, *The Millennial Sovereign*, 73.

22. Aubin, *Matériaux*, 107.

23. Ibid., 316–17.

24. Eaton, *A Social History of the Deccan*, 63.

25. See, for instance, Jowzjani, *Tabaqat-i Nasiri*, 160–67; Tabataba, *Burhan-i maʾasir*, 12–13; Digby, "The Sufi Shaykh and the Sultan," 78.

26. Manz, *Power, Politics and Religion*, 277; DeWeese, "Yasavī Šayhs in the Timurid Era," 173–75; Digby, "The Sufi Shaykh and the Sultan," 77.

27. McChesney, *Central Asia*, 103.

28. Astarabadi, *Tarikh-i Fereshteh*, 356.

29. Ibid., 358–59.

30. Eaton, "A Social and Historical Introduction to the Deccan," in Haidar and Sardar, *Sultans of the South*, 6.

31. Eaton, *A Social History of the Deccan*, 58.

32. Astarabadi, *Tarikh-i Fereshteh*, 409–10, 414–18; Tabataba, *Burhan-i maʾasir*, 88, 92–94.

33. Eaton, *A Social History of the Deccan*, 63; Philon, "New Considerations on the City of Bidar," 109.

34. Eaton and Wagoner, *Power, Memory, Architecture*, 28–31.

35. Subrahmanyam, "Iranians Abroad," 342–45; Alam and Subrahmanyam, "Iran and the Doors to the Deccan," in Overton, *Iran and the Deccan*, 78–79; Fischel, "Ghariban in the Deccan," in Overton, *Iran and the Deccan*, 128–30.

36. ᶜIraqayn is the area made up of ᶜIraq-i ᶜAjam (western Iran) and ᶜIraq-i ᶜArab (present-day Iraq).

37. Michell and Zebrowski, *Architecture and Art of the Deccan Sultanates*, 2; Haidar and Sardar, *Sultans of the South*, 304; Eaton, "From Bidar to Timbuktu," 12; Flatt, *Courts of the Deccan Sultanates*, 133–34; Subrahmanyam, "Iranians Abroad," 342–43; Gavan, *Riyaz al-Inshaʾ*, 207; Aubin, "Le royaume d'Ormuz," 134–35.

38. Also recorded as Khujandi: Astarabadi, *Tarikh-i Fereshteh*, 382–83.

39. Samarqandi, *Tazkirat al-shuᶜara*, 449.

40. Astarabadi, *Tarikh-i Fereshteh*, 374–75.

41. Ibid., 375–76.

42. Binbaş, *Intellectual Networks*, 96.

43. On Ahmad Shah as a successor of Shah Neᶜmatullah, see Aubin, *Matériaux*, 308. For the list containing the *Risala-yi khirqa*, see Neᶜmatullah Vali, *Divan*, Garrett no. 1469Y, f. 393a.

44. Aubin, "De Kūhbanān a Bidar," 233–61. See also Flatt, *Courts of the Deccan Sultanates*, 145.

45. Aubin, "De Kūhbanān a Bidar"; Flatt, *Courts of the Deccan Sultanates*, 145, fn. 114; Graham, "The Niᶜmatullāhī Order," 167; Babaie, "Sacred Sites of Kingship," 227–28.

46. Flatt, *Courts of the Deccan Sultanates*, 145.

47. Astarabadi, *Tarikh-i Fereshteh*, 462; Sherwani, *Mahmud Gawan*, 26; Flatt, *Courts of the Deccan Sultanates*, 133–34; Subrahmanyam, "Iranians Abroad," 341.

48. Flatt, *Courts of the Deccan Sultanates*, 81; Siddiqi, "The Pro-alien Policy of Ahmad Shah," 179–203.

49. Aubin, *Matériaux*, 287–88.

50. Ibid., 110, 308.
51. Connell, "The Nimatullahi Sayyids," 12–22.
52. Aubin, *Matériaux*, 302–305.
53. Tabataba, *Burhan-i maʾasir*, 75.
54. Ibid., 96, 107–108. There seems to be no records of the family's involvement in the Bahmanids' coronation after this date.
55. Ibid., 68.
56. Ibid., 137–38.
57. Fereshteh offers a different interpretation, however, noting that with these intermarriages, the Neʿmatullahis reached the highest temporal status in the Deccan: Astarabadi, *Tarikh-i Fereshteh*, 384.
58. Flatt, *Courts of the Deccan Sultanates*, 128.
59. For an earlier Tughlugh example, see Ahmad, "The Sufi and Sultan," 151.
60. Tabataba, *Burhan-i maʾasir*, 92–93.
61. Peacock, "ʿIyani," 175.
62. Tabataba, *Burhan-i maʾasir*, 97, 123.
63. The *Burhan-i maʾasir* mentions the donations once, ʿAbd al-Razzaq Kermani's biography of Shah Neʿmatullah and the *Jamiʿ-i Mufidi* twice each, and the *Tarikh-i Fereshteh* three times.
64. Astarabadi, *Tarikh-i Fereshteh*, 382–83.
65. In this instance Fereshteh does not mention any gifts, but Tabataba does: Tabataba, *Burhan-i maʾasir*, 65; Astarabadi, *Tarikh-i Fereshteh*, 383–84.
66. Ibid., 384.
67. Aubin, *Matériaux*, 108.
68. Tabataba, *Burhan-i maʾasir*, 68.
69. Astarabadi, *Tarikh-i Fereshteh*, 384.
70. Tabataba, *Burhan-i maʾasir*, 75.
71. Astarabadi, *Tarikh-i Fereshteh*, 384.
72. Ibid., 384.
73. Samarqandi, *Matlaʿ-i saʿdayn*, 513.
74. Tabasi, *Athar-i Darwish Muhammad-i Tabasi*, 334–35.
75. For later accounts of the circulation and significance of Indian and Indian Ocean furniture, see Um, "Chairs, Writing Tables, and Chests," 721–25.
76. Aubin, *Matériaux*, 201.
77. Peacock, "ʿIyani," 176–77.
78. Astarabadi, *Tarikh-i Fereshteh*, 336–37.
79. On the Sayyid dynasty khutba, see Schimmel, *Islam in the Indian Subcontinent*, 36.
80. Anooshahr, *Turkestan and the Rise of Eurasian Empires*, 141.
81. Binbaş, *Intellectual Networks*, 62.
82. Binbaş, "Sharaf al-Dīn ʿAlī Yazdī," 65. See a detailed discussion of these conflicts in Dekkiche, "New Source," 248–55.
83. Tabasi, *Athar-i Darwish Muhammad-i Tabasi*, 335. As Binbaş has discussed, Sharaf al-din ʿAli Yazdi was tasked with taking the kiswa from Yazd to Herat before it was sent to Egypt: Binbaş, "Sharaf al-Dīn ʿAlī Yazdī," 63–65.
84. Manz, *Power, Politics and Religion*, 243; Binbaş, *Intellectual Networks*, 63. See also Aubin, "De Kūhbanān a Bidar," 242–43.
85. Tabasi, *Athar-i Darwish Muhammad-i Tabasi*, 335.

3

Shrines, Cosmos, Territory

The Making of the Taft Khanaqah

"Two kings cannot coexist in one city."

Waʿizi, *Treatise on the Virtues of Shah Neʿmatullah Vali*, 123.

Attributed to Timur, the founder of the Timurid dynasty (1370–1507), the epigraph of this chapter is recorded in the earliest biography of Shah Neʿmatullah Vali, written by ʿAbd al-ʿAziz b. Shir Malik Waʿizi in the first half of the fifteenth century.[1] The statement is said to have been made in a conversation between Timur and Shah Neʿmatullah in Samarqand. Worried about the Sufi's growing popularity, Timur asked him to leave the city. In doing so, Timur goes so far as to equate Shah Neʿmatullah's status with his own by the use of the same title (king, *padshah*). The passage stands at several layers of remove from the event it narrates, representing the biographer's perception of the court's perception of the Sufi's power. However, regardless of whether Timur said these words or not, the anxieties surrounding the Sufi's proximity to the court, and the resulting assertion of a need for distance—as this and the following chapters will show—exerted a decisive impact on both the movement of Neʿmatullahi Sufis across regions and the formation of their architectural network.

This chapter accounts for the absence of Timurid patronage at the shrine at Mahan as noted in the discussion of its portal in chapter 1. To do so, it turns its attention away from Mahan to engage with the early history of the Neʿmatullahi network as told through their earliest major architectural complex, the Shah Vali khanaqah, located in Taft, a village near the central Iranian city of Yazd. The Shah Vali khanaqah predates the transformation of the Mahan shrine from humble structures into a monumental funerary tomb in the 1430s. Both Mahan and Taft contain significant potential for tracing the early history of the Neʿmatullahis' architectural network. While Mahan represents a complex with preexisting history that gathered momentum with the patronage of the Bahmanids of India, the complex at Taft, located about four hundred kilometers to the southeast of Mahan, was developed from scratch through the patronage of the Timurids. In telling the story of this lesser-known and largely lost complex of the Neʿmatullahi Sufis in Taft, I also aim to shed light on the agency of the Sufis in bringing about this grand project.

Drawing on surviving architectural elements of the complex in Taft, this chapter first offers hypotheses on what the khanaqah of Taft constituted at the time of its inception and what significance it held for the Neʿmatullahis. Examined alongside hagiographies and poetic descriptions, the physical remains reveal how an anthropocentric idea of the universe was articulated in the space of the khanaqah. This hypothetical reconstruction of the architecture raises questions about the extent and significance of the patronage of the Sufi network in Iran between the 1410s, when the Taft complex started to take shape, and the death of Shah Neʿmatullah in 1431. This is followed by a contextualization of the patronage of the khanaqah within broader patterns in the Timurids' patronage of Sufism, focusing specifically on the Timurid prince, governor of Fars, and patron of the Taft khanaqah Iskandar b. ʿUmar Shaykh (r. 1409–15). I examine the contentious alignments between courtly circles and Sufis that brought the Taft complex into existence: Timurid patronage and their interest in a sacral model of kingship, which played out against the backdrop of internal conflicts and imperial ambitions, as well as the pursuit, negotiation, and justification of these acts of patronage by the Neʿmatullahi Sufis.

Combining historical and philological questions around a hypothetical reconstruction of a complex that is largely lost, this chapter is guided by two principles: first, that the absence of patronage can be as important as its presence for our understanding of material culture and its political functions; second, that the study of patronage needs to expand beyond the finished product, the actions of the patron, and their possible motives. If we want to understand the intricacies of relationships between Sufism and materiality, the study of patronage should extend to the political alignments and social formations that initiated it, the negotiations that facilitated it, and its consequent reception. This expansive view makes it possible to examine the role of Sufis as active agents in the making of their own built environment. As such, this chapter positions architecture as a material entity that stands at the intersection of collaborative and at times competing visions among the patron, the Sufi network, and their audiences. Significantly, in the Taft khanaqah, these notions of collaboration and competition were inscribed onto the building as a rationale for its construction. The Sufis' encounter with the patron, and their broader engagement with patronage, was encapsulated in the epigraphy so as to frame the devotees' encounter with the building.

Placing these stories of patronage in central Iran alongside those in the Deccan from the previous chapter elucidates the privileges and opportunities that the Sufi network's geographical expansion provided for their architectural complexes. Taking note of these opportunities, the final section of the chapter turns to the potential challenges that transregionality posed, not only to the maintenance and financial management of their sacred sites but also to the self-representation of the Neʿmatullahis in Iran.

I. Architecture, Text, and Ambiguity

Home to the Shah Vali khanaqah, Taft is a village about twenty-six kilometers to the southwest of the central Iranian city of Yazd, on the route to Shiraz. The village is situated in a small valley on the northern skirt of Mount Shirkuh (fig. 3.1). Supplied with abundant water resources from the mountain, Taft's *qanat*s (underground water channels) provide one of the main sources of water for Yazd and the wider region.[2] The Shah Vali complex is situated in a key location by the old seasonal river of Taft and on the route of principal qanats (fig. 3.2).

Today, the Shah Vali khanaqah survives in an extremely fragmentary and heavily restored state. There is a stand-alone domed structure from the complex's first phase of construction in the fifteenth century, since restored and converted into a small museum (fig. 3.3). There is also a mosque, attributed to the Safavid period (1501–1736), that contains earlier elements as well as a bazaar, a cistern, and a *husayniya* (a structure for Shiʿa commemorative ceremonies) datable to the Qajar period (1796–1925) and later (figs. 3.4 and 3.5). Based on Safavid chronicles such as the *Jamiʿ-i Mufidi* and a poem on Taft written in the late seventeenth century by the poet and vizier of Yazd Mirza Mohsen Taʾthir, we know that the complex still stood in that period

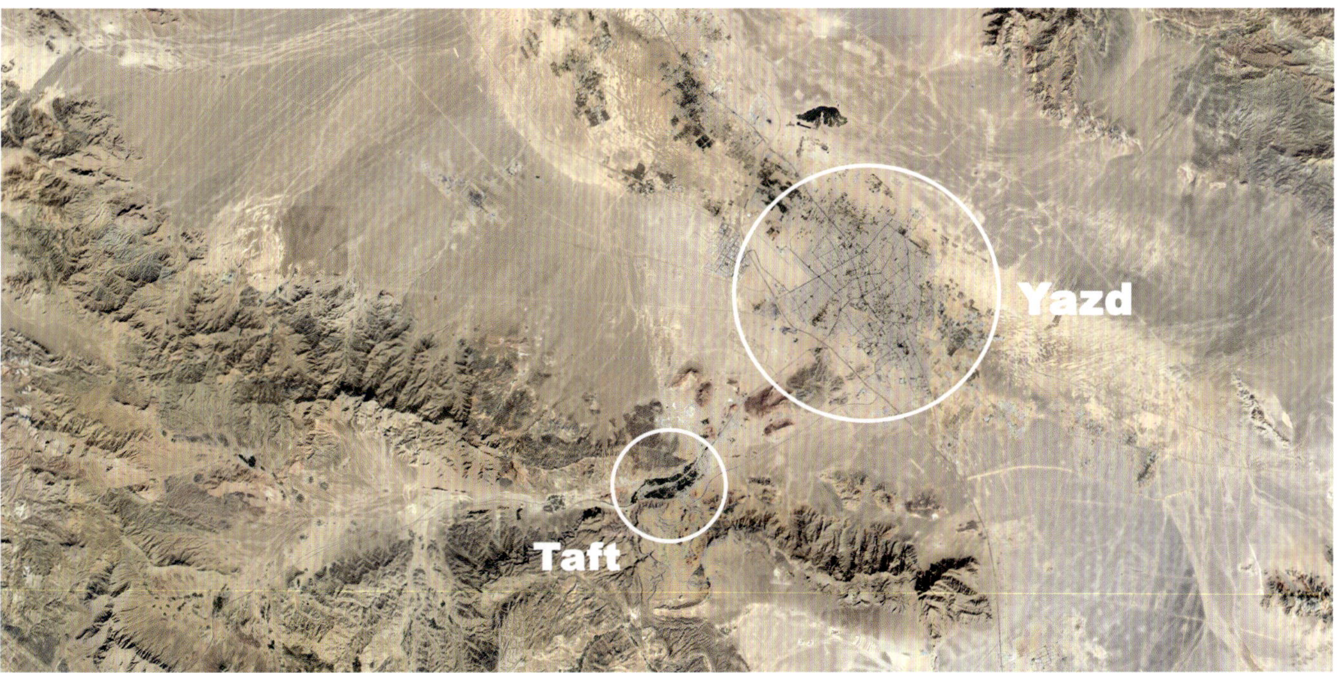

FIGURE 3.1. Taft and the Shirkuh Mountain in relation to Yazd. *Google Earth Pro; with additions by author.*

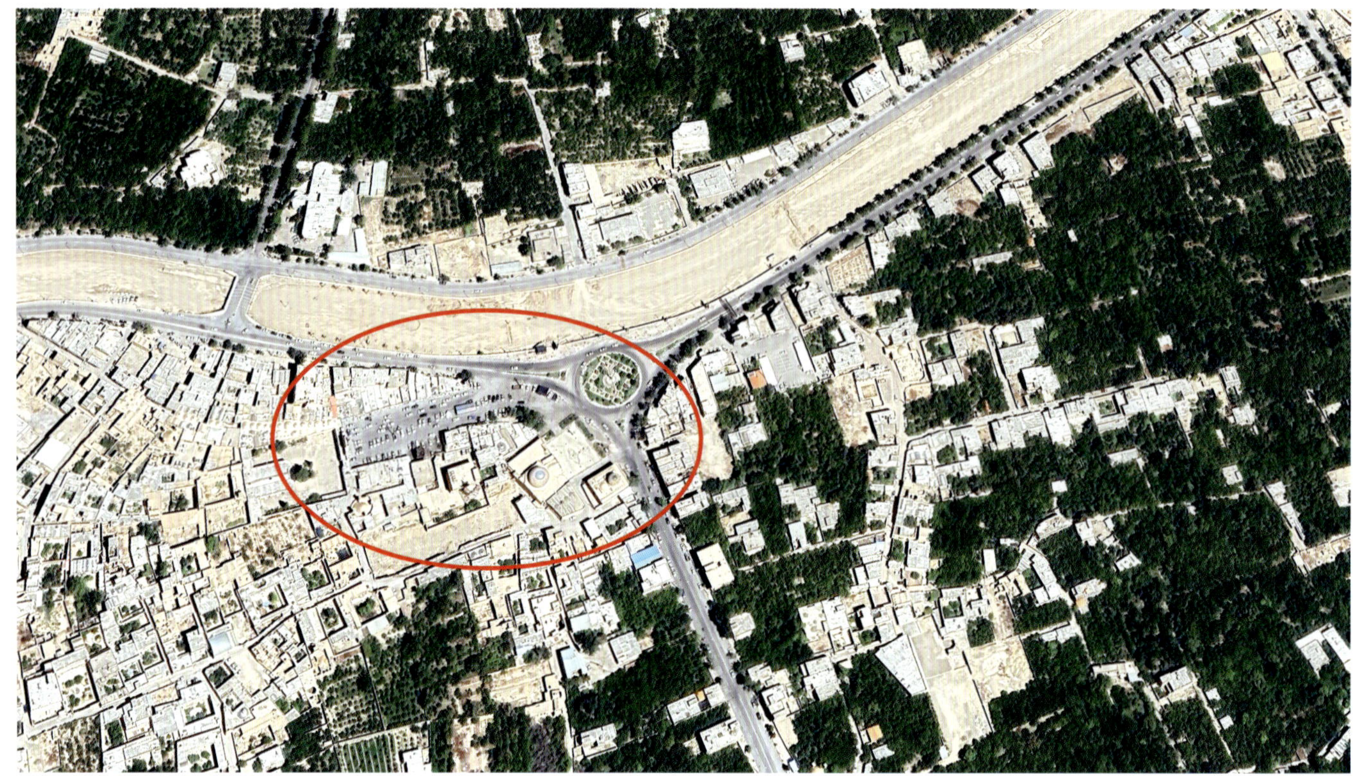

ABOVE, FIGURE 3.2.
Aerial view of the Shah Vali complex in Taft, with the Yazd-Taft Road to the right. The two domes are the Shah Vali Mosque (*left*) and the mausoleum (*right*). The open space and the facade to the west (*left*) of the mosque are the Qajari additions. *Google Earth Pro; with additions by author.*

FACING TOP, FIGURE 3.3.
The stand-alone structure converted into the Museum of Anthropology at the Shah Vali complex in Taft. *Photograph by author, 2013.*

FACING BOTTOM, FIGURE 3.4.
Shah Vali complex in Taft, the Museum of Anthropology (*left*) and the Shah Vali mosque (*right*). *Photograph by author, 2014.*

as it was built and developed in the fifteenth and sixteenth centuries. While some destruction occurred in the Qajar period, the majority likely dates to the twentieth century, mainly in order to make way for new roads and the small square built in front of the Shah Vali complex.[3]

The construction of the Shah Vali khanaqah was prompted by patronage from the Timurid prince Iskandar Mirza, later known as Iskandar Sultan. While governor of Shiraz, he offered land and tax relief to Shah Neᶜmatullah for the purpose of building the khanaqah, which consisted of a *kushk* (lit. kiosk; palace), a soup kitchen, a holy mausoleum, a bath, and lodges for the poor and Sufis.[4] Since only one of these initial structures is extant today, the nature of the fifteenth-century complex is shrouded in ambiguity and can be inferred only on the basis of textual and spatial speculations. Apart from several structures that are lost, some elements have been moved around or otherwise removed from the site. In this first section of the chapter, I combine the fragmentary material in situ with textual sources, such as local histories and biographies of Shah Neᶜmatullah, in order to establish hypotheses about the khanaqah's form, construction process, and relation to the natural and built environments.

The earliest account of the khanaqah at Taft appears in a chapter on sources of water in Yazd in Katib's *Tarikh-i jadid-i Yazd*—a local history that covers events up until 1457–58.[5] Katib gives an account of the different elements of the complex and their spatial arrangement:

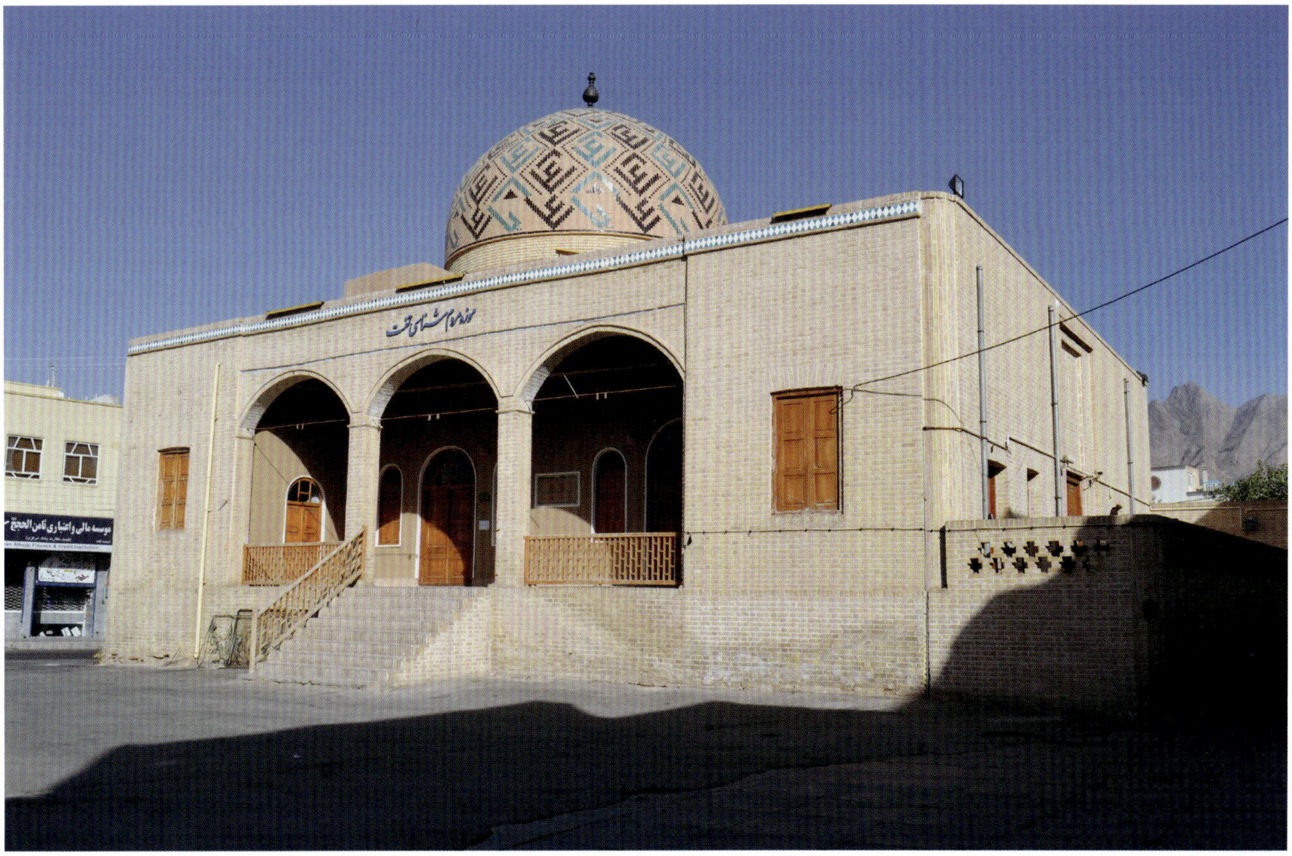

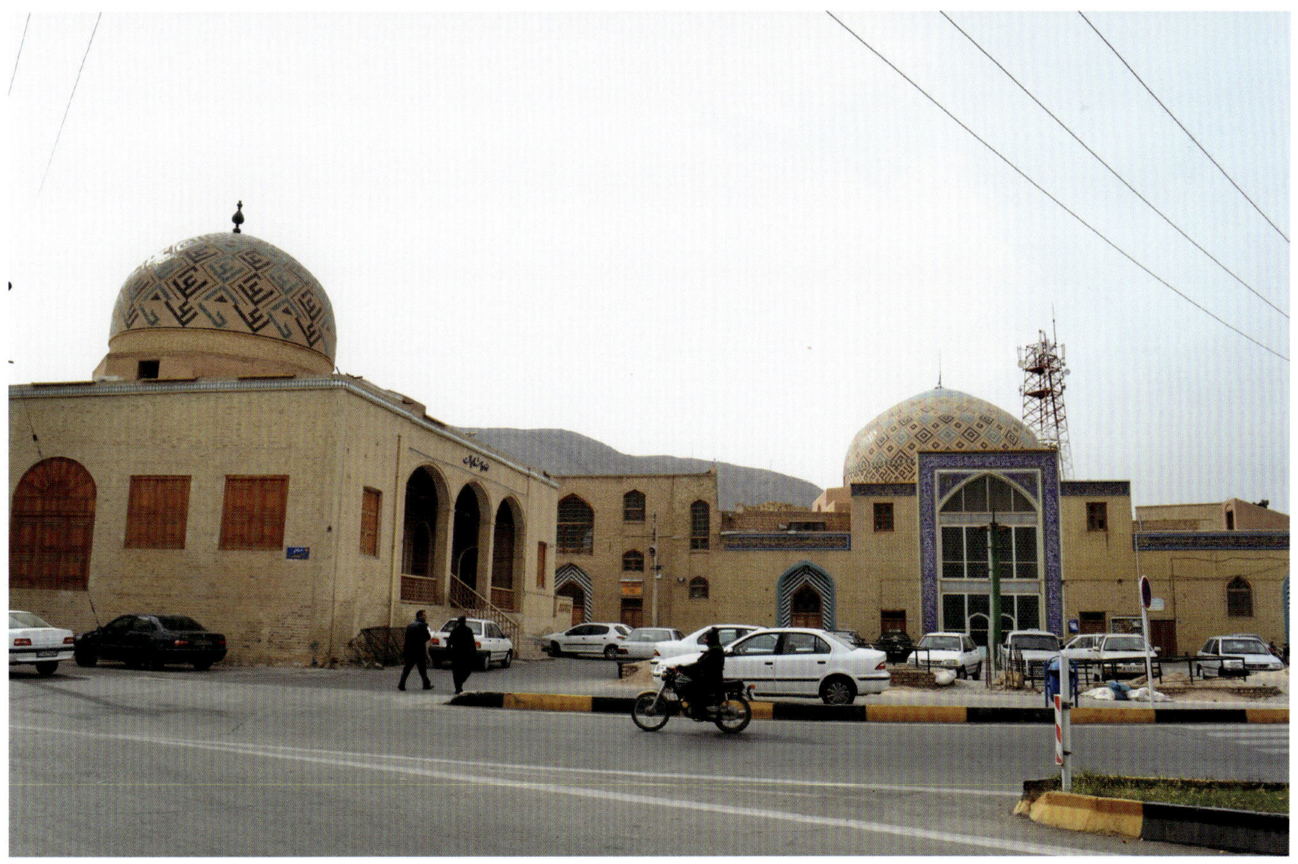

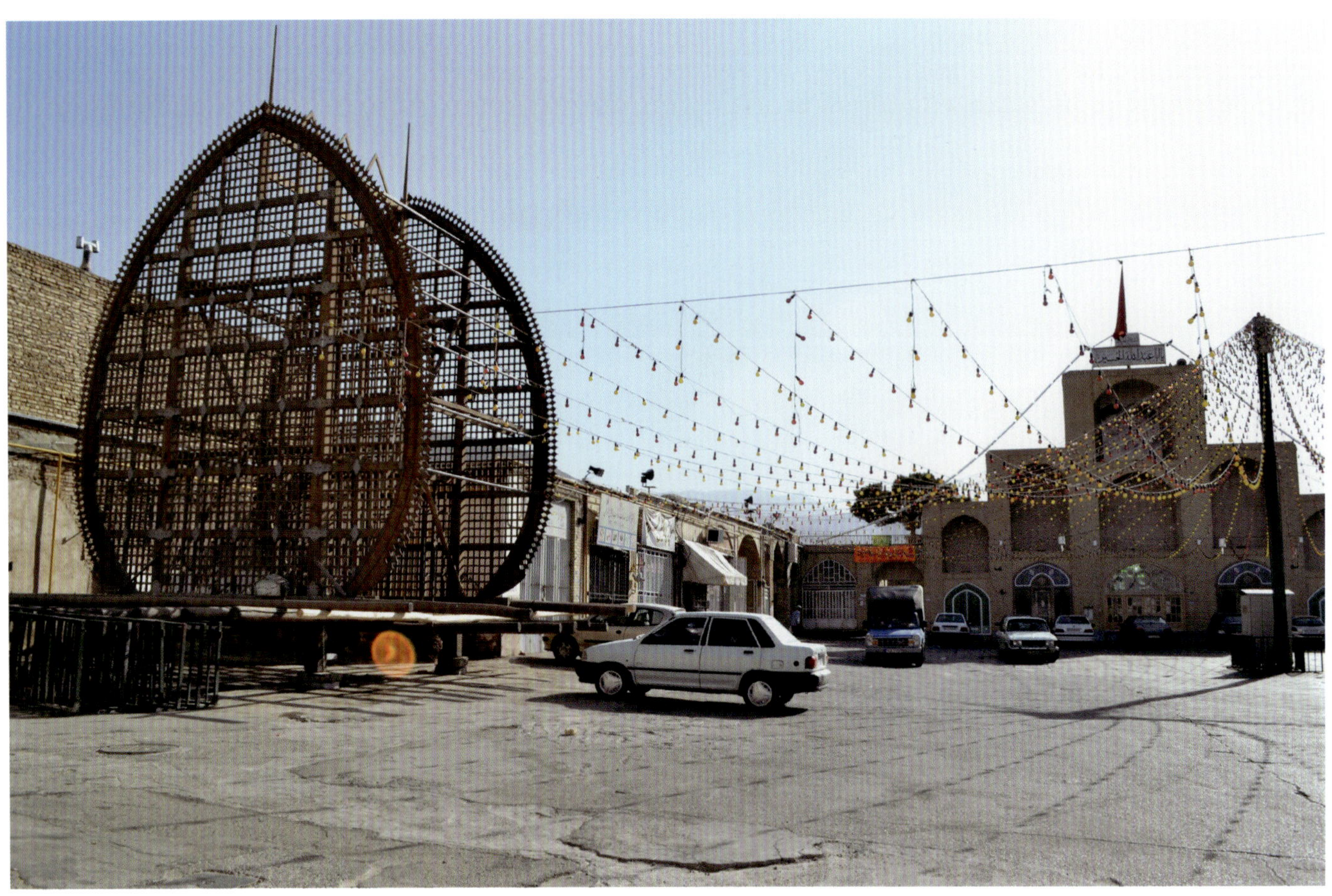

FIGURE 3.5. Shah Vali complex in Taft, Qajar expansions with the husayniya in the background. *Photograph by author, 2013.*

The founder (*bani*) of this khanaqah was . . . Amir Nur al-din Sayyid Ne^cmatullah, who was the pole (qutb) of the saints of his time and model of the people of faith, the sunlight of the heavens of gnosis (*^cirfan*), master of the world and its inhabitants. The truth is that this khanaqah is the envy of the garden of paradise. . . . It was built as a square (*murabba^c*), and in the middle of it there is a high, lofty kushk. Surrounding the khanaqah, lodges were built for the indigent and the renunciates (*fuqara wa masakin*), and a beautiful kitchen (*matbakh*) was constructed where day in and day out food was prepared for the poor and the wealthy.

The following verses, from the extraordinary poems of Ne^cmatullah, are inscribed over the entrance of the dome chamber:

If you should wish to host Ne^cmatullah,
the tablecloth must stretch all the way around the sphere of the world.
And if you should build a small palace to match his magnanimity,
the four walls must enclose the seven climes.

On one side of the mazar, a magnificent *suffa* is built. On the side of the suffa, from one direction, water from [the qanats of] Sa^cdabad and Nasiri flow into the khanaqah and divide into two streams: one stream flows all around the courtyard of the khanaqah and [the other?] around the *shadurwan* (foundation, fountain, or water channel) of the kiosk. Then they mix together again and flow inside the *haram* (living quarters) of the great noble-borns (*makhdumzadigan*), who are the light of the eye of the earth and earthly creatures, and then into orchards and gardens.

Behind the kushk, which would be the back of the khanaqah, a blessed tomb (mazar) with a high cupola was built. The sanctified sarcophagus was cut from marble, and a crypt was dug. However, his blessed body found tranquility in the luminous tomb at Mahan.

And on the corner of the khanaqah an excellent *hammam* (bathhouse) was built, endowed as *waqf* to travelers. On the side of the aforementioned suffa is the *khalwat khaneh* (residence, retreat chamber) of . . . Maulana Sharaf al-din Yazdi. . . .

When Amirzadeh Iskandar b. ʿUmar Shaykh gave the village of Taft as *suyurghal* to the aforementioned one [i.e., Sharaf al-din Yazdi], he settled in Taft and in the year 821 [1418–19] [and] built this excellent [khalwat khaneh].[6]

There are several points to make about this extensive description. Here, I am mainly concerned with the general layout of the khanaqah and its significance as the earliest major complex of the Sufi network. I will return to the poem cited in the middle of the description later in this chapter and to specific key elements of the complex in the following chapters. One major element of the khanaqah highlighted in the account above, for instance, is a funerary structure (mazar). What Katib emphasizes in his description of the mazar is a caveat about its function: "However, his [Shah Neʿmatullah's] blessed body found tranquility in the luminous tomb at Mahan."[7] This point is repeated in Mufid's description as well and perhaps aims to clarify a common misconception about the burial of Shah Neʿmatullah in the Taft complex.[8] As such, the importance of the funerary element of the Taft khanaqah, and the intended functions of the complex for the family of Shah Neʿmatullah, can best be discussed in close dialogue with the shrine at Mahan, a topic I will treat in chapter 4. The Safavid developments of the site, which postdate the account above, will be discussed in chapter 6.

Thinking through the layout of the khanaqah based on Katib's textual description, we are confronted with a perennial problem in the relationship between space and language. How much can we gather from words like *behind* and *beside* in reference to a space that no longer exists? To what extent does the fluidity of architectural terminology and its historicity contribute to these uncertainties? It is with these ambiguities in mind that I attempt to spatialize the text, approaching Katib's description of the khanaqah in relation to both later descriptions and architectural remains on the site.

The first and most straightforward element of the khanaqah's layout in Katib's account is a rectangular courtyard (sahn) built as a square (murabbaʿ). Around this courtyard, lodges as well as a soup kitchen (matbakh) were built. A bathhouse (hammam) occupied one corner. The next significant element is a kushk (generally meaning a kiosk or a palace) built in the middle of the courtyard. Based on Katib's spatial clues, the kushk should be a stand-alone kiosk-type building. Katib uses the term elsewhere in his history to describe another garden, called the Kushk Garden in Taft, referring to a building open on all sides with a marble pool in the middle and water channels around, surrounded by trees.[9]

In later textual descriptions of the khanaqah, the kushk seems to merge with another element, the suffa. When Katib refers to a suffa in his accounts, he is usually referring to an *ivan* (vaulted space).[10] Suffa could also mean a raised platform or building. Both of these features likely overlapped in the design of a kiosk. When ᶜAbd al-Razzaq Kermani, the author of a hagiographical treatise of Shah Neᶜmatullah (completed in 1506), commented on the khanaqah of Taft, the suffa was the only element of the complex he singled out, referring to it as "*suffa-yi ba safa*" (the pleasant ivan).[11] Later, in a seventeenth-century account of the khanaqah in the *Jamiᶜ-i Mufidi*, the author, Mufid, opens his description of the khanaqah by referring to a lofty kushk in the middle of the complex, known as Suffa-yi Safa.[12] Were the suffa and the kushk the same? According to Mufid, they were, but according to Katib, they were two different structures. Are we dealing with loose or inaccurate descriptions?

Both the *Jamiᶜ-i Mufidi* and the *Tarikh-i jadid-i Yazd* are local histories with a commitment to the region of Yazd and its architecture, especially regarding questions of patronage. In another chapter of the *Jamiᶜ-i Mufidi*, based on the seventeenth-century hagiography written by Sunᶜullah, Mufid locates the construction of his Suffa-yi Safa in a later period, in the sixteenth century. He refers to a descendant of Shah Neᶜmatullah, Amir Nizam al-din ᶜAbd al-Baqi (d. 1514), who built a Suffa-yi Safa in the khanaqah of Taft.[13] One possibility is that Mufid confused two separate and significant elements of the khanaqah with each other. Another plausible explanation is that Mufid inflated the extent of constructions materialized closer to his time: as I will show about another part of the complex in chapter 6, it is possible that Mufid was conflating the act of mere refurbishment with constructing an architectural element from scratch in order to augment and praise Safavid-era patronage.[14]

While Mufid's account offers an update on the development of the khanaqah between the mid-fifteenth and seventeenth centuries, his account is not as detailed as Katib's on the earlier structures of the site. Katib walks the reader through the complex, as he does with other major urban structures on the path of the main qanats of Taft, allowing water and its movement to guide the reader's imagination through space. He distinguishes between the kushk and the suffa, noting that water from the two main qanats of Taft enters the complex from the side of the suffa; one stream circulates around the courtyard, and the other goes to the shadurwan of the kushk. *Shadurwan* could mean the foundation of a structure, a fountain, or a water channel in this context. Elsewhere, when Katib uses the term *shadurwan* to describe the kiosk in the middle of the Garden of Kushk in Taft, he seems to be referring to water channels around the foundation of the kiosk.[15] If the kushk in Katib's description was a stand-alone building with water channels around it, then his kushk and suffa would be separate entities. If, as implied by one of Mufid's accounts, the two were the same, a feasible possibility is that one or more suffas in the khanaqah were referred to as Suffa-yi Safa over time. This would explain the

FACING, FIGURE 3.6. Shah Vali complex in Taft, view of the two domes covering chambers of the current museum building. *Photograph by author, 2014.*

inconsistent location of the suffa in the writings of the two authors: Mufid's suffa was part of, or the same as, the kushk in the middle of the courtyard and was called Suffa-yi Safa as a whole while Katib's suffa was a separate structure that defined the urban territory of the khanaqah in relation to its surroundings (i.e., where the qanats entered the complex). The last part of Katib's account suggests that this main layout of the complex, the courtyard with the kushk in the middle and the suffa on the one side of it, was in place by 1418–19 when Timurid historian and vizier Sharaf al-din ʿAli Yazdi built his khalwat khaneh and took up residence in the khanaqah.[16]

II. Reading the Architecture: Reconstructing the Khanaqah at Taft

Apart from the Shah Vali Mosque, which is a later addition to the early fifteenth-century core of the complex, the only other building extant on the site today is a highly restored stand-alone domed structure housing Taft's Anthropology Museum (fig. 3.3).[17] The building consists of a chamber with a double-shell dome covered with plain bricks, some glazed blue and green and others unglazed, that form large inscriptions of the name of the first Shiʿa Imam and son-in-law of the Prophet Muhammad, O' ʿAli (ya ʿAli) in *bannayi* (square kufic) script. A low smaller dome covers another room to the south of the main chamber (figs. 3.6 and 3.7). The building is raised on a platform

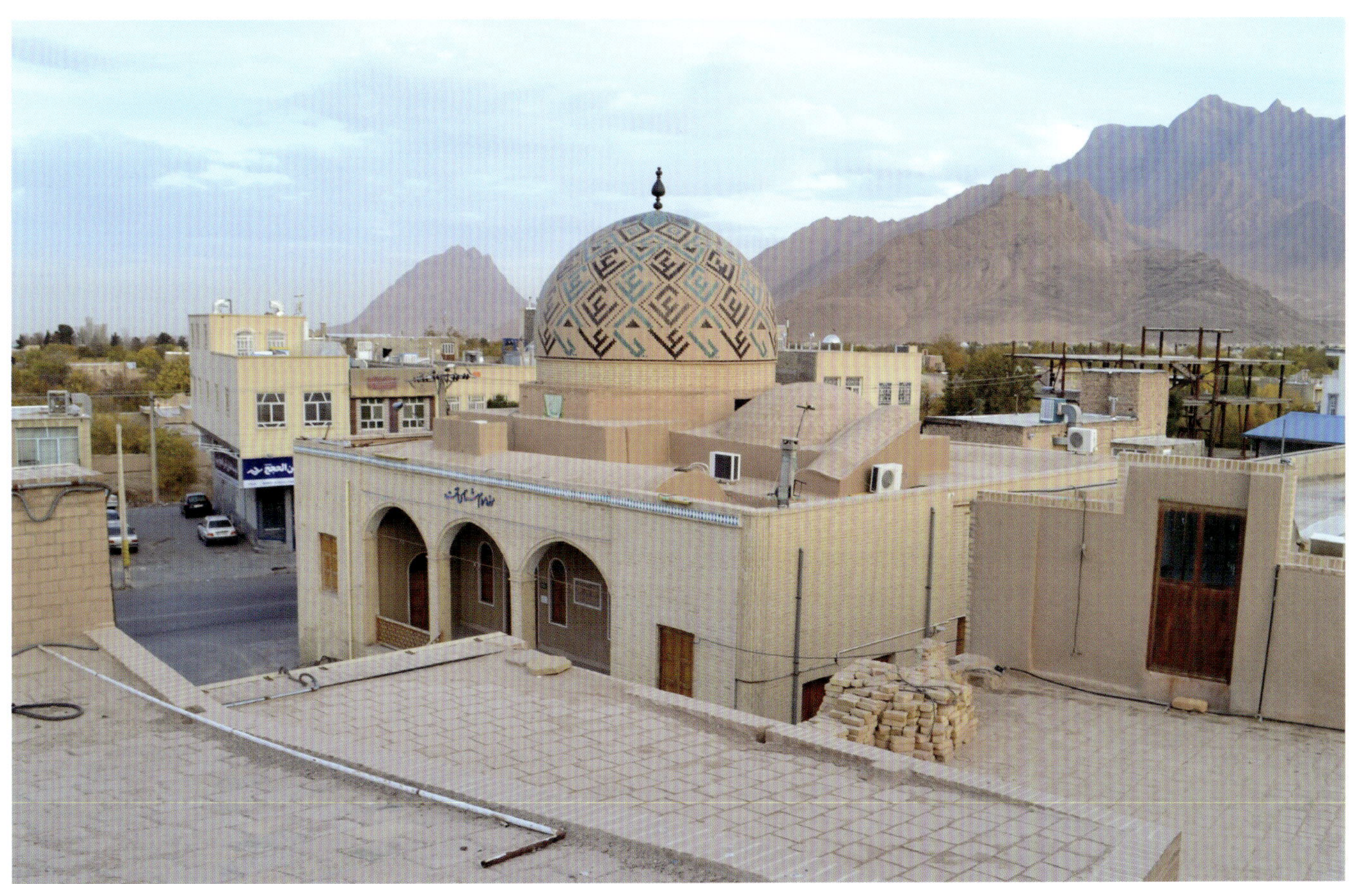

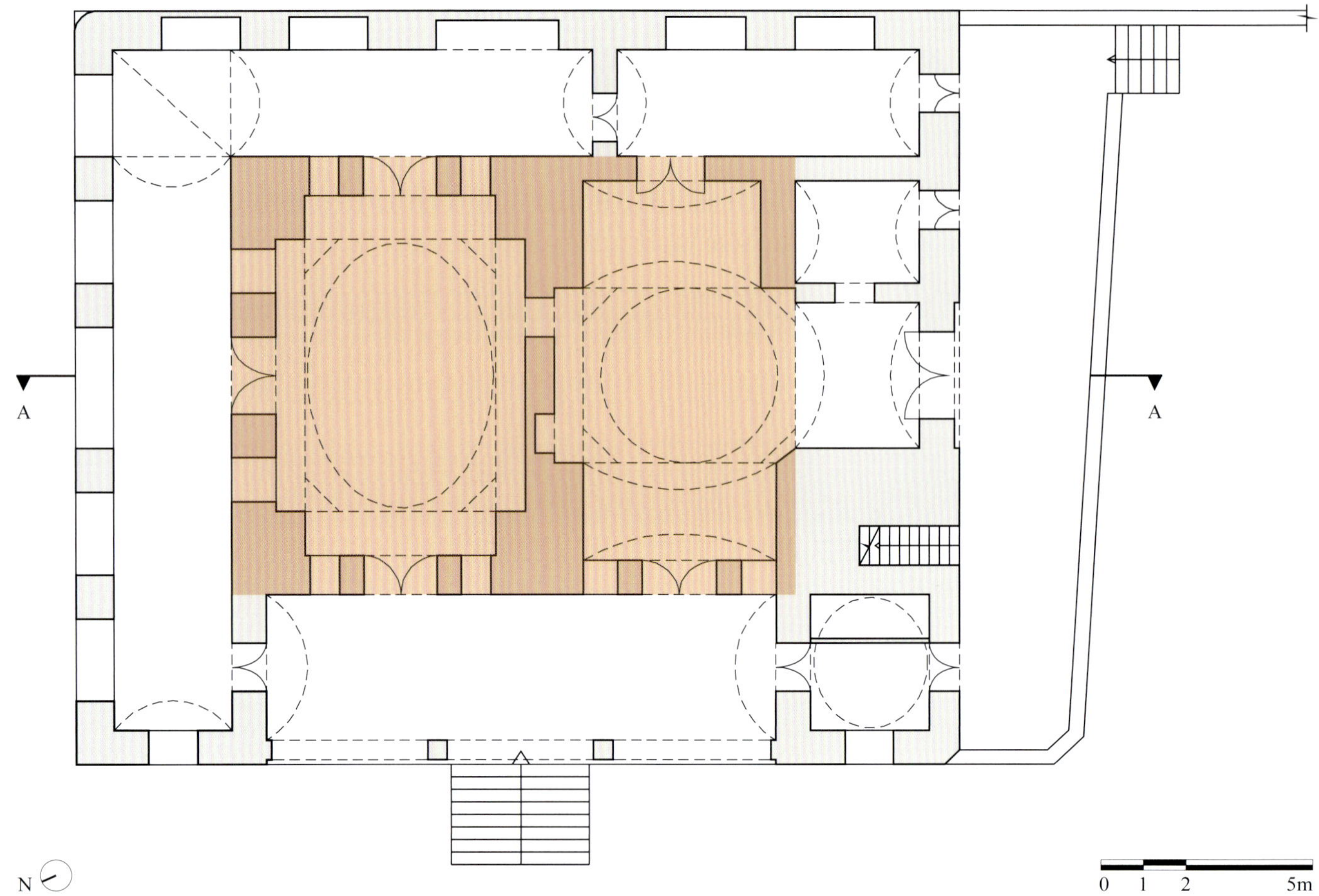

FIGURE 3.7. Plan of the current museum building at Taft. *Drawing by Farah Michel, after plans by Iran's Cultural Heritage Organization in Yazd.*

and accessed via steps. A crypt can be entered from the south of the building. A corridor wraps around the two domes on the north and east sides. On the west, an arcade, consisting of three arches, contains the current entrance of the building (figs. 3.3 and 3.4).

Three features of this building correspond to Katib's description of the fifteenth-century tomb (mazar): the dome, the crypt, and the fact that it was used as a funerary structure at some point in its history, based on burials that were discovered in a recent restoration.[18] In the southern dome chamber there is an anonymous tombstone, the sole remnant of a group dating from the mid-fifteenth to sixteenth century that Iraj Afshar recorded in situ (fig. 3.8).[19] Many of these are now kept at the office of the local branch of Iran's Cultural Heritage Organization in Taft.

In addition to these tombstones, the funerary function of the building is affirmed in a twentieth-century inscription band inside the main dome chamber, recording a restoration project during the Pahlavi era (1925–79). A tile inscription in nastaʿliq script, dated 1944–45 and written by Ibrahim Buzari, scribe of the Iranian parliament and royal court at the time, refers to the building as *buqʿa-yi Khalilullah-i Thani* (tomb of Khalilullah II).

We know almost nothing about Khalilullah-i Thani except that he was a descendant of Shah Neʿmatullah and that based on the chronogram on his

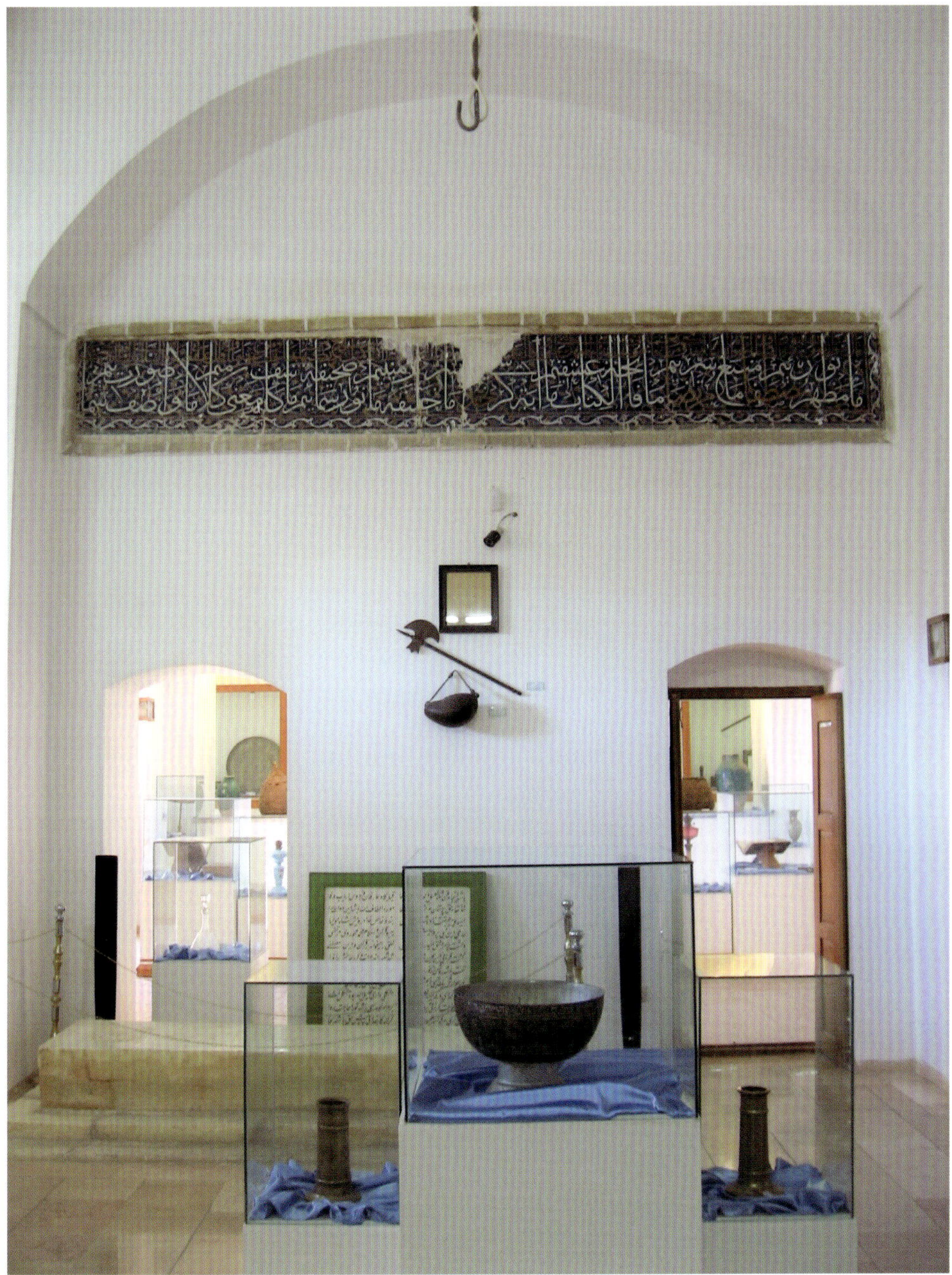

FIGURE 3.8. Interior of the southern dome chamber at the complex in Taft with the remaining tombstone. *Photograph by author, 2012.*

tombstone, "*shahid-i Herat*" (martyr of Herat), he died in Herat in 925/1519–20. His tombstone is among the group recorded in the building by Afshar and later moved to the Cultural Heritage office of Taft. To my knowledge, the aforementioned inscription on the interior is the only reference to this building being named after Khalilullah-i Thani. In any case, if we accept it as a highly restored version of the funerary structure mentioned in Katib's account, this means the building was associated with Khalilullah-i Thani about a century after its construction. This, of course, raises the question of the function of the building prior to Khalilullah's death in 1519–20, a question I will return to in chapter 4.

FIGURE 3.9. Arcades on the northeast and northwest sides of the current museum building in Taft, rendered as partially open on the northeast in the drawing after a photograph by Iraj Afshar (*top*) and completely closed in its current state (*bottom*). *Drawing by Farah Michel, photograph by author, 2014.*

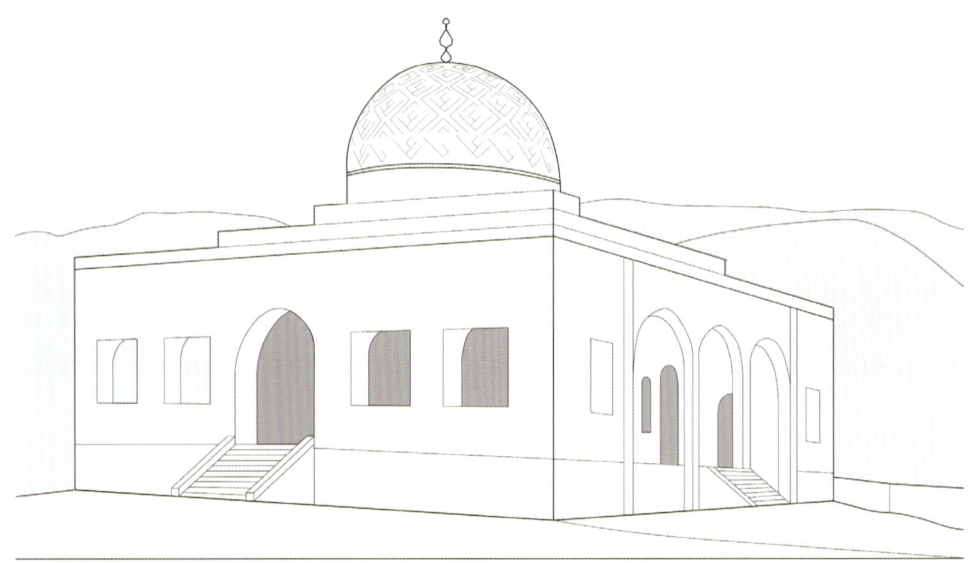

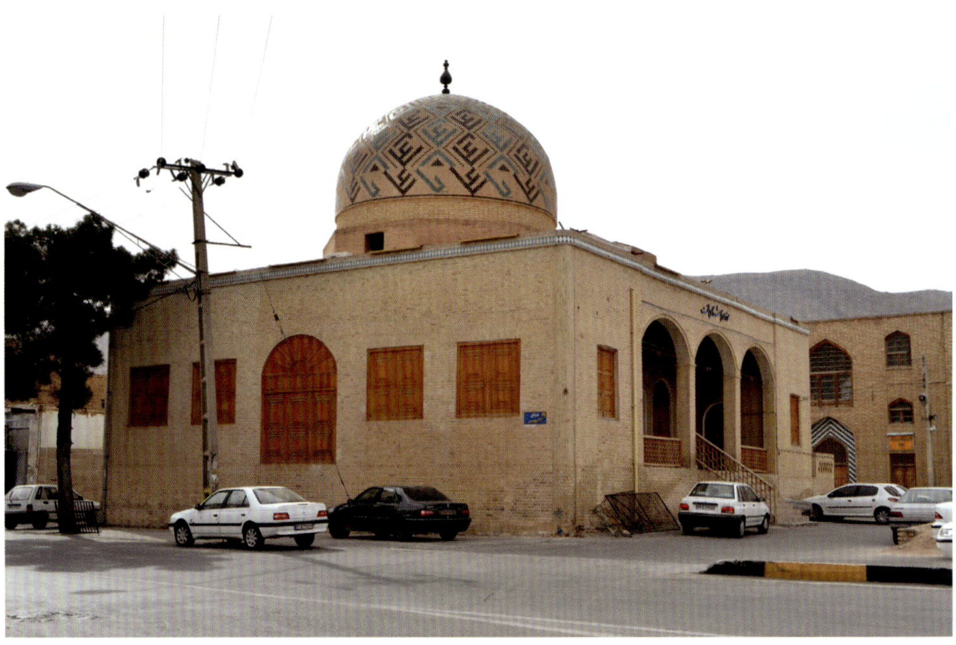

A photograph published by Iraj Afshar in *Yadgarha-yi Yazd* (*Monuments of Yazd*) raises interesting points about the function of the museum building and about the relationship between the mazar and the kushk in Katib's description (fig. 3.9). The photograph shows two sides of the building, northeast and northwest, both with open arcades accessed through stairs.[20] The northwest arcade is still open, offering the only entrance to the museum, while the northeast arcade is now closed and incorporated into the museum's interior space. The photograph raises the possibility that similar openings existed on all four sides of the building. In fact, clear traces of similar alterations can be seen on the northeast and southeast facades (figs. 3.9 and 3.10). Together with the

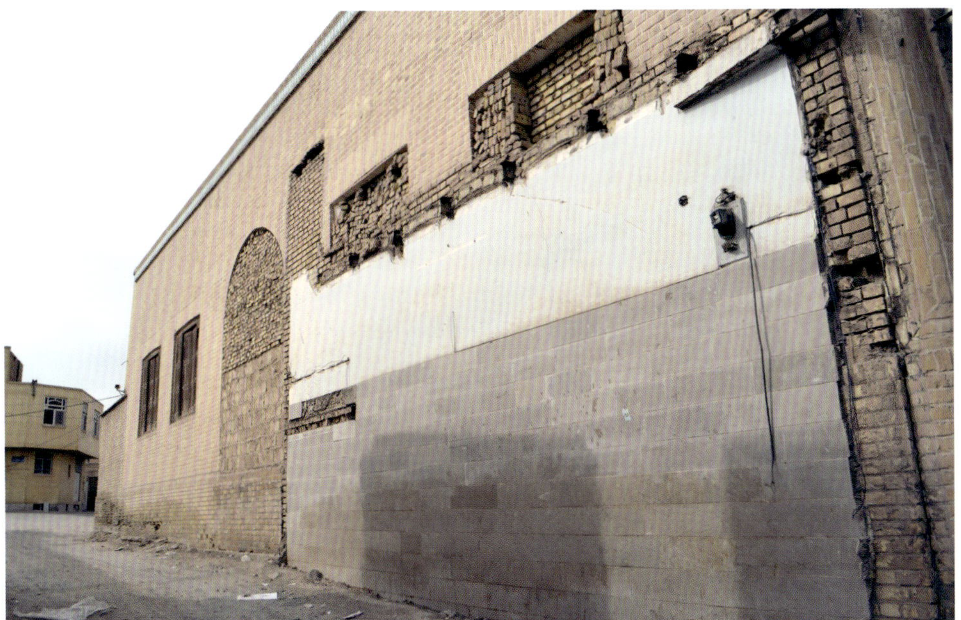

FIGURE 3.10. Closed arcades on the southeast side of the current museum in the Taft complex. *Photograph by author, 2014.*

terrace that exists on the southwest side, these arcades wrapped around the two domed chambers of the building and provided an entrance on different sides (likely three, save the *qibla* side on the southwest, which indicates the direction of Mecca). This spatial arrangement suggests that the building was a stand-alone semiopen structure and that the current museum could be the fifteenth-century kushk in the middle of the courtyard of the khanaqah.

Are we then dealing with two funerary structures—a mazar and a kushk built in the fifteenth century and later adapted as a funerary structure—one of which has since been lost? Or did the mazar and kushk both occupy the same structure as the current museum? Revisiting the accounts of Katib and Mufid in this light, two possibilities arise. Katib notes a lofty kushk built in the middle of the khanaqah's courtyard. Later, he locates the mazar behind the kushk.[21] Was the mazar a stand-alone structure behind the kushk or attached to it? I mentioned a low dome behind the main dome chamber of the surviving building on the site (figs. 3.6 and 3.7). This is the domed room housing the remaining tombstone. Furthermore, this smaller dome chamber is on the same side of the building where the crypt can be accessed. These observations together introduce the possibility that the mazar and kushk in Katib's account were joined.

Different parts of Mufid's description both support and contradict this hypothesis. Right after mentioning the mazar, Mufid notes that at a later time, on the qibla side—that is, most probably the qibla side of the mazar—a mosque was built.[22] The surviving mosque is almost behind the qibla side of the current museum, confirming the possibility that the two interconnected parts of the museum were the kushk and mazar. But Mufid's description runs contrary to this hypothesis when he describes the mazar opposite (*dar barabar-i*) the

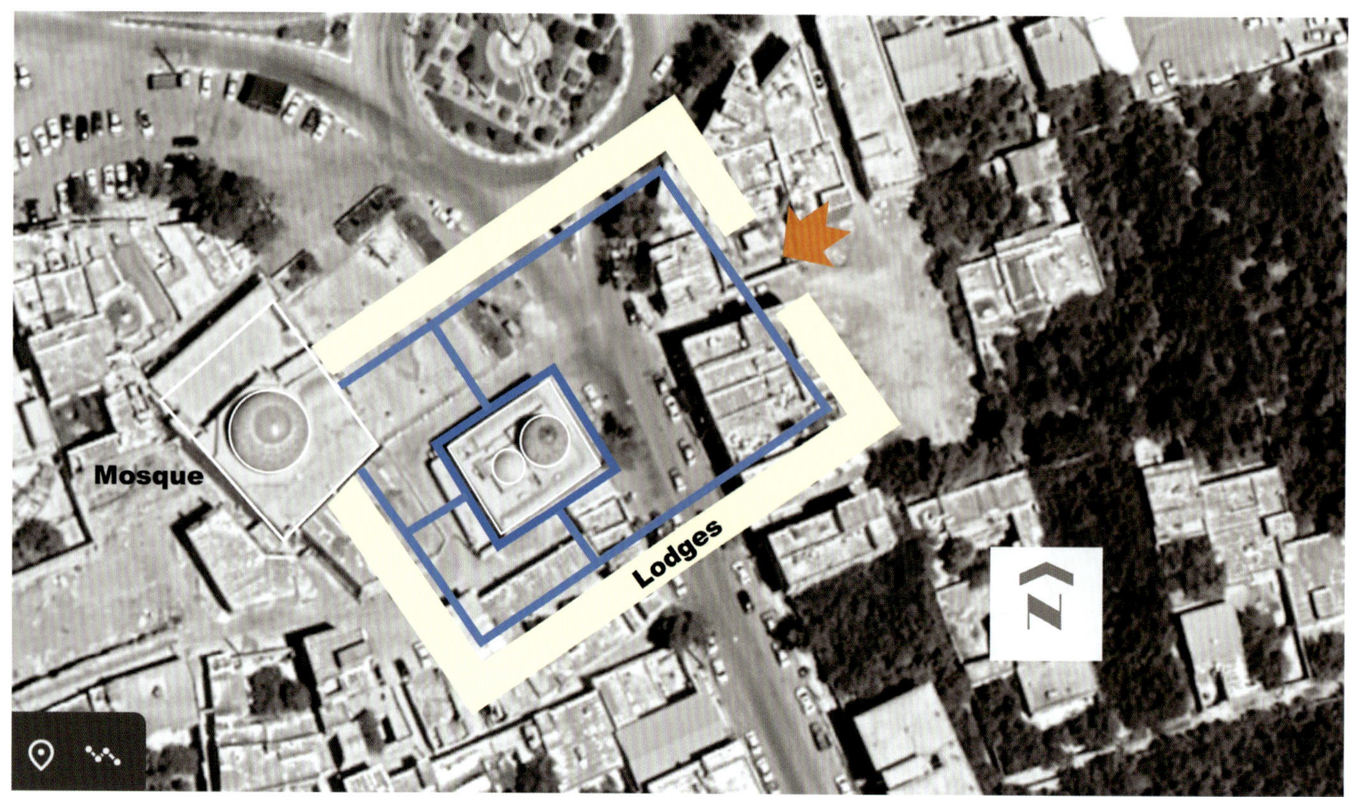

FIGURE 3.11. Schematic plan of the khanaqah of Shah Vali in Taft. *Map © Google Earth Pro; drawing by author.*

kushk, which could imply detachment. Is it possible that another now-lost structure was placed just opposite the current museum, perhaps even mirroring it, as suggested by the connotation of the phrase *dar-barabar*? Are Mufid and Katib both accurate without offering us the full picture? In either case, the openness of the current museum, whether it corresponds with the mazar alone or with the mazar and kushk together, suggests it was a central element in the courtyard of the khanaqah.

Another point that I want to draw on is the directionality of the complex according to Katib and Mufid. One would expect some degree of orientation toward the qibla in a funerary structure. If the current museum was in fact the mazar-kushk, as I suggest, the area around the southern chamber defines the back of the complex, as noted by Katib. When the mosque was added, the complex extended in the direction of the qibla. This suggests an axis running northeast and southwest for the courtyard and the complex as a whole. This orientation corresponds to Katib's description in two ways: first, it matches the direction of the two qanats in Taft that he mentions, which, according to his account, flowed directly from there into the Kushk Garden, presumably located to the northeast of the complex.[23] Second, such an orientation also matches the course of the qanats of Taft toward Yazd, which corresponded to the Shiraz-Taft-Yazd road on which most travelers would be arriving. Standing on the southern side of the river occupied by several gardens (as opposed to the residential texture of the town on the northern side), the once colossal body of this architectural complex would stand out both in contrast to the gardens and due to its proximity to the main road. A sketch of this viable layout for the spatial configuration of the complex can be seen in figure 3.11.

III. The Khanaqah and the Cosmos

In the context of descriptions of a khanaqah, the juxtaposition of the words *suffa* and *safa* (Persian: lightness, purity) in both Mufid's and Kermani's accounts presents an interesting dialogue between architectural terminology and the etymology of Sufism. Indeed, historically, each term played a role in etymological debates around the word *Sufi* itself.[24] Although not as widespread as *Suf*, the woolen material from which Sufis' cloaks were made, both suffa and Safa were historically discussed as possible, although unproven and grammatically unlikely, etymological roots of the word *Sufi*—connotations that, regardless of their accuracy, were probably enshrined in popular imagination.

The connection between the words *Sufi* and *suffa* is premised on the likening of Sufis to Ashab al-Suffa, a group of Prophet Muhammad's companions who, upon migration from Mecca to Medina, took refuge on the suffa of the Prophet's mosque—a raised platform or a sheltered area.[25] Given the khanaqah's accommodation of travelers and the poor, the title was thus appropriate for the kushk, which was a significant section of the complex. It was customary in architectural descriptions to associate suffas with accommodation for the poor and dervishes. Katib, for instance, refers to four suffas built in the madrasa of Dar al-Safa (also known as Qutbiyya) of Yazd for the accommodation of the poor—an example that brings the juxtaposition of the words *safa* in the name of the complex and *suffa* together with the charitable function of the space.[26]

The word *safa* was connected to the word *Sufi* in a variety of different ways, building on the connotation of safa as light and purity.[27] The pairing of suffa and safa was common in poetry.[28] Also common was the trio *Sufi-yi suffa-yi safa*, which further resonated with the pictorial image of a Sufi seated in an ivan, or on a sheltered raised platform, as found in paintings of Sufis across the Islamic world (fig. 3.12). By pairing suffa and safa in their descriptions of the khanaqah at Taft, authors Kermani and Mufid conjure up architectural images that overlap with conventional topoi in the popular reception of Sufis. Writing in the seventeenth century, the aforementioned Mirza Mohsen-i Taʾthir, who held the position of vizier in Yazd, utilizes the phrase "Sufi-yi suffa-yi safa" when describing Shah Vali's khanaqah in his poem about Taft.[29] By far, however, the most relevant example of this combination is found in the poetry of Shah Neʿmatullah himself.

> All that is known [lit. named] in the universe
> are servants to humankind, the king.
> [the universe is] like a khanaqah in six directions;
> the human is the Sufi of the suffa-yi safa.[30]

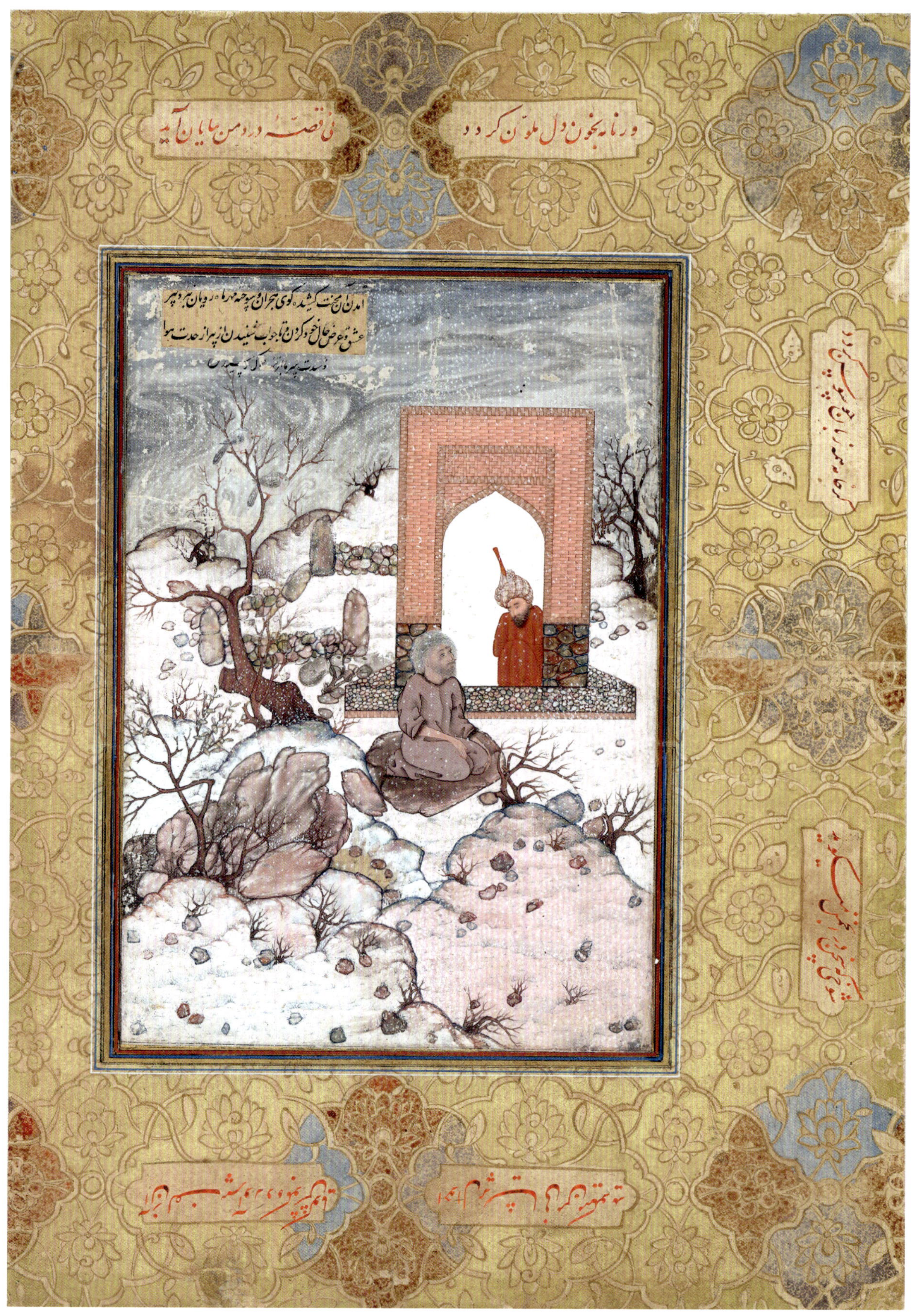

There are several metaphors at play in these lines. First is the metaphor that equates the khanaqah with the universe. Building on this equation, Shah Neʿmatullah argues for the centrality of humans in the universe through the metaphor of the centrality of the suffa-yi safa in the khanaqah and its role in sheltering Sufis. His use of the spatial configuration of the khanaqah, and the role of suffa-yi safa within it, to illustrate a theological point hints at the familiarity of both the architectural arrangement and terminology in the intellectual and literary circles at the time.

FACING, FIGURE 3.12. A Sufi and courtier conversing at a shrine. Album folio, Iran, Safavid period, mid-sixteenth century. Opaque watercolor and ink on paper, 32.8 × 22.6 cm. © *National Museum of Asian Art, Smithsonian Institution, Freer Collection, Purchase—Charles Lang Freer Endowment, F1946.13.*

Going back to the remaining parts of the complex in Taft, if we focus on the consistencies between the textual accounts of the Shah Vali khanaqah, we confront the possibility that the current museum constituted the one central element of the khanaqah, encompassing the three ambiguous elements of the kushk, suffa, and mazar. If so, the multidirectionality of the khanaqah in Shah Neʿmatullah's poem speaks to the open design of the kushk (current museum) within the courtyard of the Taft complex (fig. 3.11). The kiosk would thus stand as a literal counterpart to Shah Neʿmatullah's poetic invocation of the khanaqah complex as a metaphor for the centrality of humans in the universe: so, too, in the khanaqah complex, the central element is the suffa-yi safa, an architectural space that, through its funerary function, embraces the body of the Sufi at its center. Even though the body of Shah Neʿmatullah was not eternally enshrined in the khanaqah, it was substituted by his representation: the carved marble tombstone—the sarcophagus to which Katib refers and its likely physical match, one of the marble tombstones found in situ.

My aim here is not to argue that Shah Neʿmatullah's poetry served as some sort of manual for the construction of the khanaqah or that he was describing the layout of his own khanaqah in the poem. What I am suggesting is a traffic of shared notions between the anthropocentric idea of the universe articulated in his poetry, literal and metaphorical ideals of how a khanaqah should be arranged, and the terms that writers used to describe architectural spaces associated with Sufism. The resonances of this notion—across a variety of different genres, in verse and prose, from hagiography to local history—coalesce in the khanaqah of Taft through the agency of both its makers and its observers, both architecture and text.

IV. Patronage of the Dead and the Living: Sufi Shrines Under the Early Timurids

The central question of why a given work of art or architecture was planned, commissioned, and funded usually remains unanswered, not least because written sources do not directly address such motives, and when they do, the use of standard formulas—which remain largely understudied—dominates the language. Unsurprisingly, the socioreligious motives of court patrons are mentioned in chronicles and endowment documents more often than hagiographies. Frequently, motives for the patronage of the built environment were described as purely religious, referencing the Qurʾan or sacred *hadith* (sayings of the Prophet Muhammad). Sociopolitical motives were less likely to be explicitly documented in a revealing manner: rulers seeking to legitimize their power, governors seeking popularity in the eyes of the elite, and rich merchants seeking respectability by supporting the foundation of charitable institutions. Beyond these kinds of immediate intentions, however, analysis of the historical, social, and political circumstances of patronage can also open up wider and more specific hypotheses on how patrons and Sufis envisioned their relationship to one another as well as the role that architecture played in forging that relationship.

Regardless of how we read the details of the textual sources discussed above and whose descriptions we prioritize, one thing is clear: the khanaqah at Taft, the first major architectural project of the Neʿmatullahi Sufis, was a grand multipurpose complex capable of performing a variety of urban functions as well as accommodating travelers and dervishes. Moreover, it seems to have been designed as such from the outset rather than growing gradually from a funerary core. Many of its elements—the courtyard, surrounding lodges, tomb, kiosk, bathhouse, and kitchen—were in place by at least the mid-fifteenth century when Katib recorded the layout of the complex. I will deal with Shah Neʿmatullah's possible visions for the construction of the khanaqah in chapter 4. In the rest of this chapter, I will take a step back to explore the religiopolitical circumstances in which this structure came about, addressing the question of who financed it and in what context.

Patronage or lack thereof played a crucial role in determining where and when a Sufi network's earliest complexes were constructed as well as how they later evolved. Apart from a few passing hagiographical notes, no surviving documents discuss the Neʿmatullahi network's early sources of financial support except in the instance of court patronage. It is crucial to bear in mind that these narratives of court patronage cannot explain the whole institution of the network's endowments. In the earliest phases, there must have already been financial sources other than the donations, lands, and tax exemptions offered by ruling authorities. Yet, on the basis of surviving sources, we do not know what other landed properties the family possessed apart from those where their buildings stood in Taft, Mahan, Abarqu, and Kuhbanan, or how much they depended on charity from the laity. In what follows, I will first offer a brief overview of the patronage of Sufi networks by early Timurids and then attend to the questions around the patronage of Iskandar, the Timurid prince and governor of Fars and Yazd, for the Shah Vali khanaqah in Taft.

The relationship between Timur and Shah Neʿmatullah Vali is recounted as a series of confrontations, culminating in the banishment of Shah Neʿmatullah from Samarqand, a city he had chosen to settle in to spread his teachings after he left Mecca and after Timur ascended the throne, as mentioned in the beginning of the chapter.[31] The biographies of Shah Neʿmatullah offer a variety of reasons for these conflicts. ʿAbd al-Razzaq Kermani, for instance, attributes the roots of the confrontation to Timur's vulnerability at the beginning of his rule, contrasting it with Shah Neʿmatullah's rising popularity. Kermani notes that a group of advisers enticed Timur to ask the Shaykh to move elsewhere and has Shah Neʿmatullah reply in a flattering manner: "Wherever I traveled or settled was your kingdom."[32] The Sufi's reply implies an effort on his part to de-escalate the conflict by asserting Timur's temporal power, although an overtone of sarcasm, too, can be detected.

Another version of the encounter appears in Sunʿullah's biography of Shah Neʿmatullah (as recorded by Mufid). Here Timur is portrayed differently, as more trusting of Shah Neʿmatullah and wary of his own circle. First we are given more details about the cause of the threat to Timur and his court. Mufid mentions that while Shah Neʿmatullah was on a retreat in the mountains of Samarqand, a large group of Mongol tribes, who were described as armed rebels, paid homage to him. When this news spread, some ill-intentioned people persuaded Timur to ask the shaykh to leave Turkestan. In Sunʿullah's version, Timur sent the following message to Shah Neʿmatullah: "Although you are completely trusted, the corrupt ones do not leave me alone. It is advised that you leave."[33] While accounts of this encounter vary, they all result in Shah Neʿmatullah's submission to Timur's request; he left Samarqand and made his way to the southern regions of Kerman, Shiraz, and Yazd.[34]

This confrontation must be understood in the context of Timur's broader attitudes toward Sufis. There are several recorded instances of Timur's connections with contemporary Sufis: his ties with his spiritual adviser, Sayyid Barakah (d. 1403), and the prominent Naqshbandi Sufi Baba Sangu (d. 1386), as well as his relocation of several prominent Sufis—such as Saʿd al-din Taftazani (d. 1390), Sayyid ʿAli Jurjani (d. 1413), and Shams al-din Muhammad Jazari (d. 1429)—to his capital Samarqand.[35] Some of these relationships resulted in architectural patronage. One notable example is Timur's endowment of two khanaqahs to the shrine of Shaykh Ahmad-i Jam (d. 1141), a renowned Sufi from the tenth and eleventh centuries, in Turbat-i Jam, prompted by a letter from a contemporary Sufi, Shaykh Zayn al-din Taybadi (d. 1389).[36] Another example is Timur's uncompleted restoration and expansion of the shrine of Ahmad Yasawi (d. 1166), the main figure in the Yasawiyya Sufi network who lived in the eleventh and twelfth centuries, as recounted in Timur's biography, the *Zafarnama* (*Book of Victories*).[37] As Matthew Melvin-Koushki, Azfar Moin, and Kazuo Morimoto have argued, by the second half of the fifteenth century, Timur's association with the Yasawiyya had been translated into a genealogical narrative as well. Such genealogical narratives align with claims about Timur's direct descent from ʿAli ibn Abi Talib—as recorded on Timur's tombstone in Gur-i Amir—and his immaculate conception by Alanqo'a, the legendary princess-mother of the Mongols. Together, these genealogical assertions cast a retrospective image of Timur as the shah of both the temporal and spiritual realms.[38]

Timur's successor, Shahrukh, appears to have assumed a more definitive religious stance than his father in light of several religiously charged episodes during his reign.[39] Shahrukh's seemingly clear religious attitude was combined with a cautious approach in relation to individuals among the ʿulama and Sufis. As Beatrice Manz has shown, Shahrukh tried to maintain a safe distance from them—especially those his father did not favor—in an attempt to avoid any conspicuous preference for one group over another.[40]

When translated into architectural patronage, Shahrukh's approach resulted in the restoration and expansion of already revered sites in the region. Shahrukh and his wife, Gowharshad, embarked on a large-scale building project at the shrine of the eighth Shiʿa Imam (d. 817 or 819) at Mashhad, already a thriving and highly venerated site at the time. Shahrukh visited the shrine several times while Gowharshad constructed a Friday mosque (finished in 1418) and later set up a waqf (endowment) for it in 829/1426.[41] Shahrukh further built a madrasa and contributed endowments and gifts to the shrine, most notably a magnificent gold lamp.[42] At the shrine of ʿAbdullah Ansari (d. 1089) in Gazur Gah, Shahrukh undertook a rebuilding campaign in 1424–25. He also honored ʿAbdullah Ansari's teacher, Khwaja Abu ʿAbdullah Taqi (d. 1025–26), a revered figure among the Kartids (r. 1244–1381), by constructing a tomb over his grave.[43]

Manz argues that too little is known about Shahrukh's doctrinal orientation to draw assumptions about the motives for his policies toward religious figures and Sufis.[44] A few religious challenges might have played roles in the shaping of his policies and possibly his architectural patronage. The messianic and millenarian expectations of the time—on which Timurid rulers occasionally capitalized to claim cosmic kingship—posed challenges to the central government.[45] The movements of Khwaja Ishaq-i Khatlani, the Kubrawi shaykh who declared himself *Mahdi* (messiah) in 1423–24, and similar claims by Muhammad Nurbakhsh (d. 1464–65), who was exiled to central Iran, are examples of such challenges.[46]

A significant moment of crisis came in 1427 with an unsuccessful attempt on Shahrukh's life by Ahmad-i Lur, a member of the Hurufi network (from *huruf*, literally meaning "letters").[47] This was followed by a wave of interrogations, arrests, executions, and punishments for intellectuals, religious figures, and at times artists who were suspected of affiliations with Hurufism.[48] No direct links have been established between Shah Neʿmatullah and the Hurufi incident. However, the involvement of Shah Neʿmatullah and his network with intellectual trends associated with the science of letters (*ʿilm-i huruf*), which approached the logic of letters as a way to unlock the secrets of creation, especially given Shah Neʿmatullah's direct engagement with works of Hurufi leaders such as ʿAli Hamadani (d. 1385), might have led to speculation.[49] Against this background, Shahrukh's attitude toward the Neʿmatullahis was not so different from his father's: he never commissioned any buildings for the Sufi network, made a donation, or visited Shah Neʿmatullah or any of his affiliates, despite Neʿmatullahi efforts to cultivate such a relationship, as I discussed in chapter 2.

Two observations can be made from this analysis of Timur, Shahrukh, and Gowharshad's architectural patronage of Sufism, both of which suggest that the Neᶜmatullahis were not unique in the kind of treatment they received from the early Timurids in the central government.[50] The first observation is related to the venerated funerary sites that received Timurid attention. Their patronage indicates a tendency to support long-demised Sufi shaykhs and not Sufis who were alive and influential at the time.[51] It is arguable that Shahrukh and Gowharshad erred on the side of caution by sponsoring previously revered sites such as Mashhad or local holy places like the shrine of Bibi Setti in Herat, the shrine of ᶜAbdullah Ansari in Gazur Gah, as well as the shrine of Ahmad-i Jam in Turbat-i Jam.[52]

The second observation is based on the khanaqahs and madrasas sponsored by Timur, Shahrukh, and Gowharshad. The first major religious complex built during the reign of Shahrukh in Herat, the madrasa-khanaqah designed by the architect Qavam al-din Shirazi, was completed in 1411 under Gowharshad's patronage.[53] Maria Subtelny and Anas Khalidov have suggested this was the court's main tool to promote doctrinal orthodoxy.[54] Interestingly, this khanaqah did not belong to a particular Sufi network. Rather, it was a communal space for Sufi networks and closely connected to the central government, with officials appointed by Shahrukh himself.[55] Similar examples were the khanaqah that Tuman Aqa, Timur's wife, had sponsored in Samarqand and the madrasa-khanaqah of Muhammad Sultan (completed 1401–2) that was later developed into the funerary complex of the Gur-i Amir.[56] The administrative aspects of these institutions speak to the Timurid tendency to centralize religious appointments and exert control over Sufi networks.[57]

While Shahrukh and Gowharshad did not directly patronize contemporary influential Sufis, their courtly circle took an active role in patronizing contemporary and historical figures, although their efforts were mostly concentrated in the Khurasan region, especially in Taybad and Turbat-i Jam, two important sacred towns that, alongside Mashhad, were royal pilgrimage destinations frequented by Timurid princes.[58] In Taybad, vizier Ghiyath al-din Pir Ahmad-i Khwafi (d. 1453) commissioned the mausoleum of Zayn al-din Khwafi (d. 1435) and the funerary mosque of Zayn al-din Abu Bakr-i Taybadi (d. 1389) while sons of Amir Firuzshah, a chief courtier of Shahrukh, patronized the mausoleum of Baha al-din ᶜUmar (d. 1453–54).[59] In Turbat-i Jam, Amir Firuzshah built a mosque and a madrasa (probably 1440–41), and Shah Malik, governor of Khwarazm, and Mir Chaqmaq, governor of Yazd, each added a madrasa and mausoleum.[60]

The policy of building mainly for long-deceased Sufis was not necessarily practiced by subsequent Timurid princes. An example is the case of Iskandar b. ᶜUmar Shaykh, which will be discussed in the following section. Also noteworthy is an unpublished waqf document from the fifteenth century recording that the Timurid prince Mirza Sultan Muhammad b. Baysunghur (r. 1447–51 in Fars) made endowments for the restoration of the Muhammadiyya khanaqah in Bam in southern Iran.[61] The khanaqah belonged to Sayyid Tahir al-din, son of Sayyid Shams al-din, a contemporary of Shah Neᶜmatullah. More importantly, both Baysunghur (d. 1433) and Muhammad b. Baysunghur, son and grandson of Shahrukh, are known to have had a good relationship with the Neʿmatullahis. This is implied by Baysunghur's welcoming attitude to Shah Neʿmatullah's son during his visit to Herat, as recorded in biographies of the Sufi and a letter written by Amir Ziaʾ al-din Nurullah (grandson of Shah Neʿmatullah) to congratulate Muhammad on his reign.[62]

While a confluence of political and ideological factors might have led Timur and Shahrukh to avoid favoring one Sufi network over others, the subsequent Timurid princes viewed the connection to Sufi shaykhs as a means of establishing themselves and gaining support in regions where they governed or had political ambitions. This accords with the appanage system and power-sharing strategies on which the governance of Timurid territories was based. As İlker Evrim Binbaş has shown, the policy of joint sovereignty resulted in the partition of Timurid territories among family members. For instance, by 1413, Shahrukh in Khurasan and Iskandar in Fars marked two main poles of Timurid politics, each with different regional dynamics and policies.[63] It is in this partitioned geographical and political landscape that the local sociopolitical and sacral authority of Sufi shaykhs came to be seen as an important force to be reckoned with.

V. Iskandar b. ʿUmar Shaykh and the Neʿmatullahis

There is no epigraphical evidence for Iskandar's patronage of the khanaqah in Taft. Neither Katib nor Mufid mentions anything about Iskandar's financial support for it either. Among the four known hagiographies of Shah Neʿmatullah, only one mentions Iskandar's patronage in Taft: the treatise completed by ʿAbd al-Razzaq Kermani (finished in 1506). Kermani writes, "When exploring Taft, he [Shah Neʿmatullah] chose a location in the middle of the river, envisioned a khanaqah, and planned it. With the help of . . . Sultan Sikandar, son of the late highness Mirza ʿUmar Shaykh, it was finished. And for four years, all the revenue of Taft and its dependencies were allocated by that successful owner of government [i.e., Iskandar] for its construction. And whatever the Lord of the Auspicious Conjunction (*sahib qiran*) of the realm of certainty [probably referring to Shah Neʿmatullah] demanded was given to him and he ordered the establishment of that foundation."[64]

Iskandar's patronage of the Neʿmatullahis is significant for both the Timurids and the Neʿmatullahi network. For the Timurids, its significance lies in Iskandar's departure from earlier Timurid conventions in supporting a Sufi who was both influential and alive. For the Neʿmatullahis, it marks the first known case of any ruler financially supporting them. In what follows, I will offer several hypotheses regarding Iskandar's investment in the Neʿmatullahi network by looking into his relationship with Shah Neʿmatullah and other intellectuals in the region as well as broader patterns in Iskandar's patronage and their relationship to his short-lived political ambitions.

In the previous section, I briefly mentioned the duality of Timurid political powers in the early fifteenth century. While Shahrukh was gaining power in Khurasan, sons of his brother ʿUmar Shaykh and Malikat Agha, who held the governorship of Fars and adjacent regions, had been fighting within their realm after the death of ʿUmar Shaykh in 1394. For a short period, Iskandar b. ʿUmar Shaykh emerged out of these political struggles having gained sufficient power to challenge Shahrukh.[65] Iskandar started with the governorship of Yazd and later rose to significant power in the region with the murder of his brother Pir Muhammad in 1409. For a brief period from 1412–13 to the beginning of 1414, Iskandar's power was recognized in Hamadan, Isfahan, Shiraz, Yazd, and Kerman. Yet, in 1414, his rebellion against Shahrukh in pursuit of independent rule sparked major conflicts between the two, leading Shahrukh to confront and defeat Iskandar in Isfahan. Iskandar was subsequently killed in 1415 by his brother Rustam b. ʿUmar Shaykh, from whom he had seized control of Isfahan, and Shahrukh appointed his own son, Ibrahim Sultan (r. 1415–35), as governor of the region.[66]

Iskandar was deeply involved in cultural patronage even before he could claim regional power but became even more so during his stay in Shiraz after 1409–10. This was when he emerged as a patron of book production with a wide range of interests, including albums, anthologies of scientific and historical literature, and poetry in Persian, Turkic, and Arabic.[67] As Priscilla Soucek has noted, all dated and fully documented manuscripts linked to him were produced within the years 1410–13, although attributed examples as early as 1407 and 1397 also exist.[68] When Iskandar took Isfahan and made it his capital, he undertook a major building campaign and began to mint coins.

Iskandar gathered major religious figures at his court, including a number of intellectuals who were unhappy with the Khurasan-based Timurids. As Binbaş and Melvin-Koushki have shown, he relied on the support of the intellectual networks in the region such as those of Muhammad al-Jazari (d. 1429), Sayyid Sharif Jurjani (d. 1413), Ibn Turka (d. 1432), and Shah Neʿmatullah Vali to argue for a conjuncture of kingship and sainthood in his reign.[69]

The rise of political discourses around sacral power (*wilaya*) has been connected to the post-Mongol termination of the caliphal system of control in the Islamicate world. In constructing the ideals of sacral power in the political realm, apart from identification with the House of the Prophet and especially ʿAli, two other vehicles were most effective: Sufism and occultism. Iskandar made use of them all.[70] By fashioning himself as a saint-philosopher-king, Iskandar strategically utilized the patronage of theology, philosophy, astronomy, astrology, Sufism, and especially the occult sciences (*al-ʿulum al-ghariba*), the latter facilitated by his access to a hub of occultist scholars in Shiraz in the fifteenth century.[71] Ibn Turka, for instance, wrote his first lettrist treatises for Iskandar.[72]

Eventually, this reliance on sainthood and the simultaneous move toward absolutist models of kingship would result in a competition between sultans and saints over sacral kingship in the early modern era. Sufis rose to political power and became kings, as in the case of the Safavids, and kings adopted saintly personas, as in the case of the Mughals and Ottomans.[73] As I will show in the following chapters, both the Bahmanid rulers of Deccan India and the descendants of Shah Neʿmatullah in the Safavid period attempted to establish themselves as saint-kings within the framework of this model.

This backdrop can help us make sense of Iskandar's relationship with Shah Neʿmatullah on a theological and ideological basis. Apart from Iskandar's patronage of the khanaqah in Taft, there are a few recorded instances of their relationship. In 1412, Iskandar sent a set of theological questions to Shah Neʿmatullah as well as Sayyid Sharif Jurjani. The response that Shah Neʿmatullah wrote to those questions is listed among his main treatises by hagiographers.[74] The questionnaire addressed a range of theological issues "on the primary cosmological distinction between the realm of human beings and the realm of God."[75] Binbaş makes the point that Iskandar's own work, the *Jamiʿ al-Sultani* (*Compendium of the Sultan*), complements the debate between Jurjani and Shah Neʿmatullah Vali around these questions in order to define the parameters of his constitutional program and argue for the embodiment of both kingship and heavenly sovereignty in his own persona.[76]

Apart from this epistolary exchange, three out of the four extant hagiographies of Shah Neʿmatullah record a face-to-face meeting between him and Iskandar in Shiraz a few years earlier. Kermani, Mufid (following Sunʿullah), and Sadid al-din all note that Shah Neʿmatullah visited Shiraz during the reign of Iskandar, probably around the time the latter gained power over the city in 1409, and that the two attended Friday prayer at the ʿAtiq (old) Mosque in Shiraz. At the prayer service, Iskandar stood to Shah Neʿmatullah's right while to his left was Sayyid Sharif Jurjani, who, like Neʿmatullah, would respond to Iskandar's theological questionnaire a few years later. The prayer's spatial arrangement suggests both a public display of the interdependence between kingship and Sufism and the hagiographers' concern to represent a hierarchy between the two religious figures.[77] There might also have been a connection between Iskandar's ambitions to gain control over Kerman and Shah Neʿmatullah's presence and spiritual authority in the region.[78]

Hagiographer Kermani holds that for four years Iskandar allocated all the revenue of Taft and its dependencies to the completion of the Shah Vali khanaqah.[79] Accepting this time frame, and given 1414 as the end of Iskandar's reign in the region, the decision to support a khanaqah for Shah Neʿmatullah was probably made no later than 1410. The decision could thus fall into a specific chain of events involving the two figures, succeeding Shah Neʿmatullah's visit to Shiraz shortly after 1409 and preceding Iskandar's dispatch of the questionnaire to Shah Neʿmatullah in 1412.

While Iskandar's level of involvement in patronizing the khanaqah of Taft ultimately remains an open question, it is important to consider a few points raised by the choice of terminology in textual sources. In Katib's fifteenth-century history of Yazd, Shah Neʿmatullah—not Iskandar—is recorded as the bani (founder) of the complex.[80] According to Kermani's aforementioned hagiographic account, Iskandar did not build or commission the khanaqah for the Neʿmatullahis himself but granted funds for it to Shah Neʿmatullah. This level of authority is emphasized through Kermani's choice of terminology, which asserts that Shah Neʿmatullah chose the site, "envisioned" the khanaqah (*dar khatir-i ʿatir-ishan ihdath-i bana-yi khanaqah amad*: literally, "[the idea] of constructing the khanaqah entered his bountiful mind," implying both his initiative and power of imagination) and "planned" or "designed" (*tarh afkand*) the complex.[81] On the one hand, the terminology attributes a high level of freedom and control to the Sufi over the building process, similar to the patronage they later received from Ahmad Shah Bahmani for the construction of Shah Neʿmatullah's mausoleum in Mahan. On the other hand, in lieu of long-lasting endowments, maintenance of the Taft complex depended on tax privileges that were not guaranteed to continue after Iskandar's death.[82] The vulnerabilities to which this lack of long-term provisions exposed the Neʿmatullahi network will be discussed in the final part of this chapter.

Iskandar's patronage of Shah Neʿmatullah was in stark contrast to the central Timurids' attitude and shaped a turning point in the architectural history of the Neʿmatullahi network. The construction of khanaqahs or madrasa-khanaqahs dedicated to charitable functions or the veneration of specific Sufi shaykhs was common in the Timurid period, but a distinction must be made in the case of the Neʿmatullahis. When the Shah Vali khanaqah was built in Taft, it was not common for Timurid rulers to grant this kind of open patronage to a living Sufi shaykh, particularly with such freedom to design and govern the institution. In this respect, the project points to the considerable status that the Neʿmatullahis must have held in the region. It also points to the specificity of Iskandar's religiopolitical agenda that distinguished his relationship with the Sufis from the relationships of Timur, Shahrukh, and other Timurid rulers with Sufi shaykhs in Samarqand and Herat.

Although his reign was short-lived, Iskandar's importance for the Neʿmatullahi network must not be overlooked. He supported the construction of their very first khanaqah *complex* and thus facilitated its transition from humble to monumental structures. Before the construction of the khanaqah at Taft, all the buildings related to the Sufi network, although spread widely throughout the region, were either residences or gardens, lacking the grand urban and charitable elements of the Taft complex. This monumental turn in effect contributed to the institutionalization of the Neʿmatullahis in the following decades of the fifteenth century.[83]

VI. The Other Side of Patronage: Sufis as Interlocutors

The sacral power of Sufis could play a significant role in the making or breaking of a sovereign's image in the post-Mongol era, whether rulers styled themselves as upholders of organized religion or claimed more immediate connections to supernatural forces.[84] This dynamic was amplified by the millenarian aspect of state-making in the fifteenth and sixteenth centuries, when anticipation of the end of first millennium in the Islamic calendar in 1591 ushered in relations of both competition and interdependence between kings and Sufis.[85] As noted earlier, shared titles were a testament to intersections between the worlds of Sufis and kings in this period. Early modern kings adopted the title *qutb* (pole) while the title *shah* (king) was common for Sufis.[86]

In this charged, uncertain environment, rulers needed to manage their relationships with Sufis as either allies or competitors. As allies, Sufi shaykhs had the cultural and political power to lend credibility and popularity to a regime, especially on the local level, due to their perceived intimacy with the divine and the resulting sway they held among the public. As Moin argues, it is exactly because of their intermediary role in controlling "social knowledge and opinion formation" that Sufis proved effective in local politics.[87] Sufis had access to the mental life of a regionally diverse polity to an extent that a ruler based in a capital could not gain otherwise.

Sufis took on the role of representing communities in their relationship with rulers, negotiating with the local or central government on a variety of issues including taxation. This was a crucial role in determining the fate of the population, especially in times of shifting power dynamics. Hagiographies suggest that in some communities the grandees may have expected Sufis to assume such responsibilities.[88] They could also provide a refuge for the community in case of a siege or a clash with rulers—such as in the case of Sayyid Shams al-din, a fifteenth-century Sufi from Bam who negotiated his residence as a shelter for the population during the siege of the city by the same Iskandar who supported the construction of the khanaqah at Taft.[89]

In other cases, Sufis came to be involved with the state on a managerial level, assuming official positions in government, religious and otherwise. The posts of *muhtasib* (inspector of market practice and city morality), *qadi* (judge), *shaykh al-Islam* (chief judge), and *sadr* (vizier) were commonly held by religious figures, especially during the reign of the Timurid ruler Shahrukh.[90] An example is Saʿd al-din Taftazani (d. 1390), whose family was influential in Herat under Shahrukh and who came to hold the office of shaykh al-Islam.[91] This way, it was possible to make administrative use of religious figures' knowledge and expertise and to keep Sufis under control.[92]

VII. Contentious Alignments and the Politics of Encounter

Alongside material evidence from surviving buildings and documentary records of patronage, textual (and later visual) accounts of personal encounters between kings and Sufis offer an invaluable point of reference, replete with symbolic hints—some subtle, others not—about how each side understood and sought to define itself in relation to the power of the other. These encounters, some examples of which have already been discussed, range from epistolary contacts to real or imagined face-to-face meetings for ceremonial blessings, the bestowal of kingship on new rulers, and predictions of the geographical regions they would control.[93]

The historicization of these encounters, whether contemporary or retrospective, involved a wide spectrum of people from courtly to Sufi circles: rulers and viziers, hagiographers and historians, and calligraphers and artists who wrote inscriptions for buildings and depicted these encounters in album paintings—the latter especially common in early modern India.[94] The details of the powerful religiopolitical narratives that were shaped around these encounters vary drastically between different types of sources—for example, between dynastic histories and hagiographies. The frequency with which these encounters were described points to their power and significance and, in the case of hagiographic sources, to the anxieties faced when communicating them to different audiences.

Hagiographical sources usually portray Sufis as agents who defined the limits of their relationship with the court while also conforming to acceptable norms of diplomacy. The distance between the court and the khanaqah could be staged through the design of meetings between the two sides. Both parties would go to great lengths to reach an agreement about such details as who should pay a visit to whom and where—in the khanaqah, at court, or in a third more neutral place. One key to a nuanced understanding of the Sufis' strategies toward worldly matters is that there was rarely a blanket policy on how the khanaqah connected to the court, whether in the case of a single Sufi network, a single Sufi shaykh, or in their relations to a single dynasty.

In chapter 2, when discussing the imagined meeting between the Bahmanid ruler Ahmad Shah I and the Neʿmatullahis, I focused on the symbolism of the objects exchanged during these meetings. Here, I want to explore the politics of the encounters between the Neʿmatullahis and Timurids in more detail—in particular, how the mechanics of their negotiations manifest themselves in the process of proposing, accepting, and planning the details of an encounter and, most importantly, in its poetic representation in the epigraphic program of the Taft khanaqah.

The most relevant and significant instance is the initial encounter between Timur and Shah Neʿmatullah after Timur assumed power in Samarqand. According to Mufid's recounting of Sunʿullah's hagiographic treatise, when Shah Neʿmatullah left Mecca and arrived in Samarqand, Timur sent a messenger to the Sufi asking whether he was interested in visiting the king or if Timur had to pay a pilgrimage to his threshold. Shah Neʿmatullah left the decision to Timur but implied that it was advisable for Timur to visit him, a suggestion that the latter respected.[95] By detailing these negotiations, the hagiographical treatise signals the superiority of the Sufi's authority in both determining the location of the meeting and accepting the Timurid ruler into his own spatial realm. This dynamic perhaps aimed to neutralize the tensions that were to arise between the two figures over the course of the story.

For context, it was not uncommon for Sufis to refuse meetings with rulers or to deny them permission to enter a khanaqah. There is an abundance of such instances in medieval and early modern texts.[96] Within the Neʿmatullahi hagiographic traditions, an account from the seventeenth century relays this sentiment. When Mirza Shah Abu'l Mahdi (fl. second half of seventeenth century), a descendant of Shah Neᶜmatullah, arrived in Basra (in modern-day Iraq) while on pilgrimage to Mecca, he was invited to the residence of the governor, Husayn Pasha. Abu'l Mahdi refused the invitation on the basis that he needed to refrain from visiting impure worldly rulers on his pilgrimage to the holy site and asked the governor to visit him instead. The governor was not content, and in the end the negotiations resulted in their meeting on a pilgrimage to one of the holy sites of Basra.[97] Alongside narratives like this, we know that contemporary relatives of Mirza Shah Abu'l Mahdi in the Neᶜmatullahi family held high positions in the Safavid court, attesting to the diversity of the Sufi network's political strategies.

When attempting to portray themselves as spiritual authorities detached or distanced from worldly matters, Sufi figures and their hagiographers were also responding to the criticism of Sufi-sultan relations in intellectual networks of the region, among their followers, and within the general population. Writing in the fifteenth century in his *Maqamat* (*Anecdotes*) of the Sufi ᶜAbd al-Rahman Jami, ᶜAbd al-Wasiᶜ Nizami Bakharzi openly criticizes Sharaf al-din ᶜAli Yazdi, historian and vizier to the Timurid prince Ibrahim Sultan and a figure in the Neᶜmatullahi network, for finding comfort at the court of the Timurids: "Throughout his life, Yazdi was attached to the courts of the sultans of the time as an attendee and expert. [In contrast,] Jami's threshold, which is the refuge of the truth, is and will always be the deserved place that the kings of the world will unreservedly kiss."[98]

It is in the context of these tensions that we should interpret the subtleties of the relationship between Shah Neᶜmatullah and Timur. After Timur's aforementioned visit to Shah Neᶜmatullah in Samarqand, the king held a feast and requested the Sufi's attendance. Shah Neᶜmatullah responded with a poem that is recorded in Sunᶜullah's hagiography.

> If you should wish to host Neᶜmatullah,
> the tablecloth must stretch all the way around the sphere of the world.
> And if you should build a small palace (*sara*) to match his magnanimity,
> the four walls must enclose the seven climes.[99] (app. 3.1)

Despite the reluctance conveyed in the poem, Shah Neᶜmatullah eventually accepted Timur's invitation. But that outcome does not override the construction of Sufi-sultan power dynamics that is effected in the poem. In these verses, Shah Neᶜmatullah plays with the literal meaning of his own name—Neᶜmat Allah, "bounty of God"—to relay a sense of grandiosity in relation to Timur. The first line ponders Timur's ability to provide a feast that matches the bounty of God: what gift can one offer to one who is a gift from God himself? Shah Neᶜmatullah's self-aggrandizement is also evident in architectural metaphors employed here: the four walls of the palace ought to contain the whole world—returning to the notion of the khanaqah as cosmos discussed earlier in this chapter. At the same time, the verses try to maintain a modicum of humility through the use of the adjective *small* before what is described as an all-encompassing abode.

The relationship between these verses and the Neʿmatullahi network's architecture goes beyond the level of poetic metaphors, for as noted above, it is exactly these same verses of poetry that used to adorn one of the main facades of the khanaqah at Taft. Here I am returning to Katib's description of the complex recorded in his chronicle in the middle of the fifteenth century and discussed in the first section of this chapter.[100] As Katib notes, these verses were inscribed over the entrance of the dome chamber that likely occupied the center of the complex's courtyard. What seems to have been an occasional poem, written in the midst of or in response to a political encounter between Shah Neʿmatullah and Timur, is solidified in architecture patronized by another Timurid ruler in Taft—even though the occasional nature of the poem does not seem to have been a point of reflection by Katib.

What does it mean to emblazon the politics of the Sufi's encounter with a ruling authority over the publicly visible facade of one of the most prominent elements of the khanaqah, accessible to anyone who would enter the complex? Although there is a gap of about two decades and thousands of kilometers between Timur "spreading his tablecloth" in Samarqand and Timur's grandson, Iskandar, "building a small palace" for Shah Neʿmatullah in Taft, the sentiment in accepting the gifts remains the same. These verses are a metaphor for how the Neʿmatullahis set the terms in accepting the gifts of Timurid courts in both architecture and convivial encounters: what they were offered in both cases was short of their status, but they accepted it anyway. The ambiguity of the word *sara* in the verses above, whose meaning ranges from a residence to a palace, is also relevant here and coincides with the ambiguities of the term *kushk* in the Taft complex, which was likely used to refer to the building on which these verses were inscribed. Both terms could simultaneously denote a small structure and a grand monument that entailed convivial festivities—a convenient ambiguity given the broader ambivalent relationship between Sufism and materiality.

To those passing through the khanaqah in Taft, reading these lines on their own, unaware of the hagiographical tradition, this meaning was clearly communicated: the "small palace," the dome chamber onto which these words were inscribed, both occupied the center of the constructed universe of the khanaqah and "contained the seven climes within it." This spatial and metaphorical overlap ties in with the poetics of the equation between the khanaqah and the universe in Shah Neʿmatullah's divan that I discussed earlier. Here, through the projection of Shah Neʿmatullah's verses onto architecture, the poetic and political intersect.

Some readers might have known more about the verses and their connection with Shah Nimatullah's encounter with Timur, perhaps through oral narratives spread in the community. To those in the Neʿmatullahi network who were familiar with these narratives, the verses were laden with even more meaning. They signaled an iconic moment in defining their relationship with

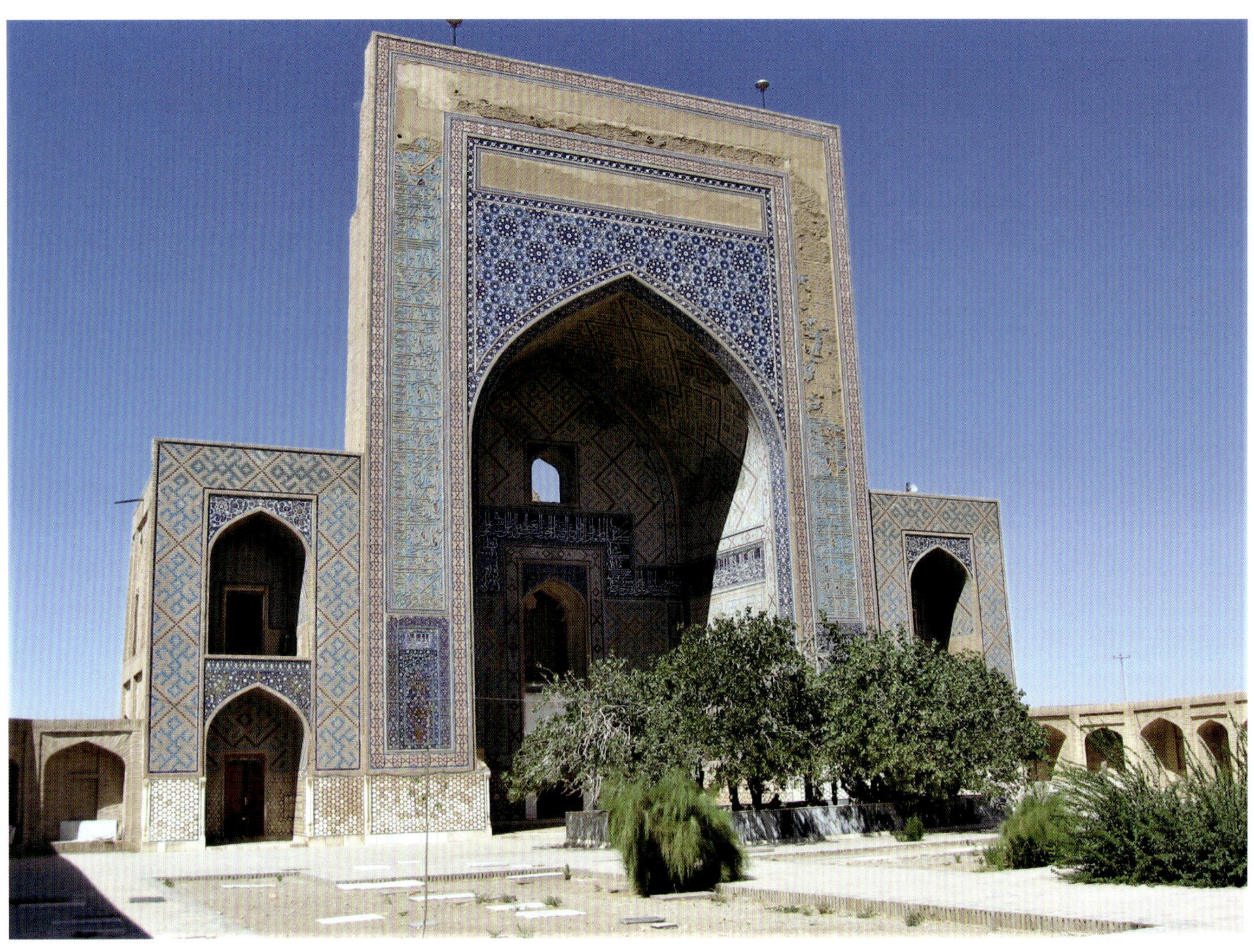

FIGURE 3.13. Open-air burial at the shrine of Shaykh Zayn al-din Abu Bakr-i Taybadi, Taybad, Iran. *Photograph by author, 2012.*

the Timurid court and temporal power, historicized in text and materialized in stone. For the insiders, these verses also addressed the tension between spirituality and materiality by claiming the inconceivable submission of the spiritual to the limits of the material, even if that inconceivability had to be communicated through the materiality of their convergence in the brick and mortar of the khanaqah.

One of the common manifestations of anxieties over court-shrine relations usually revealed itself in the process of accepting patronage for and constructing monumental architecture, especially the Sufis' mausoleum. Early stages of several comparable shrines in Khurasan, such as the shrine at Gazur Gah, the tomb of Shaykh Ahmad-i Jam, and that of Shaykh Zayn al-din Abu Bakr-i Taybadi, epitomize the prohibitions against the construction of monumental funerary structures over Sufis' graves even though such prohibitions were not observed in later expansions of these complexes (fig. 3.13). It is easy to look at the Neʿmatullahis' monumental architecture (or that of other premodern Sufi networks) and associate the mere existence of these monuments with a lack of austerity among them. Yet, at the Taft khanaqah, reading the architecture against the sum of textual evidence from different genres (poetry, hagiography, local history), as discussed above, it becomes clear that the monument does not simply manifest a lack of anxieties over the intertwining of court and shrine—rather, the architecture and its epigraphy openly exhibit those concerns.

This balance between the spiritual and material images of the Sufi network would not necessarily be sought through the existence or form of a given building complex. In the long term, broader patterns of architectural development in the Neʿmatullahi network reveal attempts to separate the spiritual and worldly activities of the network between distinct Neʿmatullahi centers, as will be shown in chapter 4. However, anxieties over the separation between the spiritual and material reached a peak with the family's reception of gifts from Deccan India, necessitating a balance in their allegiance to the rulers in Iran and the Deccan as well as new strategies for managing the multiplying centers of their growing transregional networks. In a way, the poem's tablecloth stretching "all the way around the sphere of the world" foreshadows the network's ambition for transregional expansion. It alludes to the subjective mechanics of worldmaking through which the Sufis understood and imagined themselves at the center of the globe. As rhetorical as this notion may seem in the poem at Taft, it also unfolded in tandem with the literal physical expansion of their network across the ocean as reflected in the foundation inscription in Mahan.

VIII. The Curse of Transregionality

Having discussed the privileges provided by the Sufi network's patronage and mobility in the Deccan, and both the opportunities and complexities of the Neʿmatullahis' relationship with the Timurids, this final section of the first part of the book and the current chapter addresses the challenges posed by both the metaphorical and geographical renditions of Neʿmatullahis' transregional imagining. Alongside the financial, political, and symbolic privileges that the Neʿmatullahis gained as a result of their geographical expansions, it is easy to overlook the intrinsic struggles of building a transregional Sufi network. The invitation from the Deccan certainly presented an opportunity for the Neʿmatullahis, especially given the financial and political challenges they were facing in Iran at the time. They approached this opportunity cautiously and pragmatically, maintaining their bases and fiscal interests in central Iran while simultaneously navigating the sea routes between Iran and the Deccan; accepting what the Bahmanid court had to offer, they concurrently negotiated for better financial conditions from the Timurids.[101] However, sea travel also brought trials and tribulations of its own as well as the emotional burdens of distance between family members. Letters of the Neʿmatullahi family from Iran to India convey a sense of longing for the members of the family who at times spent years in the Deccan before their return.[102]

It was perhaps in response to these travel anxieties that accounts of Shah Neᶜmatullah's miracles as a savior of ships in the ocean found their way into his hagiographies.[103]

The network's transregionality also gave rise to financial complications. The cross-regional popularity of Shah Neᶜmatullah and the multiplication of patronage across Iran and India seems to have become a source of anxiety, intensifying the need for financial negotiations with the local and central governments in Iran amid a complicated episode in the economic history of the region. One specific hagiographical account of gifts sent to Shah Neᶜmatullah from the Deccan reveals the Timurids'—in particular Shahrukh's—conflicted reception of the Sufi network's transregional connections. Sunᶜullah records that when bountiful gifts and donations from the Deccan arrived in Kerman, the governor, Amir Ghana Shirin (r. 1416–36), faced the dilemma of whether to tax the gifts.[104] Relinquishing the tax (*tamgha*), which was seventy *tuman* (*tuman-i kapiki*), could invite the reprimand of Shahrukh whereas imposing a tax could offend Shah Neᶜmatullah.[105] Ghana Shirin therefore chose to present the case to the central government in Herat. What eventually resolved the issue seems to have been a matter of symbolism and economic rivalry between Iran and India rather than financial gain. Shahrukh consulted Gowharshad, who believed that taxing the gifts would damage Shahrukh's image: if he taxed the gifts, people would forever say that the king of Hindustan sent so many gifts to the Sayyid that Shahrukh, the king of the world (*khaqan-i zaman*), could not exempt him from taxes. Shahrukh wrote to Kerman and ordered Ghana Shirin to forgo taxation.[106]

The delicacy of the Neᶜmatullahis' relationship with the Deccan and Timurid rulers at this time—which could have motivated Shah Neᶜmatullah's gifts to Shahrukh in Herat, including the Hindustani takht discussed in the previous chapter—has in part to do with the fiscal management of Kerman. Amir Ghana Shirin was appointed governor of Kerman in the aftermath of Shahrukh's campaign against the Timurid prince Iskandar in 1416 in central and south Iran.[107] Under Ghana Shirin, Kerman lost much of its fiscal independence, and this meant that major decisions about tax issues were made at Herat, a change that had a considerable impact on the Neᶜmatullahis, especially after the death of Shah Neᶜmatullah Vali.[108] We can sense such tensions in the movements of his son, Shah Khalilullah, as well as in letters exchanged among the members of the family in Taft and the Deccan and with the Timurids.

Two hagiographies of Shah Neᶜmatullah recount Shah Khalilullah's visit to the court of Shahrukh in Herat.[109] Mufid (after Sunᶜullah) reports that when Khalilullah visited Shahrukh's court, Amir Firuzshah, one of Shahrukh's great *amir*s, confronted Khalilullah for not paying the *kharaj* (agricultural tax) on properties in Kerman.[110] The fact that the case was taken to Herat could hint at a considerable sum of money involved or perhaps the souring of the relationship between the family and the Timurid court. Khalilullah responded by comparing the situation to the conflict between the grandson of the Prophet Muhammad, Husayn b. ʿAli (d. 680), and the Umayyad caliph Yazid (r. 680–83), which resulted in the massacre of Husayn and most of his family in Karbala in 680.[111] The symbolic moral weight imposed by the analogy was not lost on Shahrukh, who in response took Khalilullah's side, reprimanded the great amir, and lifted the taxes.[112] After this visit to Herat, Khalilullah appointed his son Shah Shams al-din Muhammad as the head of the astana at Mahan and left for the Deccan with two other sons.[113]

The positioning of this otherwise unrecorded encounter in Sunʿullah's text is highly suggestive. Juxtaposed with Khalilullah's departure for the Deccan, the text implies a causal relationship between the two episodes, as if the Timurids' treatment of the family motivated Shah Neʿmatullah's successor to undertake his journey to the Deccan. This implication, however, must be measured against the broader sociohistorical context. Shahrukh's government faced a wide array of problems around 1436–37, owing, in Manz's words, to a "combination of Shahrukh's increasing age and illness, the death of his most senior amirs and the early death of most of his sons"—a predicament that could itself have contributed to Khalilullah's decision.[114]

Another instance of disputes over taxes is indicated by a group of petitions from a descendant of Shah Neʿmatullah to the Timurid ruler Sultan Muhammad, who had been appointed governor of central and western Iran in 1443 by Shahrukh. These petitions are recorded in a fifteenth-century miscellanea called the *Munshaʾat* (*Compositions*) of Sharaf al-din ʿAli Yazdi—a collection of short treatises, prefaces written for other works, architectural inscriptions, and copies of letters and official documents written by Yazdi, the aforementioned affiliate of the Neʿmatullahi family, as well as Yazdi's brother Qavam al-din and his teacher Saʾin al-din Turka.[115] The Neʿmatullahi family seems to have been interested in cultivating a relationship with Sultan Muhammad, as indicated by a letter of congratulations from a great-grandson of Shah Neʿmatullah named Zahir al-din, written to Sultan Muhammad after his appointment as governor.[116] Several petitions from the Neʿmatullahi family asked Sultan Muhammad to mediate with the central office on their behalf.[117] Binbaş discusses these petitions in the context of conflicts between Sultan Muhammad and Shahrukh around taxes, in which western Iranian elites aligned with Sultan Muhammad pleaded for tax reduction.[118]

The struggle for a reduction of taxes appears to have worsened due to Shah Khalilullah's journey to the Deccan. The family's distress is sensed in several letters recorded in the *Munshaʾat*—their numbers attesting to the severity of the issue and the Neʿmatullahis' desperation.[119] A letter from Shah Khalilullah's grandson, the aforementioned Amir Zahir al-din, to the Timurid official Sayyid Ghiyath al-din Zayn al-ʿAbidin is a case in point.[120] Having lost the tax privileges for the Shah Vali khanaqah in Taft due to a decision made by the *nawwab* (representative) of Shahrukh's vizier, Khwaja Ghiyath al-din Pir Ahmad Khwafi, Zahir al-din pleaded to the addressee to mediate on behalf of the Sufi family and to accompany one of his own brothers, Ghazanfar al-din Asadullah, to Herat in order to resolve the issue.[121] Zahir al-din also wrote two lengthy petitions directly to Pir Ahmad Khwafi, both included in the *Munsha'at*, expressing his shock and disbelief about the matter, elaborating on the hardship the taxes had caused for the dervishes at the khanaqah, and attempting to clarify the circumstances that had led to the loss of tax privileges. In one of the petitions, written with a more practical tone, he informed the vizier of his brother's forthcoming visit to Herat, hoping that the vizier would save his father, the rest of the family, and the dervishes at the khanaqah from their distress.[122]

The circumstances to which Zahir al-din, Khalilullah's grandson, attributed the loss of tax privileges concern an interesting and rather complicated account of a failed pilgrimage to Mecca by his father, Nurullah. Recorded in the two petitions sent to Shahrukh's vizier, Pir Ahmad Khwafi, Zahir al-din's account of the journey, which brought several seaports of the Indian Ocean together, outlined the events as follows: "As you have heard . . . my father left for his pilgrimage to Mecca. Two months into the journey, his ship was wrecked in a storm and it was washed up on shore. . . . By the time the ship was repaired, the pilgrimage season had passed so they returned to [the port city of] Qalhat in [Oman]. . . . Given my grandfather's [i.e., Khalilullah's] prolonged stay in Gulbarga, Nurullah decided to pay a visit to his father to persuade him to return with him."[123]

Zahir al-din specified that when the news of Nurullah's journey to Hindustan reached Herat it was assumed that his journey was intentional, and the decision was made to annul the tax exemption (*musallami*).[124] He also stressed that his father had written a letter in his own hand from Qalhat to inform the court of the unfortunate events and his change of plans.[125]

It is plausible that once in Qalhat, Nurullah would have wanted to salvage his journey with a trip to India. Qalhat was a significant port city in Indian Ocean trade and an important stop for ships from India. But in the second letter by Zahir al-din, written three years after his father's attempted journey to Mecca, Zahir al-din completely skips over the Qalhat episode. Instead, he claims that several other ships sank in the same storm, but Nurullah's had the good fortune to wash up on the shores of Hindustan.[126]

None of these letters are dated. But among the tax-related petitions is another letter from Zahir al-din, written in response to a letter that his father, Nurullah, had sent from the Deccan. Expressing the relief granted by the arrival of his father's news, Zahir al-din notes that the letter had reached him on a Sunday, the twenty-sixth of the month of Muharram.[127] Limiting the range of dates to the 1430s and 1440s, when these letters seem to have been written, the plausible years corresponding with a Sunday falling on the twenty-sixth of Muharram are the year 839/1435 or 847/1443, as Aubin pointed out.[128] If the former, the date falls directly in the midst of the tax conflicts between Khalilullah and Shahrukh and the construction of the shrine at Mahan, which would be completed the following year when Khalilullah secured the second donation from the Deccan.

Why would Zahir al-din downplay his father's decision to head for India after the storm and emphasize that he ended up in India by accident? More importantly, why was reporting the whereabouts of the key figures of the family so important? And why would Nurullah's intent to visit India affect the Ne'matullahis' tax liability? All of this points to the possibility that the division of the Ne'matullahi family between Iran and the Deccan was held against them. The Nurullah in these letters is probably Shams al-din Muhammad Nurullah, one of Khalilullah's four sons. Khalilullah had put Nurullah in charge of the shrine at Mahan (and probably the whole Ne'matullahi network in central Iran) before traveling to the Deccan with two of his other sons, where they joined the fourth son who already resided there. Against this background, the tax exemption might well have been conditional on the head of family's presence in the region and the upkeep of their properties. Did tax officials interpret Nurullah's journey to the Deccan as a sign that Khalilullah and all of his four sons had moved permanently? An additional possibility is that the Timurid officials were skeptical of the family's involvement in trade between Iran and the Deccan, which could have earned them a fortune while avoiding taxes—hence the possible omission of Qalhat as an important trade port from Zahir al-din's subsequent letters.

The picture that emerges from the meeting between Shah Khalilullah and Shahrukh, as well as the letters and petitions on tax exemption, speaks to an unstable relationship between the Sufi family and Timurid officials. The impact of the expansion of the Ne'matullahi network between Iran and India and the possible control that the Timurid court sought to maintain over the Ne'matullahis is implied by a constant need in these letters to report the whereabouts of the head of the khanaqah in Taft. In the conflict-ridden economic landscape of central and western Iran at this time, the absence of the khanaqah's leader or the possibility of his migration to the Deccan could easily lead the family to lose the privileges they had assumed since Iskandar's patronage of the Taft complex.

The lines of thuluth calligraphy inscribed on the foundation inscription of the shrine at Mahan, binding the Ne'matullahis with their allies in the Deccan, had much more complicated implications than just lending the Ne'matullahis transregional opportunities. They also demanded strategic allocations of time, space, and human resources across the Arabian Sea. The various episodes brought together in this and the previous chapter capture the ebb and flow of transregional living. At times, the main actors discussed here—the Timurids, Bahmanids, and Ne'matullahis—appear to be in control of their finances, their whereabouts, and their image. But ultimately, the sticky, interconnected complexities of this global picture upend any illusion of control. Taking stock of these complexities sets the scene for how concerns around materiality intersected with material culture in the second part of the book. Examining those intersections sheds light on the strategies that the Sufi network adopted to make sense of and to resolve issues of proximity and distance both in terms of geography (be it regional or transregional) and the relationship between the spiritual and material.

Notes

1. Aubin, *Matériaux*, 281.
2. Katib, *Tarikh-i jadid-i Yazd*, 214–16.
3. Afshar, *Yadgarha-yi Yazd*, I:399–401; Mardomi and Dehghani Tafti, "Baztab-i sayr-i muwajiheh ba tasawwuf-i Neᶜmatullahi," 152.
4. Aubin, *Matériaux*, 48.
5. Katib, *Tarikh-i jadid-i Yazd*, 216–17.
6. Ibid., 216–17; later quoted in Mufid, *Jamiᶜ-i Mufidi*, III:685–87. For a slightly different translation, see Mancini-Lander, "Memory on the Boundaries of Empire," 445–46.
7. Katib, *Tarikh-i jadid-i Yazd*, 217.
8. Mufid, *Jamiᶜ-i Mufidi*, III:686.
9. Katib, *Tarikh-i jadid-i Yazd*, 218, compare with 211.
10. Ibid., 116, 118, 137, 142–45, 156, 203, 218.
11. Aubin, *Matériaux*, 49.
12. Mufid, *Jamiᶜ-i Mufidi*, III:685.
13. Aubin, *Matériaux*, 218; Mufid, *Jamiᶜ-i Mufidi*, III:56.
14. See chapter 6, section III, "Safavid Women as Interlocutors: The Case of Shah Vali Mosque in Taft."
15. Katib, *Tarikh-i jadid-i Yazd*, 218.
16. Binbaş, *Intellectual Networks*, 44, 49, 51, 68, 70–71.
17. Qaraʾizadeh, *Report*, 3.
18. "The Discovery of 15 Old Coffins in Shah Vali Khanaqah," *Yazd Farda*, October 27, 2007, http://www.yazdfarda.com/news/af/8056.
19. Afshar, *Yadgarha-yi Yazd*, I:414–17.
20. Ibid., I:632.
21. Katib, *Tarikh-i jadid-i Yazd*, 216–17.
22. Mufid, *Jamiᶜ-i Mufidi*, III:686.
23. Katib, *Tarikh-i jadid-i Yazd*, 217–18. For the approximate location of the Kushk Garden, see Mardumi, Nughsanmuhammadi, and Dehghani Tafti, "An Inquiry in Historical Evolution," 92–102. The layout and orientation that the authors suggest differ from my hypothesis: Mardomi and Dehghani Tafti, "Baztab-i sayr-i muwajihi ba tasawwuf-i Neᶜmatullahi," 139–58; Nughsanmuhammadi and Dehghani Tafti, "Majmuᶜih Shah Vali," 141–54.
24. For medieval debates, see Al-Qushayri, *Al-risala al-Qushayriyah*, 468; Al-Samᶜani, *Al-ansab*, 8:346.
25. Tottoli, "Ahl al-Ṣuffa."
26. Katib, *Tarikh-i jadid-i Yazd*, 144.
27. Al-Qushayri, *Al-risala al-Qushayriyah*, 468; Al-Samᶜani, *Al-ansab*, 8:346.
28. Examples include verses by the twelfth-century poet Anvari, ᶜAttar (d.1221), and Shah Neᶜmatullah Vali. For the latter, see Neᶜmatullah Vali, *Divan*, 321, 391, 396.
29. Afshar, *Yadgarha-yi Yazd*, I:414–17.
30. Neᶜmatullah Vali, *Divan*, 396.

31. Aubin, *Matériaux*, 13–14, 281; Paul, "Scheiche Und Herrscher Im Khanat Čaġatay," 307–18.

32. Aubin, *Matériaux*, 12–15, 123; Algar, "Naḳshband"; Algar and Burton-Page, "Niʿmat-Allāhiyya." On Neʿmatullah's response, see Aubin, *Matériaux*, 42.

33. Aubin, *Matériaux*, 166–67.

34. For an expression of his discontent and lament for having to leave the heart of Sufi gatherings at Samarqand and Herat, see Neʿmatullah Vali, *Divan*, 337.

35. McChesney, *Waqf in Central Asia*, 30; Paul, "Scheiche Und Herrscher Im Khanat Čaġatay," 302; Manz, *Power, Politics and Religion*, 215–16.

36. Navayi, *Asnad wa mukatibat-i tarikhi-yi Iran*, 1–3; Mahendrarajah, "A Revised History," 117–19. On tensions between Timur and Shaykh Zayn al-din Taybadi, see Manz, *Power, Politics and Religion*, 196.

37. Yazdi, *Zafarnama*, 861–62.

38. Melvin-Koushki, "Early Modern Islamicate Empire," 356–58; Moin, *The Millennial Sovereign*, 37–39; Morimoto, "An Enigmatic Genealogical Chart of the Timurids," 145–78; Golombek and Wilber, *The Timurid Architecture*, 260–63.

39. Manz, *Power, Politics and Religion*, 28.

40. Ibid., 243–44.

41. Farhat, "Islamic Piety," 82; McChesney, *Waqf in Central Asia*, 42.

42. Farhat, "Islamic Piety," 86.

43. Manz, *Power, Politics and Religion*, 219–20.

44. Ibid., 219–20.

45. Melvin-Koushki, "Early Modern Islamicate Empire," 360–62.

46. Binbaş, "Timurid Experimentation," in Mir-Kasimov, *Unity in Diversity*, 277–307; Bashir, *Messianic Hopes and Mystical Visions*, 29–75.

47. Binbaş, *Intellectual Networks*, 14, 119–21; Melvin-Koushki, "The Occult Challenge," in Mir-Kasimov, *Unity in Diversity*, 247–76.

48. Binbaş, "The Anatomy of a Regicide Attempt," 391–428; Binbaş, *Intellectual Networks*, 17, 91–92; Algar, "Horufism"; Roxburgh, *The Persian Album*, 87.

49. Binbaş, "The Anatomy of a Regicide Attempt," 20; Nasiri Jami, "Du shah dar yik iqlim," 87; Aubin, *Matériaux*, 115.

50. For similar cases, see DeWeese, "The Eclipse of the Kubraviyah in Central Asia," 57–58; Graham, "The Niʿmatullāhī Order," 185.

51. See also Subtelny, *Timurids in Transition*, 200.

52. Manz, *Power, Politics and Religion*, 243–44; Subtelny, *Timurids in Transition*, 201–205, 208–12; Mahendrarajah, "A Revised History," 119; McChesney, *Waqf in Central Asia*, 31–32.

53. Babaie, "Qavam Al-Din Shirazi," 32.

54. Subtelny and Khalidov, "The Curriculum of Islamic Higher Learning," 211.

55. Manz, *Power, Politics and Religion*, 59, 74.

56. Yazdi, *Zafarnama*, I:988–89; Golombek and Wilber, *The Timurid Architecture*, 260–63.

57. For a similar approach in Ottoman Istanbul, see Green, *Sufism*, 134.

58. Golombek, "The Chronology," 28, 42–44.

59. Manz, *Power, Politics and Religion*, 206.

60. Golombek, "The Chronology," 28, 39–40; Golombek and Wilber, *The Timurid Architecture*, 440–55; Mahendrarajah, "A Revised History," 117–26.

61. Rezaʾi, *Fihrist-i asnad-i mawqufat-i Iran*, II:48.

62. Aubin, *Matériaux*, 201–202; Yazdi, *Munshaʾat*, 139–40.

63. Binbaş, *Intellectual Networks*, 170, 192–93.

64. Aubin, *Matériaux*, 48.

65. Manz, *Power, Politics and Religion*, 29; Binbaş, *Intellectual Networks*, 185.

66. Binbaş, *Intellectual Networks*, 41, 185, 198; Manz, *Power, Politics and Religion*, 157–68.

67. Sims, "Ibrahim-Sultan's Illustrated Zafarnama," 132–43; Sims, "The Illustrated Manuscripts of Firdausī's 'Shāhnāma,'" 43–68; Wright, *The Look of the Book*, 102–103.

68. Soucek, "The Manuscripts of Iskandar Sultan," 116.

69. Binbaş, *Intellectual Networks*, 185; Binbaş, "Timurid Experimentation," 281, fn.12; Melvin-Koushki, "In Defense of Geomancy," 391.

70. Melvin-Koushki, "Powers of One," 130.

71. Melvin-Koushki, "In Defense of Geomancy," 392; Binbaş, "Timurid Experimentation," 281–93; Binbaş, *Intellectual Networks*, 260–61; Melvin-Koushki, "Early Modern Islamicate Empire," 360–61

72. Melvin-Koushki, "Powers of One," 160–61.

73. Melvin-Koushki, "Early Modern Islamicate Empire," 354; Moin, *The Millennial Sovereign*, 1–3.

74. Noted as the *risala-yi as'ala-yi Sultan Iskandar wa ajwabi-yi hazrat-i muqaddasa* and *risala-yi so'alat va jawabat-i Iskandar Sultan padishah*: Aubin, *Matériaux*, 115, 311.

75. Binbaş, *Intellectual Networks*, 253.

76. Ibid., 195.

77. Aubin, *Matériaux*, 74, 86–87, 180–81; Neʿmatullah Vali, *Divan*, Garrett no. 1469Y, ff. 367a–368a.

78. On Iskandar's campaigns against Kerman, see Manz, *Power, Politics and Religion*, 157–68; Binbaş, *Intellectual Networks*, 189.

79. Aubin, *Matériaux*, 48.

80. Katib, *Tarikh-i jadid-i Yazd*, 216. On bani, see Qayyumi Bidhendi, "Patronage and the Hidden Aspects," 5–7.

81. Aubin, *Matériaux*, 48.

82. Binbaş, *Intellectual Networks*, 77.

83. On the institutionalization of Sufi networks, see Binbaş, *Intellectual Networks*, 7; Firouzeh, "Between the Spiritual and Material," 124–25.

84. Manz, *Power, Politics and Religion*, 192; Moin, *The Millennial Sovereign*, 33.

85. Moin, *The Millennial Sovereign*, 34; Subrahmanyam, "Connected Histories," 739.

86. On the title *qutb al-aqtab* (Supreme Pole) given to Sultan Bayezid II (r. 1481–1512), see Melvin-Koushki, "Early Modern Islamicate Empire," 359.

87. Moin, *The Millennial Sovereign*, 69.

88. See, for instance, Nafisi, "Maqamat," 110–13.

89. Ibid., 157–61, 195–96.

90. Manz, *Power, Politics and Religion*, 210.

91. Ibid., 58. On Sufi shaykhs in charge of 120 khanaqahs endowed by Sultan Firuz Shah Tughluq (r.1351–88) in Delhi, see ʿAfif, *Tarikh-i Firuz Shahi*, 300.

92. Manz, *Power, Politics and Religion*, 109.

93. See a variety of examples in Digby, "The Sufi Shaykh and the Sultan," 75; Samarqandi, *Matlaʿ-i saʿdayn*, II:518; Nafisi, "Maqamat," 110–13.

94. Safi, "Bargaining with Baraka," 265.

95. Aubin, *Matériaux*, 164–65.

96. See Digby, "The Sufi Shaykh and the Sultan," 72; Ahmad, "The Sufi and Sultan," 147.
97. Aubin, *Matériaux*, 253–54.
98. Binbaş, *Intellectual Networks*, 69, 80.
99. Aubin, *Matériaux*, 165.
100. Katib, *Tarikh-i jadid-i Yazd*, 216–17.
101. For comparative seventeenth-century examples, see Subrahmanyam, "Iranians Abroad," 354.
102. Yazdi, *Munshaʾat*, 157–59.
103. Aubin, *Matériaux*, 168.
104. Ibid., 189–90.
105. For comparison, Baysunghur's landed properties under Shahrukh were worth 600 *kapaki* (currency common under the Ilkhanids, Timuirds, and Safavids). The annual taxes collected from Tabriz and the surrounding countryside amounted to 100 tumans under Uljaytu: Blair, *Text and Image*, 129.
106. Aubin, *Matériaux*, 189–90.
107. Manz, *Power, Politics and Religion*, 37.
108. Aubin, *Deux Sayyids de Bam*, 51; Subtelny, *Timurids in Transition*, 198–99.
109. Dates vary and might refer to multiple meetings: Kermani, writing in the early sixteenth century, notes a visit happening in the same year as Shah Neʿmatullah's death in 1431 while Sunʿullah, writing in the seventeenth century, records a visit a few years after Shah Neʿmatullah's death following a request from Shahrukh: Aubin, *Matériaux*, 68 and 199.
110. Ibid., 199–201.
111. Ibid., 200–201.
112. Ibid. On Shiʿa-Sunni debates around this account, see Firouzeh, "Between the Spiritual and Material," 141–44.
113. His first visit can be dated roughly between 1431 and 1435. Aubin, *Matériaux*, 202–203.
114. Manz, *Power, Politics and Religion*, 14.
115. Yazdi, *Munshaʾat*, 149–55; Binbaş, *Intellectual Networks*, 10–11, 45, 75–76. For a comparative example of letters exchanged among Mevlevi Sufis in relation to the patronage of Seljuqs of Anatolia, see Peacock, "Sufis and the Seljuk Court," 206–26.
116. Yazdi, *Munshaʾat*, 216–18. See also Binbaş, *Intellectual Networks*, 57–59.
117. Yazdi, *Munshaʾat*, 216–18.
118. Binbaş, *Intellectual Networks*, 56–57.
119. Yazdi, *Munshaʾat*, 140–55.
120. Aubin, "De Kūhbanān a Bidar," 248.
121. Yazdi, *Munshaʾat*, 149.
122. Ibid., 151–54.
123. Ibid., 152–54. Also see Aubin, "De Kūhbanān a Bidar," 247–48.
124. Yazdi, *Munshaʾat*, 151–52.
125. Ibid., 152–54.
126. Ibid., 151–52.
127. Ibid., 147–48.
128. Aubin, "De Kūhbanān a Bidar," 248.

PART TWO

Distance, Intimacy, Substitution

Strategies of Self-Representation

4

Betwixt and Between

The Sacred and Material in Taft and Mahan

The eastward expansion of the Neʿmatullahi network across the Arabian Sea and into the Deccan has at times been interpreted as a definitive act of migration, casting the part of the family who still resided in Iran as a "headless" Sufi network.[1] Historical sources, however, tell a different story. While there were difficult decisions to be made in the process of this transoceanic mobilization, the movement of the Neʿmatullahi Sufis and the circles of artists and intellectuals connected with them was more fluid than the notion of permanent migration would suggest. Furthermore, the network's architectural and material histories in Iran or India cannot be explained solely in light of their transregional dimension. To demonstrate this, the present chapter brings the conversation back to the local level, foregrounding how the key to understanding a transregional Sufi network like the Neʿmatullahis can at times lie in their local and regional material histories.

This chapter focuses on the relationship between the two central Iranian sites of the Neʿmatullahis: the khanaqah of Shah Vali in Taft and the complex in Mahan. The loss of major parts of the complex at Taft, the complete loss of pre-funerary structures in Mahan, and the scarcity of scholarly attention to the relationship between them have resulted in a fragmentary view of the history of the Sufi network and its material culture in Iran in the fifteenth century—one that is overly dominated by transregional relations. Building on the previous chapters, the goal here is to examine how these two important centers of the network in Taft and Mahan evolved against and in relation to each other, both before and after Mahan's transformation into the most significant funerary site of the Neʿmatullahi Sufis in the 1430s.

Swinging between Mahan and Taft, the overarching aim of this chapter is to show how the existence of two distinctive centers associated with the Sufi network in the same region made room for a distance between the spiritual and material affairs of the family. This separation was at times a key strategy in crafting an image of the Neʿmatullahi qutb as an auratic spiritual figure distanced from worldly matters and engaged in seclusive practices at Mahan, especially in the last decades of his life. This image, promoted in the Mahan complex, contrasts with that of Shah Neʿmatullah's descendants, who were actively engaged in the urban, mercantile, and educational agenda of the khanaqah in Taft (and later in the Deccan). At the same time, the divide between the spiritual and material aspirations of the Mahan and Taft centers was by no means absolute. As I show toward the end of the chapter, a range of aesthetic, spatial, and epigraphic strategies were adopted to account for this divide and soften its edges.

I start with textual accounts that highlight the family's preoccupation with creating a spiritual buffer around the qutb of the Sufi network, which would in turn allow other members of the family to maneuver between their spiritual and worldly roles as needed. A series of architectural and textual observations then highlight the portrayal of the Mahan complex as a holy site and of Taft as the worldly working khanaqah of the network. In the last sections of the chapter, I introduce nuances that emphasize the khanaqah at Taft as a sacred space despite the conspicuous corporeal absence of Shah Neʿmatullah Vali from the site both during and after his lifetime. The culmination of these shifts between the spiritual and material shows us how the lines between the two were redrawn and reimagined when and where needed.

I. Crafting a Sacred Distance

Before getting to the relationship between the complexes in Mahan and Taft, I want to focus on two textual accounts that highlight the importance of the division between spiritual and material affairs as viewed by the Neʿmatullahi Sufis. It is important to emphasize at the outset that accounts like these, which consciously draw a line between the two realms, are rare. Yet, their occasional appearances in hagiographical narratives and official correspondence point to an underlying current in the shaping of the family's decisions at critical points in their history.

The first account has to do with the reception and distribution of gifts arriving from the Deccan—a source mentioned briefly in chapter 3 as it pertained to Shah Neʿmatullah's relationship with Timurid rulers and their conflicts over taxation.[2] Appearing in Sunʿullah's biography of Shah Neʿmatullah, the account corresponds with Ahmad Shah's second invitation of Shah Neʿmatullah to the Deccan and his sending of gifts to the Sufi in Mahan.

> [For the second time] the Sultans of Hind sent more valuable and numerous gifts to Mahan which the bringer left in the middle of the river in front of the khanaqah. Because Shah Neʿmatullah was on a retreat (khalwat), no one had the courage to [interrupt and] inform him. Three days later, when Shah Neʿmatullah finished the retreat, he noticed the gifts and asked about them. They told him the truth of the matter and mentioned the value of the gifts, which was as much as the tax value of the region. He ordered that they

> divide the gifts into three shares, all equal, and said: "one should go to Mirza Shahrukh, whose army is large in numbers; one should go to [my son] Khalilullah, for he likes a fortune (*jah*), and the third share should be spent on the expenses (*ikhrajat*) of the shrine (astana) at Mahan. . . ." And there was a piece (*zarᶜ*) of *karbas* (white cotton cloth) on the baggage. [Shah Neᶜmatullah] picked it up and said [referring to himself]: "so that the dervishes, too, can wipe their sweat."[3]

Apart from its reference to the Timurid ruler Shahrukh that was mentioned in chapter 3, this account reveals the intentional divisions drawn between the sacred and the material. It highlights the groundwork that Shah Neᶜmatullah—or the retrospective image of him in his biography—laid for the subsequent development of the Sufi network: the equal importance of enhancing political ties with the ruling powers, empowering his heir financially, and promoting the architecture of the network and its maintenance. His role as the decision-maker for the material affairs of the Sufi network, however, is contrasted with his ascetic disinterest in worldly matters, comparable to many of his counterparts in the history of Sufism.[4] This becomes evident both in his disciples' fear of intruding on his retreat and in the final gesture, emphasizing that no material possessions except for the bare essentials (i.e., the piece of Indian cotton) were kept for his personal use. In his capacity as the decision-maker, he diverts material possessions away from himself and delegates their management to others. There is a stark contrast between the image of Shah Neᶜmatullah and his son as projected in this account. Shah Khalilullah is excluded from the "dervishes" category in this instance and is instead portrayed as interested in dealing directly with financial matters. More importantly, he is sanctioned by the leader of the Sufi network to do so.

This ascetic aura was not exclusive to Shah Neᶜmatullah but rather passed down to some, though not all, of the descendants who later took on the leadership of the Sufi network. Letters exchanged between the descendants of Shah Neᶜmatullah and Timurid elites, as recorded in the fifteenth-century collection the *Munshaʾat* (a source discussed in chap. 3), draw an interesting picture.[5] In a letter from Amir Zahir al-din b. Nurullah (a great-grandson of Shah Neᶜmatullah) to a Timurid elite on the issue of tax exemption, he informs the addressee that his father, Amir Nurullah, who was in the Deccan at the time, had sent two dervishes with letters and ordered one of his sons to accompany them to Herat to acquire approval on previous tax terms. It is made clear in the letter that this was an important and urgent issue that had to be resolved by a specific deadline, for if the tax exemption was withheld, it would have appeared as if the reason for Amir Nurullah's upcoming visit to Herat was to sort out this matter. Instead, Nurullah preferred that his journey be "completely free from the impurities of the material world."[6] In what follows, I contend that similar anxieties about the material affairs of the network came to be mapped onto the duality between the two centers in Taft and Mahan in the first few decades of the fifteenth century.

The relationship between Taft and Mahan is obscure not only due to the losses that both sites have endured but also due to the ambiguity of the textual accounts about them. In discussing the relationship between Taft and Mahan during their early history, to distinguish the two phases of the Mahan complex from one another, especially in light of the loss of the pre-1430s structures, I will refer to them as the *khanaqah at Mahan* prior to the construction of Shah Neʿmatullah's tomb in the 1430s and the *shrine at Mahan* afterward.

The khanaqahs in Mahan and Taft are never explicitly discussed in relation to each other in textual sources. The references are found either in local histories of Yazd, which do not deal with Mahan, or hagiographies that do not describe in detail the architecture or the relationship of the buildings to one another. The majority of these textual references were written retrospectively, after the death of Shah Neʿmatullah. They may therefore have more to do with the reception and development of these sites in later centuries than with their initial relationship. Nevertheless, these sources, which contain several place-centric narratives, offer a rare and incisive perspective on the Sufis' approach to materiality, alluding to distinct moods, functions, and agendas promoted in Taft and Mahan.

II. The Sacral Aura of the Khanaqah at Mahan

The choice of a small village like Mahan as one of the major sites of the Neʿmatullahis conforms with a broader pattern: what Lisa Golombek describes as the growth of "little cities of God" such as Bastam, Natanz, Qum, Ardabil, and Mashhad in the fourteenth century, some of which would turn into major shrine cities in the following centuries.[7] Textual narratives often associate these locations with holy people, miracles, and preexisting venerated sites near and far—elements that would guarantee the auspiciousness of the newly erected structure.[8] Hagiographical accounts of Mahan reveal similar conventions. In one such narrative, after traveling around Kerman, Shah Neʿmatullah reaches the water mill of Mahan, where he meets an old white-haired individual (*pirzal*) who shares bread and yogurt with him. This person's generosity and sincere attitude kindle Shah Neʿmatullah's desire to stay in Mahan, where he builds the khanaqah and gardens of Khayrabad. Subsequently, he divides his time between Kerman and Mahan.[9]

Nearby pilgrimage destinations, alongside textual narratives that emphasize their sacredness, elevate Mahan's auspiciousness. One holy site was the now-lost tomb of Khwaja ʿAlamdar in Jupar, a village about twenty-five kilometers to the west of Mahan.[10] En route to Jupar was an even more frequently visited pilgrimage site in the village of Langar, one and a half kilometers to the northwest of Mahan: the tomb of the fourteenth-century Sufi Shaykh Qutb al-din ʿAbd al-Salam-i Mahani, presumably a teacher of Shah Neʿmatullah (fig. 4.1). Surviving at the site today are a principal double-domed chamber featuring light- and dark-blue tiles and a band of Kufic inscription on the outer dome. A second chamber contains the tomb and a mihrab.[11] These structures are datable to the fifteenth century, and it is likely that the

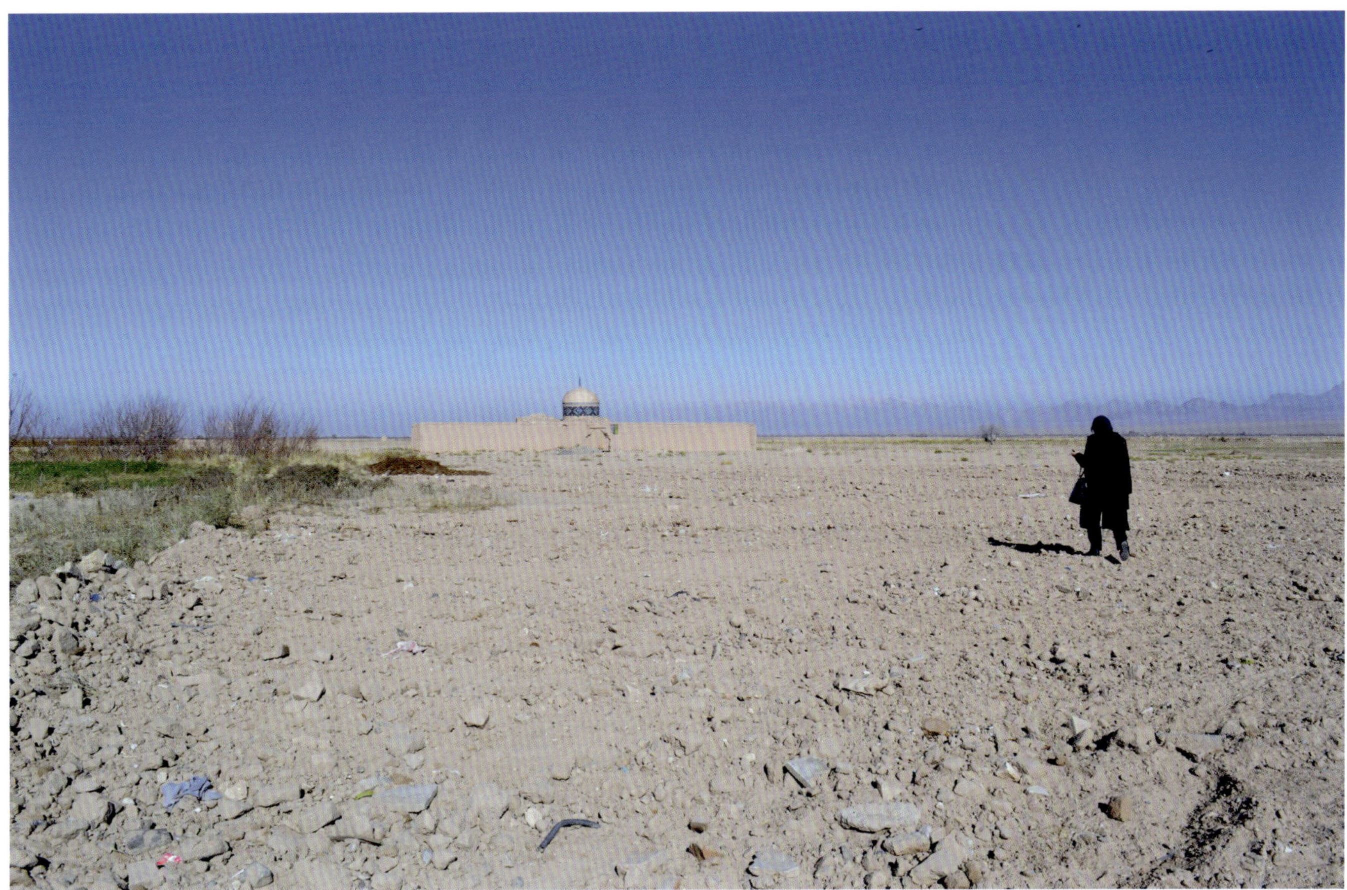

FIGURE 4.1. Tomb of Shaykh Qutb al-din ᶜAbd al-Salam-i Mahani in Langar, near Mahan, view from the south. *Photograph by author, 2014.*

constructions or restorations on the site in this period were instituted due to heightened pilgrimage activities in Mahan and its surroundings following Shah Neᶜmatullah's settlement there. Hagiographical narratives relate that on his visits, Shah Neᶜmatullah would wait for hours at the entrance of Shaykh ᶜAbd al-Salam's tomb and at times would return home without going inside, saying that so many holy spirits were engaged in circumambulation of the blessed tomb that there was no room for him to enter.[12]

The *Mazarat-i Kerman* (*Tombs of Kerman*), written by Mihrabi Kermani in the first half of the sixteenth century, notes Shah Neᶜmatullah's regular visits to the tomb of another holy figure, Muhammad b. ᶜAli Muhammad Dibaj (a descendant of Imam Jaᶜfar Sadiq, the sixth Shiᶜa Imam) in Khabis (today's Shahdad), situated to the northeast of Mahan and Kerman. A pilgrimage account similar to the aforementioned discussion of Langar relates that every time Shah Neᶜmatullah reached Khabis, he would get off his steed, remove his shoes, and walk toward the mausoleum barefoot, saying that there were so many rows of angels surrounding the building that moving through them was difficult.[13]

While these sources situate Mahan in a blessed landscape of holy spirits and white-haired sages, there are no such hagiographical narratives about Taft.[14] The chronological ambiguities that surround the two centers might be relevant to this issue. Some hagiographical sources grant chronological precedence to Taft over Mahan, noting that Shah Neᶜmatullah initially split his time between Kuhbanan and Taft, shifting to Mahan and Kerman later on.[15] What complicates this image, and has likely resulted in the perceived hierarchy of Mahan over Taft, is the regularly quoted note that Shah Neᶜmatullah spent the last twenty-five years of his life in Mahan.[16] Considering his death date of 1431, this reference suggests 1406 as the initial date of his move to Mahan—just a few years before the inception of the khanaqah at Taft, prompted by donations from the Timurid ruler Iskandar b. ᶜUmar Shaykh. How can we make sense of this seeming tension, this emphasis on Mahan as the more long-standing residence of Shah Neᶜmatullah that does not quite fit into the above-mentioned chronological narrative?

Chronological precision is not high on the list of priorities in hagiographical sources, and this could account for the existing ambiguities. It is also possible that this lack of precision was intentional for a figure like Shah Neᶜmatullah, affording him an aura of omnipresence in different locales associated with his family and disciples. For instance, his fleeting presence in Taft, right around the offer of patronage by Iskandar (as noted in chap. 3), earned Taft an association with the Sufi saint but, at the same time, granted him distance from notions of wealth and court patronage as well as the hustle and bustle of construction.

As for Mahan, it is likely that hagiographical sources exaggerated the length of Shah Neᶜmatullah's stay there to emphasize its sanctity as the place blessed with the prolonged presence of the Sufi toward the end of his life and the place chosen for his burial after his death. Such efforts could have been geared toward winning financial support for the development of the site at Mahan, which, after the completion of the mausoleum and a restoration in the fifteenth century, remained almost unchanged until the late sixteenth century.[17] With the continued architectural developments in the khanaqah at Taft, it is conceivable that there was no need to create that aura of sanctity through hagiographical narratives in Taft, a point that—as I will discuss later in the chapter—should not be mistaken for Taft's lack of spiritual significance. Nevertheless, the sources present a clear contrast. On the one hand was Mahan, mapped within preexisting venerated pilgrimage sites and blessed with the presence of the Sufi master; on the other was Taft and its connection to the state, power, and wealth. The Neᶜmatullahis would benefit from association with both types of textual and architectural narratives.

III. Modesty and Solitude: The Khanaqah at Mahan

Among the four biographies of Shah Neᶜmatullah, there are scarce references to the buildings in Mahan during his lifetime. When discussed, they are usually, but not always, described as humble structures dedicated to a limited range of organized activities. Waᶜizi's biography from the fifteenth century stands out in this regard. While he gives some space to the khanaqah at Mahan, he does not mention the Taft complex, which, architecturally speaking, normally received more detailed mentions in biographies: "[Shah Neᶜmatullah] installed a garden and madrasa in Mahan and all the money that would reach him by way of donations (*futuhat*) were used for charity and God's sake. And he made a residence (*qasr*) for his own occupation so that he could stay there in solitude with peace of mind and dedicate himself to his occupation."[18] Waᶜizi adds that the aforementioned residence was on the upper level of the madrasa, and no one knew what went on there during the Shaykh's night prayers, nor could anyone interrupt him.[19] During the day, Shah Neᶜmatullah would reserve a time for assemblies (*majlis*) to meet his students and followers, presumably in the madrasa downstairs.[20] Elsewhere, Waᶜizi describes the kitchen at the Mahan khanaqah as a busy place where an abundance of food was served every day and where, by way of charity, many donations of cash, clothes, and edibles were brought to Shah Neᶜmatullah.[21]

Waᶜizi's rather expanded description of Mahan, with no mention of Taft, is probably related to the patronage of the Bahmanids: both the support that they offered to the Neᶜmatullahis—as discussed in chapters 1 and 2—and their patronage of Waᶜizi's biography of Shah Neᶜmatullah. The Bahmanids' donations by Ahmad Shah I were sent to Mahan, both during the lifetime of Shah Neᶜmatullah and after his death—the later donations specifically for the construction of his mausoleum. Although not dated, the possible timing of Waᶜizi's biography could be crucial in this regard. Ahmad Shah I died during the construction of Shah Neᶜmatullah's mausoleum in Mahan, and Waᶜizi's biography is dedicated to Ahmad Shah I's son and successor, Ahmad II.[22] Since the initial donation by Ahmad Shah I was not enough to complete the mausoleum (as I mentioned in chap. 3), Waᶜizi's expansive accounts of Mahan—including both Shah Neᶜmatullah's extended stay there and descriptions of Mahan as a thriving center—could be seen as an attempt to encourage the Bahmanids to continue their patronage of the mausoleum. At times, Waᶜizi even seems to transfer descriptions of the khanaqah at Taft, including epigraphic features recorded in contemporary local histories of Yazd, into his description of the khanaqah in Mahan.[23]

Setting aside the politics of Waᶜizi's account, his and other hagiographical texts show that several structures did exist in Mahan and were frequented by Shah Neᶜmatullah's followers during his lifetime. Waᶜizi portrays the khanaqah of Mahan as a site representing the common Sufi notion of "solitude within society" (*khalwat dar anjuman*), denoting the lack of an ideological conviction for a complete detachment from the world.[24] The solitude and the restrained presence of the Sufi master among his followers, as described in Waᶜizi's account, correspond to accounts by later biographers, such as Sadid al-din, writing at the beginning of the sixteenth century. But Sadid al-din emphasizes that such dynamics represent one phase of Shah Neᶜmatullah's career as a Sufi teacher.[25] As time went by, it seems, the balance between the *khalwat* (seclusion) and *anjuman* (communal presence) changed in favor of the former in Mahan.

In describing the architectural setting of the shrine at Mahan, biographer Sadid al-din relates an eyewitness account by Neʿmatullah-i Thani, a distinguished descendant of Shah Neʿmatullah and patron of Sadid al-din's biography in the early sixteenth century. Neʿmatullah-i Thani was in Mahan during the lifetime of Shah Neʿmatullah Vali, and his account offers an interesting glimpse of how the Sufi's growing seclusion over time could have been reflected in the architectural layout of the khanaqah at Mahan. While the earlier account by Waʿizi describes Shah Neʿmatullah's place of retreat as located on the upper floor of his madrasa, Sadid al-din describes two separate buildings: one close to the gate of the garden and another at a far distance, deep in the middle of the garden. The building in the middle of the garden was "where the Shaykh would spend all his time in prayer and no one from his circle was allowed to visit him without a personal request by the Shaykh. Outside the door, young men from the age of eight to twelve would attend to his needs if he required water for ablution."[26] The building by the gate was where "some of his attendants and followers gathered, but it was not customary for them to interrupt the Shaykh no matter who came to visit him, whether a king or a beggar, and no matter how big or small the matter was."[27]

Regardless of their precision, these two architectural accounts of the layout of the Mahan khanaqah, which seem to relate to two different periods of Shah Neʿmatullah's life, require us to see the distance between spiritual and material engagements not as a primordial phenomenon in Sufism but as something that could fluctuate even within the lifetime of a given Sufi master. The accounts also remind us that such a distance could manifest itself in material culture and its textual description. Both text and architecture could mark out ideals of distance and in fact were imagined to do so.

Another record that offers insight into the kinds of functions imagined for the khanaqah in Mahan is a note about lodging arrangements from Mahmud al-Waʿizi al-Hasani, a follower of Shah Neʿmatullah who stayed in his company in Mahan for two months. Accompanied by his brother, he notes that during their stay, they had to divide their time between Mahan and Kerman because there was no arrangement for long-term stays in the Mahan khanaqah: "We would stay one week or ten days, more or less, and every evening we would see him [Shah Neʿmatullah]. Then we would go to Kerman to earn some money. My brother would work as a scribe and I would serve, and then we would go back [to Mahan] and stay for another few days."[28] The limited stays described by the disciple do in fact correspond to the convention of accommodating travelers observed in many khanaqahs of the premodern period. It was common for travelers to be allowed to stay in khanaqah lodging for a short period, perhaps three days, but there were also provisions in place for residents, who would have to provide some sort of service to the khanaqah in return for long-term lodging.[29] What the disciple in the above account indicates is that unlike Taft, which seems to have been provisioned for longer stays (as I will discuss below), the lodging in Mahan was mostly short term and dependent on donations.

The distinction between the khanaqahs at Taft and Mahan reflected the functions taking place in them as well as visions of the role they could play in the future of the Sufi network. In order to maintain "solitude within society" at Mahan, the Neʿmatullahis allowed other centers in the region to bear the weight of hospitality and teaching.

IV. Convivial, Commercial, Educational: The Khanaqah at Taft

The Shah Vali khanaqah at Taft is portrayed as a place of gathering "dedicated to high-status guests" (*jahat-i mihmanan-i vala*), according to Kermani's biography of Shah Neʿmatullah.[30] Another biographer of the Sufi, Sadid al-din, describes the khanaqah of Taft as a building fit for the magnanimity of Shah Neʿmatullah: "World travelers agree that there is nowhere as pleasant and spacious as the Khanaqah." He notes that at the time of writing the biography, thanks to the efforts of the aforementioned Shah Neʿmatullah-i Thani (Sadid al-din's own patron), the khanaqah was improving day by day, flourishing as a communal space for the region's elite as well as travelers from all walks of life who arrived there and enjoyed its bounty.[31] A note in Katib's fifteenth-century local history of Yazd confirms this provision for the gathering and lodging of travelers and residents at the khanaqah from the early phases of the complex. In his description of the Taft khanaqah, as discussed in chapter 3, Katib mentions that the revenue of the bathhouse within the complex was dedicated to travelers.[32] Given that aside from donations the bathhouse was essentially the main revenue-producing element of the khanaqah, the statement suggests the frequency of visitors at the complex and the need for a financial provision to support them.

The hierarchy of architectural elements arranged in and around the courtyard at Taft affirms this sense of openness and reception (fig. 3.11). The central position of the *kushk* (kiosk) in the courtyard, a freestanding structure surrounded by arcades, embodies the ceremonial and convivial character of the complex, receptive not only to Sufis and travelers but also to traders and high-status guests. The fresh water that flowed from the mountains into the complex and gardens surrounding the khanaqah added to this sense of conviviality. The complex's relationship to its natural environment was celebrated in textual sources, such as a poem written in the late seventeenth or eighteenth century by the governor of Yazd. The verses describing the khanaqah proceed from the trees and fruits in the garden surrounding the complex to the melon farms in the village, then back into the water pool at the khanaqah and off to the winds blowing through the region. The khanaqah was thus mapped onto a sensorial landscape of pleasant smells, tastes, and temperatures.[33]

The design and textual descriptions of the Taft khanaqah represent an ambition to partake in the social, financial, and political affairs of the time, speaking to the identity that the Sufi network was constructing for itself. Similarities between the Shah Vali khanaqah at Taft and a few multipurpose charitable complexes built in the fourteenth and fifteenth centuries in the region of Yazd help contextualize the multiplicity of functions that took place at the khanaqah and, by extension, the variety of roles that members of the family assumed as urban elites. One such comparative example is the khanaqah complex of ʿAli Baniman (d. 1379–80) in Bidakhvid.[34] Another, though larger in scale, is the Mir Chaqmaq complex in Yazd, built in the first half of the fifteenth century, which similarly brought together mercantile, charitable, and religious elements including a caravansary, cistern, mosque, and khanaqah.[35]

A connection between the khanaqah at Taft and trade networks has been proposed speculatively by Jean Aubin, as noted in chapter 3. He points out the proximity of Yazd, which was an important center of textile making in the fifteenth century, and the accessibility of the silk-weaving workshops in the city to argue for the possibility of silk cultivation and industry as a family business.[36] It was not uncommon for Sufi shrines to engage with mercantile networks. Kishwar Rizvi, for instance, speaks of the economic viability of Shaykh Safi's shrine in Ardabil in northwest Iran, where the caravans arriving from Anatolia paid homage to the cult of Shaykh Safi when passing through the city.[37]

Although I have not located any historical or visual references to the silk trade among the Neʿmatullahis, a metaphorical reference to silk in Kermani's biography of Shah Neʿmatullah alludes to this possibility. It occurs in his account of a Sayyid Nizam al-din Mahmud al-Waʿiz, who dreamed of a *chartaqi* (a dome sitting on four vaults) by a stream of water where an old man sat, stitching fabric—probably a reference to the making of a stitched Sufi cloak (*khirqa*). The man in the dream is identified as the Sufi Bayazid Bastami (d. 848 or 875), who tells Waʿiz, "The stitching was first the job of Sultan Ibrahim-i Adham. In his hands, it was [made of] wool. When it was my turn [Bastami referring to himself], it turned to a string [of cotton?] and now that it is Neʿmatullah's turn it has transformed into silk."[38]

Generally speaking, textual references to the relationship between silk weaving and Sufism were not uncommon.[39] In the context of Shah Neʿmatullah's hagiography, what this specific account is likely implying is the chain of prominent early Sufis such as Ibrahim b. Adham (d. 777–78) and Bastami passing the honor of qutb-ship down to Shah Neʿmatullah through the possession of the cloak—a key item of clothing signifying Sufi initiation and transferal of permission for teaching. The transformation of the material in the Sufi's hands from wool to silk could be interpreted metaphorically as the refinement of Sufi teachings over time under these leading figures, culminating in the figure of Shah Neʿmatullah. However, this metaphorical interpretation does not rule out the possibility of a parallel literal connection, hinting at the Neʿmatullahis' involvement in the silk trade and interest in economic profit. Despite its generic quality, the combination of a chartaqi structure and a stream of water as the setting of the dream bears an interesting resemblance to the architectural configuration of the kiosk in the khanaqah at Taft.

The possibility of Taft's role as a trade center becomes even more plausible when considered in the context of Iran-Deccan mercantile connections in the fifteenth century. While there is no specific reference to the mercantile activities of the family in the fifteenth century, they traveled between central Iran and the Deccan on ships that carried goods between the west Indian ports, Qalhat, and Iran, making it easy to imagine the family's involvement in trade given the frequency of their journeys.[40] As mentioned in chapter 2, in the sixteenth century, a Neʿmatullahi khanaqah in Saghar in Deccan India provided lodging for merchants.[41] Several letters in the *Munshaʾat* draw a vivid picture of the influx of the Neʿmatullahi family members traveling between Iran and the Deccan, and interestingly, in almost all cases, they mention Taft and Yazd as opposed to Mahan.[42]

One specific letter from the *Munshaʾat* also reveals that a considerable number of the Neʿmatullahi family members resided in Taft. Offering his apologies for being unable to travel to Herat, Amir Zahir al-din b. Nurullah, the great-grandson of Shah Neʿmatullah, mentions his many responsibilities in Taft. He notes how his father, Nurullah—who was in the Deccan—had left under his watch "a few houses with a large group of people in each, and a khanaqah where different classes of people from the wealthy and the poor (dervishes) stop," and how he, "with his own family [who depended on him], had to maintain and manage all these [properties]."[43]

Allusions to the responsibilities of notable figures at the khanaqah of Taft also point toward the complex as a place of education for both the descendants and the followers of Shah Neʿmatullah. Biographer Sadid al-din relates an anecdote about a gathering that took place in 868/1463 in the khanaqah at Taft. Present in that gathering were the biographer himself; his patron, the aforementioned Shah Neʿmatullah-i Thani, who was in charge of the khanaqah at Taft at the time; and Maulana Haji Ikhtiyar al-din, one of the successors (*khulafa*) of Shah Neʿmatullah and an esteemed figure who had been in the service of the family for sixty years, back to the time of Shah Neʿmatullah. Based in Taft, Ikhtiyar al-din worked as a teacher to the children of the Neʿmatullahis, revealing that an important function of the complex was the training of the next generations of the family.[44] Another *Munshaʾat* letter written by Amir Ahmad Isfahani, a resident *hafiz* (Qurʾan reciter) in Taft, to his mother adds to such witness accounts about teaching activities. He relates to his mother that he was among a group of reciters who ensured that the Qurʾan was recited at all times daily. He was responsible for the period between the two evening prayers, and the rest of the day he was engaged in attending classes.[45] Although he does not specifically mention the khanaqah, given the prominence of the khanaqah in the small village of Taft at the time, it is safe to assume that he was a long-term resident and student at the khanaqah complex.

The teaching component of the khanaqah of Taft was in line with the vision that Shah Neʿmatullah is said to have had for other centers of the Sufi network in the region. Given the multiplicity of their bases and Shah Neʿmatullah's choice to spend most of his time in retreat toward the end of his life, this was a critical decision for the transmission of the network's teachings. The Neʿmatullahi base in Abarqu, near Yazd, which was built at the same time as the khanaqah of Taft, had a similar teaching focus, albeit on a smaller scale. Sadid al-din notes that Shah Neʿmatullah installed one of his followers in Abarqu to reside in the garden so that "when the Neʿmatullahi dervishes from all around arrive they can stay there and dedicate themselves to educating followers."[46]

A long-term view of the khanaqah at Taft, gleaned through fragmented architectural and epigraphic evidence, attests to the importance of the complex as a center that constantly changed and expanded in response to the multiple needs of its growing community. This chronological snapshot shows a continuity in refurbishment and expansion campaigns of different scales after the khanaqah's initial phase of construction in the early decades of the fifteenth century. Through architectural inscriptions recorded in the *Munshaʾat* of Sharaf al-din ʿAli Yazdi, we know of constructions that a Neʿmatullahi descendant, Amir Ziaʾ al-din Nurullah, patronized two decades after its inception, in 846/1442–43.[47] Tombstones found in situ suggest the possibility of a burial on the site of the khanaqah a few years later, in 848/1444–45.[48] A mihrab on the site is dated 873/1468.[49] Around the same time, in 876/1471–72, a large tile inscription panel was added somewhere in the complex, mentioning the name of another Neʿmatullahi descendant, Zahir al-din, probably as patron of an architectural structure.[50] The year 889/1484 marks another burial on the site as well as the construction of an elaborate inscription band, currently installed around the wooden door of the khanaqah's mosque.[51] The political landscape of Kerman, too, must have played a role in the Mahan-Taft equation and the concentration of architectural activities in Taft. Michael Connell suggests that the rise of Taft was due in part to the fact that the Timurids used Kerman as a base for military operations against the Qara Qoyunlu. Kerman was ravaged during those wars and never fully recovered.[52]

Taft seems to have maintained its role as the primary working khanaqah of the Sufi network during the Safavid period, when a few of Shah Neʿmatullah's descendants forged marriage allegiances with the Safavid family and rose to positions such as governor of Yazd and sadr.[53] The connections between the Safavids and the Neʿmatullahis and the positions to which they were appointed in Yazd could have also contributed to the volume of architectural development in Taft prior to the last decades of the sixteenth century. One such example is the addition of an ivan to the khanaqah in Taft by Amir Nizam al-din ʿAbd al-Baqi, who held the position of sadr at the Safavid court for a few years until 1514, when he was killed in the Battle of Chaldiran.[54] More importantly, when Khanish Begum (d. 1564), sister of Shah Tahmasp (r. 1524–76), who had married the Neʿmatullahi descendant Nur al-din Neʿmatullah Baqi, decided to support the construction of a building associated with the Sufi family, it was not at the shrine at Mahan but in Taft that she invested in the significant development of the khanaqah's mosque (fig. 3.4).

The involvement of notable artists and descendants of Shah Neʿmatullah as well as elite patrons allude to the continuous political and religious authority held by the site in Taft. While the priority for architectural development would traditionally be given to the venerated tomb of the deceased Sufi, it seems that most of the Sufi network's architectural investments had gone to their working khanaqah in Taft until 1590, when Mahan's century-long architectural inactivity came to an end with the addition of the dar al-huffaz (recitation hall) (fig. 1.5).[55] This concentration of architectural activities in Taft emphasizes the significance of the complex, which, compared to Mahan, is less easily discernible today due to its greater material losses.

In discussing the relationship between the Neᶜmatullahi sites in Taft and Mahan, Connell describes the period after the death of Shah Neᶜmatullah as characterized by "the eclipse of Mahan by Taft."[56] This is true to some extent, as the chronological evidence above suggests. But there are two points to consider here: first, that the importance of Mahan for the Sufi network and among pilgrimage networks of regional and transregional scale cannot be overlooked, even with the relative architectural inactivity in the century following the Sufi's death. Second, as I contend in this section and the rest of the chapter, a discrepancy of functions between Taft and Mahan had been envisioned from early on, possibly from the time of Shah Neᶜmatullah himself, and this distinction only grew in the following decades. The distance between them was motivated by concerns to balance the competing demands of worldliness, materiality, and the sacred.

V. Mahan as a Site of Pilgrimage: A View Through Endowment Documents

The spatial layout of the shrine at Mahan and its chronology—especially after the death of Shah Neᶜmatullah—indicate that it was not immediately developed as the working center of the network but rather prioritized as a site of veneration and pilgrimage. Over time, even with the addition of lodging provisions, the layout of the shrine at Mahan has emphasized the monumentality of the axis that the pilgrims take to reach the sacred tomb (figs. 1.2 and 1.3). The addition of the vaulted gallery and courtyard in the Safavid period lent a greater sense of directionality to the site in relation to the pilgrimage routes from Kerman, a city that had assumed significant political and economic roles during the reign of Shah ᶜAbbas I and under the governorship of Ganj ᶜAli Khan (d. 1625).[57] This focus on the axiality of the shrine was maintained throughout the Qajar-era expansions, even with the change of orientation discussed in chapter 1.[58] That spaces for teaching and hosting travelers and dervishes were at most minimally present in Mahan prior to the expansions around 1590 is also proven by an analysis of the documents on the maintenance of the Mahan shrine.

The oldest known endowment to the shrine at Mahan is recorded in a Bahmanid farman dated 870/1465, from the reign of Muhammad Shah Bahmani (r. 1463–82). It bears the seal of Khwaja Mahmud Gavan (d. 1481), the influential Iranian figure at the Bahmanid court, vizier to several of the dynasty's rulers, a disciple of the Neᶜmatullahi family, and patron of the grand madrasa in Bidar, which brought together scholars from Iran and other parts of the Islamic world.[59] The farman specifies that a sum of the revenue of lands in the suburbs of Muhammadabad (Bidar) had to be handed to Amirza Muhibbullah (d. ca. 1505), grandson of Shah Neᶜmatullah and the qutb of the Sufi network in the Deccan at the time. In the decree, Muhibbullah is referred to as "the superintendent (*mutiwalli*) of the blessed mausoleum (*rawza-yi mutibarrika*) of Shah Neᶜmatullah Vali," meaning the shrine at Mahan. He had to oversee the endowment's expenditure on the building of the shrine.[60] Inherent in these specifications are the arrangements needed for the money to be brought to Mahan from the Deccan annually, confirming regular traffic between the two regions. A similar farman dated 894/1489 and corresponding to the reign of Muhammad's successor, Mahmud Shah Bahmanid (r. 1482–1518), shows that the endowment was still in place a few decades later.

Falling in the period between the two Bahmanid farmans is a fifteenth-century endowment document (*waqfnama*) by Shah Neᶜmatullah-i Thani (d. after 1500), the distinguished descendant of Shah Neᶜmatullah whose name has come up several times in this chapter as the patron of Neᶜmatullahi hagiographies. According to the document, Neᶜmatullah-i Thani endowed the revenue of two qanats (underground water channels) in Mahan, named "darb-i ab" and "Tahirabad," to Shah Neᶜmatullah's mausoleum (called *buqᶜa* in the document).[61] The waqfnama is dated 884/1479–80 and is supposedly kept at the provincial *awqaf* (Islamic endowments) office of Kerman.[62] Elsewhere, I have shown that this endowment document is likely to represent the only known official endowment on the Iranian side that was made to the shrine at Mahan in the fifteenth century.[63] Between this document and the later Qajar endowment documents (the earliest of which is dated 1255/1839), there is a long gap of about 350 years.

While the fifteenth-century documents discussed above are valuable sources on the financial resources of the shrine at Mahan, they tell us little about the functions taking place at the shrine. Among the later documents, some can shed light on the possibility of earlier endowment documents that have not survived. The importance of these later documents thus lies in highlighting how fragmented our view of the shrines and their financial resources is.

A number of lists dating from the first half of the twentieth century kept at the National Archives in Tehran record all the known prior endowments made to the shrine at Mahan, referring to those prior to the Qajar era as "old endowments."[64] The ten "old endowments" listed contain revenues from lands, water rights, gardens, shops, and a water mill. Seven of these are from properties located in Mahan and the other three in Guk, Langar, and Jupar, all small villages around Mahan.[65]

The most important implication of these endowment documents regards an absence: in none of the early documents is there any mention of teaching or hospitality taking place at the Mahan shrine. There is no mention of any funds for the common positions such as a *qari* (reciter), *talaba* (student), or *mudarris* (teacher). Qajar-era documents share this absence of teaching activities, but among the positions and expenditure that they list, new activities emerge such as lodging offered to Sufis and religious ceremonies held at the shrine. In addition to the salary of the superintendent (mutiwalli) and attendants (*mustakhdamih*) and the building and renovation activities, the endowments to the shrine were to be spent on dervishes and the poor (*fuqara*) including their clothing, annual commemoration of Imam Husayn (the third Shiʿa Imam), passion plays (*taʿziya*), dishes, lighting, and the coffeehouse of the shrine.[66]

I am not suggesting that the lack of evidence on teaching and lodging activities in the endowment documents of Mahan prior to the nineteenth century should be taken as definitive proof of the absence of such activities at the shrine. However, when read alongside textual and architectural evidence indicating the existence of such spaces and activities in the khanaqah in Taft from early on (i.e., *hujras* built for the poor and shaykhs), a predominantly pilgrimage-oriented image of Mahan emerges. With a bath, a soup kitchen, lodges, teaching positions, and later a mosque, the khanaqah at Taft was well equipped as the working center of the Sufi network as well as a charitable institution—a priority that was strengthened by the development of the khanaqah in the early Safavid period.

Despite this distinctive set of functions, the separation between the holiness of the shrine at Mahan and the worldliness of the khanaqah at Taft that I have so far highlighted was not absolute. Rather, it suggests different ways of prioritizing the agenda and activities of each center. Alongside this strategic division, there is also evidence of several spatial and textual strategies in the khanaqah at Taft that blur the division of sacral and worldly functions between the two complexes. In the remaining sections of the chapter, I will focus on strategies employed to create a sacred aura around the khanaqah at Taft, connecting it with both the body of Shah Neʿmatullah and the most significant site of pilgrimage for Muslims in Mecca.

VI. The Empty Mausoleum in Taft: Antemortem or Pseudo-funerary Structure?

In opposition to the emphasis on Mahan as a venerated pilgrimage site blessed by the burial of the Sufi, the khanaqah of Taft is marked by the stark absence of Shah Neʿmatullah—an absence embodied above all by the site's mausoleum. In chapter 3, I pointed out the ambiguities surrounding the "holy mausoleum" in Taft when discussing Katib's description of the khanaqah in the fifteenth century and suggested that this mausoleum could correspond with the kushk (kiosk) or the surviving freestanding building that is now Taft's Anthropology Museum (fig. 3.3).[67] While the existence of a mausoleum is known as a part of the first phase of construction in Taft, there is no mention of any burials in it at the time. Katib's description suggests that a carved tombstone was placed there, but he merely cautions that this tombstone did not mark Shah Neʿmatullah's burial (rather, he was buried in Mahan).[68] What, then, was the purpose of this building at the time of its construction?

Emic terminology cannot shed much light on this question. Textual sources, when referring to the Taft complex as a whole, describe it as either a khanaqah or *buqʿa-yi mubaraka* (the blessed building).[69] The term *buqʿa* can refer to a variety of architectural structures ranging from generic meanings such as "building" and "house" to the more specific "tomb" and "khanaqah." The funerary usage of the term was quite common and has a long history since at least the tenth century.[70] In the khanaqah at Taft, this common usage is attested to by the use of the term *buqᶜa-yi Shah Khalilullah-i Thani* to refer to the kiosk, after a descendant of Shah Neᶜmatullah who was buried there in the sixteenth century. In Katib's history, on the other hand, the term *buqᶜa* is repeatedly used to denote nonfunerary structures. When describing a fourteenth-century madrasa named Ghiyasiya in Yazd, Katib refers to the "buqᶜa-yi thilatha" (the three buqᶜas), pointing to the three structures of madrasa, khanaqah, and mosque within the complex.[71] Even more relevant and specific is Katib's use of the word *buqᶜa* in the new Friday mosque in the Chahar Minar quarter of Yazd, where he describes a building known as the buqᶜa-yi Murshidiyya as a place Sufis used as a residence, for gatherings, for offering food, and for performing rituals of samaᶜ (musical session, lit. listening).[72] In this light, it is important to remember that while it is not impossible that the "blessed buqᶜa" in the Taft khanaqah was a reference to the funerary element of the complex, it could have had much broader connotations.

To explore the function and meaning of the mausoleum built in the first phase of the Taft khanaqah, a more productive path is the chronology of burials on the site. At least three funerary structures were associated with the khanaqah at Taft in hagiographies of Shah Neᶜmatullah and in a sixteenth-century endowment document. The first is the "holy mausoleum" in question, mentioned in Katib's account and dissociated from Shah Neᶜmatullah. Another, mentioned in the Safavid period, was the "ᶜimarat-i Mansuriyya," named after a descendant of Shah Neᶜmatullah, Shah Ghiyath al-din Mansur (d. before 1590), who was buried there.[73] In *Jamiᶜ-i Mufidi*, its location is vaguely identified as "on the other side of the mosque."[74] The deceased was the Neᶜmatullahi descendant and son of Ghiyath al-din Mirmiran (d. 1590), a governor of Yazd who had strong connections with the Safavids: his father, two of his sons (although not the one buried in Taft), and one of his daughters married into the Safavid family.[75] The third concerns a burial mentioned in an endowment document that records the patronage of Khanish Begum, sister of the Safavid ruler Shah Tahmasp, who married into the Neᶜmatullahi family. The burial, referred to as a *maqbara* (tomb, sepulchre), belongs to Sultan ᶜAli Mirza, son of the aforementioned Khanish Begum and Shah Nur al-din Neᶜmatullah Baqi (Neᶜmatullah III) (d. 1563).[76]

In addition to these textual references, a group of tombstones were found in Taft's mausoleum, recorded by Iraj Afshar in *Yadgarha-yi Yazd*. He noted that three dated tombstones among the nine found in the dome chamber dated back to 848/1444–45, 889/1484–85, and 925/1519–20, the last one belonging to Shah Khalilullah-i Thani, after whom the mausoleum has been called at times (fig. 4.2 and app. 4.1).[77] Given all the change and damage undergone by these tombstones and the khanaqah complex, it remains an open question whether they all belonged here or not. Nevertheless, considering them alongside the textual accounts, the evidence of the earliest known burial on the whole site

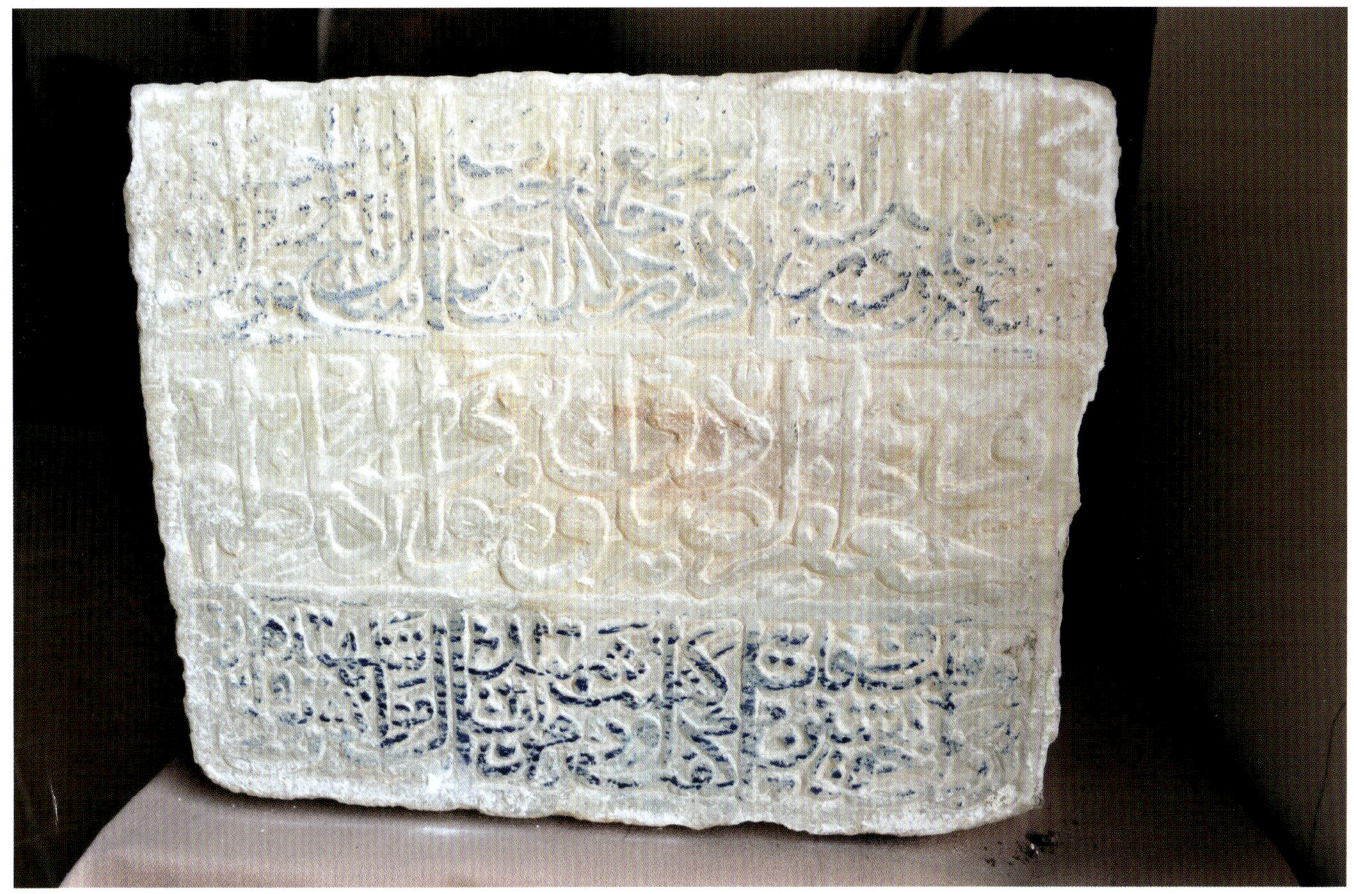

FIGURE 4.2. Tombstone of Khalilullah Thani in Taft, dated 925/1519–20. Unregistered, office of the Cultural Heritage Foundation in Taft. *Photograph by author, 2014.*

would go only as far back as the tombstone of 848/1444–45. This date leaves us with a gap of about thirty years after the completion of the khanaqah at Taft and over a decade after the death of Shah Neᶜmatullah, in which time there were no known burials in the building.

Considering the chronological priority of Taft in the primary sources discussed earlier in this chapter and that Shah Neᶜmatullah was over eighty years old at the time of the completion of the khanaqah there, is it possible that the holy mausoleum was built as an antemortem structure to house Shah Neᶜmatullah's body? The construction of antemortem mausoleums was a common practice for notable individuals in the region at the time. And yet, if this was the arrangement at Taft, why was Shah Neᶜmatullah buried in Mahan? It would have been perfectly feasible to carry his body to Taft from Kerman, where he died. One possibility is that the intention to bury Shah Neᶜmatullah in Taft was weakened by the growth of Mahan's sacred aura in the last decades of the Sufi's life. At the same time, it was not unprecedented to bury Sufi shaykhs in places other than where they desired (i.e., if there was an explicit wish), especially in their place of residence. This was the case for the Safaviyya Sufi network's leading figure, Shaykh Safi, who was buried in his own khanaqah in the fourteenth century despite his request to be buried in a graveyard west of Ardabil.[78] In the absence of any evidence of Shah Neʿmatullah's desire for his burial place, it is possible that the decision was made by his descendants and followers to bury him in Mahan, which, after all, was the place where he had spent a considerable number of years toward the end of his life. This decision also meant that the family could still hold on to their base in Mahan and develop it as a place with a venerable status and presumptive, though also contested, tax privileges on landed property.

Alongside these possibilities for the construction of the mausoleum as an antemortem structure, it is also important to consider an alternative reading. The lack of any mention of burials in Katib's account led Michael Connell to suggest that this building could be a pseudo-mausoleum built for the purpose of completing the khanaqah complex with an indispensable venerated element—namely, the funerary dome chamber.[79] The importance of Katib's account about the mausoleum, however, goes beyond his silence about burials. Given that he was writing around 862/1457–58, at least one burial seems already to have taken place in the khanaqah, corresponding with the tombstone dated 848/1444–45. After mentioning the mausoleum in Taft, Katib notes that "however, his blessed body found tranquility in the luminous tomb at Mahan." This disclaimer seems to allude not just to common misconceptions but also to an expectation: the mausoleum in Taft led visitors to imagine Shah Neʿmatullah's body in the building.

The line between whether the mausoleum contained or did not contain Shah Neʿmatullah's body was at times blurry in the elite and public spheres. Writing in the seventeenth or early eighteenth century, Mirza Mohsen Taʾthir, poet and governor of Yazd (r. 1650–1716), touched on such imaginings. In his lengthy poem on Taft and its virtues, which contains a section on the Shah Vali khanaqah, Taʾthir praises the countless bounties of the khanaqah "as long as Shah Vali is buried in it."[80]

Whether the mausoleum in Taft was built as an antemortem tomb or a pseudo-mausoleum must remain an open question due to the lack of unambiguous textual or archaeological evidence. However, based on the discussion above, I would take Connell's hypothesis a step further and suggest that the emptiness of the mausoleum served to acknowledge and embrace Shah Neʿmatullah's absence from the site—in life and in death. If so, the aim was perhaps to construct an architectural narrative around the memory of the Sufi's rather brief presence on the site and to manifest a longing for such presence. As Shahzad Bashir notes about the broader logic of Sufi shrines, "What was needed for the shrine to be established was not a freshly dead body but narratives about a body."[81] In Connell's reading, the mausoleum in Taft visualized such a narrative.

Over time, the site was blessed with the burial of the Sufi's descendants, an act that established Taft's image as the legacy of Shah Neʿmatullah. But prior to those burials, the empty mausoleum was the representation of a *presence in absence*, substituting architecture for the body of the Sufi. This possible architectural surrogate for the mausoleum and body of the Sufi collapsed the geographical distance between Taft and Mahan.[82] This substitution is reminiscent of Shah Neᶜmatullah's poetry inscribed on the portal at Mahan, which was discussed in chapter 1. As I will show in the last chapter of the book, a similar effort to instantiate the Sufi's body in space was taken up about two centuries later in Mahan itself. Substitution was an important strategy of creating genealogies among works of art and architecture. Here, in the Taft complex, it was used concurrently to create familial genealogies, not only connecting the future lineage of the Neᶜmatullahi family with the site as the burials in Taft would do but also to connect the family line with a venerated past.

VII. The Khanaqah at Taft: Architecture and Familial Legacy

The presence in absence instated by the mausoleum at Taft was complemented by its epigraphic program. An inscription panel that still survives in situ in the khanaqah alludes to the characterization of the site as the legacy of Shah Neᶜmatullah. The tile panel, which can be dated to the fifteenth century on stylistic grounds, is made in the mosaic faience technique with vegetal motifs set against a dark-blue background (fig. 3.8). The text is organized in three registers of prose and poetry in thuluth script. There is some damage in the upper central part of the inscription panel, such that certain parts are difficult to read (fig. 4.3).

The inscription panel is rather large. It measures 428 centimeters in length and 58 centimeters in width. Although it is currently fitted into an interior wall of one of the dome chambers in the kushk/buqᶜa, Iraj Afshar noted that—according to the keeper of the buqᶜa—the panel was previously installed at

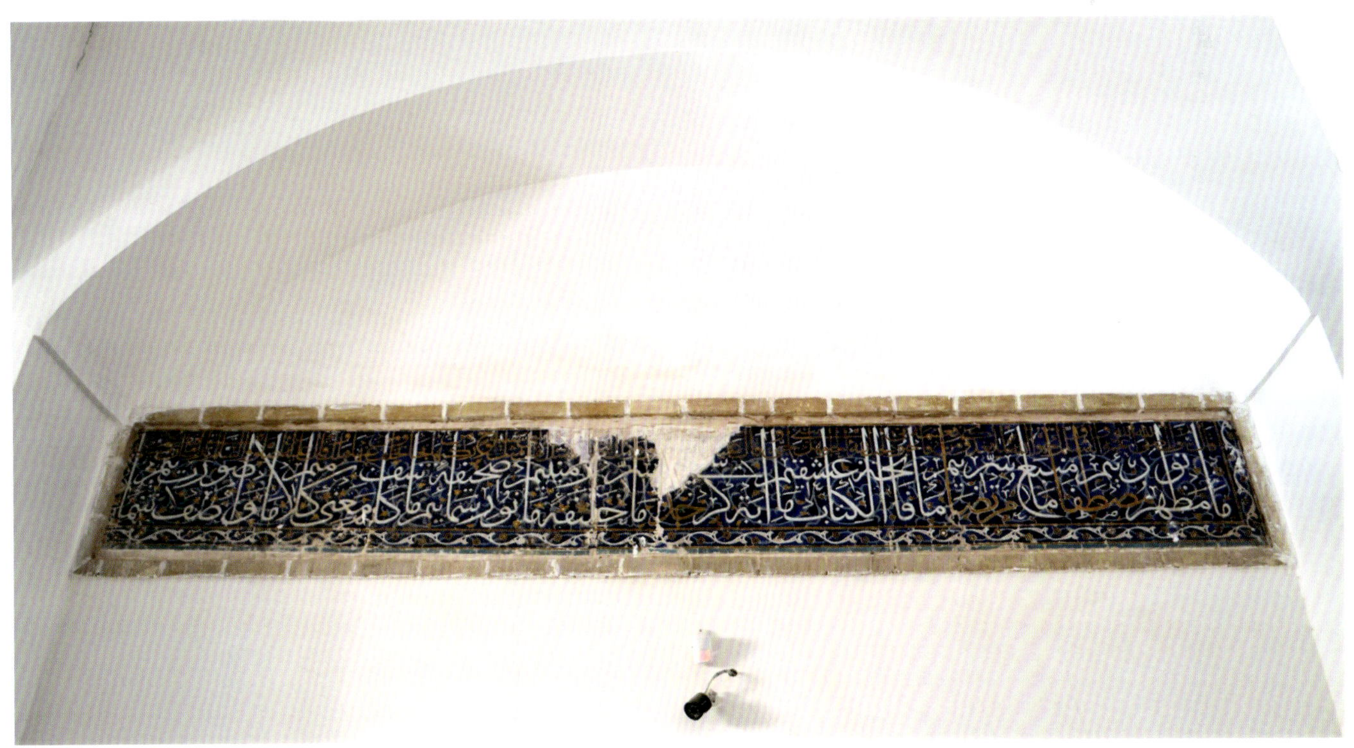

FIGURE 4.3. Tile inscription panel in the dome chamber of the Taft complex. *Photograph by author, 2014.*

the entrance of the building and moved inside the buqʿa only during recent restorations (probably referring to the 1944–45 restoration).[83] The inscription panel thus stood in a visible and easily accessible position in the courtyard of the khanaqah, adorning the facade of the mausoleum.

The first line is written in amber, in a smaller size compared to other registers, and includes three hadiths (sayings) of the Prophet Muhammad (fig. 4.3 and app. 4.2): "Said the messenger of God peace be upon him and his family: Love God for what He nourishes you with from His Blessings, love me for the love of God, and love the people of my house for the love of me. Said [the messenger of God] . . . my family is like the Ark of Noah; to ride it is to gain deliverance, to oppose it is to drown in destruction. Said [the messenger of God] peace be upon him and his family: I am leaving amongst you, as long as you hold onto them."

All three hadiths from the Prophet Muhammad are on the importance of the *Ahl al-Bayt* (people of the house). The latter two are among the most widely quoted sayings: the second is known as the *safinat al-nijah* (Means of Salvation, also known as the Ark Hadith), and the third, only part of which is quoted here, is known as the Hadith al-Thaqalayn. The *thaqalayn*, or "two valuable things," refer to the two sources of guidance—namely, the Qurʾan and the people of his house that the Prophet left behind for Muslims.

The quotation of Qurʾanic verses or hadith was a common epigraphic strategy for the crafting of lineage in the premodern Islamic world. One relevant example is the appearance of the Ark of Noah—the same hadith featured in the inscription panel in Taft—on one of the facades of Shaykh Safi al-din's shrine in Ardabil. Its juxtaposition with a farman (decree) by his descendant, the Safavid ruler Shah Tahmasp, bears a resemblance to the strategies at play in the khanaqah at Taft, resonating with the familial dimensions of the two shrines.[84]

A fascinating detail in the inscription in Taft is what it leaves out. Here, the Hadith al-Thaqalayn ends before the introduction of the two sources of guidance—namely, the Qurʾan and the people of the house. Although the inscription panel may at first seem to have been cut short to fit into its new location within the niche, several factors suggest that the omission of the Qurʾan and the Prophet's family was intentional—not a result of later alterations. First, alterations to the length of the inscription panel must have been minimal, as the poetic verses on the lower register end here too. Second, the text itself presents irregularities: the specific rendition of the hadith that seems to have been the source of the inscription translates as "I am leaving amongst you two valuable things: the Qurʾan and my family. As long as you hold onto them . . . ," but the inscription on the panel *skips over* "the Qurʾan and my family." Since the first two hadiths in the panel emphasize the family of the Prophet, the phrase "holding on to them" in this cliff-hanger of a last sentence comes to refer back to the Prophet's family as well, resulting in the stark absence of any reference to the Qurʾan in the tile panel.

The intent of the omission is emphasized even more by the verses of poetry that follow the hadiths on the inscription panel. Authored by Shah Neᶜmatullah Vali, the verses of poetry are inscribed in the lower two lines of the panel in a larger size than the hadiths above. The lines of poetry are set off in white, distinguishing them from the amber words of the prophet—only the words *God* (*khuda*), *Mustafa* (referring to the Prophet Muhammad), and *Murtiza* (Imam ᶜAli's title) are written in amber as well (fig. 4.3). Both the choice of color (contrasting white against dark blue) and the larger size of the script in the poems make them the more visible part of the inscription. The function of the verse lines is also similar to that of the lower, larger, and usually white lines of architectural foundation inscriptions, which was to communicate a message specific to the patronage and context of a building's construction.

The poem at the bottom of the Taft tile panel reads as follows (app. 4.2):

> We are the manifestation of the light of Mustafa [the Prophet];
> We are the source of the secrets of Murtaza [Imam ᶜAli];
> We are the opening chapter of love;
> We are the Throne Verse of God;
> We are the secret of the caliph of the earth;
> We are the light of the celestial book;
> We unlock the meaning of the word [i.e., the Qurʾan];
> We are the praiser of your outward form (surat).[85]

Shah Neᶜmatullah's verses take on an unambiguous meaning as they are repurposed for this architectural setting. The prophetic hadiths quoted in the inscription panel were already fitting choices for a site with familial associations. In concert with the poem, their emphasis on the notion of family becomes even more prominent. While the use of the pronoun *we* was a common feature in Sufi poetry, the content and architectural context of the inscription panel allows it to be read as a reference to the collective family of Shah Neᶜmatullah as an extension of the family of the Prophet. The poem thus becomes a statement of the family's significance as a medium of connection with the Divine, the Prophet Muhammad, and his house.[86] While in the first hadith the prophet was calling on Muslims to love and hold on to his family because of their love for him and to love him for the love of God, in the poem by Shah Neᶜmatullah, he and his family are introduced as "the manifestation of the light [guidance] of Mustafa [the Prophet Muhammad]" on earth.

Even more interesting is how the conspicuous absence of the Qurʾan from the hadith is juxtaposed with several metaphorical allusions to the Qurʾan in Shah Neᶜmatullah's poetry. The term "opening chapter" (Fatihat al-Kitab) in line three, for instance, refers to the opening chapter of the Qurʾan. In line four, the "Throne Verse" (Ayat al-Kursi) refers to the 255th verse of the Surat al-Baqara (Chapter of the Cow), which emphasizes that nothing and nobody compares to God. While the verse indicates that the "throne encompasses heavens and the earth," some Sufi traditions place the throne of God in "the lowest or seventh heaven." The Sufi's hearth is regarded as "a microcosm of God's Throne" in its capacity to "encompass all things."[87] It is in this spirit that Shah Neʿmatullah refers to himself, and by extension to his family, as the "Throne Verse of God." Finally, in lines six and seven, the "celestial book" and "word" both refer to the Qurʾan. Given these multiple allusions to the Qurʾan, and the collective *we*, the poem becomes about both the family and the Qurʾan. In a way, Shah Neʿmatullah's verses substitute the omitted part of the Hadith al-Thaqalayn in the panel. Here, the epigraphical substitution in tilework creates a venerated genealogy for the Neʿmatullahi family that does not necessarily have a claim on the family of the Prophet and the Qurʾan as their true likeness but as their surrogate in their function in guiding the community.[88]

This alignment of references to the people of the house in the first two hadiths, the omission of the Qurʾan from the last, and Shah Neʿmatullah's verses bring the importance of familial legacy and the role of Shah Neʿmatullah's descendants as the "corporeal continuity" of the Sufi to the forefront.[89] Through this playful instantiation of text, the makers of the inscription panel analogize the role of the prophet's family among the *ʿumma* (community of Muslims) after his death to that of the family of Shah Neʿmatullah among his followers and the broader community after the Sufi's death. Here also lies another possibility for the function of the holy mausoleum in Taft: in addition to the alternative readings that would cast the mausoleum as an antemortem or pseudo-funerary structure, it is also feasible, in light of the inscriptions discussed here, to interpret it as a mausoleum provisioned for the descendants of Shah Neʿmatullah Vali.

Whereas the early khanaqah in Mahan was represented as the seat of Shah Neʿmatullah's spiritual authority and the blessed site of his burial, the khanaqah at Taft was seen to bear a legacy left behind by the founder, embodied by both the building of the khanaqah and the "people of his house," many of whom were physically present there. The highly visible words on the exterior of the central structure of the khanaqah were perhaps aimed at securing respect, gratitude, and support for the Sufi's family among the public, and the architectural complex played a significant role in transmitting that message.

VIII. Replicating the Kaʿba

Whether the mausoleum was intentionally built as an empty chamber from the beginning or not, the absence of the body of Shah Neʿmatullah lends the khanaqah's layout and the position of the kiosk/mausoleum within it another layer of significance, which can be clarified by textual sources. In his early sixteenth-century biography of Shah Neʿmatullah, ʿAbd al-Razzaq Kermani describes the khanaqah of Taft as a place built "on the style of the Kaʿba" (*bar uslub-i khaneh-yi Kaʿba*).[90] This passing note sets a new image of the khanaqah before our eyes in which the design of the site invoked the House of God in Mecca. An assertive attempt was thus made to inscribe the khanaqah of Taft onto the map of sacred sites in the Islamic world.

Another textual reference to Taft as an invocation of the Kaʿba suggests that this notion represents more than a retrospective hagiographic interpretation. The reference occurs among fifteenth-century poems recorded in the *Munshaʾat* of Sharaf al-din ʿAli Yazdi as inscriptions written for a building (*ʿimarat*) that a Neʿmatullahi descendant named Amir Ziaʾ al-din Nurullah was constructing in Taft in 846/1442–43, very likely at the Shah Vali complex.[91] Amid metaphorical descriptions of architectural elements in the poem, the building is also compared to "the house of God" (i.e., the Kaʿba), "a qibla to which masses of angels prostrated," cautioning visitors that "whoever turns their face from this qibla will be punished with an eternal curse."[92] This poem is even more significant compared to Kermani's note above: while the account was accessible to the rather limited audiences of the hagiography, the poem was designed as an architectural inscription with a much wider audience and was likely inscribed in the very complex to which it was referring.

The comparison of holy sites with the Kaʿba was a common trope in the Islamic world despite the occasional controversies that the practice provoked.[93] A relevant comparative example is the dynastic Sufi shrine of the Safavids in Ardabil, which was equated with the Kaʿba as a site of mandatory pilgrimage. Similar to the poetic inscriptions written for the complex in Taft, a poem in the *Khulasat al-tawarikh* (*Summary of the Histories*, completed 1590–91) by Qazi Ahmad (Munshi Qumi) calls the shrine of Shaykh Safi a Kaʿba and a site for *tawaf*—the circumambulation ritual performed by pilgrims around the near-cubical building of the Kaʿba.[94]

As common as these analogies were, several aspects of the Taft complex reveal a connection with the Kaʿba that amounts to more than a merely rhetorical device. It is true that neither the shrine of Shaykh Safi in Ardabil nor the kiosk/mausoleum in Taft bears much formal resemblance to the cuboid structure of the Kaʿba, draped over with the kiswa (the cloth covering the Kaʿba). This lack of immediately identifiable physical resemblance between a holy site and its replications was a common phenomenon of medieval architecture as recognized in the mid-twentieth century by Richard Krautheimer and developed more recently by Finbarr Barry Flood specifically in relation to the Kaʿba.[95] As Krautheimer points out, the medieval concept of architectural comparisons, especially those involving a "highly venerable prototype," was rather fluid: writers felt "perfectly justified in comparing buildings with one another as long as some of the outstanding elements seemed to be comparable."[96] These ranged from similarities in architectural features and layout to less visible aspects such as measurements and building materials.

These points make it possible to see how the Shah Vali complex at Taft could in fact have served to replicate the Kaʿba. As discussed in detail in chapter 2, the mausoleum in Taft is a square-shaped structure consisting of two domed chambers connected to one another, although one of the two is more dominant in both size and height (fig. 3.6). On the exterior, while the mausoleum is not a pure cube in shape, the squareness of its plan combined with its status as a freestanding structure bears a resemblance to the form

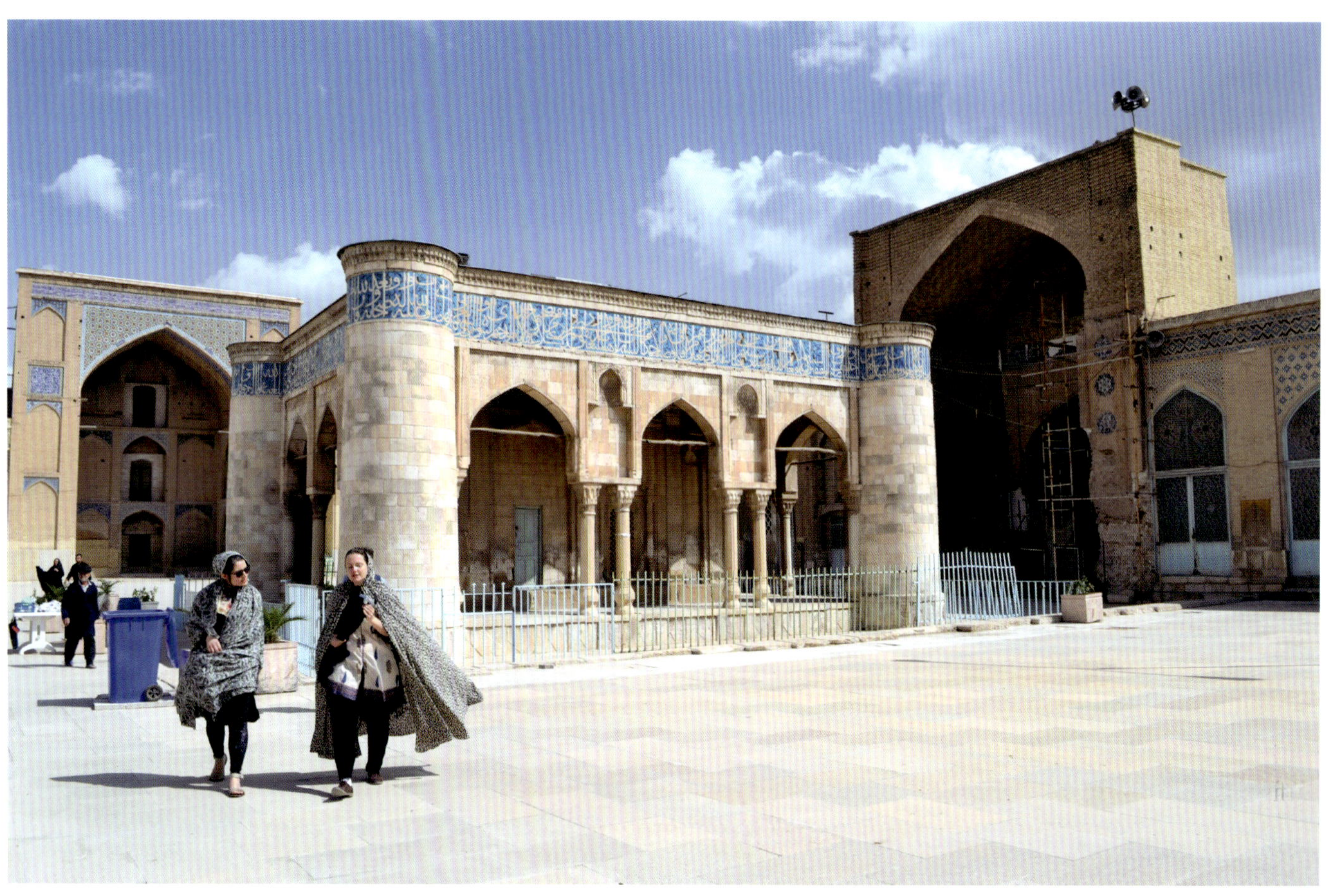

FIGURE 4.4. Khuday-khaneh (House of God) in the ʿAtiq Mosque in Shiraz, Iran. *Photograph by author, 2016.*

and physical configuration of the Kaʿba. Arcades that once existed around the chamber and are now incorporated into the interior space would have created a circumambulatory movement around the building in Taft (figs. 3.7 and 3.9). Moreover, like the Kaʿba, the mausoleum in Taft is built on a raised platform. A subtle connection also lies in the bipartite interior arrangement of the mausoleum, similar to the interior of the Kaʿba, which is divided in two by a row of three pillars.[97]

A local and near-contemporary spatial configuration in a southern Iranian complex strengthens the Taft-Mecca connection. Built in the ninth century, and rebuilt and expanded repeatedly thereafter, the old Jamiʿ mosque (Masjid-i ʿAtiq) of Shiraz includes a kiosk in the middle of its courtyard that, according to its dated inscription, was built in 752/1351 by the Injuid ruler Mahmud Shah (r. 1325–36).[98] The small kiosk has three arched bays on each side that create a circumambulatory passage and is built on a raised platform—features all shared with the kiosk in Taft (fig. 4.4). The Shiraz structure was referred to as a Bayt al-Mashaf (House of the Book) for its storage of Qurʾan manuscripts dating back to the thirteenth century and thereafter, from which recitations were performed in the mosque.[99] The kiosk was also known as the *khuday-khaneh* (House of God), referencing the Kaʿba in ways similar to the khanaqah of Taft. In addition to the spatial connections between the mosque in Shiraz and the Taft complex, it is important to recall that the Jamiᶜ mosque of Shiraz is one of the recorded locations for the meeting between Shah Neᶜmatullah Vali and the first patron of the Taft khanaqah, Iskandar b. ᶜUmar Shaykh, who was the appointed Timurid governor of Shiraz and the region at the time.[100]

Most intriguing of all these connections between the Kaᶜba and the mausoleum in Taft, however, is their shared assumption of absence. Neither of the two buildings were ever entirely devoid of objects and architectural features, and in fact the question of what was inside the Kaᶜba is a complex matter of debate.[101] Nevertheless, the absence of material representations of God in the Kaᶜba does recall the absence of the body of Shah Neᶜmatullah in the mausoleum at Taft. Indeed, the notional emptiness of the two buildings could have prompted Neᶜmatullahi Sufis or their visitors to imagine a relationship between the Taft complex and the Kaᶜba.

IX. The (Trans)regional Entanglements of Sacred and Material

Recent scholarship has shown through extensive examples that Sufi networks did not necessarily espouse detachment from or even lack of interest in material favors. For example, Andrew Peacock, Omid Safi, and Hamid Algar have made this point in the case of Sufis in the Seljuq period and the Naqshbandi Sufis in Transoxiana, to name just two.[102] The notional separation between the complexes in Taft and Mahan that I laid out in the first few sections of this chapter offers a useful methodological paradigm for understanding the relationship between the material and spiritual in Sufi material culture, suggesting that this separation is not an entirely etic construction. The implicit tension between the two sites can be charted out more explicitly in the thinking, writings, and processes of place-making among the Neᶜmatullahi Sufis. Even though a complete detachment was never practiced among the Neᶜmatullahi network, this chapter shows how sensitivity toward associations with the court and grand monumental architecture could motivate the Sufi network to create a humbler parallel institution in Mahan during Shah Neᶜmatullah's lifetime.

This chapter reminds us that in dealing with the relationship between spirituality and material cultures in Sufism, it is crucial to think beyond the bounds of unidirectional causality. Viewed in and of itself, a work of monumental architecture can at times obscure the depth of questions concerning materiality that guided its design. It is only in the dialogue between the family's two architectural complexes in Taft and Mahan, and in reading between the lines of letters penned by the Neᶜmatullahi family, that their sensitivity toward the relationship between materiality and transcendence comes to light. Seen from another angle, a considerable extent of the ingenuity, risks, and imaginative solutions that characterize the spatial and epigraphic design of the complex in Taft are bound up with such sensitivities.

The micro-level connections between the complexes in Taft and Mahan also highlight an important point about global Sufism and its relationship to materiality: in studying the material culture of Sufi networks, we find that the transregional is entangled with the regional. Without understanding the regional relationship between Taft and Mahan, for instance, the material history of the Neʿmatullahis might seem to be overwhelmingly governed by the dynamics of Iran-Deccan connections. To push it even further, the regional can be the key to a deeper understanding of the transregional. Although the discussion in this chapter has focused on the relationship between Mahan and Taft, a similar dynamic between the material and the spiritual can be extended to the relationship between Mahan and the Deccan as well. In this broader picture, Mahan can be seen as the spiritual node against which the communities in Taft and the Deccan shaped their identities as the working institutions of the network—free to engage with political and financial affairs while maintaining claims on spirituality. The key to understanding the dualities between Neʿmatullahi activities in Taft and Mahan, as well as Iran and the Deccan, lies in looking beyond the axis of patronage to consider the agency of the Sufi network in crafting stages on which they could project sacred and worldly images of themselves.

Notes

1. Graham, "The Niʿmatullāhī Order," 167.
2. See chapter 3, section VIII, "The Curse of Transregionality."
3. Aubin, *Matériaux*, 190. While I interpret "*ikhrajat-i astana-yi Mahan*" in its broad sense for the maintenance of the shrine here, Michael Connell interprets it as expenses for the needy in Mahan: Connell, "The Nimatullahi Sayyids," 35–36.
4. For a short review of comparative examples, see Bashir, *Sufi Bodies*, 59, 63.
5. See chapter 3, section VIII, "The Curse of Transregionality."
6. Yazdi, *Munshaʾat*, 154–55:
و اگر مسلمی موقوف باشد موهم آن بود که باعث بر توجه درویشان کفایت آن مهم است و دلخواه
آن است که آن عزم از شوایب اغراض دنیوی معرا و مبرا باشد.
7. Golombek, "The Chronology," 43.
8. On the importance of miracles versus natural features in the shaping of holy landscapes, see Mulder, *The Shrines of the ʿAlids in Medieval Syria*, 254.
9. Aubin, *Matériaux*, 178–79.
10. Mihrabi Kermani, *Mazarat-i Kerman*, 177.
11. Golombek and Wilber, *The Timurid Architecture*, 395.
12. Mihrabi Kermani, *Mazarat-i Kerman*, 174–75.
13. Ibid., 122–24.
14. On narrative strategies around Kuhbanan, Shah Neʿmatullah's residence before Mahan, see Aubin, *Matériaux*, 46–47.
15. Ibid., 49, 52.
16. Ibid., 182, 288; Aubin, "De Kūhbanān a Bidar," 235.
17. For similar patterns in Bektashi shrines, see Yürekli, *Architecture and Hagiography*, 79.
18. Aubin, *Matériaux*, 288.
19. Ibid., 289.
20. Ibid., 291.
21. Ibid., 303.
22. Ibid., 272.

23. Compare Aubin, *Matériaux*, 288–91; Aubin, "De Kūhbanān a Bidar," 236; and Katib, *Tarikh-i jadid-i Yazd*, 216–17.

24. This was common practice among many Sufi networks including the Naqshbandis: Algar, "The Naqshbandī Order," 132.

25. Ne^cmatullah Vali, *Divan*, Garrett no. 1469Y, ff. 361b–362a.

26. Ibid., f. 362a.

27. Ibid.

28. Ibid., ff. 380b–381a. Biographer Wa^cizi, on the other hand, noted that travelers arriving in the khanaqah of Mahan could stay for three days and on the fourth would seek permission to continue their travels. It is important to distinguish between passing travelers and those who visited Mahan to benefit from the Sufi's teachings and assemblies. For Wa^cizi's note, see Aubin, *Matériaux*, 304.

29. Blair, *The Ilkhanid Shrine*, 26.

30. Aubin, *Matériaux*, 49.

31. Ne^cmatullah Vali, *Divan*, Garrett no. 1469Y, ff. 380b–381a and 371a–372a.

32. Katib, *Tarikh-i jadid-i Yazd*, 217. See chapter 3, section I, "Architecture, Text, and Ambiguity."

33. Katib, *Tarikh-i jadid-i Yazd*, 214.

34. Afshar, *Yadgarha-yi Yazd*, I:261–62.

35. Holod-Tretiak, "The Monuments of Yazd," 100–21.

36. Aubin, "De Kuhbanan à Bidar," 235. Also see Graham, "The Ni^cmatullāhī Order," 167, 180: fn. 40. On Yazd as a center for textiles in the fifteenth century, see Floor, "Economy and Society," in Bier, *Woven from the Soul*, 20.

37. Rizvi, *The Safavid Dynastic Shrine*, 12.

38. Aubin, *Matériaux*, 82.

39. On the relationship between silk weaving, Sufism, *futuwwatnama*s, and prophetic narratives, see Sayadi, "Prophets and Caterpillars," 41–65; Munroe, *Sufi Lovers*, 123–24.

40. Aubin, "De Kūhbanān a Bidar," 235.

41. Flatt, *Courts of the Deccan Sultanates*, 145.

42. Yazdi, *Munsha'at*, 143–47.

43. Ibid., 154–55.

44. Ne^cmatullahVali, *Divan*, Garrett no. 1469Y, ff. 362b–363a.

45. Yazdi, *Munsha'at*, 182–84.

46. Ne^cmatullahVali, *Divan*, Garrett no. 1469Y, f. 386a.

47. Yazdi, *Manzumat*, 63–65.

48. Afshar, *Yadgarha-yi Yazd*, I:414–17.

49. See chapter 6, section III, "Safavid Women as Interlocutors: The Case of Shah Vali Mosque in Taft."

50. See chapter 5, section V, "Weaving an Epigraphic Network."

51. See chapter 6, section III, "Safavid Women as Interlocutors: The Case of Shah Vali Mosque in Taft."

52. Connell, "The Nimatullahi Sayyids," 122. See also Nafisi, "Maqamat," 124.

53. Aubin, *Matériaux*, 219–31; Mir Khwand, *The rowzat al-safa*, VIII:573; Mufid, *Jami^c-i Mufidi*, III:66–67.

54. Mufid, *Jami^c-i Mufidi*, III:55–56.

55. Comparable with the architectural inactivity in the shrine of shaykh Jam in Turbat-i Jam: Golombek, "The Chronology," 43.

56. Connell, "The Nimatullahi Sayyids," 37.

57. Babaie, "Sacred Sites of Kingship," 193–99.

58. See chapter 1, section I, "The Mahan Shrine and Its Development."

59. On the madrasa, see Blair and Bloom, "From Iran to the Deccan," in Overton, *Iran and the Deccan*, 175–202; Merklinger, "The *Madrasa* of Maḥmūd Gāwān," 145–57.

60. Khan, *Faramin wa Asnad-i Salatin-i Deccan*, 3–4.

61. Reza'i, *Fihrist-i asnad-i muqufat-i Iran*, II:267.

62. Despite several attempts, I have not been able to consult this specific document.

63. Firouzeh, "Between the Spiritual and Material," 146–48. There are a number of structures associated with the Safavid ruler Shah ʿAbbas in later documents, but neither the structures nor the relevant documents have survived (or come to light). See Eisazadeh, "Tak-negari," 135–36, also noted in chapter 6.

64. Most important of them are no. 297-23600-1 and no. 297-23600-3: Firouzeh, "Between the Spiritual and Material," 146–48.

65. For a later waqfnama of Muhammad Shah Qajar (r. 1834–48), see Bastani Parizi, "Haram-i Shah Vali," in Pazuki, *Majmuʿih maqalat*, 158–59.

66. Document no. 297-23600-3, National Archives of Iran. In the late nineteenth century, Percy Sykes notes a "permanent population of dervishes" at the shrine at Mahan as well as free lodging for pilgrims: Sykes, *Ten Thousand Miles*, 149.

67. See chapter 3, section I, "Architecture, Text, and Ambiguity."

68. Katib, *Tarikh-i jadid-i Yazd*, 217.

69. For references to the Shah Vali complex as *khanaqah*, see Katib, *Tarikh-i jadid-i Yazd*, 216–17; Aubin, *Matériaux*, 49; Mufid, *Jamiʿ-i Mufidi*, III:685–87. As *buqʿa-yi mubarakih*: Aubin, *Matériaux*, 207; Neʿmatullah Vali, *Divan*, Garrett no. 1469Y, ff. 371a–372a.

70. Blair, *The Ilkhanid Shrine*, 24–25.

71. Katib, *Tarikh-i jadid-i Yazd*, 140.

72. Ibid., 122.

73. Aubin, *Matériaux*, 235.

74. Mufid, *Jamiʿ-i Mufidi*, III:687.

75. Aubin, *Matériaux*, 220, 227.

76. Mufid, *Jamiʿ-i Mufidi*, III:687; Khaziʿin, "Waqfnama-yi Khanish Begum," 495–99.

77. Afshar, *Yadgarha-yi Yazd*, I:414–17.

78. Rizvi, *The Safavid Dynastic Shrine*, 46; Rizvi, "Its Mortar Mixed," 332. On the burial of religious figures in their residences, see Blair, *The Ilkhanid Shrine*, 49.

79. Connell, "The Nimatullahi Sayyids," 169–70. See also Mancini-Lander, "Memory on the Boundaries of Empire," 447–48.

80. Afshar, *Yadgarha-yi Yazd*, 399.

81. Bashir, *Sufi Bodies*, 210.

82. On the "substitutional system" and the function of art and architecture within it, see Nagel and Wood, *Anachronic Renaissance*, 32.

83. Afshar, *Yadgarha-yi Yazd*, I:418.

84. Rizvi, *The Safavid Dynastic Shrine*, 98. See also the inscription at the shrine of Fatemeh Maʿsumeh in Qum: Rizvi, *The Safavid Dynastic Shrine*, 159.

85. Persian transcription published in Afshar, *Yadgarha-yi Yazd*, I:418. See also Neʿmatullah Vali, *Divan*, 391.

86. For similar later claims in the Qajar era, see Scharbrodt, "Anti-Sufism in Early Qajar Iran," in Tabandeh and Lewisohn, *Sufis and Their Opponents*, 344–45.

87. Elias, "Throne of God."

88. On surrogacy and true likeness, see Nagel and Wood, *Anachronic Renaissance*, 29–30.

89. On "corporeal continuity," see Bashir, *Sufi Bodies*, 188.

90. Aubin, *Matériaux*, 49.

91. Yazdi, *Manzumat*, 63–65.

92. Ibid., 64.

93. On the commonality of such examples, see O'Meara, *The Kaʿba Orientations*, 17–18, 86–87, 123; Zarcone, "Pilgrimage to the 'Second Meccas,'" 251, 253, 265–66. For examples of controversies around such imitations, see Flood, *Technologies de dévotion*, 39–41, n.28–33.

94. Rizvi, *The Safavid Dynastic Shrine*, 51; Morton, "The Ardabil Shrine," 52.

95. Krautheimer, "Introduction to an 'Iconography of Medieval Architecture,'" 2–19; Flood, *Technologies de devotion*, 29–71.

96. Krautheimer, "Introduction to an 'Iconography of Medieval Architecture,'" 15–16.

97. Shalem, "Four Faces," 142.

98. Wilber, *The Masjid-i ʿAtiq of Shiraz*, 1, 3, 6–7, 22–23, 25–26; Wilber, *The Architecture of Islamic Iran*, 183; Golombek and Wilber, *The Timurid Architecture*, 200.

99. Wilber, *The Masjid-i ʿAtiq of Shiraz*, 6; Wilber, *The Architecture of Islamic Iran*, 183. On pavilions used as *kitabkhana*, the space for both making and storing manuscripts, see Emami, "Royal Assemblies and Imperial Libraries," 63–81.

100. See chapter 3, section V, "Iskandar b. ʿUmar Shaykh and the Neʿmatullahis."

101. See Shalem, "Made for the Show," 269–83; and compare with O'Meara, *The Kaʿba Orientations*, 116.

102. Peacock, "Sufis and the Seljuk Court," 206–26; Safi, *Religion and Politics in Saljuq Iran*, esp. chaps. 5 and 6; Algar, "The Naqshbandī Order," 123–52.

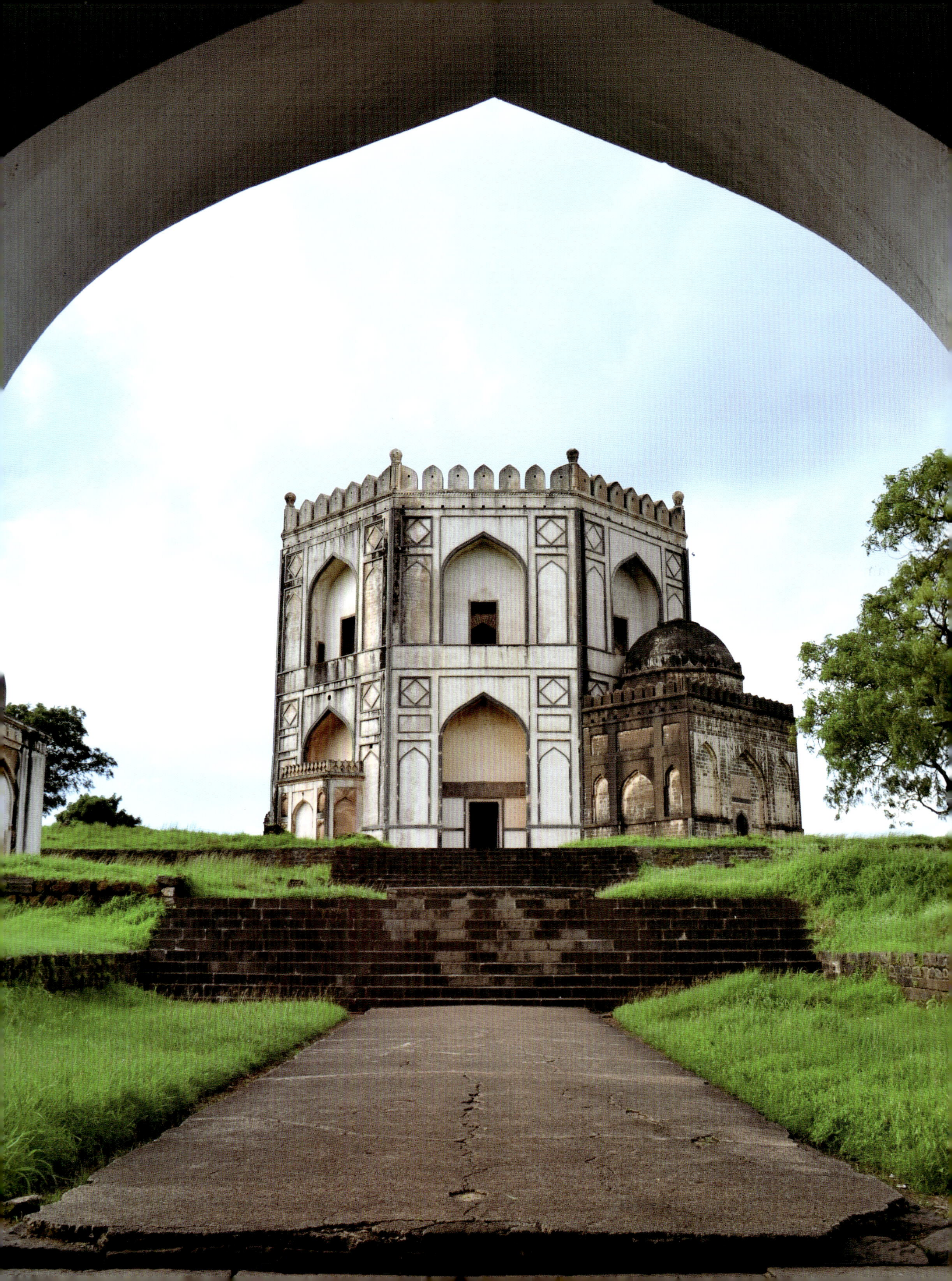

5

Inscribing as Belonging

Architecture, Textile, Ritual

FACING, FIGURE 5.1. Mausoleum of Shah Khalilullah, Ashtur, near Bidar, Karnataka, India. *Photograph by author, 2013.*

This chapter deals with a network of epigraphic programs in architecture and textile in and around the innermost sacred spaces of the Neʿmatullahi family's shrines in Bidar, Mahan, and Taft. Taking up the theme of distance and proximity from the previous chapter, the aim is to understand the act of inscription as a transregional means of self-representation by the Sufi family. The chapter considers the making, content, and spatial arrangement of these inscriptions to show how the Sufis orchestrated intimate rituals of grave visitation that struck a balance between devotional experience and dynastic politics in Iran and India.

Like commissioned hagiographies, the use and reuse of poetry, Qurʾanic verses, and the hadith (sayings attributed to Prophet Muhammad) played an important role in the crafting of spiritual and familial identity. The epigraphic programs in these shrines form a transregional network built around the power of allusions in poetic and Qurʾanic verses. Analyzing this network reveals a closely knit relationship between the Sufis and their architecture. In the picture that emerges, the selection of epigraphic content is laden with devotional and political significance, setting familial genealogies into the backdrop of Qurʾanic citations or commissioned poetry while also, on another level, communicating a cosmic understanding of sacred space to their audiences through lines of calligraphy carved into stone or woven in thread.

Starting with the family's funerary site in Bidar, the first three sections lead us through the most intensely inscribed surfaces of the shrine: liminal spaces in which the Sufis presented the complex as a place of their own, personalized by a subtle, intricate web of text and image, replete with cosmic, transregional, and political messages. Sections IV and V take us back to the shrine at Mahan, into the interior of the sacred tomb of Shah Neʿmatullah Vali and the methods of self-representation employed in the architecture there and in Taft. In the last part of the chapter, sections VI and VII show how this architectural ensemble was reinforced and extended by textiles. I draw on fragments of a group of carpets designed for the Mahan mausoleum and inscribed with personalized verses of poetry to illustrate the interconnections between textile and architecture in the formation of devotional experience and a system of kinship. The study of this textile as an integral part of the architecture reveals an evolving program of inscribing that created a sense of belonging for the Sufi family and their disciples. This program was based on a measured sense of distance: the Sufis never shared an inscribed surface with ruling patrons in the innermost parts of their sacred spaces—an absence that becomes all the more conspicuous due to its consistency across the broader transregional network of Neʿmatullahi shrines.

I. Khalilullah's Funerary Site and Its Chronology in Bidar

The mausoleum of Shah Khalilullah (d. before 1454), the only son of Shah Neʿmatullah Vali, is located in the village of Ashtur, approximately four kilometers to the east of the fort of Bidar in Karnataka, India (fig. 5.1). Begun most likely in the first half of the fifteenth century, when the first members of the Neʿmatullahi family arrived in the region, the shrine complex is one of the many nodes in the sacred landscape of the Deccan—and South Asia more broadly—that commemorated migrant Sufis.[1] The architecture, the buried bodies of itinerant Sufis, and the narratives around their mobilities blended the local and the global in the medium of words and stone.[2]

Khalilullah's complex plays with the notion of proximity and distance in several ways, ranging from minute details in the layout of the funerary site to a larger urban and transregional scale. Before delving into the inner workings of the space and its epigraphic program vis-à-vis this dynamic, this section will offer an overview of the site and its chronology.

The site of Khalilullah's mausoleum is a composite containing several structures built over the centuries (fig. 5.2). The central building on the site is an octagonal enclosure that contains a square dome chamber within it, associated with Shah Khalilullah and roughly dated to the mid-fifteenth century (figs. 5.1 and 5.3). This dating rests on stylistic grounds, and the date of Khalilullah's death is itself a matter of debate.[3] The only unambiguous point of reference for his death date is a dedication note in a Persian calligraphic treatise called the *Tuhfat al-muhibbin* (*The Bounty of the Lovers*), written by the renowned calligrapher Siraj al-Shirazi in 858/1454 in Bidar. The author grants Shah Khalilullah eulogizing titles and dedicates the treatise to his son and successor in Bidar, Muhibbullah (d. ca. 1505).[4] This dedicatory note places Shah Khalilullah's death date prior to the completion of the manuscript in 1454.

Since Khalilullah was the most senior member of the Neʿmatullahi family in the Deccan and the only son of the Sufi saint, it is unsurprising that the site came to be known after him. The complex is referred to as Khaliliyya-yi shahr-i Deccan (Khaliliyya of the city of Deccan) by biographer Sunʿullah and as the maqbara (tomb) of Shah Khalilullah in *Tarikh-i Fereshteh*.[5] Locally, the building is known as the *chaukhandi*: a Dakhni term that could mean

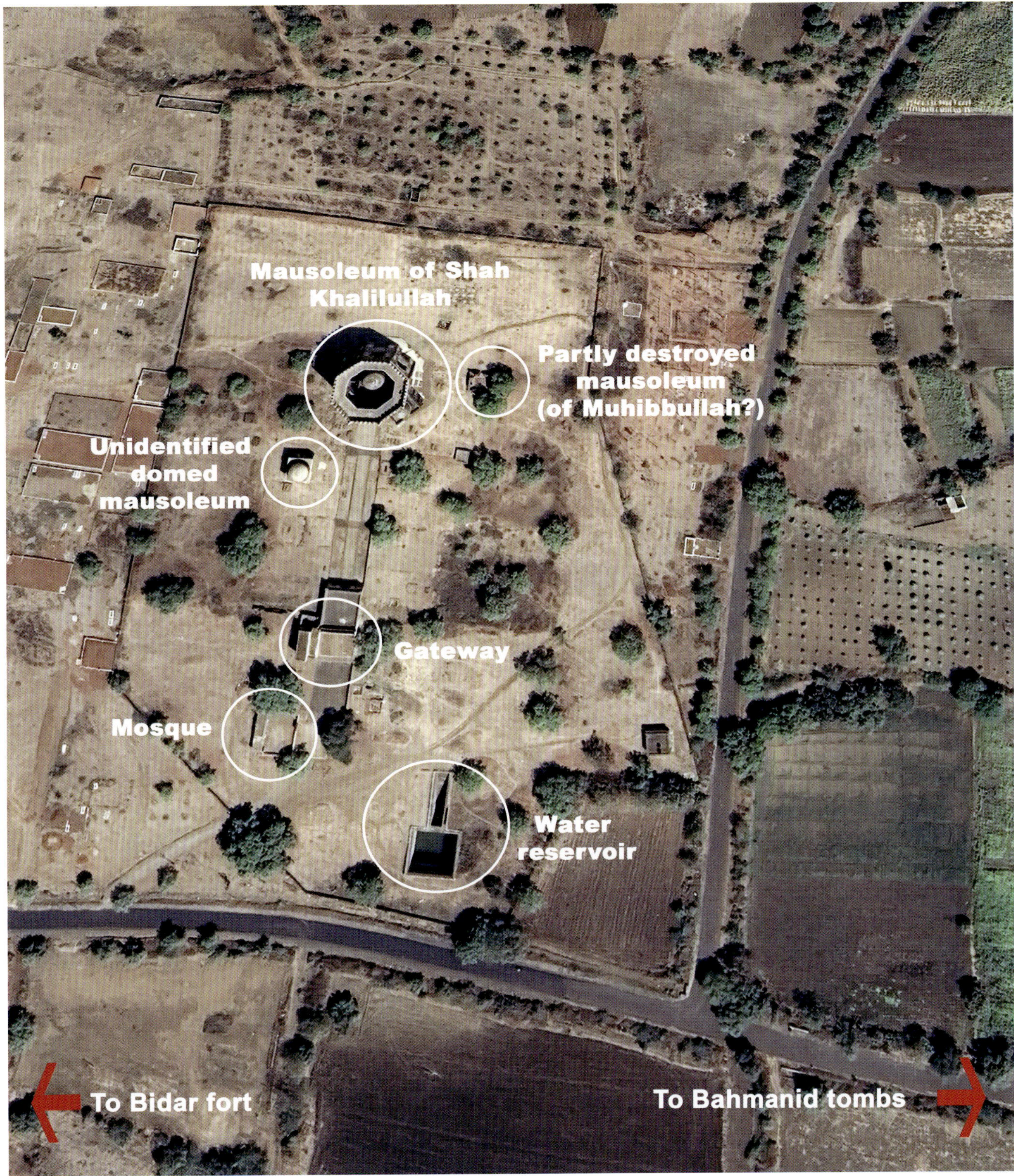

FIGURE 5.2. Site plan of Khalilullah's mausoleum complex in Ashtur. *Google Earth Pro; with additions by author.*

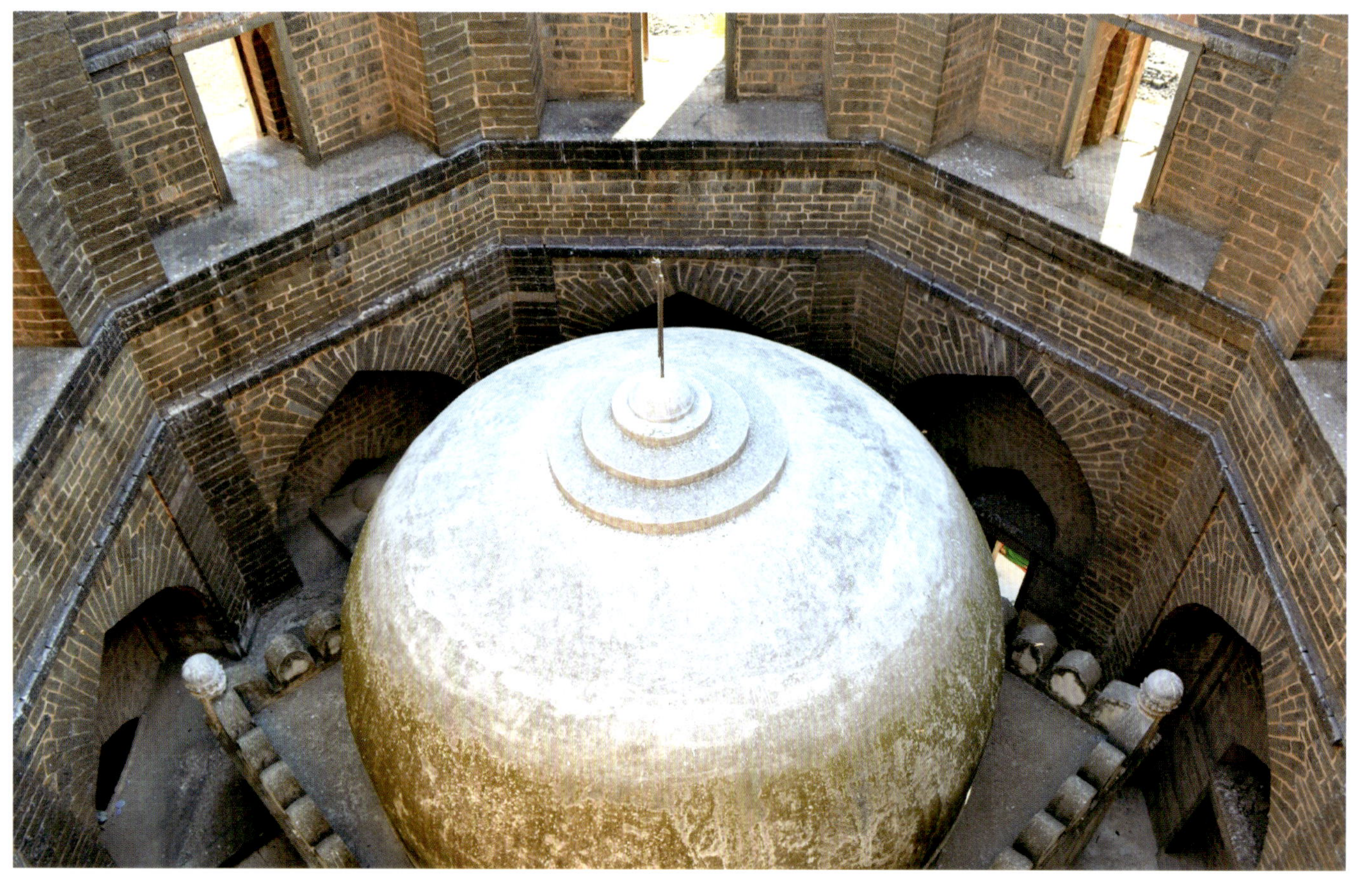

FIGURE 5.3. Mausoleum of Shah Khalilullah in Ashtur, central dome chamber within the octagonal shell. *Photograph by author, 2017.*

a mausoleum; a four-segmented, four-story, or square-shaped structure; or an enclosure of uncovered walls around a venerated grave—the latter being especially fitting for the site's octagonal enclosure, open from above.[6]

Apart from the octagonal enclosure that forms the focal point of the site, other surviving structures from the fifteenth century include a water reservoir, dated to 850/1446 by a loose tablet inscription found in its vicinity, and a mostly ruined domed chamber to the east of the octagonal structure (figs. 5.2 and 5.4). This latter domed structure once had an inscription that mentioned the name of Mahmud Shah, most likely the Bahmanid ruler Sultan Mahmud (r. 1482–1518), placing the building in the second half of the fifteenth century or the early sixteenth century.[7] Based on the death date of Shah Muhibbullah, son of Khalilullah, which falls under the reign of Mahmud Shah, Ghulam Yazdani suggested that the tomb could have belonged to Muhibbullah.[8] This is plausible, as according to biographer Sunᶜullah, Shah Muhibbullah was buried next to his father in the Khaliliyeh of the Deccan, although this could also imply his burial next to his father's grave in Khalilullah's dome chamber inside the octagon.[9]

Later structures, likely dating from the Baridi (1487–1619), Adil Shahi (1490–1689), and Mughal (1526–1857) periods, include another stand-alone dome chamber to the southwest of the octagon (fig. 5.5), a double-story gateway

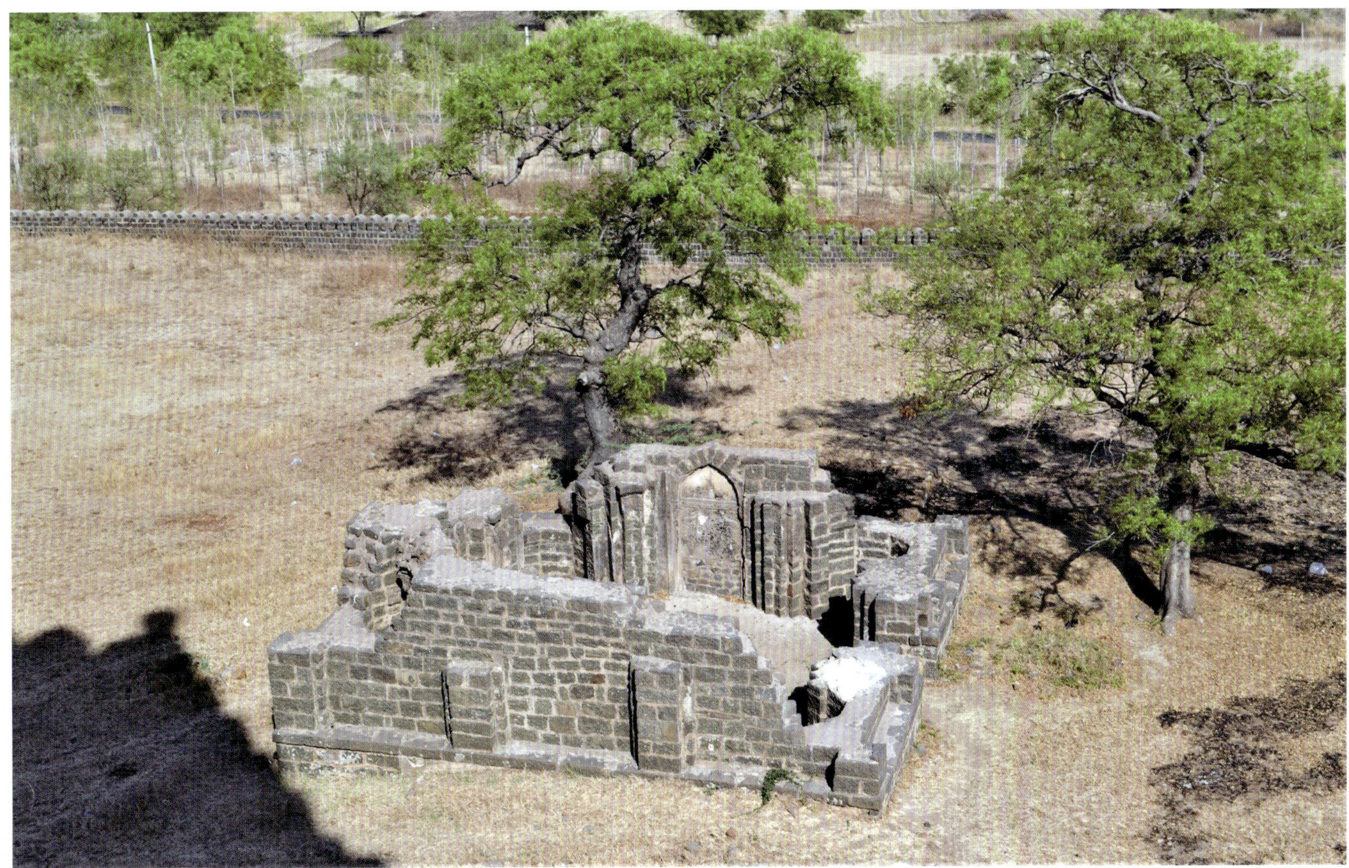

FIGURE 5.4. Remains of a dome chamber located to the east of the octagonal structure in Khalilullah's complex in Ashtur. *Photograph by author, 2017.*

with a three-tiered facade inscribed with the Throne Verse (Q 2:255), and a two-story building to the west of it (fig. 5.6).[10] The latter structure has a double vaulted hall on the lower ground and an open hall on the upper ground that Yazdani described as a ceremonial hall for musicians (fig. 5.7).[11] The rooms on the lower floor could have been used as lodging for travelers and pilgrims, but in the absence of spatial clues and sources, their function remains obscure. A small mosque with an adjacent courtyard is located to the south of the gateway (fig. 5.8).[12] Scattered graves in the open air or under trees punctuate the site.[13] In the northern part of the site, to the west of the octagon, there is an enclosure of perforated stone walls containing two graves, indicating their heightened status compared to the ones lying in the open (fig. 5.9).

The patronage of the early phase of the complex is attributed to ʿAla al-din Ahmad Shah II (r. 1436–58), son and successor of Ahmad Shah Bahmani I, who was a supporter and follower of Shah Neʿmatullah Vali.[14] Neither epigraphic sources nor Deccani chronicles from the sixteenth and seventeenth centuries record this possible act of patronage by Ahmad II. But this attribution is likely due to the location of the complex in proximity to the Bahmanid royal necropolis; the style of the architecture and its ornamentation, which bear similarities to the Bahmanids' own tombs nearby; and the sociopolitical status of the Neʿmatullahis at the Bahmanid court (fig. 5.10). Ahmad II

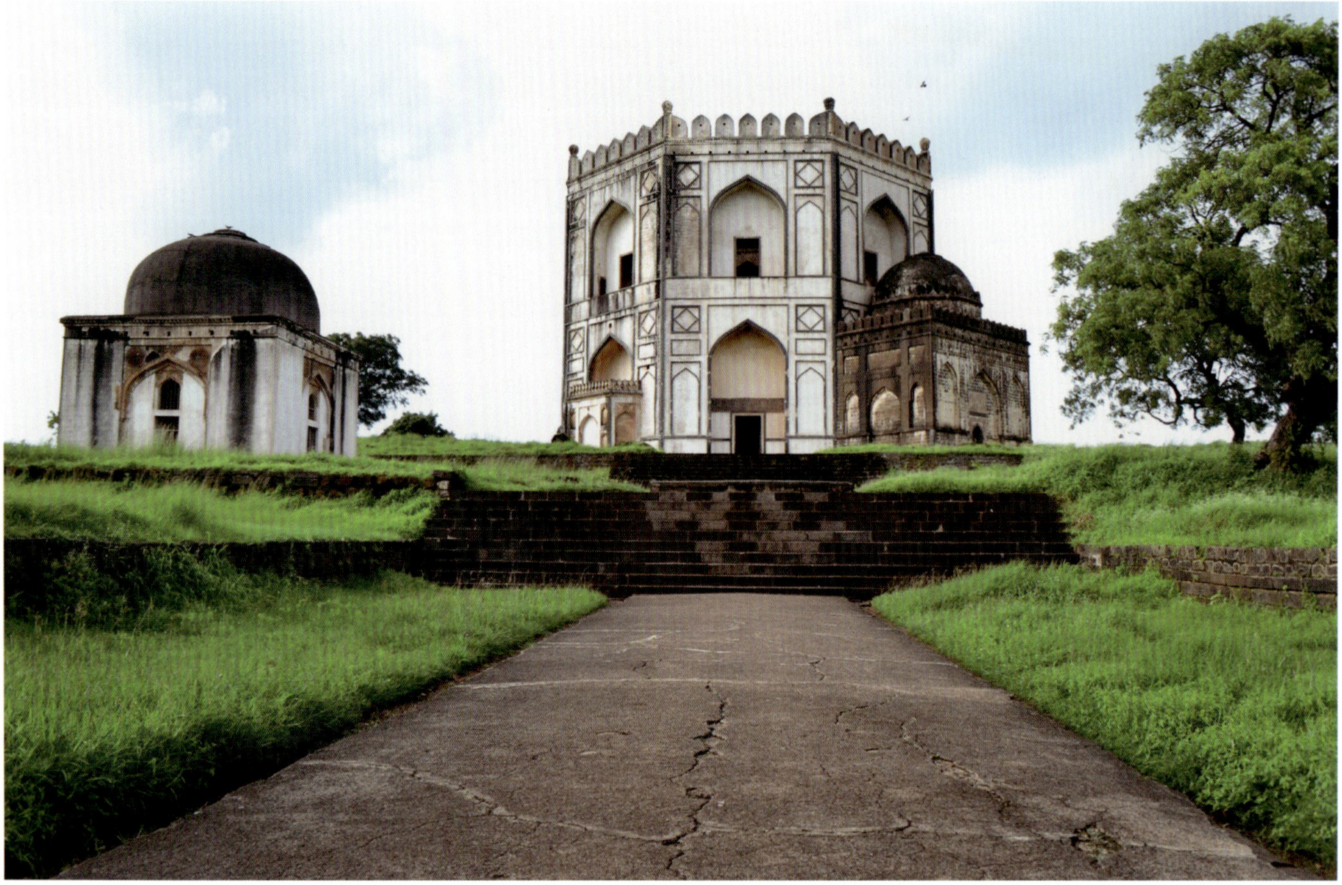

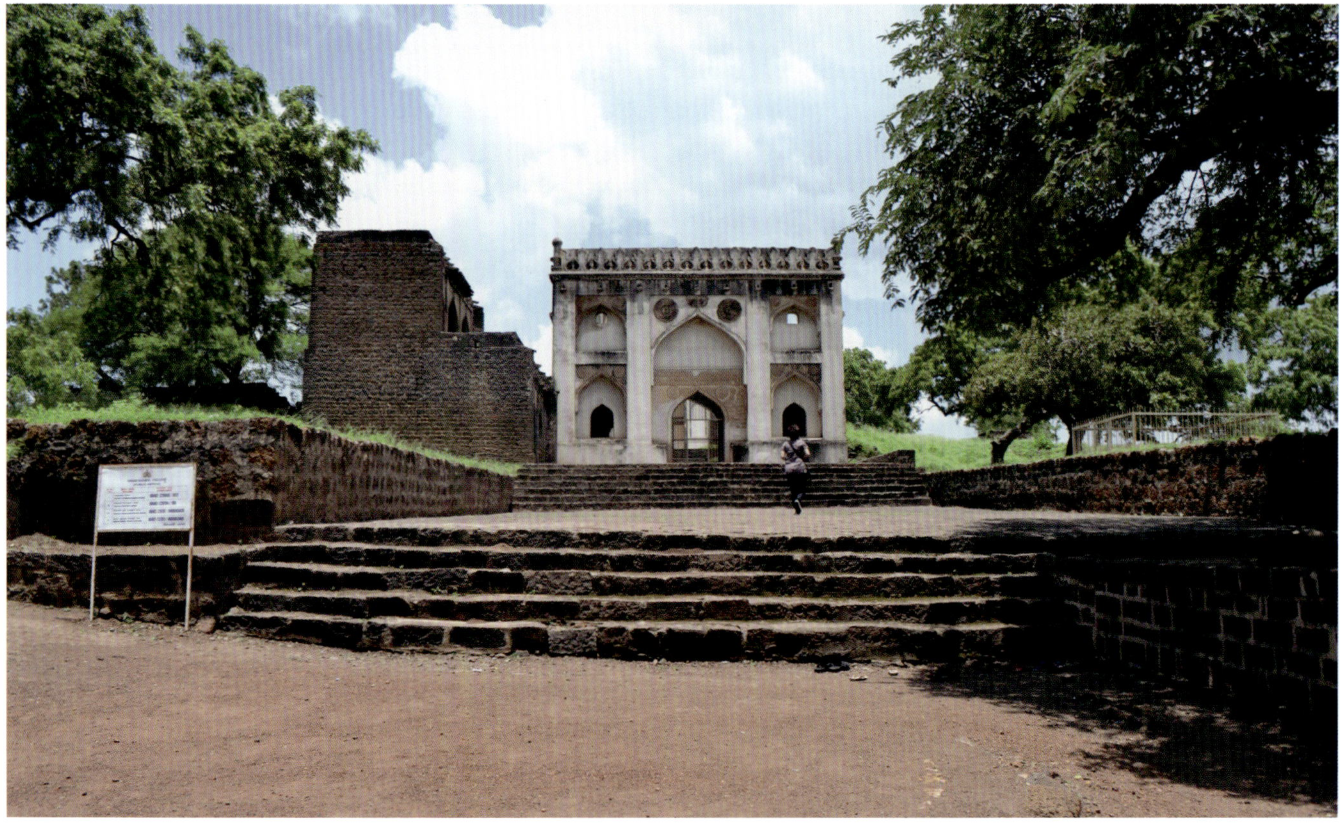

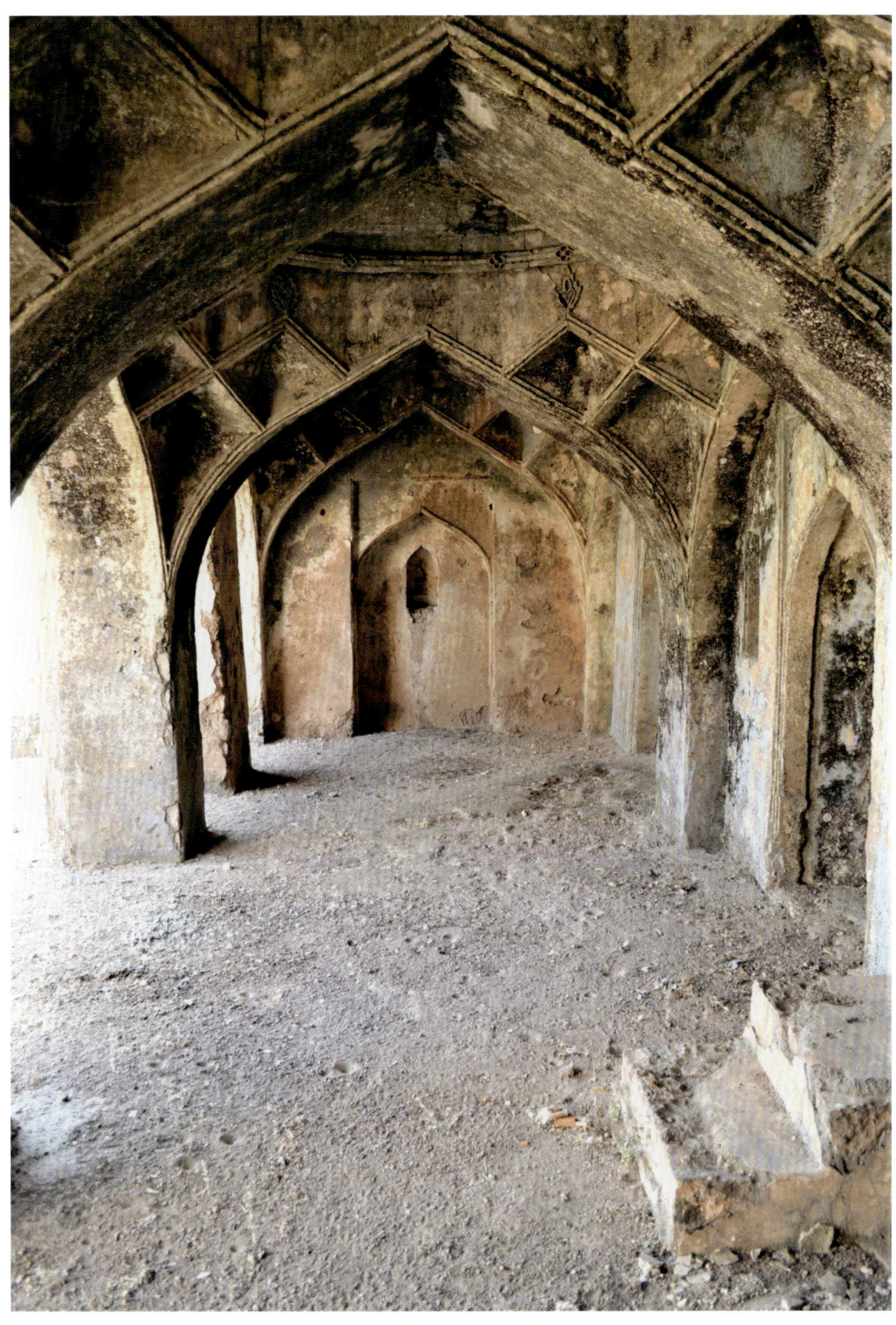

FACING TOP, FIGURE 5.5.
The single-dome chamber to the southwest of the octagonal structure in Khalilullah's complex in Ashtur. *Photograph by author, 2013.*

FACING BOTTOM, FIGURE 5.6.
View of gateway and two-story building from the south of Khalilullah's complex in Ashtur. *Photograph by author, 2013.*

LEFT, FIGURE 5.7.
Interior of the upper-ground hall of the two-story building next to the gateway in Khalilullah's complex in Ashtur. *Photograph by author, 2017.*

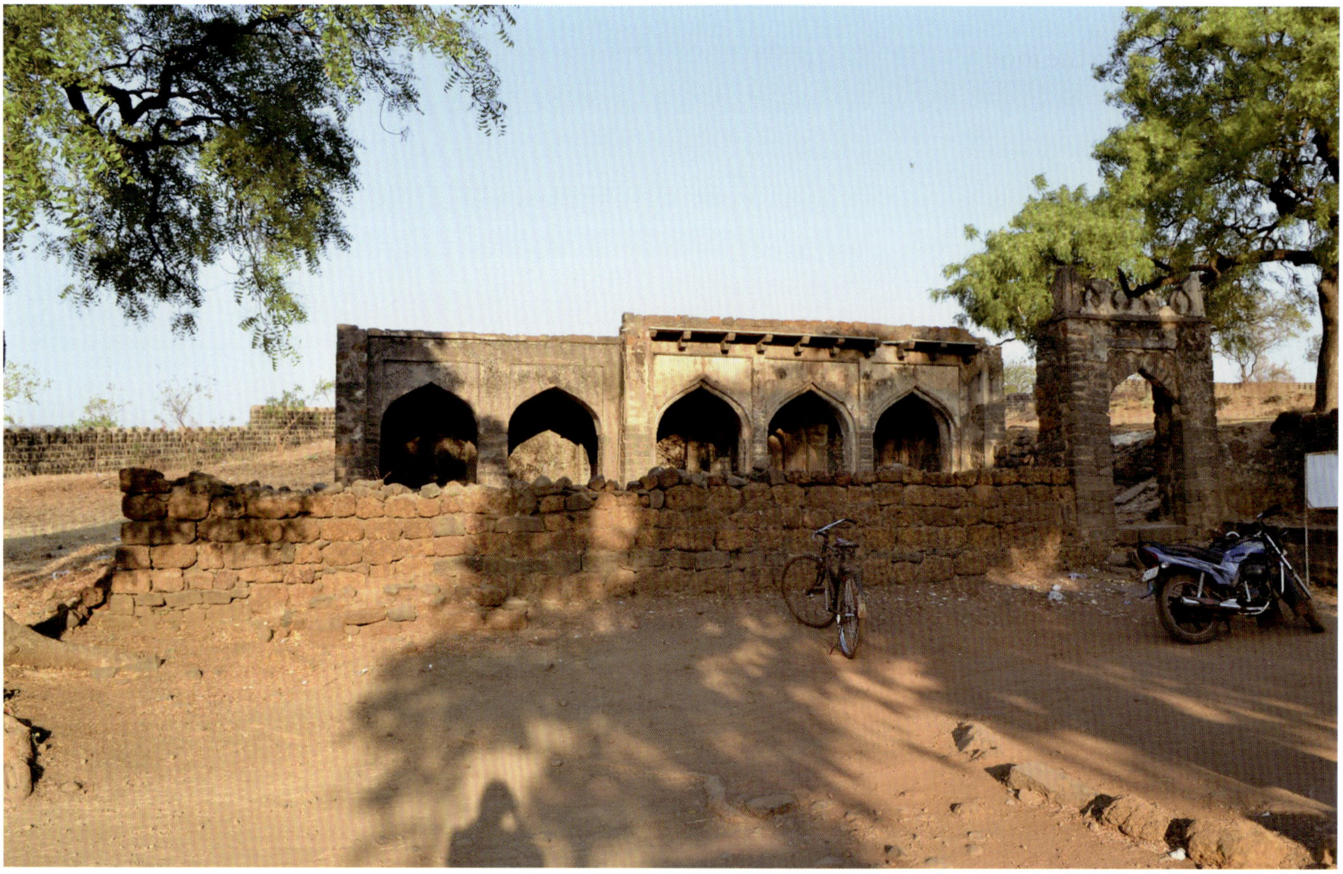

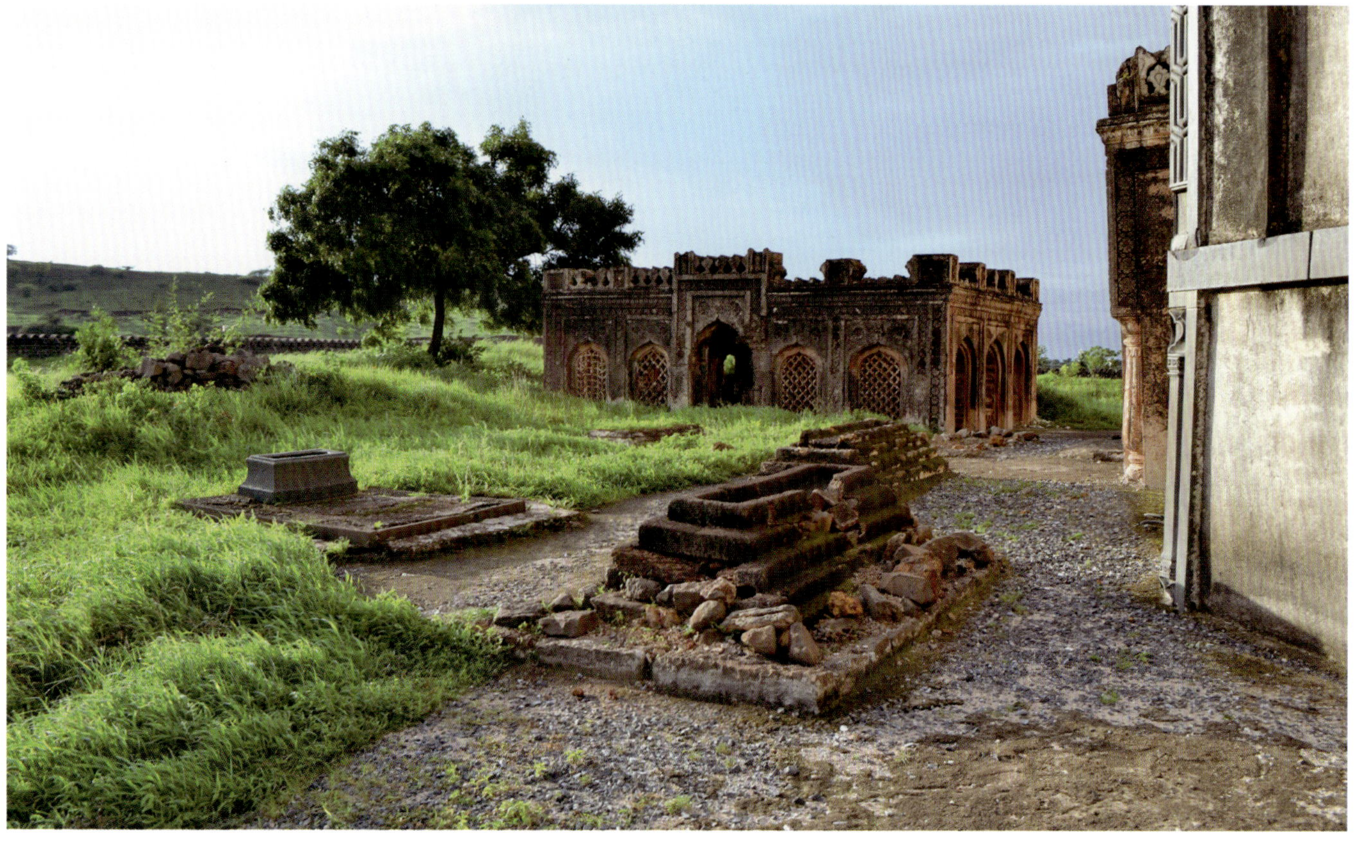

had also supported the construction of Khalilullah's father's mausoleum in Mahan, following in the footsteps of his own father—a relationship that makes his patronage of the site in Bidar more plausible.

The site of the mausoleum seems to have been associated with the Neʿmatullahi family well before Shah Khalilullah's death. An inscribed tablet whose current location is unknown was recorded by Yazdani as lying in the vicinity of Shah Khalilullah's shrine. The epigraph, in *naskh* (a small round calligraphic script), consists of a chronogram in verse and five lines of Persian prose recording the date of the demise of a Nurullah-i Husayni. The chronogram reads "*jannat al-firdaws*" (garden of Heaven), which, according to the *abjad* system (letters assigned with numerical values), amounts to the date 834/1431.[15] The prose section of the inscription indicates that Nurullah's tomb "was broken" during the time of the Baridi kings (1487–1619 in Bidar) but was restored by Asadullah Khan, one of the descendants of Nurullah, during the reign of a Muhammad Shah. Yazdani read the date of this inscription as the year 1196/1781–82 (and elsewhere as 1195/1780–81), but it is more probably 1157/1744–45 or a date in 1150s (app. 5.1).[16] I have not been able to locate and consult this panel. Therefore, my suggestion is based on Yazdani's published image. However, the date I suggest above fits the historical context of the Neʿmatullahi family that I explain below and indeed falls within the reign of the Mughal ruler Muhammad Shah (r. 1719–48), who is probably the person mentioned in the panel's inscription.

FACING TOP, FIGURE 5.8. View of the mosque to the south of the gateway in Khalilullah's complex in Ashtur. *Photograph by author, 2017.*

FACING BOTTOM, FIGURE 5.9. Open-air graves and the grave enclosure to the west of octagonal building in Khalilullah's complex in Ashtur. *Photograph by author, 2013.*

BELOW, FIGURE 5.10. Aerial view showing the location of Khalilullah's complex (*left*) in relation to the Bahmanid tombs (*right*) in Ashtur. *Google Earth Pro; with additions by author.*

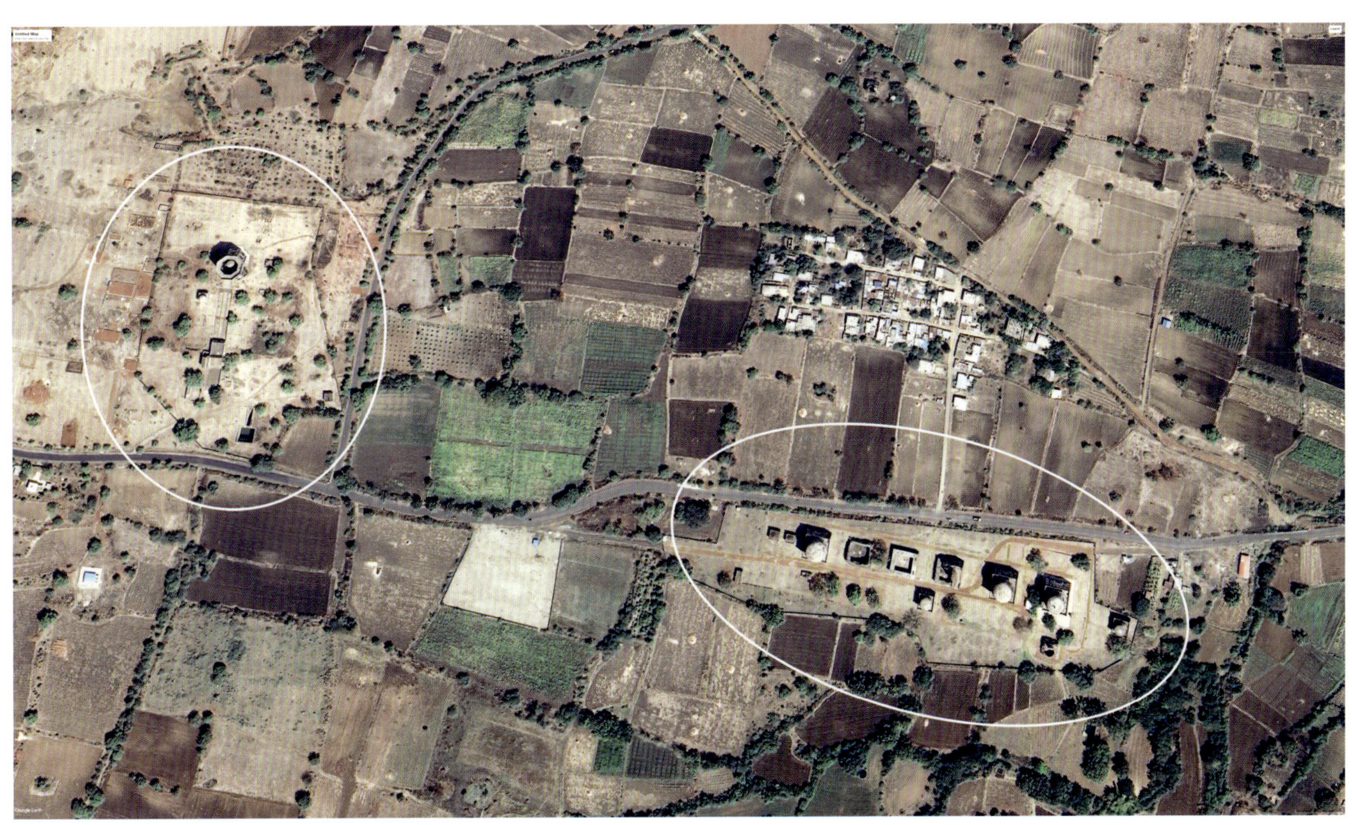

Assuming that the eighteenth-century inscribed panel is quoting the historical data from the original tomb, it is plausible that the deceased was the Neʿmatullahi descendant Shah Nurullah, son of Shah Khalilullah and the first member of the Neʿmatullahi family who traveled to the Deccan before the death of Shah Neʿmatullah in 834/1431, following Ahmad Shah I's invitation. As recorded in the *Burhan-i maʾasir*, Nurullah died in 834/1431—the same year as his grandfather—shortly after his arrival in the Deccan, matching the date on the tablet above. It is worth mentioning, however, that Nurullah's death date is not free from discrepancies in textual sources.[17]

Asadullah, the name of the descendant responsible for the reconstruction of the tomb, was a common name in Shah Nurullah's lineage.[18] A likely candidate is a Neʿmatullahi descendant by the name of Asadullah (d. 1745–46), son of Mirmiran Mir Khan-i Kabuli (d. 1698), who was appointed governor of Kabul by Aurangzeb (r. 1658–1707).[19] Kabuli's brother (and Asadullah's uncle), Ruhullah Khan (d. 1691–92), was a key figure in the success of Aurangzeb's campaigns against the Deccan and was installed as the governor of Bijapur and Golkonda by the Mughal emperor.[20] Asadullah himself was a noted amir.[21] As I will discuss in chapter 7, these Neʿmatullahi figures were among a branch of the family who migrated to Mughal India, and it is likely that with their renewed political authority in the Deccan they undertook the restoration of their ancestors' funerary complex.

The language used on the tablet establishes some parameters regarding the significance of this structure and, as a result, the site's prominence from the earliest years of the Neʿmatullahis' arrival in the Deccan. The term *reconstruction* and the act of *finishing* it, used on the tablet, relay a sense of longevity in the process of construction (app. 5.1). The mention of the reigning monarch, Muhammad Shah, adds to this significance, pointing to a structure that was likely more than just a tombstone built to commemorate a death in 1431 on the site and subsequently lost.[22]

Returning to the whole complex, Khalilullah's funerary site has received attention for its "peculiar shape" in the works of Ghulam Yazdani, George Michell and Mark Zebrowski, Elizabeth Merklinger, and, more recently, Helen Philon.[23] This "peculiarity" is rooted in the question of the relationship between the square-plan sepulchre and the octagonal walls surrounding it (figs. 5.3 and 5.11). Octagonal structures were common in the architecture of Islamicate societies, and comparable contemporary examples existed across Iran and India and in the vicinity of Bidar (fig. 5.12).[24] Setting the question of scale aside, thinking of Khalilullah's mausoleum alongside the Dome of the Rock in Jerusalem, the monumental tomb of Sultan Uljaytu in Sultaniyeh, and the tomb of Rukn-i ʿAlam in Multan helps locate the mausoleum in Bidar as part of a long genealogy of octagonal funerary (or commemorative) architecture in the Islamic world.[25] Yet it is the juxtaposition of the dome chamber, the roofless octagon, and the circumambulatory space between the two that make the structure in Bidar unique.

Based on structural observations, Yazdani proposed that the building of a dome over the octagon was not part of the original scheme of the

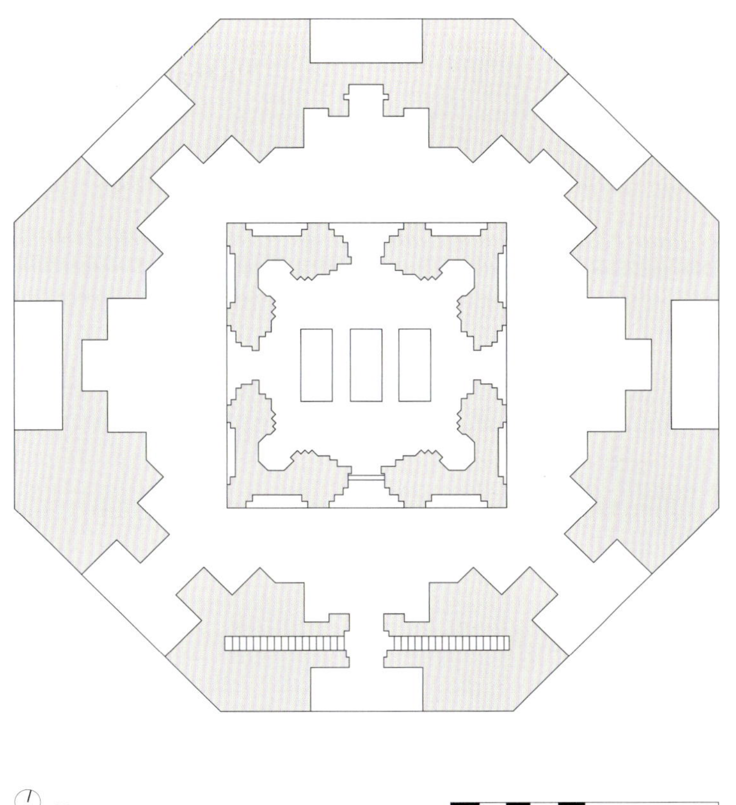

FIGURE 5.11. Plan of Khalilullah's mausoleum in Ashtur, before the Mughal-era expansion. *Drawing by Farah Michel after Michell and Zebrowski.*

FIGURE 5.12. Tomb of Dilawar Khan (fifteenth century) in Holkonda, Karnataka, India. *Photograph by author, 2017.*

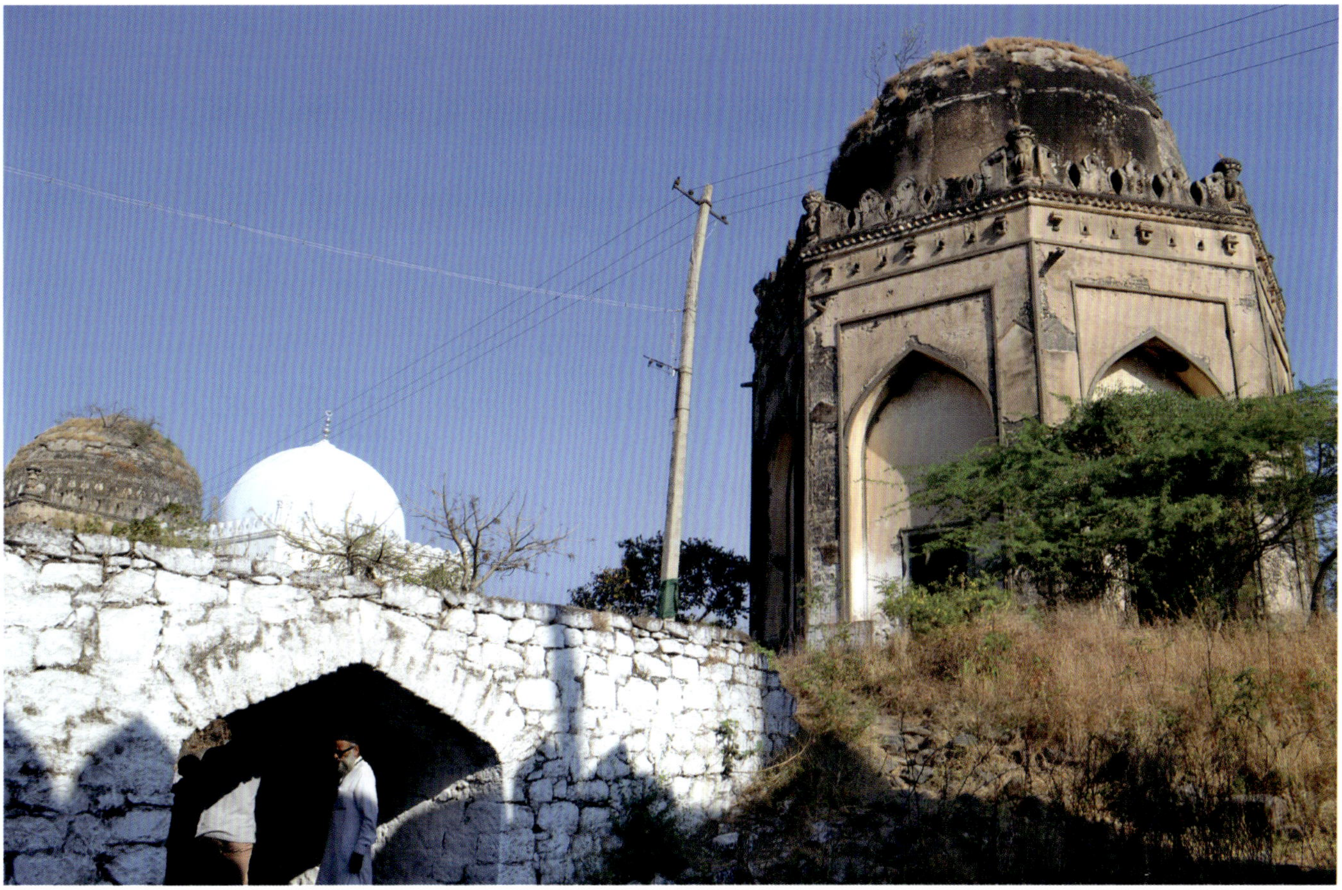

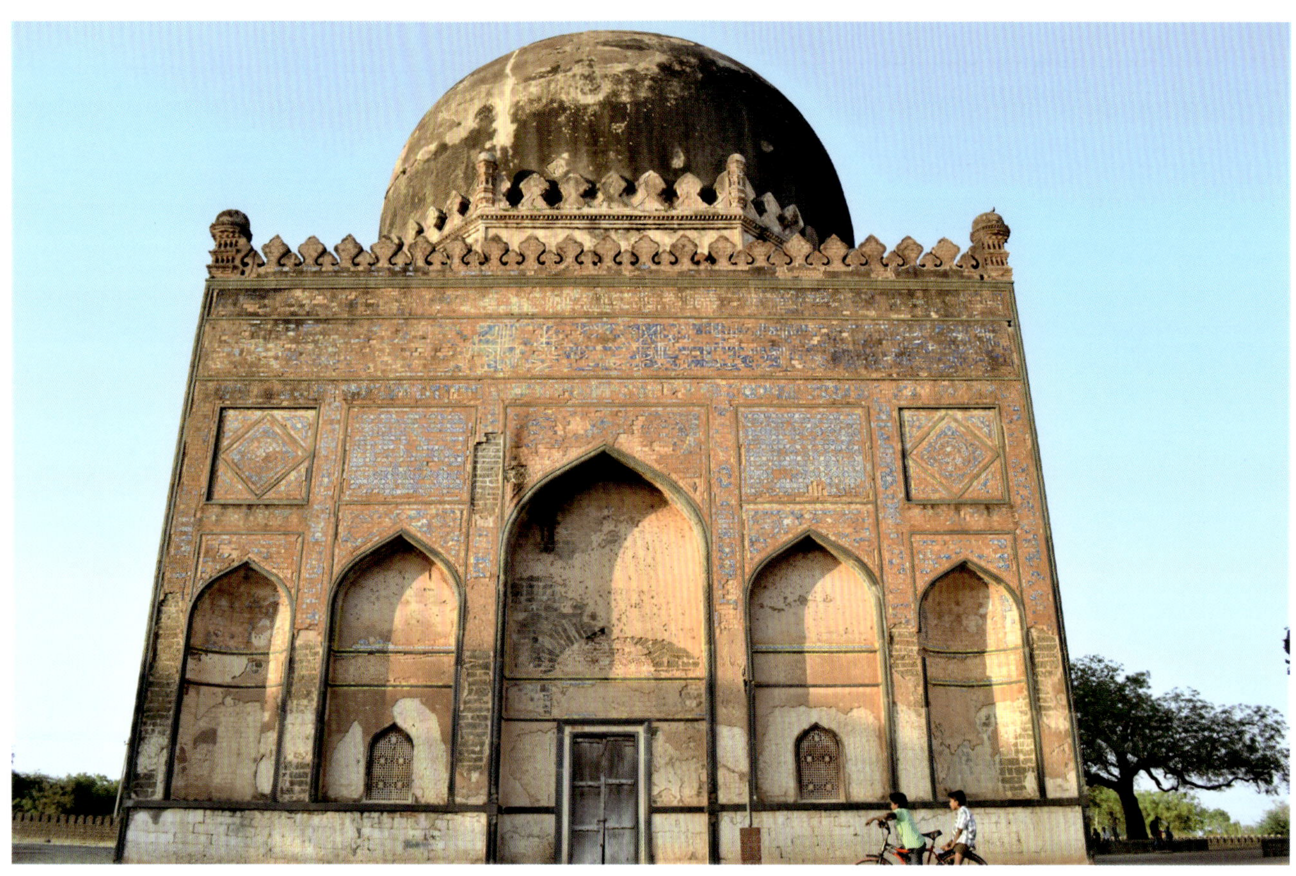

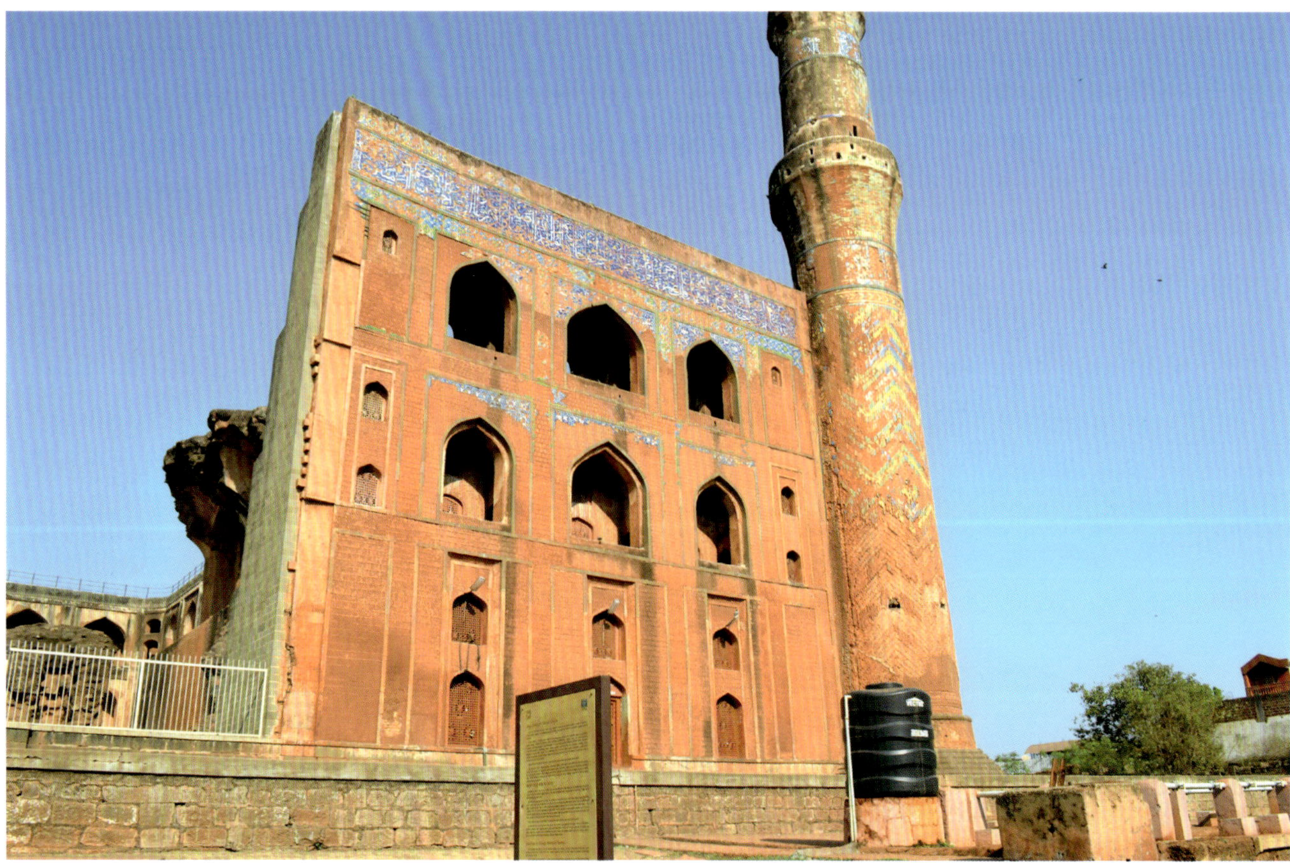

architecture.[26] Building on this suggestion, Philon offers a hypothesis that brings the structure to life: that the roofless space could have been covered with textile awnings.[27] This textile arrangement, which could have covered the bare walls of the octagon's interior as well, likely created a connected aesthetic experience between the interior and exterior of the structure, which seems to have featured polychrome tiles.[28] The few remnants of the tiles that were in place on the facade of the octagon when Yazdani examined the building in the early twentieth century are now lost, but he compares them in style and quality to those surviving on the exterior of Ahmad Shah II's tomb in the royal necropolis nearby and that of the madrasa of Mahmud Gavan in Bidar (figs. 5.13 and 5.14).[29]

FACING TOP, FIGURE 5.13. Remnants of polychrome tiles on the facade of Ahmad Shah II's tomb in Ashtur. *Photograph by author, 2017.*

FACING BOTTOM, FIGURE 5.14. Remnants of polychrome tiles on the facade of the madrasa of Mahmud Gavan, Bidar. *Photograph by author, 2017.*

On the chronology of the two structures—the octagon and the dome chamber—Philon offers an unlikely hypothesis, proposing that the octagonal walls were built first and the dome chamber was later inserted within the octagon.[30] Her reasoning proceeds from both formal and theological points of reference. Though a square dome chamber on the outside, the mausoleum is internally shaped into an octagon by means of projections inserted into the corners (fig. 5.11). Philon connects this type of plan with the late fifteenth- and early sixteenth-century tombs in Bidar, including later Bahmanid tombs in the nearby necropolis and the aforementioned ruined dome chamber on the site of Khalilullah's mausoleum. Based on these affinities, she suggests a later date for the dome chamber compared to the possible death date of Shah Khalilullah around the mid-fifteenth century. On theological grounds, Philon notes that Khalilullah's grave in the chaukhandi was originally open to the sky "in accordance with the precepts of Islam," which "may have even been dictated by the express wishes of the saint himself."[31]

Contrary to Philon's hypothesis, I suggest that the central dome chamber came first, likely built around the time of Khalilullah's burial on the site—that is, sometime before 1454. First, the facades of the dome chamber represent the familiar decorations of Bahmanid architecture and, specifically, the funerary architecture of the time: three-tiered facades with recessed arches, medallions of carved stucco flanking the apex of the arches, and vegetal carvings right above the apex of the arch (fig. 5.15). This ornate exterior suggests that the building was meant to stand alone and be visible at the time of its construction. It seems neither practical nor logical to insert a domed chamber within the limited space of the octagonal enclosure and then decorate its facades in the fashion typical of earlier Bahmanid tombs, since the viewers' proximity to the facades of the building would severely limit their visibility.

Second, it is not entirely clear why Philon suggests a later fifteenth- or early sixteenth-century date for the octagon-in-square plan of the dome chamber. She observes how Khalilullah's mausoleum could have been the model for later Bahmanid tomb plans of this type, but this does not preclude an earlier date. As Philip Wagoner and John Henry Rice suggest, the general concept of the octagon-in-square plan has a long history in sultanate architecture. Although Khalilullah's dome chamber in Bidar lacks features such as a mandapa-type

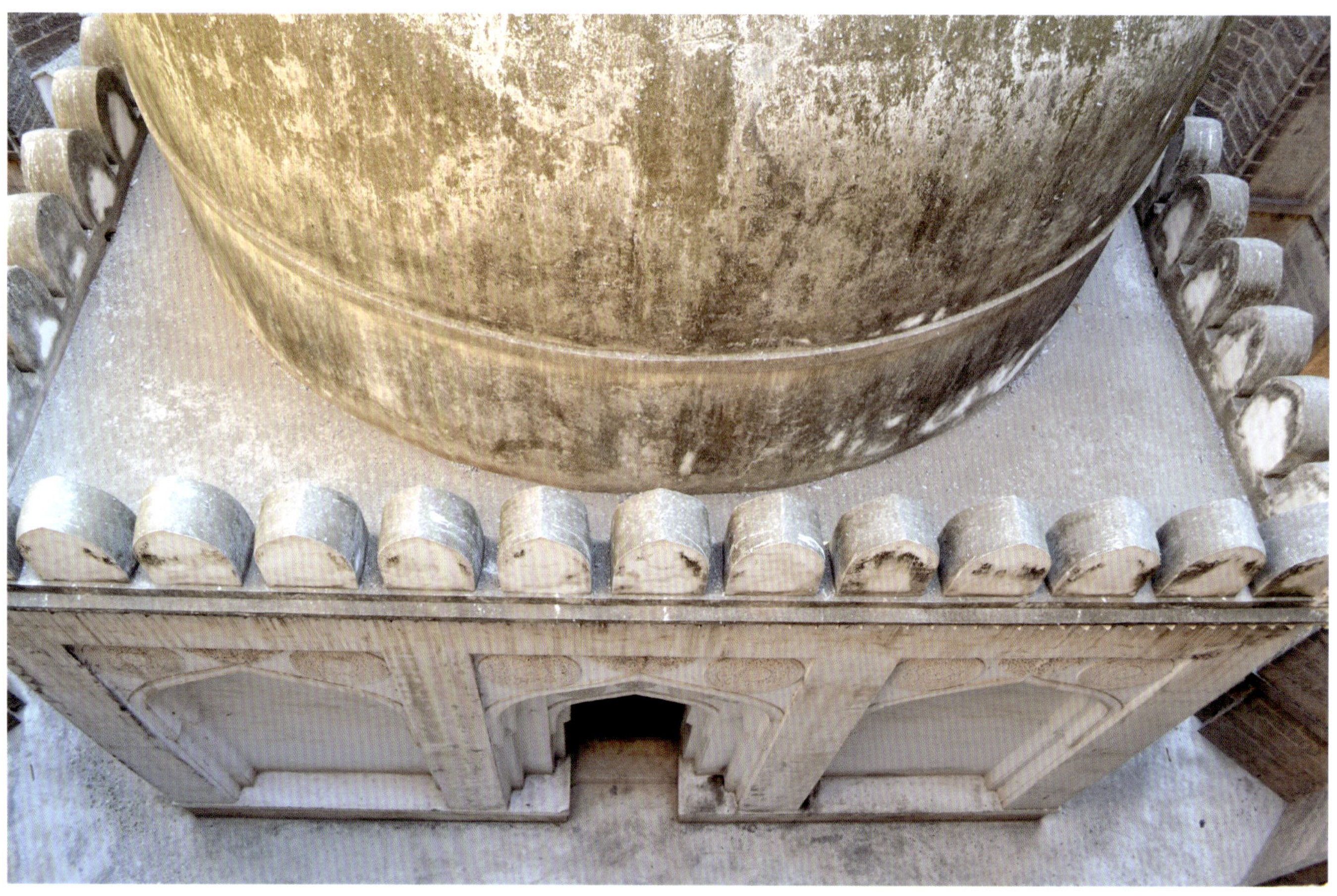

FIGURE 5.15. Northern facade of the dome chamber inside the octagonal shell at Khalilullah's mausoleum in Ashtur, as seen from the upper floor of the octagon. *Photograph by author, 2017.*

internal space and the use of temple spolia, it shares formal and structural similarities with the plan type discussed by Wagoner and Rice. For example, they associate the plan type with "conquest mosques" built partially from mandapa spolia from temples, including the fourteenth-century Jamiᶜ mosque of Warangal-Sultanpur.[32]

Finally, prohibitions against erecting monumental architecture for Sufi networks, of which Philon speaks, were by no means practiced by all Sufis across Islamicate societies. The lack of such prohibitions in the funerary buildings built for the Neᶜmatullahi network is evident in the case of the fifteenth-century structures in Taft and Mahan, some built during the lifetime and under supervision of the Sufi Shah Neᶜmatullah.[33] Shah Khalilullah himself oversaw the construction of his father's domed mausoleum in Mahan.

It is more likely that Khalilullah's mausoleum gradually expanded outward from the inner core of the dome chamber. The next stage was the addition of the freestanding octagonal shell around the sepulchre, measuring 15.54 meters in height, which elevated the monumental dimensions of the structure. The negative space between the dome chamber and the octagonal shell created a defined corridor that likely had a circumambulatory function (fig. 5.16). This kind of ambulatory arcade was common in Islamic funerary and temple architecture of India in a variety of forms. In a semiopen configuration, it

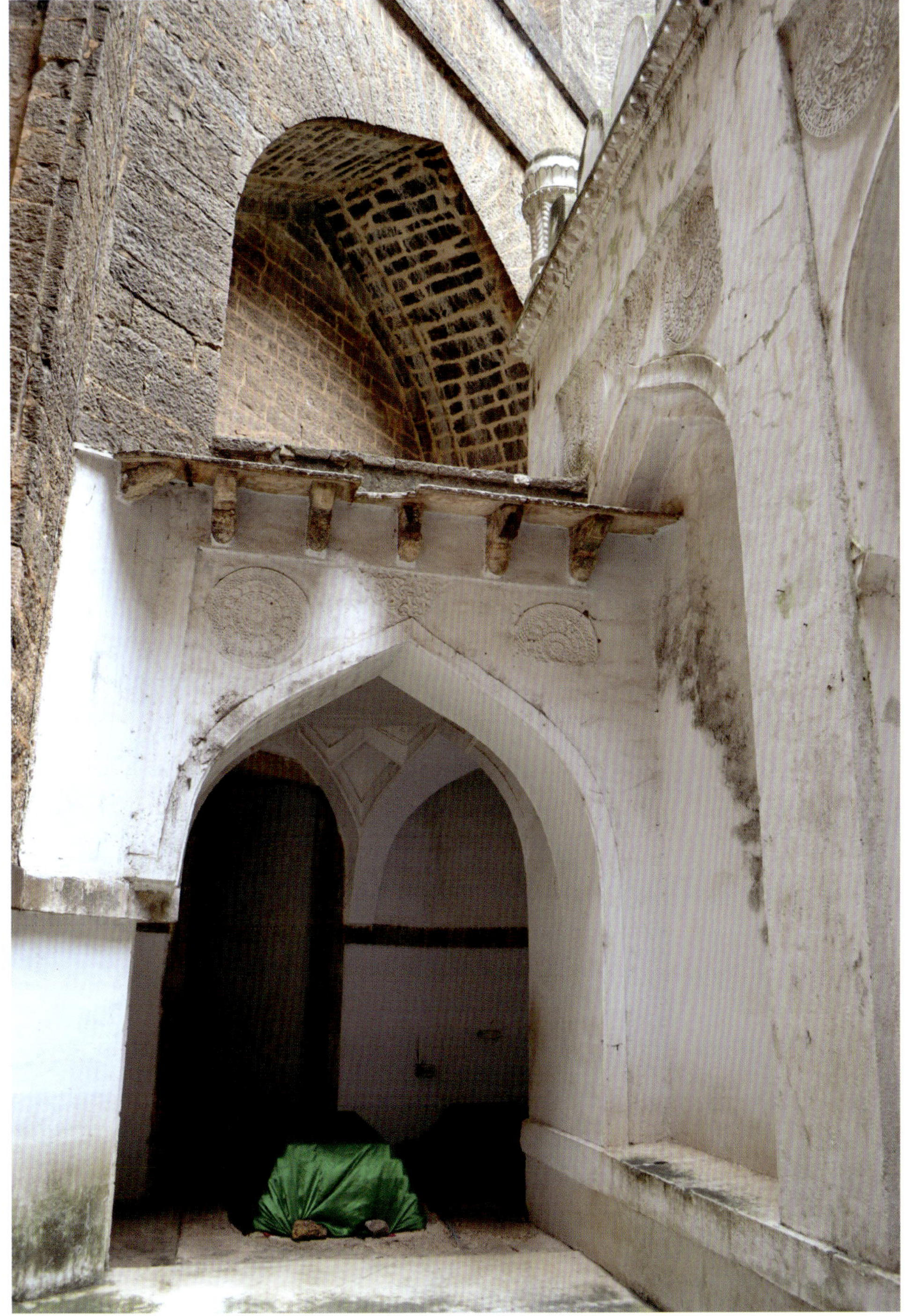

FIGURE 5.16. The corridor created between the dome chamber and the octagonal shell at Khalilullah's mausoleum in Ashtur. *Photograph by author, 2013.*

was visible in the arcades of the royal tombs of Muslim rulers of the Delhi Sultanates or those later in the Deccan, such as that of ʿAli ʿAdil Shah II (d. 1672) in Bijapur, for which Khalilullah's mausoleum can be considered a Deccani predecessor.[34] The circumambulation ritual around deity images and sacred objects was also an integral part of Hindu devotional practices. Given how often sacred landscapes were shared between Muslim and non-Muslim populations in Deccan India, the circumambulatory space at Khalilullah's

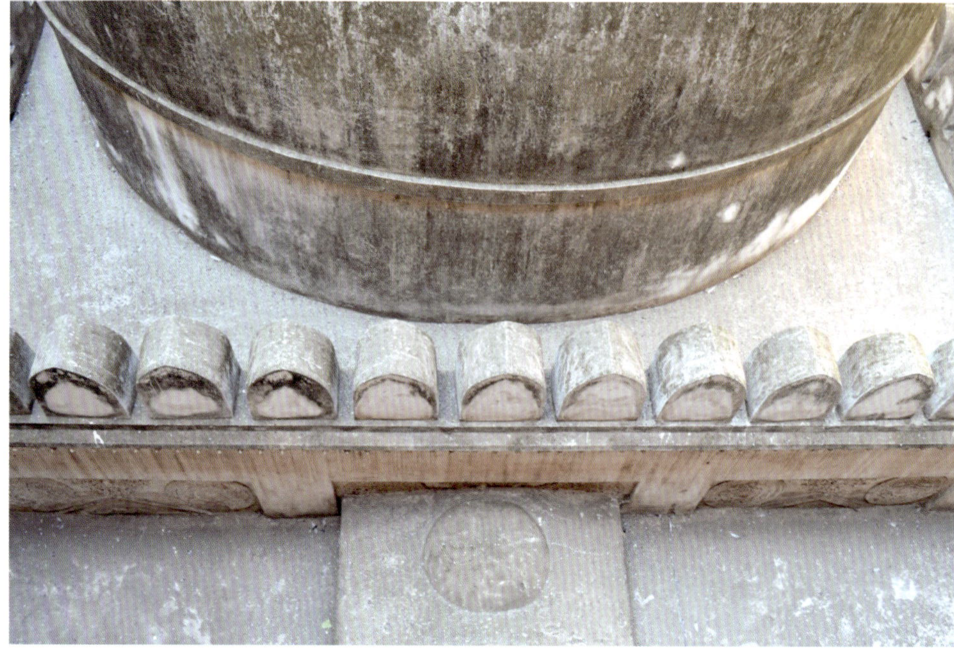

FIGURE 5.17. Southern facade of the dome chamber at Khalilullah's mausoleum in Ashtur, as seen from the upper floor of the octagon. *Photograph by author, 2017.*

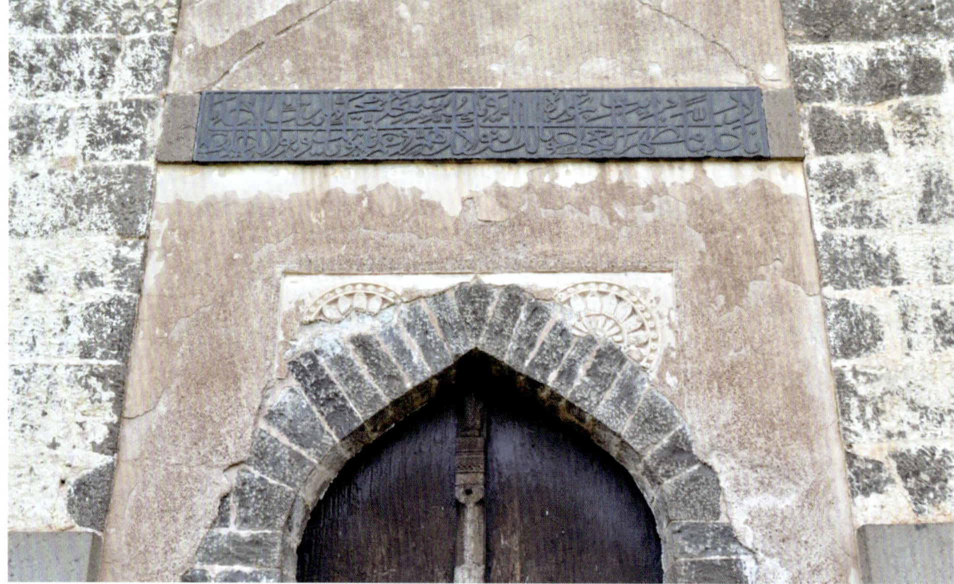

FIGURE 5.18. Inscription panel on the facade of the dome chamber annexed to the octagonal shell, dated 1086/1675–78 in the lower register. *Photograph by author, 2013.*

mausoleum could have contributed to establishing a familiar scene for non-Muslim pilgrims to the site.[35]

The construction of the octagonal shell was later followed by several other alterations: the addition of a roofing system with transverse vaults over the southern sections of the corridor (figs. 5.16 and 5.17), the conversion of facade niches of the octagon into enclosures on the southwest and west sides of the octagon (fig. 5.1), and the addition of a dome chamber to the southeast of the octagon dated 1086/1657–58 on its exterior, indicating its construction after the annexation of the Deccan to Mughal territories by Aurangzeb (figs. 5.1 and

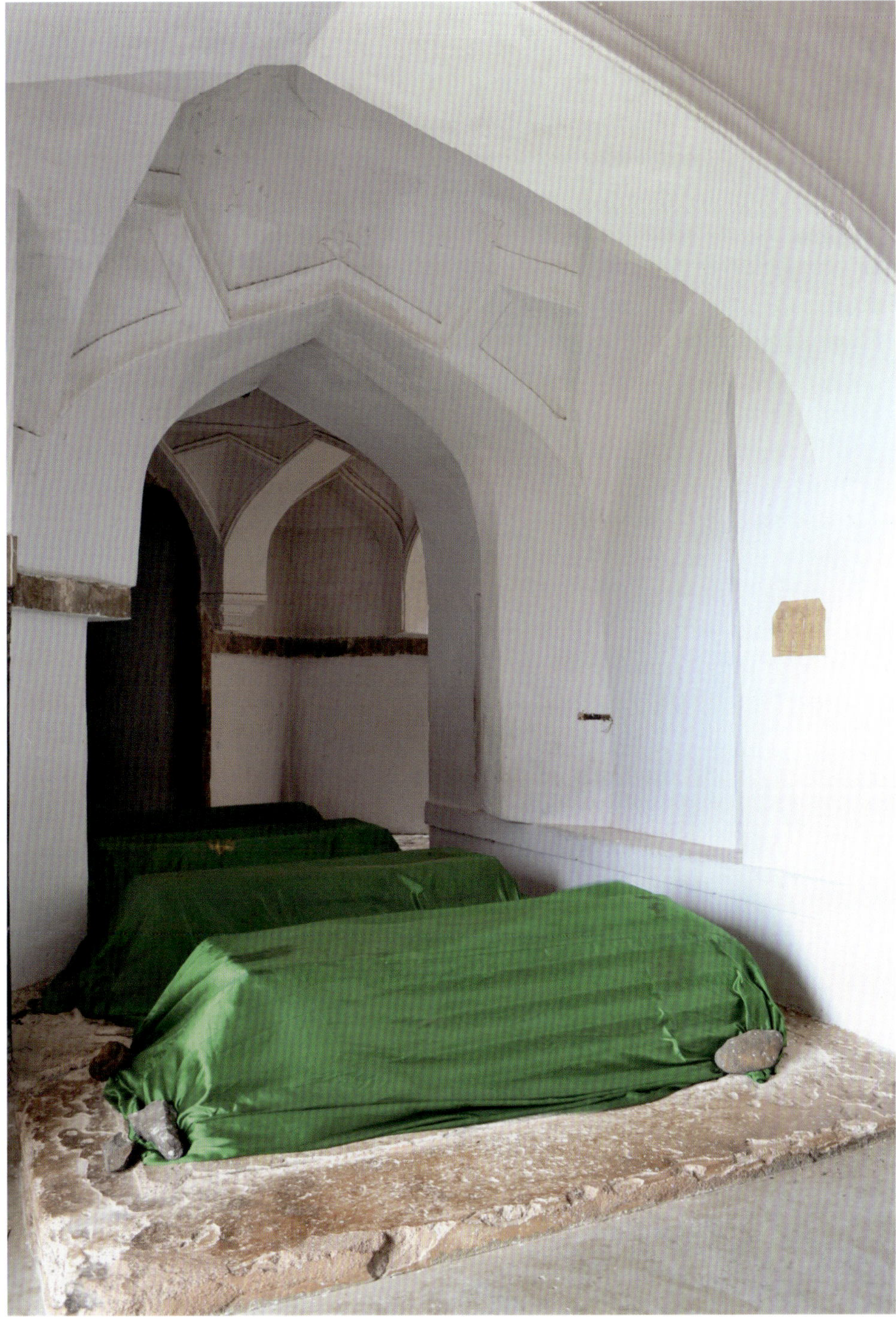

FIGURE 5.19. Burials in the covered portion of the corridor between the dome chamber and the octagonal shell at Khalilullah's mausoleum in Ashtur, view from entrance of the octagon. *Photograph by author, 2013.*

5.18).[36] While these alterations interrupt the coherence of the octagon's facade, they provided more burial space around the main dome chamber, maximum proximity to the three graves within it, and easy access to the main entrance (figs. 5.11 and 5.19). This architectural intervention may have been a response to the increased presence of the Sufi family in the Deccan by way of their involvement in Mughal campaigns in the region.

II. The Inscribed Gates of Heaven

The facades of the octagon are marked by lines of black basalt rods in different shapes: arched borders, framed square panels, and twisted carved strings that break up the surface of the building and accentuate its structural lines (fig. 5.1). A locally abundant material, black basalt was commonly used in Deccani architecture, as in the carved columns of Hindu temples, the strings on the facades of Bahmanid tombs, or, later, the inscribed and polished architectural panels and cenotaphs in Qutb Shahi buildings.[37] In this light, its use on the surface of the monumental unroofed octagon in Bidar alongside the tiled surfaces that once might have punctuated it represents a blending of familiar and new forms and materials.

Walking around the octagon, we again find black basalt in the form of polished monochrome inscription panels across recessed arches of the facade (fig. 5.20). These panels are extant only on the south, southwest, and west sides of the octagon. But it is likely that all sides of the octagon once featured similar inscribed panels, as suggested by the black basalt rods that define the upper and lower borders where the panels would have been located. Whether these have been lost or moved to another location remains unknown. Among the three surviving panels, only two are visible from outside: those above the main entrance of the octagon on the south and on the west facade (figs. 5.20 and

FIGURE 5.20. Black basalt inscription panel on the south wall (main entrance) of the octagonal shell at Khalilullah's mausoleum in Ashtur. *Photograph by author, 2013.*

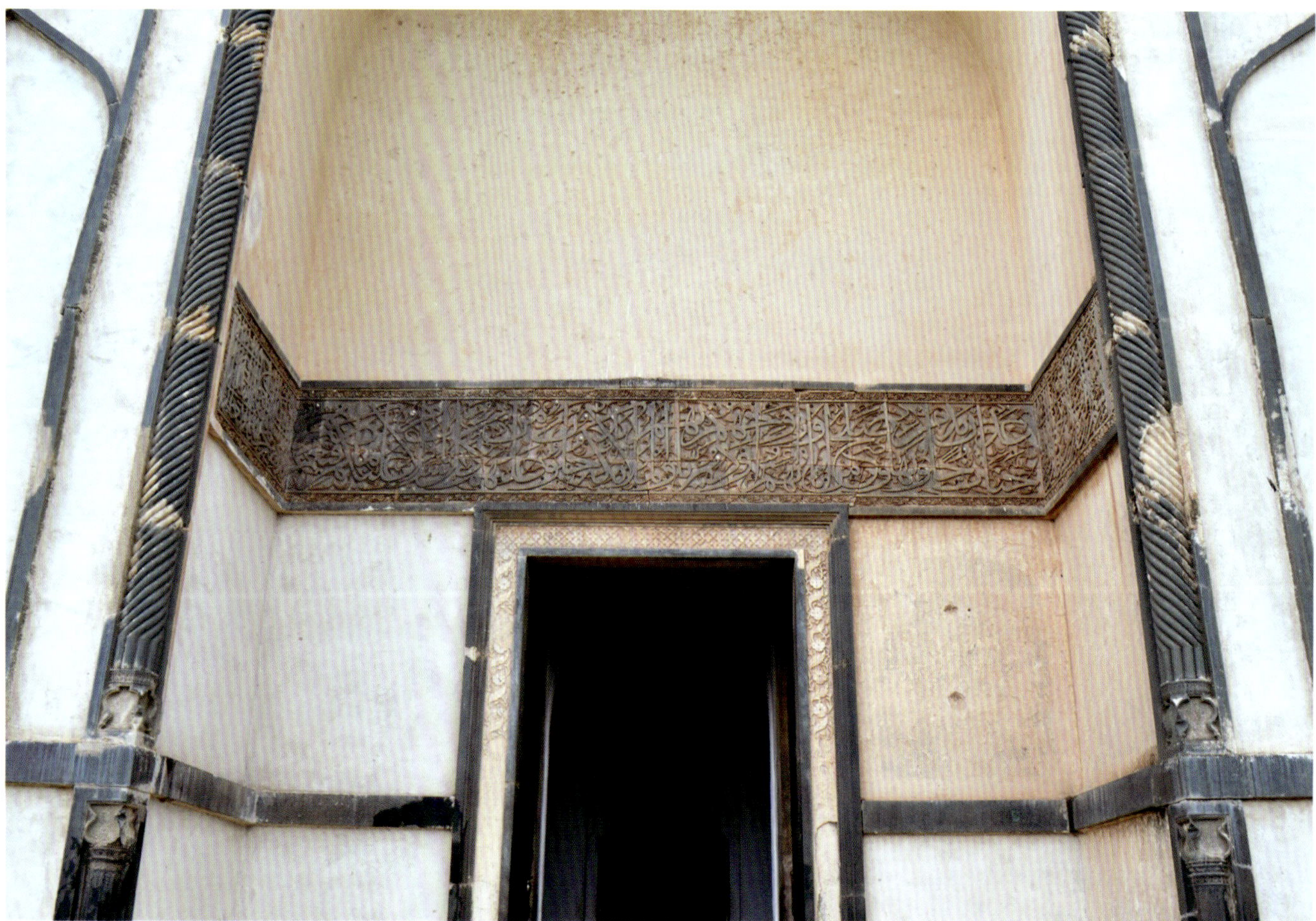

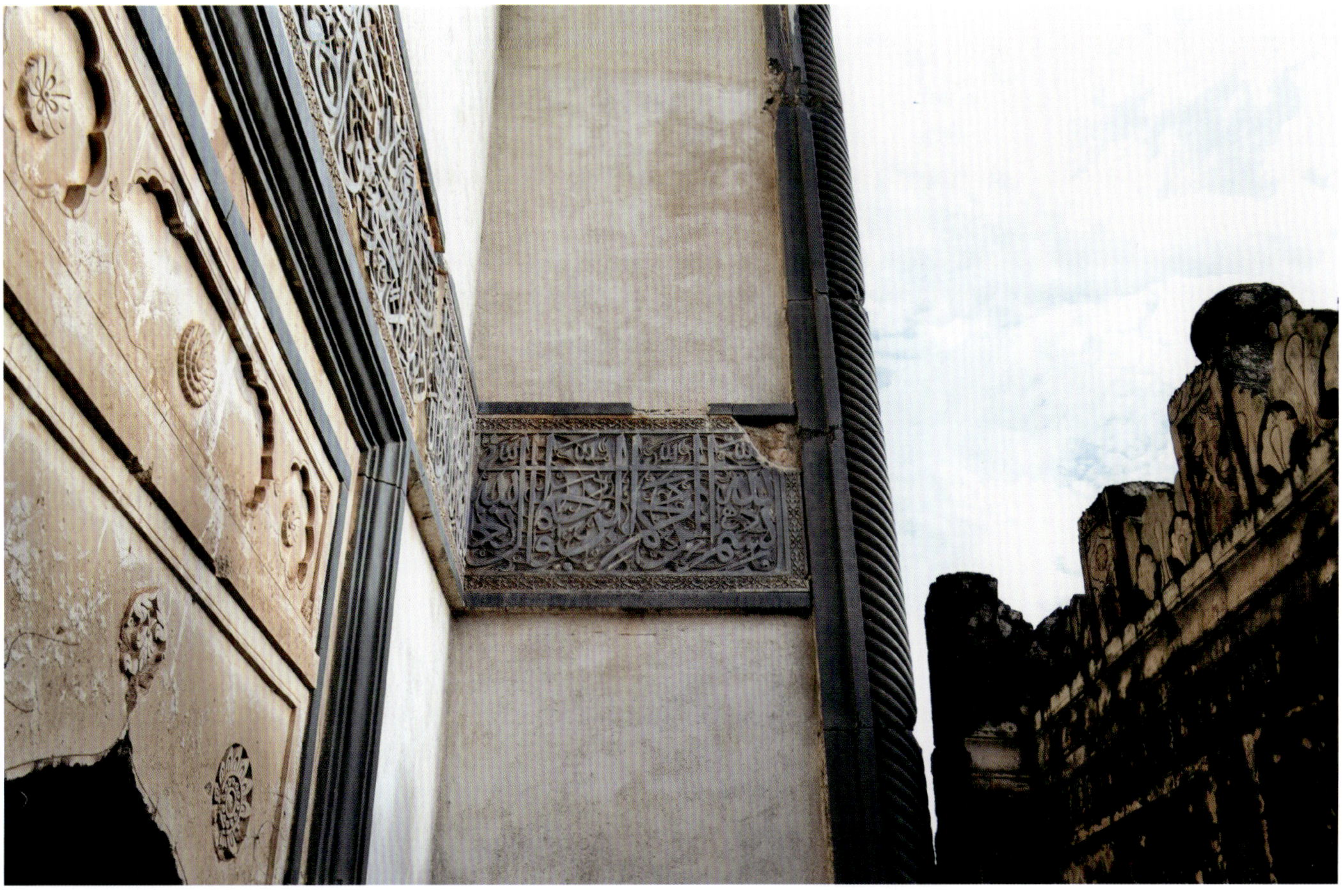

ABOVE, FIGURE 5.21.
Black basalt inscription panel on the west wall of the octagonal shell at Khalilullah's mausoleum in Ashtur.
Photograph by author, 2013.

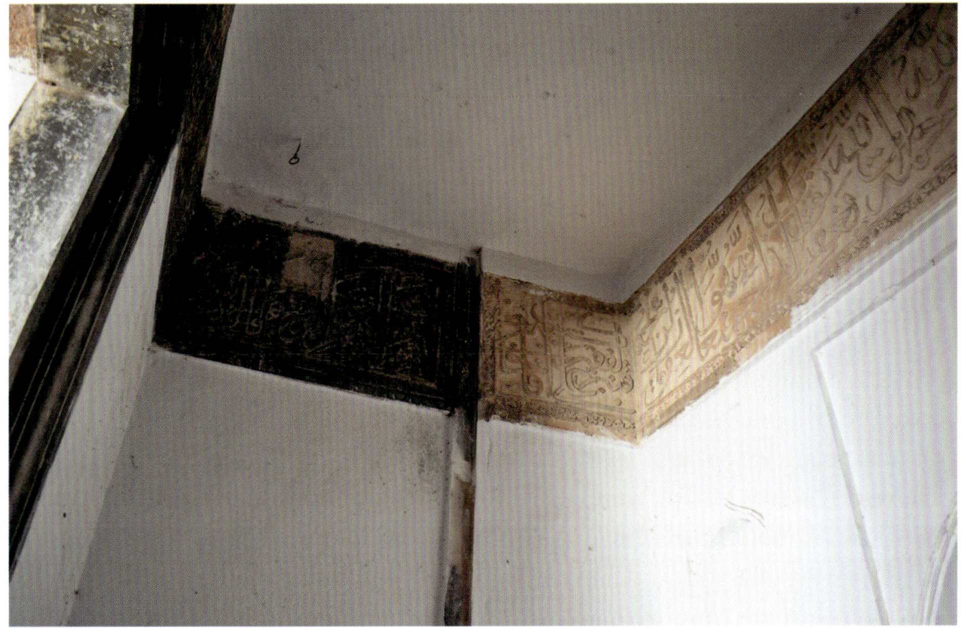

LEFT, FIGURE 5.22.
Black basalt inscription (*left*) on the southwest wall of the octagonal shell at Khalilullah's mausoleum in Ashtur, now located in an enclosed room, with the later inscription mirroring it (*right*).
Photograph by author, 2013.

5.21). The southwest panel, now concealed from the facade, can be accessed only in the interior of an annexed room. A later inscription band mirrors it on the opposite wall that was added to create an enclosed room for burials (fig. 5.22).

The monochrome inscription panels are written in thuluth script, and the crisp, polished carving of the letters is superimposed on floral scroll designs (figs. 5.20, 5.21, and 5.23). This is a configuration that points to intermedial connections with other architecture of the period. The forms are similar to those of inscriptions commonly rendered in tile and, more specifically, to the nearby polychrome tile inscriptions on the facades of the tomb of Ahmad Shah II (fig. 5.13) or the madrasa of Mahmud Gavan in Bidar (fig. 5.14).[38] Carved in basalt stone, the text at the Chaukhandi is distinguished from its background by volume rather than colors. These layers give the panel a three-dimensional quality, comparable in design to stucco counterparts across India.

The inscribed panels consist of Qurʾanic verses. Although some space is reserved for the signature of the artist on the return wall of the southern recessed arch (fig. 5.23), there is no marker dedicated to the Bahmanid rulers or their officials. Instead, such markers are pushed to the outer boundaries of the site, a distinction that finds several parallels in the Neʿmatullahi shrine network.

The Qurʾanic verses inscribed on the panels were chosen not only in relation to the function and context of the building but also to connect its form with cosmic meanings and to guide the experience of the reader through those connections. The Qurʾanic text that appears on the southern wall of the octagon contains verses from Surat al-Raʿd (Q 13:23–24) (fig. 5.20): "In the name of God, the Compassionate, the Merciful. Says God: the Gardens (*Jannat*) of Eternity, which they will enter along with the righteous among their parents, spouses, and descendants. And the angels will enter upon them from every gate, [saying] (23) 'Peace be upon you for your perseverance. How excellent is the ultimate abode!' (24)."

These verses thematize the act of entering while standing over the very entrance of the building. This is an act that concerns both the bodies of the Sufis buried within and the pilgrims who visit them.[39] By referring to kinship relations ("parents, spouses, and descendants"), the verses also speak to the strong familial context of the funerary structure, reflecting the relationships between those whose graves occupy the interior of the dome chamber.

Several features of the verses work together to relay a strong sense of orality. There are intimations of orality in the phrasing of the inscription on this panel and others still in situ. They all start with the phrase "says God"—a common textual and auditory strategy in quotations of the Qurʾan to distinguish the word of God from other texts, especially relevant here as the text of each panel shifts from one chapter of the Qurʾan to another.[40] This auditory element is echoed toward the end of the south wall inscription where the righteous entering heaven—and by extension the visitor entering the tomb—receive

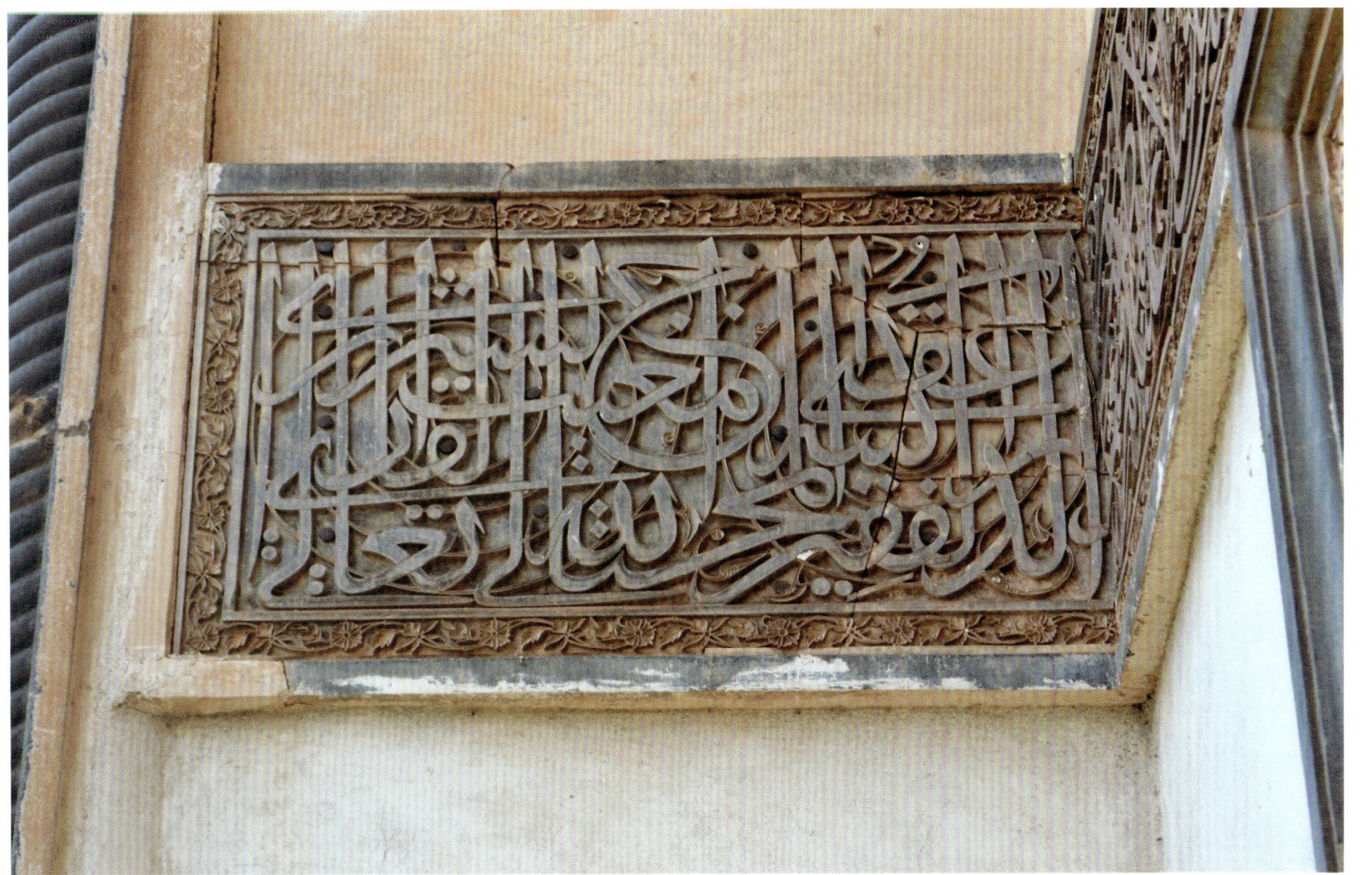

FIGURE 5.23. Side section of the inscription panel on the south wall of the octagonal shell at Khalilullah's mausoleum in Ashtur, containing the signature of Mughith al-Shirazi. *Photograph by author, 2013.*

salutations from angels. The verses on the west wall (Q 33:41–43) emphasize the remembrance of God as a means of guiding believers out of darkness and into the light: "O you who have believed, *remember* Allah with much *remembrance*" (Q 33:41; emphasis added by author). Confirming the oral dimension of the ensemble, two words in this verse, *udhkuru* and *dhikran*, share a root with the word *dhikr* (remembrance, utterance), an oral Sufi ritual grounded in the act of remembering God and verbalizing that memory, especially through the tireless repetition of God's name or short phrases of prayer.[41] This auditory mode of engagement with the word of God accompanies the visual description of paradise in the verses. Together, they bring the company of the dead and invisible cosmic beings to the visitor's imagination. This sensorial act of entrance, activated by the verses of the Qurʾan, could have been intensified by the recitations of the Qurʾan, or dhikr rituals, around the graves inside the octagon.

Multisensory perception of paradise is, as Sebastian Günther points out, a common trope in Qurʾanic descriptions of heaven. Here it finds an architectural resonance in the form of the octagonal shell with its common paradisial associations, which suggest the eight gates or doors of paradise.[42] The Qurʾanic verses inscribed on the panels likewise mention the "gates" from which the

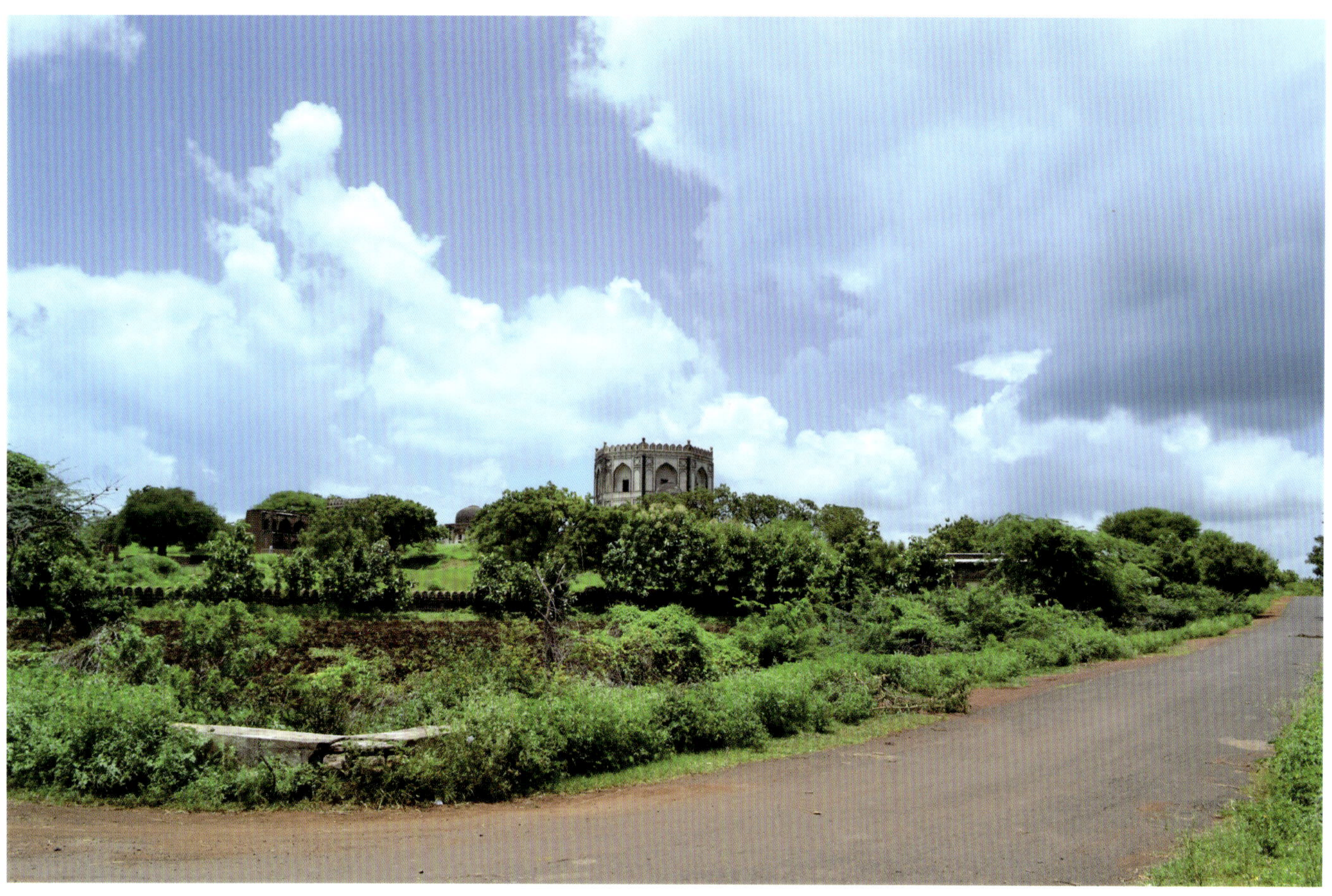

ABOVE, FIGURE 5.24. Surroundings of Khalilullah's mausoleum in Ashtur. *Photograph by author, 2013.*

FACING, FIGURE 5.25. Flyleaf with the octagonal seal of the Neᶜmatullahi descendant Valiullah or Muhibbullah, Bidar, mid- to late fifteenth century. From a manuscript of the *Mataliᶜ al-anzar fi sharh-i tawaliᶜ al-anwar*, copied by Jaᶜfar al-Riza al-ᶜUrayzi al-Husayni and dated 3 Rabiᶜ I 861/January 29, 1457. The manuscript later entered the Bijapur library, as the dated inscription indicates.

angels enter, descending on the believers. The result is a mirroring effect in which the text and the architecture magnify the paradisial connotations of one another. This characterization of the octagon as a combination of gates is further reinforced by its lack of a roof. Separate from the actual dome chamber, the octagon is a threshold whose main function, not unlike the walls of a city and its gates, is to define a boundary. Here at the tomb, it is presented as the boundary between the heavenly and terrestrial realms. To cross this boundary is to enter an architectural image of heaven, just as the voice of the angels announce in the inscription panel.

The term *jannat* on the south panel is the most frequently used word for paradise in the Qurʾan. The lush surroundings of the complex in the village of Ashtur resonate with the literal meaning of *janna*: "garden" (fig. 5.24). But another sense of the word *janna* could also be relevant here, for it has also been defined by Muslim commentators as "to cover, to conceal, to protect."[43] From the outside, the original funerary dome chamber appears to be completely concealed by the gates of the octagon (fig. 5.1). It is only by crossing the threshold of the octagonal shell that the core of the building reveals itself to us.

The word *janna* commonly appears in combination with other words that have paradisial connotations.[44] The south wall, for instance, features the phrase *Jannat-i'adn* (Eden), a combination that occurs six times in the Qurʾan.

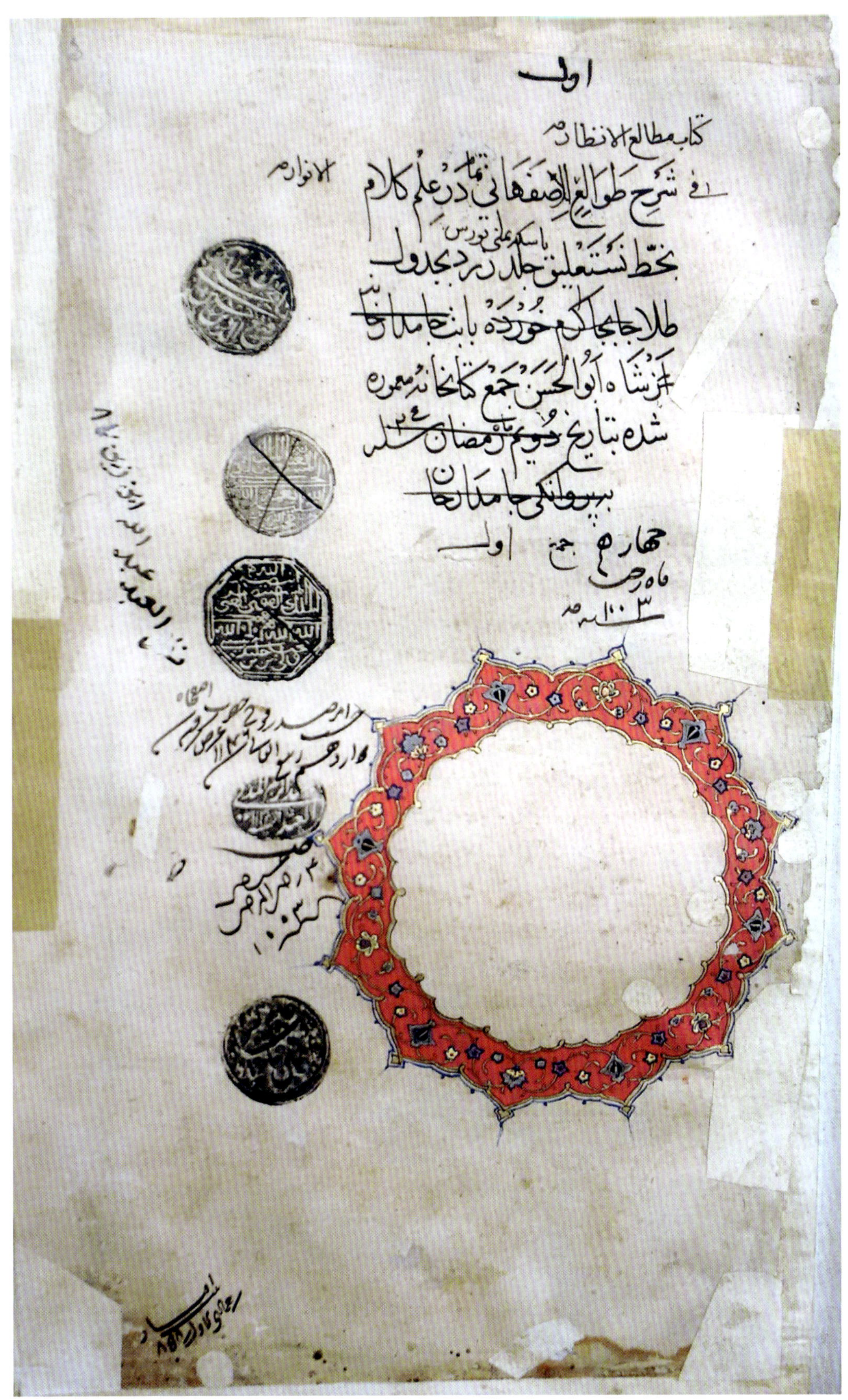

The panel on the southwest wall (Q 18:107), now located inside the annexed room, features another variation of Qurʾanic paradise terminology: jannat al-firdaws (gardens of paradise). This phrase, which also appears above the mihrab of the nearby tomb of the Bahmanid ruler Ahmad Shah I, has a special connection with the Neʿmatullahi family.[45] As a chronogram, it amounts to the year 1431, which marks the death of not only Shah Neʿmatullah but likely also his grandson Nurullah, the first member of the family who traveled to the Deccan. This is the Nurullah discussed earlier in this chapter, whose tomb could correspond to a structure reconstructed on the site in the eighteenth century (app. 5.1). The chronogram jannat al-firdaws was noted in hagiographies of Shah Neʿmatullah and elsewhere in the Neʿmatullahis' network of architectural epigraphy.[46] Given that the verse inscribed on the southwest wall contains the only occurrence of the phrase *jannat al-firdaws* in the Qurʾan, the familial context may have provided another rationale for its selection.

Wrapped around the sacred bodies of Sufis, the octagonal shape of the enclosure established a visual identity for the Neʿmatullahi family in the Deccan. The addition of the octagonal shell distinguishes the mausoleum from all other funerary buildings in the nearby royal necropolis, but it finds resonances in visual materials associated with the Neʿmatullahi descendants—particularly in seals appearing on works on paper. An example of such seals can be found in a mid-fifteenth-century manuscript of the *Mataliʿ al-anzar fi sharh-i tawaliʿ al-anwar* (*Horizons of Logical Reasoning, Commentary on the Rays of Dawn*) now kept at the British Library (IO Bijapur 223A). Dated 861/1457, the colophon of the manuscript contains the signature of the copyist Jaʿfar al-Reza al-ʿUrayzi al-Husayni, who, according to the manuscript's dedication note as well as his titles and signature formula, was a disciple of the Neʿmatullahis. The colophon further records that the volume was dedicated to Shah Muhibbullah, son of Shah Khalilullah.[47]

The manuscript's flyleaf bears two Neʿmatullahi seals: a circular example that belongs to Shah Muhibbullah and an octagonal seal that belongs to either Shah Muhibbullah or one of his sons named Valiullah (fig. 5.25).[48] This twenty-five-millimeter double-ruled octagonal seal features a braided knot in the center dividing the Arabic inscriptions written in thuluth script into two upper and lower registers. The lower register contains a short genealogy of the descendant that likely reads "Valiullah b. Allah b. Khalilullah al-Husayni."[49] Jake Benson has also noted the numbers nine and five on the two sides of the letter *lam* in *al-husayni* and has suggested that this could be part of a date, presumably 895/1489.[50] Shah Muhibbullah (d. ca. 1505) was still alive at this time, but given that the manuscript was completed in 861/1457, it is possible that it had already passed to his son by the time the seal was added, thirty-two years later.

What is interesting in the design of both the octagonal shell in Khalilullah's mausoleum and the seal is their shared function of containment. Just as the octagonal shell wraps around the bodies of the family's descendants buried within and around the dome chamber, the lines making up the outline of the octagonal seal wrap around the names of members of the family. Bodies in the architectural octagon turn into names calligraphed into the seal. The knotted lines in the middle of the octagonal seal resonate with the core of the architecture on the site where the graves are laid out (fig. 5.11). In both cases, the lines of the octagon create a threshold around the space occupied by the Sufi family, like a skin that marks a space of their own.

III. The Many Dimensions of Epigraphy: Cosmic, Transregional, Temporal

The connection between the site of Khalilullah's burial and the art of writing noted above is not an isolated example. Ideas about the mystical aspects of calligraphy circulated in Bidar, as in many other centers of cultural production. In Bidar's case, they were frequently entangled with the Neʿmatullahi network.[51] Such connections are epitomized by a treatise on the forms, aesthetics, and spiritual connotations of calligraphy, titled *Tuhfat al-muhibbin*. According to internal textual evidence, it was completed in fifteenth-century Bidar, but the earliest surviving copy is an eighteenth-century manuscript.[52] The itinerant author of this treatise, Yaʿqub b. Hasan b. Shaykh, known as Siraj al-Husayni al-Shirazi (fl. 1436–54), was a well-known calligrapher connected with the Timurid court workshop in Shiraz. He was the scribe of two copies of the famous *Zafarnama*, a panegyric text on the life of Timur commissioned by his grandson and governor of Shiraz Ibrahim Sultan.[53] Given the demand for bookmaking and the art of writing in fifteenth-century Bidar, which I have outlined elsewhere, the calligraphic treatise could have been an important asset not only in training calligraphers for an increasingly expanding collection of manuscripts and building projects in the fifteenth-century Deccan but also for its contribution to intellectual conversations around the mystical dimensions of calligraphy that were an important aspect of the connections between Deccan India and Iran at the time.[54]

Two threads connect the *Tuhfat al-muhibbin* to the Neʿmatullahi circle and their funerary site in Bidar. First, the author, Siraj al-Shirazi, was a Neʿmatullahi disciple and dedicated the treatise to Shah Muhibbullah, son of Shah Khalilullah. The author enumerates all the spiritual characters of Muhibbullah that made him a suitable patron for the treatise, a narrative all the more significant because it makes no references to the Bahmanid rulers of Bidar at the time.[55] The second thread lies in broader connections with Shiraz: both Siraj al-Shirazi and the calligrapher of the inscription at Khalilullah's mausoleum, whose name is recorded in the panel as Mughith al-Qari al-Shirazi (fig. 5.25), had a Shirazi *nisba* (affiliation). Siraj is also documented as having worked at the Timurid atelier in Shiraz.[56]

The same monsoon winds that facilitated the mobility of Sufis across the Indian Ocean allowed these artists, alongside literary scholars, historians, and merchants, to travel extensively between various parts of the Indian Ocean rim and the Deccan. The Deccan's artistic and literary productions in this period are characterized by such an intensity of movements.[57] The artistic and political connections of a Sufi network like the Neʿmatullahis both enabled such mobilities and in turn came to be amplified by them. With regard to Shiraz, there was also a particular diplomatic context that worked in tandem with the transregional agency of Sufi networks. Diplomatic letters and gifts, including manuscripts, were exchanged between the Timurid prince and governor of Shiraz Ibrahim Sultan (r. 1415–35) and the Bahmanid ruler Ahmad Shah I, as recorded in the *Munshaʾat* of Sharaf al-din ʿAli Yazdi.[58] Ibrahim Sultan, who was recognized for his calligraphic skills in writing Qurʾans and designing architectural inscriptions, wrote a personal note in a Qurʾan manuscript that was sent to the library of the Bahmanid sultan in Bidar as a gift.[59] In one of his letters, Ibrahim Sultan gives us a glimpse of these oceanic connections, describing the water as a connecter. As he puts it, his territories and those of the Bahmanid sultan were "united by the sea between them."[60]

In this light, the function of the inscriptions at the mausoleum of Shah Khalilullah in Bidar was not only to invest the inner workings of the architecture with cosmic meanings. They also had an earthly, outward-looking function that highlighted Bidar's transregional connections in this period. Such connections are evident in the most basic purpose of the structure as a container for the bodies of itinerant Sufis, which linked Bidar to their places of origin as well as all other sacred nodes that they had visited or inhabited. But they can also be seen in the transregional networks of artists who contributed to the making of these carved stone inscriptions and left their marks on the structure, even though many aspects of these artistic collaborations have since been lost to us.[61]

This display of transregional genealogies of art making and devotion finds a parallel in another panel in Khalilullah's funerary complex, which likely marked the outermost boundary of the site. The panel's inscription links the significance of water for sacred sites with transregional narratives of patronage and shared Persianate genealogies of kingship. Featuring seven Persian couplets written in two columns of naskh script, the tablet records another construction on the site in the first half of the fifteenth century. Found about 460 meters to the northwest of the octagonal shell by Yazdani, the panel is currently kept at the Bidar Fort Museum (fig. 5.26).[62] Through the content of these verses, we know that the tablet was connected to the construction of a *baʾin* during the reign of the Bahmanid ruler ʿAla al-din Ahmad II, son of Ahmad Shah I (app. 5.2). The structure was completed on the 9th of Rajab 850 / September 30, 1446, by the patron Nasir b. ʿAla Khanshah, who is praised in the poem. The term *baʾin* (in Dakhni) could be synonymous with *baoli* (stepwell).[63] It is therefore reasonable to assume that this tablet is the foundation inscription of the reservoir located in the southern part of the site, or at least an earlier iteration of it (fig. 5.27). Nasir b. ʿAla Khanshah, the patron of the structure, could be the same person as Nasir Khan, who, according to chronicler Fereshteh, was the ruler of Asir (Asirgarh, to the north of Burhanpur) and whose daughter married ʿAla al-din Ahmad Shah II in 1428–29.[64]

With minor changes to Yazdani's translation, the inscribed lines read as follows (app. 5.2):[65]

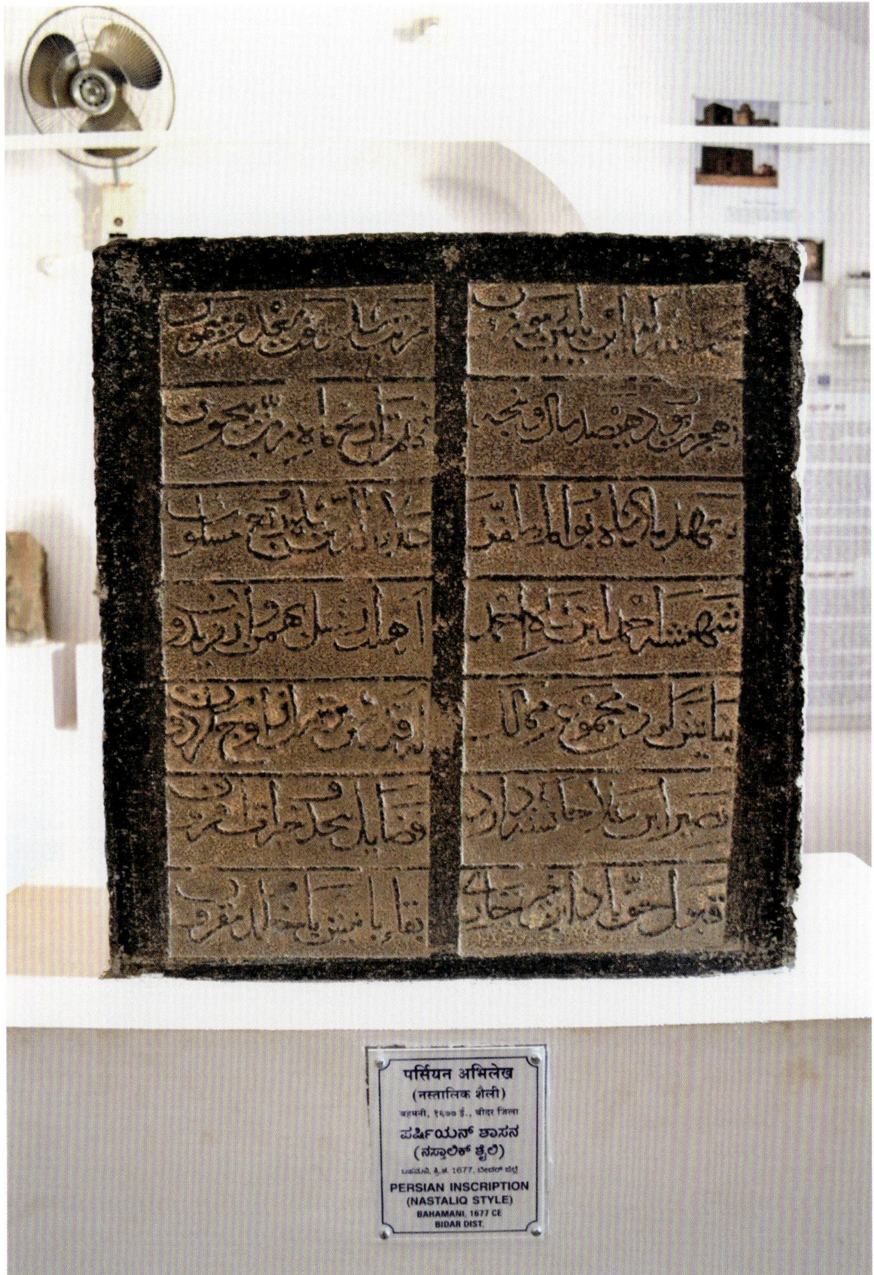

FIGURE 5.26. Inscribed tablet found on the site of Khalilullah's mausoleum in Ashtur, currently at the Bidar Fort Museum. *Photograph by author, 2017.*

Praise be to God, this delightful baʾin was built in an auspicious and happy time,
the hijri year was 850 and it was the 9th of the month of Rajab,
during the reign of the victorious king, ʿAla al-din, the sovereign of the inhabited [quarter of the] world,
the emperor Ahmad, son of King Ahmad, who is the descendant of Bahman and Faridun,
who built whole kingdoms, higher than the Heaven.
Nasir, son of ʿAla Khanshah, who possesses innumerable virtues and whose charity is increasing,
may God accept this flowing (*jari*) charity and may its builder enter Heaven.

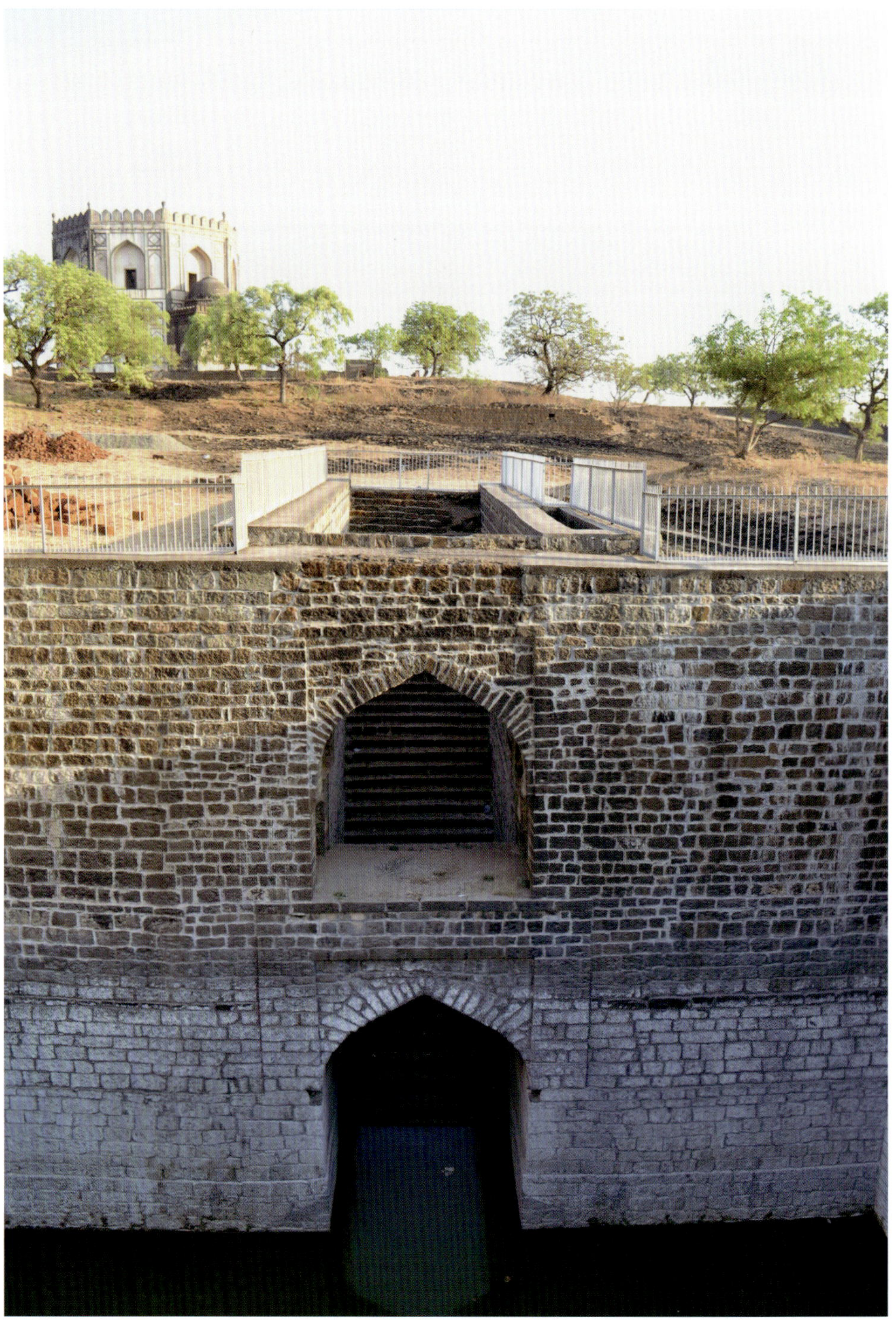

FIGURE 5.27. Stepwell in the southern part of Khalilullah's funerary site in Ashtur. *Photograph by author, 2017.*

Although a modest structure within the broader complex, Nasir Khan's "flowing" endowment—a nod at it being a water structure—is symbolically important for several reasons.[66] First, his act of charity, which is undertaken under the name of his son-in-law, the Bahmanid ruler, and documented in their shared foundation inscription, provided the site with access to water throughout the year. Stepwells were common in Bidar, and, given the efficiency of Bidar's soil in holding water, they were an appropriate method of storage.[67] Since the complex was already associated with the Neʿmatullahi family by the time of the stepwell's construction, this endowment could be an indication that the site received a considerable number of pilgrims and visitors.

Second, for the Bahmanid ruler and his official, whose names are inscribed on the tablet, the endowment offered a point of access and representation in a site that possessed spiritual and political authority. Transregional connections also played into this act of image making for the Bahmanids. Written in Persian and installed on a site associated with an Iranian Sufi family, the tablet glorifies the Bahmanid king by referring to his "ancestors," Bahman and Faridun, ancient Iranian kings and *Shahnama* (*Book of Kings*) heroes with whom the dynasty connected their lineage. This, of course, was one of several strategies of self-fashioning for the dynasty and a common genealogical trope in India.[68] In this respect, the sacred site embodied an appropriate landscape for both the spiritual and the genealogical claims on which the Bahmanids were building their models of kingship.[69] Yet, most importantly for the discussion in this chapter, Bahmanid efforts to build on the genealogical roots of the Neʿmatullahi Sufis and their spiritual power were predicated on considerations of distance and proximity. The inscription's representation of kingship appears on the outermost boundary of the site, at a measured distance from its core and from inscriptions that mark connections with the Sufi family.

As a whole, Khalilullah's funerary site exists in an intriguing dialogical relationship with the Bahmanid royal necropolis located a short distance to the east (fig. 5.10).[70] This proximity mimics the pattern established in the Bahmanids' earlier capital of Gulbarga, where tombs of the early Bahmanids are positioned near the burial of the Sufi Shaykh Siraj al-din Junaydi (d. 1379–80), who is said to have blessed the reign of Hasan, the founder of the dynasty. The later Bahmanids of Gulbarga are buried near the Sufi shrine of the Chishti Sufi Gisu Daraz (d. 1422).[71] This is a very different configuration compared, for instance, to the later Mughal emperors who were buried *inside* the shrine of Sufi masters.[72] In the Bahmanid examples, this carefully controlled distance creates a space for a dialogue between the royal and Sufi funerary structures. In Ashtur, in addition to their distance from one another, the height of Khalilullah's mausoleum in relation to the Bahmanid tombs is noteworthy: the Sufi's tomb is situated on a hill about fifty meters higher than the Bahmanid tombs, which gives the mausoleum a significant topographical position in relation to the royal necropolis.[73] This dominant position is especially evident in vistas opened onto the royal tombs from the upper-floor balconies of Khalilullah's mausoleum or from different vantages throughout the surrounding landscape (figs. 5.28 and 5.29).

On an even larger scale, there is the relationship between Khalilullah's complex and urban nodes of power. In Bidar, like the earlier capital of the Bahmanids, Gulbarga, the shrines of Sufis closely affiliated with the court are located just outside the capital (fig. 5.30). The location of the Neʿmatullahis' funerary architecture in Bidar reflects the sociopolitical roles that members

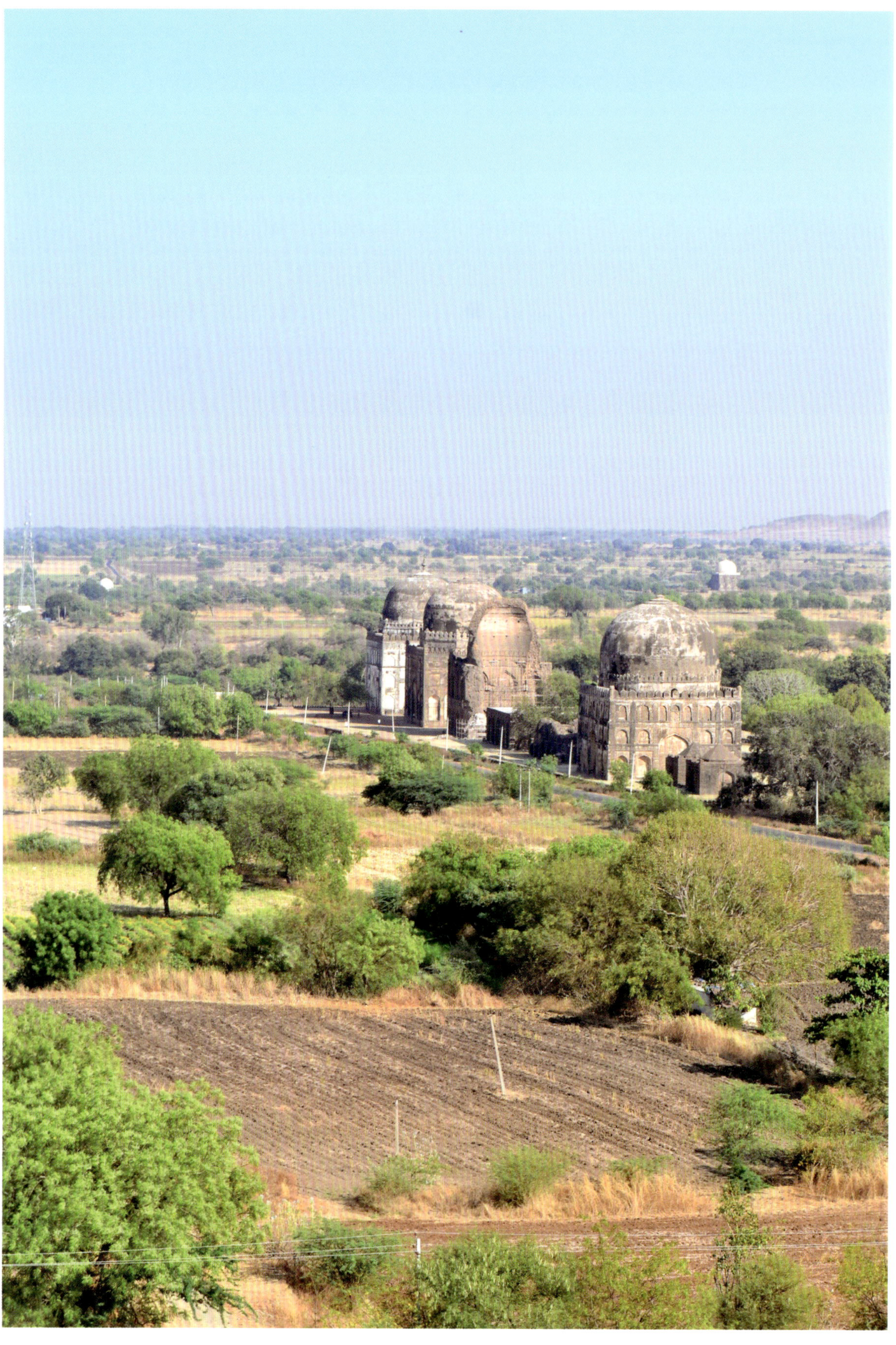

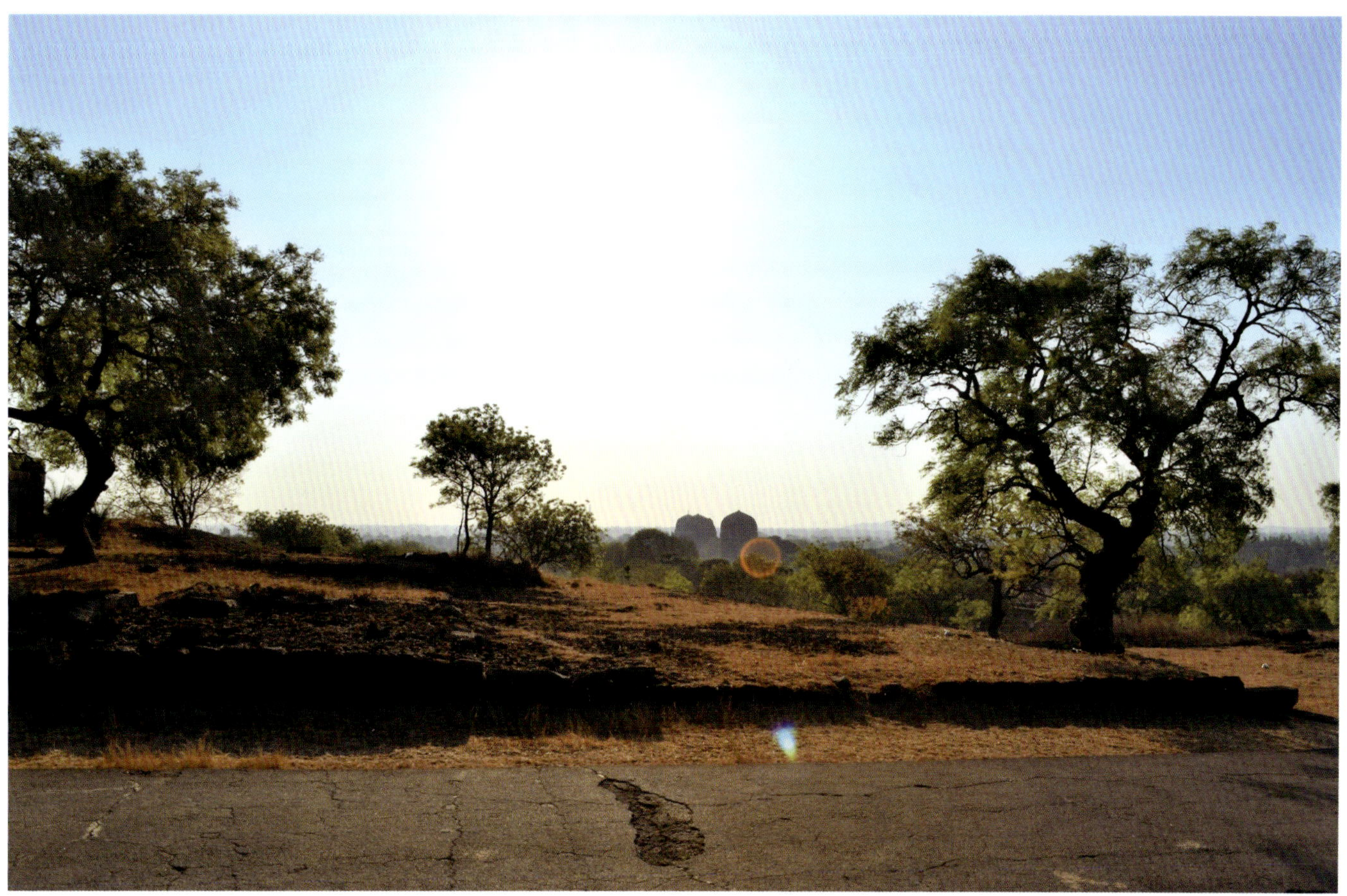

of the family held vis-à-vis their patrons in the Deccan, different from their links with the courts in the central-western regions of today's Iran. While the khanaqahs of the Neᶜmatullahis in Taft and Mahan were located at a distance from the seat of power or even from secondary capitals such as Yazd (similar to other Sufi shrines under the Timurids, such as the complex in Turbat-i Jam), buildings that the Bahmanids commissioned for the Chishti and Neᶜmatullahi Sufis were located in or just outside the capitals of the time.[74] This urban configuration between the court and the shrines in Bahmanid capitals, which also entailed certain challenges, should be read as a strong political and religious statement on the parts of both the Sufis and the rulers in Iran and Deccan India.[75]

How did these notions of distance and proximity play into the sacred sites of the family in Iran? Several threads connect the strategies adopted to create a sense of belonging in the Neᶜmatullahi shrines in Iran and Deccan India. Similar to Khalilullah's mausoleum in Bidar, there seems to be an aversion to sharing intimate spaces with ruling patrons in the shrine at Mahan. Surfaces that bore marks of patronage beyond the Neᶜmatullahi circle were strategically positioned on the outsides of buildings. On the other hand, on many inner surfaces of the Mahan shrine, there are pointed efforts to stamp the building with the names of family members, claiming the space as their own.

FACING, FIGURE 5.28.
View of the Bahmanid royal tombs from the upper floor of the octagonal shell at Khalilullah's mausoleum in Ashtur. *Photograph by author, 2017.*

ABOVE, FIGURE 5.29.
View of the Bahmanid royal tombs from Khalilullah's funerary site in Ashtur. *Photograph by author, 2017.*

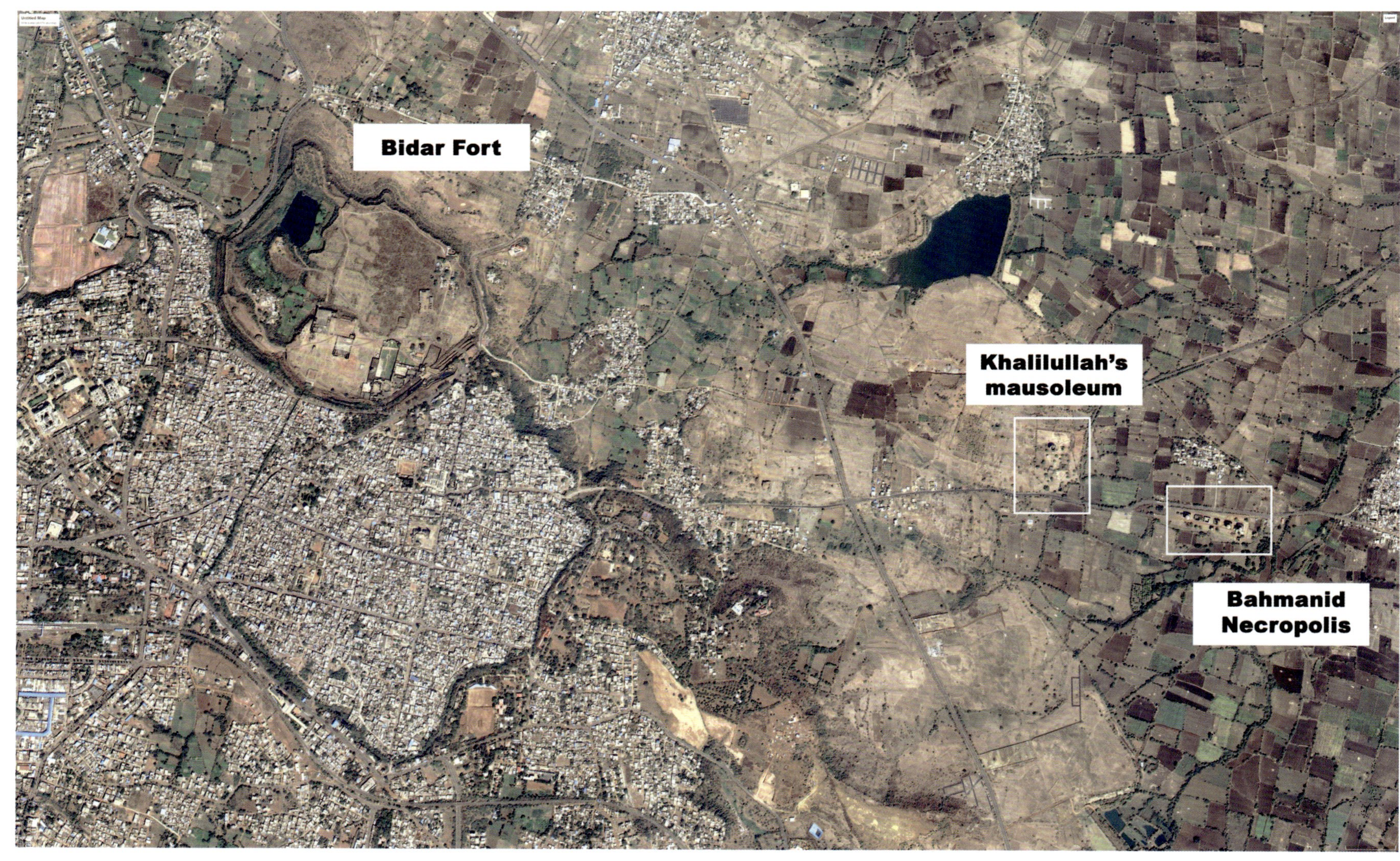

FIGURE 5.30. Aerial view of Bidar and its environs, showing the relationship between the Bidar Fort, Khalilullah's mausoleum, and the Bahmanid necropolis in Ashtur. *Google Earth Pro; with additions by author.*

IV. The Art of Citation: Inside the Sacred Mausoleum in Mahan

Entering the innermost part of the shrine at Mahan, the dome chamber housing the cenotaph of Shah Neʿmatullah Vali, is an optic and haptic exercise in adjusting to scale. Due to the dominating height of the space, the eyes' initial point of concentration on the cenotaph is drawn upward along the vertical axis into the dome (fig. 1.13). In between, painted motifs dot the surfaces of the white plastered walls: teardrop medallions flanking shallow recessed niches, small eighteen-pointed stars on the spandrels, and alternating four-piece palmettes and eight-lobed flowers on the borders between the niches on the walls. Beneath the zone of transition, these paintings may not be original.[76] Regardless, the relative density of the patterns above the zone of transition leads the eye of the beholder toward the dome. There, painted motifs dominate the white surfaces. These paintings resonate with the few surviving wall paintings from the fourteenth and fifteenth centuries, textual descriptions of Timurid murals of gold and lapis pigments, and wall paintings depicted in architectural spaces within manuscript illustrations from the period.[77]

The space's upward visual trajectory facilitates the pilgrim's encounter with the epigraphic bands arranged in two registers on the walls of the chamber (fig. 5.31). The lower of these two registers appears across the four recessed arched niches on each side of the dome chamber, topping the four entrances

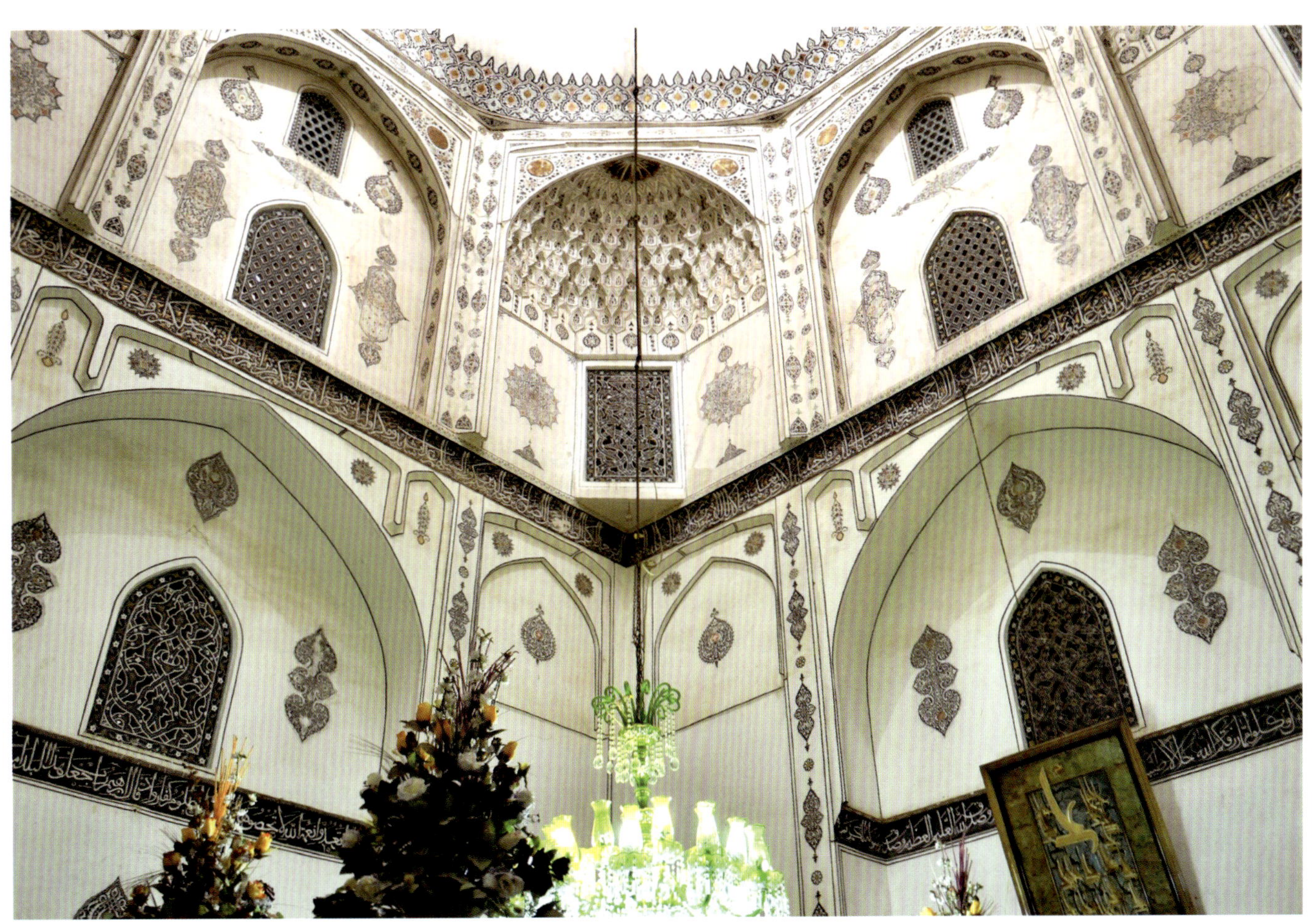

FIGURE 5.31. Inscription bands in the interior of Shah Neʿmatullah's tomb in Mahan, Iran. *Photograph by author, 2013.*

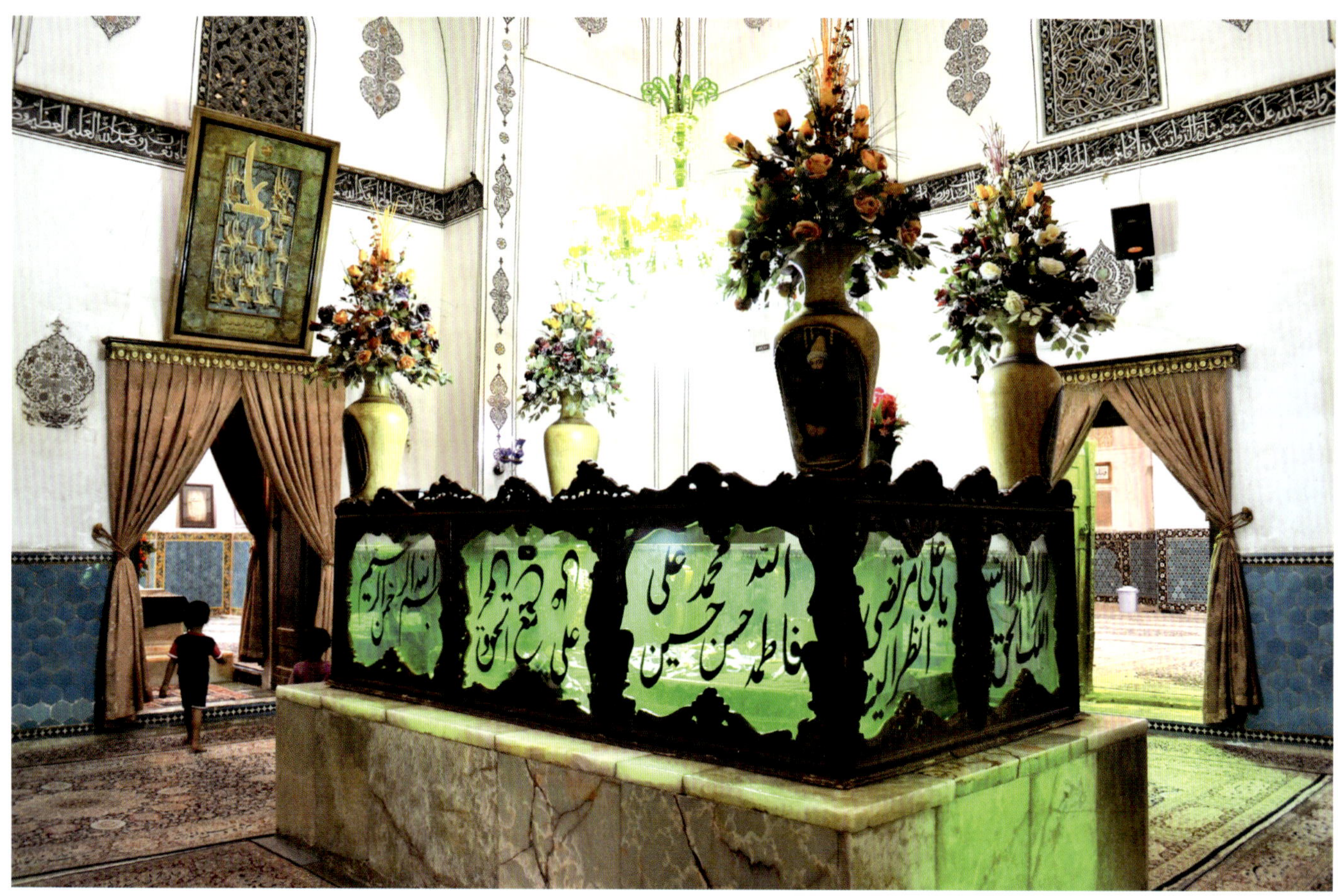

FIGURE 5.32. Interior view of Shah Neʿmatullah's tomb in Mahan, showing his cenotaph and the lower register of inscription bands above the doors. *Photograph by author, 2013.*

of the room (fig. 5.32). Painted over plaster, the words are written in white thuluth script against a dark-blue background, adorned by scrolls and leaves in light blue and amber, mimicking the aesthetics of tile inscription panels. All of these panels contain verses from various chapters of the Qurʾan. From the southern panel, moving counterclockwise back to the main entrance on the western wall, these include verses from Surat al-Nahl (Q 16:114), al-Ibrahim (Q 14:34–35), al-Nahl again (Q 16:18–21), and al-Maʾidah (Q 5:7).

Far more than a patchwork of quotations from the Qurʾan, these verses create a narrative that unfolds as the pilgrim walks around the cenotaph upon entry from the west.[78] The themes range from the worship of God (south wall) to prayers for protection from the worship of idols (east), the inability of idols to create or save their followers on the day of resurrection (north), and a reminder to believers of their covenant with God and his all-encompassing knowledge of what is hidden in their hearts (west). Although plucked from different chapters of the Qurʾan, each panel manifests careful deliberation, as the themes echo and respond to those in each preceding panel.

The emphatic presence of God's word in the space is established both by positioning these inscriptions in visually accessible locations on the walls and by crafting a sensory experience for the viewer that extends beyond the visual. Qurʾanic verses on the west wall (Q 5:7) remind the reader of "the covenant God made with you when you said, we hear and obey." In the Qurʾan, hearing and deafness are tightly woven into themes of knowledge and obedience. Emphasizing this direct quotation, a version of the phrase "said God the Almighty" is added at the beginning of every single inscription panel on the four walls, similar to the panels in Bidar. In both places, the reminder that one is encountering the word of God is intensified by the auditory sensation implied by the word *qala* (Arabic for *said*) as it reverberates across each wall.

The blessing and prosperity bestowed by God is a unifying theme across the chosen verses, tying each thread into a coherent program. Without exception, all four panels dedicate noticeable space to commenting on God's blessing: "eat from the good, lawful things which God has provided for you, and be grateful for God's blessing" (Q 16:114); "if you tried to count God's blessings, you would never be able to number them" (repeated in Q 14:34 and 16:18); and "remember God's blessing upon you" (Q 5:7). The phrase "God's blessing" in all these verses is none other than "Neʿmat Allah"—the most widely used title of Shah Neʿmatullah Vali. This self-referential quality of the interior program arrives at an even more sacred plane in that it is "God the Almighty" who repeats Neʿmatullah's name, reminding the visitor that the Sufi himself is God's blessing upon his followers, one whose greatness cannot be measured.

This rationale for the choice of verses is echoed in the mausoleum's tent band: the longest inscribed space in the interior of the tomb, which follows a similar but busier aesthetic in comparison to the smaller panels below (fig. 5.31). Quoting verses from the Surat al-Fatir (Originator) (Q 35: 3–11), the panel opens with a reminder: "Remember God's favor (Neʿmat Allah) upon you"—a message that is followed by another reminder of the unity of God.

The intent of the choice of verses for the five epigraphic panels in the chamber becomes even more evident when we look at them in the context of their source, the Qurʾan. The combination of the words *Neʿmat* and *Allah* appears in nineteen verses in total, spread over eleven different chapters. Surat al-Nahl (Bee) contains the highest frequency (five in total), which also happens to be the only chapter quoted twice inside the Mahan mausoleum. Of these verses, some are reminders of the blessings of God to believers; some invite them to count God's blessings, implying their abundance; and others comment on the denial of God's blessing. All the chosen verses in Shah Neʿmatullah's tomb are from the first two categories, leaving out Qurʾanic usage of the phrase *Neʿmat Allah* in a negative context.

This web of self-referential inscriptions, investing Shah Neʿmatullah's name with Qurʾanic metaphors, was a subtle yet forceful strategy by which the Sufis marked the space as their own. The humility of veiling the Sufi's name in a network of quoted texts is balanced by the power of inscribing family members into the sacred space and, indeed, of appropriating the word of God for this purpose. In many instances, the names of the family members were chosen for their Qurʾanic connotations in the first place. Nevertheless, this intricate appropriation of Qurʾanic texts has the effect of lending an air of predestination to the connection between the text, the architecture, and the Sufi commemorated in it.

This power of naming was brought to fruition through architecture and the work of people who parsed these verses out of the Qurʾan. The latter involved either memorized knowledge of the text or digging through large bodies of physical books, then selecting appropriate citations, writing them in calligraphy, painting them onto plaster, or transferring them to tiles. Reversing that process has been made easy for the modern scholar through the emergences of databases, encyclopedias, and search engines. But it is important to recognize the significance of such a slow, labor-intensive process of architectural citation, which required a wealth of textual and practical knowledge and has not received the attention it deserves in past scholarship.

These citations transform the inner skin of the architecture into a network of belonging, claiming the space through inscriptions of the Sufi's name and metaphors that weave the sacred word into the material of the walls. In this way, the interior substantially differs from the portal marking the outer border of the dome chamber. If the facade of the portal offered a slate of text and image for the collective representation of patrons and artists (fig. 1.1), the interior of the dome chamber is not a space to be shared between the Sufis and their patrons. The interior remains an intimate space of their own.

V. Weaving an Epigraphic Network

The web of metaphors inside the Mahan mausoleum also connects the architecture to other sacred sites of the Sufi network. The interior of the tomb of Ahmad Shah I in Bidar builds on this self-referential dynamic between text and architecture. Ahmad Shah's tomb, as I will discuss in the next chapter, translates Mahan's hierarchical relation between the word of God and the Sufi into one between the poetry of the Sufi and the praise of the king-disciple, appropriating Shah Neʿmatullah's own poems. Descendants of Shah Neʿmatullah continue this technique of self-representation as well, as surviving epigraphy from the Taft khanaqah attests.

An extant inscription panel from Taft offers a close parallel to the strategies adopted in the interior of the Mahan mausoleum (fig. 5.33). The inscription in question appears on a tile panel now kept at the National Museum in Tehran (no. 3279). Featuring high-quality calligraphy and tilework execution, this panel has been a prized object in the National Museum since its inauguration. Arthur Upham Pope's 1946 publication in *Bulletin of the Iranian Institute*, which aimed to contextualize the collection of the National Museum among international collections of Persian art, shows this panel fixed into a wall at the National Museum, a display strategy that has remained unchanged although the panel has since moved to the adjacent building of the Museum of Islamic Archaeology and Art of Iran.[79] Pope attributes the inscription panel to "a Sufi monastery from Taft," and Iraj Afshar notes that while the original location of the panel is unknown, it probably came from the Taft khanaqah.[80] A study

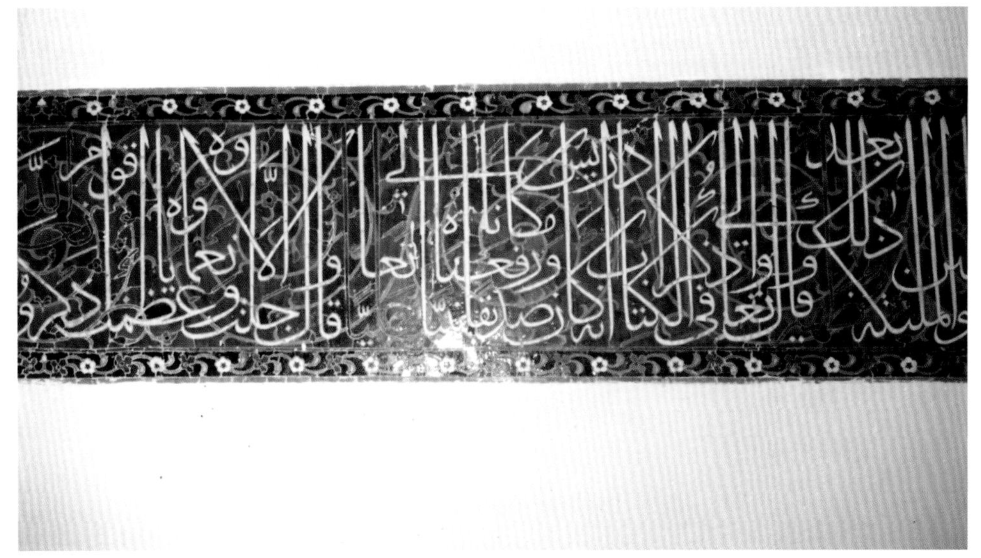

FIGURE 5.33. Section from a tile panel from the Shah Vali complex in Taft, containing the inscription of the name Zahir in amber (*right*). © *National Museum of Iran, no. 3279.*

of the content of inscriptions confirms the panel's provenance from the Shah Vali khanaqah in Taft.

Dated 876/1471–72, the panel contains quotations from three different chapters of the Qurʾan (Q 66:4; 19:56–57; and 5:20–21), followed by a hadith on grave visitation as well as the signature of the scribe Mahmud (app. 5.3).[81] Similar to the inscriptions in Mahan, those on this panel bear the name of Neʿmat Allah, reminding believers of God's blessings upon them by way of quoting two verses from the Surat al-Maʾidah (Q 5:20–21)—a chapter that is also cited in Mahan. All words are inscribed in the thuluth script in white against a dark-blue background, except a few that are singled out and written in amber: *Allah*, *nabi* (Prophet), *ʿAli*, and, most relevant to the panel here, *Neʿmat Allah* and *Zahir* (supporter). Apart from its Qurʾanic meaning, the word *zahir* is an allusion to Zahir al-din ʿAli, son of Nurullah (one of the grandsons of Shah Neʿmatullah). Zahir al-din was an active member of the Neʿmatullahi family, as is evident from his letters on tax negotiations to the Timurid court at Khurasan and to other members of the family in the Deccan.[82] After the death of the Timurid ruler Shahrukh (r. 1405–47), Zahir al-din visited Sultan Muhammad ibn Baysunghur (r. 1447–51) in Isfahan as one of three representatives of Yazd and was given suyurghal—a financial source that may relate to the structure(s) he patronized in Taft, for which we have no attributable architectural and textual evidence other than this panel.[83]

On the panel, Zahir's name appears in a quotation of verses from the Surat al-Tahrim (The Prohibition) that comment on repentance and penance in an episode that refers to the wives of the Prophet, ending with the line "and Gabriel, the righteous believers, and the angels are his [the Prophet's] supporters (zahir) as well." On first glance, the verses that allow for the appearance of the name Zahir do not seem to bear a link with the architecture. It is important to note, however, that the word *zahir* appears only twice in the Qurʾan. The other instance (Q 34:22), involving themes of heaven, earth, and false claims to divinity, renders zahir in a negative light: "None of them is a helper (zahir) to God." These limited choices for a Qurʾanic reference to the name Zahir could explain the choice of quotation in the panel at Taft. Here, an appropriate reference to the Neʿmatullahi patron was prioritized over the relationship between the content of the verse and the architecture.

The network of epigraphic self-references offers an interesting intersection of the Qurʾan and poetry in several Neʿmatullahi sites. In Taft, alongside the above-cited Qurʾanic panel, a poem attributed to Sharaf al-din ʿAli Yazdi, written for an inscription at the Taft khanaqah, engages in wordplay on the name of Ziaʾ al-din Nurullah, another descendant of Shah Neʿmatullah and a patron of the site.[84] Qurʾanic quotations in Mahan and Taft also bear an intriguing yet subtle connection with the poetic inscriptions that once adorned a facade at the Taft complex and are now known only through textual descriptions. The Qurʾanic verses in question are 5:7 (Mahan) and 5:20 (Taft) from the Surat al-Maʾidah (meaning The Table, or The Table Spread with Food), reminding believers of God's blessings. Lost poetic inscriptions in Taft, which have survived in both local histories and the Sufi's hagiography, play with the double meanings of the words *Neʿmat Allah* and the idea of a cloth spread with food (Persian *sofreh* and Arabic *maʾidah*). The poem, which was discussed in chapter 3 in relation to the Neʿmatullahi network and Timurid politics, gains another level of significance in light of the web of Qurʾanic citations in Taft and Mahan discussed in this chapter (app. 3.1).[85] The first couplet indicates that if one "wishes to host [Shah] Neʿmatullah," or, in an alternate reading of the phrase, "wishes to hold a banquet with God's blessings," "the tablecloth (sofreh) must stretch all the way around the sphere of the world." In this way, the poetic verses reference the chapter Maʾidah through a mention of its name—albeit in a different language. The poem also offers a response to and a poetic translation of both Qurʾanic verses from the Maʾidah inscribed in Mahan and Taft, which denote the inability of the created to enumerate God's blessings.

Much like the engagement between Shah Neʿmatullah's poetry and the prophetic hadith in the Taft inscription, as discussed in chapter 4, the reuse of Qurʾanic verses and the Sufi's poetry becomes a veritable language of its own through architecture. It is the juxtaposition of the two—self-referential language and architecture—that allowed the Neʿmatullahis to claim these spaces and speak directly to the beholder, then and now.

The "tablecloth" spread around the globe in the poem becomes a metaphor for the network of Neʿmatullahi shrines interwoven across the Arabian Sea. This metaphor and the textile connotations of the sofreh also point toward a range of textiles—real, imagined, and imitated in architecture—that linked these sacred spaces together. Like many other Sufi networks, textile items worn on the body or used as furnishing, such as the taj (hat), khirqa (cloak), and various types of carpets, played a crucial role in the strategies of self-representation among the Neʿmatullahis. Tactile and intimate encounters around woven stuffs were at the heart of their Sufi rituals and symbolic encounters with kings and elites as textual sources—several of which have been discussed so far—elucidate. Yet material remains and representations of these textiles and woven items are quite rare before the nineteenth century.[86] In chapter 8, I will discuss an architectural representation of the Neᶜmatullahi taj from the seventeenth century.[87] Returning to Mahan, the next section focuses on a literal corpus of carpets that looms large in this devotional network.

VI. The Mahan Carpet Fragments

In the middle of the seventeenth century, a group of luxurious inscribed carpets was commissioned for the dome chamber of the shrine at Mahan. Though the carpets were removed from the shrine in the nineteenth century, seven fragments survive in the collection of the National Museum of Bosnia and Herzegovina (BiH).[88] Based on the surviving pieces, it is likely that the complete set comprised three carpets that fitted together around the cenotaph of Shah Neᶜmatullah in the Mahan dome chamber (figs. 5.34 and 5.35).[89]

The Mahan fragments are woolen-pile carpets woven in the so-called vase technique style, common among carpets of central Iran and Kerman from the Safavid period (fig. 5.36). Such carpets included both vase and animal designs. They were objects of fascination among Europeans who described them in accounts of their travels through Iran in the early modern period.[90]

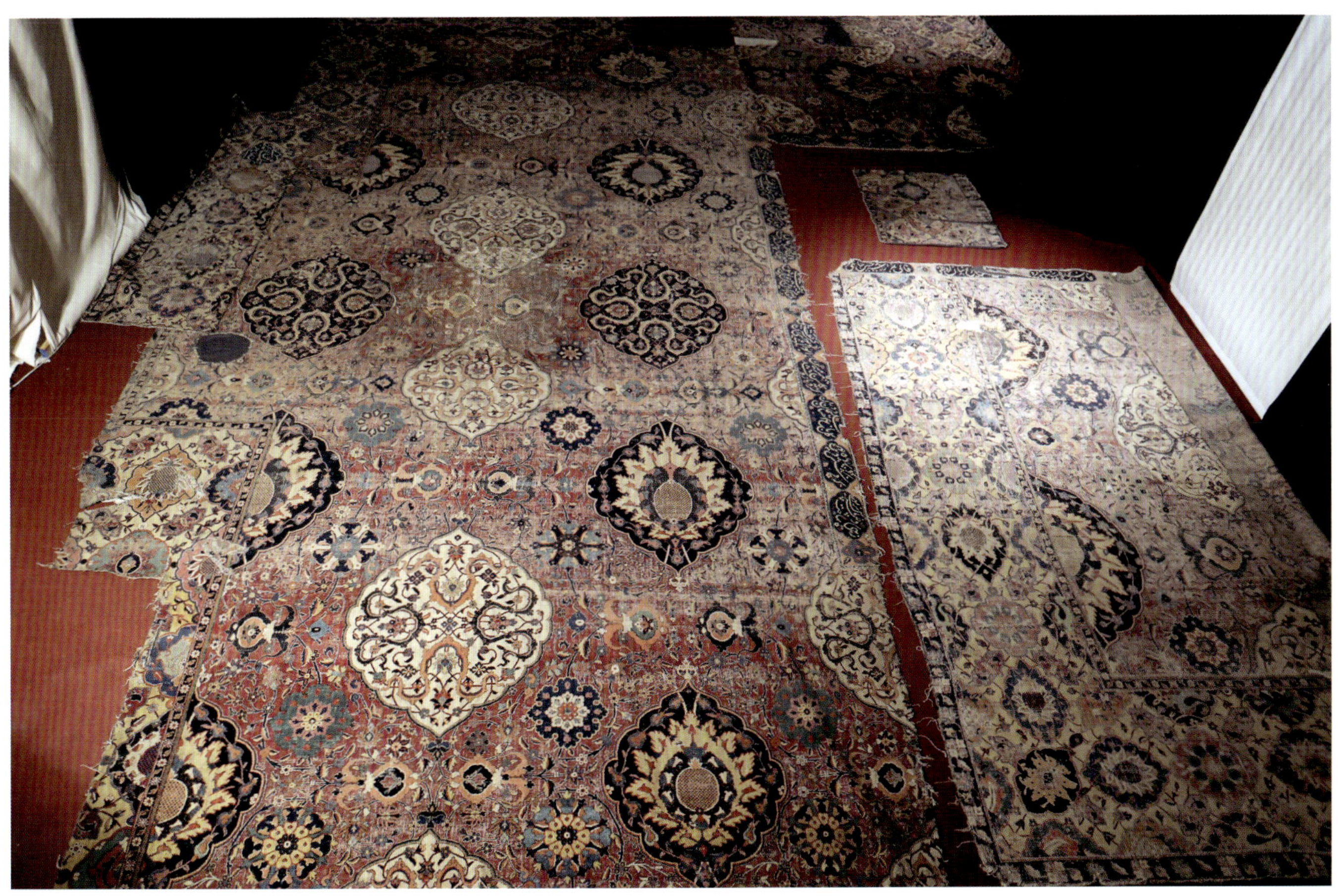

FIGURE 5.34. Surviving fragments of the Mahan carpets made for the mausoleum of Shah Neᶜmatullah in Mahan. *Photograph by Azra Becevic. © The National Museum of Bosnia and Herzegovina, no. 1049.*

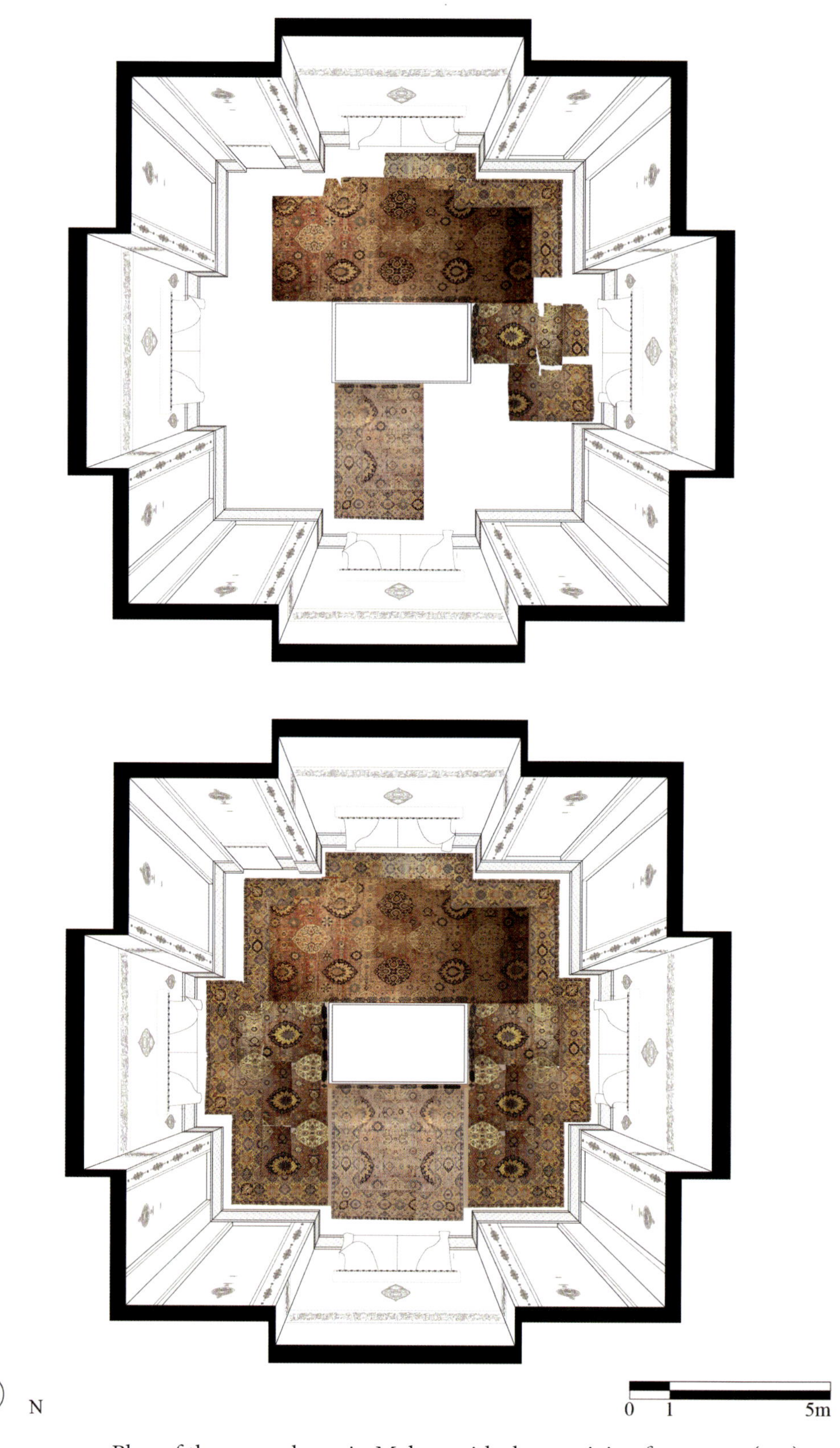

FIGURE 5.35. Plan of the mausoleum in Mahan with the surviving fragments (*top*) and a reconstruction of the lost fragments alongside the surviving ones (*bottom*). Reconstructed by the author, in collaboration with Farah Michel. *Drawings by Farah Michel.*

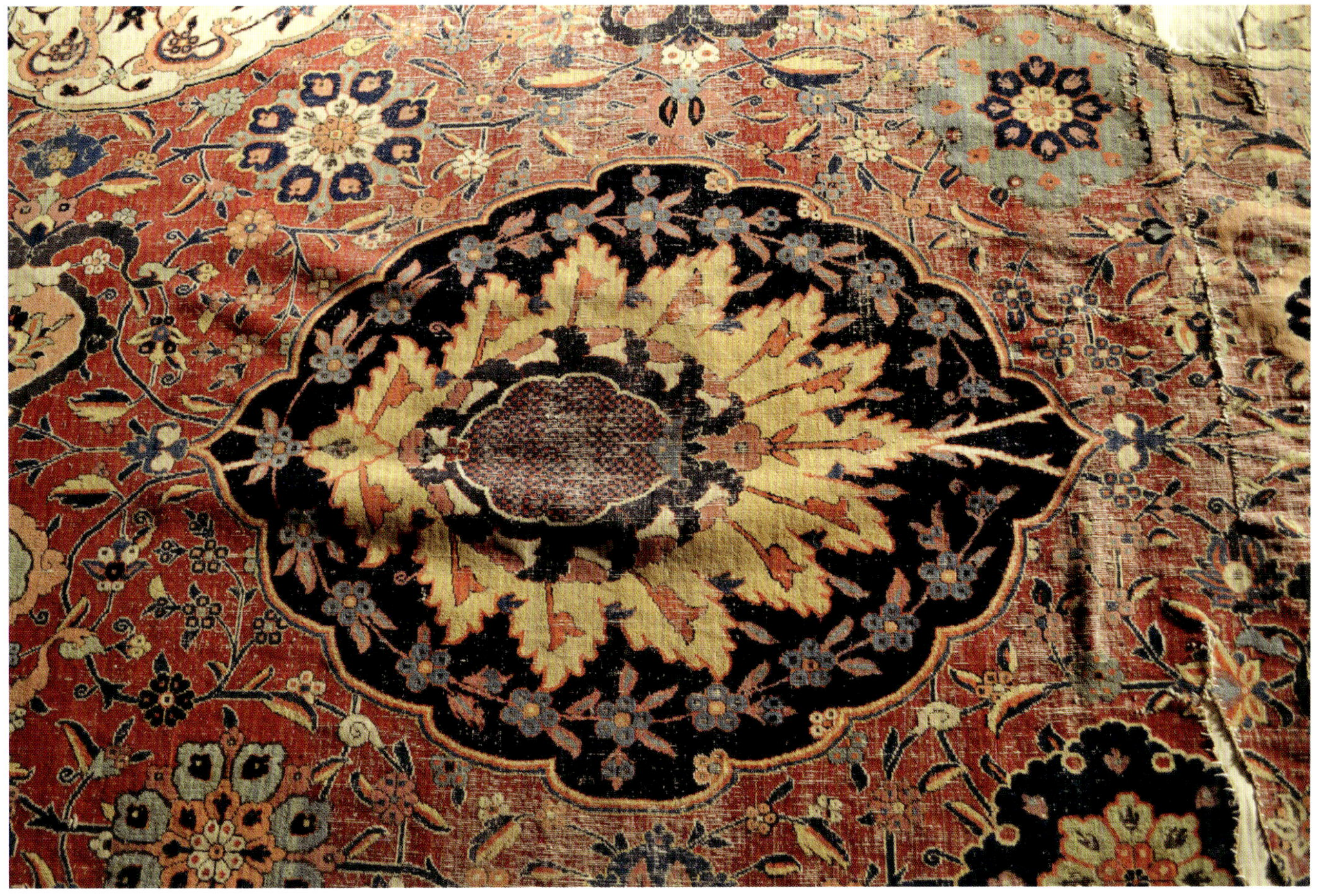

FIGURE 5.36. Detail of the medallions on Mahan carpet fragments. *Photograph by author, 2016. © The National Museum of Bosnia and Herzegovina, no. 1049.*

In the Mahan fragments, the main field—a crimson background, which was a common feature of carpets attributed to Kerman—is filled with offset ogival medallions and vase motifs of varying designs, all surrounded by wide margins in a distinct yellow (fig. 5.37).[91] The Mahan carpets are among the few vase technique–style carpets that feature interwoven inscriptions.[92] Their poetry was specifically commissioned for the site.

Two of the Mahan carpet fragments are dated: once in figures (1067/1656–57) and twice in chronograms (1066/1655–56 and 1067/1656–57) (fig. 5.38 and apps. 5.5 and 5.6). At least one other fragment was dated through a chronogram, but the cartouche containing the relevant verse has been lost (fig. 5.39 and app. 5.4). Although the dates have been debated in the past, recent personal examination of the fragments confirms the dates as given above.[93] One fragment is signed by a master weaver from or associated with the town of Mahan, *ustad-i muʾmin* (faithful master) Qutb al-din b. Mahani (fig. 5.40).[94]

The Mahan carpet fragments are significant for several reasons. First, as they are signed and dated, they occupy a special place in the canon of Persian carpets from the seventeenth century. Since relatively few Safavid carpets are dated, examples like this have been used to establish chronology and

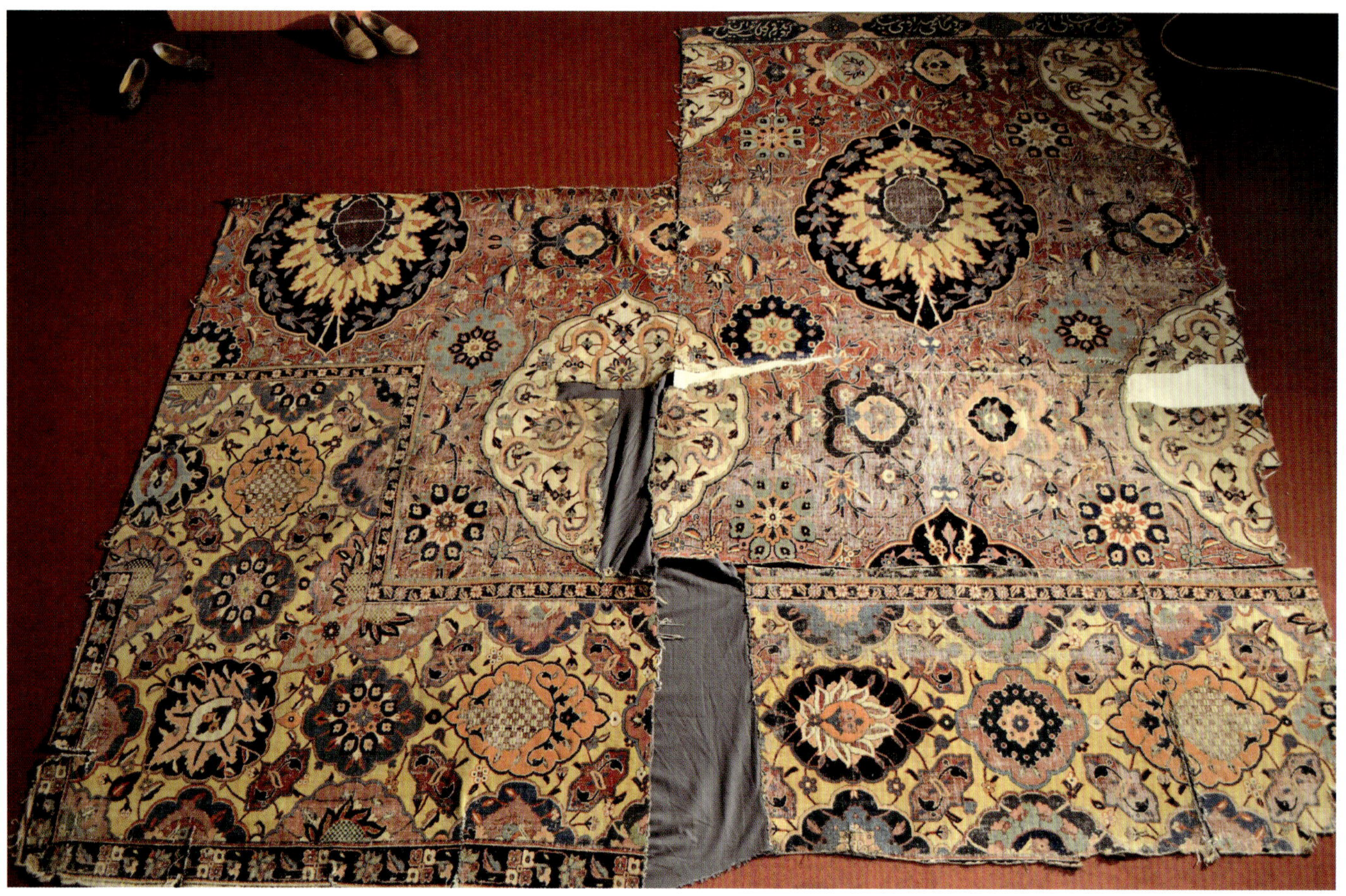

FIGURE 5.37. Fragments of the Mahan carpets. *Photograph by author, 2016. © The National Museum of Bosnia and Herzegovina, no. 1049.*

FACING TOP, FIGURE 5.38. One of the Mahan carpet fragments with four surviving inscribed cartouches and a chronogram in the far-left cartouche. *Photograph by author, 2019. © The National Museum of Bosnia and Herzegovina, no. 1049.*

workshop connections for other undated carpets with similar stylistic features—a method that has not proven immune to debate. Second, devotional carpets with irrefutable links to Sufi shrines are rare. A comparable example is the inscribed Ardabil carpets made for the shrine of Shaykh Safi al-din in the northwestern Iranian city of Ardabil.[95] The Ardabil carpets have endured a similar fate in terms of their removal from the shrine context in the 1890s and subsequent musealization.[96] Finally, the Mahan carpets shed light not only on the local networks of art making that were operating within Sufi shrines but also on the sense of belonging instilled by devotional objects that is the subject of this chapter.

Since the publication of the Mahan carpets' photographs and a brief discussion by Arthur Upham Pope in *A Survey of Persian Art*, scholarship on the Mahan carpets has focused on dating them, their possible connection with Safavid royal workshops, the reconstruction of the fragments in their original configuration, and, more recently, their provenance.[97] Iván Szántó's 2013 article engages with the complicated provenance of the carpets in the nineteenth century, bringing to light the carpets' journey to Sarajevo. He shows how collecting policies informed by orientalist narratives tied to the Austro-Hungarian occupation of Bosnia prompted the acquisition of these

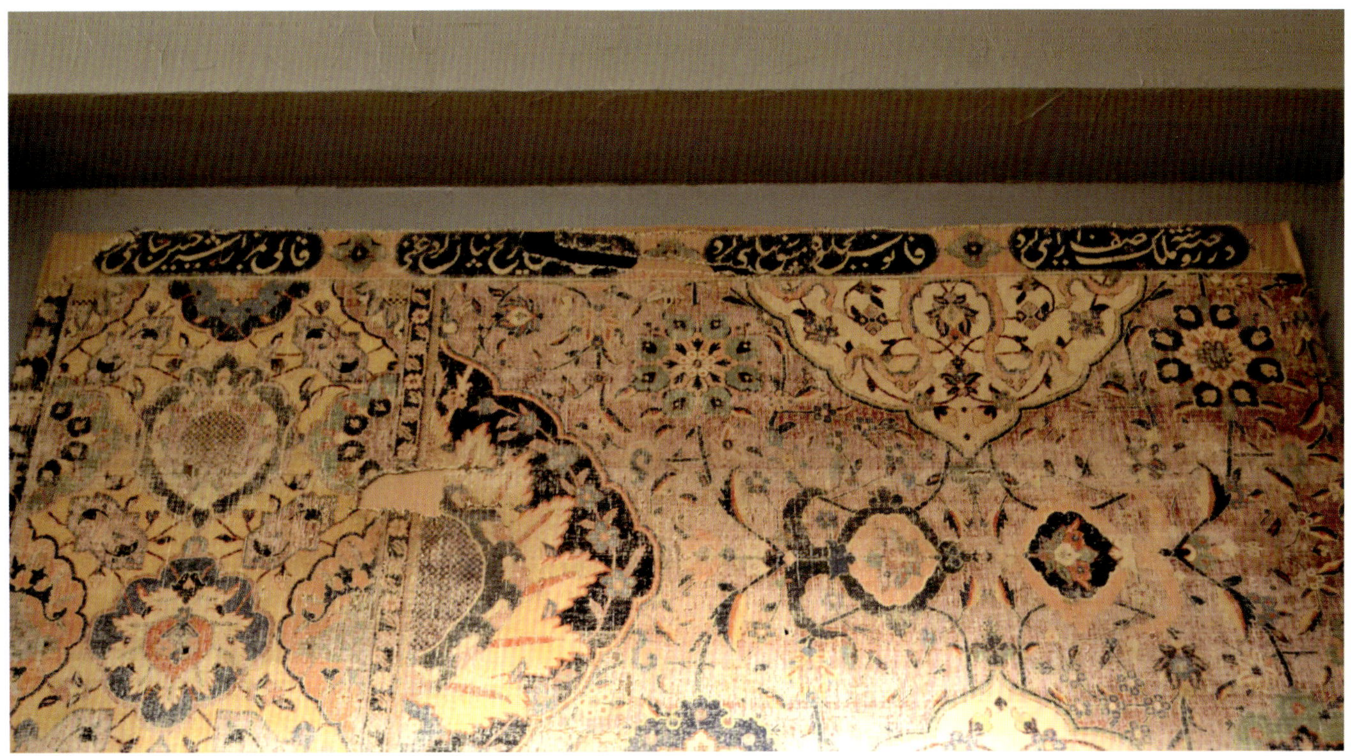

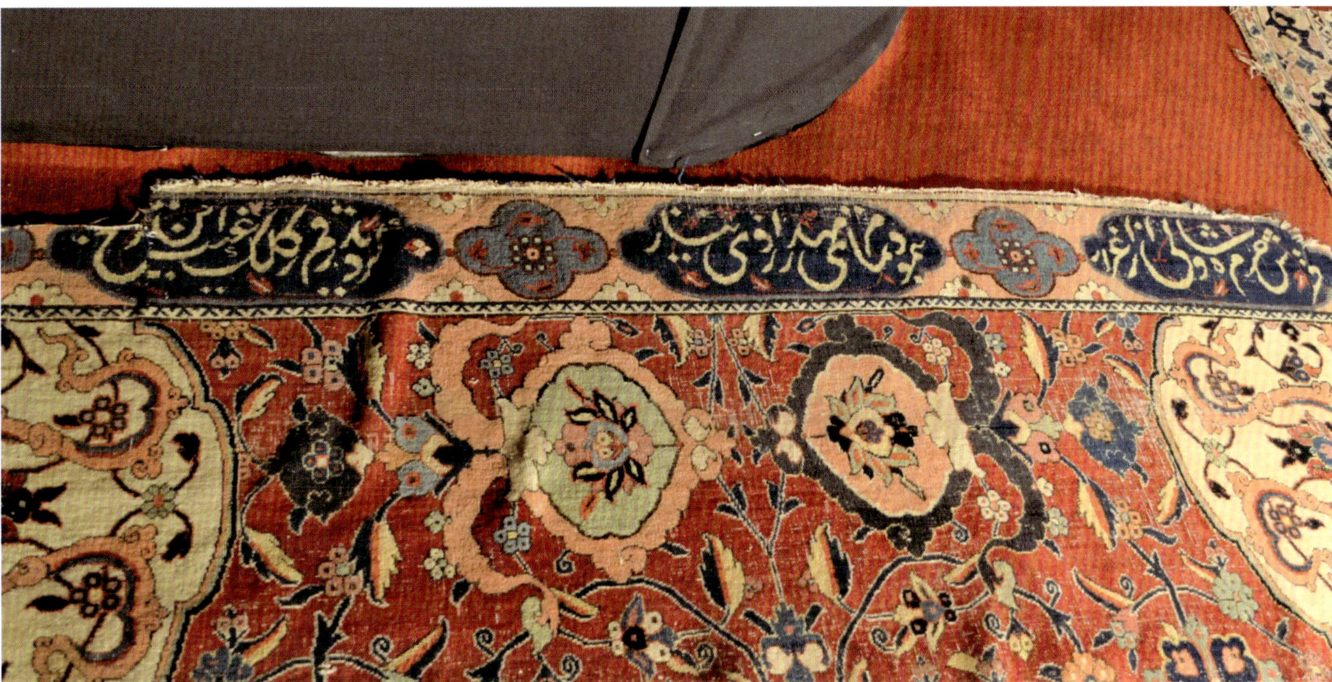

FIGURE 5.39. One of the Mahan carpet fragments with three surviving inscribed cartouches. The missing cartouche containing the chronogram would have been placed next to the far-left cartouche. *Photograph by author, 2016. © The National Museum of Bosnia and Herzegovina, no. 1049.*

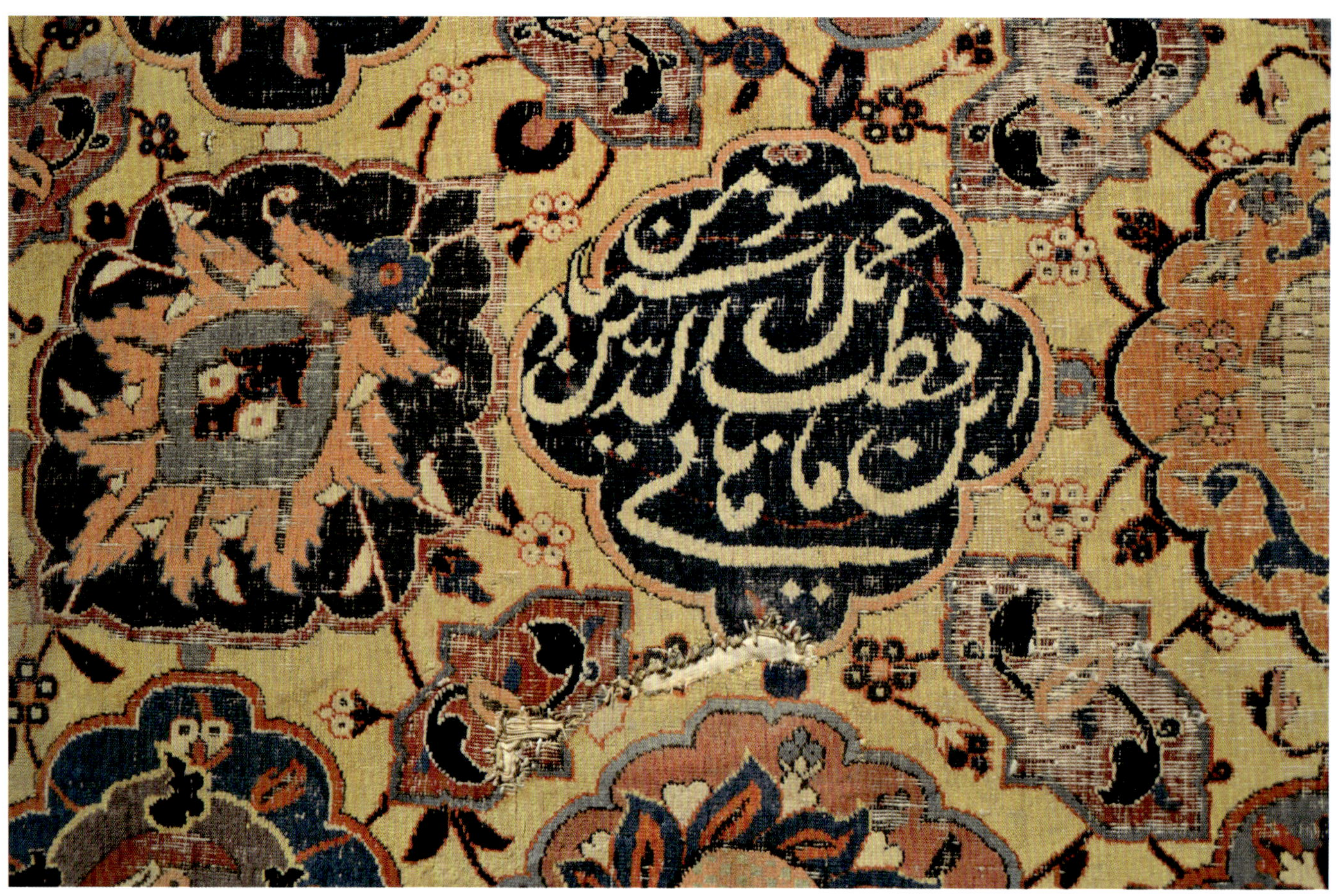

FIGURE 5.40. Detail of the signature of Qutb al-din b. Mahani on one of the Mahan carpet fragments. *Photograph by author, 2016. © The National Museum of Bosnia and Herzegovina, no. 1049.*

carpets—among other objects—by Baron Albert Béla Rakovszky (d. 1916), a longtime diplomat and the first to occupy Vienna's diplomatic mission in Tehran from 1888 to 1892.[98] According to Szántó, "the ideological uses of Persian art in the historical context of South-East European colonialism," although short-lived and not universally supported by Austro-Hungarian politics, aimed to foster a "new Islamic-inspired outlook" for Bosnia with a measured distance and consequent detachment from the Ottoman Empire.[99]

The purchase of the carpets took place in the context of Rakovszky's 1894–95 mission to collect art objects for the exhibition pavilion of Bosnia in the international exposition in Budapest in 1895.[100] His purchase of the carpets is recorded in the accounts of Ella Sykes (d. 1939), the British traveler and writer, and her brother, Percy Sykes (d. 1945), a scholar, a diplomat, and the first British consul for Kerman and Persian Baluchistan, appointed in 1894.[101] More broadly, the acquisition of the Mahan carpets fits within the context of global interests in "original" and "antique" Safavid carpets in the nineteenth century.[102]

Despite their significance as provenanced shrine textiles, little has been written about the Mahan carpets' role as devotional objects in the context of a sacred space. This is in part due to their inaccessibility, lack of exhibition opportunities, and unknown condition status in postwar Bosnia, compounded by the more recent closure of the museum between 2012 and 2015 due to funding constraints.[103] Historiographic approaches to carpet studies, however, have played a significant role in this scholarly gap too. The carpets have tended to be treated as documents, even with regard to their relationship to the shrine, rather than living objects at the center of human lives and devotional rituals.

Of the roughly thirty Mahan carpet fragments that Ella Sykes notes—that is, if we take this number as accurate—only seven are in the collection of the museum at Sarajevo while the fate of the rest is unknown.[104] In addition to these actual missing fragments, several broader factors have been left out of the scholarship on the carpets, especially in the second half of the twentieth century. In 1955 Cvetko Popović wrote on the Mahan carpets, focusing on their inscriptions and dating. Piecing together some of the fragments, and based on the location of the inscriptions, he suggested the carpets were designed to fit *a* structure.[105] Jenny Housego then connected the carpets with the shrine at Mahan in an essay published two decades later in conjunction with the exhibition *Carpets of Central Persia* (1976).[106] However, the nature and significance of the spatial connection between the carpets and the shrine have yet to be deeply explored.

Since the reopening of the National Museum of BiH, a small exhibition was dedicated to the carpets, generating a renewed interest in the fragments. Despite that and the history of fascination with the carpets' inscriptions and patronage, their epigraphy and its close connection with the Sufi family have been neglected or misunderstood. The visual and contextual entanglements between the carpets and the shrine space are many, and these played a key role in the experience of pilgrimage. The design of the carpets and their epigraphic program even allowed them to become active participants in the rites of grave visitation—a topic I discuss elsewhere.[107] My goal here is to establish their familial connection and explore its implications, both for the spatial relationship of the carpets with their architectural setting and for the question of patronage. As I contend in the next section, among their many functions, the poems created a woven lineage, a system of kinship, that embedded the carpet in a genealogical relation with its surroundings.

VII. Lost in Translation: Sufi Lineage in Threads

Four out of the seven surviving fragments of the Mahan carpets are inscribed. Except for the signature of the weaver, Qutb al-din b. Mahani, which occupies one of the lobed medallions on a small fragment, other inscriptions are located on the borders, arranged in oval cartouches (figs. 5.34–5.39). Each cartouche contains a hemistich of poetry in Persian, rendered in the cursive nastaʿliq script. The poetic inscriptions would tightly frame the cenotaph while the signature would fall at a location close to an entrance of the dome chamber (fig. 5.35).

The verses of poetry on the carpets have been translated several times in past scholarship, yet their historical referentiality and close connection to the building and its rituals have not been detected in previous interpretations. As mentioned earlier, the poems were specifically commissioned to be inscribed on these carpets—a common practice in the period, alongside the citation of preexisting poetry by well-known poets such as Hafiz (d. 1390).[108] At times these verses were written by the weavers themselves.[109] In the case of the Mahan carpets, the otherwise-unknown poet's pen name, Ghani (bountiful), is distinguished from the likely weaver (or supervisor of the weavers) of the carpets and appears in one of the inscribed cartouches (fig. 5.38 and app. 5.5). Beyond what is contained in their signature, we know nothing about the life of the weaver or the poet, or the nature of their relationship with the Neᶜmatullahis. Although there is no evidence to support this, it is not impossible that they were integrated into the Neᶜmatullahi circle. Both poets and weavers were among the professions accepted into Sufi networks at this time, and as chapter 8 will show, artists from within the Neᶜmatullahi family were actively involved in artistic projects at their shrines.[110]

In the case of the poems inscribed on the Mahan carpets, we know at least one other contender who hoped to receive a commission for these verses. A letter written by the seventeenth-century scholar and poet Maulana Muhammad Amin Vaqari (d. after 1686–87) to Neᶜmatullahi descendant and patron of the Mahan carpets Abu'l Mahdi, includes a *qitᶜa* (lit. piece or fragment) penned by Vaqari whose content bears similarities to the verses by Ghani that appear on the Mahan carpets, including a chronogram that similarly amounts to the year 1067/1656–57.[111] A qitᶜa was a monorhyme poetic form commonly employed in occasional poetry, at times for requests of patronage and after the fifteenth century "as the typical form for the chronogram."[112] Given the status of Vaqari, the preference for an otherwise-unknown poet such as Ghani to pen the carpet inscriptions may point to the latter's belonging to an inner circle.[113] In any case, the fact that the commission of these carpets was a known event among the cultural elite and that their poetic inscriptions brought out competitive efforts among poets highlights the importance of the making of these carpets as an artistic project.

When Percy and Ella Sykes saw these carpets around the time of their removal from the shrine, they described them as gifts "presented to the shrine by Shah ᶜAbbas."[114] This royal attribution for the patronage of the carpets, for which there are no historical records, has generally been accepted in previous literature.[115] The inscriptions, however, tell a different story of patronage and belonging. As I argue, these carpets are instead connected to a phase of interventions in the Mahan shrine conducted by descendants and disciples from within the Neᶜmatullahi Sufi network. With a few departures from previous readings, I translate the verses on the longest surviving fragment, measuring 6.80 × 3.50 meters and containing ten inscribed cartouches, as follows (fig. 5.34 and app. 5.6):

How excellent is the pure illuminated threshold of this tomb,
its carpet worthy of the Sun's pupil.[116]
The flower of the garden of benevolence, *Sulayman* of [our] time,
from whom the flower garden of *Mirmiran* was freshened,
Abu'l Mahdi, that gem of the sea of truth,
having the fortune of finishing this carpet,
spread this excellent carpet in the tomb.
When I asked after the date of the carpet's completion,
the coveted date came [through] a voice from the invisible world:
The angel's wing is to serve the carpet as a broom.
Year 1067

These verses engage directly with the relationship between the carpet and the shrine, ending with a chronogram in the last hemistich that calculates to 1067/1656–57, matching the date recorded in figures at the end of the poem. There are several direct references to the shrine at Mahan, comparable to those in verses of poetry inscribed on the Ardabil carpets.[117] On the Mahan carpets, words such as *rawza* (garden, but also tomb) and *sahat* (courtyard, threshold) have at times escaped translation in previous scholarship.[118] The same goes for several instances in the verses where there are references to the members of the Neʿmatullahi family (in italics above)—one of whom, Abu'l Mahdi (d. unknown), is introduced as the maker or patron of the carpets. Admittedly, names such as Sulayman and Mahdi could in fact be nods to well-known religious and political figures.[119] References to Shiʿa imams and the promised Mahdi were common tropes in Safavid poetry and epigraphy and could be alluded to here in the Mahan carpets as well. But the fact that these poems were commissioned for the carpets, as opposed to being selected from a pre-existing source, alongside the successive line of the names of Neʿmatullahi descendants leaves no doubt that the verses in fact aimed to frame the story of the carpet's making in terms of a genealogical narrative. Metaphors of kinship that link the figures in the poem strengthen this hypothesis (i.e., "freshening a garden with a new flower," referring to Mirmiran's child).

In previous translations, Mahdi's act of making the carpets is communicated in a passive voice, detached from his name.[120] Symptomatic of the broader issue of privileging royal patronage and neglecting Sufi agency in devotional material culture, this seemingly straightforward matter of translation takes away the patron's active role—and by extension that of the Sufi network—in the creation of this devotional object.

The individuals mentioned in the verses above—Mirmiran (d. 1589), his son Sulayman (d. 1640, Taft), and his grandson Mahdi—were all influential figures in the family during the Safavid period. The family intermarried with the royal house several times, and Mirmiran himself was the son of the Safavid prince Khanish Begum, sister of Shah Tahmasp (r. 1524–76). The three received suyurghals and endowments from several Safavid rulers—Shah Tahmasp, Shah Safi (r. 1629–42), and Shah ʿAbbas II (r. 1642–66)—and were appointed to positions such as governorship of Yazd.[121]

The attribution of the carpets' patronage to Abu'l Mahdi is reinforced in another fragment of the carpet, with three surviving cartouches of poetry (fig. 5.39 and app. 5.4).

> The carpet of Shah Vali's tomb,
> Was completed by Mahdi out of supplication and respect.

Abu'l Mahdi was an active patron of architecture, and we know of him and his activities from a hagiography of the Sufi network written in the seventeenth century.[122] Mahdi built gardens, residences, and qanats (underground water channels) in Yazd, Taft, and Meybod. His death date is not known, but he was actively involved in architectural patronage around 1070/1659–60.[123] He was given similar suyurghals as his father and grandfather and was appointed as the *kalantar* (headman) of Yazd by the Safavid king Shah ʿAbbas II.[124] The context in which he commissioned the carpets could be related to a pilgrimage to Mecca. He embarked on his pilgrimage in 1065/1654–55; on the 12th of Muharram 1066/1655, he left for Yathrib, continued to Medina and Basra, and, in the same year, returned to Isfahan, where he offered gifts to Shah ʿAbbas and then left for Yazd.[125] In that same year, 1066, the first of the carpets was commissioned (or completed) for the shrine in Mahan, most likely as a gift to the shrine of his ancestor, commemorating the successful completion of his pilgrimage to Mecca.[126]

Carpets were particularly appropriate as gifts to Sufi shrines due to their strong association with the inheritance of spiritual authority. The term *sajjada-neshin*, which could be translated as the "occupant of the prayer carpet," was commonly used in the context of transitions of authority in Sufi lineages, distinguishing among descendants of Sufi masters in terms of the sociospiritual and political roles assigned to them.[127] Sheila Blair has argued that the donation of the Ardabil carpets by the Safavid ruler Shah Tahmasp to the shrine of his ancestor Shaykh Safi was a way of justifying his spiritual inheritance.[128] In the Neʿmatullahi network, too, *sajjada neshini* seems to have a connotation of spiritual inheritance combined with sociopolitical responsibilities, as I discussed in chapter 2 in the context of Deccan India.[129]

Alongside their strong genealogical connection with the Neʿmatullahi family, the inscriptions on the Mahan carpets could have also been perceived as an allusion to the family's ambitions and political rivalry with the Safavid family, a point that I will explore in more detail in chapter 6. "Sulayman-i duran," or "the Solomon of our time," inscribed on the largest carpet fragment, is an interesting term in this regard (app. 5.6) and one that could have acquired new meaning in the decade after the production of the carpets. In the context of the broader web of familial references, the name refers to Sulayman, a Neʿmatullahi descendant within the Safavid bloodline. However, for viewers who could read the inscriptions in the late 1660s, it could also have been perceived as a reference to the eighth Safavid ruler, whose second coronation under the name Sulayman I took place in 1668—over a decade after the dates appearing on the Mahan carpets. This unintentional allusion could have granted the carpets a new level of anachronistic political significance in which the Neʿmatullahi Sulayman was presented as the true Solomon of our time, in competition with the Safavid Sulayman.

The line of succession woven into the carpets, from Mirmiran to Mahdi, visualizes the Neʿmatullahi lineage in the Safavid period, commemorating the family's presence—albeit short term—on the center stage of south-central Iranian politics. This inscribed lineage ties into the many layers of work by patrons, poets, and craftspeople whose contributions were memorialized through foundation inscriptions and signatures at Mahan—an architectural genealogy that extends throughout the interior and exterior of the tomb. Similar strategies of incorporating familial genealogies into epigraphic programs can also be witnessed in other spaces in the shrine at Mahan. The most important example of these, a retreat cell, will be discussed in chapter 8 in relation to Sufi rituals and artistic production.

It is important to remember that by the time the carpets were commissioned for the mausoleum, the shrine had already expanded from a stand-alone dome chamber into a complex with a vaulted gallery and an adjacent courtyard (fig. 1.2). Due to the layers of construction around the sacred tomb of Shah Neʿmatullah, an immediate proximity to his cenotaph was no longer possible through architectural patronage. In this regard, the making of the carpets was a creative solution by a descendant of the family to patronize a devotional work of art: an intimate tactile object set at the very heart of the shrine (fig. 5.41). The carpets not only overcame the distance from the most sacred part

FIGURE 5.41. Reconstruction of the Mahan carpet fragments inside the mausoleum of Shah Neʿmatullah Vali. *Reconstructed by the author, in collaboration with Farah Michel. 3D rendering by Farah Michel.*

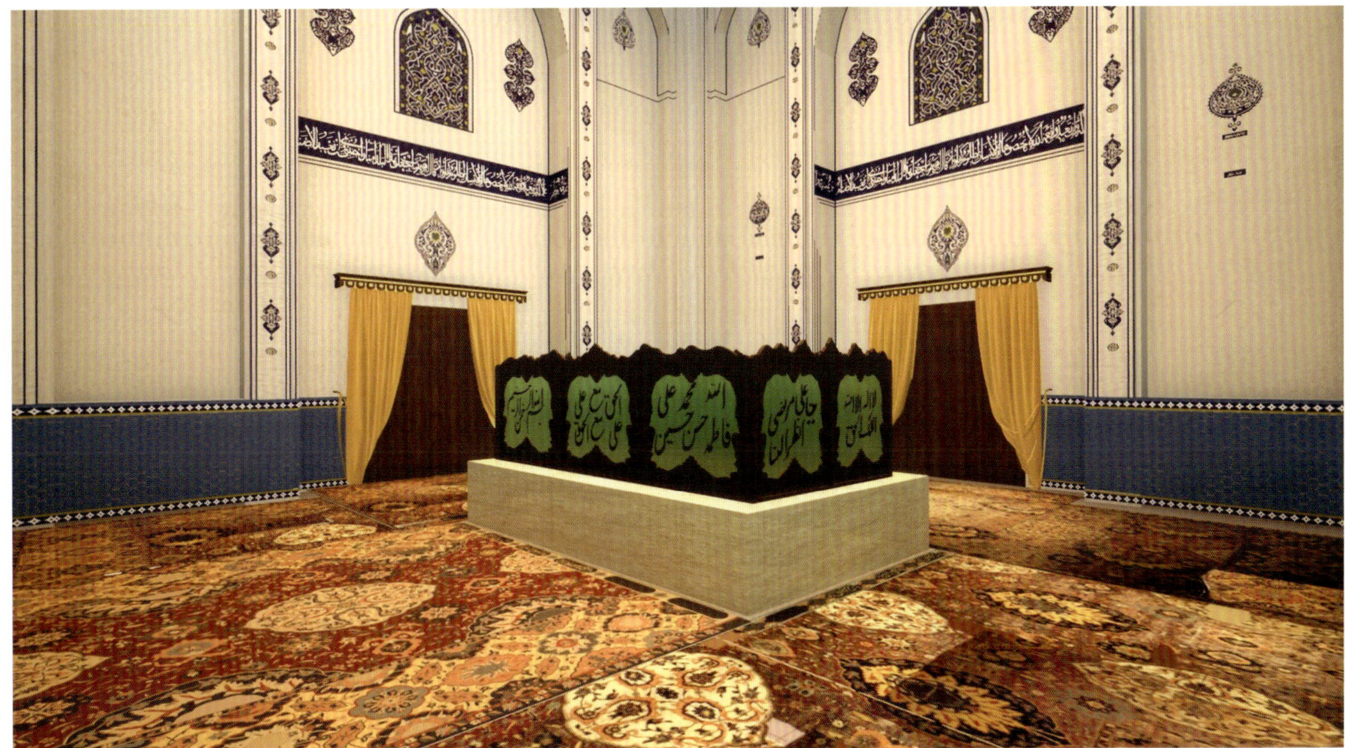

of the shrine that accrued through architectural patronage but also extended the established tradition of self-referentiality and lineage making from the tomb's epigraphy into the fabric of the textile. Directly surrounded by references to the name of Shah Neʿmatullah in the Qurʾanic verses on the interior walls of the tomb, the carpets' poetry reinforces the continuity of the familial lineage into the seventeenth century. Alongside contemporary hagiographies that emphasized this continuity, the dialogue between the architecture and the textile added a more publicly visible layer to that narrative for anyone who could read the inscriptions or was made aware of such connections.

Finally, a point of reflection on the historiography of the carpets in relation to the Sufi family. The lack of acknowledgment of the Neʿmatullahi family's patronage of the carpets reveals two interrelated sets of biases in art historical discourse: first is the overreliance on royal attributions in the study of high-quality textiles and carpets, as evident in the previously unchallenged attribution of the carpets to the Safavid king. The consensus has been that intricacy, precision, and good draftsmanship points to court patronage.[130] This is not a completely unfounded claim, as I explain below, but one that needs to be nuanced. The obsession with royal patronage could be a result of the historical circumstances around the Safavids' establishment and control over royal weaving workshops in places such as Kerman.[131] However, as Willem Floor has pointed out, the existence of royal workshops in the Safavid era did not result in a complete monopoly over textile production.[132] In this regard, the Mahan carpets open up a much-needed glimpse into the socioeconomic role of textiles beyond royal patronage.

Second, this tendency toward assuming royal patronage is also symptomatic of the broader marginalization of Sufis' role in the active creation of art and material culture. This is not to deny the possibility that these carpets could have been woven in existing royal workshops, utilizing court resources. After all, the Neʿmatullahi Sufis had strong connections with the royal family and were linked to the Safavid court. The expertise of weavers who were employed by royal patrons, too, might have contributed to the making of these carpets, although the affiliation of the Mahani artist who signed the work speaks to a claim on localization. In sum, there are crucial distinctions in the variety of societal affiliations at play here that need to be made explicit. In acknowledging this nuance, the patronage of the carpets becomes a field of political and aesthetic competitions. By demonstrating patronage of this high-quality work, the Neʿmatullahi patrons concretize their status as contenders in both regional politics and the realm of art making. To consider the patronage of the carpets under the blanket category of *royal* is to write the Neʿmatullahis out of their own history, to deprive them of agency in the making of their spaces—an agency they repeatedly insist on in the carpets themselves through both subtle metaphors and unambiguous references.

The spatial design of the carpets offers a striking metaphor for the gap between what the carpets want to tell us and what has been said about them in past scholarship. Inscribed carpets of the period would usually, although not without exceptions, orient inscriptions toward a reader seated in the middle of the carpet, establishing a compositional center of gravity within. In the Mahan carpets, this center of gravity is instead located outside the carpets, in the position of the cenotaph (fig. 5.35). Everything in the design of the carpets—from their remarkably wide margins to the orientation of their inscriptions and the overall spatial configuration of the fragments—work in tandem to direct one's gaze toward an empty center, occupied by the grave. All of the fragments thus point, quite literally, to the centrality of the Sufi's body. By contrast, historiographic approaches to these carpets have consistently centered them around royal weaving workshops and royal patronage, ignoring the labor, intention, and devotion that Sufis invested in their creation. Shifting the locus of patronage and art making from the ruling dynasty to the Sufi circle allows us to see the making of these carpets as an intimate endeavor that also makes a claim on artistic and political autonomy.

The Mahan carpet fragments are pivotal objects in defining the thematic direction of the chapters in the final part of the book. The kind of genealogical epigraphic networks that the carpets develop in dialogue with the architecture are similar to the epigraphic strategies that would be appropriated by the royal patrons of the Neʿmatullahi in several instances throughout their history. One such example is the tomb of the Bahmanid ruler Ahmad Shah I, outside Bidar, which will open the next chapter. The Mahan carpets are also crucial case studies for challenging the marginalized role granted to Sufis as patrons of art and architecture—a thread that I pick up in chapter 7 by exploring further evidence of the Neʿmatullahis' significant but understudied role as urban patrons of small and large projects beyond their own shrines. Finally, both the signature and poetic inscriptions of the Mahan carpets point to a local and intimate system of patronage and art making, which will come to the fore in the last chapter of the book.

Notes

1. Another monument associated with the Neʿmatullahi network that awaits further research is the Takht-i Kermani in Bidar. See a brief discussion in Philon, "New Considerations on the City of Bidar," 110–11.
2. Green, "Migrant Sufis," 496–97.
3. Helen Philon and Elizabeth Merklinger date the main mausoleum based on the death date of Shah Khalilullah, which they offer as 1459–69. Philon, "The Chaukhandi at Ashtur," 52; Merklinger, *Indian Islamic Architecture*, 114. Terry Graham mentions Khalilullah's death date once as 1447 and elsewhere as 1455: Graham, "The Niʿmatullāhī Order," 173, 174. Nasrollah Pourjavady notes the death date as 1455–56 and Michael Connell as 860/1455: Pourjavady, "Khalil Allāh Shāh"; Connell, "The Nimatullahi Sayyids," 116. Tabataba and Fereshteh recorded only that Shah Khalilullah died during the reign of ʿAla al-din Ahmad Shah II, which ended in 862/1458: Tabataba, *Burhan-i maʾasir*, 81; Astarabadi, *Tarikh-i Fereshteh*, 409. See also Firouzeh, "Between the Spiritual and Material," 150, fn.2.
4. "*Al-wasil-u ila rahmat Allah*" translates to "[the one] who joined the mercy of God": Shirazi, *Tuhfat al-muhibbin*, 52.

5. Aubin, *Matériaux*, 204; Astarabadi, *Tarikh-i Fereshteh*, 429.

6. See for "chaukhandi" as unroofed wall enclosures: Baloch, "Kalmati Tombs," 244–45; Zajadacz-Hastenrath, *Chaukhandi Tombs*, 8–10; as four-section building: Yazdani, *Bidar*, 141. The term *chaukhandi* was used for another tomb in Bidar, a square dome chamber associated with Mir Kalan, governor of Bidar under the Mughals and later under Asaf Jah I (r.1724–48): Yazdani, *Bidar*, 190. Textual sources prior to Mughal and Asaf Jah I period do not use the term *chaukhandi* for Khalilullah's mausoleum.

7. Yazdani, *Bidar*, 144.

8. Ibid., 144. Yazdani also noted another tomb, near the village of Malkapur outside Bidar, attributed to Shah Muhibbullah: Ibid., 212–13.

9. Aubin, *Matériaux*, 206–207.

10. Yazdani, *Bidar*, 145–46. Philon dates the dome chamber to the late fifteenth and sixteenth centuries: Philon, "The Chaukhandi," 52.

11. Yazdani, *Bidar*, 145.

12. Ibid., 145.

13. On Sufi burials under trees across South Asia, see Green, "Migrant Sufis," 498.

14. Merklinger, "The *Madrasa* of Maḥmūd Gāwān," 155–56.

15. Yazdani, *Epigraphia Indica*, 20; Yazdani, *Bidar*, 146.

16. The date has been read as 1196 in Yazdani, *Bidar*, 146, and as 1195 in Yazdani, *Epigraphia Indica*, 20.

17. His possible death date is recorded as 1431 in Tabataba, *Burhan-i maʾasir*, 65, but Fereshteh places it during the reign of ʿAla al-din Ahmad Shah II (r. 1435–58): Astarabadi, *Tarikh-i Fereshteh*, 409. A letter attributed to an Amir Ziaʾ al-din Nurullah b. Amir Khalilullah during the reign of Muhammad ibn Baysunghur (r. 1447–51) pushes the death date to 1450s: Yazdi, *Munshaʾat*, 139–41. However, the later could be another descendant of Shah Neʿmatullah with the same name and not his grandson Nurullah, a point also made in Graham, "The Niʿmatullāhī Order," 179.

18. Aubin, *Matériaux*, 319.

19. Connell, "The Nimatullahi Sayyids," 250, 260–61; Muʿtamid Khan, *Tarikh-i Muhammadi*, II:9.

20. Connell, "The Nimatullahi Sayyids," 259–60; Muʿtamid Khan, *Tarikh-i Muhammadi*, II:3.

21. Muʿtamid Khan, *Tarikh-i Muhammadi*, II:131.

22. There was in fact a now-lost anonymous mausoleum on the site: Yazdani, *Bidar*, 145.

23. Ibid., 141–46; Michell and Zebrowski, *Architecture and Art of the Deccan Sultanates*, 73–77; Merklinger, *Indian Islamic Architecture*, 16; Philon, "The Chaukhandi," 51–56.

24. Merklinger, "The *Madrasa* of Maḥmūd Gāwān," 155–56; Merklinger, "Seven Tombs at Holkonda," 194–95.

25. On the legacy of Sultaniyeh, see Blair, *Text and Image*, 153, 252; Wilber, *The Architecture of Islamic Iran*, 139. On the mausoleums of Rukn-i ʿAlam (after 1335) in Multan and Muhammad Shah Sayyid (1446) in Delhi, see Porter, *The Glory of the Sultans*, 54–55, 66–67. For later examples in Delhi, Bihar, and the Deccan, see Porter, *The Glory of the Sultans*, 82–85, 91–92, 146–48.

26. Yazdani, *Bidar*, 142–43; Philon, "The Chaukhandi," 52.

27. Ibid., 52. On the customary use of embroidered textiles in funerary architecture, see Daneshvari, *Medieval Tomb Towers*, 9–11.

28. Philon, "The Chaukhandi," 52.

29. Yazdani, *Bidar*, 142; Blair and Bloom, "From Iran to the Deccan," in Overton, *Iran and the Deccan*, 192–93. Philon and Michell note in their recent publications that these tiles were likely never added to the facade: Michell and Philon, *Islamic Architecture of Deccan India*, 181.

30. Philon, "The Chaukhandi," 52–54.

31. Ibid., 53–54.

32. Wagoner and Rice, "From Delhi to the Deccan," 90–92, 104.

33. On the lack of legal issues against the erection of domed mausoleums, see Subtelny, *Timurids in Transition*, 195; Leisten, "Between Orthodoxy and Exegesis," 16.

34. Porter, *The Glory of the Sultans*, 66–67, 82–85; Alfieri, *Islamic Architecture of the Indian Subcontinent*, 50–59; Hutton, *Art of the Court of Bijapur*, 45.

35. On shared sacred spaces, see Khalidi, "Sacred Spaces and Objects," 330. On the nearby examples of the shrine complex of Gisu Daraz in Gulbarga and the tomb of Ahmad Shah in Ashtur, see Mondini, "Architectural Heritage and Modern Rituals," 129–42.

36. Philon, "The Chaukhandi," 53; Yazdani, *Bidar*, 143.

37. Michell and Zebrowski, *Architecture and Art of the Deccan Sultanates*, 118–19, 121–22. On basalt and the occasional use of the harder and more expensive granite, see Philon, *Gulbarga, Bidar, Bijapur*, 26.

38. Yazdani, *Bidar*, 142; Blair and Bloom, "From Iran to the Deccan," 192–93.

39. On entering the paradise and architectural thresholds, see Quraishi, "'This Is Makkah for Me!,'" 277.

40. The inscription panels on the southwest and west walls contain verses 106–107 from Surat al-Kahf (Q 18:106–107) and 41–43 of Surat al-Ahzab (The Coalition) (Q 33:41–43), respectively.

41. On dhikr and architectural epigraphy, see Quraishi, "'This Is Makkah for Me!,'" 277–78.

42. Daneshvari, *Medieval Tomb Towers*, 18–20, 27–30; Günther, "The Poetics of Islamic Eschatology," 208–10; Quraishi, "'This Is Makkah for Me!,'" 276–77.

43. Kinberg, "Paradise."

44. Ibid.

45. See chapter 6, section I, "Ahmad Shah's Tomb in Bidar: Architecture as Transoceanic Dialogue," and Yazdani, *Epigraphia Indica*, 20.

46. Aubin, *Matériaux*, 194–95.

47. Firouzeh, "Dynastic Self-Fashioning," in Overton, *Iran and the Deccan*, 162–66, 170 n.66; Loth, *A Catalogue of the Arabic Manuscripts*, I:111; Overton, "Book Culture," 116; Overton and Benson, "Deccani Seals and Scribal Notations," 565–66.

48. On the ambiguities around the reading of the seal, see Firouzeh, "Dynastic Self-Fashioning," 170–71 n.67; Overton and Benson, "Deccani Seals and Scribal Notations," 566–67; Overton, "Book Culture," 116, 149 n.164. I thank Keelan Overton and Jake Benson for discussing this seal with me.

49. Firouzeh, "Dynastic Self-Fashioning," 170–71 n.67; Overton and Benson, "Deccani Seals and Scribal Notations," 566–67.

50. Firouzeh, "Dynastic Self-Fashioning," 170–71 n.67.

51. On Bidar's networks of Neʿmatullahi Sufis and calligraphers, see ibid., 145–74.

52. Afshar's introduction to Shirazi, *Tuhfat al-muhibbin*, 24; Blochet, *Catalogue des manuscrits persans*, II:302–303. Afshar also notes that ʿAbd al-Hayy Habibi

listed another copy of the manuscript (date unknown) at the Khuda Bakhsh Oriental Library (no. 1086), Patna: Habibi, *Hunar-i ʿahd-i Teymuriyan*, 215, 518–19.

53. Sims, "Ibrahim-Sultan's Illustrated Zafarnama," 132–43; Richard, "Nasr al-Soltāni," 92–93.

54. Firouzeh, "Dynastic Self-Fashioning," 155–65. See, for instance, Fereshteh's account about the three thousand books that were kept at the library of the madrasa of Mahmud Gavan: Astarabadi, *Tarikh-i Fereshteh*, 466.

55. Shirazi, *Tuhfat al-muhibbin*, 48–52.

56. Firouzeh, "Dynastic Self-Fashioning," 147–55. See also Desai, "Sahm-i hunarmandan-i Irani," 138; Ghelichkhani, *Daramadi bar khushnivisi-yi Irani*, 263.

57. Overton, "Introduction to Iranian Mobilities," in Overton, *Iran and the Deccan*, 3–48; Alam and Subrahmanyam, "Iran and the Doors to the Deccan," in Overton, *Iran and the Deccan*, 77–104; Fischel, "Ghariban in the Deccan," in Overton, *Iran and the Deccan*, 127–44.

58. Yazdi, *Munshaʾat*, 120–38; also discussed in Firouzeh, "Dynastic Self-Fashioning," 157–61.

59. Yazdi, *Munshaʾat*, 112; Firouzeh, "Dynastic Self-Fashioning," 159. For later Qurʾan manuscripts traveling between Iran and the Deccan, see Farhad and Rettig, *The Art of the Qurʾan*, 293.

60. Yazdi, *Munshaʾat*, 125; Firouzeh, "Dynastic Self-Fashioning," 158–59.

61. Firouzeh, "Dynastic Self-Fashioning," 153–55.

62. Yazdani, *Epigraphia Indica*, 20.

63. Khan and Nath, *Monuments of Delhi*, 45.

64. Astarabadi, *Tarikh-i Fereshteh*, 377–78.

65. Yazdani, *Bidar*, 147.

66. *Khayr-i jari* in this inscription could also be a reference to *sadaqa jariya*, an act of charity with continuous benefits for the community, even after the endower's death.

67. Philon, *Gulbarga, Bidar, Bijapur*, 12–13.

68. On the use of the *Shahnama* by Ghurids and Tughluqs, see Flood, *Objects of Translation*, 251, 255; O'Kane, *The Appearance of Persian*, 95.

69. On the relationship between the Bahmanids' Persianate and Sufi claims, see Eaton and Wagoner, *Power, Memory, Architecture*, 30.

70. For a comparative example, ʿAla al-din Ahmad Shah II's garden and main residence in the village of Neʿmatabad, which was connected to and named after the Neʿmatullahis, see Tabataba, *Burhan-i maʾasir*, 76–77.

71. Sardar, "Golconda through Time," 107–10; Sardar, "The Bahmanis and Their Artistic Legacy," in Haidar and Sardar, *Sultans of Deccan India*, 29–30.

72. Green, *Making Space*, 23–25; Dadlani, "The City Built," in Rizvi, *Affect, Emotion, and Subjectivity*, 156; Ernst, "Khuldabad," 109; Ernst, *Eternal Garden*, 206–207.

73. Yazdani, *Bidar*, 143.

74. Potter, "Sufis and Sultans," 83; Subtelny, *Timurids in Transition*, 200; McChesney, *Central Asia*, 81; Sardar, "Golconda through Time," 107–10.

75. For the disputes between Gisu Daraz and Firuz Shah Bahmani, see Astarabadi, *Tarikh-i Fereshteh*, 348–49.

76. Bernard O'Kane informed me that these did not exist during his visit to the tomb in the 1970s. Photographs by Sheila Blair and Jonathan Bloom taken in 1984 demonstrate this: https://archnet.org/sites/1637/media_contents/42364, accessed on

August 18, 2021. It is also possible that some paintings under the zone of transition were previously over-painted.

77. O'Kane, *Timurid Architecture in Khurasan*, 62–63; Lentz, "Dynastic Imagery," 253–65; Pugachenkova, "'Ishrat-Khāneh and Ak-Saray," 177–89.

78. For Robert Hillenbrand's discussion of the rarity of architecturally relevant quotations from the Qur'an on buildings, especially mosques, see Hillenbrand, *Studies in Medieval Islamic Architecture*, I:308, 323, 326.

79. Pope, "The National Museum in Teheran," 97.

80. Ibid., 89; Afshar, *Yadgarha-yi Yazd*, I:421.

81. Afshar, *Yadgarha-yi Yazd*, I:421.

82. Yazdi, *Munsha'at*, 147–55. See also chapter 3, section VIII, "The Curse of Transregionality," and chapter 4, section I, "Crafting a Sacred Distance."

83. Suyurghal was a reward, a designation for an often-hereditary grant of immunity from taxation. On Zahir al-din's suyurghal, see Katib, *Tarikh-i jadid-i Yazd*, 249.

84. Yazdi, *Manzumat*, 63–65.

85. Aubin, *Matériaux*, 165. See chapter 3, section VII, "Contentious Alignments and the Politics of Encounter."

86. A number of figural carpets and painterly representations of Neʿmatullahi Sufis survive from the nineteenth century. For examples of paintings, several of which include a representation of the Neʿmatullahi taj, see Ekhtiar, "Ahl al-Bayt Imagery Revisited," 80–93.

87. Chapter 8, section V, "A Vaulted Initiation Hat."

88. Old museum number: 1049; new number: 2111/I: a, b; 2112/I: a, b; 2113/I: a, b, c. p.

89. On the commonality of fitted carpets being made in two or more pieces, see Beattie, *Carpets of Central Persia*, 16.

90. Examples include the Portuguese traveler Pedro Teixeira around 1605 (traveling from Goa); Chardin in 1670s; Olfert Dapper, a Dutchman, around the same time; and the German traveler Engelbert Kaempfer: Beattie, *Carpets of Central Persia*, 1.

91. Beattie, *Carpets of Central Persia*, 15; Housego, "Kirman," 16.

92. Beattie, *Carpets of Central Persia*, 16.

93. On different readings of the date and chronogram of the Mahan carpet fragments, see Blair, "The Ardabil Carpets in Context," 137–38, where the date in figures is noted as 1047 (as opposed to 1067) and the two readings of the chronogram as 1056/1646–47 and 1066/1656–57. See similar readings in Szántó, "Persian Art for the Balkans," 144; Dervišević, "Sarajevska kermanska halija," 286–88; Housego, "Kirman," 16–17, although in the catalogue of the same exhibition published in 1976, May Beattie refers to the date in figures correctly as 1067: Beattie, *Carpets of Central Persia*, 16. Earlier, Popović had read the chronogram in such a way that it would account to 1047: Popović, "Fragmenti persiskih ćilima," 42–43. On the contrary, Pope had read the date correctly as 1067: Pope, *A Survey of Persian Art*, 2381. Recently, Žutić noted the date correctly: Žutić, "Safavid Number Games," 77; Žutić, "Tri safavidska tepiha," 310–11. For a detailed summary of the dating debates, see Firouzeh, "Ritual Personification."

94. The signature could also be read as "Ustad, Mu'min b. Qutb al-din Mahani."

95. Blair, "Texts, Inscriptions, and the Ardabil Carpets," 142; Blair, *Text and Image*, 233–34, 249–56, 266.

96. Weaver, "The Ardabil Puzzle," 43; Blair, *Text and Image*, 228.

97. The Mahan carpet fragments, among other Safavid carpets, are being studied in an ongoing PhD dissertation at the Courtauld Institute of Art by Margaret Squires, titled "Woven Ground: The Site-Specific Carpet in Safavid Iran, 1501–1722." While this dissertation was not available to me during the writing of this book, the author's analysis of the relationship between architecture and similar carpets, as well as her technical analysis of the carpets, promises to shed crucial new light on the Mahan carpets.

98. Szántó, "Persian Art for the Balkans," 140; Blair, "The Ardabil Carpets in Context,"137–38.

99. Szántó, "Persian Art for the Balkans," 130–35, 137–39, 141.

100. Ibid., 136, 143.

101. Sykes, *Through Persia*, 83–84.

102. Carey, *Persian Art*, 182, 198; Baker, "Safavid Carpets," 77–82.

103. Szántó, "Persian Art for the Balkans," 146.

104. Sykes, *Through Persia*, 83–84; Sykes, *Ten Thousand Miles*, 149.

105. Popović, "Fragmenti persiskih ćilima," 36.

106. Housego, "Kirman," 16.

107. Firouzeh, "Ritual Personification."

108. Erdmann, *Seven Hundred Years of Oriental Carpets*, 163.

109. See, for instance, Clinton, "Image and Metaphor," in Bier, *Woven from the Soul*, 7–11.

110. On weavers within Sufi networks, see Munroe, *Sufi Lovers*, 125.

111. Abouʾi Mehrizi, *Sadat-i Neʿmatullahi*, 188–89, 203. Interestingly, Vaqari notes in the poem that Abu'l Mahdi had arranged for the making of *five* carpets for the shrine of his ancestor. Whether all these five pieces were to sit around the cenotaph, within the domed mausoleum, or elsewhere in the shrine is unknown.

112. Losensky, "Qitʿa," 1136.

113. On Vaqari's status and works, see Abouʾi Mehrizi, "Muʿarrifi-yi Guldasteh-yi Andisheh," 256–62. On the importance of artists in the inner circle of the Neʿmatullahis, see also chapter 7, section III, "Who Wrote it Better? Connoisseurship, Patronage, and Collecting Book Arts."

114. Ella Sykes seems to have confused Shah ʿAbbas I (r.1588–1629) and Shah ʿAbbas II (r.1642–66) as she notes that the gifting of the carpets happened in the sixteenth century. Sykes, *Through Persia*, 83–84; Sykes, *Ten Thousand Miles*, 149.

115. See, for instance, Blair, "The Ardabil Carpets in Context," 137–38; Žutić, "Safavid Number Games," 77; Beattie, *Carpets of Central Persia*, 16; Housego, "Kirman," 17. A recent article written by Devicevic suggests the possibility of a joint patronage between the Safavid court and the Mirmiran family of Yazd, but the connection with the Neʿmatullahi family is not discussed: Dervišević, "Sarajevska kermanska halija," 291–93.

116. In the past, the words in this first line have been read in the wrong order. The word *sahat* has sometimes been read as *sakht* (from *sakhtan*, building): Popović, "Fragmenti persiskih ćilima," 49; Housego, "Kirman," 16; Žutić, "Tri safavidska tepiha," 310. For a discussion of this reading as "the Sun's pupil," see Firouzeh, "Ritual Personification."

117. Blair, "Texts, Inscriptions, and the Ardabil Carpets," 141; Blair, *Text and Image*, 235.

118. Popović, followed by Housego, translated *sahat* and *rauza* as "park": Popović, "Fragmenti persiskih ćilima," 49; Housego, "Kirman," 16.

119. Popović, for instance, considers Mahdi a reference to the twelfth Shiʿa imam and Sulayman as the Ottoman ruler Suleiman the Magnificent: Popović, "Fragmenti persiskih ćilima," 43.

120. See, for instance, Žutić's translation of the line concerning Mahdi: "When the worthy carpet was finally completed, it was thrown on the tomb": Žutić, "Safavid Number Games," 79. Housego connects the act of spreading, but not the completion, of the carpets with Mahdi: "He spread this carpet in the shrine, so that it may achieve completion as it ought": Housego, "Kirman," 16–17.

121. See Aubin, *Matériaux*, 219–58.

122. Ibid., 261–67.

123. Ibid., 261–64.

124. Ibid., 246–48.

125. Ibid., 251–58.

126. On gift donations to shrines, see Blair, *Text and Image*, 241–49.

127. For such divisions in the Safavid Sufi network, see ibid., 246.

128. Ibid., 246.

129. See chapter 2, section IV, "The Making of a Transregional Sufi Network"; Tabataba, *Burhan-i maʾasir*, 92–93.

130. Beattie, *Carpets of Central Persia*, 17; Žutić, "Safavid Number Games," 77.

131. Beattie, *Carpets of Central Persia*, 9; Steinman, "Sericulture and Silk," in Bier, *Woven from the Soul*, 12.

132. Floor, "Economy and Society," in Bier, *Woven from the Soul*, 22–23.

PART THREE

Patronage *and* Authorship Inside Out

6

The Architecture of Intimate Alliances and Competitions

The aesthetic and epigraphic strategies at the Neʿmatullahi sites in Bidar, Mahan, and Taft linked these spaces through markers of kinship and belonging. Subtle strategies of naming created a spatial network for the followers of the Sufi network but also an opportunity for royal patrons connected to the family to appropriate the spatial authority constructed at these sites for their own purposes.[1] This chapter explores how early modern regimes—from local governors to reigning kings—made interventions into existing Neʿmatullahi sites or constructed new ones, utilizing architecture, epigraphy, and texts associated with the Sufi family to consolidate their dynastic power and to position themselves as divinely ordained rulers. Building on the questions raised in the discussion of thc Mahan portal in chapter 1, the case studies brought together in this chapter enumerate examples of royal patronage that can be understood as appropriations of the Neʿmatullahi authority. While the previous chapter focused on how the Sufi network created a distance from the court through spatial representations, my goal here is to take a deeper look at instances where the realms of the court and the shrine became entwined.

The chapter moves from Bidar to Mahan and Taft. The section on Bidar concerns the tomb of the Bahmanid ruler Ahmad Shah I—a royal funerary structure turned into a shared space commemorating the king and his Sufi teacher, Shah Neʿmatullah Vali. Through its spatial arrangement and its epigraphy, the tomb utilizes a dialogue with the Mahan shrine to cast Ahmad Shah as a divine king engaged in transregional conversations at the crossroads of art making and Sufism. Moving to Mahan, the Safavid-era Qurʾan recitation hall tells the story of an unsuccessful uprising, providing material evidence for several alliances—at times conflicting—that brought about this structure. The final case study in this chapter takes us to the complex in Taft and its expansion campaign by a royal Safavid patroness. Royal women who married into the Neʿmatullahi network played a pivotal role in the history of both households. They facilitated, on the one hand, the adoption of Sufi shrines outside of the Safaviyya network by the ruling elite as the locus of their power, and on the other, the Neʿmatullahi family's intermingling with elite and royal circles of art making.

This chapter has two main goals. First, while my examples are centered on court patronage, I aim to look at them from a specific angle: not only how they represent the patrons' investment in regional and transregional politics but also how the act of patronage acknowledges the established power of the Neʿmatullahis as spiritual and political interlocutors. Second, beyond notions of appropriation and intervention, this chapter highlights the strategies of intimate alliance that enabled patrons to engage with the spiritual authority of Neʿmatullahi Sufis. This subtle shift of viewpoint will allow us to understand these acts of patronage not just as the stamping of power and control onto monumental buildings but also as a process that entangled patrons into intimate connections with the Neʿmatullahi family as they formed master-disciple relations or marriage bonds, or worked together as rebellion leaders.

I. Ahmad Shah's Tomb in Bidar: Architecture as Transoceanic Dialogue

Located in the village of Ashtur outside the city of Bidar (figs. 5.10 and 5.30), the tomb of the Bahmanid ruler Ahmad Shah I (r. 1422–36) epitomizes how courts and courtly circles drew on the spiritual authority of Sufis to construct local and transregional narratives of kingship.[2] The interior program of the tomb is a visual manifestation of the Bahmanids' attempt at inscribing themselves into transoceanic dialogues with Iran and the broader Islamic world. It also demonstrates how these transregional connections were localized in the Deccan.

The tomb dates to the reign of Ahmad I's son and successor ʿAla al-din Ahmad Shah II (r. 1436–58) and is a venerated site for Muslims and Hindus in Deccan India.[3] It is part of the latest Bahmanid royal necropolis, preceded by two sites in Gulbarga, the earlier Bahmanid capital.[4] A simple domed chamber, the exterior of Ahmad Shah's tomb, is marked by carved stucco medallions and rods of black basalt accentuating the profile of the building and divisions of the facades (fig. 6.1).[5] Ahmad's tomb and its companions in the Ashtur complex are part of an architectural lineage that connects them to the variations of cubic domed structures with sloped walls and arched openings found in the two necropolises in Gulbarga as well as the Tughluq tombs of Delhi and, more broadly, what has been generally referred to in past scholarship as sultanate funerary architecture (figs. 6.2–6.4).[6]

Despite these shared architectural genealogies, the extent of surviving paintings and calligraphic inscriptions in Ahmad Shah's tomb give it a special status among its counterparts.[7] The interior of Ahmad Shah's tomb, measuring about 23.5 meters on each side of the plan and approximately 32.8 meters in height, is entirely covered by elaborate paintings (fig. 6.5).[8] This massive three-dimensional canvas of sharp contrasting colors creates an all-encompassing optic experience for the viewer—an experience sharpened by the limited light in the space. On each corner, two perforated stone windows above the dadoes allow light into the building (fig. 6.6). Except for the western wall, where the

FIGURE 6.1. Tomb of the Bahmanid ruler Ahmad Shah I in Ashtur, view from the southeast. *Photograph by author, 2013.*

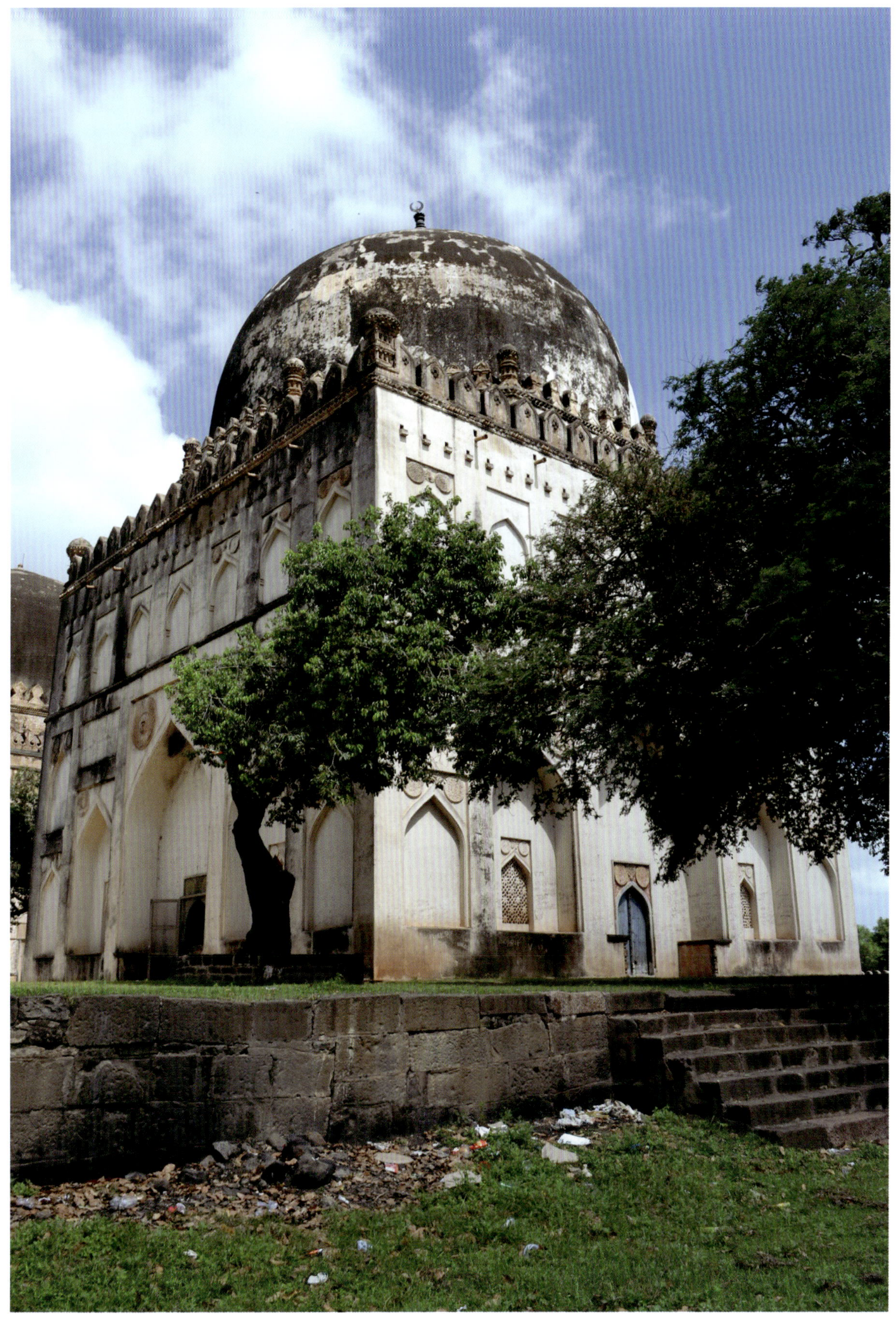

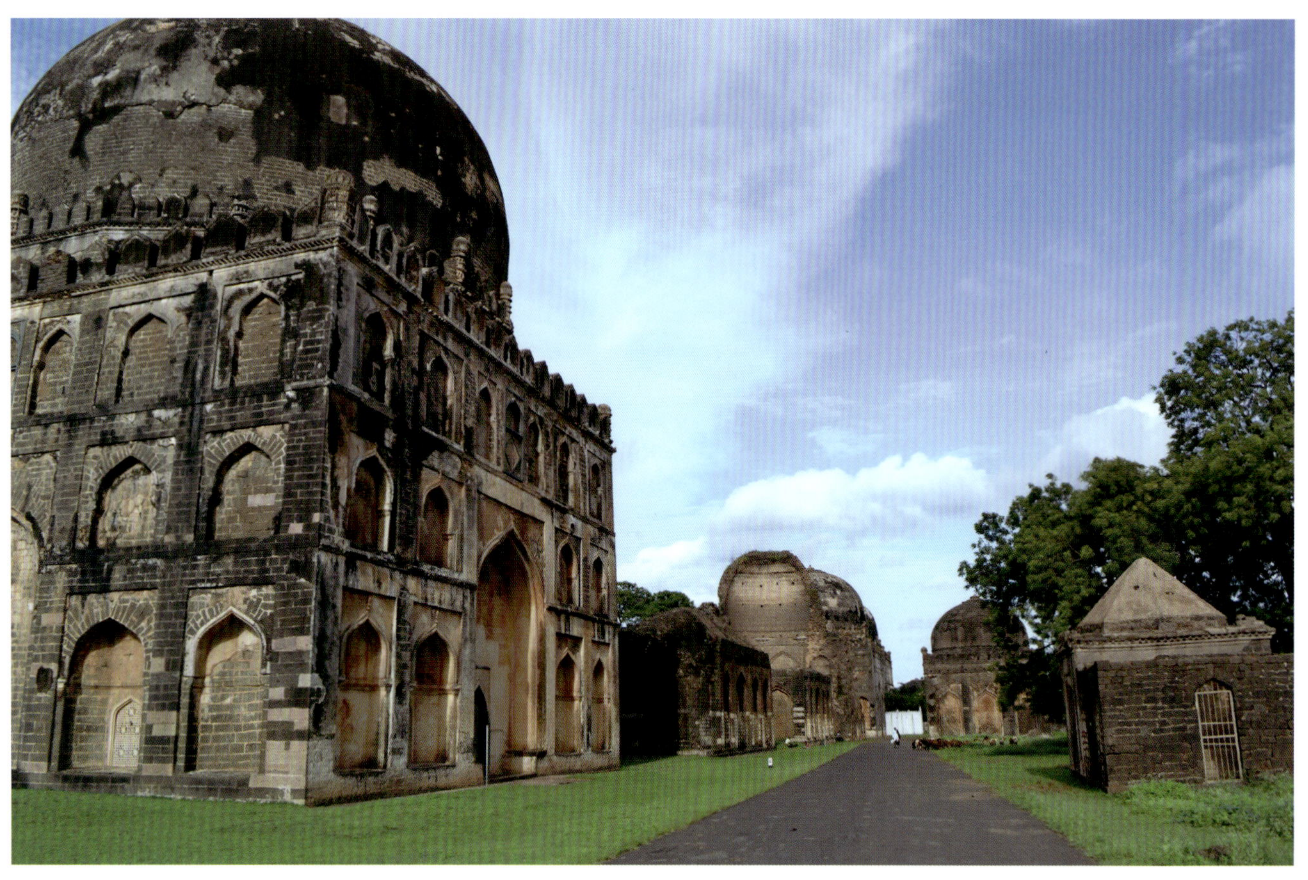

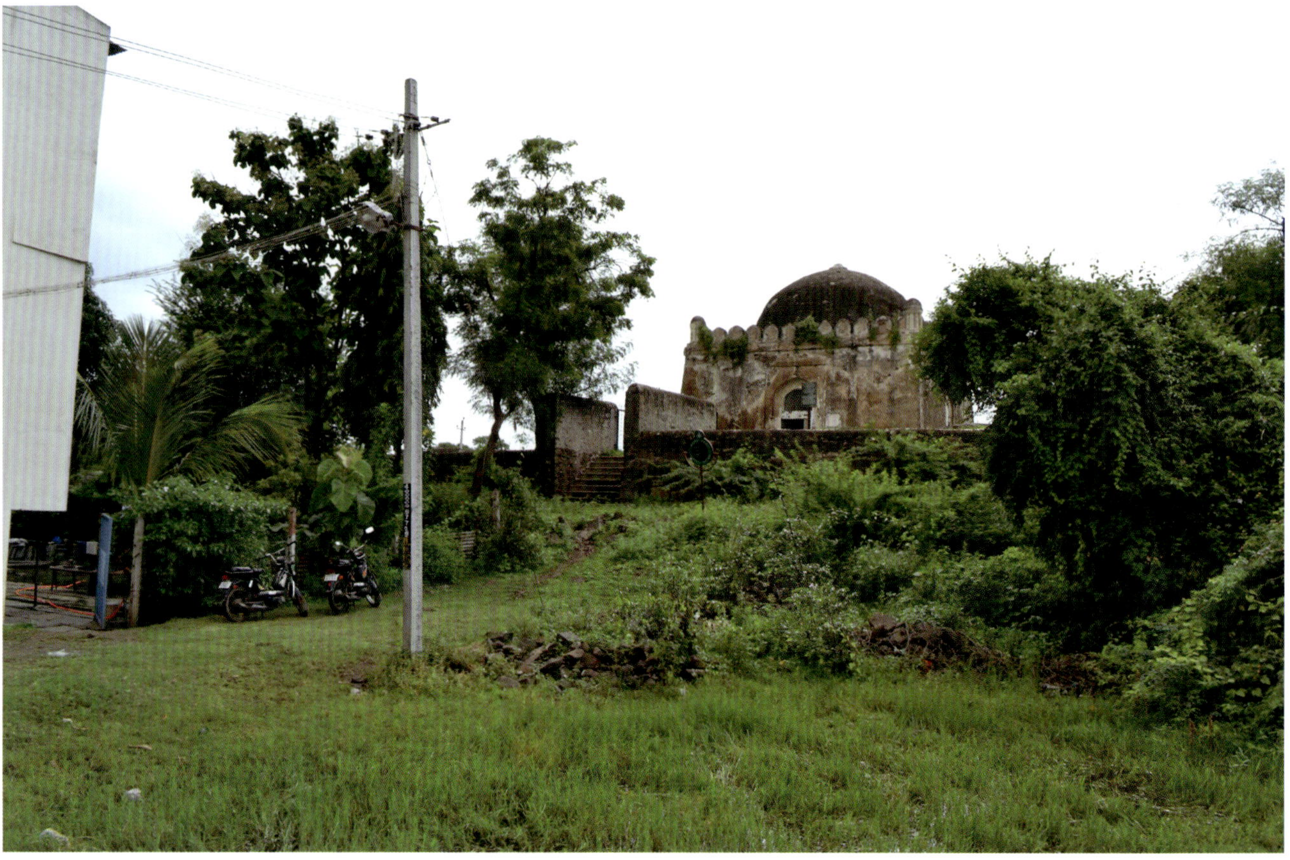

tomb's mihrab is located, arched openings give access to the chamber and, when open, allow more light in (fig. 6.5). Once the viewer's eyes are adjusted to the level of light and darkness, a wide range of designs and inscriptions can be taken in. Painted motifs range from stylized vegetal cartouches to geometrical patterns, roundels, and vases of cypress trees dotting tightly inscribed surfaces (figs. 6.5 and 0.1). Epigraphic panels, calligraphic and teardrop medallions, and concentric bands under the dome define and mark the structural lines of the architecture, its corners, and transitory spaces.

The interior is like a picture gallery showcasing a variety of experiments with intermediality. Designs that are familiar from the media of portable objects such as manuscripts, textiles, or tilework are translated into paint and plaster: corners of the tomb resemble manuscripts open to their illuminated frontispieces; wall surfaces look like carpets and wall hangings that would cover architectural surfaces; portions of the walls with their hexagonal motifs or the combination of pentagon-and-star configurations look like architectural surfaces with glazed tiles from the period (fig. 6.5).[9]

The interior's inscriptions commemorate Ahmad Shah himself but also feature names of God, blessings to the Prophet Muhammad and the twelve Shiʿa Imams alongside poems and genealogies of Ahmad Shah's Sufi guide, Shah Neʿmatullah Vali. The latter group dominates the interior space to the extent that if not for the mention of Ahmad Shah's name or the building's

FACING TOP, FIGURE 6.2. The Bahmanid royal necropolis in Ashtur, view from the west. *Photograph by author, 2013.*

FACING BOTTOM, FIGURE 6.3. Tomb of ʿAla al-din Hasan Bahmani, founder of the Bahmanid dynasty, in Gulbarga, India. *Photograph by author, 2013.*

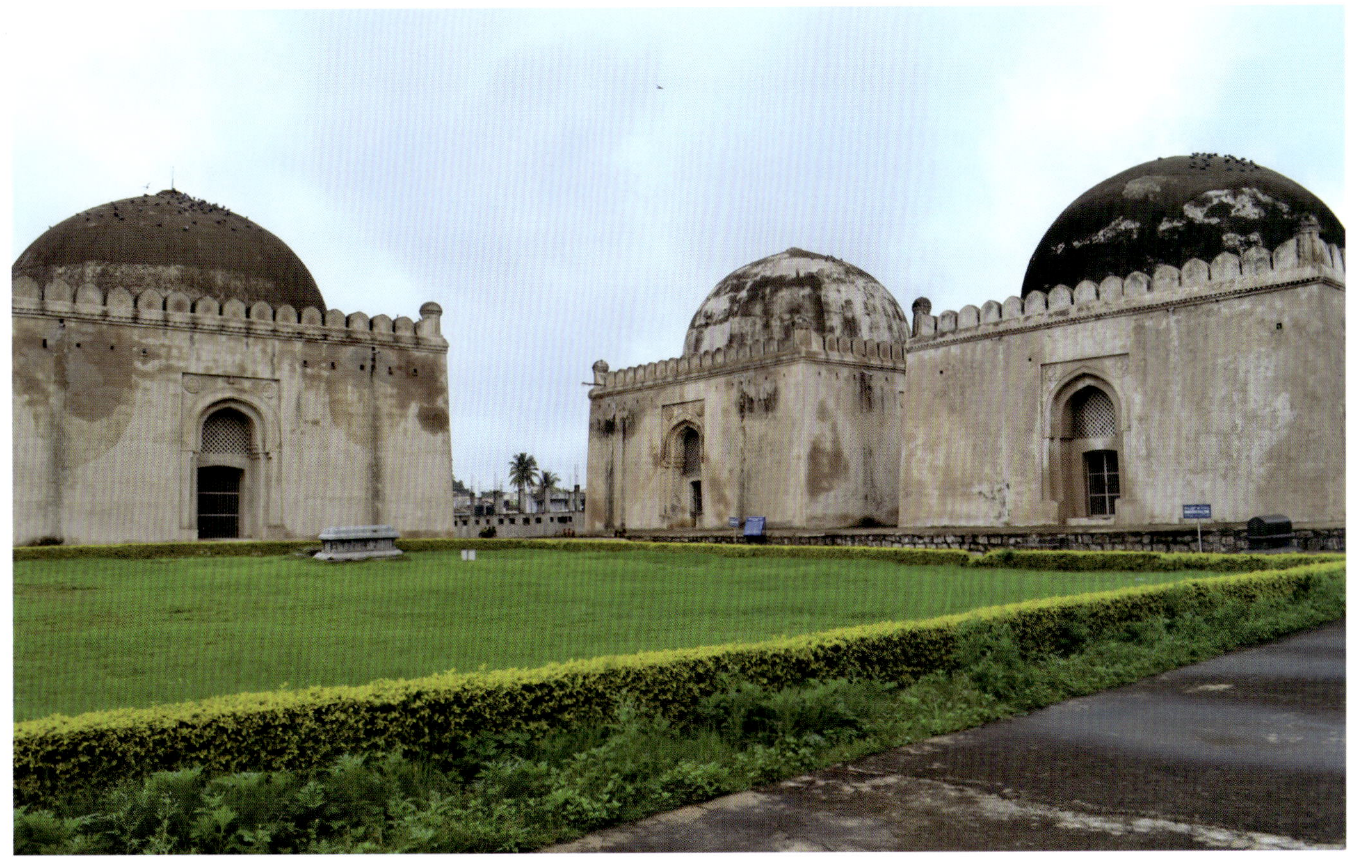

BELOW, FIGURE 6.4. The Bahmanid tombs in the Haft Gombad necropolis in Gulbarga. *Photograph by author, 2013.*

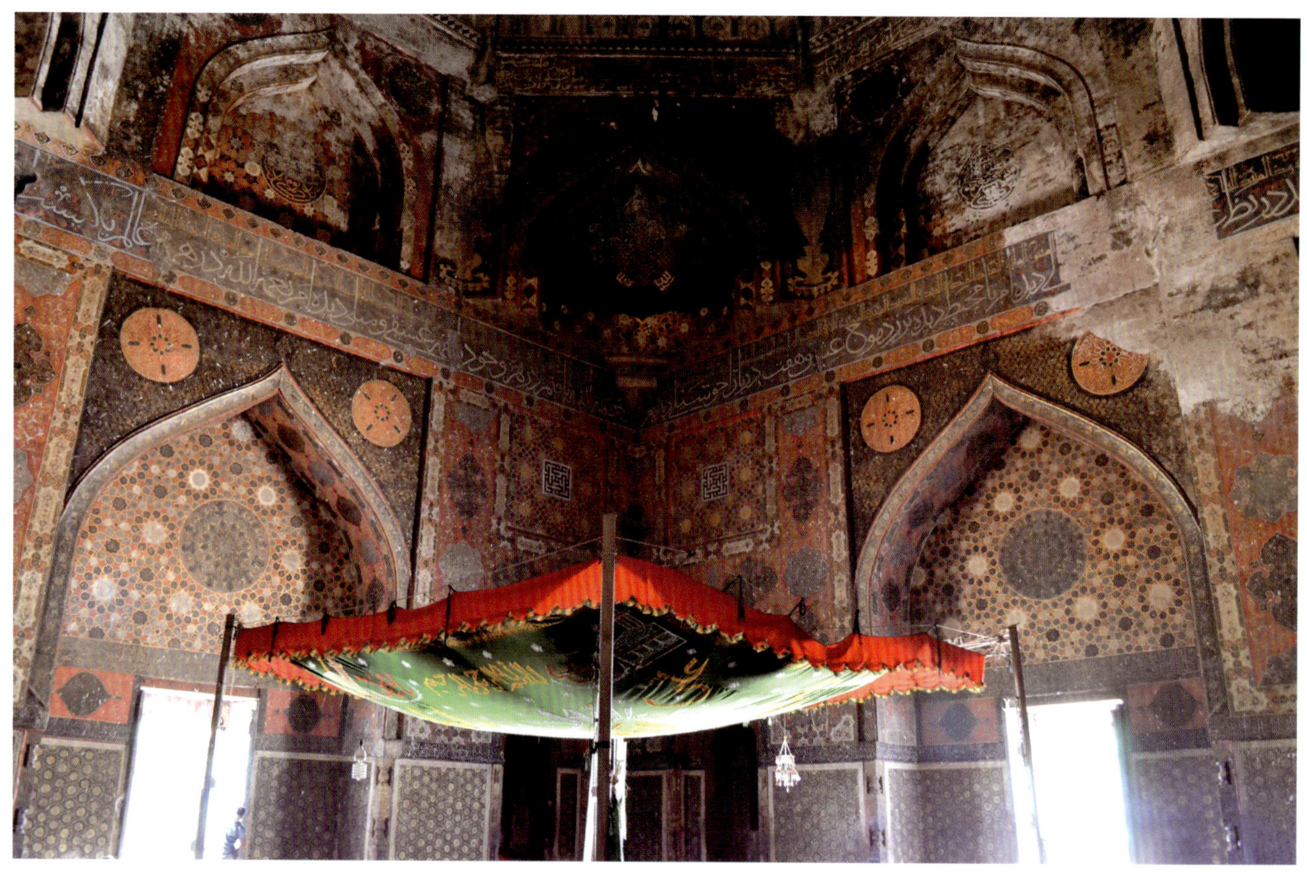

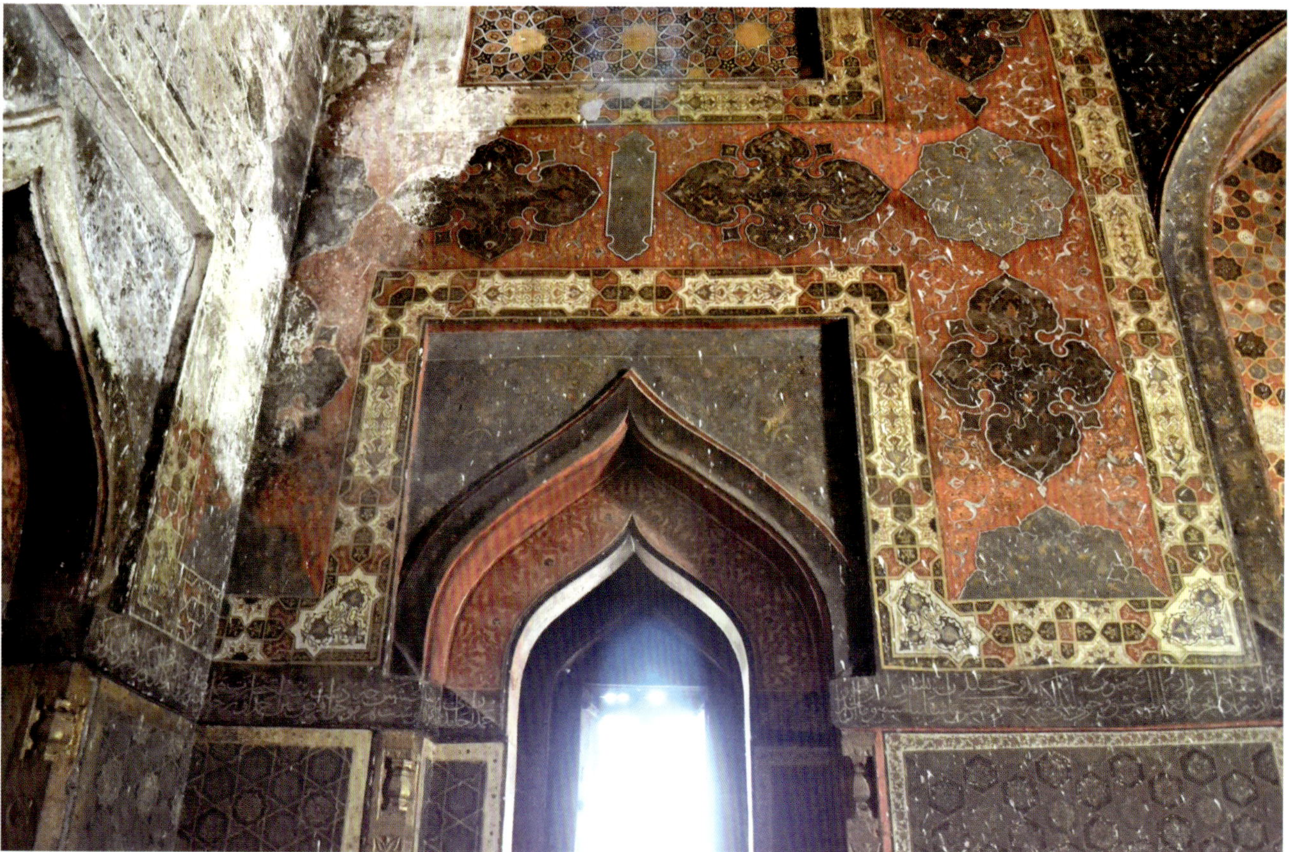

location within the Bahmanid royal necropolis, it could have been considered a commemorative space for the Sufi.

There is an overall vertical hierarchy in the interior's epigraphic program, starting with poetic inscriptions from the divan (collection of poems) of Shah Neᶜmatullah at the lowest register to the tent band marking the chamber's zone of transition where the square-shaped plan converts into an octagon (fig. 6.7).[10] The different registers of inscriptions in this area bracket four inscription panels above the doors that associate the building with the Bahmanid ruler Ahmad Shah.[11] Above the panel topping the eastern entrance of the tomb is a twelve-pointed star featuring the signature of the otherwise-unknown artist Shukrullah al-Qazvini-yi Naqqash (the painter), an itinerant artist associated with the northern Iranian city of Qazvin who worked at the Bahmanid court and was likely responsible for at least parts of the tomb's internal program (fig. 6.8).[12]

From the tent band moving upward, the inscriptions transition from poems of Shah Neᶜmatullah to his Sufi lineage as well as names of the Prophet Muhammad's descendants and God's name under the apex of the dome (fig. 6.9). The overall position of each inscription group in the chamber roughly corresponds with its symbolic and theological status: we move upward on a visual journey from the disciple to the Sufi guide and on to the Prophet Muhammad and his household before culminating in the name of God.

The epigraphic program of Ahmad Shah's tomb has been studied with great scrutiny. Ghulam Yazdani deciphered many of the inscriptions of this space, and I read and discussed the remaining ones elsewhere in the context of their spatial hierarchy within the tomb as well as transregional connections between Iran and Deccan India.[13] Here, I want to focus on two groups of inscriptions in the tomb that encapsulate the Bahmanids' appropriation of and intervention into the Neᶜmatullahi poetic and hagiographic traditions through architecture.

The first group of inscriptions, which were invoked in the introduction of this book, are from the widest inscription panel in the interior of the tomb—the tent band running around the whole space just above the main recessed arches (figs. 6.5 and 6.7 and app. 6.1). Two different inscriptions are juxtaposed on this panel: the lower line, in larger white letters in thuluth script, contains poems from the divan of Shah Neᶜmatullah Vali (figs. 6.7 and 6.10). The poetic verses are topped by superscriptions of smaller letters in (now much faded) gold in Kufic script. These superscriptions, which Yazdani referred to as religious texts, are in fact the ninety-nine names of God (*asmaʾ al-husna*).[14] The aesthetics of the tent band draw on the familiar visual features of Persianate foundation inscriptions: all texts are written against a blue background, reminiscent of dark-blue tiled surfaces. The juxtaposition of the two lines of calligraphy, one in Kufic, which is usually reserved for Qurʾanic verses in foundation panels, and one in thuluth containing information about the foundation of the structure, are replaced here by the ninety-nine names of

FACING TOP, FIGURE 6.5. Interior of Ahmad Shah I's tomb in Ashtur. *Photograph by author, 2013.*

FACING BOTTOM, FIGURE 6.6. One of the perforated windows in the interior of Ahmad Shah I's tomb in Ashtur. *Photograph by author, 2013.*

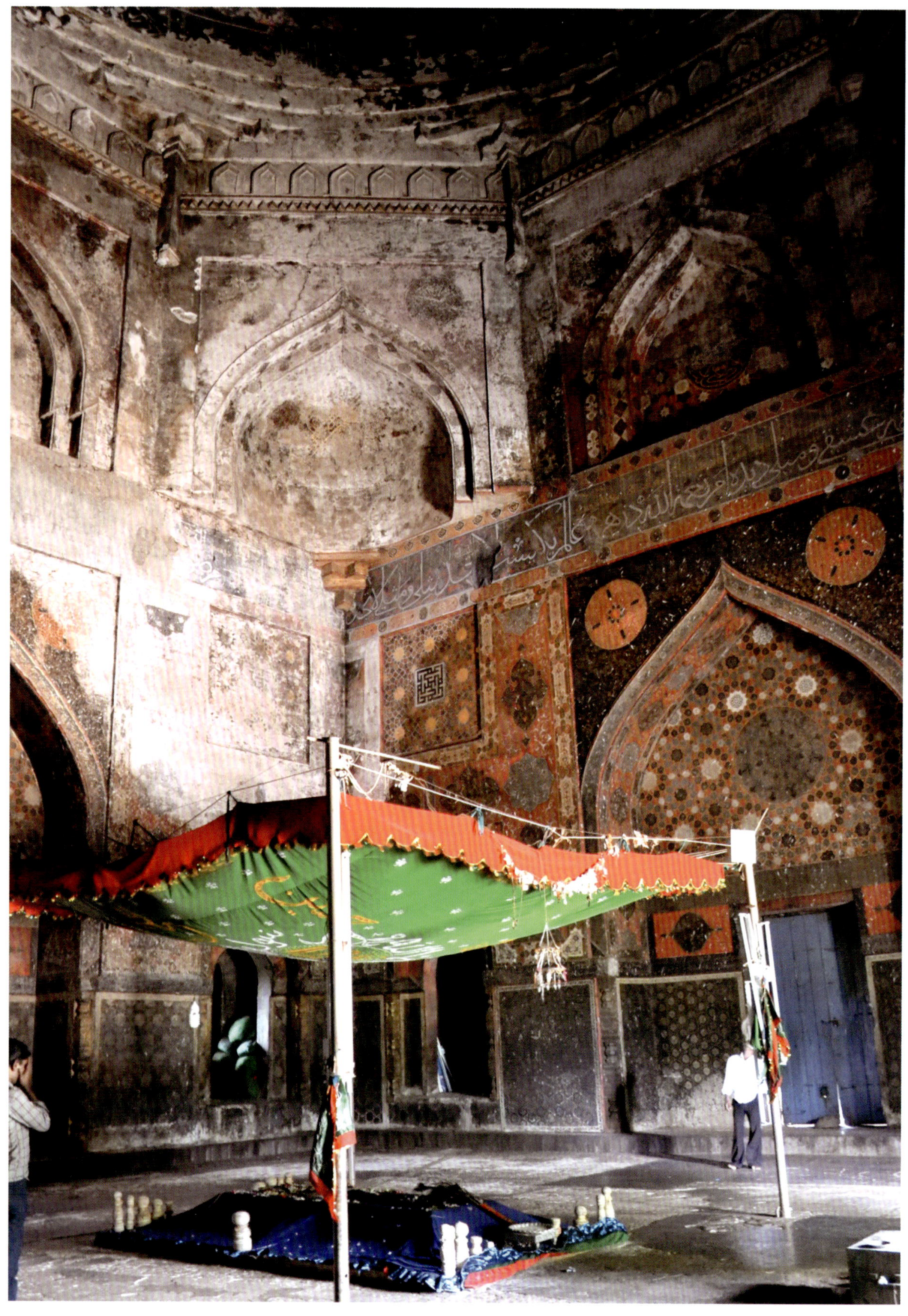

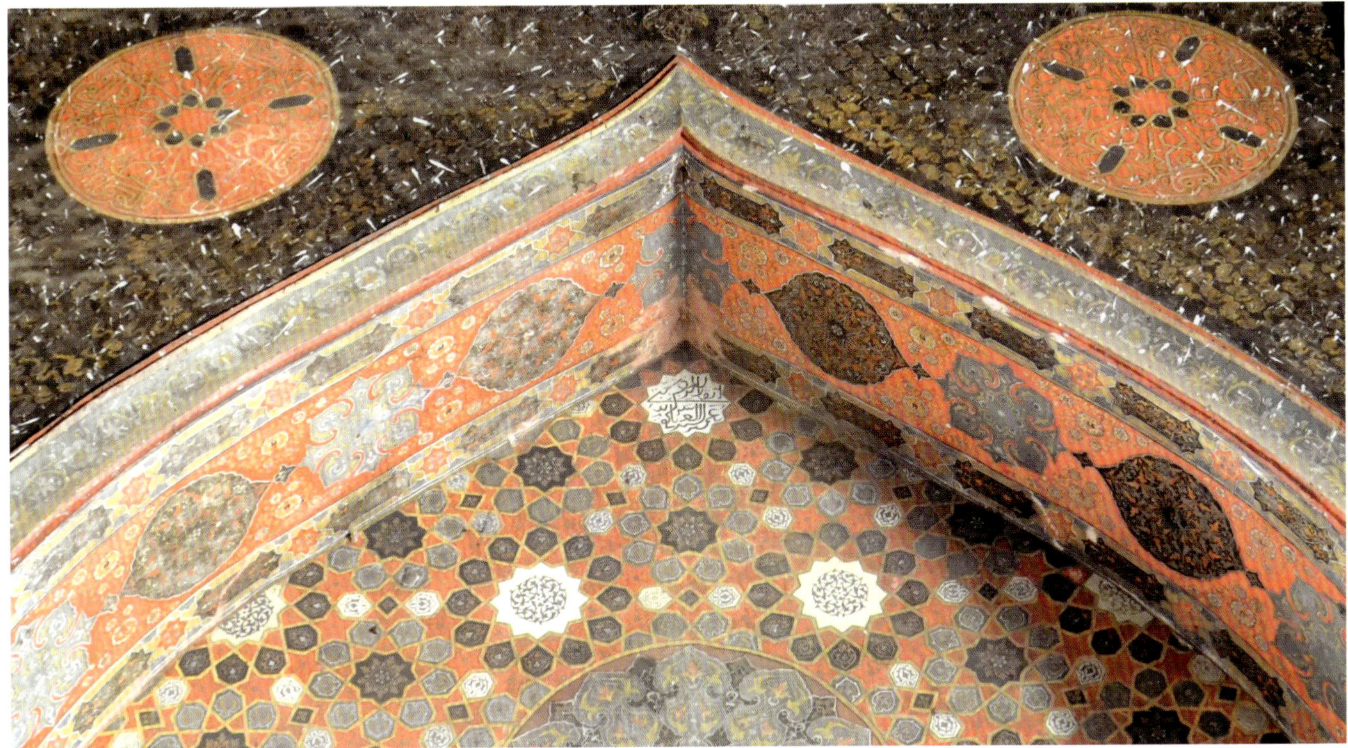

God and poetry of Shah Neᶜmatullah, respectively. There is perhaps a subtle suggestion here that the Sufi's verses of poetry *are the foundation* of this tomb.

Even more suggestive is the choice of poetic verses on this band and their connection with the Sufi's tomb in Mahan. The tent band verses on two out of the four walls in Bidar are rendered illegible due to water damage (figs. 6.7 and 6.10).[15] The verses that survive on the southern and eastern walls were not from the same poem but were chosen purposefully from two different poems for their content. Both feature the title "Neᶜmat Allah," meaning "Grace of God" (fig. 6.7). The process to select these verses replicated that of the verses in Mahan's sepulchre, which—as a reminder—was finished in 1436 with donations from Ahmad Shah and his son, around the same time as the construction of the Bidar tomb (fig. 1.13). The main difference is that in Mahan's interior, the inscriptions invoking the name Neᶜmat Allah are citations from the Qurʾan and not the poems of Shah Neᶜmatullah. An act of substitution is at work here: where the interior of the teacher's tomb is adorned with the word of God, the disciple's tomb depends on the words of the Sufi guide. This substitution echoes the hierarchies evident in the vertical arrangement of the tomb's epigraphic program, from the cenotaph of Ahmad Shah to the apex of the dome.

Through this substitution a collapsing of the geographical distance between the tombs in Mahan and Bidar is also at work, linking the lineages constructed in the two spaces. The relationship between the two tent bands in Mahan and Bidar creates a transoceanic dialogue. Where the disciple adopts the voice

FACING, FIGURE 6.7. Interior of Ahmad Shah I's tomb in Ashtur, view toward the northeast corner. *Photograph by author, 2013.*

ABOVE, FIGURE 6.8. Signature of Shukrullah al-Qazvini-yi Naqqash in the apex of the niche on the eastern wall of Ahmad Shah I's tomb in Ashtur. *Photograph by author, 2013.*

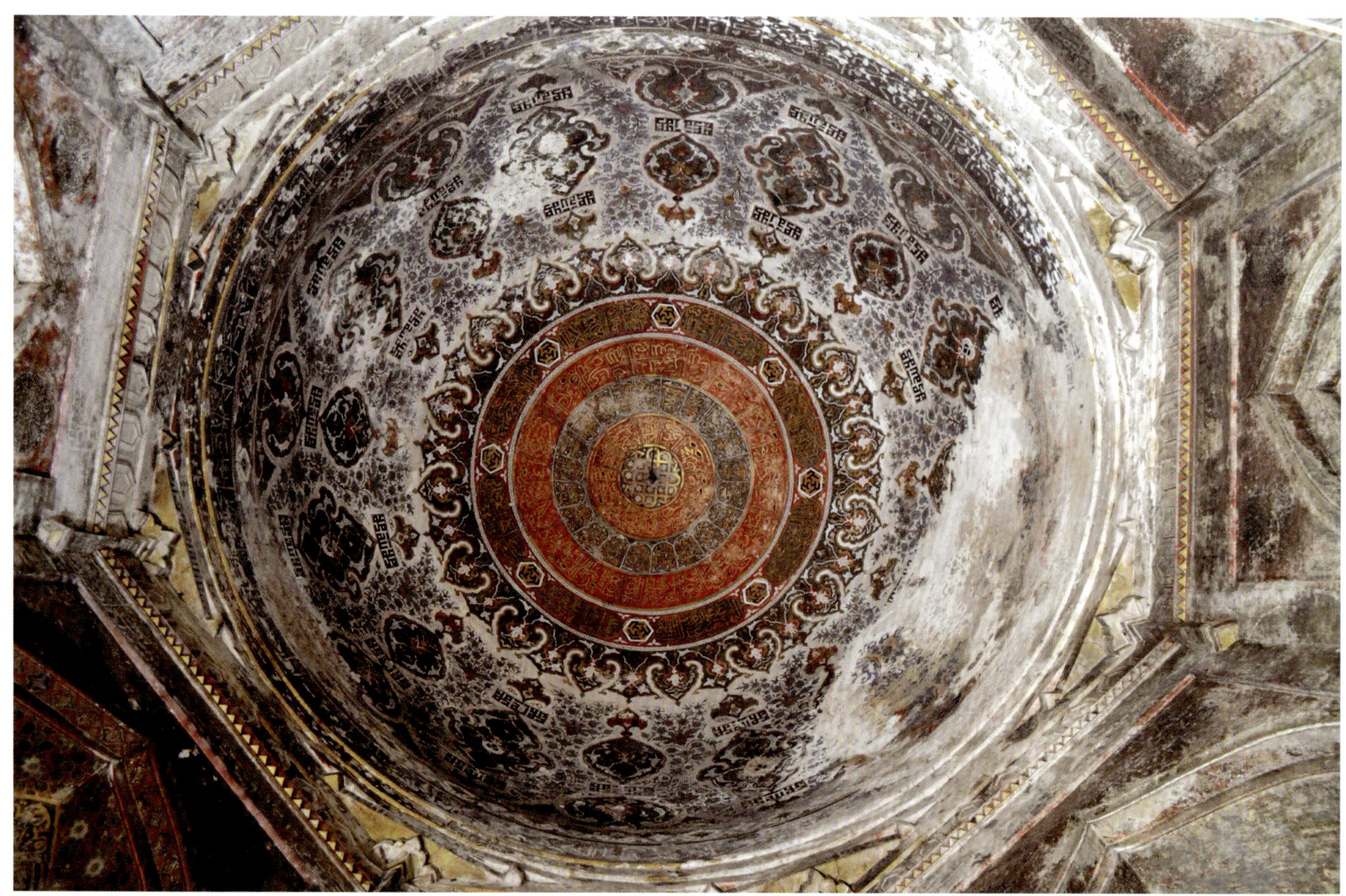

FIGURE 6.9. Interior of Ahmad Shah I's tomb in Ashtur, looking up toward the zone of transition and the dome. *Photograph by author, 2013.*

of the Sufi to call on him, the Sufi speaks by drawing on the words of God. In doing so, the two architectural structures and their dialogue become a spatial rendition of the literary genre of *javab*—philosophical questions and responses exchanged between Sufis and their disciples. In this dialogue, the disciple and the Sufi master are represented by the corporeality of their mausoleums on the two sides of the ocean.

This dialogic notion of the building reverberates in other inscriptions in the tomb at Bidar. As I have discussed elsewhere, some epigraphic segments of the tomb are meant to resonate with the historical and imagined elements of the relationship between Ahmad Shah and his Sufi teacher.[16] One such example is the poem inscribed on the rim of the dome in Ahmad Shah's tomb, sourced from the Sufi's collection of poems (fig. 6.9).[17] In its new architectural setting, what was written as a poem on divine love comes to echo the sense of longing between a teacher and a disciple who never actually met. The poem's theme of encounter can here be interpreted in light of the pivotal role of dreams in the Sufi-disciple relationship. As noted previously, Ahmad Shah dreamed of an unnamed Sufi shaykh who—as he later learned, according to some hagiographic traditions—was none other than Shah Neʿmatullah Vali, who promised the kingdom of the Deccan to the future ruler.[18]

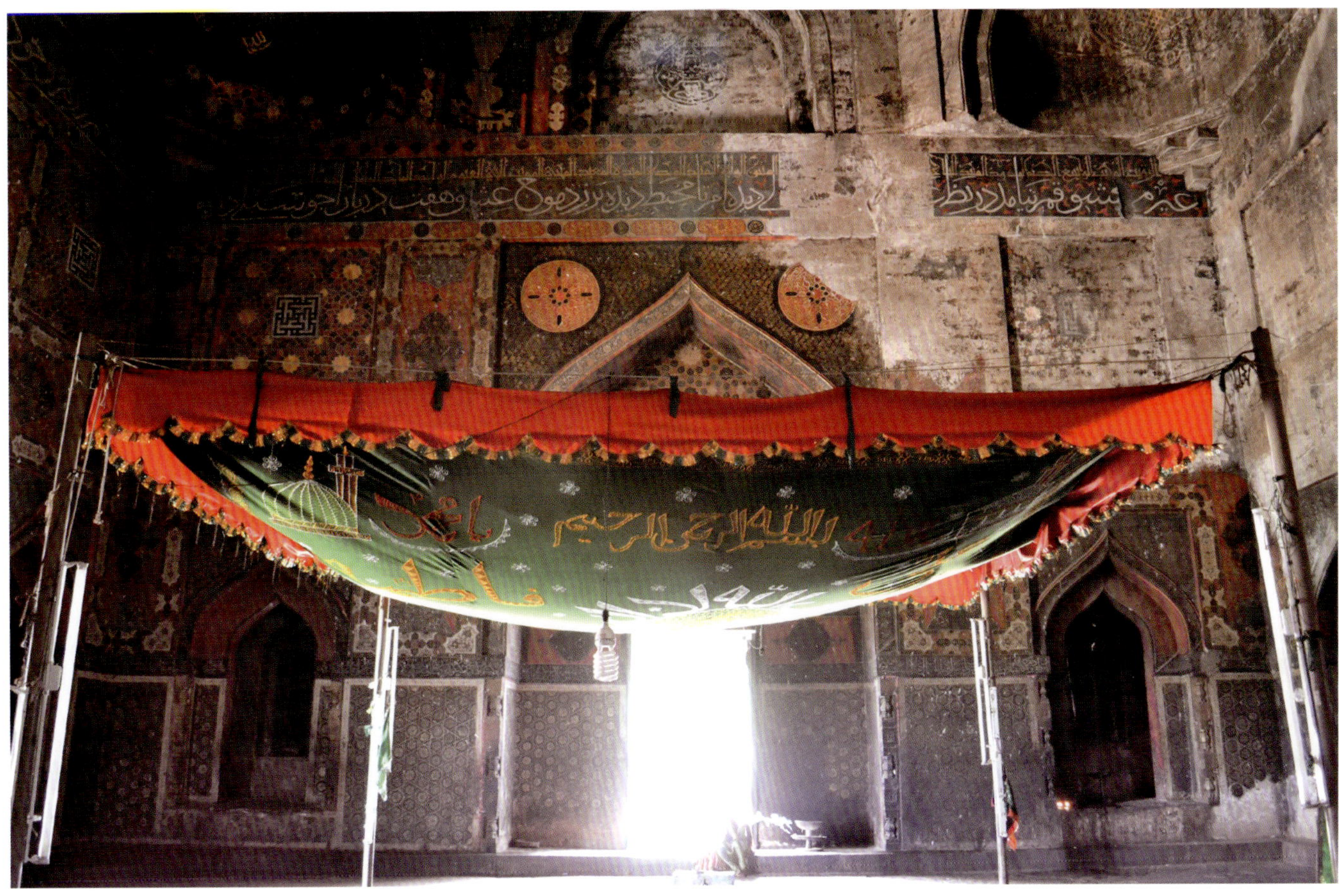

FIGURE 6.10. Tent band inscription on the southern wall of Ahmad Shah I's tomb in Ashtur. *Photograph by author, 2013.*

The anonymity of the Sufi in the dream and the two figures' longing for one another—themes that dominate the poem on the rim of the dome—are common tropes in Sufi poetry, but the choice of Shah Neʿmatullah's poem for an inscription in the Bidar tomb is also laden with historical specificity. The poem relates a sense of eternal anticipation for a reunion, one that is also noted in historical narratives of their relationship, which claim that Shah Neʿmatullah was awaiting the king as his future disciple.[19] The two were thus destined to meet, and while this reunion never took place in real life, Ahmad Shah's tomb becomes a materialization of their union where the body of the king and the words of his Sufi master are laid together. Multiple self-referential inscriptions echo this intimacy, emphasizing time and again that the king's tomb is a Sufi khanaqah. The tomb becomes the meeting place for a meeting that never occurred—a dreamscape built out of stone, mortar, and poetic verses.[20]

A second group of inscriptions weaves the history of the Bahmanids into the lineage of the Neʿmatullahi Sufis in an even more pointed manner. Under the apex of the dome are four concentric bands of inscription fringed with a series of palmettes (figs. 6.9 and 6.11).[21] The outermost band, arranged in cartouches, contains invocations to the Prophet Muhammad and his family. The next two bands are inscribed with the silsila (Sufi lineage) of Shah Neʿmatullah

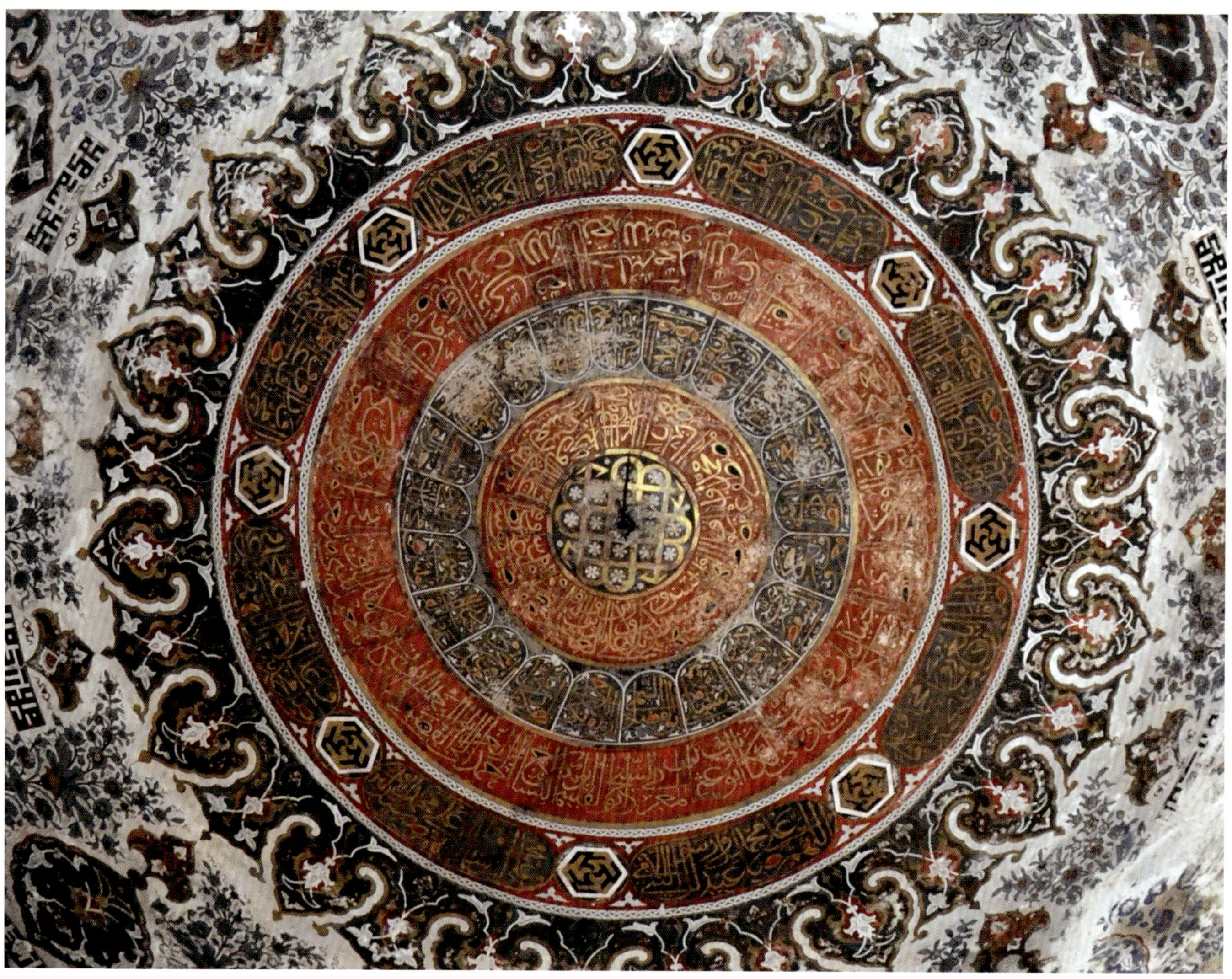

FIGURE 6.11. Concentric inscriptions under the dome of Ahmad Shah I's tomb in Ashtur. *Photograph by author, 2013.*

Vali (app. 6.2).[22] In the innermost band with the vermilion background are the names of and blessings to the Prophet Muhammad, his daughter Fatima, and the twelve Shi^ca Imams. Finally, the concentric bands culminate in a roundel under the apex of the dome that contains a monogram device amounting to the word *Allah* (God) inscribed in four directions.[23] This concentric configuration with the notion of the divine at its center resonates across visual cultures of painting the cosmos.[24] More specifically, it is echoed in numerous examples of Sufi poetry as well as in poems attributed to Shah Neʿmatullah that equate God, as the pole of the universe, with a dot in the middle of the circles that comprise the world.[25]

Among the concentric bands in Ahmad Shah's tomb, the two dedicated to the silsilas of Shah Neʿmatullah are particularly significant here. In general, silsilas record the Sufis' chain of initiation, accounting for the status of a Sufi master in a wider system of spiritual authority.[26] The silsila traces the official reception of permission (ijaza) by a disciple from their Sufi teacher, authorizing them to accept followers and pass their knowledge and teachings on to them. The reception of ijaza could entail a ritual in which a khirqa (patched cloak) or taj (hat) was bestowed on the disciple from the hand of the master; the tactile element of both the textile and the act of exchange signified the transmission of permission to the body of the disciple.[27] While the ritual was an ephemeral event, the objects exchanged, and the historicizing silsilas in hagiographies, had a lasting effect. Most influential Sufis had more than one silsila. Since disciples endeavored to travel around and benefit from the teachings of authoritative contemporary Sufis from different networks, they could receive permission from multiple teachers, inevitably leading to the existence of numerous silsilas for a Sufi, some more popular than others.

What we see in the circular inscription bands under the dome of Ahmad Shah's tomb in Bidar are only two of the many possible variations of Shah Neᶜmatullah's silsilas (fig. 6.11). These variations are recorded in a contemporary hagiographical text on the life of Shah Neᶜmatullah written by Shir Malik Waᶜizi in the first half of the fifteenth century. As mentioned before, the hagiography was written in the Deccan and dedicated to ᶜAla al-din Ahmad Shah II, son of Ahmad Shah I, during whose reign his father's tomb was completed. The two lineages inscribed in Ahmad Shah's tomb appear as two of the main silsilas recorded in Waᶜizi's hagiography.[28] Both silsilas, as was common, start with Shah Neᶜmatullah and move backward, recording the chain of his teachers and their teachers, ending the lineage with the Prophet Muhammad.

Another section of Waᶜizi's hagiography sheds further light on the significance of the silsila inscriptions in Ahmad Shah's tomb. In a chapter on matters of succession and spiritual authority, Waᶜizi specifies some of the "perfect mystics" (*ᶜurafa-yi kamil*) and "seekers of truth" (*tullab-i haq*) whom Shah Neᶜmatullah had chosen as his most righteous successors, granting them permission to spread his teachings. While the silsilas map the history of the Sufi network's authority across time and space, moving back in time through Sufi teachers in different locales, the following section of Waᶜizi's text gives us a glimpse of a vision for the *future* of the Neᶜmatullahi network. The author lists the main successors of Shah Neᶜmatullah as follows:

> [His] son, the owner of his prayer mat (*sahib-i sajjada*), the successor on his path (*khalaf-i bar jadda*), agreeable to his posterity, hazrat-i Amir Shahab al-din Khalilullah; the great noble-born (*makhdumzada*), the essence (*zubda*) of the family, hazrat-i Amir Nurullah; the agreeable great noble-born, hazrat-i Samad Amir Shams al-din Muhammad; the great noble-born, Amir Habibullah; the great noble-born, Amir Muhibbullah.[29]

The five successors named thus far include Shah Neᶜmatullah's only son, Khalilullah, buried in proximity to the Bahmanid necropolis outside Bidar, and his four sons. The account then continues to name a sixth successor:

> . . . the honorable caliph, the legitimate successor, the most virtuous of the sultans, the most perfect of the mystics, who seeks victory in God—the Self-Sufficient—the father of conquests, Shahab al-dunya wa'l-din Ahmad Shah Abi al-Bahmani—may God enlighten his grave.[30]

This is a powerful and unambiguous narrative of the transmission of spiritual authority from the Sufi family to the Bahmanid household. Unsurprisingly, given the Bahmanid context of this hagiography and its dedication to Ahmad I's successor and patron of the Neʿmatullahis, Ahmad Shah II, this extract is unique among the hagiographies of Shah Neʿmatullah. In other hagiographies, Ahmad Shah is mentioned only in the capacity of a patron of the Sufi network. The circumstances of the text clarify questions of when, where, and why Sufi hagiographies were commissioned. For the Bahmanids, it served the purpose of assuming the status of "perfect mystics" within a Sufi network of their choice. For the Neʿmatullahis, it facilitated the establishment of their network in a new locale.

In the account above, the Bahmanid king is portrayed as a ruler who has combined *saltanat* (worldly sovereignty) with *wilayat* (spiritual authority)—a "sacred king" whose tomb is a shared space between the temporal and the spiritual, a royal tomb as well as a khanaqah. Ahmad Shah's adoption of the title *vali* (or *wali*, meaning friend of God), which was allegedly given to him by Shah Neʿmatullah, is absent from the coinage of Ahmad Shah I but recorded in that of his successors.[31] The coinage thus bears witness to a sustained claim in the Bahmanid house.

Ahmad Shah's inclusion among the core group of successors of Shah Neʿmatullah, all of whom were close family members, was not a natural affair given the lack of both direct contact and blood relations between the two figures. Hagiography and architecture filled this gap. What the hagiographic text verbalizes in such unambiguous terms, the architecture of Ahmad Shah's tomb achieves metaphorically through its spatial organization. Sitting right underneath the concentric bands inscribed with the primary silsilas of Shah Neʿmatullah, the cenotaph of the Bahmanid ruler occupies the last loop in the chain of the Sufi's lineage. Although elusive due to the absence of a direct mention of Ahmad Shah's name, the architectural inscriptions under the dome widen the audience of the legitimacy narratives, inscribing them in a more public arena than the hagiographies. Like official public documents, the contextual meaning of these inscriptions in the space is to affirm the Bahmanid's belonging in the chain of Neʿmatullahi Sufis. We need to remember that the building of the new capital in Bidar and its urban program, which included the Bahmanid necropolis, were carried out in a moment of political and spiritual legitimacy crises that were precipitated, on the one hand, by the violent transition of power from Ahmad's brother and predecessor to himself and, on the other, by the loss of Ahmad Shah's spiritual guide, Gisu Daraz. Against this background, the public depictions of legitimacy narratives gain an urgent level of significance.

In Ahmad Shah's tomb we are confronted with a sacral model of kingship that is constructed through a transregional dialogue, drawing on the spiritual authority of a Sufi who never set foot in the Deccan, borrowing verses of poetry that were penned on the other side of the ocean at the khanaqahs of the Sufi in Iran. The inscription of the silsilas under the dome intensifies this transregional dimension, linking the tomb to a wide range of geographical locations associated with the chain of Sufi masters from many great centers of learning in the Islamic world. To borrow Nile Green's words, the physical location of this tomb in the Deccan was displaced by the "hagiographical or devotional eye" that saw this space lying on a route connecting it to places like Mecca, Baghdad, and Mahan.[32] And yet, as transregional as this notion of divinely ordained kingship may be, it is also firmly localized in Ahmad Shah's tomb, a building made of locally sourced stones, following the Deccani style of funerary architecture, and with interior decorations that in design and color scheme were the product of the cosmopolitan locale of the Bahmanid capital.

II. The Dar al-Huffaz in Mahan: Time Capsule of a Rebellion

There is a subtle yet critical relationship between the Neʿmatullahi hagiographic traditions in fifteenth-century Bahmanid Deccan and sixteenth-century Safavid Iran. These moments represent the two historical periods in which the surviving biographies of Shah Neʿmatullah were written. Like the fifteenth-century hagiography written in the Deccan, those from the sixteenth and seventeenth centuries fulfilled a need for the Sufi family: the reestablishment of their power and status in a new political environment, this time in Safavid Iran.

In the Safavid era, this hagiography-writing impulse worked in tandem with the Neʿmatullahi descendants' reinterpretations of the Sufi saint's corpus of poetry to cast an image of themselves as believers in the spiritual authority of the Safavid rulers and as their loyal supporters.[33] At first glance, such historiographic alignments stand in contrast with challenges that other Sufi networks endured or presented to the Safavids, in particular Shah ʿAbbas I (r. 1588–1629).[34] The Neʿmatullahis were not unique in this regard, neither in their favorable treatment by the Safavids nor in the challenges that accompanied such close connections with the royal household.[35]

Contemporary with the reworkings of Neʿmatullahi writings were expansions at the shrine in Mahan (fig. 1.3). This architectural campaign was led by local authorities accompanied by a nod to the support from the central Safavid government. While the Neʿmatullahis' role in Safavid historiography and in the service of empire building has received attention from historians, my goal here is to connect the textual evidence with the architectural.[36]

As discussed in chapter 1, the mausoleum of Shah Neʿmatullah in Mahan developed from a single-dome chamber to a multilayered complex during the reign of the Safavid ruler Shah ʿAbbas I. A vaulted hall known as the dar al-huffaz (hall of [Qurʾan] reciters) or riwaq-i ʿAbbasi, adjoined by a courtyard, was added to the western side of the fifteenth-century dome chamber (figs. 1.5 and 1.6).[37] A foundation inscription inside the vaulted hall records this phase of construction, dated Shawwal 998/August–September 1590 (figs. 1.16, 1.28, and 6.12). This date is also inscribed in a roundel on the other side of the recitation hall (fig. 1.18). A tent band inscription, running around the entirety of the vaulted hall and featuring the Surat al-Fath (Victory) of the Qurʾan, is

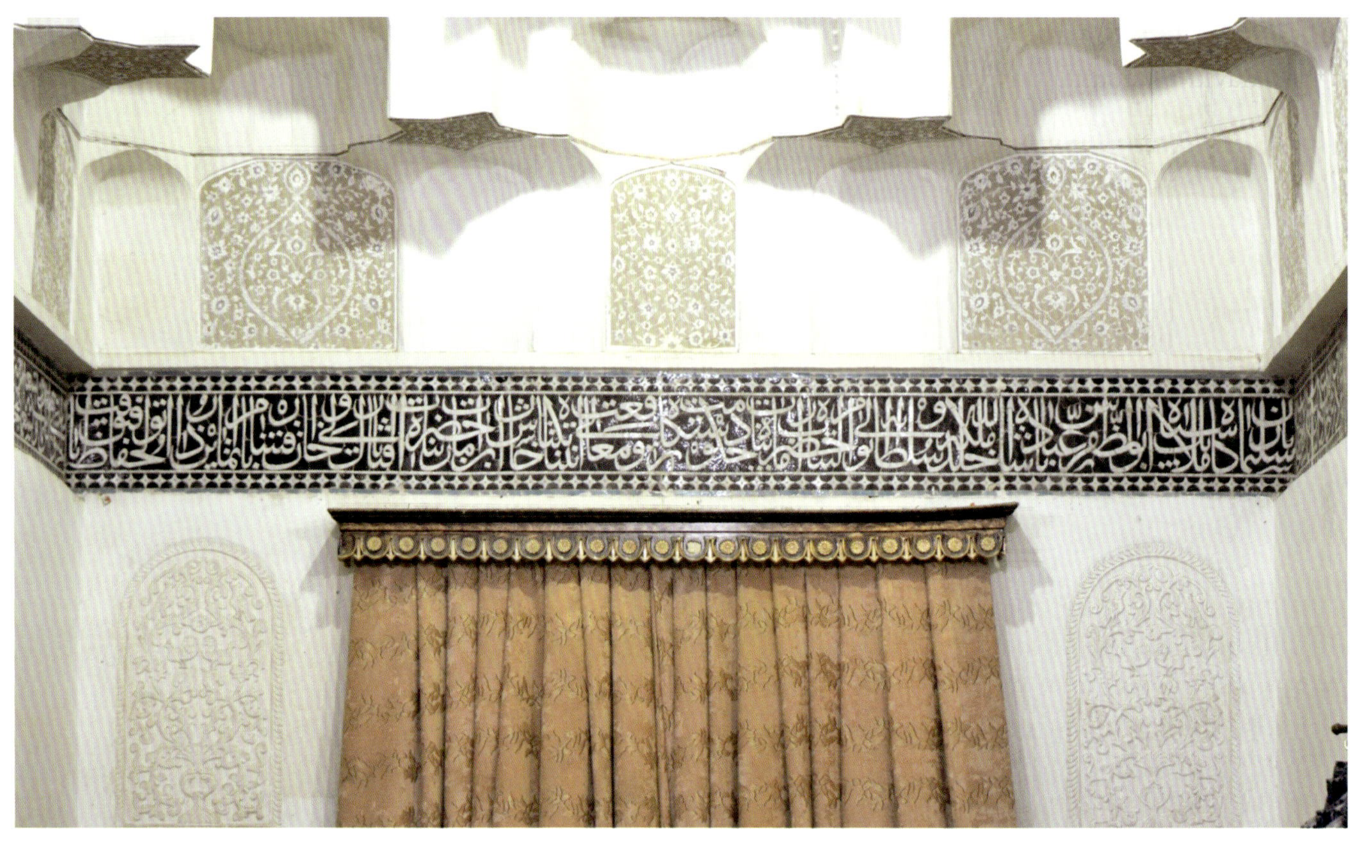

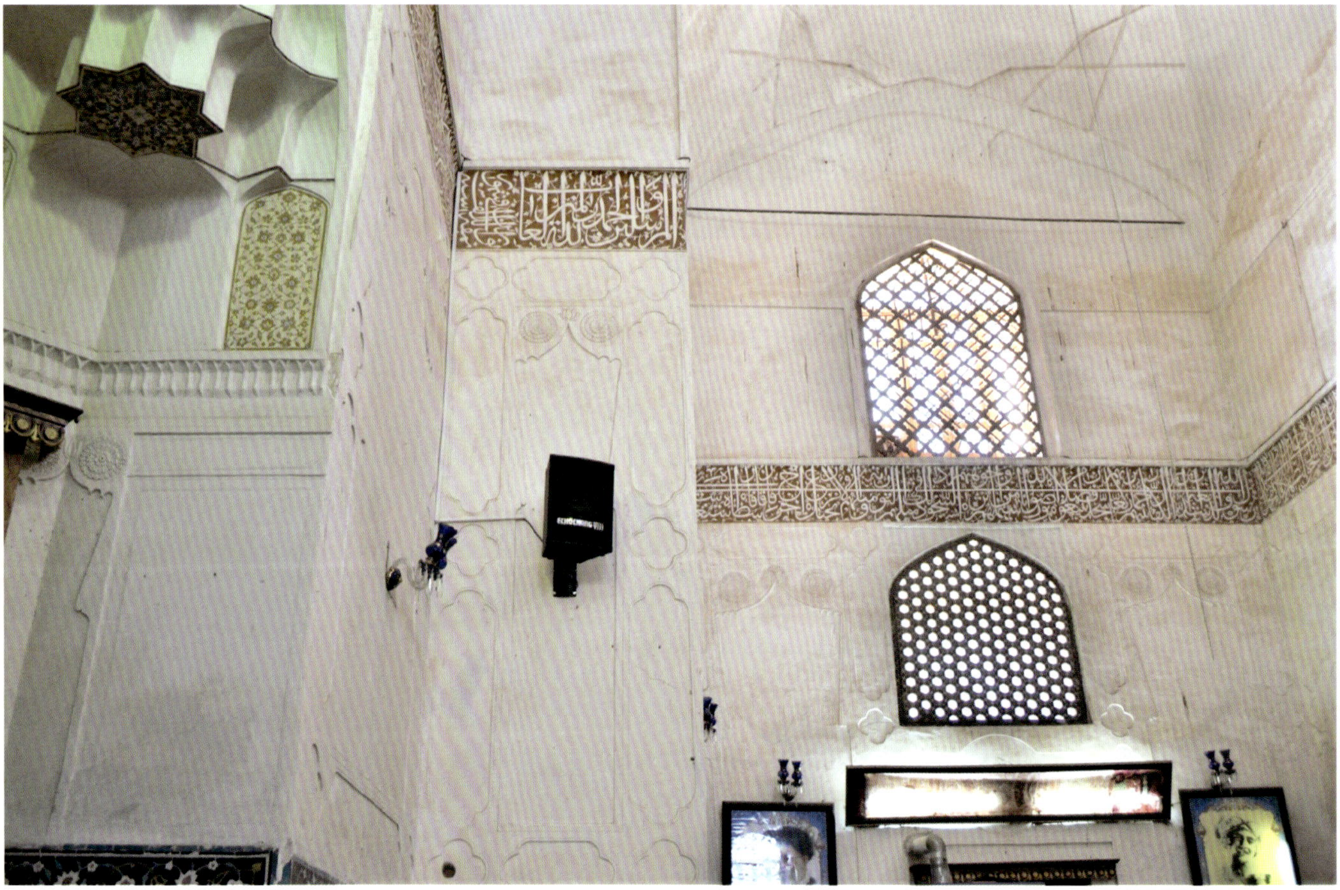

signed by a Nur al-din in the year 1000/1592–93, two years after the completion of the Safavid-era foundation inscription (fig. 6.13).

The foundation inscription attributes the patronage of the vaulted hall to Bektash Khan-i Afshar (d. 1589), the governor of Kerman and Baluchestan in the sixteenth century. He shares this inscribed space with Shah ʿAbbas I, whose name precedes the governor (fig. 6.12 and app. 1.3).[38] The inscription specifies that the building was finished "in the reign of" (*dar zaman-i khilafat*) the Safavid king. This formula does not normally suggest a direct involvement of the reigning king, but here it is immediately followed by introducing the patron, Bektash Khan, as the "*vali-yi ʿamr*" of the Safavid king—his representative or executer of his commands. The combination suggests the Safavid ruler's oversight—however hands-off—of this architectural campaign.

This was a highly significant moment in time. It was only a few years before the Safavid capital was officially moved from Qazvin in the north to Isfahan and just two years before the year 1000 in the hijri calendar (corresponding to the years 1590–91), a year laden with millenarian expectations around the return of the Mahdi (messiah); it thus also falls on the cusp of civil rebellions around Safavid territories, several of which had millenarian motivations.[39] Particularly relevant within this context were the violent conflicts between the Afshar and Zu'l-qadr tribes in central Iran, which involved all the players in the construction of the dar al-huffaz at Mahan: Bektash Khan-i Afshar, Shah ʿAbbas I, and prominent figures of the Neʿmatullahi network who took sides in these conflicts. This highly charged political context will throw some light on the circumstances around the architectural intervention into the shrine at Mahan, especially the contradictions posed by the epigraphic evidence within it.

The expansion of the shrine at Mahan fits perfectly in two broader historical patterns. First, the early Safavid era corresponds to the increase in return or resettlement of members of the Neʿmatullahi network who had migrated to Deccan India or were moving between the centers of the network in Iran and India in the fifteenth century.[40] While the family maintained some presence in the Deccan, this new wave of migration was incentivized by the gradual disintegration of the family's major patrons, the Bahmanid dynasty of Deccan India, in the late fifteenth and early sixteenth centuries.[41] This resurgence in the presence of influential members of the family in Iran led to a renewed attention toward hagiography writing in Iran and construction at the shrine at Mahan as well as the Taft complex, as I will discuss in the next section.

The second relevant context for understanding the architectural campaign in the shrine at Mahan is the Safavid program of shrine renovations. As Kishwar Rizvi has noted, Shah ʿAbbas I oversaw an architectural campaign that developed a number of sacred landscapes and townscapes in Iran in order to shift the focus from the key holy sites of Muslims—namely, Mecca, Medina, and Jerusalem, which were under Ottoman control at this time.[42] This surge in architectural patronage, which coincided with urban developments in the

FACING TOP, FIGURE 6.12. Detail of the Safavid-era foundation inscription in the dar al-huffaz at the shrine at Mahan, Iran. *Photograph by author, 2018.*

FACING BOTTOM, FIGURE 6.13. Southern segments of the tent band in the dar al-huffaz at the shrine at Mahan. The signature of Nur al-din and the year of completion, 1000/1592–93, can be seen written vertically in the corner. *Photograph by author, 2013.*

Safavid's new capital in Isfahan, marked the end of a period of relative architectural inactivity and a revitalization of the court's investment in economic and religious endeavors after a long period of warfare with the Uzbeks and Ottomans.[43]

The Mahan shrine's development also bears similarities to patterns of renovation and development at the shrine of the Safavids in Ardabil in this period. Like the dar al-huffaz in Ardabil, the vaulted hall in Mahan had an elongated form and was a later addition to a preexisting funerary structure (fig. 1.3).[44] Similar to the dar al-huffaz in Ardabil, the one in Mahan contained rooms for solitary meditation and a large hall for communal activities (figs. 1.5 and 1.6).[45] Although the idea of adding a nave-like hall for reciters to a preexisting tomb was far from unique, its precedence in the Ardabil shrine is significant given its status as the Safavid dynastic shrine and its continued renovations and alterations during the period of Mahan's refurbishment.[46] The dar al-huffaz in Ardabil was built in the fourteenth century but was renovated by Shah ʿAbbas I about three decades after Mahan's dar al-huffaz.[47] As Rizvi notes, the renovations at the Ardabil shrine followed "an emerging imperial aesthetic which called for a coherent and monumental spatial arrangement."[48] This statement can be applied to the enlargement of the shrine at Mahan as well, which transformed the structure from a single tomb into a monumental complex in ways that maintained a coherent spatial dynamic between the old and the new on both the macro and micro levels, from the overall structure of the tomb and the vaulted hall to the minute details of tilework and ornaments, as I discussed in chapter 1.

In thinking about the relationship between the shrines of Mahan and Ardabil, the architectural evidence should be considered alongside textiles. The patronage of the Mahan carpets in the seventeenth century reminds us of the earlier Safavid patronage of the Ardabil carpets. While the Mahan shrine differed from the Ardabil shrine given the latter's imperial hierarchy, these new developments in Mahan could be understood as gestures of connecting with and mimicking the status of the Safavid dynastic shrine—a point that is crucial in understanding the juxtaposition of local and imperial authorities on Mahan's 1590 foundation inscription in the dar al-huffaz.

The history of organized Sufi orders under the Safavids is usually characterized by a pattern of gradual decline.[49] Previous scholarship has argued for a case of Neʿmatullahi exceptionalism but also for a Neʿmatullahi decline narrative specifically in the seventeenth century.[50] There is certainly a foundation for this latter argument, partly as a result of textual sources of different natures and agendas that offer patchy and, at times, contradictory views of the family—a point to which I will return later.

Against the broader decline narratives, however, historical sources enumerate evidence of the Neʿmatullahi family's rise in the sociopolitical order of the realm alongside their marriage alliances with the Safavids, which merged the two households. Amir Nizam al-din ʿAbd al-Baqi (d. 1514), an influential Neʿmatullahi descendant in Yazd, became Shah Ismaʿil's (r. 1501–24) sadr, the highest religious office in the Safavid household, and later his *vakil* (viceroy).[51] He also led the center of Shah Ismaᶜil's forces at the Battle of Chaldiran (1514) against the Ottomans, where he was killed along with several other high-ranking members of the Shah's inner circle. Nizam al-din ᶜAbd al-Baqi's own son, Shah Naᶜim al-din Baqi (d. 1563–64), also held high office. He married a sister of Shah Tahmasp (r. 1524–76) named Khanish Begum (d. 1564). Upon Tahmasp's accession, Naᶜim al-din Baqi was confirmed as the *naqib* (chief) and given the governorship of Yazd. He owned a mansion and a garden within the Saᶜadatabad Garden quarter of Qazvin, an area dedicated to the Safavid palace as well as residences of the royal family and the elite of the Safavid capital at the time.[52] In 1554–55, Tahmasp's future successor, Shah Ismaᶜil II (r. 1576–77), married a Neᶜmatullahi woman, Pari-Paykar Begum (d. unknown), either a granddaughter or a daughter of Khanish Begum from her marriage into the Neᶜmatullahi family.[53] One of Shah Tahmasp's daughters, another Khanish Begum (d. 1590–91), and a Khadija Sultan Begum (d. unknown), a daughter of either Shah Tahmasp or Shah Ismaᶜil II, married sons of Amir Ghiyath al-din Muhammad Mirmiran (d. 1590–91), who was also appointed as vizier and *darugha* (mayor) of Yazd and played a key role in Bektash Khan's rebellion.[54] The importance of these marriages lies not only in the mere fact of connecting the two households but also in their reception and popularization in Safavid histories.[55]

In her erudite studies of Safavid historiography, Sholeh Quinn has shown how certain fourteenth-century hagiographical narratives of Shaykh Safi al-din (d. 1334), head of the Safavid Sufi network, were rewritten into Safavid chronicles to argue for the spiritual, Shiᶜa, and even messianic legitimacy of Safavid rulers.[56] The Neᶜmatullahis' prominent social and political standing in the Safavid era was a result not just of their acceptance of the Safavids' messianic claims but also of their active role in contributing to this socioreligious construct. Mobilizing the divinatory reception of Shah Neᶜmatullah Vali's poetry, his disciples now argued that Shah Neᶜmatullah "had predicted the rise of the Safavids as the expected messianic order."[57]

Returning to the dar al-huffaz in Mahan, it is important to consider how the life circumstances of the two patrons, Bektash Khan-i Afshar and Shah ᶜAbbas I, resonated through their documented intervention into the fabric of the shrine. For the Safavids, and especially for Shah ᶜAbbas I, the civil wars inside their territories, as well as serious external threats from the Ottomans and Uzbeks, meant that relying on local notables in areas with high potential for rebellion—like Yazd and Kerman—was especially advantageous before the move of their capital to Isfahan. For Bektash Khan, the stakes were even higher: the patronage of the dar al-huffaz was the material manifestation of his tribe's alliance with the Neᶜmatullahi family, which held considerable sociopolitical and spiritual status in the region. The Mahan shrine also offered the canvas for a foundation inscription that proclaimed the loyalty of the Afshar tribe to the Safavids alongside the Neᶜmatullahi Sufis as their mutual supporters and allies.

But the Safavid-Neʿmatullahi-Afsharid alliance rendered on the inscription panel at Mahan is far from a straightforward story of loyalty and architectural patronage. The key moment of the story takes place less than a year before the completion of the foundation inscription, in the month of Safar 998/December 1589, when Bektash Khan started a rebellion against the Safavids.[58] Shah ʿAbbas had appointed Bektash Khan in Kerman, but instead he decided to install himself around Yazd, leading to a conflict with Yazd's governor, ʿAli Quli Beg Karamatlu from the Shamlu tribe.[59] Bektash Khan's supposed disobedience was also met by resistance from Yaʿqub Khan-i Zu'l-qadr (d. 1590), a Qizilbash official from the Zu'l-qadr tribe in Fars.[60] Eventually, the conflict resulted in the execution of Bektash Khan.[61]

The violent episode between the Afshar and Zu'l-qadr tribes was narrated by several Safavid historians, and the details vary based on the personal sympathies and official agendas of the chroniclers. While many of these narratives of conflict do not assign a role to the Neʿmatullahis or mention them only in passing, some feature them as central players in the making of the Afshar rebellion. One example is the work of Afushta-yi Natanzi (d. after 1599), Safavid poet and historian and author of *Nuqawat al-athar* (*Selection of Antiquities*, completed in 1598), which covers the early years of Shah ʿAbbas I's reign and its challenges. At the beginning of his account of the Afshar-Zu'l-qadr conflicts, Natanzi draws a link between Bektash Khan's presence in Yazd and his "submission to the tariqa and friendship of the silsila of Neʿmatullahiyya." He also adds a crucial detail to the story: that the two tribes' armies met in Taft, where one of the Neʿmatullahis' major complexes was located.[62] The unknown author of the *Tarikh-i ʿalam-ara-yi ʿAbbasi* (*History of Shah ʿAbbas*), characterizes the distinguished Neʿmatullahi descendant Mirmiran-i Yazdi as a "divisive figure" who approved of Bektash's rebellious tendencies.[63]

Another Safavid chronicle that highlights the role of the Neʿmatullahi family in the conflict is the *Rawzat al-Safaviyya* (*The Garden of the Safavids*, completed ca. 1630s), written by Husayni Junabadi, a Safavid court functionary about whose life we know very little.[64] Junabadi grants an even more central role to the Neʿmatullahi family, in particular to the head of the Sufi network at this time: Mirmiran-i Yazdi, whose daughter was married to Bektash Khan. When discussing Taft as the scene of the Afshar-Zu'l-qadr battle, the Neʿmatullahis made a forceful entrance into the scene. Once Bektash Khan saw himself losing the battle to Yaʿqub Khan-i Zu'l-qadr, he escaped from the battlefield and took refuge in Mirmiran's house. Junabadi even goes so far as to ground Bektash's revolt in Mirmiran's ambition for an Afshar-Neʿmatullahi confederation, through which his grandson, Sanjar (born to the Safavid princess Khanish Begum and a son of Mirmiran) was to seize power in the region.[65] It is important to remember, as Maria Szuppe points out, that while the "tradition of succession by the eldest son" was a strong contender, competing traditional theories on the right to the throne were popular under the Safavids. This included the "Turkic pattern of succession," which granted the right to the throne to "all members of the family, including those descending from the female line."[66] It is plausible that the possibility of the right to a regional throne was a temptation that the Neʿmatullahis and their Afsharid allies were reckoning with in this moment. Decades later, the murder of the Neʿmatullahi-Safavid descendant Sanjar (d. 1632–33) alongside other Safavid family members at the hand of Shah Safi (r. 1629–42) to eliminate his competitors might attest to such prospects.[67] The historical events of the late sixteenth century seem to recapitulate elements of the Safavids' original rise to power about a century earlier, much like the relationship between the Neʿmatullahi shrine in Mahan and the Safavid shrine in Ardabil.

Little information survives on the life and political inclinations of the authors of the Safavid chronicles mentioned above. For that reason, speculations about their motives for including the Neʿmatullahis' involvement in these clashes must await further research. What is more, the texts patronized by the Neʿmatullahis themselves in this period (such as the one penned by Sunʿullah in the seventeenth century) pass over the whole Bektash-Yaʿqub episode in silence—a decision that is to be expected given their hagiographical and biographical nature.[68] Against this lacuna in sources written from the Sufi family's perspective, the vaulted hall in Mahan stands like a time capsule, condensing the ongoing power struggles and their aftermath. The contradictory political messages it contains challenge straightforward perceptions of early modern Sufi patronage and allegiances.

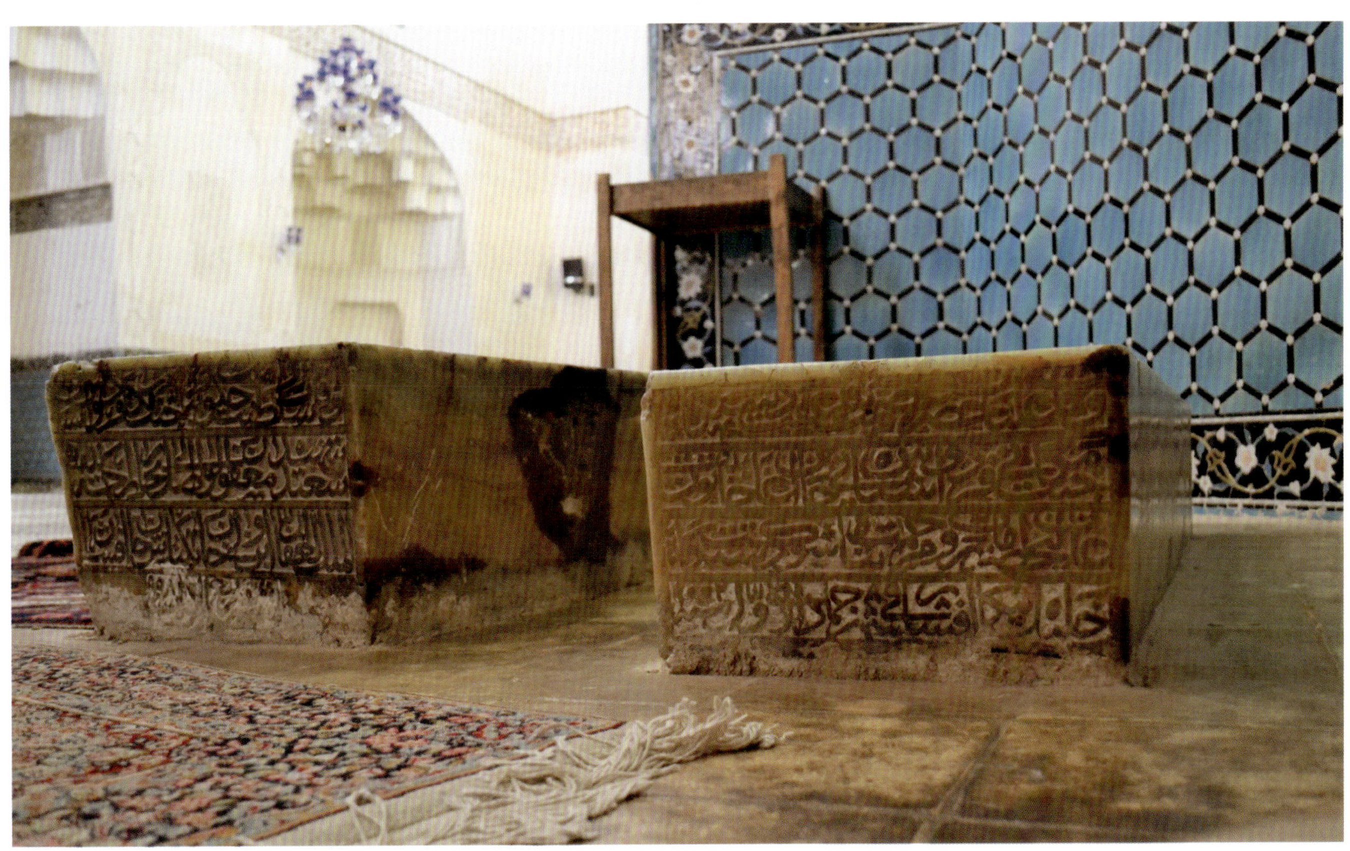

FIGURE 6.14. Bektash Khan's tombstone (*left*) in the dar al-huffaz at the Mahan shrine. A section of the Safavid-era foundation inscription can be seen in the background. *Photograph by author, 2013.*

Across the hall from the Safavid foundation inscription, Bektash Khan's tombstone serves as a reminder of how the construction of the recitation hall took place in the very midst of these violent clashes (fig. 6.14). The dar al-huffaz's foundation inscription indicates that the construction of the hall finished in Shawwal 998/August–September 1590. This was months after the conflicts and the death of Bektash Khan in Rabiʿ I 998/January 1590. In the inscription on Bektash's tombstone on the other side of the hall, he is referred to as a *shahid* (martyr), signifying the sympathetic attitude toward his cause and its memory, despite his unsuccessful attempt at securing power (app. 6.3). This epigraphical loyalty to the patron of the shrine and the juxtaposition of his name with the Safavid ruler against whom he rebelled demonstrate the multidirectional alliances of the local authorities and keepers of the shrine after the conflicts. The Afshars' patronage of Mahan and their involvement in the management of the shrine continued after Bektash's death and well into the Safavid period, despite the control exerted over the region by other tribes—including Yaʿqub Khan's short-lived dominion over the region before his death and Ganj ʿAli Khan's (d. 1625) subsequent appointment as the governor of Kerman by Shah ʿAbbas I.[69]

Alongside projects such as the commissioning of the Mahan carpets, an early eighteenth-century waqfnama of the family of Quli Beg Afshar, dated 1114/1702–3 and kept in the awqaf office of Kerman, shows that the shrine at Mahan had flourished in the seventeenth century. Under the patronage of the Afshars, a number of gardens and farmlands in Mahan as well as twenty-seven shops and part of the revenue of the caravansary next to the shrine complex of Shah Neʿmatullah were endowed for upkeep, salaries of the employees, and purchases of clothes for the poor in the madrasa of the family of Quli Beg in Kerman.[70] Other funds gathered from the shrine at Mahan went into the restoration of two important mosques in the city of Kerman: the Malek Mosque and the Muzaffari Jamiʿ Mosque. The fact that part of the revenue of the shrine was used for purposes other than the upkeep of the shrine makes it seem that the new patrons were pumping cash out of the Mahan complex, but on another level it also speaks to the agreeable financial conditions of the complex in the preceding decades. The waqfnama also highlights the connections between Mahan and Kerman, which were strengthened with the latter's becoming an important center on world trade routes and with architectural developments under the governorship of Ganj ʿAli Khan during the reign of Shah ʿAbbas I.[71]

It is important to note that the Neʿmatullahi family's response to the Bektash rebellion was far from homogenous. Both the Neʿmatullahis and the Afshar tribe were divided in their support or lack thereof for Bektash Khan. Yaʿqub Khan had convinced some of Bektash Khan's own tribesmen, including Yusuf Khan-i Afshar, to join him in breaking Bektash's siege. On the Neʿmatullahi side, Mirmiran's son, Khalilullah III, also opposed his father's support of the disobedient Bektash Khan, preferring the Afshar tribesmen loyal to the Safavid Shah and opening up communication with Yaʿqub Khan-i Zu'l-qadr and Yusuf Khan-i Afshar.[72] After Bektash's death, the Afshars who had been loyal to him were plundered, and fines were executed on Mirmiran.[73] In contrast, Yaʿqub Khan treated Khalilullah (Mirmiran's son) with honor.

In 999/1590–91, shortly after the Bektash-Yaʿqub episode, Shah ʿAbbas visited Khalilullah, who was married to a daughter of Shah Ismaʿil II. The visit took place in Yazd, on Shah ʿAbbas's way to Isfahan to attend the funeral of Khanish Begum, daughter of Shah Tahmasp, who had married into the Neʿmatullahi family.[74] While most texts mention this event in passing or completely leave it out, Mufid describes it in elaborate detail, suggesting Shah ʿAbbas's restoration of security after a period of upheaval in the region.[75] In Mufid's account, the Neʿmatullahi family stands at the center of this restored order. Their centrality is enacted through a lavish ceremony that they hold to host the Safavid king—an interesting angle taken by the author, given his omission of the whole Bektash episode, similar to other biographies of the Sufi family.[76]

Accounts in the *Jamiʿ-i Mufidi* also note that Khalilullah III and other members of the Neʿmatullahi family visited the royal capital of Isfahan.[77] Terry Graham has interpreted the family's presence in Isfahan as a form of exile—an attempt by Shah ʿAbbas to keep the family under the court's close watch.[78] This is a plausible scenario given the changing loyalties of the family and the political landscape of central Iran at the time. Further, the inclusion of a state-sponsored Neʿmatullahi convent on the famed Chaharbagh avenue in Isfahan may suggest an attempt by the Safavid ruler to exert a sense of control over the Sufi network.[79] But there is no evidence to suggest that the Isfahan visit itself should be interpreted as the direct backlash of the Bektash rebellion, as the decline narrative for the Sufi family might suggest.

I propose that the Safavid sponsorship of the Chaharbagh structure was a rather notional attempt at showcasing their control over and patronage of the Neʿmatullahis and simultaneously reiterating the Sufi network's allegiance to them. After all, the Neʿmatullahis, alongside the Haydaris, were the only two Sufi networks to receive such theatrical patronage in the Safavid capital against the backdrop of the state's suppression of other Sufis. There is no evidence to suggest that a large-scale forced migration of the family to Isfahan took place at this time. As Derek Mancini-Lander has noted, the little information we have about what went on in Isfahan concerns Shah Khalilullah's dissatisfaction with Shah ʿAbbas's preference of a rival Sayyid, which was eventually remedied by the king, though reluctantly.[80] What is certain is that a souring of the relationship between Khalilullah III and Shah ʿAbbas took place and likely led to the former's migration to Mughal India, as I will discuss in the next chapter.

Despite the fragmentary, contradictory nature of the textual sources, the Afshar-Neʿmatullahi episode is a significant moment for clarifying the nuances of the relationship between the Sufi network and the Safavid government. It challenges two prominent historiographical narratives around the Sufi family: first, the narrative of Neʿmatullahi exceptionalism that attributes the family's survival under the Safavids to their unwavering support of the dynasty's political and spiritual authority, and second, the narrative of the family's decline in the seventeenth century.

The image of the Neʿmatullahi Sufis as loyal supporters of the Safavids appears in a number of sources. Quinn identifies two distinct historiographic approaches in documenting the Neʿmatullahi Sufis in Safavid chronicles. The first consists of early and official Safavid sources that focus on the political alliances the Neʿmatullahi family forged with the Safavid court as well as their intermarriages and important positions held by individuals from the Neʿmatullahi family, without discussing the Sufi network in detail.[81]

By contrast, the second strand contains later Safavid historical writings from the seventeenth century that draw on popular and oral traditions. This later group of chronicles, while discussing the same events as the first group, elaborates on Neʿmatullahi individuals and their heroism, projecting an image of them as loyal supporters of the Safavid family.[82] Quinn speculates that this reimagination of earlier Safavid history around the central role given to the Neʿmatullahi family could be the result of the authors' personal choices: they might have originated from Yazd and Tabriz—cities where Neʿmatullahi Sufis had a strong presence and a working institution during the Safavid period. It could also be the result of the intensified loyalties of the population following clear divisions and feuds between the Neʿmatis (followers of Shah Neʿmatullah) and Haydaris (followers of Shaykh Qutb al-din Haydar Tuni, d. ca. 1426) in city neighborhoods, sometimes encouraged by Safavid authorities.[83] Farshid Emami's reconstruction of two facing convents belonging to the Neʿmatis and Haydaris on the two sides of the Chaharbagh as part of Shah ʿAbbas's constructions in Isfahan demonstrates such sentiments, alongside constructing a sense of government surveillance over the two factions.[84]

As this section has shown, alongside these two strands of Neʿmatullahi historiography that Quinn has identified—one documenting individuals and their prominent positions, the other foregrounding elaborate stories of Neʿmatullahi heroism in support of the Safavids—it is possible to see a third (although less extensive) approach in the work of chroniclers like Junabadi and Afushta-yi Natanzi, who point toward the family's *disloyalty* to the central government. In other words, the Bektash rebellion, in and of itself, throws into question the narrative of Neʿmatullahi exceptionalism.

The Afshar rebellion is usually seen as a point of disruption in the Neʿmatullahis' longer history, inaugurating the marginalization of the family's political influence even though individual members continued to hold high, albeit local, positions such as kalantar in Yazd in the seventeenth century.[85] As Quinn points out, the "standard accounts of the Nimatullahiyya explain how after the falling out between Shah ʿAbbas and Mirmiran-i Yazdi, the Nimatullahis ceased to exist as an active Sufi order and it was only after Maʿsum ʿAli Shah Dakkani went from India to Iran in the late eighteenth century and reintroduced the order that a resurgence took place."[86] Pushing against this assertion, Quinn uses the evidence of the seventeenth-century popular chronicles—as outlined above—to suggest that "the Neʿmatullahi historiographical legacy continued to be extremely strong even into the late seventeenth century."[87]

Other historical and material evidence supports Quinn's suggestion: the flourishing state of the Mahan shrine in the seventeenth century, as indicated by the endowment document cited above; the completion of the dar al-huffaz; the mid-seventeenth-century carpets made for the sepulchre of Shah Neʿmatullah; and the evidence of a functioning Neʿmatullahi *tekke* (Sufi lodge) in the Safavid capital of Isfahan in the second half of the seventeenth century, as recorded by Jean Chardin.[88] The rather localized status of the Neʿmatullahis can be attributed to broader Safavid policies in the seventeenth century, such as "the absorption of Yazd into Crown Lands" and the resulting diminishment of governors' power, as Mancini-Lander has shown.[89]

I argue that the decline narrative is symptomatic of two broader historiographic tendencies: first, the overreliance on dynastic textual accounts and second, the straightforward interpretation of architectural scale in relation to political power. Quinn's work has already shown that once we look at popular chronicles (as opposed to dynastic ones), the decline narrative starts to crumble. There is also a point to be made about the importance of considering the textual and material evidence in a transregional context. Following the Bektash-Yaʿqub episode and the move of the Safavid capital to Isfahan, both in 1589, a change is surely sensed in the Neʿmatullahis' status and the scale of their architectural projects. What may seem like a decline of the Sufi family in the seventeenth century is partially a result of the energy they were devoting to establishing themselves in Mughal India (more on this in chap. 7).

While projects such as the expansion of the shrine at Mahan and the construction of *maydan*-i Shah (royal square) in Yazd (a case study in the next chapter) mark the height of the status of the Sufi network in the sixteenth century, projects of smaller scale characterize the seventeenth century for the Neʿmatullahi family. But as the recitation hall in the Mahan shrine reminds us, scale is not always an accurate measurement of political authority. The construction process of this monumental hall encapsulates both the family's venture to seize power and the ensuing conflicts and failures that defined the landscape of regional politics for the following decades. The Bektash Khan rebellion was a significant moment in the history of the Neʿmatullahis not because it led to their decline but because its reverberations can be seen in other artistic and urban projects of the Sufi network in both Iran and India. The scale of seventeenth-century projects such as the making of the Mahan carpets or the design of the *chelleh khaneh* (retreat cell), which I will discuss in the last chapter of the book, should not be interpreted as mere decline. Instead, they should be read as local and intimate projects that stand for an inward-looking period in the history of the network when they processed their conflicts and competitions with Safavid authorities while making a new home for themselves at the Mughal courts of Lahore and Delhi.

III. Safavid Women as Interlocutors: The Case of Shah Vali Mosque in Taft

The construction of the dar al-huffaz at Mahan was not the Safavids' only architectural intervention into the network of Neʿmatullahi shrines. Decades before Shah ʿAbbas's name was written on the foundation inscription at the shrine of Mahan, architectural campaigns at the Shah Vali khanaqah in Taft were attributed to a Safavid princess. The patron, Khanish Begum (d. 1564), whose name came up in the previous section, was a sister of Shah Tahmasp.[90] Khanish Begum married Shah Nur al-din (Naʿim al-din) Neʿmatullah-i Baqi, a descendant of Shah Neʿmatullah who became the governor of Yazd.[91] The extent of Khanish Begum's involvement with the site is not entirely clear as there are discrepancies between textual sources and epigraphic material in situ. In the textual accounts, she is credited with the construction of a mosque in the complex. The visual and epigraphic evidence, on the other hand, suggest a role in renovating the mosque and possibly other structures on the site.

The Shah Vali Mosque in Taft is not listed among the structures that were built in the first phase of the khanaqah's construction during Shah Neʿmatullah's lifetime.[92] The mosque today consists of a dome chamber, with a vaulted entrance on the north, flanked by a rectangular hall on the west and two halls on the east (figs. 3.4 and 6.15).[93] The dome chamber has a large bay at each side on two levels, with open galleries on the upper level (fig. 6.16).[94] The

FIGURE 6.15. Plan of the mosque at the Shah Vali khanaqah in Taft before the addition of the late twentieth-century hall to the east. *Drawing by Farah Michel, after plans by Iran's Cultural Heritage Organization in Yazd.*

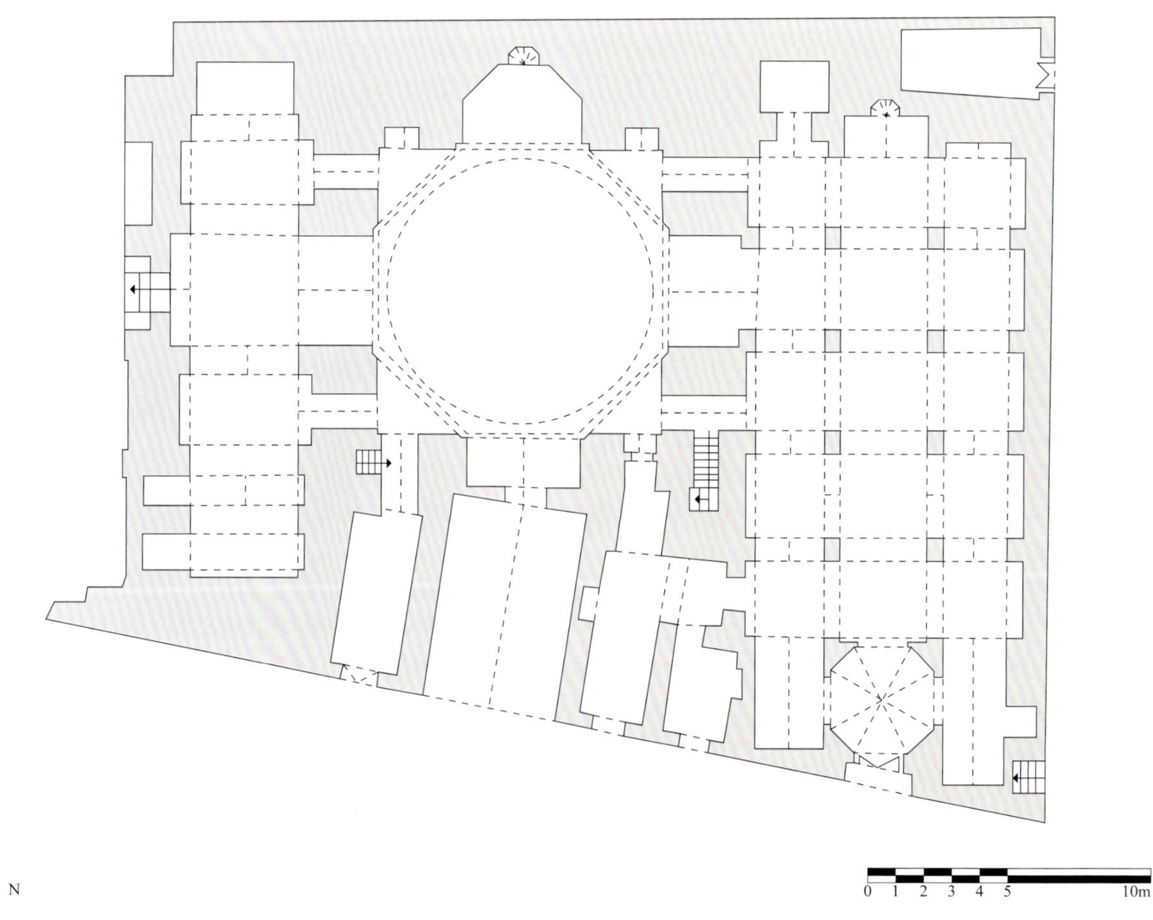

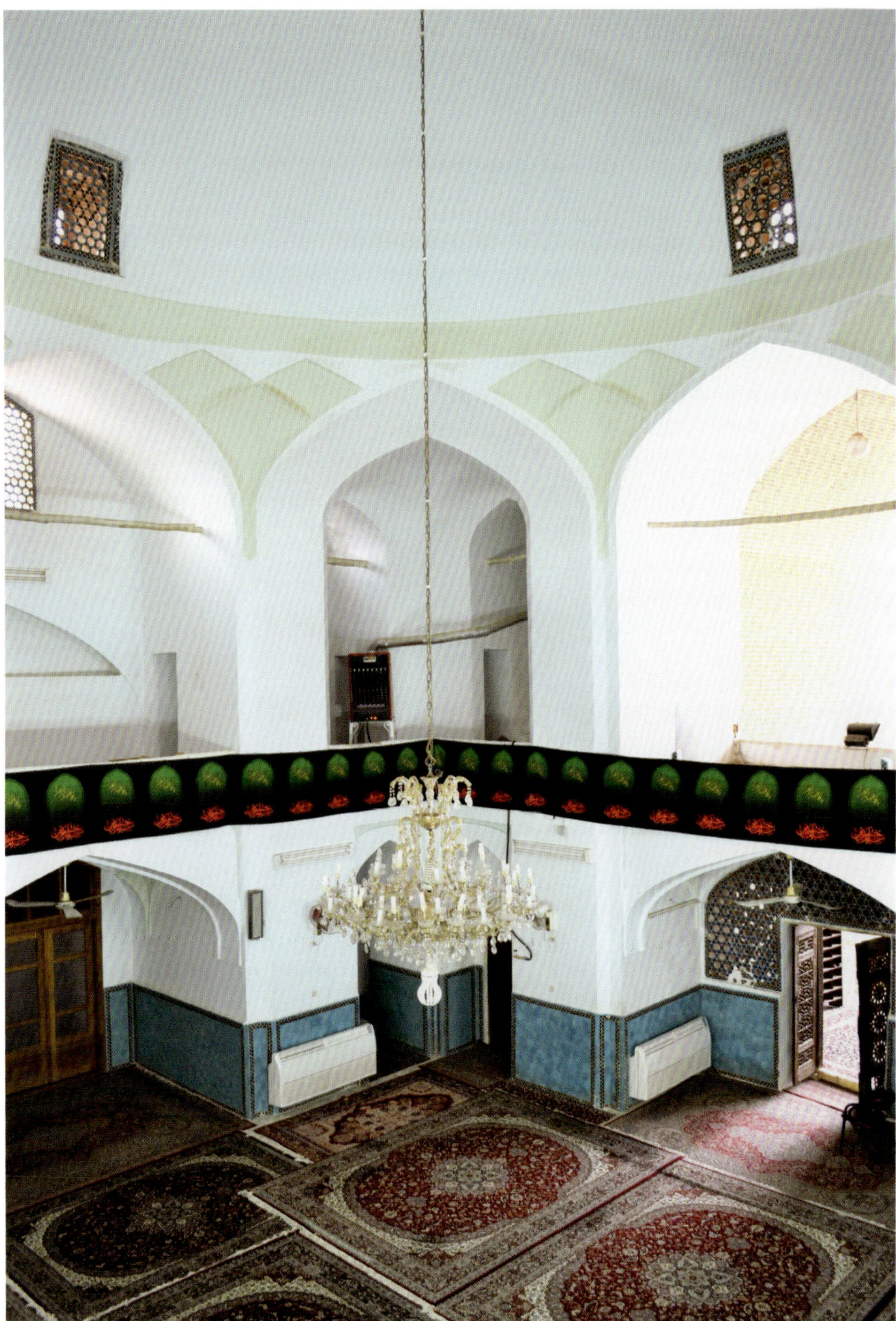

FIGURE 6.16. View of the dome chamber of Shah Vali's Mosque in Taft from the upper-floor gallery. *Photograph by author, 2014.*

dome sits on eight massive piers and arches. Except for light-blue hexagonal tiles covering the walls at the dado level, the surfaces are mostly whitewashed, occasionally interrupted by carved and molded plaster or perforated windows (fig. 6.17).[95]

At least three phases of construction are recognizable in the architecture of the mosque: the dome chamber and two long rectangular halls to the east

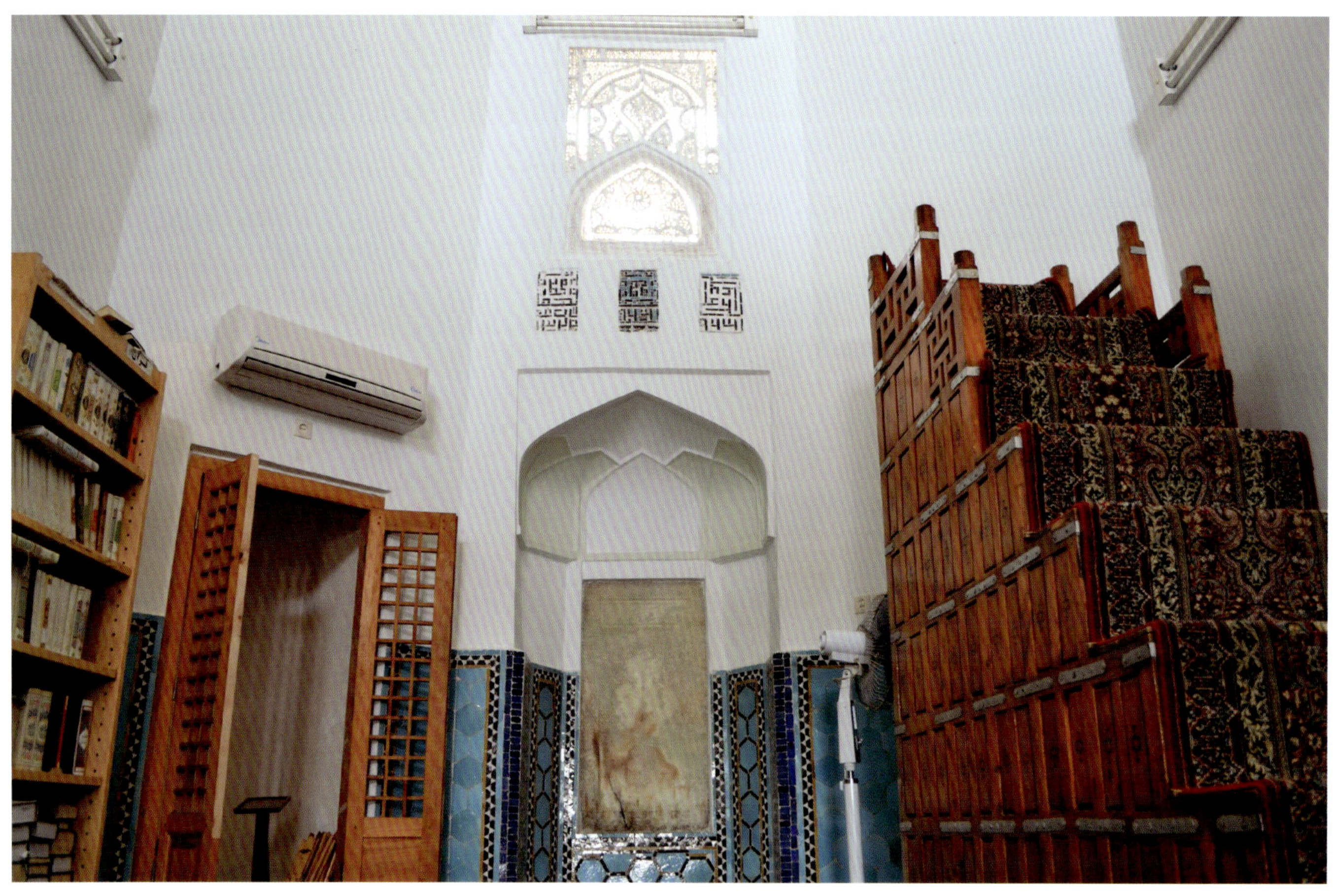

FIGURE 6.17. Tilework and perforated windows in the mihrab area of the Shah Vali Mosque in Taft. *Photograph by author, 2013.*

and west were probably built together (figs. 6.15, 6.18, and 6.19). Lisa Golombek and Donald Wilber suggest that the columned winter hall to the west of the dome chamber was a later construction, probably replacing an earlier original hall (fig. 6.19).[96] Finally, the larger and easternmost hall was built recently, after 1983, as indicated by a report of Iran's Cultural Heritage Foundation and photographic evidence (figs. 6.15 and 3.9).[97]

Most of the elements on the facade of the mosque are recent additions (fig. 6.20).[98] The main entrance, for instance, is framed by inscription panels dated 1386/1966. The exterior of the dome is covered in a combination of unglazed as well as turquoise- and blue-glazed bricks that on the stem of the dome make up the words *Allah*, *Muhammad*, and *Shah Vali* in kufic script. These were added in a restoration in 1999, but it is unclear whether the intention was to re-create an earlier state of the dome's ornamentation.[99]

The construction of the mosque is attributed to Khanish Begum in two textual sources. Sunᶜullah Neᶜmatullahi, who wrote on the life of Shah Neᶜmatullah and his descendants in the Safavid period, includes this information in his *risala* (treatise), which was later included in Muhammad Mufid's seventeenth-century chronicle, the *Jamiᶜ-i Mufidi*.[100] The account provides

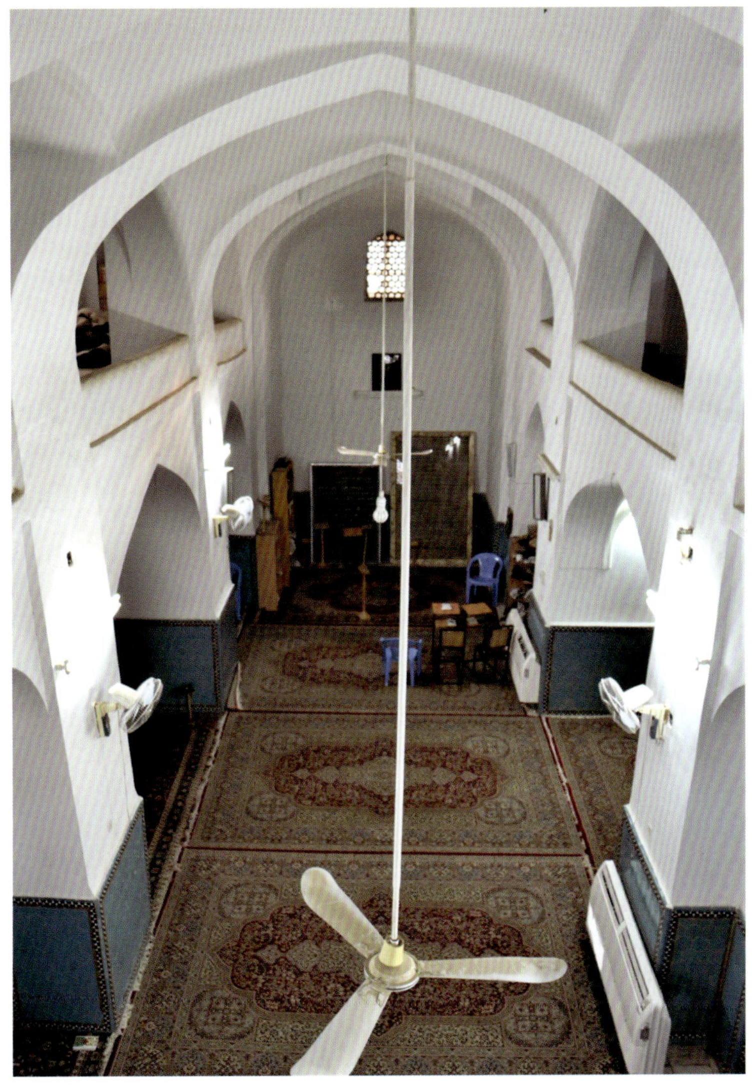

FIGURE 6.18. View of the elongated hall on the east side of the dome chamber at the Shah Vali Mosque in Taft. *Photograph by author, 2014.*

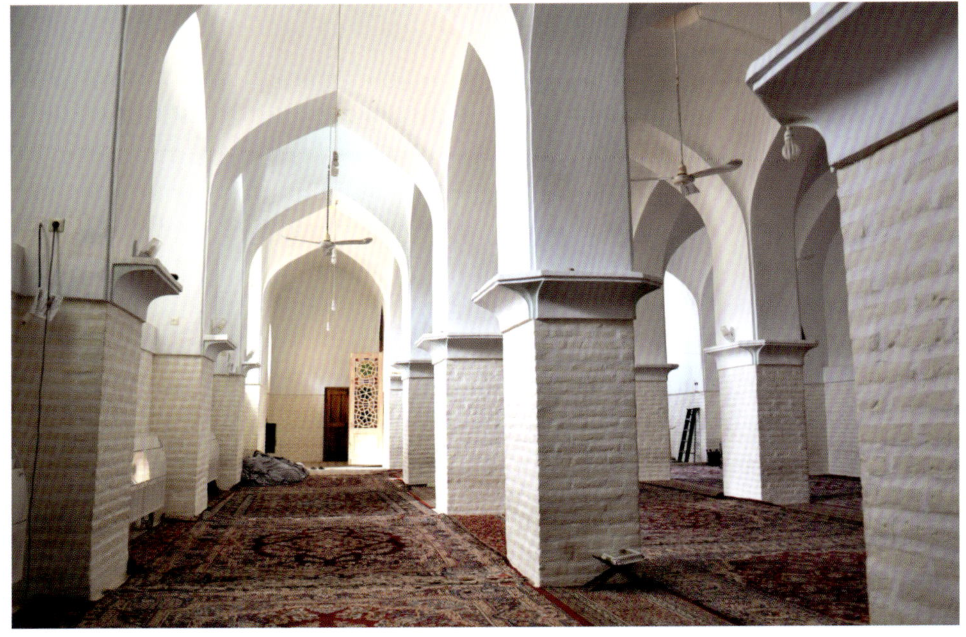

FIGURE 6.19. View of the columned hall to the west of the dome chamber at the Shah Vali Mosque in Taft. *Photograph by author, 2013.*

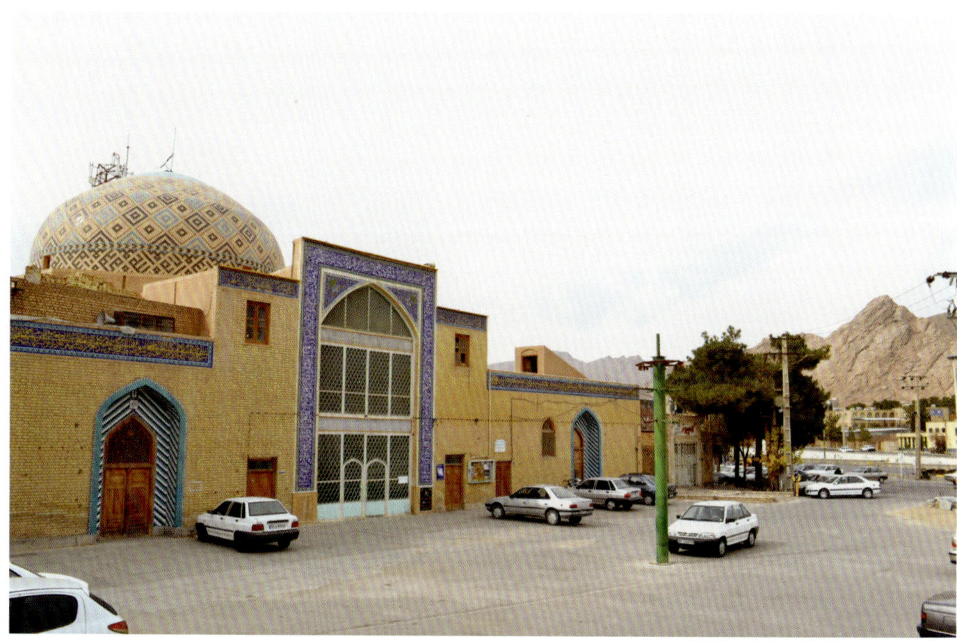

FIGURE 6.20. Facade of the Shah Vali mosque in Taft, view from the southeast. *Photograph by author, 2014.*

little detail about the mosque but describes it in language that aggrandizes this act of patronage and the status of the site. Sunʿullah notes that Khanish Begum "ordered artful engineers (*muhandisan*) and skillful knowledgeable masters to design an excellent mosque and erected a lodge in each of its four corners. . . . Its gate invited the devout [Muslims] of the seven climes to the *dar al-salam* of Taft. Around its walls, panels were adorned with inscriptions and the light of letters and words of the holy Qurʾan shone on them."[101] The inscription panels described were perhaps installed on the exterior walls of the dome chamber and are lost now. The location of the four lodges mentioned in the description matches the ones in the dome chamber today (figs. 6.15 and 6.16).

Contrary to this textual reference, the material evidence in situ and an endowment document of Khanish Begum suggest that this attribution is far from conclusive. Two areas of the mosque are of special interest here: a composite entrance panel now located behind the modern entrance of the mosque and the mihrab in the main dome chamber. These will be considered alongside Khanish Begum's endowment document and a textile made for the mihrab area of the mosque around the same time as her patronage of the site.

The earliest architectural element of the mosque is its marble mihrab stone, located in a semioctagonal niche in the qibla wall of the dome chamber (fig. 6.17). The mihrab stone features a mosque lamp (*qandil*) in relief, surrounded by floral motifs in the form of trefoil (fig. 6.21)—a configuration also found in contemporary examples from the region, such as the Mir Chaqmaq Mosque in Yazd. Framing the mihrab stone in Taft is an inscription band in thuluth script containing verses 78 and 79 of Surat al-Isra' (The Night Journey)—a common inscription on mihrab stones emphasizing the virtue of prayer—followed by

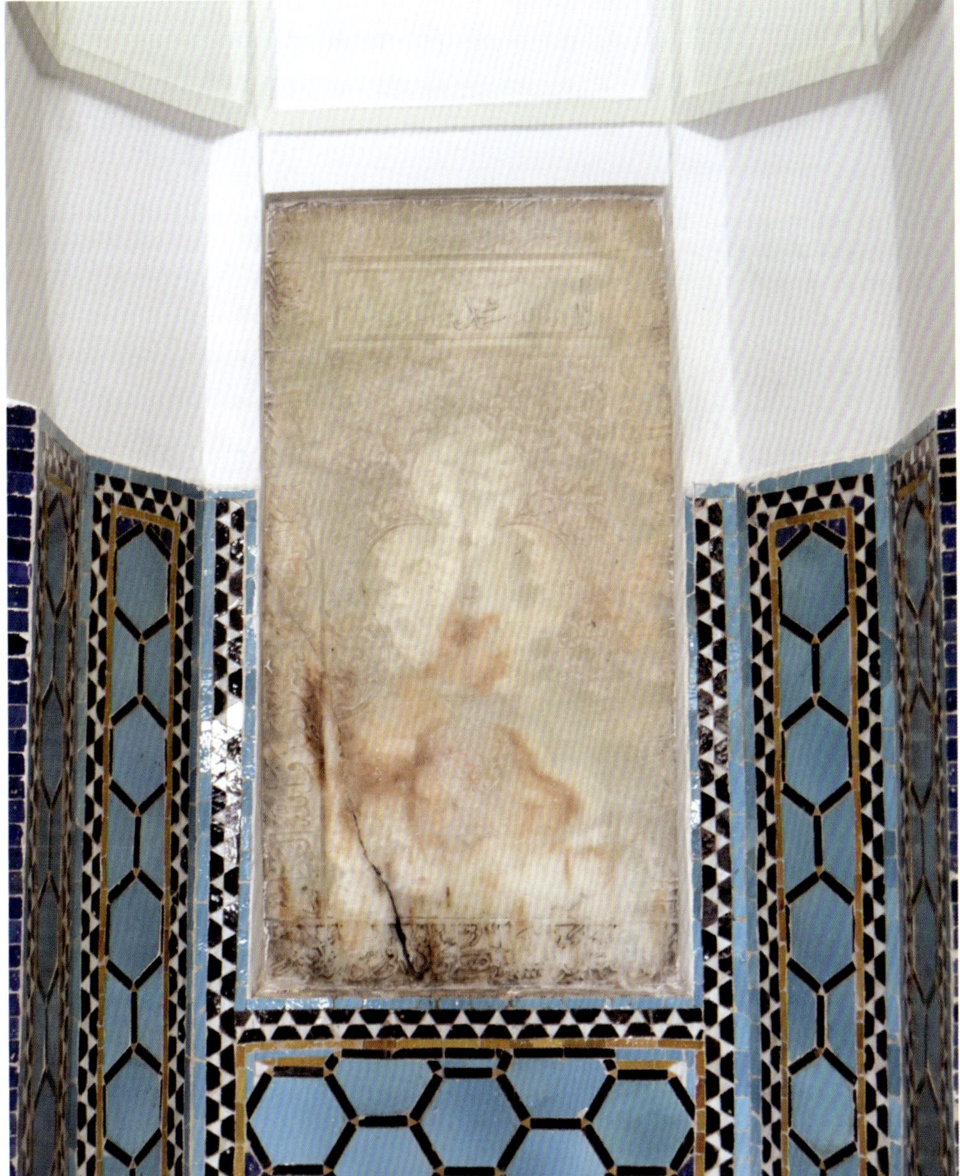

FIGURE 6.21. The mihrab stone at the Shah Vali Mosque in Taft. *Photograph by author, 2013.*

part of a hadith from the Prophet and the date 873/1468 (app. 6.4). As the date suggests, the mihrab was made many decades prior to the time of Khanish Begum.

Passing through the current entrance to the mosque, a small, vaulted hall leads to the dome chamber through an entrance panel composed of wooden and tile elements that contain another dated fragment, made about two decades later than the mihrab stone (fig. 6.22). The lower half of the panel consists of a latticed wooden door and is surrounded by a glazed tile inscription band, flanked by perforated glazed tile panels in cobalt blue, turquoise, and amber (fig. 6.23). These are topped by a triangular panel of carved wood surrounded

FIGURE 6.22. Tile panel at the portal opening onto the dome chamber at the Shah Vali Mosque in Taft. *Photograph by author, 2014.*

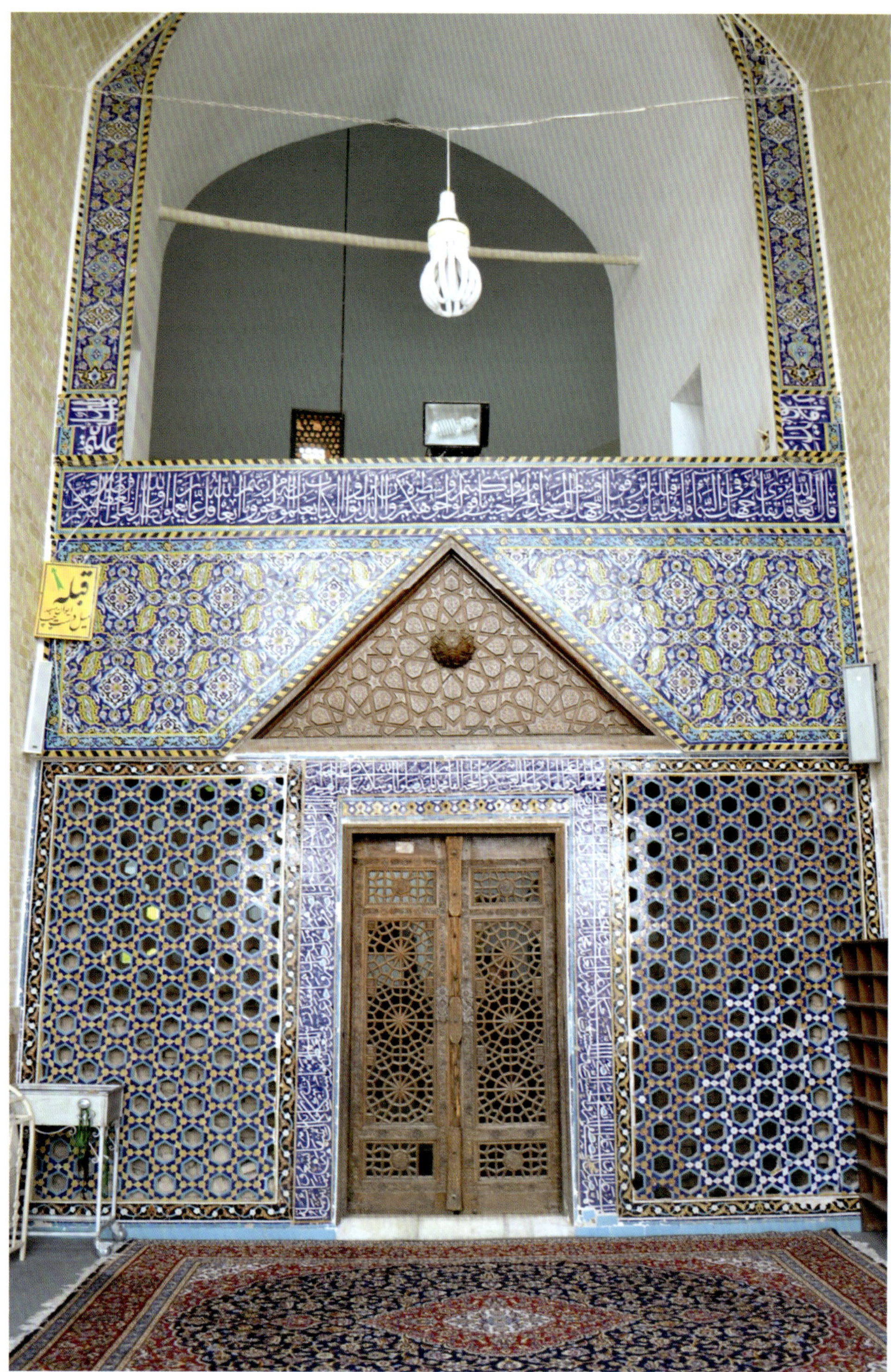

FACING, FIGURE 6.23. Inscription band around the entrance of the Shah Vali Mosque in Taft. Kamal's signature and the date 889/1484 can be seen on the bottom left. *Photograph by author, 2014.*

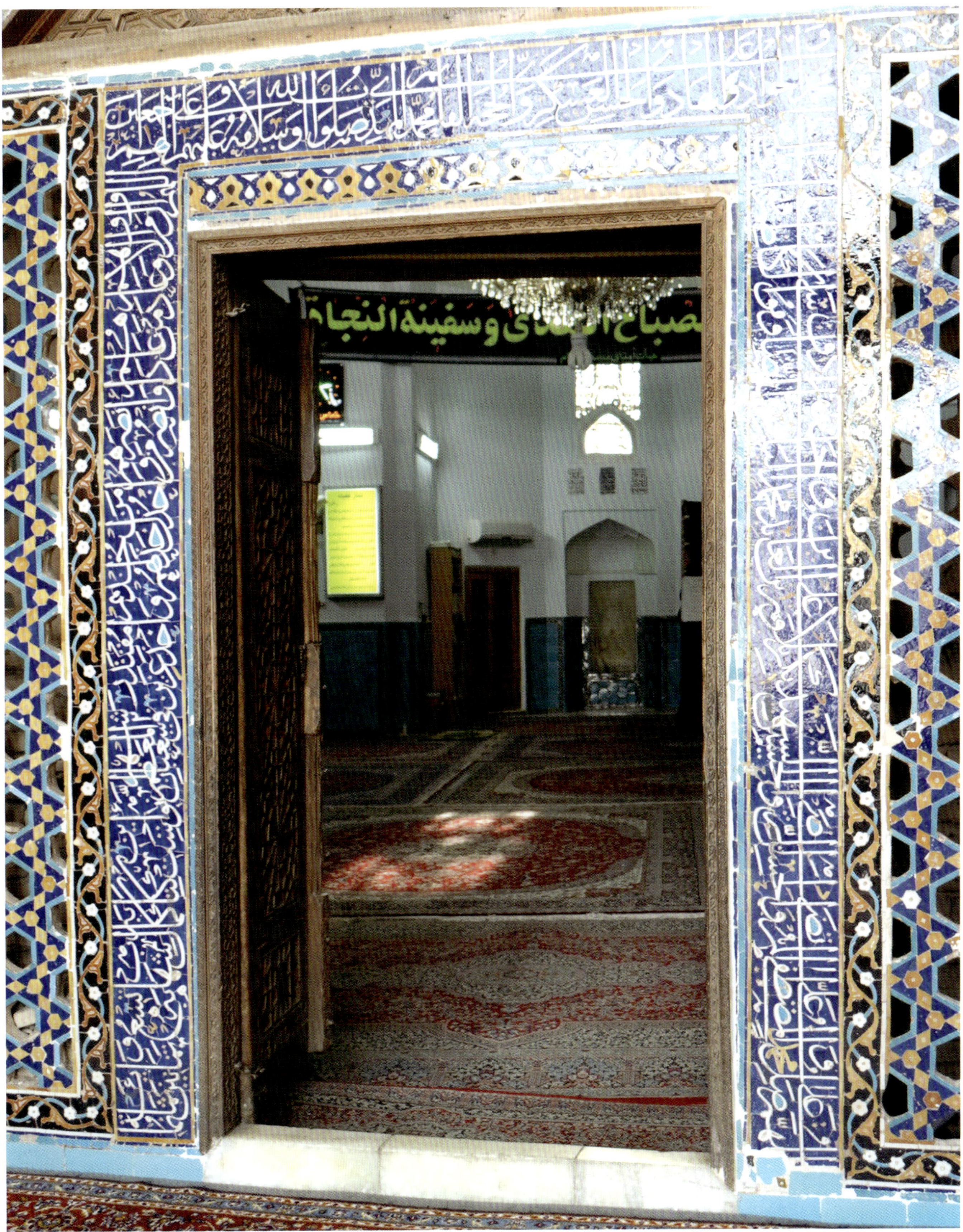
وسفينة النجاة

by another tile panel, some elements of which seem to be contemporary with the modern parts of the facade (fig. 6.22). The upper half of the panel contains mismatching elements that have been randomly put together.[102]

On the lower half of the panel, the inscription band that runs around the doorframe is written in thuluth script and contains the names of the twelve Shiʿa Imams, the date Shaʿban 889/August 1484 on the left margin, and the signature of Kamal Shahab—a calligrapher well known in central Iran in the second half of the fifteenth century (fig. 6.23 and app. 6.5). As Golombek, Wilber, and more recently Sandra Aube have noted, the calligrapher's signature is found in several other inscriptions in Isfahan and Yazd.[103] The most outstanding of them are at the Jamiʿ mosque of Yazd, including an undated mosaic faience in the mihrab, a mosaic panel in the vestibule dated 863/1459, and a carved stone slab in the vestibule dated 875/1470–71. The last two contain information on granting tax relief.[104] In both inscriptions, the name of the Qara Qoyunlu ruler Jahanshah (r. ca. 1438–67) is inscribed.

How do we read these earlier fifteenth-century fragments in the mosque alongside its sixteenth-century attribution to Khanish Begum in textual sources? Golombek and Wilber accept that this building is probably the sixteenth-century mosque built by Khanish Begum and suggest that the fifteenth-century dated elements are reused materials from other buildings.[105] On the contrary, based on the date of the mihrab and the mosque's stylistic features, Aube dates the architecture of the main structure to the Qara Qoyunlu period. While it was not unusual to repurpose important segments of earlier or lost architecture such as a mihrab, the dome, with its corner pillars, does structurally resemble fifteenth-century Qara Qoyunlu architecture, as Aube argues through a comparison to the Masjid-i Kabud in Tabriz (1465).[106] Similarly, Karim Mardomi and Mohsen Dehghani Tafti suggest that the mosque was a Qara Qoyunlu construction, although they do not mention their reasoning for this attribution. It seems they find a plausible date for the construction of the mosque in the intermarriage between the daughter of the Qara Qoyunlu ruler Jahanshah and a descendant of Shah Neʿmatullah known as Shah Neʿmatullah-i Thani in the middle of the fifteenth century, as well as the date of calligrapher Kamal's inscription.[107] Kamal Shahab's involvement in other projects for Jahanshah strengthens this possibility, but at the same time, it was common for artists to move between courts with a regime change. Whether under court or urban patronage, Kamal's work in the khanaqah at Taft highlights both the stature and the quality of architectural work carried in Taft and the khanaqah's connectedness with important places of worship in the region through artist networks.

Another mosaic tile inscription from the Taft complex, dating from 876/1471–72 and currently kept at Iran's National Museum (discussed in chap. 5), suggests there were some ongoing architectural activities at the complex around this time (fig. 5.33).[108] Overall, the architectural evidence around this period dates from the 1460s to the 1480s, represented by the mihrab, the entrance tile panel, and the National Museum panel. These architectural fragments may have coalesced around the construction of a new mosque.

A few other pieces of evidence support the possibility of the construction of the mosque prior to the time of Khanish Begum. Her patronage of the Taft complex must have fallen sometime after her marriage to the Neʿmatullahi descendant. While the date of their marriage is missing from Sunʿullah's biography of the Neʿmatullahi family, it is recorded as 943/1536–37 in a manuscript of the *Tarikh-i Qutb Shahi*, dated Shawwal 1038/June 1629 and kept in the Salar Jung Museum in Hyderabad (MS.3534–71). We also know that Khanish Begum was actively involved in architectural patronage in the region of Yazd around Rabiʿ I of 963/February 1556 based on her dated waqfnama (endowment document).[109]

The purpose of Khanish Begum's document is to specify several endowments from the revenue of her properties in and around Yazd and Meybod to three different funerary sites of significance: the shrine of Imam Husayn in Karbala, the shrine of Imam Reza in Mashhad, and the khanaqah of Taft, where her son, Sultan ʿAli Mirza, and one of her daughters were buried, although her daughter's burial was later transferred to Mashhad.[110] The conspicuous absence of any mention of a mosque in the endowment document raises the possibility that the extent of Khanish Begum's patronage did not include building the Shah Vali Mosque from scratch.

A contemporaneous piece of textile, a *zilu* (reversible cotton floor spread) donated to the mosque, supports this possibility. Although not as precious as silk and woolen-pile carpets made in central Iran, zilus were considered to be of better quality and more expensive than felt. Zilus were preferable textiles in mosques and shrines in southern and central Iran, where the dry climate would preserve the material intact.[111] The semioctagon zilu purpose-made for

FIGURE 6.24. Zilu made for the mihrab area of the Shah Vali Mosque in Taft, displayed in the adjacent Museum of Anthropology. *Photograph by author, 2014.*

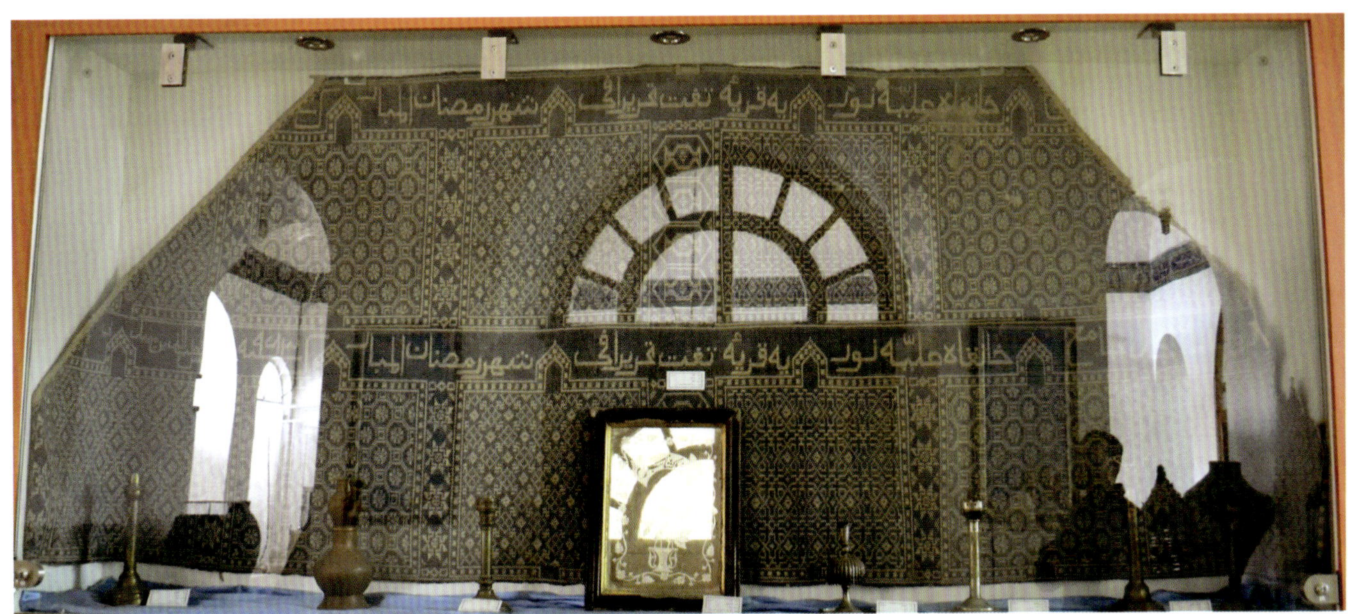

the mihrab area of the Shah Vali Mosque is dated Ramadan 963/July 1556 and is still kept on-site in the adjacent building of the Museum of Anthropology (no. 58) at the buqᶜa of Khalilullah-i Thani (fig. 6.24 and app. 6.6).

The zilu's inscriptions indicate that it was endowed to the "Masjid-i Jamiᶜ-i Khanaqah-i Nuriya-yi ᶜilliya" in Taft, suggesting the mosque was in place six months after the date of Khanish Begum's waqfnama. Shaped textiles were usually commissioned for architectural spaces that were complete. If correct, this timeline would suggest that the mosque should have been near completion, or at least under construction, when the waqfnama was written, making the absence of the mosque in the endowment document even more noticeable. While it is arguable that there could have been a separate waqfnama for the mosque that has not survived or is not yet known to us, the conjunction of the circumstances above suggests that the mosque's dome chamber was likely in place before Khanish Begum's patronage. It is likely that given her investment in the site after the burial of her son in the khanaqah, Khanish Begum refurbished the mosque and expanded it, perhaps by adding the western hall to the dome chamber. It is also likely that the zilu was commissioned in conjunction with this refurbishment campaign.

It was not uncommon in epigraphic and textual sources to conflate architectural refurbishment with new construction.[112] Or perhaps writing in the Safavid era, in an attempt to embellish the patronage of a member of the royal family, Sunᶜullah inflated Khanish Begum's architectural project in his biography, describing the preexisting dome chamber of the mosque in Taft that he had seen or heard about.

Setting aside the degree of Khanish Begum's contribution to the Taft complex, how should we interpret the significance of her patronage? And how do we understand the inherent power, as well as the gender dynamics, of her patronage as a Safavid woman and as the wife of an influential figure in the Neᶜmatullahi family? While it is true that Khanish Begum's marriage into the Neᶜmatullahi family prompted her choice of the Taft complex as a site of patronage, I also want to emphasize her natal genealogy in order to evaluate her project as Safavid patronage.[113] Scholars have made a strong case for the power that Safavid women carried as highly educated individuals and political players.[114] Khanish Begum was a woman of power married into a family of power, and both sides of her identity should be equally taken into account. Her patronage in Taft strengthened the royal family's alliance with the Sufi family, benefiting the Safavids by exerting surrogate authority in central and southern Iran—an authority the Safavid government increasingly depended on in the following decades. As Szuppe has shown, such marital bonds were extremely important to the Safavids in frontier provinces where royal women married to local rulers would consolidate dynastic power and "promote Safavid interests."[115]

For the Neᶜmatullahi family, on the other hand, Khanish Begum's contribution to the khanaqah complex lent imperial legitimacy to the working institution of the Sufi network by expanding its most orthodox element—namely, the mosque, which the Mahan complex lacked.[116] This could be read as a sign of approval from a dynasty known for its complicated relationships with Sufism, including the suppression of many Sufi networks.[117] Khanish Begum's endowment to Taft, alongside the shrines at Karbala and Mashhad, implied a symbolic equation of these sites, reconfiguring the hierarchy of the Taft complex alongside such significant sites of pilgrimage and Shiʿa veneration. The importance of Karbala and Mashhad as Shiʿa centers of religiosity for the Safavids helped to establish a Shiʿa narrative around the site in Taft and, by extension, around the Neʿmatullahis' own adherence to Shiʿism.

Khanish Begum's patronage of the Shah Vali Mosque in Taft—regardless of its extent—was followed by her construction of another mosque a few years later, this time in Yazd. The mosque in Yazd later became part of a major but now-lost sixteenth-century urban complex. It is important that during a time of limited mosque building for the Safavids, it was in the region of Yazd, rather than in the Safavid capital, and through collaborations with the Neʿmatullahi family, that their architectural campaigns retained a presence in central Iran.

The prominent patrons considered in this chapter—the Bahmanid king, the Safavid princess, the Afsharid governor, and the Safavid king—as different as the circumstances of their patronage may be, were all drawing on the popular, spiritual, and political authority of the Neʿmatullahi network. Just as it is important to think through the agency of the Sufi network in negotiating such patronage, it is crucial to consider how they built on the layers of architecture that each of these patrons added to their sites. From this point of view, the sacred sites are palimpsests where the different layers at times concealed, dominated, or responded to one another. Khanish Begum's project in Yazd, which I will turn to in the next chapter, elucidates this back-and-forth relationship well.

Notes

1. Ethel Sara Wolper argues for the notion of "visual authority" in Bektashi shrines, the buildings' increased importance as markers of status—which has inspired my use of the term *spatial authority* here: Wolper, *Cities and Saints*, especially chapter 1.

2. On Ahmad I's tomb, see Gupta, "Interpreting the Eye," 189–208; Mondini, "Vague Traits," 155–80; Firouzeh, "Sacred Kingship," 187–214; Mondini, "Architectural Heritage and Modern Rituals," 134–41; Philon, "The Murals," 3–10; Yazdani, *Bidar*, 114–29.

3. Yazdani, *Bidar*, 115–16; Merklinger, *Indian Islamic Architecture*, 11–16; Michell and Zebrowski, *Architecture and Art of the Deccan Sultanates*, 72–73; Mondini, "Architectural Heritage and Modern Rituals," 134–41; Michell and Philon, *Islamic Architecture of Deccan India*, 175.

4. Michell and Zebrowski, *Architecture and Art of the Deccan Sultanates*, 67–68.

5. For traces of the now-lost painted areas on the exterior surfaces, see Yazdani, *Bidar*, Pl.LXXV.

6. Michell and Zebrowski, *Architecture and Art of the Deccan Sultanates*, 67–68; Merklinger, *Indian Islamic Architecture*, 11.

7. Although traces of paintings can be found in other tombs in the Ashtur and Gulbarga necropolises. On later imitation of the Bahmani paintings in the mausoleum of Gisu Daraz in Gulbarga, see Green, "Auspicious Foundations," 73.

8. Merklinger, *Indian Islamic Architecture*, 16.

9. Michell and Zebrowski, *Architecture and Art of the Deccan Sultanates*, 141; Philon, "The Murals," 9. On parallels between architectural decorations and loom-woven textiles, see Golombek, "The Draped Universe of Islam," 34–35.

10. For the inscriptions, see Yazdani, *Bidar*, 115–27; Firouzeh, "Architecture, Sanctity, and Power," 219–24. On the circulation of Shah Neᶜmatullah's divan in the Deccan, see Firouzeh, "Sacred Kingship," 205.

11. Ahmad Shah's death date is inscribed as 839/1436 while in written sources it is recorded as 838/1435: Tabataba, *Burhan-i maʾasir*, 65; Astarabadi, *Tarikh-i Fereshteh*, 382.

12. Yazdani, *Bidar*, 124–25. See also Desai's article in Nayeem, *Studies in History of the Deccan*, 216–22. On the practice of calligraphers signing themselves as *naqqash* (painter), see O'Kane, *Timurid Architecture in Khurasan*, 39.

13. Yazdani, *Bidar*, 115–27; Firouzeh, "Sacred Kingship," 209–11.

14. Yazdani, *Bidar*, 127; Firouzeh, "Sacred Kingship," 207.

15. Yazdani, *Bidar*, 119–27.

16. Firouzeh, "Sacred Kingship," 209–11.

17. Ibid., 209, 211.

18. Aubin, *Matériaux*, 107, 316–17; Astarabadi, *Tarikh-i Fereshteh*, 354, 382–83. See also chapter 2, section I, "The Iconography of Encounter: Sufis in the Sacred Landscape of the Bahmanid Deccan."

19. Astarabadi, *Tarikh-i Fereshteh*, 382–83.

20. Firouzeh, "Sacred Kingship," 209–12.

21. Michell and Zebrowski, *Architecture and Art of the Deccan Sultanates*, 141.

22. Yazdani, *Bidar*, 115.

23. Merklinger reads this as the name of Allah and the *panjtan*: Merklinger, *Indian Islamic Architecture*, 113.

24. Philon, "The Murals," 8–9; Gupta, "Interpreting the Eye," 202–203.

25. Saberi, *Majmaᶜ al-rasaʾil*, 304.

قطب عالم چو نقطه بر کار است   دایره گرد او به پرگار است

26. Green, "Migrant Sufis," 500.

27. Flood "Bodies and Becoming," 463.

28. Aubin, *Matériaux*, 293–301.

29. I read this part of the extract with a slight difference from Aubin's reading. Aubin read "Nurullah" as "nawwar Allah" and added "*marqadahu*" ("his grave") in brackets to refer to Shah Neᶜmatullah. I believe that "Nurullah" here is meant to refer to Shah Neᶜmatullah's grandson and successor. This reading would also mean that the title "makhdumzada" is not used twice to refer to Shams al-din Muhammad. Aubin, *Matériaux*, 307–308.

30. Ibid., 308.

31. On the title, see Astarabadi, *Tarikh-i Fereshteh*, 382–83.

32. Green, "Migrant Sufis," 501, 506.

33. Aubin, *Matériaux*, 136–39.

34. Newman, *Safavid Iran*, 51.

35. A comparative example would be the case of the Nurbakhshiyya: Mitchel, *The Practice of Politics*, 100–101.

36. Quinn, "Rewriting Niʿmatu'llāhī History," 201–22; Mitchel, *The Practice of Politics in Safavid Iran*, 50.

37. Based on a twentieth-century document, Eisazadeh notes the structures around the astana known as the Shah ʿAbbas buildings: a cistern (built in 1000/1591–92), a bathhouse, and a mosque. The mosque has been highly restored, and the cistern and bathhouse, although extant until 1342/1963–64, are lost now. See Eisazadeh, "Tak-negari," 135.

38. With some minor differences from my reading, the inscription has been published in Kermani, *Zendegi va athar-i Qutb al-muwahhidin*, 129. On the politics of shared foundation inscriptions in the Safavid period, see Babaie et al., *Slaves of the Shah*, 19.

39. Babayan, "The Cosmological Order," 246; Arjomand, *The Shadow of God*, 198–99; Mitchel, *The Practice of Politics in Safavid Iran*, 30–33.

40. On patterns of movements between Taft, Yazd, and the Deccan since the fifteenth century, see Aubin, *Matériaux*, 206–207; Abouʾi Mehrizi, *Sadat-i Neʿmatullahi*, 88.

41. Eaton and Wagoner, *Power, Memory, Architecture*, 126; Speziale, "A Propos Du Renouveau Niʿmatullāhī," 91–118.

42. Rizvi, *The Safavid Dynastic Shrine*, 160.

43. Melville, "Shah ʿAbbas's Patronage," 131; Hillenbrand, *Studies in Medieval Islamic Architecture*, II:22.

44. Rizvi, *The Safavid Dynastic Shrine*, 47, 52.

45. Ibid., 121.

46. Morton, "The Ardabil Shrine," 51–52. On the dar al-huffaz at Mashhad, see Rizvi, *The Safavid Dynastic Shrine*, 133.

47. Rizvi, *The Safavid Dynastic Shrine*, 14, 121, 133; Morton, "The Ardabil Shrine," 52–54; Blair, *Text and Image*, 263.

48. Rizvi, *The Safavid Dynastic Shrine*, 75.

49. Moin, *The Millennial Sovereign*, 82–83; Quinn, "Rewriting Niʿmatu'llāhī History," 205; Böwering and Melvin-Koushki, "ḴĀNAQĀI I."

50. Arjomand, *The Shadow of God*, 112, 116–17; Connell, "The Nimatullahi Sayyids," 176; Quinn, "Rewriting Niʿmatu'llāhī History," 205–206; Moin, *The Millennial Sovereign*, 82–83.

51. Aubin, *Matériaux*, 219–31; Newman, *Safavid Iran*, 20. On sadrs, see Newman, *Safavid Iran*, 17; Arjomand, *The Shadow of God*, 125.

52. Shirazi, *Rawzat al-safat*, 54–55; Abouʾi Mehrizi, *Sadat-i Neʿmatullahi*, 137–38.

53. On the discrepancies in sources, see Abouʾi Mehrizi, *Sadat-i Neʿmatullahi*, 15, 148.

54. Aubin, *Matériaux*, 220, 227. Also discussed in Szuppe, "Status, Knowledge, and Politics," 147; Newman, *Safavid Iran*, 32–33, 45, 54; Arjomand, *The Shadow of God*, 116; Abouʾi Mehrizi, *Sadat-i Neʿmatullahi*, 146.

55. Afshar, *ʿAlam ara-yi Shah Tahmasp*, 135–38; Quinn, "Rewriting Niʿmatu'llāhī History," 217.

56. Quinn, *Persian Historiography*, 7. See also Rizvi, "Its Mortar Mixed," 324–25; Babayan, "The Cosmological Order," 252–54; Mitchel, *The Practice of Politics*, 69; Subrahmanyam, "Connected Histories," 754–55.

57. Moin, *The Millennial Sovereign*, 82–83; Abouʾi Mehrizi, *Sadat-i Neʿmatullahi*, 78; Mancini-Lander, "Memory on the Boundaries of Empire," 458, 492–97; Aubin, *Matériaux*, 136–39.

58. On Bektash Khan's rebellion, see Abou'i Mehrizi, *Sadat-i Neʿmatullahi*, 151–66; Matthee, "Loyalty, Betrayal and Retribution," 184–200; Mancini-Lander, "Memory on the Boundaries of Empire," 463–66.

59. Munshi, *Tarikh-i ʿalam-ara-yi ʿAbbasi*, 412; Mancini-Lander, "Memory on the Boundaries of Empire," 464.

60. Junabadi, *Rawzat al-Safaviyya*, 707–708; Afushta-yi Natanzi, *Naqawat al-athar*, 326–31.

61. Junabadi, *Rawzat al-Safaviyya*, 710–11.

62. Afushta-yi Natanzi, *Naqawat al-athar*, 326–31.

63. Munshi, *Tarikh-i ʿalam-ara-yi ʿAbbasi*, I:418, 421; Mancini-Lander, "Memory on the Boundaries of Empire," 464–65.

64. On Husayni Junabadi, see Blake, *Time in Early Modern Islam*, 116.

65. Junabadi, *Rawzat al-Safaviyya*, 710–11; Newman, *Safavid Iran*, 54; Matthee, "Loyalty, Betrayal and Retribution," 191, 194.

66. Szuppe, "Status, Knowledge, and Politics," 147.

67. Connell, "The Niʿmatullahi Sayyids of Taft," 235–36; Munshi and Muvarrikh, *Zayl-i tarikh-i ʿalam-ara-yi ʿAbbasi*, 98; Mancini-Lander, "Memory on the Boundaries of Empire," 478.

68. Abou'i Mehrizi, *Sadat-i Neʿmatullahi*, 22.

69. As indicated in a waqfnama of the family of Quli Beg Afshar: Reza'i, *Fihrist-i asnad-i mawqufat-i Iran*, II:133–34.

70. Reza'i, *Fihrist-i asnad-i mawqufat-i Iran*, II:133–34.

71. On Kerman in this period, see Babaie, "Sacred Sites of Kingship," 175–217; Golombek, "The 'Citadel, Town, Suburbs,'" 445–63.

72. Quinn, *Historical Writing*, 99; Arjomand, *The Shadow of God*, 116–17.

73. Munshi, *Tarikh-i ʿalam-ara-yi ʿAbbasi*, I:424–25; also discussed in Mancini-Lander, "Memory on the Boundaries of Empire," 465.

74. Aubin, *Matériaux*, 237–40. The dates of Shah ʿAbbas's visit to Yazd match his itineraries: Melville, "From Qars to Qandahar," 204–206.

75. Aubin, *Matériaux*, 237–40; Mancini-Lander, "Memory on the Boundaries of Empire," 467–74.

76. Aubin, *Matériaux*, 238–40; Mancini-Lander, "Memory on the Boundaries of Empire," 472.

77. Mufid, *Jamiʿ-i Mufidi*, III:70.

78. Graham, "The Niʿmatullāhī Order," 194–95; also discussed in Mancini-Lander, "Memory on the Boundaries of Empire," 474–75.

79. Emami, *Isfahan*, 111.

80. Arjomand, *The Shadow of God*, 117; Mancini-Lander, "Memory on the Boundaries of Empire," 475–76.

81. Quinn, "Rewriting Niʿmatu'llāhī History," 206–208, 221–22; Khwandamir, *Tarikh-i habib al-siyar*, 4:7, 517, 606.

82. From the second group, Quinn focuses on the *ʿAlam arra-yi Safavi* (1086/1675–76) and *ʿAlam ara-yi Shah Tahmasp*: Quinn, "Rewriting Niʿmatu'llāhī History," 211–19.

83. Quinn, "Rewriting Niʿmatu'llāhī History," 219; Shukri, *ʿAlam ara-yi Safavi*, xx–xxi; Afshar, *ʿAlam ara-yi Shah Tahmasp*, 15. Mancini-Lander discusses Quinn's work on the Neʿmatullahis and suggests the second strand might draw on the family's stories as advice literature for the Safavid kings: Mancini-Lander, "Memory on the Boundaries of Empire," 485–92. On the Neʿmati-Haydari battles, see Emami, *Isfahan*, 111–15. Moin, *The Millennial Sovereign*, 162; Newman, *Safavid Iran*, 59,

78, 88; Arjomand, *The Shadow of God*, 117–18; Perry, "Toward a Theory of Iranian Urban Moieties," 51–70; Sykes, *Ten Thousand Miles*, 29.

84. Emami, *Isfahan*, 102–104, 111–13.

85. On kalantars in the Safavid period, see Lambton, "The Office of Kalantar," 206–18.

86. Quinn, "Rewriting Niʿmatu'llāhī History," 220.

87. Ibid., 219. Abouʾi Mehrizi, too, argues for continuity in the history of the Neʿmatullahis in the Safavid period in spite of the Bektash Khan episode: Abouʾi Mehrizi, *Sadat-i Neʿmatullahi*, 13, 166.

88. Chardin, *Voyages*, 473; Connell, "The Nimatullahi Sayyids," 241; Emami, *Isfahan*, 111–13.

89. Mancini-Lander, "Memory on the Boundaries of Empire," 437.

90. Not to be mistaken with another Khanish Begum, daughter of Shah Tahmasp.

91. Mufid, *Jamiʿ-i Mufidi*, III:687.

92. Katib, *Tarikh-i jadid-i Yazd*, 216–17.

93. On the Shah Vali Mosque in Taft, see Golombek and Wilber, *The Timurid Architecture*, 410–12; Aube, "In Search of 'Kamāl,'" 77; Afshar, *Yadgarha-yi Yazd*, I:633–36.

94. Golombek and Wilber, *The Timurid Architecture*, 411.

95. Afshar, *Yadgarha-yi Yazd*, I:420.

96. Golombek and Wilber, *The Timurid Architecture*, 410.

97. Qaraʾizadeh, "Report," 2.

98. Ibid., 127.

99. Ibid., 15.

100. Mufid, *Jamiʿ-i Mufidi*, III:687.

101. Aubin, *Matériaux*, 224–25.

102. As evidence of alterations, see a photograph taken between 1951 and 1980 by Baroness Marie-Thérèse Ullens de Schooten (d. 1989): http://archnet.org/sites/3899/media_contents/62941, accessed on October 13, 2019.

103. Golombek and Wilber, *The Timurid Architecture*, 411; Aube, "In Search of 'Kamāl,'" 77–79.

104. Afshar, *Yadgarha-yi Yazd*, I:149–50, 143–44, 139–40; Aube, "In Search of 'Kamāl,'" 77–81.

105. Golombek and Wilber, *The Timurid Architecture*, 410.

106. Aube, "In Search of 'Kamāl,'" 77.

107. Mardomi and Dehghani Tafti, "Baztab-i sayr-i muwajiha ba tasawwuf-i Neʿmatullahi," 148.

108. See chapter 5, section V, "Weaving an Epigraphic Network."

109. Khaziʿin, "Waqf-nama-yi Khanish Begum," 489–508; Tasdiqi, "wagf-nama-yi Khanish Begum dukhtar-i Shah Ismaʿil," I:452–63.

110. Khaziʿin, "Waqf-nama-yi Khanish Begum," 495–99.

111. Afshar, "Zilū," 31–36; Blair, *Islamic Calligraphy*, 180.

112. For another case of elite women mentioned in hagiographies as patrons of buildings that they may not have supported, see Wolper, "Princess Safwat al-Dunya," in Ruggles, *Women, Patronage and Self-Representation*, 37.

113. On the power of women's natal genealogy and hagiographies, see Ruggles, *Women, Patronage and Self-Representation*, 9; Wolper, "Princess Safwat al-Dunya," 35–52.

114. Ruggles, *Women, Patronage and Self-Representation*, 10–11; Szuppe, "The 'Jewels of Wonder,'" 325–47.
115. Szuppe, "The 'Jewels of Wonder,'" 332, 336; Szuppe, "Status, Knowledge, and Politics," 144–48.
116. On the importance of mosques in shrine complexes, see Blair, *The Ilkhanid Shrine*, 18–19.
117. Arjomand, *The Shadow of God*, 112–18; Bashir, *Messianic Hopes*, 186–95; Babayan, "The Isfahani Era of Absolutism," 349–87.

7

Patronage Beyond the Court, Sufis Beyond the Shrine

Throughout this book, I have shown how the historiographical problem of detaching Sufism from materiality has resulted in the marginalization of Sufis' roles as patrons and makers of material culture. We have seen that the Neʿmatullahi Sufis did not just stand by, acting as authoritative political and social figures at the receiving end of artistic and architectural patronage—rather, they actively sought and negotiated court and urban patronage while also patronizing objects and spaces of ritual within their own shrine network. We have also seen how court patrons, for a variety of social and political reasons, drew on the artistic strategies that the Sufis had adopted in designing their spaces and objects.

This chapter develops yet another perspective on the multifaceted relationship between Sufism and patronage. The aim is to reverse standard models of power relations that, in art history, have confined nonruling Sufis to marginal roles in the making of art and architecture. To do so, I draw on three sets of examples, mainly from the Safavid and Mughal realms in the sixteenth and seventeenth centuries. This is a period when the Neʿmatullahi Sufis assumed patronage of urban and architectural projects and art collecting beyond the boundaries of their shrines.

The first and second case studies concern architectural projects that have received scant attention in past scholarship: the construction of an urban complex in Yazd, Iran, and the renovation of a sacred site belonging to another influential Sufi network, the Chishtis, in Delhi, India. Each of these examples illustrates how the Neʿmatullahi family opted for an imperial language of architectural patronage to carve out a new space for themselves as urban elites. Both sections build on the last chapter's discussion of the family's relationships with the Safavids. These relationships consolidated at a significant moment when the history of urban development increasingly buttressed the empire's standing in transregional and global politics. The last set of examples in this chapter enacts a shift in scale to focus on the Neʿmatullahi family's engagement with the collecting of works of calligraphy and the making of albums. Sixteenth-century textual sources reveal a desire on the part of the family to partake in elite circles that were engaged in the valuation and collecting of works on paper as well as a recognition among contemporaries of their standing as connoisseurs, collectors, and distinguished calligraphers.

I. Beyond the Shrine and into the Maydan: The Neᶜmatullahi Urban Project in Yazd

Khanish Begum (d. 1564), the Safavid patron of the Taft complex, was also a protagonist in a major construction project in Yazd. A few years after her patronage in Taft, she built a mosque in Yazd, which at the time was under the governorship of her husband, Neᶜmatullah Baqi (d. 1563), an appointee of her brother Shah Tahmasp (r. 1524–76). She named the mosque after her brother—the Shah Tahmasp Mosque.[1] Located adjacent to what is today the Biᶜsat Square of Yazd, in the Safavid period the mosque was one of the first structures built as part of an expanded urban complex and maydan (public square) that is the subject of this section.

While the sixteenth-century mosque has been lost, a completely new structure has been built on the site (fig. 7.1), and it still houses two elements from the original building. The first is a marble mihrab stone with a medallion of floral and scroll design, and the other is an inscribed panel installed on a column inside the mosque.[2] Inscribed in naskh script, the panel is a decree by Shah Tahmasp on tax reduction for Yazd, dated 969/1561–62. Neᶜmatullah Baqi, who is mentioned in this decree as the governor of Yazd, is tasked with "inscribing this decree onto stone and installing it in the Jamiᶜ Mosque."[3]

Referring to this mosque as a Jamiᶜ mosque bears significance on the urban level in and beyond Yazd. If this decree were in fact meant to be installed in the Shah Tahmasp Mosque, there is a suggestion here as to how this new mosque was intended to multiply the centers of the city alongside the existing Jamiᶜ mosques of Yazd. In this sense, the function and meaning of the Shah Tahmasp Mosque was not unlike its larger fifteenth-century counterpart: the Mir Chaqmaq complex, which had expanded Yazd beyond its medieval city walls and its main focal point, the old Jamiᶜ mosque and bazaar. The three mosques formed a triangle in relation to one another (fig. 7.2), representing a reorientation of urban space beyond the medieval city—a notable feature alongside other monumental Safavid projects in Qazvin and Isfahan.[4] To characterize the Shah Tahmasp Mosque as a Jamiᶜ mosque was also to underline the significance of the building and the broader urban project that came to surround it. As such, it stands as a strikingly precocious statement in light of subsequent Safavid mosque building campaigns and the theological debates around them.[5] For context, the Shah Tahmasp Mosque of Yazd was built decades before the imperial Safavid mosques in Isfahan.

Khanish Begum's choice of the site for her project in a neighborhood known as the dar-i madrasa-yi ᶜAbd al-Qadiriyya in Yazd, which was located outside the city's medieval walls, drew on the Neᶜmatullahis' existing association with this quarter. The connection revolves around a now-lost fifteenth-century

FACING TOP, FIGURE 7.1. Aerial map of the Biᶜsat Square in Yazd with the dome of the new structure of the Shah Tahmasp Mosque. © *Google Earth Pro; with additions by author.*

FACING BOTTOM, FIGURE 7.2. Aerial map of Yazd, showing the relationship between Maydan-i Shah, the Mir Chaqmaq Complex, and the old Jamiᶜ Mosque. © *Google Earth Pro; with additions by author.*

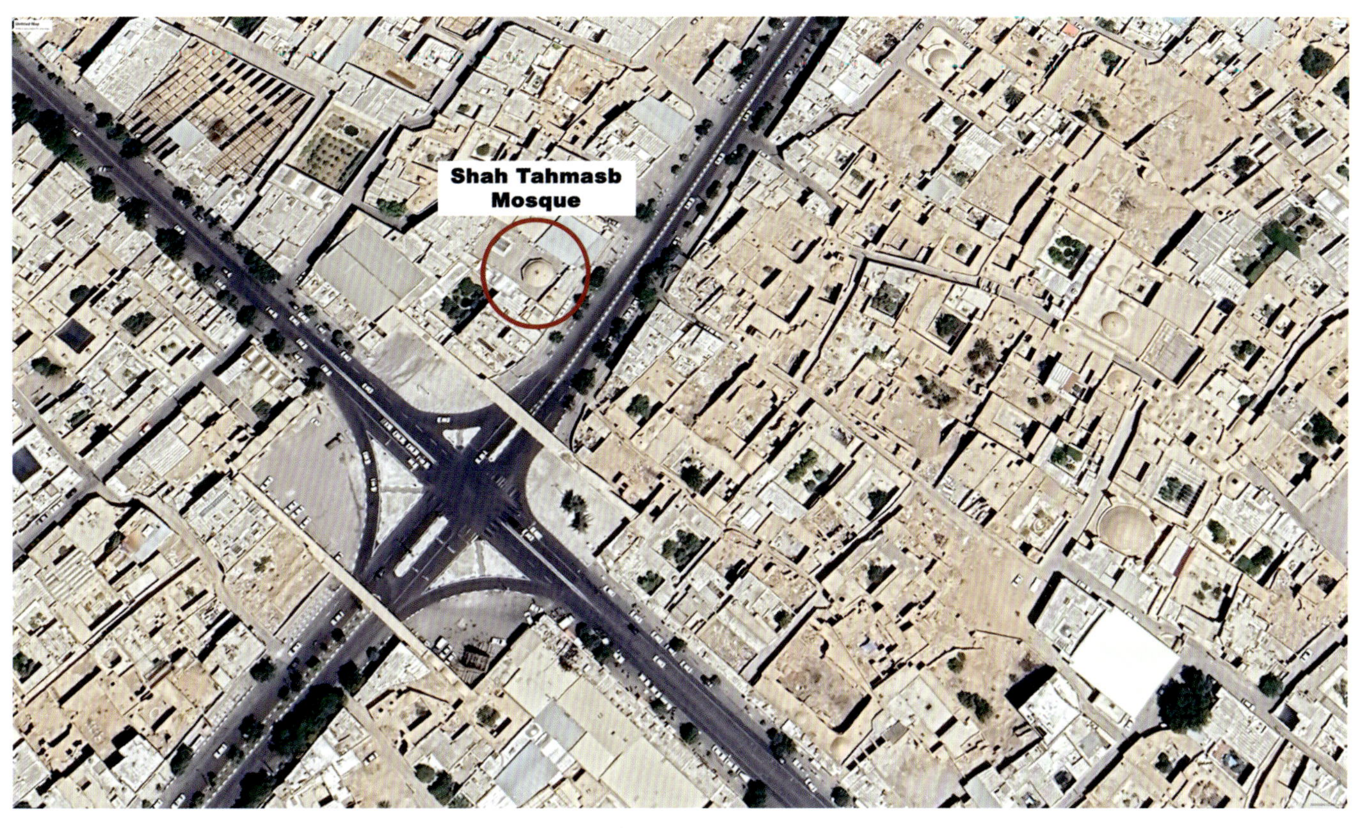
Shah Tahmasb
Mosque

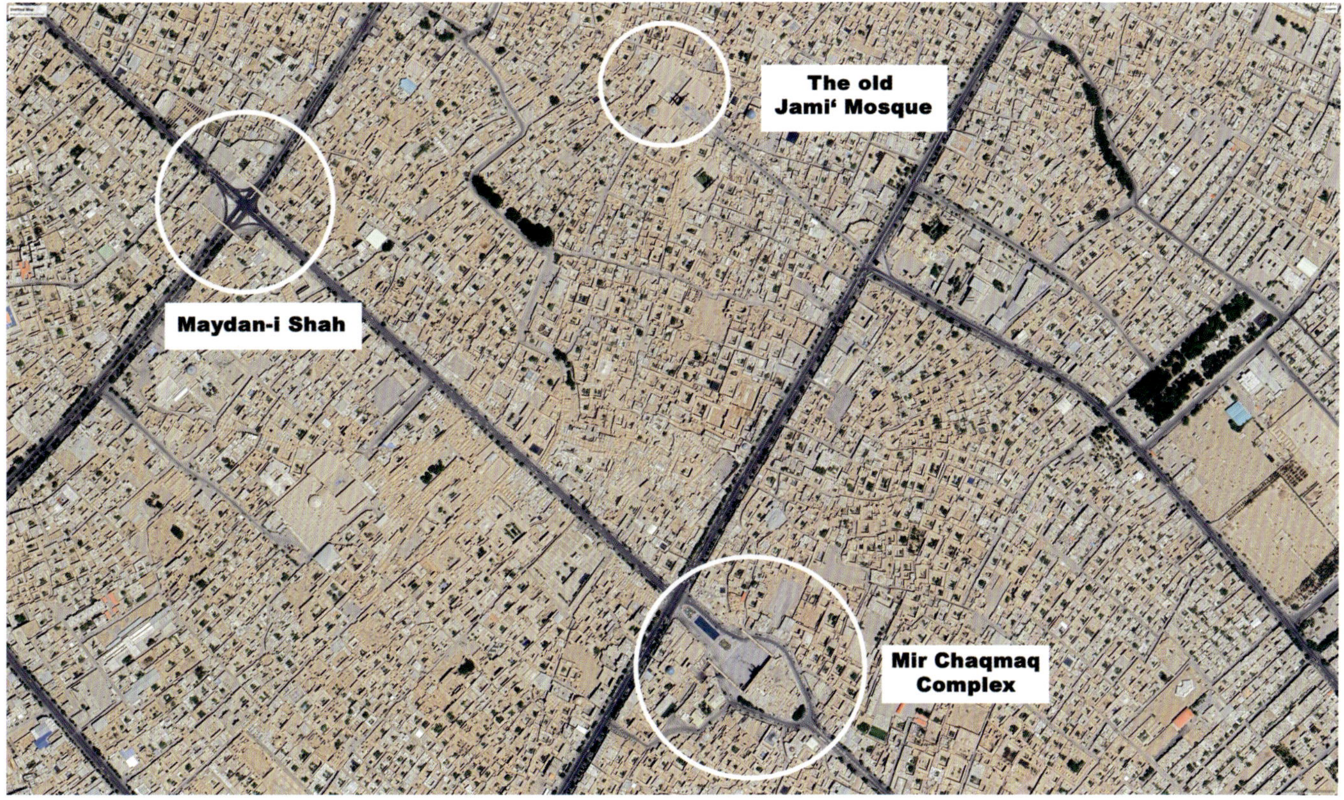
The old
Jami‘ Mosque
Maydan-i Shah
Mir Chaqmaq
Complex

residence built by a certain Sayyid Ghiyath al-din in 838/1434–35. Textual sources attest that this fifteenth-century site, on which Khanish Begum and later her son developed their project, already exuded an air of social and artistic prestige. The author of *Tarikh-i Yazd* describes this residence as a magnificent monument with a garden, a lofty wind catcher, and an excellent lower-ground hall. The famous Timurid historian and poet Sharaf al-din ʿAli Yazdi, who had a known affiliation with the Neʿmatullahi family, wrote poems in praise of the house and its wind catcher.[6] A well-known calligrapher of the time, Shams al-din Muhammad Shah-i Hakim, inscribed these verses on the walls of the building.[7] The residence was adjoined by a lavishly decorated bathhouse (hammam) featuring gilded inscriptions of verses penned by Sharaf al-din ʿAli Yazdi, which included the name of the reigning Timurid sultan, Shahrukh (r. 1405–47).[8]

In addition to these physical descriptions, the *Jamiʿ-i Mufidi* also gives us a glimpse of the house's ownership history. While there is no known record of a relationship between the original owner of the house and the Neʿmatullahi family, we know that after the owner's death, the property was transferred to the descendants of Shah Neʿmatullah generation after generation, reaching Mirza Ghiyath al-din Muhammad Mirmiran, son of Khanish Begum and Neʿmatullah Baqi, who became the governor of Yazd after his father.[9] This Mirmiran is the same Neʿmatullahi descendant who allied with Bektash Khan in his rebellion against the Safavids. By the time Mufid was reporting, the residence was known as the ʿAbbasiyeh after Shah ʿAbbas I (r. 1588–1629), and Khanish Begum had built her aforementioned mosque—named after her brother and grandfather of Shah ʿAbbas I—in the vicinity of the fifteenth-century residence. That Mirmiran devised this urban project in the name of the imperial Safavids is especially interesting in light of Bektash Khan's uprising and its aftermath for the Neʿmatullahis.

Mirmiran's architectural patronage united the fifteenth-century residence and his mother's sixteenth-century mosque around a maydan that is referred to as maydan-i Shah (royal square) in the *Jamiʿ-i Mufidi*. His additions to the existing buildings elevated the complex to an expanded urban development project that contained several public, administrative, and ceremonial elements of monumental scale.[10] During the reign of Shah ʿAbbas I, Mirmiran constructed a *dowlat-khaneh* (palace) with gilded ivans and lofty halls that had elaborate paintings on their walls and ceilings.[11] This seems to have expanded the earlier fifteenth-century residence. Mirmiran also built a massive gate for this monument, and the large open maydan that was designed in front of it was surrounded by numerous lofty arches on each side. Opposite the ʿAbbasiyeh, on the other side of the maydan, he built a *talar*, which seems to have been a multistory building serving ceremonial functions with a *naqqareh-khaneh* (kettledrum house) where kettledrums were played every morning and evening.[12]

Almost all the elements that made up this urban and administrative center are now lost. According to the *Jamiʿ Jaʿfari* (completed 1829–30), a history

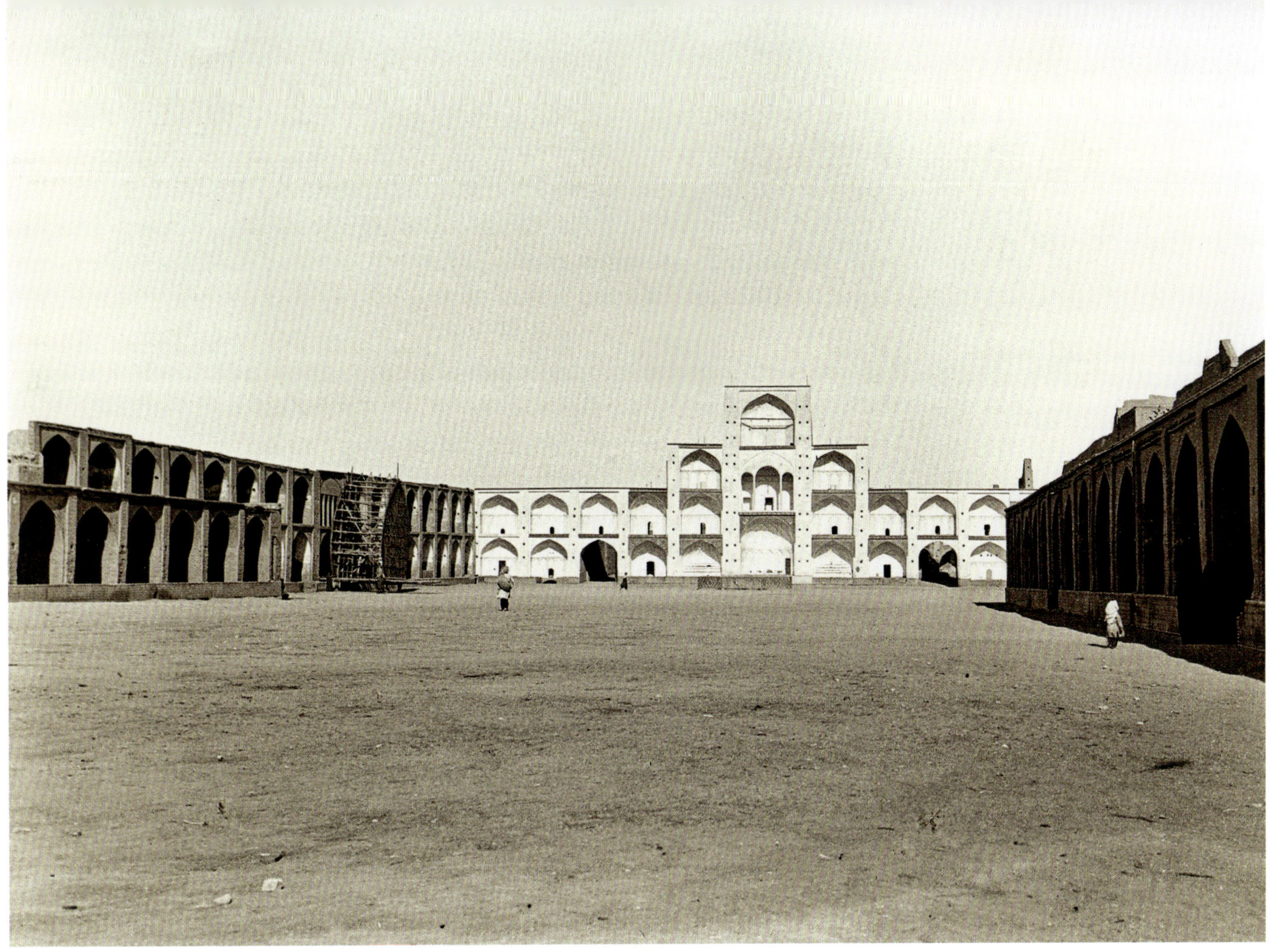

FIGURE 7.3. View of the nineteenth-century husayniya built in Maydan-i Shah in Yazd. Percy Molesworth Sykes, ca. 1900. Lantern slide, glass. © *The Trustees of the British Museum, Sykes.240.*

of Yazd written in the Qajar era, a governor of Yazd built a monumental husayniya in the maydan-i Shah around 1800 (and no later than 1805) for the ritual mourning ceremonies of Husayn—the third Shiʿa imam and grandson of the Prophet Muhammad (fig. 7.3).[13] We do not know exactly how this new construction related to the earlier maydan, but it is possible that some destruction took place to accommodate this new building—a project that was mirrored in the nineteenth-century changes made to the fifteenth-century maydan of Mir Chaqmaq. Road constructions in the twentieth century also contributed to further destruction: the Shah Street (now known as Qiyam), which was built in 1943, for instance, ripped through the Safavid maydan-i Shah (fig. 7.1).[14] Remnants of colonnades from the nineteenth-century maydan-i Shah, as well as reconstructed segments that seem to have been built recently to imitate the earlier structures, can be seen around the periphery of the current maydan in Yazd.

Despite this substantial loss, Mufid's description of the spatial configuration and functions of the structures built around the maydan recalls the imperial urban projects in Qazvin, the Naqsh-i Jahan maydan at the new Safavid capital of Isfahan and the relatively smaller project of the Ganj ʿAli Khan maydan in Kerman. The historical connections between the maydan-i Shah complex in Yazd and the development of Qazvin into a ceremonial and administrative center a few decades earlier in 1540s are worth mentioning here.[15] In Qazvin, a preexisting dowlat-khaneh (palace) had been refurbished and used under Shah Isma'il (r. 1501–24), which resonates with the development of Yazd's dowlat-khaneh in maydan-i Shah, expanding on a preexisting residence.[16] The Ne'matullahis had an established presence in the former Safavid capital of Qazvin during the development of the city under Shah Tahmasp. Mirmiran's father owned a mansion and garden in the quarter of Sa'adatabad, the neighborhood where Safavid palaces and other courtly buildings were located.[17] When the renowned poet 'Abdi Beyg Shirazi (d. 1580) was tasked with writing a work in verse on the Sa'adatabad garden quarter and its palaces, there were twenty-three private gardens around Qazvin's Arshi-khaneh palace (also known as Chehel Sotun), the Ne'matullahi palace being one of them.[18] The construction projects of Shah Tahmasp in Qazvin took about fifteen years, from 1546–47 until 1560–61, only one year before Khanish Begum's construction of the Shah Tahmasp Mosque in Yazd in 969/1561–62. These various familial and administrative connections point toward the Ne'matullahis' intimate knowledge of the construction projects in Qazvin around the time the maydan complex in Yazd was starting to take shape.

Textual sources date Mirmiran's constructions in the Yazd maydan to the reign of the Safavid ruler Shah 'Abbas I, almost three decades after Khanish Begum's patronage of the mosque in Yazd. Since Mirmiran died in 1590, two years after Shah 'Abbas's reign began, the project falls within a small window between 1588 and 1590, around the same time as the construction of the maydans in Isfahan and Kerman (and the rebellion of Bektash).[19] In addition to this contemporaneity, the Shah maydan in Yazd and the Naqsh-i Jahan maydan in Isfahan also share similar spatial configurations in bringing together the architectural elements of a religious, ceremonial, and administrative center: both incorporate an older palace or residential element, new mosques, naqqareh-khaneh, and the presence of a mercantile element, the bazaar. Though based only on textual descriptions it might seem that the commercial elements seen in Isfahan, or in Kerman as Sussan Babaie has discussed, did not have a strong presence in Yazd's new maydan, the complex was in fact connected to the older maydan of Mir Chaqmaq through the old bazaar, sections of which were in possession of Khanish Begum, patron of the Shah Tahmasp Mosque.[20] This connection between an older urban center with a new maydan through the bazaar is also an important urban design element in Isfahan, where the bazaar connected the new Naqsh-i Jahan maydan with the old center of the city, which had developed under the Seljuqs from the eleventh to the thirteenth centuries and included the old congregational mosque.[21]

In Yazd, both the old maydan of Mir Chaqmaq and the new maydan-i Shah incorporated architectural spaces that were related with Sufism. The now-lost fifteenth-century khanaqah in the Mir Chaqmaq complex seems to have been a state-controlled institution, much like the contemporary khanaqahs in Samarkand and Herat patronized by Timurid rulers and princes, which did not necessarily belong to one specific Sufi network but were administered by an official installed by the government. In Yazd's maydan-i Shah, by contrast, the physical element of a khanaqah as a separate entity is missing, although it is possible that Sufi rituals and gatherings were held in the dowlat-khaneh. Moreover, compared to the Mir Chaqmaq complex, the Shah maydan demonstrates a collapse of roles between Sufis and patrons. In the maydan-i Shah, the patron, the governor, and the Sufi are all embodied in the Neʿmatullahi Sufi Mirmiran. To some extent this is comparable to the Naqsh-i Jahan square in Isfahan—although at a much smaller urban and political scale—where the figures of Sufi and temporal authority were conflated in Safavid rule.

The constructions in the maydan-i Shah of Yazd and the connections to the Safavid imperial projects symbolize the great degree of political power that the Neʿmatullahis had achieved in Iran—from local notables in the Timurid period to members of the elite with named positions strongly connected to the main seat of power in Safavid capitals. Such political status reverberates in the architectural projects associated with the family in this period. They became influential patrons of architecture and made the decision to invest in projects that went beyond developing their own physical institutions—projects that reached a new urban and public scale. In responding to and replicating the royal precinct models of urban development from the Safavid capital of Qazvin, the Neʿmatullahi family inscribed themselves into the history of Safavid empire building, even if their project was not in an official capital. Perhaps even more significant is that the urban complex in Yazd, named after Safavid Shahs, expanded from a residential core associated with the Neʿmatullahi family: a symbolic relationship signifying the entanglement of their familial networks and histories with their political and architectural careers.

II. Not a Shrine of Their Own: The Neʿmatullahi Project in Delhi's Nizamuddin Dargah

If the patronage of the maydan complex in Yazd marks the epitome of the Neʿmatullahis' monumental urban patronage outside of their shrines, an architectural project in Delhi can be considered their most notable project in a Sufi shrine outside of their own network. In the mid-seventeenth century, one of the descendants of Mirmiran at the Mughal court left his mark on one of the most significant sacred nodes of Delhi: the dargah of the Chishti Sufi Nizamuddin Awliya (d. 1325). The evidence of Neʿmatullahi patronage at the Nizamuddin dargah opens an interesting chapter in the patronage career of the Sufi network, much of which awaits further research. While the presence of the Neʿmatullahis in Mughal India has been discussed by scholars in the past, the extent of their urban patronage and their specific role in Nizamuddin dargah has not received any attention in previous literature.[22] My goal here is simply to contextualize this project alongside other examples of the Neʿmatullahis' direct involvement in artistic patronage during the period.

The exact circumstances of the family's presence at the Mughal court require more in-depth research. Muhammadreza Abouʾi Mehrizi and Michael Connell map the Mughal sources that outline the presence of the Neʿmatullahis in Mughal India and their reception by the courts of Jahangir (r. 1605–27), Shah Jahan (r. 1628–58), and Aurangzeb (r. 1658–1707).[23] The family's earliest appearance in Mughal sources dates to the reign of the Safavid ruler Shah ʿAbbas I, less than two decades after Bektash's rebellion in central Iran, which was discussed in the previous chapter. While it is possible that migrations to Mughal India unfolded in the aftermath of the rebellion, it is important to recognize the possible nuances of this decision and the circumstances that led to it. In facilitating the departure of some members of the family from Safavid Iran, it seems a key actor was son of Mirmiran Yazdi, Khalilullah III (d. 1609), who, unlike some other members of his family, had in fact remained loyal to Shah ʿAbbas throughout Bektash's rebellion.

To understand the nuances of the family's migration to the Mughal court, it is also important to note that the Neʿmatullahis still maintained a presence in Iran as attested by figures such as Khalilullah III's own brother Sulayman (d. 1640) and the latter's son Abu'l Mahdi (d. unknown), who was the patron of the Mahan carpets among other projects. Further, as I briefly noted in the previous chapter, Shah ʿAbbas's absorption of Yazd into crown lands brought about a decrease in the power of local authorities such as the Neʿmatullahi family, which may have been a factor in the relocation of some of them to India.[24] The broader religiopolitical atmosphere of central Iran during the reign of Shah ʿAbbas and the lure of financial opportunities offered by Mughal rulers, specifically in light of the intensification of movements between the Safavid and Mughal courts in the preceding decades, provide a likely backdrop to the family's itinerary.[25] Much like their movements between Iran and Deccan India in the fifteenth century, this new wave of migrations in the seventeenth century seems to have stemmed from a decision to multiply the social and financial opportunities of the family by dividing their members in various locales.

Given the Neʿmatullahi family's historical ties with Deccan India, Deccani courts might seem like a more obvious destination for the family's descendants. Migrations to the Deccan still occurred. However, as Sanjay Subrahmanyam and Muzaffar Alam have shown in their work on biographical dictionaries such as the *Zakhirat al-khavanin* (ca. 1650) and the *Maʾasir al-umara* (or *Maʾathir al-umara*, ca. 1750), the broader landscape of movements between Iran and the Deccan started to shift from the second half of the sixteenth century. With the growth of the Mughal court as a principal attraction for Iranian elites, artists, and scholars, "a complex trajectory triangle" of migrations between Iran, Mughal India, and the Deccan started to form—sometimes leading Iranian migrants who had started their careers in the Deccan to move to North India for better opportunities and resources.[26] While this triangle starts to take shape from the reign of Shah Tahmasp (r. 1524–76), marked by the flight of prominent Sunni scholars and Sufi networks such as the Nuqtawis, it is in the last decades of the sixteenth century that the rapid intensification of these movements sets in.[27] Mughal rulers Jahangir, Shah Jahan, and Aurangzeb are noted for appointing Iranian migrants to positions such as *diwan* (chief revenue officer) and *mir bakhshi* (chief officer in charge of the military department).[28] The Iran–Deccan–Mughal India triangle offers a meaningful context for the movements of the Neʿmatullahi family between Iran and India and within India in several historical instances. Some members of the family who had migrated from Safavid Iran to Mughal India played a central role in Mughal campaigns in the Deccan in the seventeenth century and were appointed to positions in Bijapur and Golkonda by Aurangzeb.[29]

It is within this broader context of migrations between Iran and India that, during the reign of ʿAbbas I in Iran, the name of the Neʿmatullahi descendant Khalilullah III appears in the memoirs of Jahangir. Khalilullah III was received by Jahangir in Lahore in 1016/1608. His Neʿmatullahi lineage is noted in Jahangir's memoir; he is praised as belonging to the greatest family during the reign of Shah Tahmasp, and an outline of the family's marriage ties with the Safavids is offered. There is also a sense of justification for Khalilullah's departure from his home country: despite their greatness under Shah Tahmasp, the family had allegedly fallen into despair and lost properties. Jahangir offered Khalilullah III "12,000 rupees in cash, and promoted him to the rank of 1,000 personnel and 200 horses, and gave an order for a *jagir* [land grant]."[30] When Khalilullah died in India, Jahangir "ordered what he had left in cash and jewels to be sent to his children in Persia."[31]

In *Maʾasir al-umara*, the entry on Khalilullah III—or Mir Khalilullah-i Yazdi, as he is referred to in this source—immediately emphasizes his descendancy from Shah Neʿmatullah Vali, "the saint who is famed throughout the world for his miracles and expositions." The author goes on to offer an account of the life of Shah Neʿmatullah in the fourteenth and fifteenth centuries before returning to the biography of his descendant Khalilullah-i Yazdi. During this detour, he completes the Iran–Deccan–Mughal India triangle by outlining a brief history of the Neʿmatullahis under the Bahmanids (probably citing Fereshteh's text), ending with a note that some of the descendants of the Sufi still live in the Deccan and elsewhere in India, but those in Yazd and Kerman are the ones who have preserved his doctrines and lineage.[32] Here the author might be making an attempt to elevate the status of the newly arrived Neʿmatullahis from Iran to the Mughal court over those who had maintained a presence in the Deccan. After an account of the Neʿmatullahis' grandeur under the Safavids, the author delves into Bektash's rebellion and then takes us back to Khalilullah III, who, for some obscure reason other than the family's role in the rebellion, had fallen out of Shah ʿAbbas's favor and fled to India, the "abode of security," out of fear for his life.[33]

Khalilullah III's son, Mirmiran (d. 1621), who is noted as a "*qalandar* and *dervish*" in sources, was similarly received by Jahangir in Ajmer and given cash as well as "1,000 personnel and 400 horses."[34] Mirmiran's son and grandson continued to hold an array of high-status positions at the courts of various Mughal kings. Mirmiran's grandson, Amir Khan Mirmiran (d. 1698), for instance, collected many titles and positions under Shah Jahan and Aurangzeb, ranging from *mir tuzuk* (court chamberlain) and *fawjdar* (governor of a medium rank) of Jamu to the governor of Allahabad.[35] One of his sons was made governor of Patna.[36]

There are fundamental differences between Indian and Iranian textual sources in treating this episode of the Neᶜmatullahi family. In their mapping of the Neᶜmatullahis' entrance into the political landscape of Mughal India, the Mughal sources are unique. As Abouʾi Mehrizi has noted, none of the Safavid histories or biographies of the family on the Iranian side mention the family's branching into Mughal India.[37] The Safavid-era hagiographies focus on the family's status and support of the new rulers of Iran. Mufid's treatment of Khalilullah III is especially evasive. After mentioning Shah ᶜAbbas's visit to Khalilullah III in Yazd in 999/1590–91, the text moves to a brief mention of Khalilullah's visit to Isfahan, followed immediately by a notice of his death in 1016/1608 (as opposed to the year 1017/1609 mentioned in Mughal sources).[38] Mufid's text completely skips over any details of his stay in Isfahan or his subsequent migration to India.

The Safavid chronicles discuss the family as elites of Yazd who held important political positions and married into the royal family without discussing the significance of their lineage going back to Shah Neᶜmatullah Vali.[39] Most refer to them as Mirmirans of Yazd, not even mentioning the Neᶜmatullahi connection. On the contrary, it is exactly the family's lineage, their spiritual and sociopolitical status, and their geographical reach in India in the centuries prior to their presence at the Mughal court that are of great importance to the Mughal sources.

The Neᶜmatullahi patron of Nizamuddin dargah was the grandson of the first Neᶜmatullahi descendant to move to the Mughal court, Khalilullah III. He is recorded as Khalilullah Khan b. Mirmiran al-Husayni Neᶜmatullahi (d. 1662).[40] Both he and his brother Asalat Khan (d. 1648) held important posts in Delhi.[41] Apparently, when their grandfather Khalilullah-i Yazdi died in India in 1017/1609, the Mughal ruler Jahangir personally intervened by writing a letter to the Safavid ruler Shah ᶜAbbas to ask for the two young brothers, Khalilullah Khan and Asalat Khan, to be sent to India to reunite with their father, Mirmiran.[42]

Khalilullah Khan started his career with a series of positions such as "mir tuzuk (court chamberlain), *mir atish* (head of artillery), and *qur begi* (keeper of the arsenal) under Jahangir." During the reign of Shah Jahan, his status was increasingly enhanced. He rose to the ranks of mir bakhshi (head of the military department) and *subadar* (viceroy) of Shahjahanabad (Delhi).[43] In the *Tazkirat al-umara* (*Biographies of Rulers*) of Kewal Ram, he is said to have supervised the construction of the Shalimar Gardens in Lahore—a significant role that has not been corroborated in any other primary sources that I have consulted.[44] In 1061/1651 he was appointed governor of Shahjahanabad.[45] This was a particularly significant appointment given the rather recent move of the Mughal capital from Agra to Delhi.

One year after Khalilullah Khan's appointment as governor of Delhi, he embarks on the patronage of the Nizamuddin dargah by building a veranda

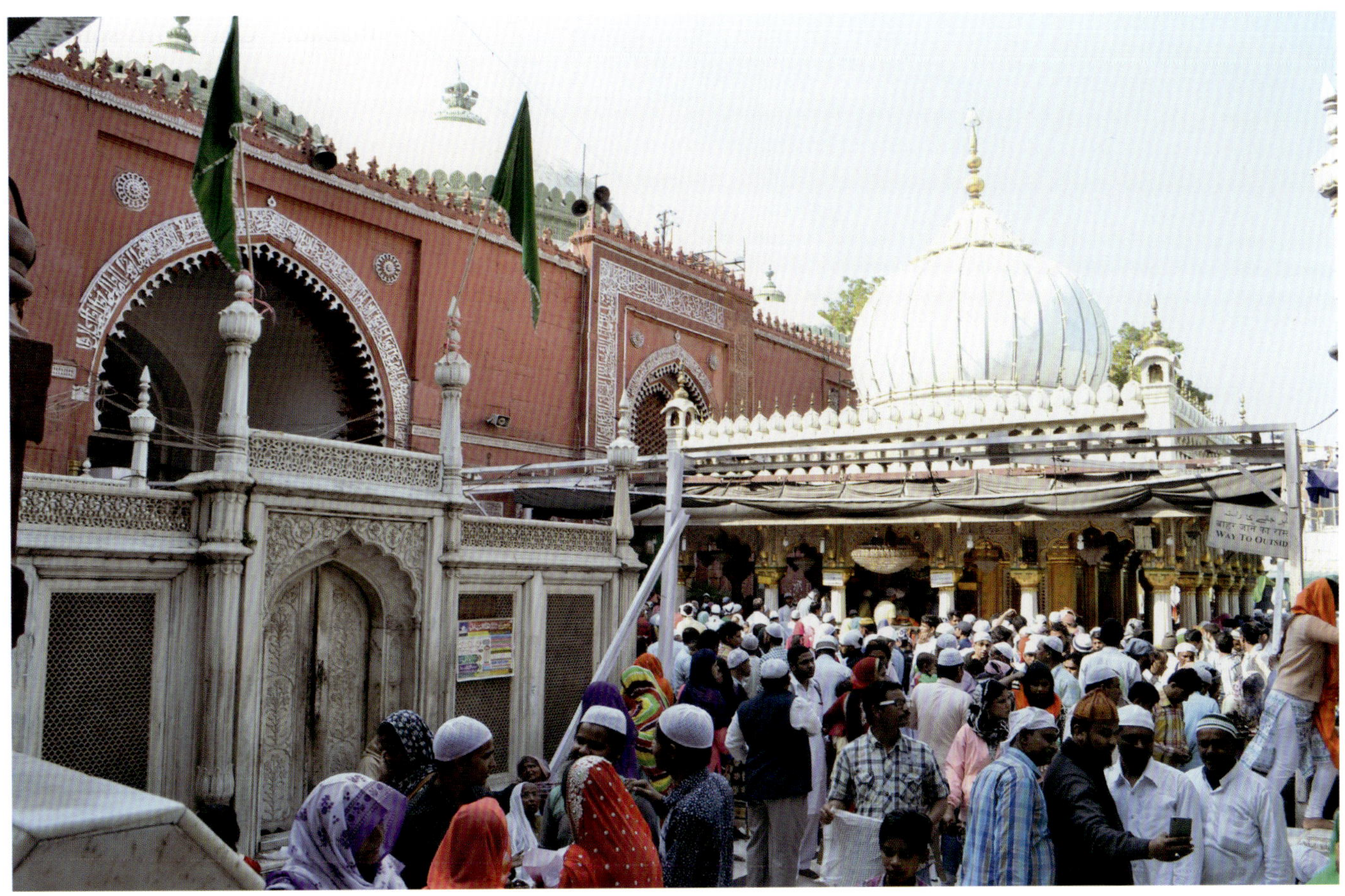

FIGURE 7.4. View of Nizamuddin's tomb on the right, with the Jamaʿat Khana Mosque to the left and Muhammad Shah's tomb in the foreground. *Photograph by author, 2017.*

around the tomb of the Sufi with multifoiled arches and a two-part prose inscription panel that records his patronage, alongside the date of the construction as 1063/1652–53 (figs. 7.4–7.6 and app. 7.1): "During the reign of his majesty the second sahib-qiran [i.e., Shah Jahan], his lowest of servants, Khalilullah Khan b. Mirmiran al-Husayni Neʿmatullahi, who was the governor of Shahjahanabad, constructed this ivan around the blessed tomb in the year 1063."[46]

Since its association with Nizamuddin Awliya in the fourteenth century, the dargah had continued to be a site of piety and patronage. Nizamuddin's tomb is part of a complex that contains the Jamaʿat Khana Mosque (completed 1315–25), a baoli (stepwell), and smaller tombs of notable figures such as Jahanara (d. 1681), daughter of Shah Jahan; the Mughal emperor Muhammad Shah; and the Sufi poet Amir Khusraw (d. 1325), who was a disciple of Nizamuddin Awliya (fig. 7.4). Nizamuddin's tomb itself has been rebuilt several times over the centuries. The current structure dates back to 1562, during the reign of Mughal emperor Akbar (r. 1556–1605), when a noble of the emperor's court named Farid al-Khan built the square-plan tomb with marble screens (*jalis*).[47] Khalilullah Khan's veranda was constructed around this tomb.

During the Mughal period, the site acted as an index of nobility for the Mughal Empire, mainly through Mughal officials who left their mark on the

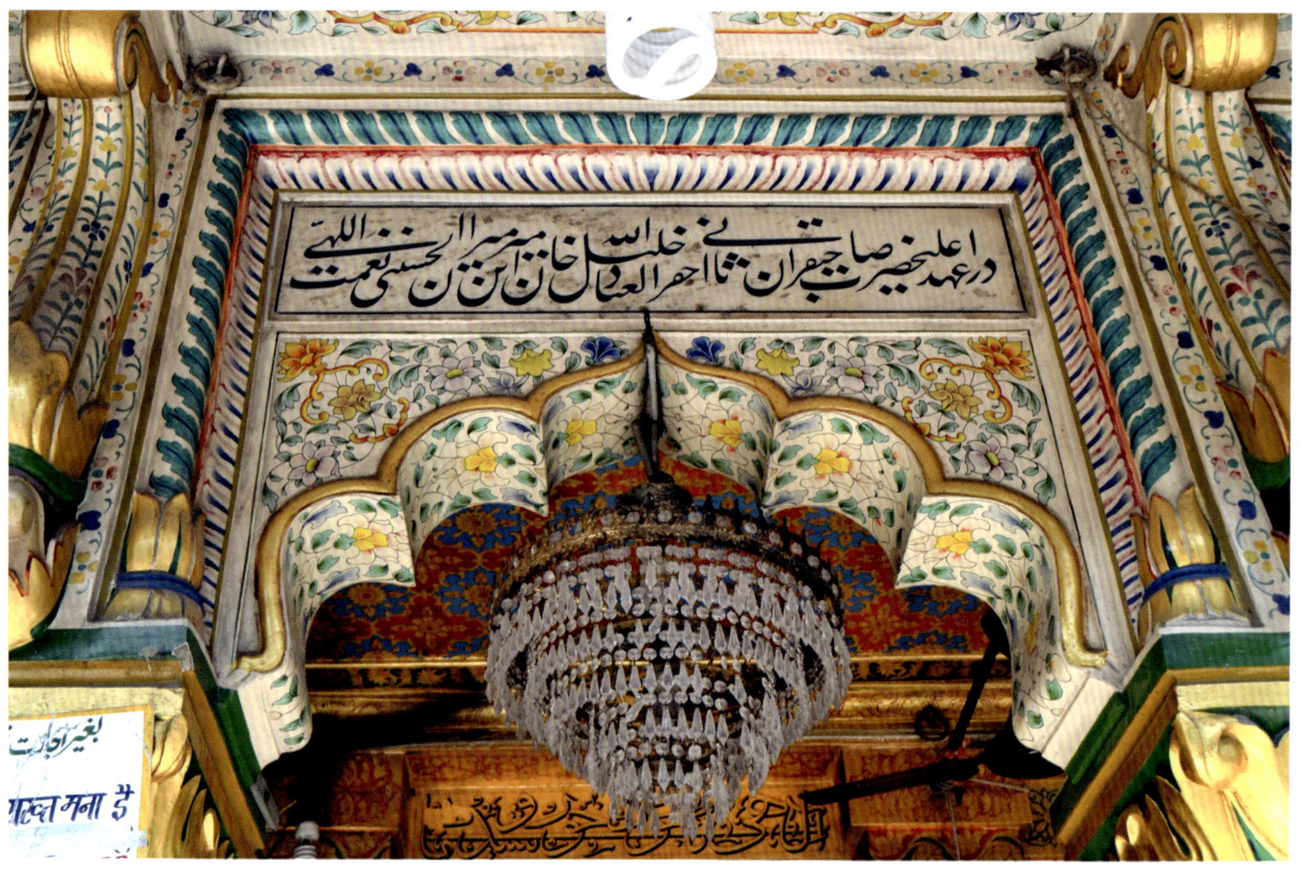

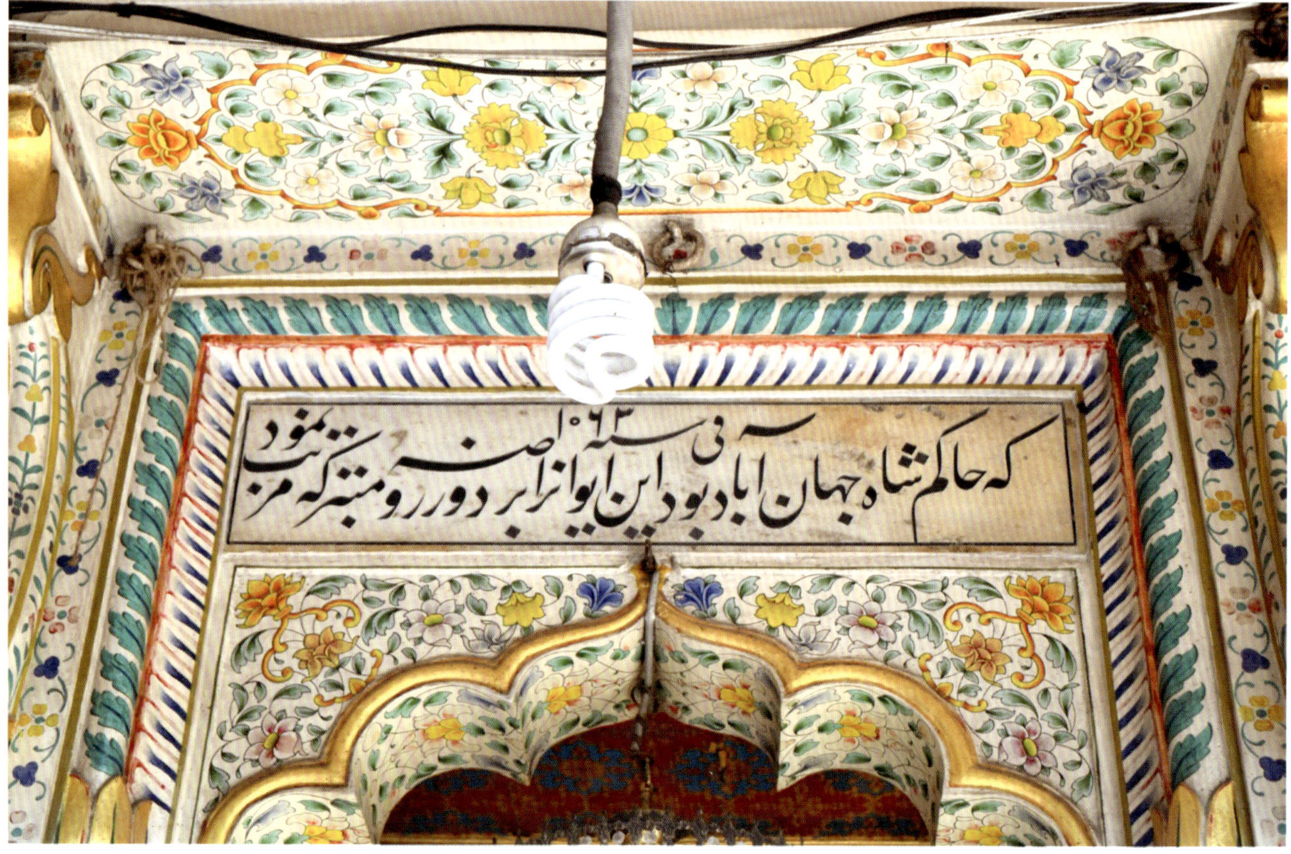

site by refurbishing and expanding it.[48] The choice of the site for Humayun's tomb in the proximity of the dargah was both a sign of its spiritual significance and a means of elevating its political prestige.[49] Mughal emperors continued to make pilgrimages to the dargah, during which they would make donations to the sacred site.[50]

Given the historical and contemporary significance of the Nizamuddin dargah, the implications of Khalilullah Khan's patronage at the site are profound. It is not just the choice of the dargah of a renowned Sufi that signals the weight of this architectural patronage but also the mechanics of the structure itself. Khalilullah Khan's patronage gets to the heart of the sacred site, as close as possible to the tomb of the Sufi, wrapping around it. At the same time, his patronage entails an outward-looking new architectural element whose presence would not be missed by any visitor. Although the project itself lacks the scale of an urban development project like the maydan in Yazd, the nature of the site as a shrine dedicated to another Sufi network makes this an intriguing project.

Khalilullah Khan's motives in the Nizamuddin dargah project are perhaps twofold. On the one hand, he is acting as the governor of Delhi and an urban patron, following suit alongside his many historical and contemporary counterparts who patronized this site of spiritual and political prominence. On the other hand, Khalilullah's lineage, including the title Neʿmatullahi, is inscribed on the panel to ensure that his identity as a descendant of a notable Iranian Sufi honoring another renowned Sufi remains visible. Here, in the meeting of the two Sufi silsilas lies an intersection of different pathways of spiritual and political authority that connect the Mughal and Safavid realms of urban patronage with the many migrants who traversed them.

FACING TOP, FIGURE 7.5. Detail of the ivans around Nizamuddin's tomb, with the first part of the inscription recording the name of Khalilullah Khan. *Photograph by author, 2017.*

FACING BOTTOM, FIGURE 7.6. Detail of the ivans around Nizamuddin's tomb, with the second part of the inscription recording the position of Khalilullah Khan as governor of Shahjahanabad and the date of construction as 1063/1652–53. *Photograph by author, 2017.*

III. Who Wrote It Better? Connoisseurship, Patronage, and Collecting Book Arts

From the fifteenth century forward, there is continuous if also scattered evidence around the Neʿmatullahi network's involvement with arts of the book. Sources highlight their artistic engagement in different capacities as artists, patrons, collectors, and connoisseurs.[51] This section has two goals. First, while the practice of calligraphy among Sufis is commonly discussed in art historical scholarship, their roles as patrons of calligraphy, collectors, or connoisseurs is less frequently explored.[52] The textual accounts in this section contribute to remedying this gap. Second, while there was certainly a meditative and devotional aspect to calligraphy that suited the pursuit of Sufism—as will be discussed in the final chapter of this book—the practice, collecting, and critique of calligraphy among Sufi networks should also be seen as a social phenomenon shaped by a deep engagement with elite circles of art making and art writing.

Shah Neʿmatullah Vali himself is known to have copied certain manuscripts on lettrism in his own hand.[53] Scattered signatures in Iran and India, alongside mentions of lost works in textual sources, offer a small corpus of

Neᶜmatullahis' artistic endeavors. According to ᶜAli Tabataba, Mawlana Sharaf al-din Mazandarani, who adorned the palace of Ahmad Shah Bahmanid in the fifteenth century with inscriptions of the poems written by Shaykh Azari, was also a disciple of Shah Neᶜmatullah.[54] In Mahan, too, there is evidence of signatures by artists who were disciples of the Sufi network and carried a Neᶜmatullahi title—a topic that will be explored further in chapter 8.

Books and anthologies were patronized by the Neᶜmatullahi family on special occasions. There is, for instance, a mention in the *Munshaʾat* of Sharaf al-din ᶜAli Yazdi of a *jung* (anthology) put together most probably in the region of Yazd in the fifteenth century on the occasion of the birth of the great-grandson of Shah Neᶜmatullah Vali, Amir Asadullah (d. unknown). Sharaf al-din himself is said to have written a preface for the anthology.[55] Two examples that were brought up in chapter 5 in the context of Deccan India have a particular significance for the discussion here. One is a fifteenth-century manuscript of the text *Mataliᶜ al-anzar fi sharh-i tawaliᶜ al-anwar*, written in Arabic and held at the British Library (IO Bijapur 223A). In the colophon, the manuscript's scribe, Jaᶜfar al-Reza al-ᶜUrayzi al-Husayni, refers to himself as a disciple of Shah Muhibbullah b. Khalilullah, grandson of Shah Neᶜmatullah Vali. Muhibbullah was the patron of the book, as is evident in a seal adorning the flyleaf of the manuscript.[56] The scribe's documentation of his Sufi affiliation alludes to the tight-knit circles of artists and patrons that converged around Sufi networks. The second example is the renowned *Tuhfat al-muhibbin*, completed in 858/1454 in the Deccan by the famous calligrapher of Timurid manuscripts Siraj al-Husayni al-Shirazi, who was a disciple of the same Shah Muhibbullah to whom he dedicated his eponymous work.[57] This example in particular speaks not only to the Sufi family's interest and investment in calligraphy and the art of writing but also to their intellectual aspects and theorization in relation to tenets of Sufism.

The rise of art writing and artist biographies in the sixteenth century makes it easier to locate the Neᶜmatullahi family in circles of art making. Their careers as poets, calligraphers, art collectors, and patrons are recorded in significant Safavid sources. In his *Tuhfa-yi Sami*, Sam Mirza Safavi (d. 1576–77), son of Shah Ismaᶜil I (r. 1501–24), praises Nizam al-din ᶜAbd al-Baqi (d. 1514), his father's sadr, as a skilled poet. Sam Mirza notes that he wrote under the pen name Baqi (immortal) and attributes a divan of ghazals to him.[58] These words of praise carry considerable weight given Sam Mirza's own status as a poet and his knowledge of contemporary literary circles.[59] However, the most important source that documents Neᶜmatullahi family members as artists, art connoisseurs, and patrons is Qazi Ahmad's renowned work the *Gulistan-i hunar* (*Rose Garden of Art*), a treatise on calligraphy and biographies of noted calligraphers, completed ca. 1595. The same ᶜAbd al-Baqi described in Sam Mirza's biography is noted by Qazi Ahmad for the quality of his *taᶜliq* (a cursive calligraphic script). Qazi Ahmad claims that "little can be compared to the maturity of his hand" and that he had seen decrees and administrative documents written by him.[60]

In Qazi Ahmad's chapter on noted calligraphers of nastaʿliq, ʿAbd al-Baqi's son, Shah Neʿmatullah Baqi (d. 1563), appears as a collector and connoisseur in the context of a debate about the quality of certain calligraphers' hands.

> Since he [Mirza Mahmud] was the *sofrehchi* (banquet supervisor) of Nawwab Shah Neʿmatullah Baqi, and the Shah was always busy making *muraqqaʿ*s (albums), Mirza Muhammad [Mahmud?] did calligraphy too. Shah [Neʿmatullah Baqi] was very fond of his handwriting. Master Maulana Malek says that one day I visited Shah Neʿmatullah [Baqi] and showed him a specimen [of my calligraphy]. Shah took out samples written by Mirza Muhammad [Mahmud?] and presented them to me and said look how he writes, and in the end said that his [i.e., Mirza Mahmud's] hand was better than Maulana Sultan ʿAli [Mashhadi] and Maulana Mir ʿAli [Herawi]. I said, my shah! He writes better than I do, but he cannot write better than them.[61]

On the face of it, this account can be read as a dismissal of Neʿmatullah Baqi's artistic judgment. However, a few contextual points should serve to modify this reading. First of all, despite the nature of the debate presented in this excerpt and the possibility of Qazi Ahmad's agreement with the narrator and opponent of Neʿmatullah Baqi, it is important that the anecdote, and the short biography of Mirza Mahmud, whose works were sponsored and praised by Neʿmatullah Baqi, found their way into the pages of the *Gulistan-i hunar*. This decision means that the calligrapher's hand was of notable quality. Even if its ranking was a matter of debate, the debate itself was worthy of inclusion in Qazi Ahmad's biography.

A second point revolves around how Neʿmatullah Baqi is pictured in the beginning of this account—that is, as someone who was constantly in the business of making albums. Although we do not know what these albums included, apart from works by the calligrapher whom Qazi Ahmad mentions, the passage implies Baqi's patronage of a variety of works of calligraphy and possibly painting, as well as his career as a collector. Putting albums together required a degree of involvement in collecting and possibly having a collector's eye for historical and contemporary works of art. Neʿmatullah Baqi's familiarity with the renowned calligraphers of the fifteenth and sixteenth centuries Sultan ʿAli Mashhadi (d. 1520) and Mir ʿAli Herawi (d. 1544) is made evident in Qazi Ahmad's account.

Most important for the significance of this anecdote is the status of the other protagonist in this debate, Maulana Malik (d. 1561–62). He was a noted calligrapher of several scripts—thuluth, naskh, and nastaʿliq, as signaled by his multipage biography in *Gulistan-i hunar*. The author Qazi Ahmad himself learned calligraphy under him in Mashhad. He notes that Maulana Malik's unsigned naskh hand was indistinguishable from that of the master calligrapher Yaqut (d. 1298), a comparison that would not be granted to just any calligrapher.[62] Maulana Malik acquired a greater reputation than anyone else during his time for his nastaʿliq skills. He was appointed to the library of the Safavid prince Sultan Ibrahim Mirza (d. 1577) and accompanied the prince in Mashhad until he was summoned to Qazvin by Shah Tahmasp in order to write the inscriptions for the building of the new capital's dowlatkhaneh. Maulana Malik is credited for multiple epigraphic projects in Qazvin's Saᶜadatabad Garden and Chehel Sotun in the 1550s, before his death in 969/1561–62.[63] Neᶜmatullah Baqi owned a residence in the same quarter in Qazvin, and it is likely that they were involved in projects there together.

Given Maulana Malik's status as a court artist and calligrapher of imperial projects, the documentation of his dialogue with Neᶜmatullah Baqi brings more weight to the Sufi's status as a connoisseur and collector. It is not just that the Sufi family had a claim on producing and possessing great works of art. While it is easy to sense a tone of rivalry and hurt pride in Maulana Malik's response to Baqi's grand comparison of his calligrapher with the renowned masters of nastaᶜliq, Malik's admission to the superiority of Baqi's calligrapher over his own hand is remarkable—even if prescribed by codes of etiquette. Finally, from Qazi Ahmad's account, it seems that Maulana Malik had come to Neᶜmatullah Baqi to present a specimen of his work. Was he seeking his judgment or hoping that Baqi would acquire some of his works or commission an architectural inscription? Or were they just engaging in a conversation around artistic skills and calligraphic genealogies? If the former, it appears that Malik's desire was unlikely to have materialized. In both cases, the calligrapher's possible intentions point toward an acknowledgment of Neᶜmatullah Baqi's status as a connoisseur, art collector, and patron in contemporary Safavid society.

This chapter has shown how the patronage of the Neᶜmatullahi family could trickle beyond their shrines into the public sphere and elite circles of artistic patronage in the sixteenth and seventeenth centuries. Alongside this outward-looking perspective, the final textual account also suggests an inward-looking aspect of the phenomenon: the Sufi's vigorous support of the work of a calligrapher who was an insider in the Neᶜmatullahi network. Neᶜmatullah Baqi's comments about the work of Mirza Mahmud the calligrapher might be entirely rooted in matters of taste and preference, but they could also point to a deeper connection between artistic patronage and Sufi affiliations. The possible loyalties and privileges that came with affiliation with a Sufi network raise interesting questions about the nature of artistic patronage in and around Sufi shrines. What did it mean for an artist to carry an affiliation with a Sufi network alongside their professional affiliations? The next chapter focuses on one such example where discipleship and artistic practice converge in a small yet enormously important devotional room.

Notes

1. Aubin, *Matériaux*, 434, 461; Afshar, *Yadgarha-yi Yazd*, II:207–209; Mancini-Lander, "Memory on the Boundaries of Empire," 458, 492–97.
2. Afshar, *Yadgarha-yi Yazd*, II:207–209.
3. Ibid., II:209; Abouʾi Mehrizi, *Sadat-i Neᶜmatullahi*, 138–39.
4. On the urban reorientation of Qazvin and Isfahan, see Babaie, *Isfahan and Its Palaces*, 48–50, 71–78, 89–90.

5. Ibid., 56–57, 86; Abisaab, *Converting Persia*, 56, 71–72.
6. Jaʿfari, *Tarikh-i Yazd*, 48–49.
7. Mufid, *Jamiʿ-i Mufidi*, I:179–81.
8. Ibid., I:180.
9. Ibid., I:180–81.
10. Mitchel, *The Practice of Politics*, 176; Graham, "The Niʿmatullāhī Order," 192.
11. Mufid, *Jamiʿ-i Mufidi*, III:65–66.
12. Ibid., III:66.
13. Husayni Naʾini, *Jamiʿ Jaʿfari*, 486, 495, 499.
14. Qalamsiyah, *Tarikh-i salshumari-yi Yazd*, 267; Modarres, *Modernizing Yazd*, 90–92.
15. On the construction of the royal precinct in Qazvin, see Babaie, *Isfahan and Its Palaces*, 33, 47–55.
16. On Qazvin's dowlat-khaneh, see Babaie, *Isfahan and Its Palaces*, 47; Mitchel, *The Practice of Politics*, 105.
17. Mitchel, *The Practice of Politics*, 105; Abouʾi Mehrizi, *Sadat-i Neʿmatullahi*, 137–38. See also chapter 6, section II, "The Dar al-Huffaz in Mahan: Time Capsule of a Rebellion."
18. Shirazi, *Rawzat al-safat*, 7, 13, 54–55. On ʿAbdi Beyg's poem, see Babaie, *Isfahan and Its Palaces*, 50–51, 53–55; Losensky, "The Palace of Praise," 1–29.
19. Inscriptions date the Ganj ʿAli Khan complex in Kerman to 1007/1598, but work was probably begun as early as 996/1587: Hillenbrand, *Studies in Medieval Islamic Architecture*, II:497.
20. On Kerman, see Babaie, "Sacred Sites of Kingship," 193–99.
21. Babaie, *Isfahan and Its Palaces*, 71–78, 89–90.
22. I am indebted to Hamidreza Ghelichkhani for drawing my attention to the epigraphic evidence that is the basis of this section.
23. Connell, "The Nimatullahi Sayyids," 249–61; Abouʾi Mehrizi, *Sadat-i Neʿmatullahi*, 172–85.
24. Mancini-Lander, "Memory on the Boundaries of Empire," 437.
25. Haneda, "Emigration of Iranian Elites," 131–35.
26. Alam and Subrahmanyam, "Iran and the Doors to the Deccan," in Overton, *Iran and the Deccan*, 89. For a case study, see Anooshahr, "Shirazi Scholars," 331–52. See also Overton and Benson, "Deccani Seals and Scribal Notations," 556; Subrahmanyam, "Iranians Abroad," 345; Flatt, *The Courts of the Deccan Sultanates*, 90–91; and Quinn, *Persian Historiography*, 73.
27. Subrahmanyam, "Iranians Abroad," 352; Moin, *The Millennial Sovereign*, 164; Flatt, *The Courts of the Deccan Sultanates*, 90–91.
28. Subrahmanyam, "Iranians Abroad," 347.
29. See chapter 5, section I, "Khalilullah's Funerary Site and Its Chronology in Bidar"; Connell, "The Nimatullahi Sayyids," 259–60.
30. Jahangir, *Tuzuk-i-Jahangiri*, I:131–32; also noted in Connell, "The Nimatullahi Sayyids," 249–51.
31. Jahangir, *Tuzuk-i-Jahangiri*, I:305.
32. Awrangabadi, *The Maāt̲hir-ul-umarā*, I:770–72.
33. Ibid., I:772–73.
34. Jahangir, *Tuzuk-i-Jahangiri*, I:305–306; also noted in Connell, "The Nimatullahi Sayyids," 251–52.
35. Awrangabadi, *The Maāt̲hir-ul-umarā*, I:246–47.
36. Ibid., I:252.

37. Abou'i Mehrizi, *Sadat-i Neʿmatullahi*, 171.

38. Aubin, *Matériaux*, 240–41.

39. See chapter 6, section II, "The Dar al-Huffaz in Mahan: Time Capsule of a Rebellion."

40. Khan, *Shah Jahannamah*, 336–50, 453, 479, 551–55.

41. Connell, "The Nimatullahi Sayyids," 254–58.

42. Awrangabadi, *The Maāṯhir-ul-umarā*, I:773.

43. Ibid., I:767–70; also noted in Connell, "The Nimatullahi Sayyids," 256.

44. Ram, *Tazkirat al-umara*, 63.

45. Khan, *Shah Jahannamah*, 453; also noted in Keshani, "Building Nizamuddin," 173.

46. Keshani, "Building Nizamuddin," 173; Hasan, *A Guide to Nizamu-d Din*, 13.

47. Dadlani, *From Stone to Paper*, 67–68; Asher, *Architecture of Mughal India*, 34–35, 41–42.

48. Dadlani, "The City Built," in Rizvi, *Affect, Emotion, and Subjectivity*, 150, 156; Dadlani, *From Stone to Paper*, 67, 78; Keshani, "Building Nizamuddin," 156–78.

49. Dadlani, *From Stone to Paper*, 59; Welch, "The Emperor's Grief," 263; Keshani, "Building Nizamuddin," 169.

50. Keshani, "Building Nizamuddin," 168–70, 173; Koch, "Shah Jahan's Visits to Delhi," 24–26.

51. As a comparative example, see a note on Mevlevi Sufis as painters: Elias, "Mevlevi Sufis," in Rizvi, *Affect, Emotion, and Subjectivity*, 185, 189.

52. On calligraphy among Sufis, see Ernst, "Sufism and the Aesthetics of Penmanship," 431–42; Ernst, "The Spirit of Islamic Calligraphy," 279–86; Blair, *Islamic Calligraphy*, xxviii, 419–20, 504–505.

53. Aubin, *Matériaux*, 115; Firouzeh, "Dynastic Self-Fashioning," 161–62.

54. Tabataba, *Burhan-i ma'asir*, 71; Astarabadi, *Tarikh-i Fereshteh*, 375.

55. Yazdi, *Munsha'at*, 75–78.

56. Loth, *A Catalogue of the Arabic Manuscripts*, I: 111; Overton and Benson, "Deccani Seals and Scribal Notations," 565–66.

57. Shirazi, *Tuhfat al-muhibbin*, 51–52; Ernst, "Sufism and the Aesthetics of Penmanship," 432–33; Firouzeh, "Dynastic Self-Fashioning," 147–55.

58. Sam Mirza Safavi, *Tazkari-yi tuhfa-yi Sami*, 31–32; see also Abou'i Mehrizi, *Sadat-i Neʿmatullahi*, 122.

59. Sam Mirza Safavi, *Tazkari-yi tuhfa-yi Sami*, X–XI.

60. Munshi-yi Qumi, *Gulistan-i hunar*, 46–47.

61. Ibid., 101–102. For Minorsky's translation, see Munshi-yi Qumi, *Calligraphers and Painters*, 148–49.

62. Munshi-yi Qumi, *Gulistan-i hunar*, 93.

63. Ibid., 93–97; Munshi-yi Qumi, *Calligraphers and Painters*, 142–44.

8

Mahan's Chelleh Khaneh and the Disciple-Artist

The Poetics and Politics of the Sufi Body

In the dar al-huffaz (recitation hall) at the Neʿmatullahi shrine in Mahan, signatures of a craftsman appear in a series of small roundels. Under the ceiling, on each side of the central *shamsa* (sunburst) motif, a roundel framed by eight-pointed stars contains the signature formula of Kamal al-din b. Husayn Neʿmatullahi, a craftsman and member of the Neʿmatullahi network (figs. 8.1 and 1.17 and app. 1.4.a). His signature also appears in a five-pointed star under the *muqarnas* (three-dimensional decorative niches) carvings on the western portal of the dar al-huffaz in the adjacent courtyard (fig. 8.2 and app. 8.1). There, his name is recorded as Kamal al-din b. Husayn tayyan-i Neʿmatullahi, adding the professional title *tayyan*, literally meaning plaster mason. While this seemingly humble title appears to suggest Kamal al-din's responsibility for the plasterwork and carvings inside and outside the dar al-huffaz, its connotations could have been more far reaching. For example, the same title, tayyan, was adopted by the famous Timurid architect Qavam al-din Shirazi (fl. 1410–38), who oversaw such prominent architectural projects as the shrine at Mashhad and the Friday mosque and madrasa in Herat, built for Gowharshad, the renowned patron and wife of the Timurid ruler Shahrukh.[1]

In both of the signatures at the Mahan shrine, the title *Neʿmatullahi* is written in amber, whereas the rest of the signature is rendered in white (figs. 8.2 and 1.17).[2] This distinction signals both reverence for Shah Neʿmatullah Vali, to whom the shrine is dedicated, and a declaration of the artist's membership in the confessional network, comparable to his declaration of membership in the guild of plaster masons, implicit in the title *tayyan*. Would the artist sign his work with the title *Neʿmatullahi* elsewhere? We do not know. Regardless, the intersection between this marker of his affiliation to the Sufi network and its spatial context adds a layer of devotional meaning—indeed, a layer of intimacy—to his labor.

The local, intimate, and devotional nature of Kamal al-din's work is entirely characteristic of Neʿmatullahi projects in the late sixteenth and seventeenth

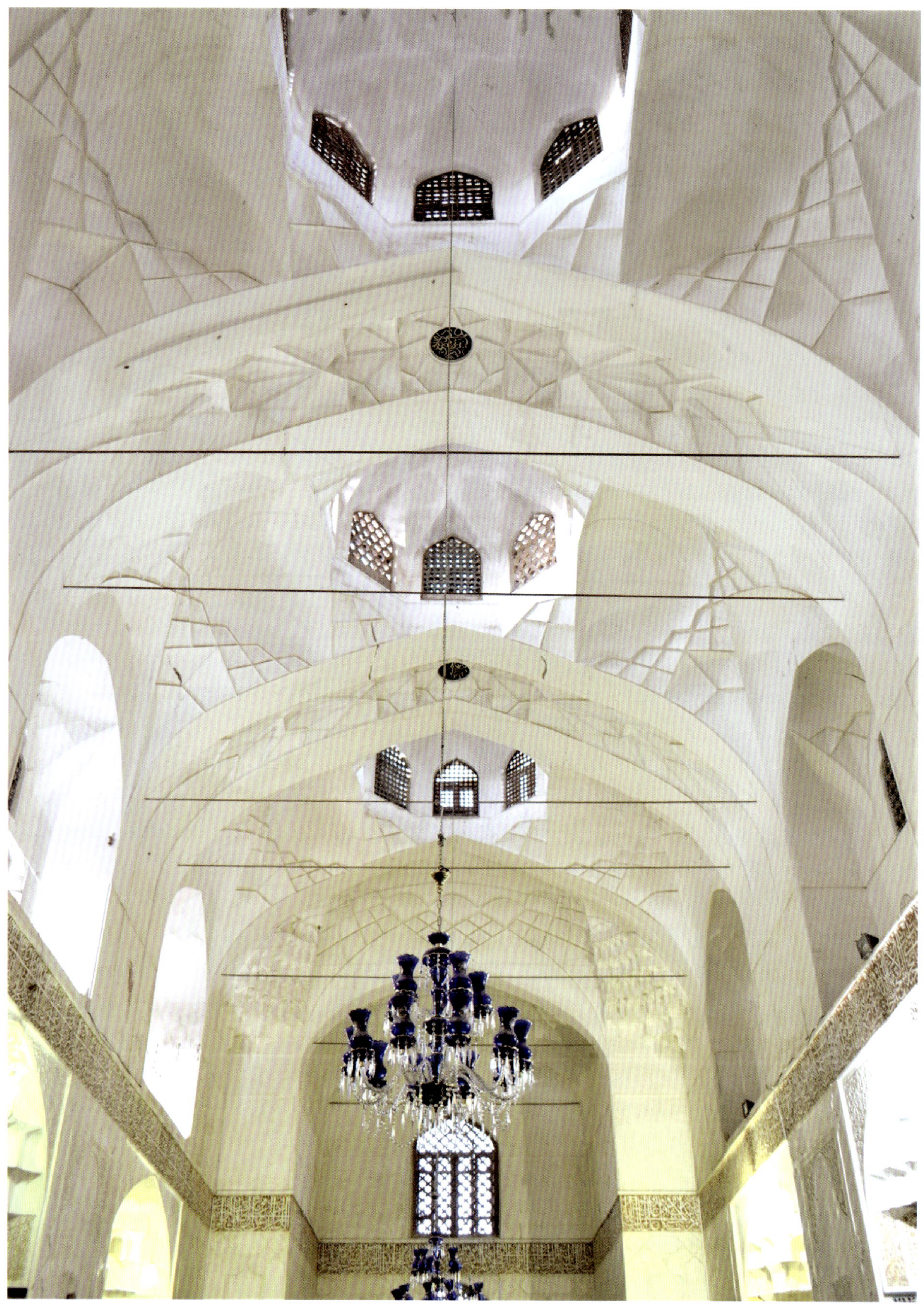

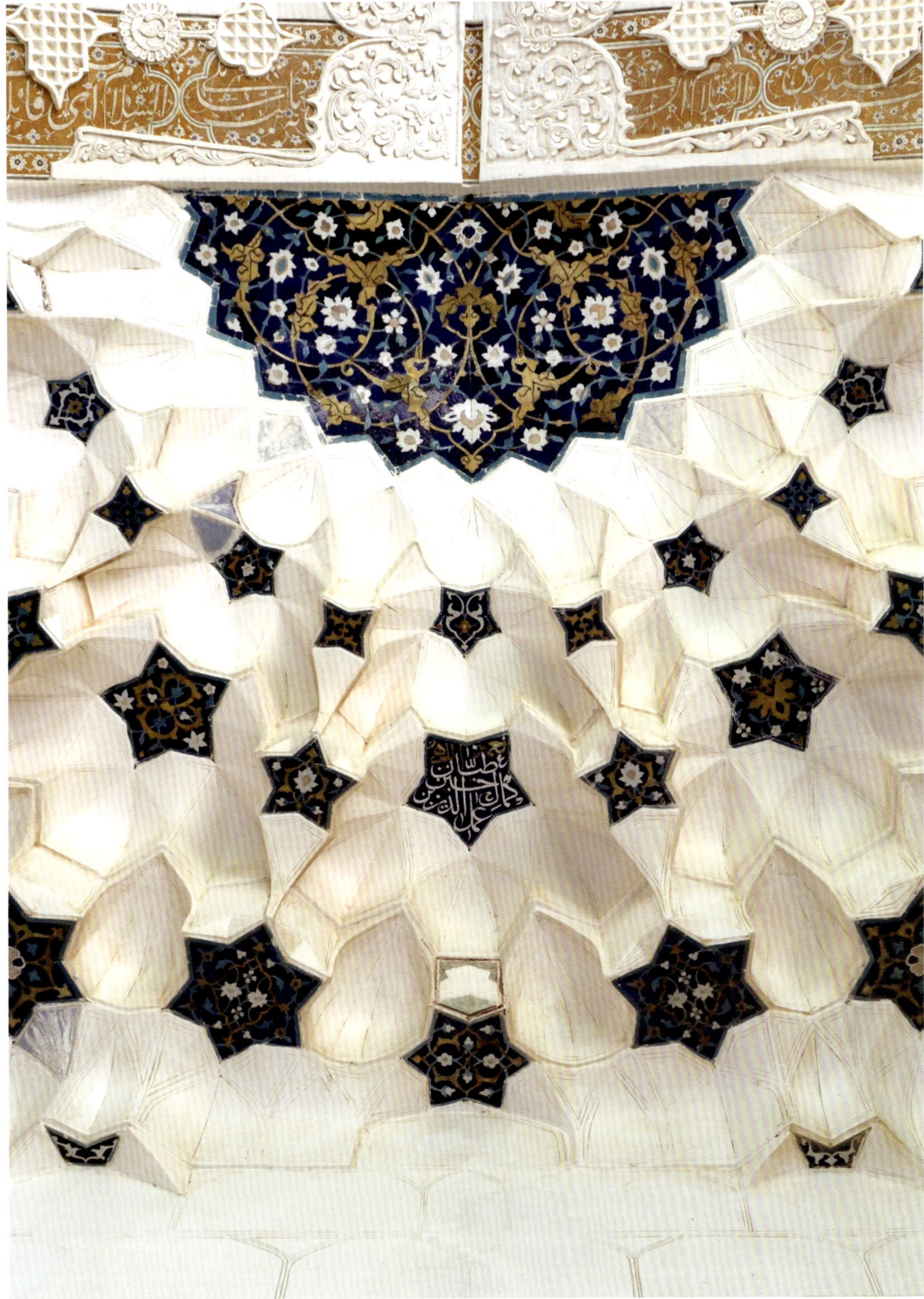

FACING, FIGURE 8.1. View of the dar al-huffaz (recitation hall) at the Mahan shrine with signature roundels under the arches. *Photograph by author, 2018.*

ABOVE, FIGURE 8.2. Signature of Kamal al-din b. Husayn Neʿmatullahi under the muqarnas carvings at the entrance of Mahan's recitation hall from the western courtyard. *Photograph by author, 2013.*

centuries within the shrine in Mahan. In this period, the surfaces of the shrine increasingly came to showcase local artists, disciples of the Sufi network, and members of the family as makers of devotional objects and spaces. Another major example of the increasing visibility of local artists—or better said, artists with local associations—is the weaver of the carpets made in the seventeenth century for the fifteenth-century sepulchre in the shrine at Mahan (figs. 5.34–5.41). As discussed in chapter 5, the signature of the maker of at least one piece of carpet from that group indicates a connection with the town of Mahan (fig. 5.40).[3]

This chapter focuses on a key element in this wave of devotional projects at the Mahan shrine: a small room dedicated to retreat (figs. 0.3 and 8.3). This room has remained understudied despite its extensive interior program of painting and epigraphy, not to mention its broader implications for the sensory richness of Sufi material culture. While there is much to be said about the room and its interior program, the embodied, sensorial analysis offered in this chapter will focus on two particular aspects of the space that tie together the intimacy and politics of devotion through spatial poetry—poetry that in this case was written for the space and can only be understood by inhabiting it.

My first aim is to understand the room as the devotional and artistic project of a disciple, one that engages the body of the viewer in order to activate a bodily representation of the Sufi master himself, Shah Neᶜmatullah Vali. My second aim concerns the relationship between this intimate mode of address and the broader political predicament of the Sufi network vis-à-vis the Safavid regime. As chapters 6 and 7 have shown, the Neᶜmatullahi network drew on the political power of the Safavid dynasty to achieve an unprecedented level of social, political, and urban power, leading to their patronage of architectural and urban projects outside the institutional framework of their shrines. Taking an inward-looking perspective, this chapter demonstrates how this newly forged political power played into the spatial program of the retreat room, merging the intimate with the political. As I will show, the decorative program of the retreat room bound Sufi bodies into a poetically structured, talismanically charged space that gave material shape to hopes and fears instilled by the uncertainties of the Neᶜmatullahi family's circumstances in this period, and the history of clashes between them and ruling authorities.

The small retreat room in the southern corner of the dar al-huffaz (recitation hall) is commonly known as the *chelleh khaneh* (house of forty-day retreat), *zawiya* (corner), khalwat khaneh (room of solitude), or the cell of Sultan Abu'l Vafa, after the artist responsible for its visual program. Khalwat (retreat, seclusion) and a number of related terms such as *riyazat* (hardship, austerity), *uzlat* (seclusion), and *chelleh* (lit. forty days) generally refer to periods of self-isolation, dedicated to meditation as well as other rituals meant to purify the soul and connect with the divine.[4] In the Islamic world, the historical practice of retreat is, in large part, shrouded in mystery, especially to those outside the circles of discipleship, and becomes only partially accessible

FACING, FIGURE 8.3. Interior of the chelleh khaneh in Mahan, view of south wall. The abstract flower in the middle of the wall contains pious invocations to the Prophet Muhammad and Shiᶜa imams. *Photograph by author, 2014.*

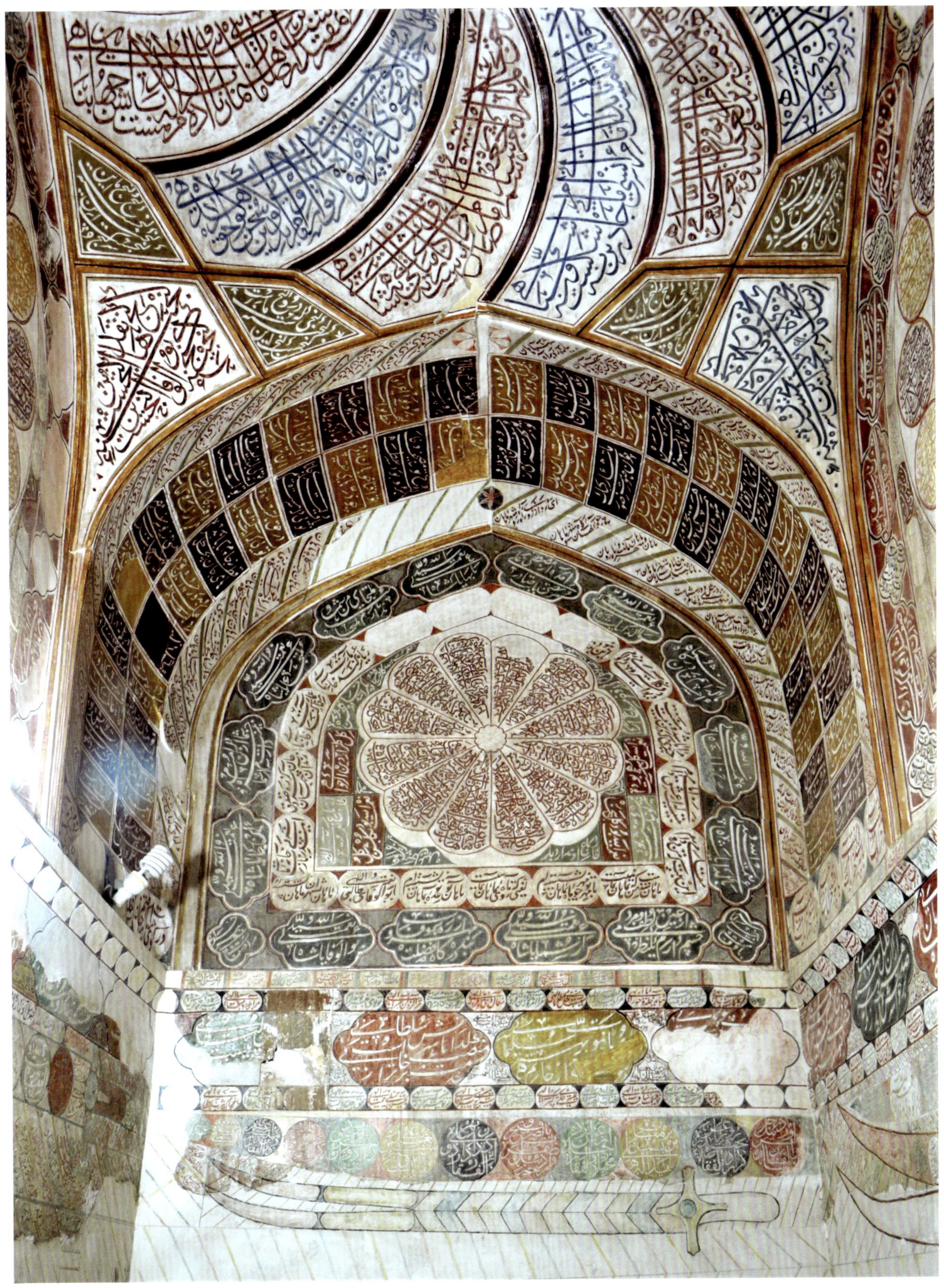

through sporadic textual and visual sources that describe it or offer guidelines.[5] Questions of materiality, bodily configurations, and sensory stimuli, which play a crucial role in the process of khalwat, have rarely been studied from an art historical perspective in the Islamic world, although they have been a more frequent subject of investigation in adjacent fields.[6] In this regard, the chelleh khaneh opens up an opportunity to explore what physical places can tell us about the intimate internal process of retreat. In the absence of textual descriptions of Mahan's chelleh khaneh, it is through the architecture and its epigraphy that I aim to offer a glimpse into the lived experience of the shrine and its meditative practices. The chelleh khaneh is also a significant example of the crossovers between artistic practice and Sufi discipleship for which we do not have many well-studied art historical examples prior to the nineteenth century.

When a specific room in a khanaqah (Sufi lodge) was dedicated to khalwat, the location usually indicated something about the rituals performed within it. Distance or some degree of separation from the most frequented areas of the shrine contributes to a sense of seclusion. The chelleh khaneh was often subterranean or located in a corner—a spatial configuration that intersects with the terminology of khalwat in Persian, which can also be called *gusheh neshini*, literally "sitting in a corner." The chelleh khaneh of Mahan aligns with this norm, occupying a corner of the recitation hall, adjacent to the qibla (west) wall of the shrine complex, which indicates the direction of Mecca. The Mahan chelleh khaneh is one of a series of cells located on the western wall of the Safavid recitation hall. It is, however, the only room accessible from the hall, as the others open only to the adjacent courtyard (fig. 1.3). This privileged access from the interior connects the chelleh khaneh to the mausoleum of the Sufi, with its entrance in the middle of the opposite side of the hall—a connection enhanced by their visual and spatial proximity within the space.

In popular belief, the chelleh khaneh is thought to be the oldest part of the shrine, where the disciples of Shah Neʿmatullah held their retreats and where Shah Neʿmatullah himself performed forty-day khalwats during his lifetime. By implication, these popular narratives imagine the room as a structure predating the fifteenth-century mausoleum as well as the recitation hall (of which the room is a part). Mehrdad Qayyumi, Lisa Golombek, and Donald Wilber speculate that this room could be a remnant of the earlier khanaqah of Shah Neʿmatullah that once stood in the garden in Mahan.[7] While possible, this hypothesis cannot be confirmed or denied on the basis of in situ architectural evidence or textual sources. It is likely that the association between Shah Neʿmatullah and the room derives from—or, rather, was encouraged by—the wider tradition of Sufi masters who blessed khanaqah rooms and performed prayers in them before assigning them to disciples.[8] Regardless, in previous scholarship, this ambiguity about the historical status of the room seems to have resulted in minimal engagement with its rich visual program. Rather than seeking to authenticate or deauthenticate these popular beliefs, this chapter investigates the visual and spatial dynamics of the room—factors that might well have guided the formation of these beliefs over the centuries of the chelleh khaneh's use.

I. Thresholds

The sixteenth-century recitation hall, where the entrance to the chelleh khaneh is located, is a space of grandeur and openness, augmented by the natural light cast in through the ceiling (fig. 8.1). Lacking windows, and fully covered by inscription bands, medallions, abstract flowers, and images of swords in colors whose vibrancy are comparable with the tomb of Ahmad Shah Bahmani (r. 1422–36) in Bidar (fig. 0.1), the chelleh khaneh marks a sharp contrast to the scale, lightness, and subdued colors of the adjacent recitation hall. It measures only about two meters deep and four meters wide, rising to about five meters at its highest point (fig. 1.3). The small room is a place to pause, a place of intense bodily engagement. Its low threshold, only slightly higher than the dadoes of the recitation hall, demands adjustment from the eyes and body of the visitor (fig. 8.4). Dwarfed by the hall, the room is reminiscent of caves or cave-like spaces known through textual and visual traditions as important places of retreat, revelation, and meeting for mystics and prophets alike. Just as the cave offers separation and seclusion from the vastness of a mountain, the retreat room offers a sanctuary of sorts, both part of and distinct from the larger open gallery and, by extension, the shrine as a whole. The fact that this room has no visual counterpart among the other blank-walled cells, which can be accessed only through the adjacent courtyard, contributes to its efficacy as a place of intensified spiritual experience.

A recessed entrance in the recitation hall leads to a door opening onto the chelleh khaneh (figs. 8.4 and 8.5).[9] This mediating space is as deep as the chelleh khaneh itself (about two meters) but much narrower, thus accentuating the orientation toward the chelleh khaneh's door. On the vertical axis, the space between the door and the high vaulted ceiling imparts a sense of openness, especially in relation to the dramatic difference between the height of the recitation hall and the first threshold. The tight space and the small door into the chelleh khaneh require another adjustment from the visitor's body, reinstating the sense of a liminal threshold, the crossing of a boundary.

The spatial experience of preparing to enter the room is structured by visual cues as well. Of all the surfaces visible to visitors as they enter the mediating space between the recitation hall and the door to the chelleh khaneh, only the one immediately in front, lying between the door and the vaulted ceiling, is covered in painted inscriptions (fig. 8.6). These are designed in diagonal bands and medallions, facilitating the transition between the subdued surfaces of the adjacent hall and the intense interior of the room lying behind this wall. The spatial-visual effect is of a temporary halt, heightening visitors' awareness of the proliferation of boundaries and preparing them visually for what they are about to encounter. Due to the broader spatial transition from large to small

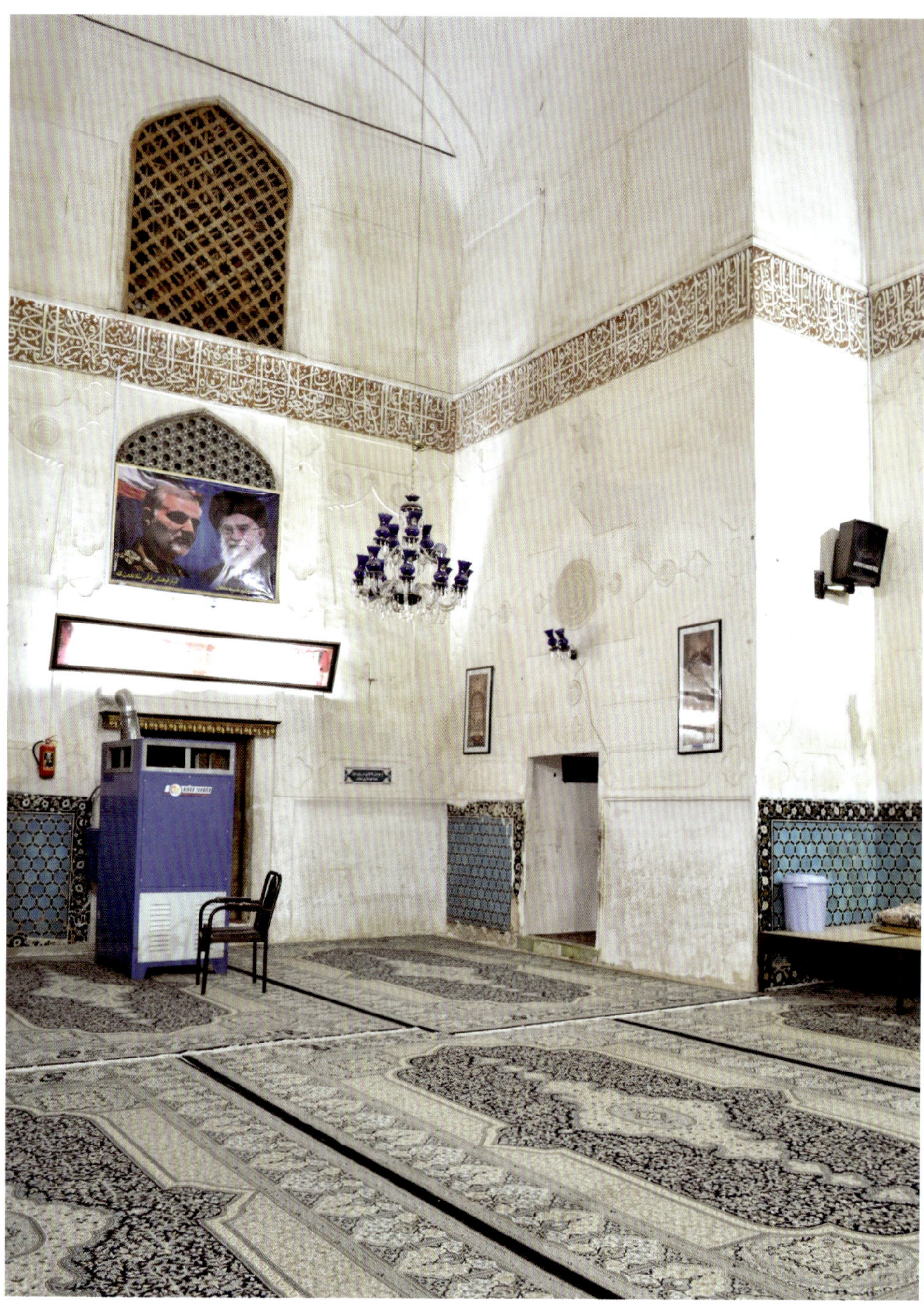

FIGURE 8.4. Opening in the recitation hall (*right*) at the shrine in Mahan, leading to the entrance of the chelleh khaneh. *Photograph by author, 2018.*

and light to dark, the visitor is likely to pause in this space while preparing to enter the main room. It is also likely that the visitor will engage with the epigraphy.

Two medallions dominate the inscribed space above the door, distinguished from the other elements by their larger size and their calligraphic script (thuluth as opposed to nastaʿliq). When read, these medallion inscriptions speak to the mediating function of the space, sharpening the visitor's encounter with the actual threshold (app. 8.2.a).

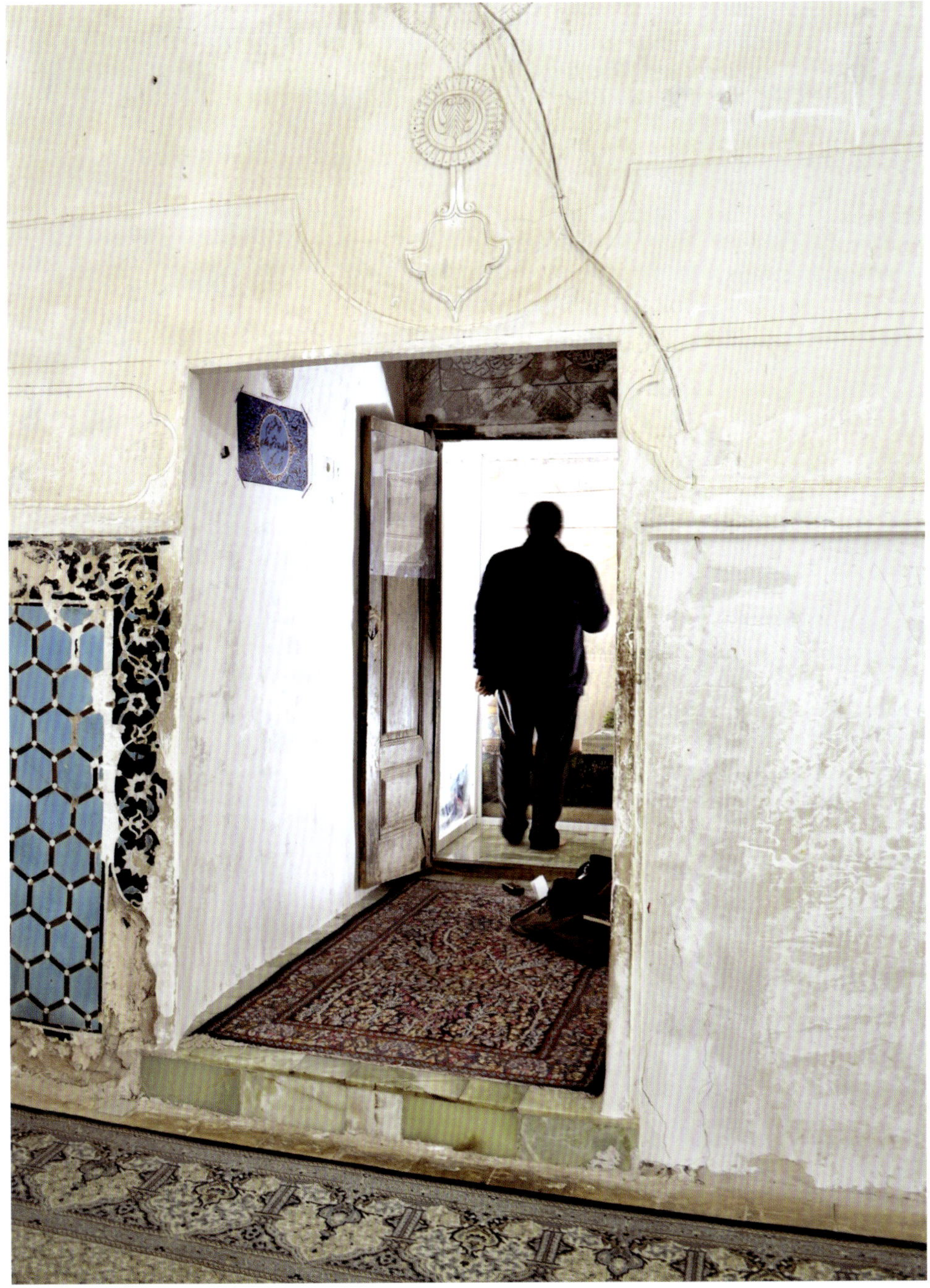

FIGURE 8.5. Entrance to the chelleh khaneh in Mahan. *Photograph by author, 2018.*

The dargah of ʿAli is the dargah of God,
the eternal dargah is the dargah of ʿAli.
God opens the door to the highest of levels,
through the dargah of Shah Neʿmatullah Vali.

The word *dargah*, repeated five times in these verses, has multiple connotations. It is commonly used to refer to a structure associated with a Sufi, funerary or otherwise. Its literal meaning, "doorway" or "portal," stems from the two parts of the word: *dar*, meaning door, and *gah*, which is a suffix indicating

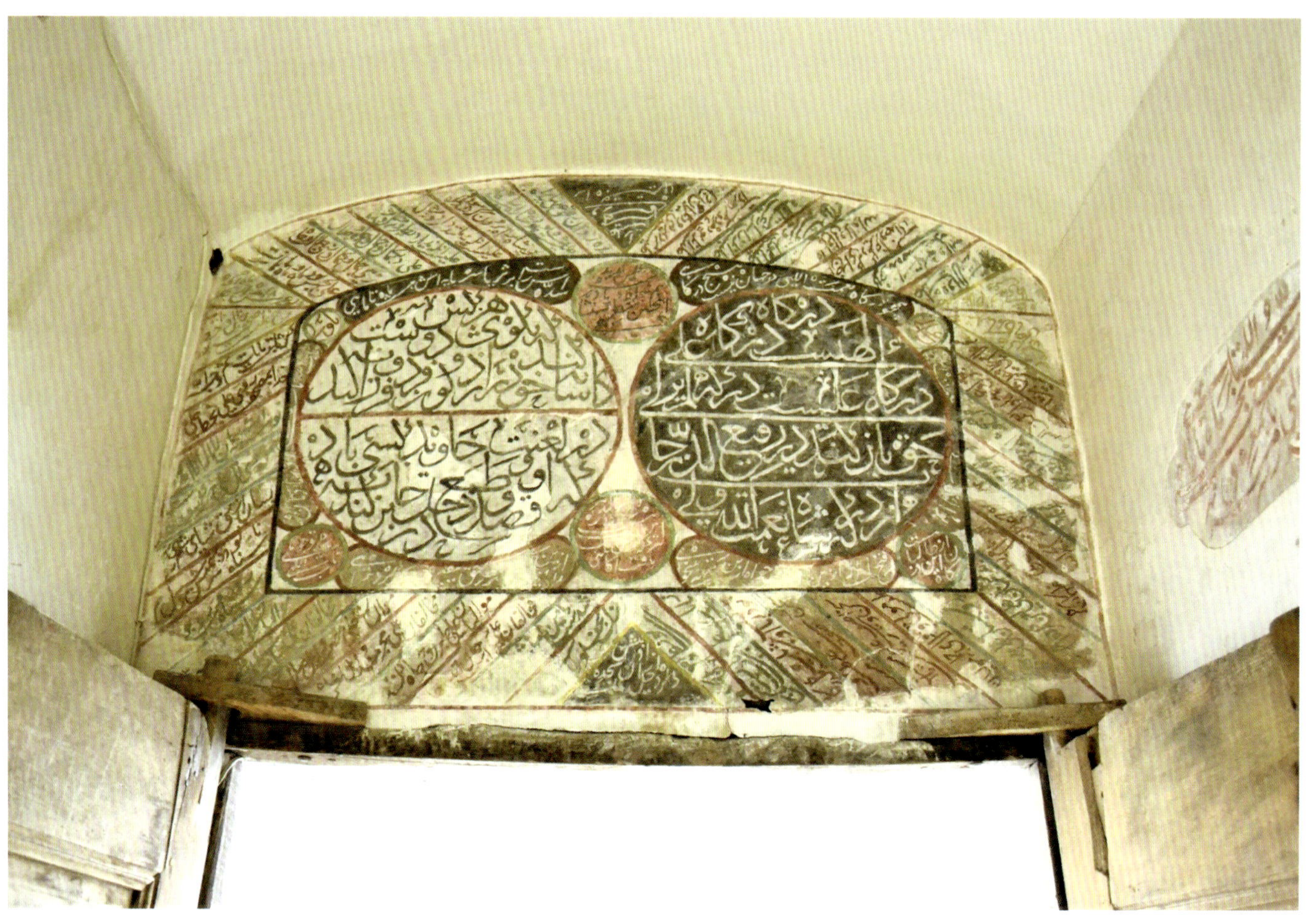

FIGURE 8.6. The inscribed surface above the entrance to the chelleh khaneh in Mahan. *Photograph by author, 2013.*

both time and space. In these verses, time, space, and language fold into one another: the word *dargah* refers both to the portal that the visitors face in the moment of reading these lines and to the shrine of Shah Neʿmatullah as a whole, as indicated in the last hemistich. The first line implies a comparison between the shrine in Mahan and the dargah (shrine) of Imam ʿAli—the first Shiʿa Imam—which itself is described as a threshold to the realm of God. The last line alludes to the shrine of Shah Neʿmatullah itself as a liminal space through which God opens pathways to himself. The place where the reader stands thus becomes a doorway that leads to another doorway, both spatially and figuratively, all within the larger doorway (astana) that is the Mahan shrine.

The analogy between the shrine at Mahan and the shrine of Imam ʿAli in Najaf creates a connected sacred landscape in which the virtues of a pilgrimage to Mahan are made comparable to those of Najaf. Poems around the medallions emphasize both the uniqueness and the interconnectedness of Mahan on this sacred map of the Islamic world (fig. 8.6). The connection with ʿAli is then brought to fruition by two smaller roundels, inscribed with the rhyming words *O' ʿAli* and *O' Vali*. The latter, literally meaning "friend" and "companion," refers to both Shah Neʿmatullah Vali and ʿAli himself, according to a title that the Prophet Muhammad gave him at Ghadir-i Khumm. In effect, the inscriptions equate the two men, suggesting the possibility of substitution, a theme to which I will return later in this chapter.

II. Authorship and Devotion, Dating and Genealogy

Alongside ʿAli and Shah Neʿmatullah, another figure stands out at the entrance of the chelleh khaneh. Inscribed twice on the side walls of the recessed threshold—once in a single medallion and again in a lobed cartouche—are the signatures of the otherwise-unknown poet and/or artist who was responsible for the design of the room: "ʿAbd al-Vafa-yi Talibi-yi Neʿmatullahi, one of the disciples of Shah Vali" (figs. 8.7 and 8.8 and app. 8.2.b). Here in the signature of the artist is a pointed connection to the Sufi network, evident not just in the title *Neʿmatullahi* but also in the word *talib* (disciple) that is turned into a nisba (affiliation) in the signature (i.e., *talibi*). The artist's disciple status is further reemphasized by spelling out that he was "one of the disciples (*taliban*)" of Shah Neʿmatullah: a short formula that tightly weaves notions of discipleship and artistic identity together.

The extent of ʿAbd al-Vafa's contributions to the room's program is not entirely clear, but his signature is the only claim to authorship in the space. This unique position suggests that the design of the retreat room could have been a personal devotional project, as indicated by the content of the interior poetic verses, which—among other things—offer up the disciple's expression of affection to the Sufi master, ʿAli, and the Prophet Muhammad. The repeated appearance of the poet's pen name in the verses inscribed inside the room remind us that self-representation occupies an important place in devotional works of art, driven perhaps by a combination of desire to gather blessings and ambition for artistic and spiritual self-promotion (fig. 8.9).[10]

The choice of medium for this devotional project is also highly significant. Apart from the general interrelations among poetry, Sufism, and the art of calligraphy, and the fact that many Sufis were accomplished poets and calligraphers, there are references in period literature to the importance of seclusion and retreat (*inziwa*, *gusheh-giri*) as part of the process for mastering the art of calligraphy.[11] The confluence of these connections makes the preponderance of calligraphy in the room's program an integral part of its devotional function.

The visual program of the chelleh khaneh is not dated, but indications of its date can be drawn from an analysis of the interior. The lower registers of paintings and inscriptions have suffered damage, most probably due to the flood of 1932–33 in Mahan, among other causes, as well as prior alterations (fig. 8.10).[12] As a result, the lower registers bear more visible traces of loss and restoration, at times featuring calligraphy of much lower quality than in the upper registers. Bearing these caveats in mind, we can situate the project roughly in the mid-seventeenth century on the basis of both textual and visual clues.

The interior of the room bears visual resemblance to the carpets woven in the seventeenth century for the mausoleum of Shah Neʿmatullah Vali across

FIGURE 8.7. Signature of the disciple ʿAbd al-Vafa-yi Talibi-yi Neʿmatullahi, on the left of the entrance to the chelleh khaneh in Mahan. *Photograph by author, 2013.*

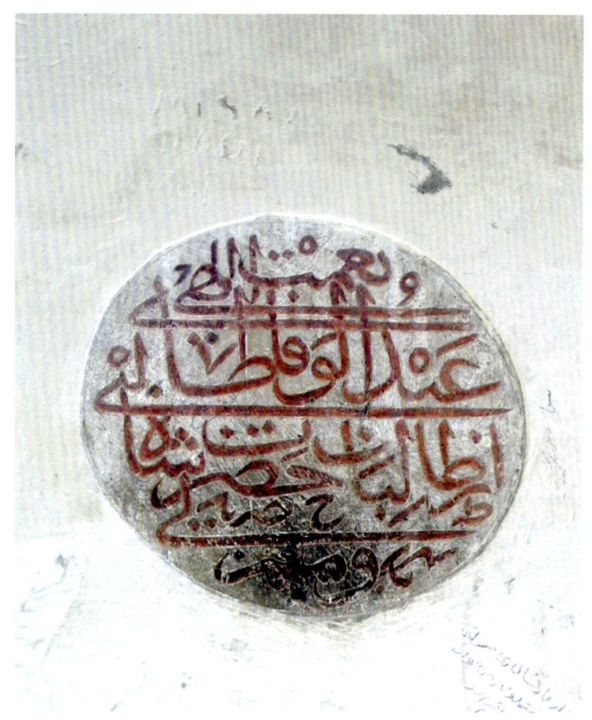

FIGURE 8.8. Lobed cartouche on the right of the entrance to the chelleh khaneh in Mahan, inscribed with a poem containing the name of the disciple ʿAbd al-Vafa-yi Talibi-yi Neʿmatullahi. *Photograph by author, 2013.*

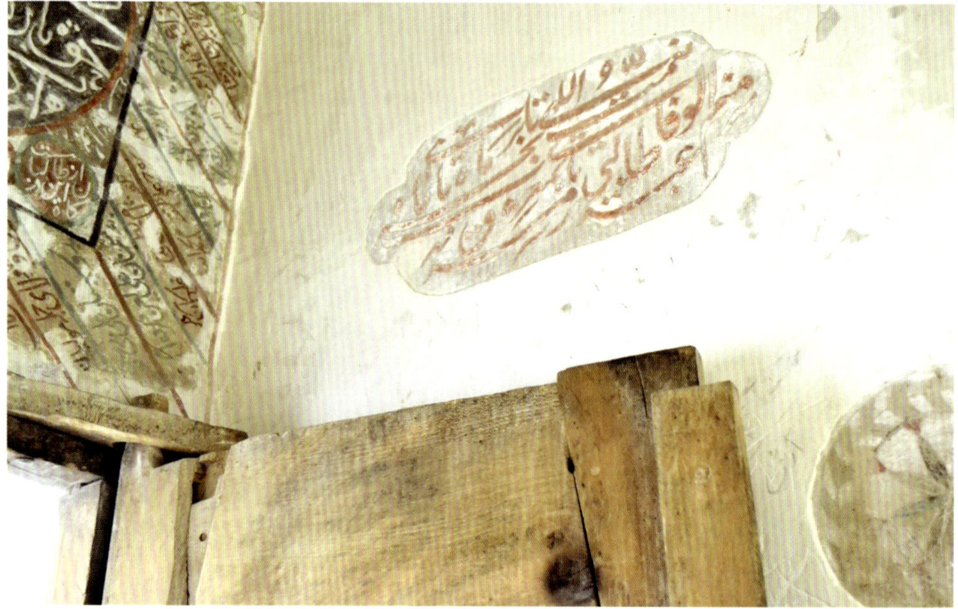

the hall in terms of both color scheme and minute visual details, such as the cartouches and their spatial arrangement, as well as their personalized epigraphic programs (figs. 5.38 and 5.39). The room also relates to the patronage and date of the carpet fragments through a textual connection. In the poetry inscribed on the interior walls of the chelleh khaneh, wordplay alludes to influential figures of the Neʿmatullahi family who were active under the Safavids, contemporary with the construction of the recitation hall and thereafter. While some of these names and titles can be read as generic revered figures

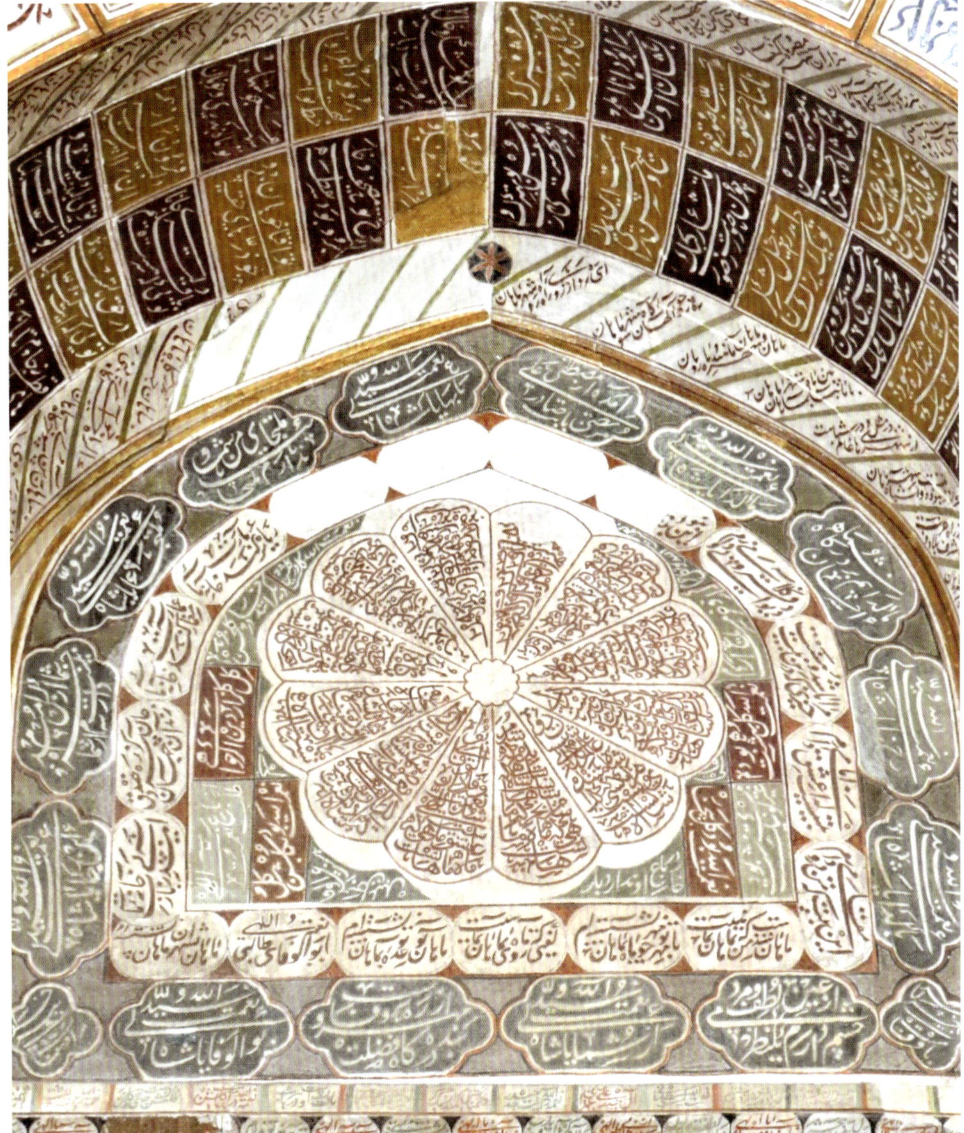

FIGURE 8.9. Partial view of the south wall of the chelleh khaneh in Mahan. The second to last green lobed cartouche on the horizontal axis and one of the oval cartouches above it contain the name of the artist. *Photograph by author, 2013.*

from Islamic history and the Safavid period, the interpretation of these names as direct references to the Sufi family becomes even more plausible due to the connections between the inscriptions of the room and those of the carpets.

These genealogical allusions appear in two different bands of inscription that run around the interior of the room. The first is composed of large lobed cartouches—similar in shape to those appearing on the borders of the carpet fragments—with large nastaʿliq inscriptions (fig. 8.11). In one of this band's cartouches on the north wall, there is a reference to a descendant of the Sufi called Neʿmatullah-i Thani (Neʿmatullah II). On the opposite wall and in the same inscription register there is another allusive reference to Sulayman (Solomon), also the name of a Neʿmatullahi descendant (fig. 8.10). The second band of inscription containing such references is much narrower, written in small nastaʿliq script and a variety of colors, each hemistich separated from

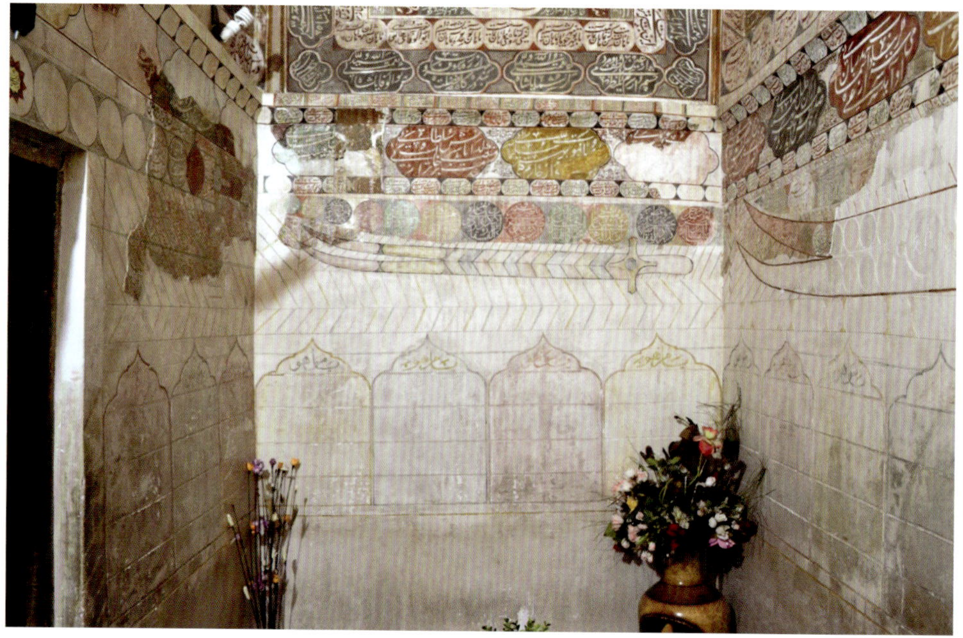

FIGURE 8.10. Lost paintings on the lower parts of the walls in the chelleh khaneh in Mahan. The large yellow lobed cartouche on the south wall (*front*) contains the name of Shah Neᶜmatullah's descendant Sulayman. *Photograph by author, 2013.*

the next by two narrow vertical lines. In this band, on the north wall, there is a verse containing the word *baqi* (lit. eternal), a title used for a few of Shah Neᶜmatullah's descendants under the early Safavids (fig. 8.11). The continuation of this band on the west wall includes a reference to the similarly used title Mirmiran, literally meaning "amir of the amirs," an honorary title given to Timurid and Safavid elites including several of Shah Neᶜmatullah's descendants whose names have come up in previous chapters (fig. 8.12).

FACING TOP, FIGURE 8.11. Partial view of the north wall of the chelleh khaneh in Mahan. The red lobed cartouche on the largest band of inscription contains the name of Neᶜmatullah II. Two bands above, the square next to the left-side edge of the photograph contains the name of Neᶜmatullah Baqi. *Photograph by author, 2013.*

FACING BOTTOM, FIGURE 8.12. Partial view of the west wall of the chelleh khaneh in Mahan. The narrowest inscription band (two registers above the largest band) contains the title Mirmiran in the middle. *Photograph by author, 2013.*

The spatial arrangement of the references to the Neᶜmatullahi family members corresponds with their lineage in this period. Shah Neᶜmatullah-i Thani (Neᶜmatullah II, also known as Naᶜim al-din Neᶜmatullah) (d. ca. 1500), featured on the north wall, was an influential figure for the consolidation of the Neᶜmatullahi network during the Safavid period, even though he died in the early years of the dynasty's formation. Apart from his endowment of water rights for the upkeep of the shrine of Mahan, which is known from an extant document, he was the patron of two of the four surviving hagiographies of Shah Neᶜmatullah, preceded only by the fifteenth-century biography written in the Deccan by Waᶜizi. In those hagiographies, a biographical sketch of Neᶜmatullah II appears right after that of Shah Khalilullah, the only son of the Sufi master—an arrangement within the text that collapses the temporal distance between Neᶜmatullah II and the Sufi's son, strengthening the family's line of descent in the sixteenth century.[13]

On the opposite (south) wall in the chelleh khaneh, the name Sulayman (Solomon), a revered prophetic figure associated with miracles and commonly invoked in protective amulets and talismans, likely belongs to a member of the Neᶜmatullahi family, possibly the latest figure mentioned in any of the room's inscriptions (fig. 8.10).[14] As I discussed in chapter 5, Sulayman's name was

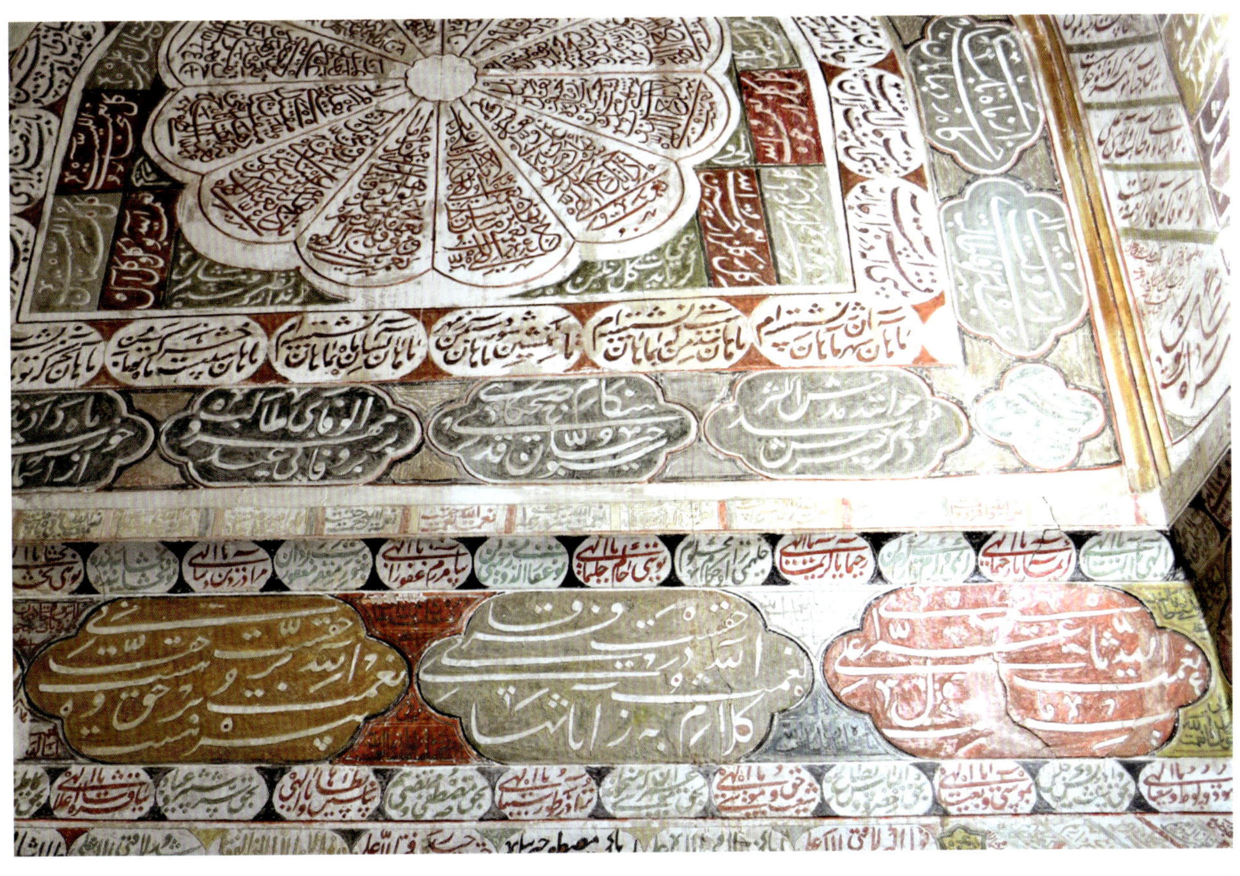

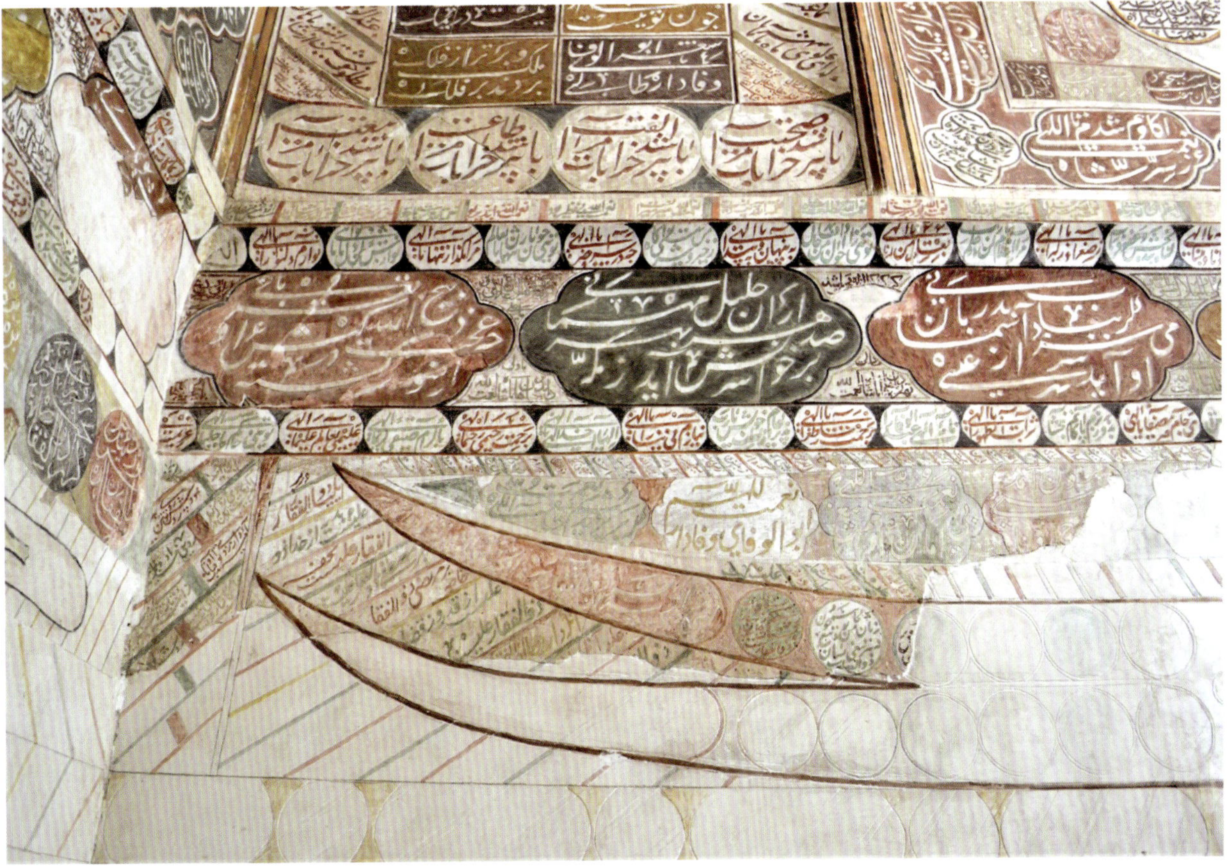

also inscribed on the carpets made for the mausoleum of Shah Neʿmatullah. On the carpet, Sulayman's positioning within an uninterrupted lineage of Neʿmatullahis makes the royal attribution of the name even less likely. Nevertheless, whether we interpret this name as the Neʿmatullahi descendant or the Safavid king Sulayman, this inscription has rather similar implications for the dating of the room, placing it in the period before and around the middle of the seventeenth century in the case of Sulayman the Neʿmatullahi descendant or the second half of the seventeenth century in the case of Sulayman the Safavid ruler.

The two other names on the narrower inscription band fall, both spatially in the room and temporally, between these bookends—that is, Neʿmatullah II and Sulayman (figs. 8.11 and 8.12). The first, Baqi, was the title of at least two influential descendants of Shah Neʿmatullah who have been discussed in previous chapters. Nizam al-din ʿAbd al-Baqi was an accomplished poet and calligrapher and the sadr (vizier, chief religious state official) at the Safavid court for a few years until his death in 1514. His son, Naʿim al-din Neʿmatullah-i Baqi (d. 1563), governor of Yazd and patron of several structures and gardens, was the descendant married to the Safavid princess Khanish Begum. At least one of their sons and a few of their grandsons were known by the title Mirmiran, referenced in the narrow inscription band on the west wall of the chelleh khaneh. Amir Ghiyath al-din Muhammad Mirmiran (d. 1590) succeeded his father as the governor of Yazd.[15] His grandson was called Mirmiran II, and his son, Sulayman, governor of Yazd, is the one most probably alluded to in the larger inscription band on the south wall of the chelleh khaneh, as mentioned earlier.[16]

Although these names appear on different inscription bands in the room, their spatial arrangement establishes a sense of succession, allowing for an intersection of temporal and spatial configurations. Reading from the right-hand corner as one enters the room, the arrangement moves chronologically and counterclockwise, corresponding with the direction of the swords depicted on the walls, moving from hilt to blade. Passing from Shah Neʿmatullah-i Thani, the figure responsible for the Safavid revival of the Neʿmatullahi family in Iran, to the Baqis and the Mirmirans with their prominent positions at the Safavid court, we reach on the left-hand side Sulayman, governor of Yazd and son of Amir Ghiyath al-din Muhammad Mirmiran. This genealogical diagram of the family embedded within the poetic inscriptions closely resonates with the carpet fragments in the domed mausoleum of Shah Neʿmatullah, which similarly sets up a sense of succession within the family from Mirmiran to his son Sulayman (who is featured in the chelleh khaneh), down to the patron of the carpet, Abu'l Mahdi (fl. second half of the seventeenth century). Due to the combination of genealogical, epigraphic, and visual connections between the carpet fragments and the chelleh khaneh, and given the dating of two of these carpet fragments by inscriptions to 1656 and 1657, a mid-seventeenth-century date for the paintings in the room is plausible.

III. Perception and Aurality

The walls and ceilings of the chelleh khaneh are covered with hundreds of verses of poetry and images painted in vibrant, ever-alternating colors (fig. 8.13).[17] There is an inherent sense of movement in the room's visual program. The epigraphy shifts between different sizes and styles (mainly thuluth and nastaʿliq) as the colors of text and background change from one band and motif to the next. Amid the inscription bands, flowers, swords, medallions, and roundels mirror each other on opposite walls (fig. 0.3). These visual elements both utilize and accentuate the architectural structure, differentiating the arches, corners, and dome from one another while weaving them together as parts of an overarching spatial program.

None of the inscriptions in the room are Qurʾanic, nor is there a single case of borrowing from preexisting poetry—not even the poetry of Shah Neʿmatullah, as was so common in Neʿmatullahi architectural inscriptions in Iran and India (see chaps. 4–6). Rather, many of the verses inscribed in the chelleh khaneh were written as spatial poetry, in dialogue with its architectural elements and imagery.

Many of these verses are pious invocations featuring the names of Shah Neʿmatullah, the Prophet Muhammad, his descendants and Shiʿa imams, with an emphasis on ʿAli. They also continue a theme taken up in the room's entrance inscriptions, situating the spiritual authority of the Mahan shrine within a broader hierarchy of sacred sites throughout the Islamic world—for

FIGURE 8.13. View of the chelleh khaneh in Mahan, looking up from the center of the room. *Photograph by author, 2013.*

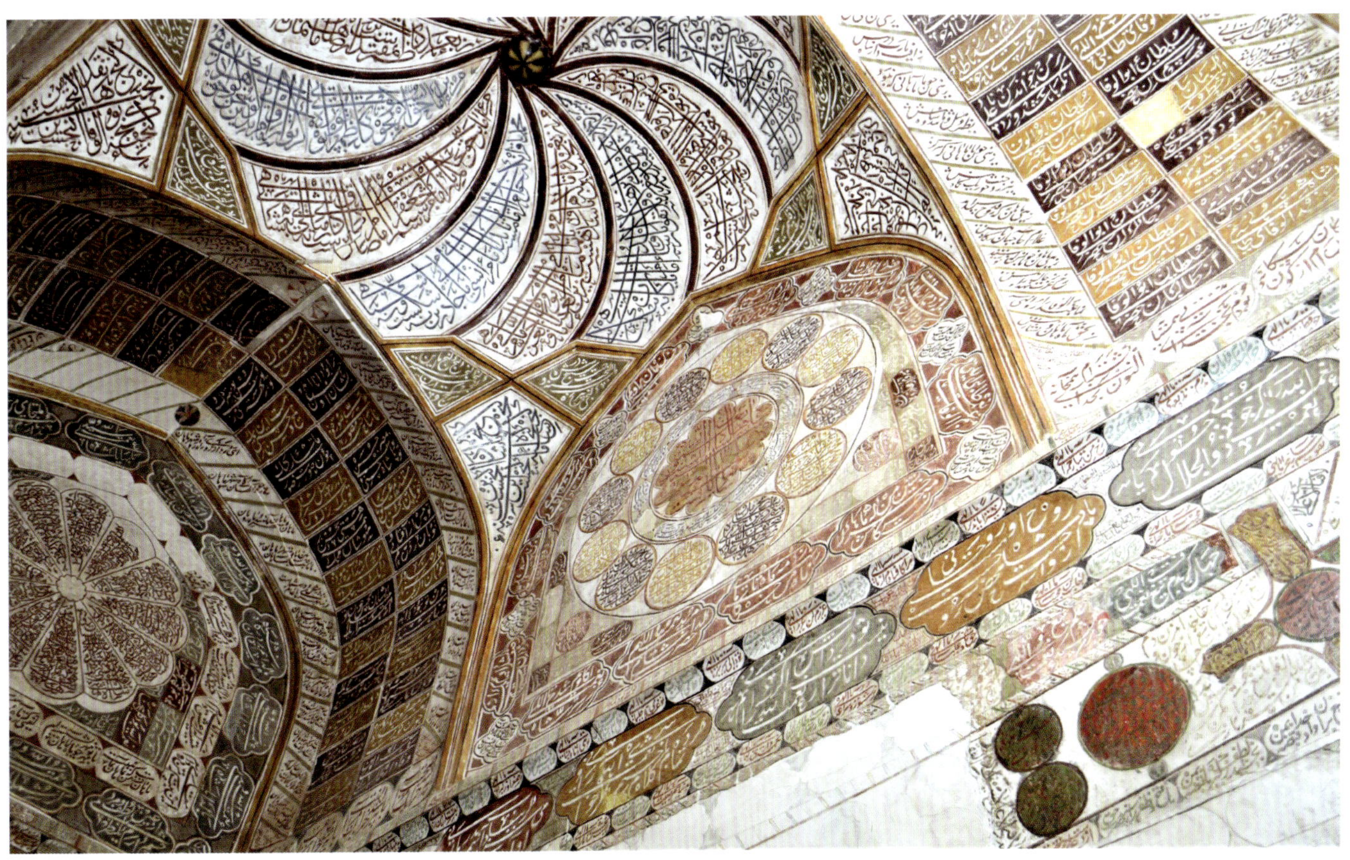

instance, Mahan is compared to Mecca and Imam ʿAli's burial place in Najaf. Examples of such comparisons can be seen in the diagonal inscriptions on the dado of the north wall.

The visual power of the interior scheme must have been intensified by its intended conditions of viewing. The retreats held in this room might have spanned from a few hours up to 40 or even 120 days, consisting of seclusion, meditation, fasting, and prayer. During that time, the words and images on the walls would have been the principal visual stimuli for participants, perhaps in combination with visual materials in manuscripts that could have been read in the room.

The chelleh khaneh would also have been experienced in different degrees of lighting. Traces of a now-blocked opening on the west wall suggest that a passage between the room and the courtyard existed at some point in the past (fig. 8.14). That door would have opened onto a small room that led to the adjacent courtyard (fig. 8.15).[18] Whether this entrance was originally part of the room and what degree of natural light was allowed through that entrance remain unclear. And yet, when natural light from all the doors was blocked out, the visual program of the room could not have been experienced all at once; rather, it had to be revealed gradually, segment after segment, by the light of oil lamps and candles, as the visitors' eyes continually readjusted to the movement of light and shadows within the surrounding dark.[19] This active zoning of light would have imparted different modes of seeing and imagining as well as recognition for visitors already familiar with the room. Other sensory inputs might also have been in play, such as the scents of oil lamps and incense burners.[20] Fasting and sleep deprivation may have heightened the senses.[21] The ingestion of psychedelics and intoxicants might also have accompanied and impacted viewers' use of the space.[22]

As an indispensable part of Sufi rituals, chanting brought aurality and bodily movements to the forefront of the room's multisensorial experience. Dhikr (remembrance, recitation, or oral supplication) is a ritual aimed at stimulating awareness of God through the repetition of short invocations, including God's names and other sacred phrases; it can be performed either silently or aloud.[23] Samaʿ is a musical session that could include singing, playing instruments, dancing, the recitation of poetry, and prayers. The Neʿmatullahi dhikr and samaʿ rituals described by the fifteenth-century hagiographer Waʿizi did not consist of "dancing, whirling, running, or moving."[24] Rather, Shah Neʿmatullah would simply sit still and move his head from side to side—a practice similar to what is commonly known as the "four beat" (*chahar zarb*) dhikr, in which a Sufi draws their head down to the level of the navel and back upright, followed by inclining the head toward their right breast and then toward the heart, pronouncing one syllable of the dhikr formula in conjunction with each beat.[25] Singing and playing musical instruments such as the pipe and *daf* were allowed for the Neʿmatullahis.[26] Footage from the documentary film *Voyage au pays des dervish sufi: l'ultime pèlerinage*, created between 1951 and 1972 by the traveler and filmmaker Marie-Thérèse Ullens de

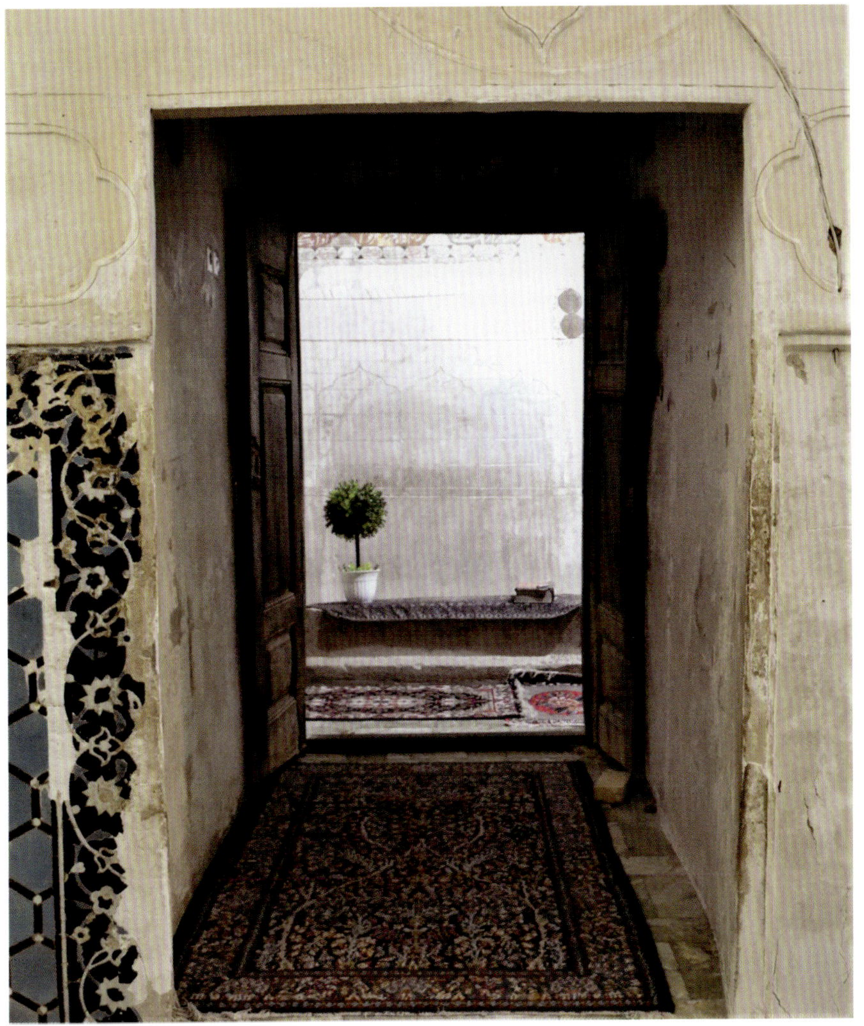

FIGURE 8.14. View of the interior of Mahan's chelleh khaneh and its cenotaph from the entrance. The blank area behind the cenotaph shows where an opening to a room in the adjacent courtyard was formerly located. *Photograph by author, 2013.*

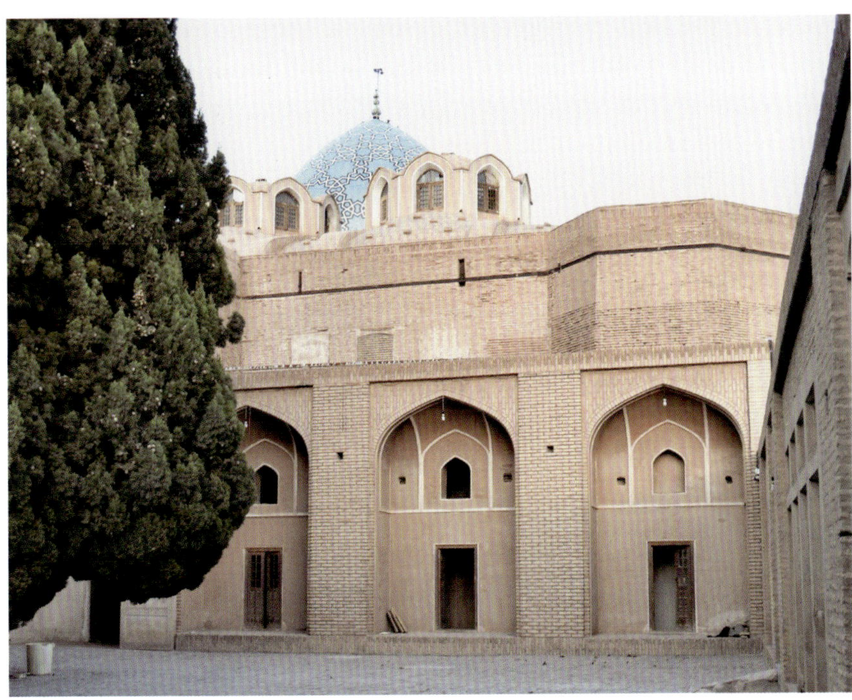

FIGURE 8.15. View of the courtyard to the west of the recitation hall in Mahan. The door to the right and the small room behind it would have had an opening to the chelleh khaneh at some point in the past. *Photograph by author, 2018.*

Schooten (d. 1989), shows Neᶜmatullahi Sufis performing the samaᶜ ritual in a manner not unlike what Waᶜizi described five hundred years earlier.[27]

Given these guidelines, the room must often have been experienced while seated on the floor. Despite this relatively static position (compared to a dance-based samaᶜ), if the Sufis' eyes were open or half-open during the dhikr, the viewer's gaze would have been kept in motion not only by the swift movements of the head but also by the alternation of colors in consecutive bands of inscriptions and the change in the direction of writing, especially in elements like the roundels and abstract flowers covering the walls. Even when the viewer was not reading the inscriptions, such varied components could lead the eye to wander over the surfaces of the room. The sense of constant motion generated by the twisting, inscribed segments of the dome would have intensified the dizzying, ecstasy-inducing effect of the ritual movement of devotees' heads (figs. 8.13 and 0.3).

There is now a cenotaph in the center of the room that is believed to belong to the disciple-artist ᶜAbd al-Vafa, although no epigraphic or historical evidence survives to support this (fig. 8.14). It is possible that prior to the addition of the cenotaph, a disciple would have occupied the center of the room during solitary retreats. It is also likely that several people partaking in a samaᶜ or dhikr ritual would sit around the perimeter of the room with their backs against the walls.[28]

There seems to be a relationship between Sufi recitation rituals and inscriptions within the room. Depending on their location and lighting, it is possible that some of the inscriptions were recited out loud, or that the nature of recitations performed during these rituals informed the composition of the room's poetry. Some of the inscriptions contain verses that build on popular invocations of Imam ᶜAli and his fabled sword Zu'lfiqar, which will be discussed in more detail in the next section of this chapter. These invocations commonly included the Arabic verses *la fata illa ᶜAli la saif illa zu'lfiqar* ("There is no hero but ᶜAli, no sword but Zu'lfiqar"), which were also inscribed on objects including swords and armor.[29] When read aloud, verses such as the following example, from the north wall of the room, induce sounds that resemble the short and commonly repetitive invocations used for dhikr, which were mostly recited by heart (fig. 8.16 and app. 8.3.a):

> The Zu'lfiqar of ᶜAli is the sword of the sublime shah [i.e., Shah Vali],
> the sword of the sublime shah is the Zu'lfiqar of ᶜAli.
> The Zu'lfiqar of ᶜAli is the most courageous warrior on the battlefield,
> the most courageous warrior on the battlefield is the Zu'lfiqar of ᶜAli.

Every second hemistich in these verses repeats the previous one in a chiasmic AB-BA format. These repetitions both simplify the message and lend it strong emphasis and rhythm.[30]

Another common trope in the formulaic phrases written or used for dhikr was to play with words derived from a given Arabic root.[31] This trait is seen

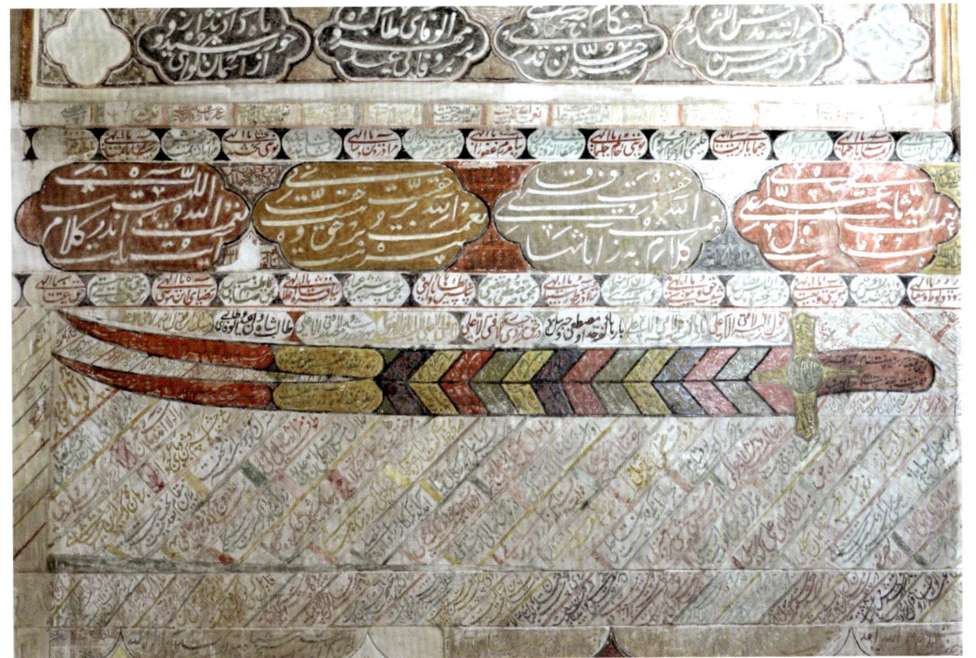

FIGURE 8.16. Dado of the north wall in the chelleh khaneh at Mahan. Inscriptions below the sword contain several references to ʿAli and his burial in Najaf and comparative references to the shrine at Mahan. The diagonal inscriptions on the body of the sword contain the chiasmic verses discussed as examples. Oval cartouches above the largest inscription band contain verses with words derived from the same root. *Photograph by author, 2014.*

in the following verse inscribed on the north wall of the room (fig. 8.16 and app. 8.3.b):

> Allah, O' Allah, O' Allah,
> O' the *Merciful*, O' the Compassionate, O' Allah,
> You are *merciful*, you have *mercy*, have *mercy* on us,
> O' the Compassionate, O' the *Merciful*, O' Allah. . . .
> You are *bountiful*, give *bounty* to your servants,
> You are *forgiving*, *forgive* O' Allah!

Apart from the repeated words and those sharing the same root (which are marked in italics above), the fast rhythm of these verses mirrors the bodily movements and breathing pattern dictated by the likes of the "four beat" format mentioned earlier, deployed during rituals in pursuit of ecstatic experience. Breath control was an integral part of dhikr, whether through intentional breathing patterns or the forceful enunciation of words and syllables in verse.[32]

Examples of this general kind are abundant in the room and demonstrate the aural potential of this space. Earlier in this chapter, I hinted at the possibility of interpreting the visual program of this room as an act of devotion by the disciple. The labor-intensive process of inscribing and painting this room would thus be understood as a meditative practice elevating him to a higher status in his path of discipleship. The poems discussed here add other layers to that reading of "art as meditation."[33] Through their aurality, these poems join the spatiovisual experience of the room to become active participants in the performance of the ritual itself. Even if these verses were not used in the rituals, their compatibility with those commonly used in dhikr and their rhythmic nature—amplified by the repetition of the visual elements on the wall—instate a sense of companionship between the architecture and its users, as if the walls of the chelleh khaneh echoed the ecstatic chanting of the disciples.[34]

Given the degree of concentration and contemplation demanded from users of the room during a retreat, the possibility of a direct, deep engagement with the poetry cannot be discounted. Nevertheless, there is a tension between aurality and legibility in the room.[35] In a space where little bodily movement was likely to take place, with limited light and some distance between the eye and certain inscriptions, such as those under the dome, the question of legibility cannot be ignored. Any of these inscriptions might have been recognized without needing to be read, akin to mnemonic aids. At the same time, as in other heavily inscribed spaces, the meaning of these words was not limited to the reading experience alone.[36] Different levels of affective response could be activated by reading or not reading the inscriptions. Regardless, their blessings and protective messages wove the political specificities of the Neʿmatullahis' near-contemporary history into the visual program of the room.

IV. Swords, Talismans, Uprisings

Among the recurrent images in the chelleh khaneh are four bifurcated swords (figs. 8.10, 8.16, and 8.17). Depicted on panels that rise from the dado of each wall to a height above the entrance door, these represent the fabled sword of ʿAli, known as the Zu'lfiqar, and thus amplify the numerous textual supplications to ʿAli written in and outside the room. The medallions, cartouches, and diagonal bands of inscriptions located within and around the sword imagery speak to its materiality and symbolic meanings as well as themes of sacrifice and *jihad* (holy war against the enemies of Islam), generating a complex spatial relationship between text and image.

The genealogy of the Zu'lfiqar is shrouded in historical and legendary narratives, including ʿAbbasid sources on the Prophet Muhammad's bestowal of the sword to ʿAli, as well as accounts of its disappearance after being relocated to Fatimid Cairo.[37] Zeynep Yürekli has shown how images of the double-pointed blade arose in the medieval period and came to be depicted in the hand of ʿAli from early fourteenth-century Ilkhanid illustrated manuscripts. Subsequently, the iconography of the Zu'lfiqar enjoyed widespread circulation beyond any specific sectarian milieu in the early modern period.[38] In contrast to the potential sectarian meaning of the Zu'lfiqar—due to its connection with ʿAli, Husayn, and the Battle of Karbala (680)—visual evidence from the Ottoman context instead foregrounds the amuletic and protective significance of the sword in the Sunni and Shiʿa contexts.[39] In Ottoman sources, for instance, the Zu'lfiqar acquires a seal-like status and appears on ceremonial banners and talismanic shirts such as that given to Murad III (r. 1574–95) by his mother in 1582—a type of clothing that warriors could have worn under their armor in hopes of activating invisible protective forces.[40] Attention to the talismanic

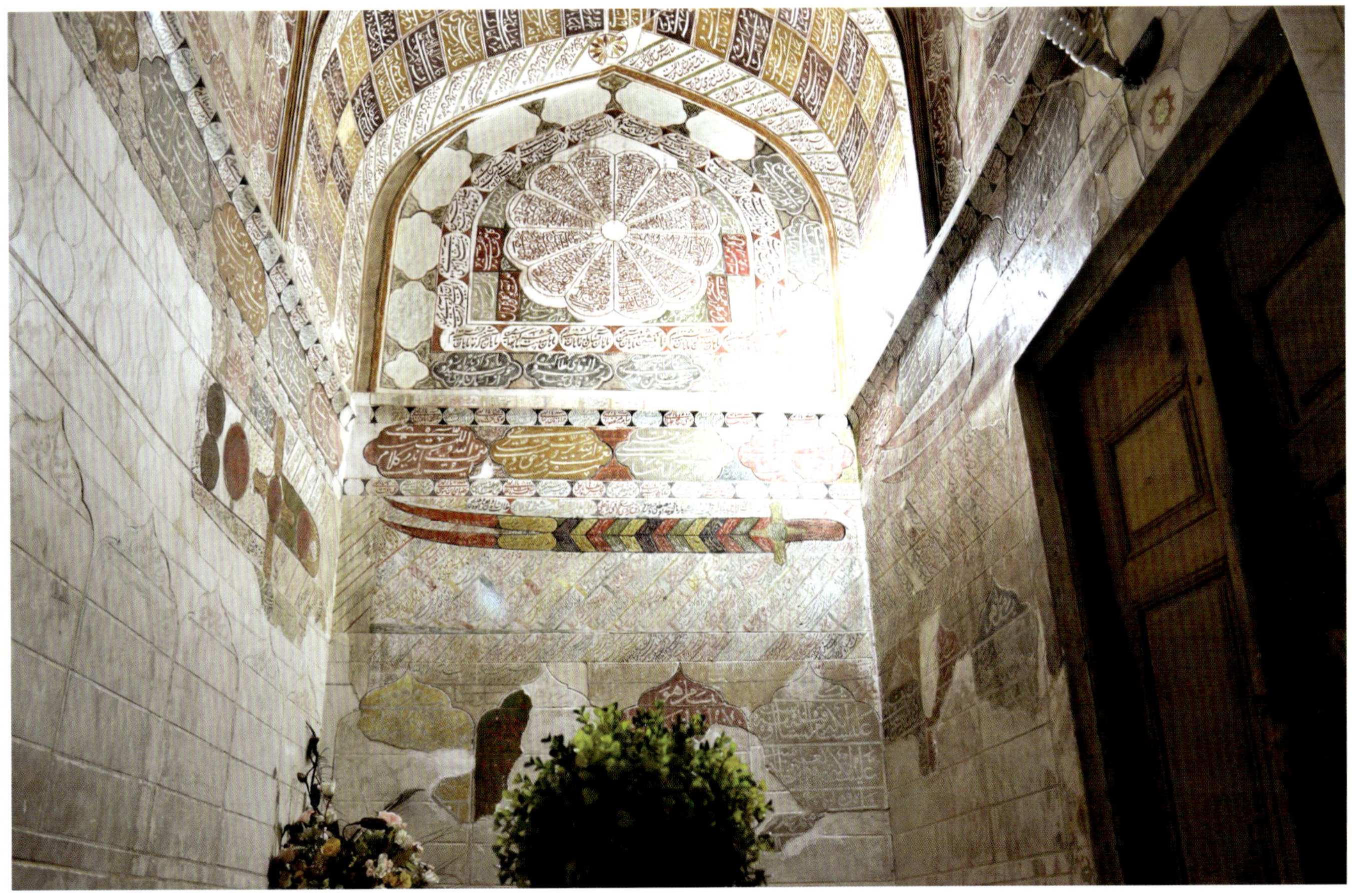

FIGURE 8.17. View of the chelleh khaneh in Mahan from the south wall, showing three of the four swords in the room around the walls. *Photograph by author, 2013.*

potency of the sword has opened up new understandings of its role in Safavid Iran as well, moving beyond sectarian readings of the object, its imagery, and inscriptions.[41]

The walls of the chelleh khaneh resonate visually with contemporary talismanic textiles, shirts, and manuscripts in their arrangements of swords and medallions, their density of inscriptions, and the intensity of their color palette (fig. 8.18).[42] As in the case of amulets and talismans, the repetition and symmetry of verbal and visual resources in the room was likely aimed to increase their devotional and protective efficacy.[43] The sword's repetition on the four walls of the room—albeit with different details and inscriptions—reinforces its potential to assume a seal-like status. An association between the room and talismanic textiles becomes all the more probable if we bear in mind just how frequently talismanic texts and imagery appeared on arms and armor and how talismanic shirts and the like featured the fabled bifurcated sword of ʿAli along with inscribed roundels.[44] That being said, there are some significant differences between talismanic textiles and surfaces of the chelleh khaneh.

Among the many differences between the room and talismanic textiles, including their scale and degree of intimacy, is the nature of the textual material inscribed on the walls of the chelleh khaneh. Unlike amulets and

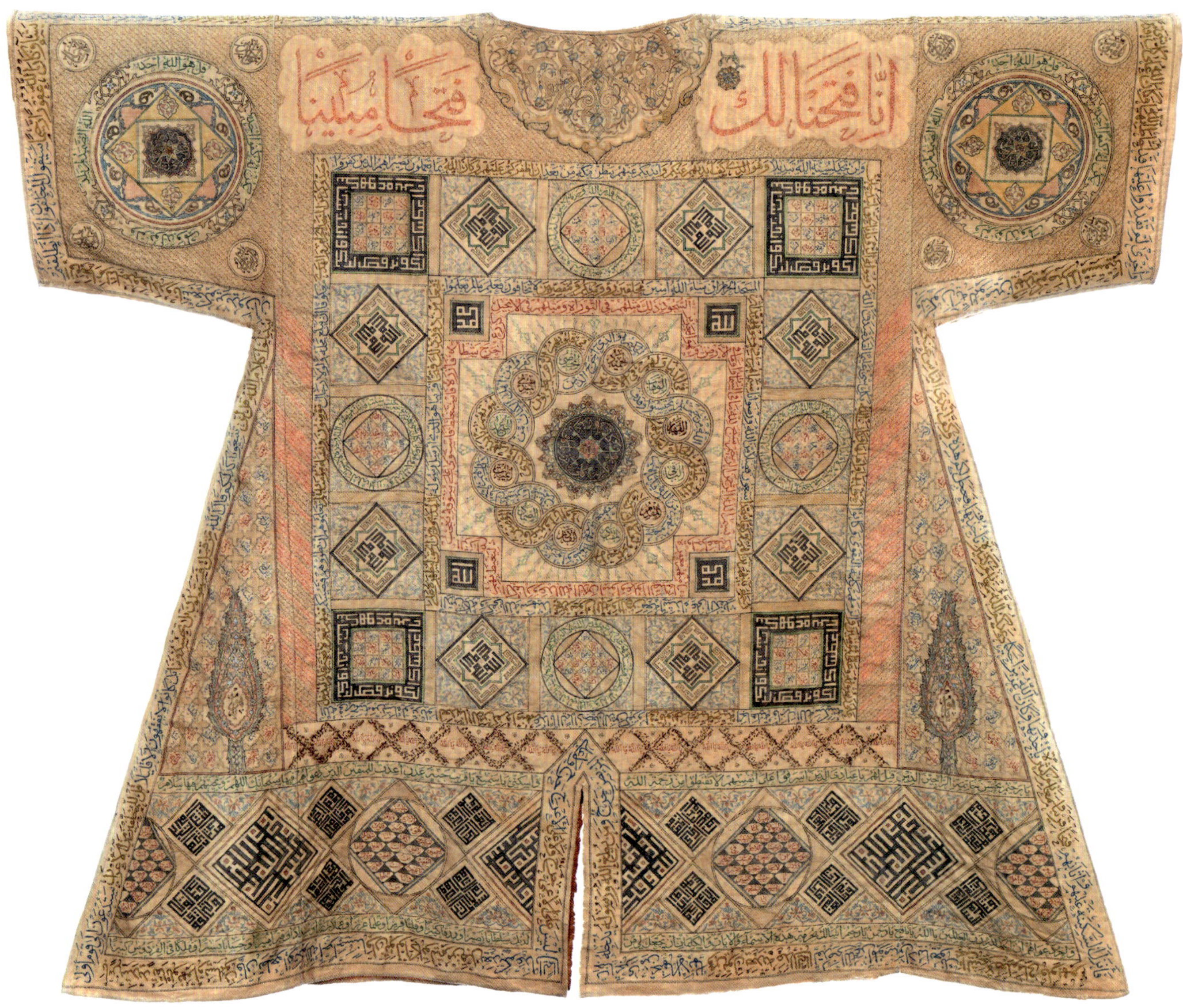

FIGURE 8.18. Talismanic shirt with Qur'anic verses, prayers, and invocations to God written in cartouches, squares, and medallions. View of the back. Turkey, seventeenth century. Cotton, inscribed in colored inks and gold, 87 × 101 cm. Hajj and the Arts of Pilgrimage. Khalili Collection, TXT 545. © *The Khalili Family Trust.*

talismanic shirts, the inscriptions in the room do not contain Qurʾanic verses, nor do they include any magical texts or numerical arrangements. However, they do contain messages of a protective nature. A second difference concerns accessibility. The high production cost of talismanic shirts likely limited their availability to prominent Sufis and court elites, but the chelleh khaneh, although far from a public space, could have been made accessible to a wider range of disciples—a difference that opens up new ways of thinking about the place of architecture as a talismanic medium.[45]

As in the case of talismanic garments and arms, the protective messages in the room could have extended to "battles" on the path of discipleship, against day-to-day sources of anxiety such as illness, hardship, or even concerns for protection during rituals and ceremonies.[46] In other words, their efficacy could extend to the prediction, understanding, and control of any hidden force that might influence human lives.[47] However, alongside the general protective effects of the room's interior program, the maker(s) of the room could have been responding to a context specific to the history of Sufi militancy—a common phenomenon in the early modern Islamic world and within the Neʿmatullahi community.[48]

Throughout the history of the Neʿmatullahi Sufis in Iran, its members had their closest ties with courtly circles in the Safavid period. Followers of the Sufi network had taken up the role of warrior-Sufis and engaged in several Safavid military campaigns, similar to their engagements with Bahmanid politics. The aforementioned leader of the Neʿmatullahis, Amir Nizam al-din ʿAbd al-Baqi, who held the position of sadr at the Safavid court and whose title is featured among the room's inscriptions, was killed while leading a faction of the Safavid army in the famous Battle of Chaldiran between the Safavid ruler Shah Ismaʿil and the Ottomans in 1514.[49]

The Safavid ruler Shah Ismaʿil himself was believed to enjoy divine powers in the eyes of the Qizilbash—a Shiʿa militant group that became his disciples.[50] Millenarian anxieties worked in tandem with the popular belief that Mahdi would return at the turn of the century as the head of a Sufi army.[51] Traces of these lines of thinking can be found among members of the Neʿmatullahi family in the sixteenth century. As discussed in chapter 6, the family had joined local governors in a civil war against the Safavid court right around the time of the construction of the recitation hall at the Mahan shrine—that is, in the year 998 of the hijri calendar (AD 1590). While the degree of the family's involvement in the uprising varies in different historical accounts, one hypothesis (discussed in chap. 6) is that they engaged in a failed attempt to install a descendant of Shah Neʿmatullah Vali as an independent ruler. This descendant, named Sanjar, was born to the Safavid princess Khanish Begum (daughter of Shah Tahmasp) and Neʿmatullah IV (son of Ghiyath al-din Muhammad Mirmiran, governor of Yazd). Given the expectations around the return of Mahdi at the end of the first millennium of the hijri calendar, with the Zu'lfiqar as one of his attributes, the depiction of the swords in the chelleh khaneh acquires another layer of significance, especially as part of a structure (i.e., the recitation hall) that was itself completed on the verge of the first millennium of the hijri calendar.[52] While some of the imagery and writings surrounding the swords could be interpreted as referring to day-to-day trials, the Neʿmati-Haydari conflicts, or as offering protection for future unrest, others—as I will demonstrate below—could be read as commemorating this recent chapter of uprising in the family's history and preparing them for any future episodes of such a kind through the active encouragement of the viewer to take up arms in the name of ʿAli and Shah Neʿmatullah.[53] After all, these were unpredictable times for the Neʿmatullahi Sufis: their relationships with the Safavids were undergoing changes as the brothers and cousins of those inscribed in the room relocated to Mughal India.

One major question that arises from these talismanesque aspects of the room is whether the text and imagery covering the walls were themselves believed to wield protective powers and, if so, how these powers were activated. In configurations that are loosely comparable to early modern inscribed swords, the inscriptions on and around the painted swords in the room contain messages of encouragement, reassurance, and protection for both the viewer and the maker—indeed, for whoever grasps onto the sword and takes part in war for the faith.[54] Drawing on these inscriptions, as I show below, devotees are invited to reimagine their physical relation to and engagement with the body of their Sufi master through the space and the objects depicted in it. In this regard, the epigraphic program of the room shares features in common with other well-known structures such as the Alhambra, insofar as the poetic epigraphy speaks to the ways in which the architecture and imagery were meant to be seen and experienced.[55] By encouraging engagement with the image of the swords, the inscriptions also recall illustrations of the "seal of prophecy" and "sandals of the Prophet" in devotional manuscripts, *hilya*s (the "verbal portraits" of the Prophet), and related text-image devices whose protective and amuletic qualities were activated by the reader's touch.[56]

In conjunction with this type of somatic engagement, the inscriptions also conflate the Zu'lfiqar with the sword of Shah Neᶜmatullah. The following verses inscribed around the hilt of the sword on the north wall are one example (fig. 8.16 and app. 8.3.c):

> We hold the sword (*qabza*) of the Shah in our hand,
> We will hold this hilt (qabza) in the palm of our hand.

The word *qabza* could refer to both the hilt of a sword and the sword as a whole. The specificity of this verse to its physical location around the hilt of the sword exemplifies a common strategy in the spatial poetry inscribed throughout the room. In this case, however, the spatial and somatic qualities of the poetry become even more entangled with one another. By connecting parts of the sword with parts of the body—not only the viewer's body but also the bodies of ᶜAli and Shah Neᶜmatullah—the poetry instills an embodied experience of viewing, reading, and "holding" the sword that merges the ordinary bodies of the viewers with these sacred bodies.

A verse inscribed underneath the hilt of the sword depicted on the western wall alludes to the role of the thumb when grasping the sword's hilt (fig. 8.19 and app. 8.4.a).

> This power in my thumb is from the thumb of ᶜAli.

Another line on the hilt itself reads (app. 8.4.b):

> I am a companion (*ham-dastan*) of the hilt of the Zu'lfiqar,
> I am hostile to the enemy of ᶜAli.

The word *ham-dastan*, which I have translated as "companion," could also mean "hand in hand," suggesting bodily contact between the hand of the viewer and the hilt of the Zu'lfiqar. The fact that the pronouns of these verses

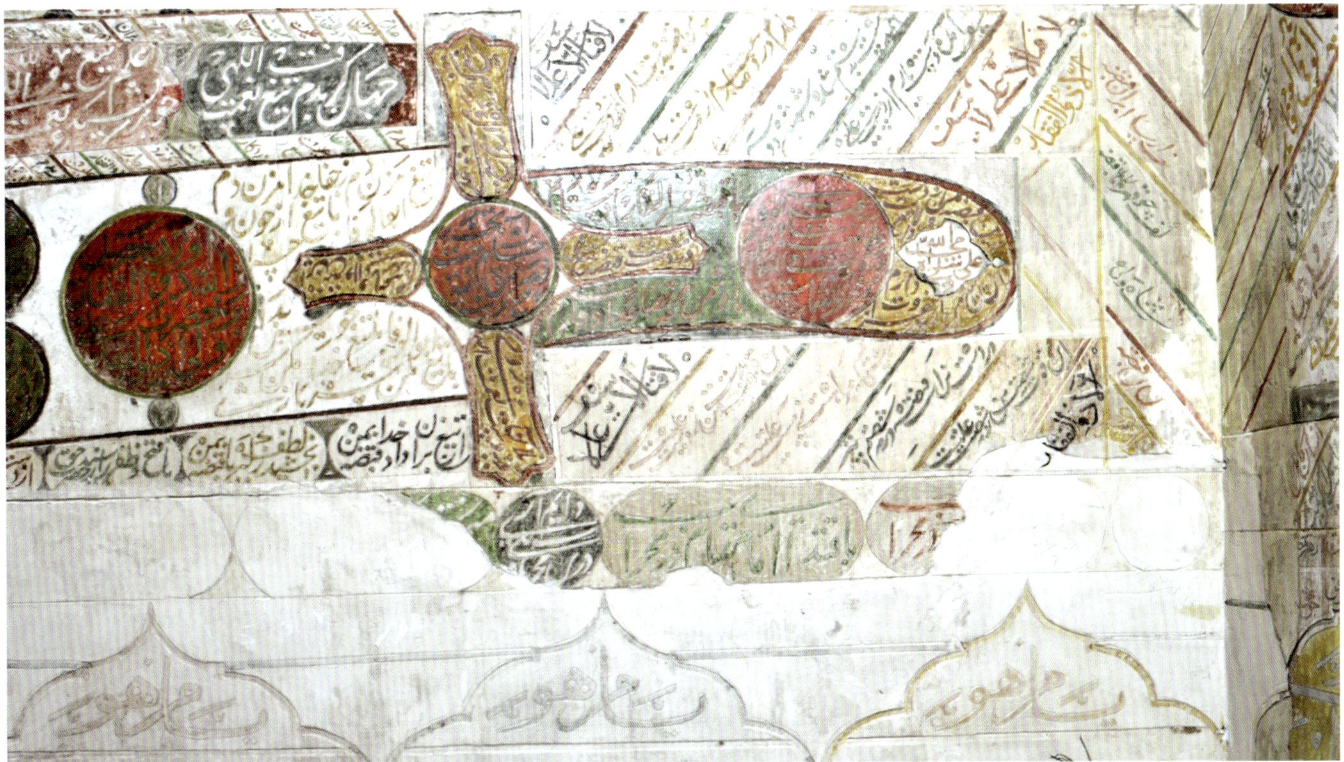

FIGURE 8.19. Partial view of the west wall of Mahan's chelleh khaneh, showing the hilt of the sword. *Photograph by author, 2013.*

have shifted to the first person adds to the intensity of this tactile experience, bringing the verses to life by projecting them onto the body of the reader.[57]

The connections drawn between the hilt of the sword and the hands of the beholder, Shah Neᶜmatullah, and ᶜAli also establish a sense of genealogical hierarchy, setting forth an imagined provenance for the Zu'lfiqar. The narratives around the history of the Zu'lfiqar relate that the sword was given by the Prophet Muhammad to ᶜAli and by ᶜAli to his sons Hasan and Husayn.[58] Taking up this chain of ownership, the inscriptions extend the political and spiritual legitimacy symbolized by the possession of the sword from the People of the Prophet's House onto Shah Neᶜmatullah and his disciples.[59] Several verses around the hilt of the sword speak directly to or on behalf of the beholder, implying that the hilt of the sword was placed in their hand by ᶜAli himself, or by Shah Neᶜmatullah as his proxy. In examples such as the verses below, located underneath the hilt on the west wall, the plaster and pigments used to depict the hilt and inscribe the poetry take on a somatic quality (fig. 8.19 and app. 8.4.a). This material quality mediates between the actual object depicted and the hand of the beholder—and, by extension, between the body of the beholder and that of ᶜAli.[60] In doing so, the image of the sword mimics the status of a contact relic.

> The existence that I have is from the existence of ᶜAli,
> This hilt in my hand is from the hand of ᶜAli.

Above the same hilt, wordplays on "hand" (*dast*) merge the hands and the hilt together (app. 8.4.c).

> The double-headed sword has become the companion (*ham-dast*) of my hand,
> This sword (*sayf*) from the hand of ʿAli has become my helper (*dast-yar*).

This combination of visual, verbal, and tactile images, with their allusions to chains of initiation and the passing down of symbolic objects through enumeration of the mentions of the "hand," restages the Prophet's gift of the sword to ʿAli and his sons. The genealogy implied by such verses is in fact stated explicitly in a cartouche on the hilt of the sword on the west wall, which features the names Allah, Muhammad, ʿAli, and Shah Neʿmatullah Vali, arranged hierarchically from top to bottom (fig. 8.19). Overt statements of such lineages can also be found elsewhere in the room: the abstract flowers, the roundels, and the twisted motif under the dome all contain twelve segments, each dedicated to the link between one descendant of the Prophet Muhammad to the next. Together, they establish a direct lineage from the Prophet to Abu'l Vafa, the Neʿmatullahi disciple who inscribed his signature in these devices (figs. 8.3 and 0.3). By inserting himself in this lineage, the maker invites the viewer to recognize his interceding status as well.[61]

The presence of Sufi bodies on the battlefield, leading a unit of the army, was a common hands-on military engagement strategy in Safavid Iran. Members of the Neʿmatullahi family who took on such roles for the Safavids—for instance, in the Battle of Chaldiran—are memorialized in the chelleh khaneh (although with no known mention of the Safavids) (fig. 8.11). Alongside invocations to Shah Neʿmatullah and ʿAli, these references could have been understood to confer protective powers to visitors. Yet, beyond this physical presence on the battlefield, there were several other strategies for the transmission of blessings and protective powers. Seeking blessings from a Sufi master before a battle was a common practice, attested to by both visual and textual accounts in the wider Islamic world. Similarly, the tactile metaphor of passing down the fabled sword of ʿAli in the chelleh khaneh could have served as a visual rite of initiation for militant Sufis, offering encouragement and protection in times of turmoil and uprising.

V. A Vaulted Initiation Hat

FACING, FIGURE 8.20.
View of the chelleh khaneh in Mahan, looking up toward the representation of the twelve-segmented initiation hat of the Neʿmatullahis. *Photograph by author, 2014.*

As in the sword motifs discussed above, the efficacy of the broader visual program of the room lies in how it weaves the protective effect of word and image together with devotional practices and embodied spatial experience. The arresting quality of this interior must be understood in terms of its small size. The proximity of the viewer's body to the words and images on the walls interacts with the height of the ceiling to create a sense of upward extension, opening into the vertical orientation in the room. As the gaze moves upward, it gravitates toward the large segmented, twisting motif under the apex of the domed ceiling (fig. 8.20). This twelve-gore swirling motif likely represents the Sufi hat of the network, the taj or crown of Shah

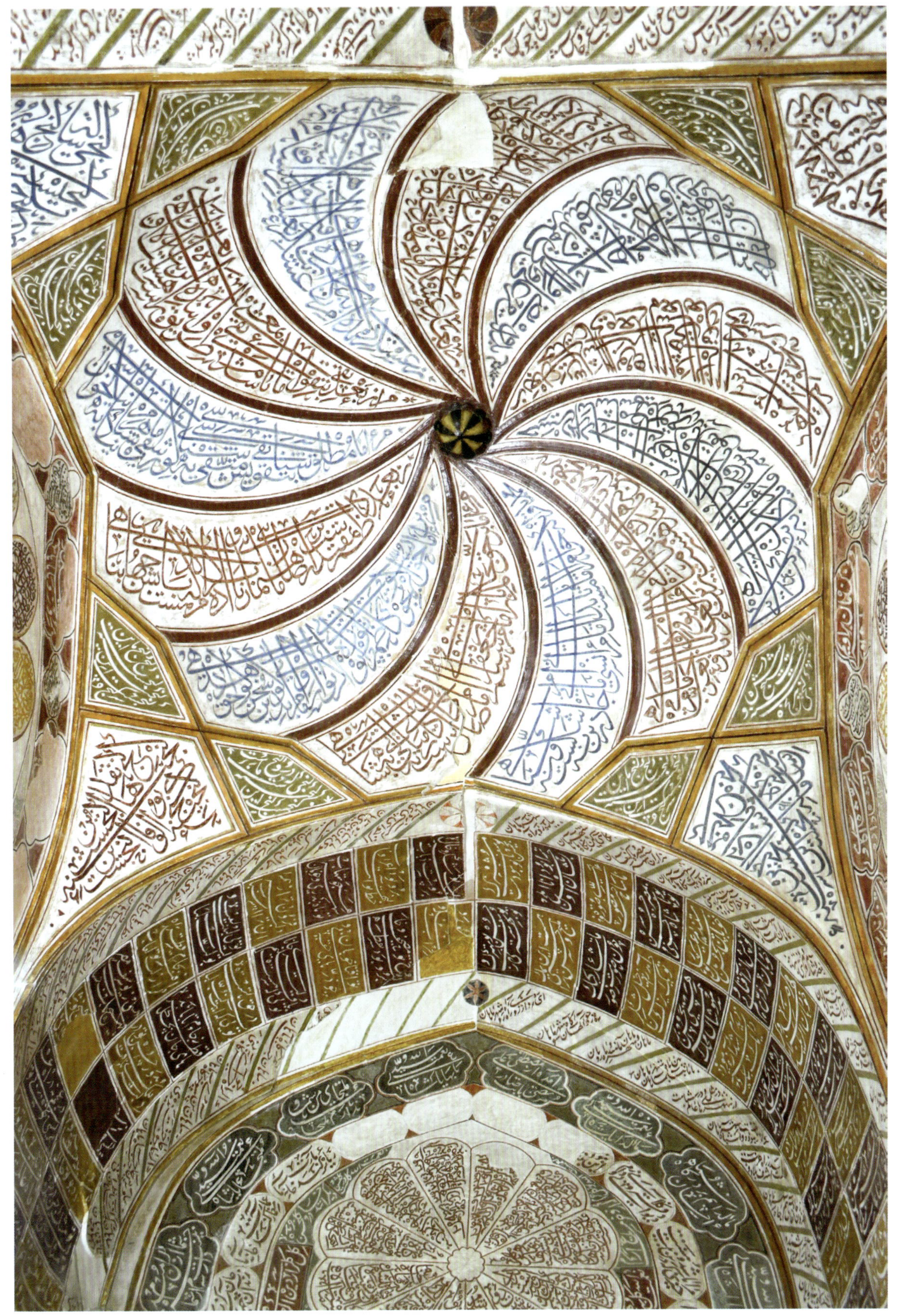

Ne‘matullah, which was placed on the head of disciples in Sufi initiation ceremonies.

The swirling segments of this motif join in the center, morphing into a smaller twelve-gore hat in relief. The poetic inscriptions within each of the twelve gores are dedicated to praise for one of the twelve Shi‘a imams, with subtle wordplays on their names. These inscriptions do not engage in the kind of self-referential games discussed above and refrain from placing the name of Shah Ne‘matullah in the succession. Rather, such tasks are reserved for the twelve-lobed abstract flowers on the walls of the room (figs. 8.3 and 8.17). Connected in both shape and arrangement to the swirling motif under the cupola, the flower motif could also be interpreted as a two-dimensional representation of a segmented hat. The inscriptions in each lobe, too, cast these flowers as Ne‘matullahi crowns while further inscriptions indicate that they have been passed down from Imam ‘Ali through his descendants, one by one, to Abu'l Vafa, the maker of the room, who thus promotes himself again as the culminating figure in the chain of initiation. As such, both the spatial and the epigraphic arrangements imply that the main taj (crown) under the dome "passes down" through the walls as initiation hats for the disciples.

No visual evidence survives from Shah Ne‘matullah's lifetime for the appearance of his taj. Prior to the spatial representation of the Ne‘matullahi crown in the chelleh khaneh, there are only textual descriptions of the hat in real or imagined accounts of Sufi initiation ceremonies.[62] The earliest mention of the Ne‘matullahi headdress appears in the fifteenth-century biography of Shah Ne‘matullah by Wa‘izi, in the context of the dream of the Bahmanid ruler Ahmad Shah I that was discussed in chapter 2. In the dream, Shah Ne‘matullah places the hat, described as the taj-i shahi (crown of kingship), on Ahmad Shah's head with his own hands.[63] While Wa‘izi's account does not offer any further details on the shape of the taj, a retrospective version of the same account from Fereshteh's early seventeenth-century chronicle of the Deccan sultanates specifies that the initiation hat—whose bestowal in Ahmad Shah's dream marked his successful ascension to the throne in the Deccan—was green and comprised twelve segments.[64] Another hagiography of Shah Ne‘matullah completed in 1503 by Sadid al-din Nasrullah Abarquyi notes that early on, the initiation hat of the Sufi network comprised five segments until a disciple made a twelve-part felt hat and presented it to Shah Ne‘matullah, who approved its production for all his followers.[65] The use of the twelve-segmented taj continued among the disciples of the Ne‘matullahis, as nineteenth-century paintings of the taj on a variety of media attest (fig. 8.21).

FACING, FIGURE 8.21. Nineteenth-century painting showing a likely representation of the Ne‘matullahi taj. The painting depicts Imam ‘Ali, his two sons, Hasan and Husayn, and his close companions with a lion. Though the figures were previously identified as Qanbar and Salman-i Farsi, Ekhtiar has recently discussed the resemblance between the figure on the left and the Ne‘matullahi descendant Nur ‘Ali Shah (d. 1801). Isma‘il Jalayir, 1860s, Iran. Ink on cardboard, 61 × 45.1 cm. *© The Metropolitan Museum of Art, New York, 2018.500. Purchase, 2017 NoRuz at The Met Benefit, 2018.*

In previous scholarship, the form and color of the hat have been interpreted as straightforward references to the Shi‘a inclinations of both the Ne‘matullahi Sufis and the Bahmanids, the number twelve connoting the twelve Shi‘a imams and green as the color commonly associated with the People of the Prophet's House—more specifically, Husayn, the third Shi‘a imam, and his campaign against the Umayyads.[66] A headdress comparable to

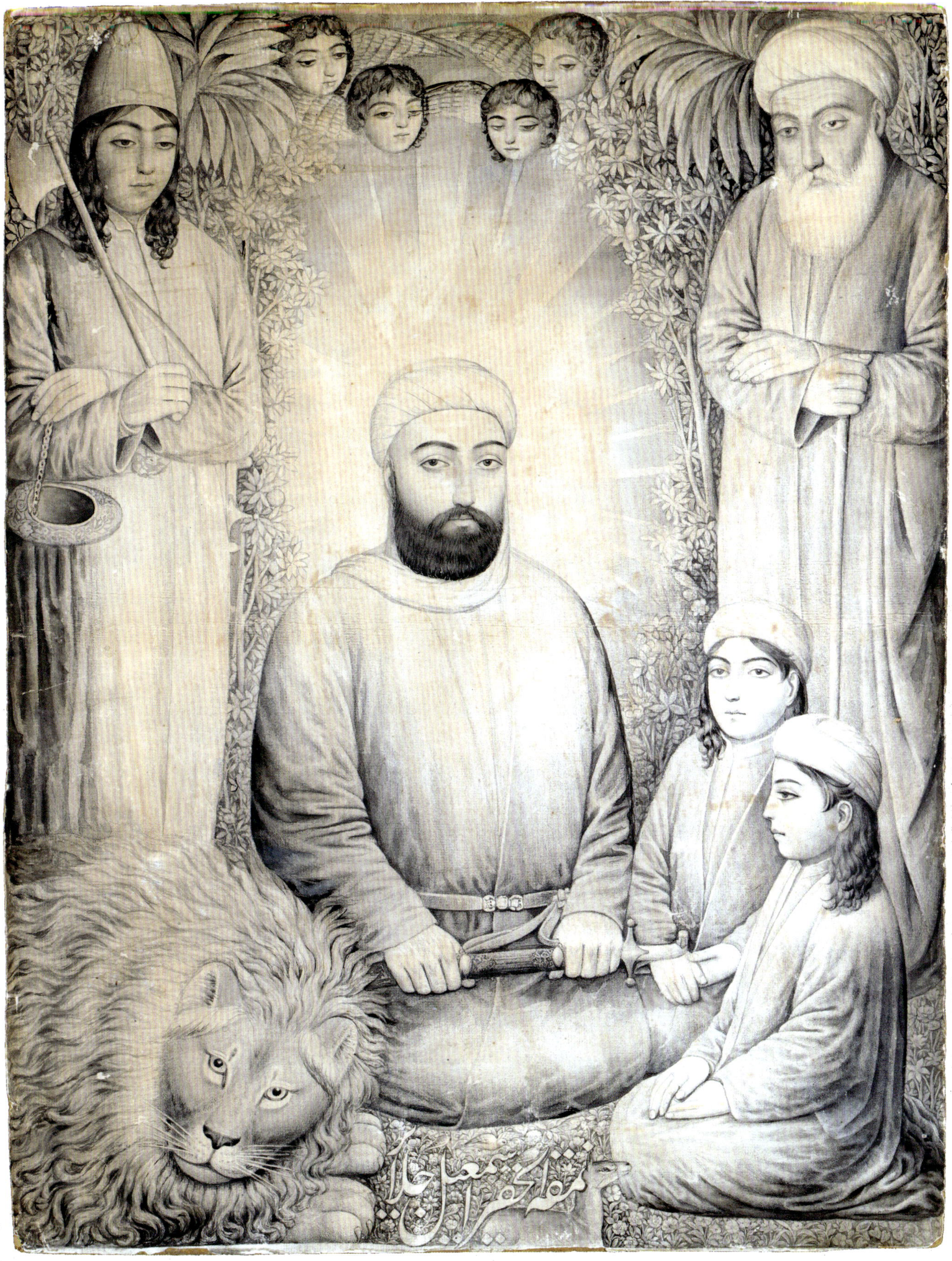

the Neᶜmatullahis' is the red twelve-gore cap (referred to as *taj-i haydari*) worn by the Qizilbash and known to symbolize Twelver Shiᶜism—a comparison that has perhaps strengthened sectarian readings of the Neᶜmatullahi hat.[67] The religious histories of both the Neᶜmatullahi Sufis and the Deccani rulers in the fifteenth century, however, are replete with confessional ambiguities and far too complicated to fit neatly into sectarian binaries.[68] In this light, despite the names of the twelve Shiᶜa imams inscribed on the Neᶜmatullahi taj in the chelleh khaneh, the established interpretation outlined above proves anachronistic, for, unsurprisingly, both color and number symbolism often refuse to settle into fixed meanings across time and religiopolitical milieus.

The picture drawn in early modern literature suggests that the colors of Sufi attire had much broader and looser connotations than binary sectarian affiliations. One such example appears in the *Futuwwatnama-yi Sultani* (*The Royal Book of Spiritual Chivalry*), a treatise on medieval chivalry, Sufism, and guild life in Iran, attributed to the Timurid-era scholar, preacher, and Naqshbandi Sufi Husayn Waᶜiz Kashifi (d. 1504–5). In the book, Kashifi lists allowable and common materials and colors for Sufi and chivalric attire. In discussing the green taj, he associates the color with grass, which "is fresh, gives rise to a sense of delight, and brings light to the eyes. Therefore, whoever wears a green taj or wraps a green cloth around it should always be cheerful . . . so that the eyes falling on the face of the wearer are filled with light." He then quotes a hemistich advising those wearing green to be "like Jesus, happy and open."[69] When discussing the khirqa (cloak), Kashifi associates the color green with water and grass, a color favored and worn frequently by the Prophet Muhammad.[70]

A more directly relevant treatise, undated and attributed to Shah Neᶜmatullah but likely from a later period, calls straightforward sectarian readings of the Neᶜmatullahi taj further into question. The short treatise, called the *Taj-nama* (*Book of the Crown*), is devoted to encoding the Neᶜmatullahi initiation hat with cosmic, ethical, and religious meanings. A key word in the treatise used to describe the shape of the hat is *tark*, which could have two meanings in Persian: as a noun tark could mean "gore" (i.e., a triangular segment of a garment), but when combined with the verb *to do* (*kardan*), it also refers to the act of renunciation or abandonment. The treatise indicates that each tark, or gore, of the hat symbolizes the act of seeking a tark—that is, the abandonment of one of the twelve sins: stinginess, hatred, vanity, lust, and so on—and replacing them with praiseworthy habits.[71] In the treatise, it is this theological connotation, rather than the possible sectarian iconography of the number twelve, that explains the shape of the hat in the first instance.

For context, neither this genre of literature on Sufi attire nor the specific treatment of the shape of the hat was unique in the early modern period. The Ottoman realm seems to be the most common context for the production of such texts, with a range of Ottoman treatises on Sufi headgear dating from the middle of the sixteenth century to the second half of the eighteenth century.[72] Similarly, the connection between initiation hats and the annihilation of sinful habits was a common thread among several Sufi networks with various confessional affiliations. For instance, for the Chishtis, an influential Sufi network in India and central Asia, the "four-gored cap [of renunciation]" (*kulah-i chahar tarki*) symbolized a fourfold state of detachment—from this world, from the hereafter (in fact everything except God), from food and sleep (beyond what was necessary for sustenance), and finally from the desires of the self.[73] In the case of the twelve-gore cap, its use among those of Ottoman Sufi networks that were considered to have Sunni affiliations shows its significance beyond the realm of strictly Shiʿa Sufis.[74]

The closest text to the Neʿmatullahi *Taj-nama* is a Safavid work titled the *Tariq al-irshad* (*The Path of Authoritative Instruction*), which has been discussed in detail by Shahzad Bashir.[75] Written by a certain Hashim b. Ahmad b. Muhammad al-Husayni al-Najafi, the work is dedicated to the red twelve-gore headgear worn by the Qizilbash, with a whole chapter on the cosmic and ethical significance of headgear and its physical attributes.[76] Like the Neʿmatullahi *Taj-nama*, Najafi's work has a section on the word *tark*, making each segment of the headgear a representative for twelve reprehensible habits that are to be replaced by twelve commendable qualities—both categories similar but not identical to those in the Neʿmatullahi *Taj-nama*.[77] Aside from this theological and ethical decoding of the hat, as Bashir has shown, the main purpose of the *Tariq al-irshad* is to inscribe the headgear as an object of sociopolitical significance that legitimized the Safavids as the rightful rulers of the state.[78] The work is concerned with the headgear's genealogy of transmission from ʿAli to the Safavid Shah Tahmasp, which, according to the Safavids' official Sayyid lineage, follows the line of Twelver imams down to the eighth imam, Reza, and from there, instead of continuing with Reza's successor, transfers to his brother and all the way to Shaykh Safi al-din, the founder of the Safavid Sufi network to Shah Tahmasp.[79]

The *Taj-nama*, on the contrary, is not directly concerned with Shah Neʿmatullah's official genealogies. These genealogies, which were in circulation in both text and image from the fifteenth century—as seen, for instance, inscribed in the tomb of the Bahmanid ruler Ahmad Shah I in Bidar—trace Shah Neʿmatullah's chain of initiation to ʿAli and the Prophet Muhammad. Instead, the *Taj-nama* takes up the task of inscribing the Neʿmatullahi twelve-gore headgear into a religiocosmic history that connects the object to the People of the Prophet's House. This connection in the *Taj-nama* is introduced only after a discussion of the twelve sins and praiseworthy habits. Compared to the latter, which takes up most of the space in the *Taj-nama* treatise, the section on the House of the Prophet is very brief. Moreover, in the treatise, unlike the depiction of the hat in the Mahan chelleh khaneh, the twelve segments are not associated with the twelve Shiʿa imams. Rather, the *Taj-nama* connects the twelve gores with the Prophet's descendants (*awlad*), starting with the Prophet's daughter, Fatima, and her sons and continuing with Husayn's descendants. ʿAli, the Prophet's cousin and son-in-law and the first Shiʿa imam, and the Prophet himself are instead represented more subtly: not by the shape of the hat as a physical object but rather by the shape of the word *taj*. In a lettrist analysis of two of the letters in the Persian word *taj*, the treatise indicates that the letter alif—the second of three letters in the word—is an allegory of the unity of God. The two dots of the letter *t* (ت)—the word's first letter—allegorize the sun and the moon, symbolizing the Prophet Muhammad and ʿAli, respectively. The descendants of the Prophet, symbolized by the gores of the taj, are likened to stars shining in the sky, guiding the path of believers.[80]

It is possible to imagine both the *Taj-nama* and the chelleh khaneh's visual program as responding to and competing not just with a text like the Safavid treatise *Tariq al-irshad* and similar works that we are unaware of but with the general ideological and confessional shifts that took place at the time. I mentioned earlier that the *Taj-nama*, although attributed to Shah Neʿmatullah (d. 1431), is undated. The *Tariq al-irshad* poses its own questions of dating. Although the single copy of the *Tariq al-irshad* kept in Berlin dates the original text to the second half of the sixteenth century, based on circumstantial evidence Bashir has suggested a seventeenth-century dating for the text. As he argues, compared to a more straightforward textual treatment of the headgear in sixteenth-century sources, the discussion of its symbolism and close connections to Twelver Shiʿism specifically gains momentum in the literature from the seventeenth century. This is also the period when Safavid chronicles start to trace the origin of the Safavid headgear to a dream by either Shah Ismaʿil, the founder of the Safavid dynasty, or his father, Shaykh Haydar.[81] By then, the highly politicized headgear is tied even more closely to the Safavids' military history due to a decree associated with Shah Tahmasp that made the red headgear compulsory for his subjects and soldiers.[82] The links I have highlighted between the contents of the *Taj-nama* and the *Tariq al-irshad*, their treatment of the twelve-gore hat in detail, the discussion of the twelve sins, and their mapping of a lineage onto the segments of the hat make a seventeenth-century dating for the chelleh khaneh suggested in the beginning of this chapter more plausible.

Reading the *Taj-nama*, the *Tariq al-irshad*, and the interior program of the chelleh khaneh together raises a range of interesting points and questions. First, this close-knit textual and visual reading of the headgear suggests that the genealogical associations of the hat, whether that of the Safavids or the Prophet's House, could have been secondary to the ethical codes of conduct expected from those wearing the hats. While reading the inscriptions of the headgear in the chelleh khaneh directly associates it with Twelver Shiʿism, the *Taj-nama* and the *Tariq al-irshad* demonstrate that the headgear was an object with multiple meanings that changed as the initiation hat moved across religious, confessional, and political boundaries both within and beyond the Safavid state.[83] Finally, the decision in the chelleh khaneh to foreground the twelve Shiʿa imams, and in the *Taj-nama* to associate the hat in its word-image form (i.e., the twelve gores as well as the shape of its letters) with the Fourteen Immaculate Ones (the Prophet, his daughter, and the twelve Shiʿa imams), seems to have been a move by the Neʿmatullahis toward aligning their confessional inclinations with the ideological shifts and pro-Shiʿa sentiments in the sixteenth- and seventeenth-century Safavid milieu, when Shiʿism had become the official religion of the state.

Bringing Shiʿa lineage to the forefront of the hat's iconography in the chelleh khaneh exemplifies how existing symbols and practices were forged anew and folded into contemporary politics—at times in apparent alignment with Safavid politics and at times against them, containing subtle messages that commemorated the family's attempts to gain independence. Given the radical political ambitions of the Neʿmatullahis and the politicized significance of the twelve-gore headgear at this time, it is possible to read the chelleh khaneh Sufi hat as an attempt to challenge the legitimacy of its Safavid counterpart. Paired with the Zu'lfiqar of ʿAli, the hat, and by extension the chelleh khaneh, could be read, in a politicized interpretation, as a visual propaganda machine casting an image of the Neʿmatullahis as even more Shiʿa than the Safavids, armed with both military power and religiospiritual authority.

VI. The Architecture of the Sufi Body

The treatise on the Neʿmatullahi initiation hat discussed above is written in a mix of prose and poetry. One couplet in particular expands the meaning of the taj by directly identifying it with Shah Neʿmatullah (app. 8.5.a).

> [He is] the crown of the wise gnostics,
> [He is] the Neʿmat Allah [lit. bounty of God], the offspring of the Prophet.[84]

This transposition of meaning from the Sufi's attributes to his very self is common to the poetics of the chelleh khaneh, which often extends it into bodily metaphors. In several of the verses inscribed in the chelleh khaneh, the sword or flower is both an attribute of the Sufi and a surrogate of Shah Neʿmatullah. Such identifications between the Sufi and the Sufi hat are reminiscent, for example, of traditions documented for the Mevlevi Sufis—followers of the thirteenth-century Sufi poet Jalal al-din Muhammad Balkhi Rumi (d. 1273) in Anatolia. A common funerary practice among the Mevlevis entailed the placement of the iconic conical Mevlevi hat (known as *sikke*) on the tombstone of a deceased Sufi to stand in for the body lying beneath.[85]

The *Taj-nama* ends with the following verse, drawing out the symbolic significance of the hat by emphasizing its tactile relationship to the head (app. 8.5.b):

> Whoever places our crown over their head,
> Will be liberated from the troubles of the two worlds.[86]

There is a functional similarity between this poetic description and the retreats meant to take place in the chelleh khaneh. The allegorical setting of the hat on one's head in the poem is akin to the purpose of entering the retreat room: a distance or liberation from matters of this world and the hereafter. In the chelleh khaneh, the disciples gathered for retreat seem to almost literally set the same hat on their heads by virtue of their position seated underneath the dome (figs. 0.3 and 8.20). The fact that the hat is represented by the hollow of the small cupola reinforces this sense, as if anyone seated in the room would be crowned by the initiation hat of the Neʿmatullahis and thus placed at the receiving end of the Sufi master's authority.

Taking a step back and reconsidering the different elements of the chelleh khaneh together, the corporeal representation of the Sufi body amounts to more than a mere array of attributes scattered around the room. Surveying the most prominent visual and verbal elements of the room from bottom to top, we first encounter the swords depicted just above the dadoes: the fabled sword of ʿAli, reminiscent of actual bifurcated swords that were made in the early modern period and would have been worn around one's belt (figs. 8.10 and 8.17). Above these are extensive architectural surfaces painted in a manner similar to talismanic textiles, costumes worn on the torso of warriors or those in need of protection (figs. 8.3, 8.13, and 8.18). Khirqas, too, could contain inscriptions of the names of God, the Prophet, and ʿAli.[87] Although the visual and textual programs of talismanic textiles are much more extensive compared to khirqas, whether patched, stitched, or simple, it is possible to imagine a relationship between them here by virtue of their participation in Sufi rituals performed for initiation into Sufi networks or before battles. Moving up, at the apex of the room is the initiation hat of the Sufi (fig. 8.20). The overall arrangement of these attributes, which the inscriptions invest with strong tactile associations, amounts to a spatial representation of the body of the Sufi master, instating his constant presence in absence, for in each case it is a hollow garment or attribute that alludes to his body.[88]

All of these elements—the swords, the textile-like surfaces, and the hat—are arranged to strike a correspondence between the architecture and the human body, as if to project each part of the Sufi's body into space, from waist to hand, torso, and head. In this way, the architecture presents itself as analogous to the body of the beloved or its substitute.[89] Activated by self-referential poetry, which in turn resonates with ritual chants, the representation of the Sufi master takes on a complex corporeal dimension whose ultimate goal is not a mimetic imitation of the sacred so much as the merging of the sacred with the viewer's own body and sense of self through metaphorically charged tactile contact. As we take up the sword, we touch what the sacred figure has touched; at the same time, by filling the space that embodies him, we take his place.

FACING, FIGURE 8.22. Hilya. Iran, nineteenth century. Ink, gold, and opaque watercolor on thin paper, 61.5 × 50.3 cm. Nasser D. Khalili Collection of Islamic Art, CAL 302. © *The Khalili Family Trust.*

This interplay of text, image, and space creates a material interpretation of the moral qualities of Shah Neʿmatullah, painstakingly recounted in the epigraphic program of the room. In this respect, the room could also be read as a spatial adaptation of the hilyas of the Prophet Muhammad. Typically laid out two-dimensionally on paper, the hilya is a genre of devotional art, also dubbed a *verbal portrait*, that represents the physical and moral qualities of the Prophet through verbal, nonfigural images and allegories (fig. 8.22). This

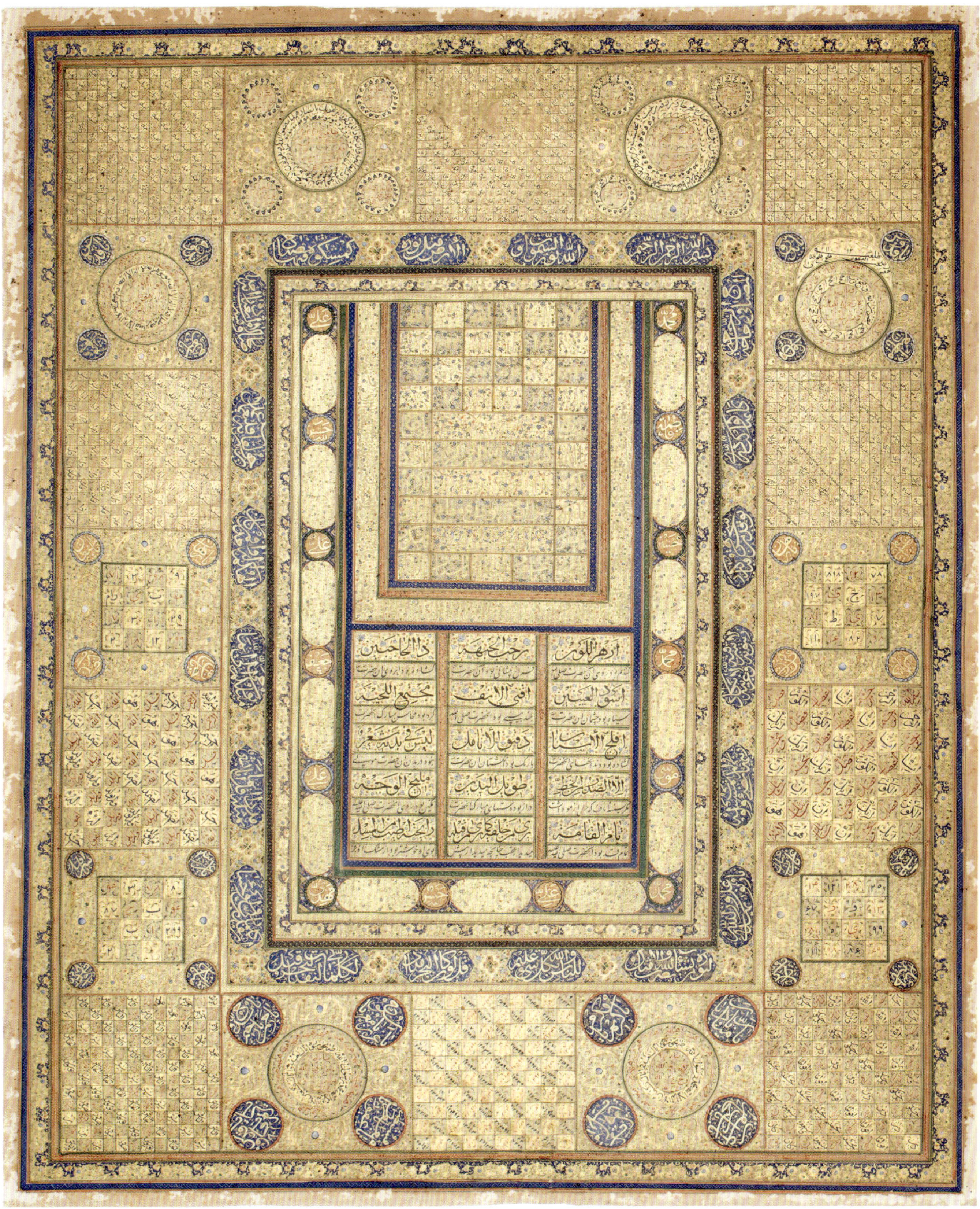

transition from two to three dimensions could already have been facilitated by common architectural configurations in the layout of the hilyas as well as the practice of attaching hilyas to the walls of private and public architecture.[90] A parallel to this understanding of the chelleh khaneh as a three-dimensional hilya-like space can be found in eighteenth-century Ottoman hilyas of the Prophet in which discrete sections of the hilya are described metaphorically as body parts.[91]

Keeping the image of the Sufi master before one's eyes during retreat and rituals of dhikr was a strategy promoted by some Sufi networks for spiritual guidance.[92] In the chelleh khaneh, by extension, the disciples would also have been enveloped by his spatial representation—his initiation hat suspended over their heads, swords passed down to a level within the reach of their hands, and protective verses inscribed on all sides in a manner reminiscent of textiles turned inside out on themselves, as if to evoke an intimate embrace, establishing a deep sense of interiority in this space. The form of the Sufi's body thus becomes a text-image-space continuum that is "legible" to, and experienced by, a variety of different senses.[93] Disciples would have entered the room believing, or hoping, that the power of this coalescence of word, image, and space would protect them on the battlefield and in their everyday life along their path of discipleship.

The virtual body of the Sufi in the chelleh khaneh created a crucial sense of proximity to the body of the Sufi master. In a sense, this practice resonates with literary and visual tropes of the Sufi masters' miraculous ability to transform their bodies and exert an omnipresent power to protect their disciples in dangerous circumstances.[94] In the Mahan shrine, the encompassing presence of the Sufi was honed by the connections drawn between the architectural and physical bodies. As such, the (absent) imagined Sufi body in the chelleh khaneh expands the possibilities of proximity to the Sufi master that, prior to the chelleh khaneh, were solely centered around the grave on the other side of the recitation hall (fig. 8.23). The similarities of the interior program of the chelleh khaneh to the vibrant compact designs and colors of the carpets furnishing the mausoleum across the hall, as well as to the interior of Ahmad Shah's tomb in Bidar across the Arabian Sea, formed a visually dense network of devotion for the transregional pilgrim, weaving these spatial invocations of the Sufi master together on a more geographically expansive level.

The need for a corporeal representation of the Sufi body was anticipated in the writings of Shah Neʿmatullah himself. In a work attributed to him, the *Risala-yi Azwaq* (*Treatise on the Distinction of Truth*), it is noted that "*ruh* [i.e., soul] . . . is contrary to the body . . . and does not need the body for its survival and strength. But, since the body is its [outward] form (surat) and the manifestation of its virtues in the realm of visibility (*shahadat*) . . . whether a king or a dervish, one is in need of their [outward] form."[95] The statement occurs amid a commentary on the relationship between the exterior (*zahir*) and interior (*batin*), a standard philosophical exercise in Islamic theology. In

FACING, FIGURE 8.23. View from the entrance of the chelleh khaneh toward the entrance of the fifteenth-century mausoleum of Shah Neʿmatullah in Mahan's recitation hall. *Photograph by author, 2018.*

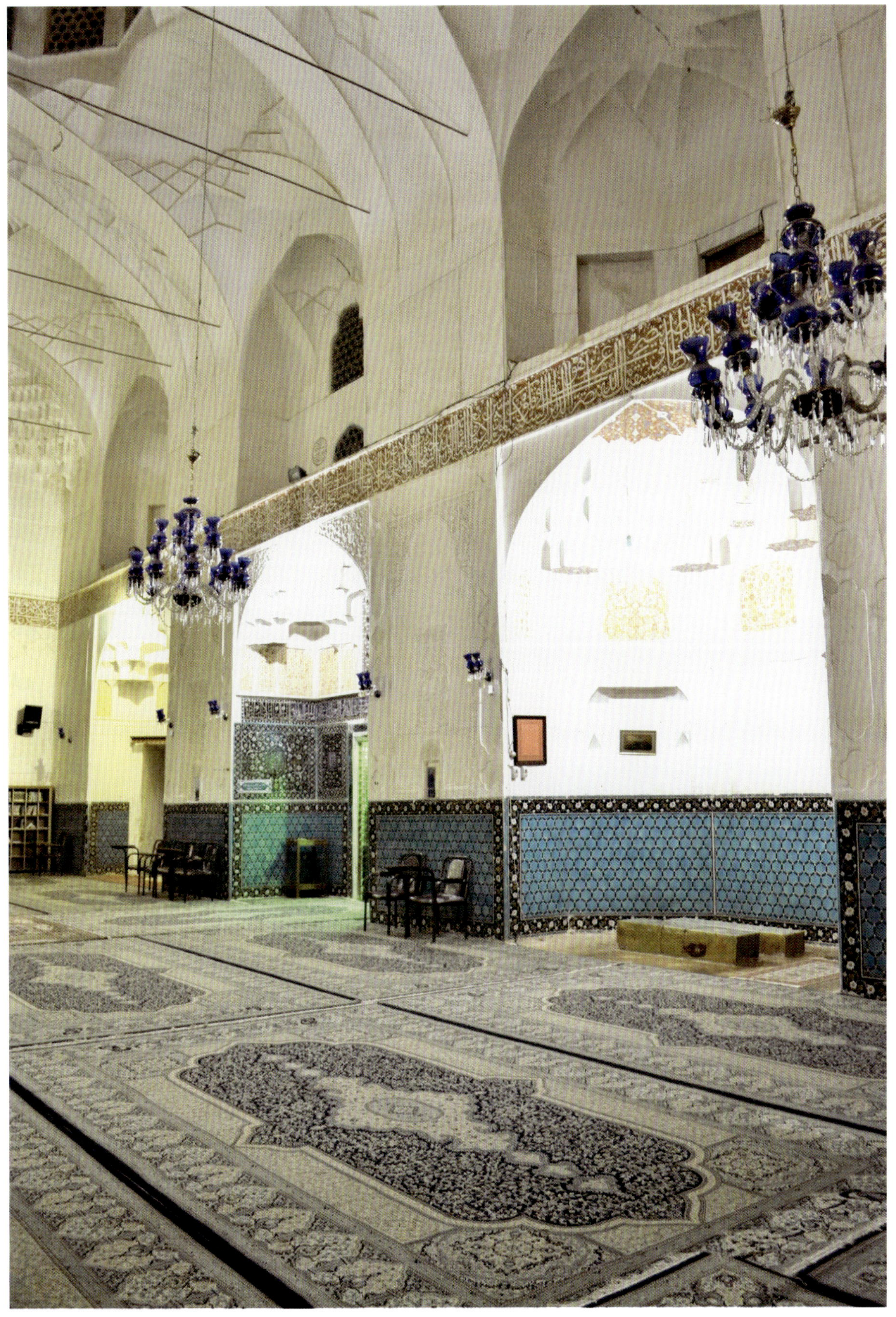

Shah Neʿmatullah's approach—by no means uncommon—the body functions as the threshold between inner and outer realms.[96] As a spatial representation that hinges on the negative space between the walls and ceiling, the image of Shah Neʿmatullah's body in the chelleh khaneh activates similar themes. The lines and surfaces of the architecture mark out a threshold, a continuous interchange between his being and nonbeing in the emptiness of the interior—an intimacy that is defined by distance. Just as the walls of this room define the boundaries between interior and exterior spaces in the shrine (i.e., recitation hall and courtyard), they also define a border between the external world and the interior (batin) of the Sufi master. This spatial mode of representation bypasses the outward representation (surat) of the Sufi's exterior in order to privilege access to his batin, surpassing the materiality of the shrine's walls.

Through this dense interplay of materiality and immateriality, the representation of the Sufi's body in the chelleh khaneh encapsulates the debates around materiality that have shaped the broader trajectory of this book. The intimacy between the disciple and the Sufi teacher is defined by distance—whether between the material and immaterial or external and internal, as was the case in the chelleh khaneh, or physical distance, as was the case in the tomb of Ahmad Shah in Bidar. This "intimacy in distance," which is akin to the notion of "presence in absence," as seen in the mausoleum in Taft or the portal at Mahan, is a type of presence that is activated through a deep fusion of space and poetry. Predicated on the poetics of distance, this is an intimacy that is at once transregional and metaphysical, collapsing boundaries between materiality, immateriality, and geographic space.

Notes

1. On the guild of tayyans and their crossover with architects, see Babaie, "Qavam Al-Din Shirazi," 29.
2. See chapter 1, section II, "Between Global and Local: Transregional Implications of an Inscription."
3. See chapter 5, section VI, "The Mahan Carpet Fragments."
4. Hofer, "On the Material and Social Conditions of Khalwa"; Schimmel, *Mystical Dimensions of Islam*, 105.
5. See, for instance, Rizvi, "Its Mortar," 325–26, 331–32.
6. For recent art historical studies dealing with such questions, see Mumtaz, *Faces of God*, especially chapter 5; Mumtaz, "Contemplating the Face of the Master," 106–28; Diamond, *Yoga*, especially the essay by Ernst, "Muslim Interpreters of Yoga," 59–68. See also Abuali, "Words Clothed in Light," 279–92.
7. Qayyumi Bidhendi, "Majmuʿih mazar," in Pazuki, *Majmuʿih maqalat*, 181; Golombek and Wilber, *The Timurid Architecture*, 395.
8. Samarqandi, *Silsilat al-ʿarifin*, 189; discussed in Bashir, *Sufi Bodies*, 210.
9. In 2018, a plexiglass structure was installed inside the door so that visitors can view the paintings in the room from behind the glass (see fig. 8.5). All other photographs were taken prior to the installation of the glass structure.
10. For comparative examples in sixteenth-century Florence, see Rubin, "Signposts of Invention," 563–99.

11. See, for instance, Munshi-yi Qumi, *Gulistan-i hunar*, 76–77.

12. On the flood, see Bastani Parizi, "Haram-i Shah Vali," in Pazuki, *Majmuᶜih maqalat*, 151–52.

13. Aubin, *Matériaux*, 199–215.

14. On Solomon, see Porter, Saif, and Savage-Smith, "Medieval Islamic Amulets," 536, 541–42; Ekhtiar and Parikh, "Power and Piety," 437–39.

15. Aubin, *Matériaux*, 220, 227; Mufid, *Jamiᶜ-i Mufidi*, 3:66–67.

16. Aubin, *Matériaux*, 261–67.

17. In its density, the design program in Mahan's chelleh khaneh is comparable to that of the shrine of Bayazid Bastami in Iran. On the Bastam shrine, see Wilber, *The Architecture of Islamic Iran*, 127–28.

18. The door opening to the adjacent courtyard still exists, but the opening between that space and the chelleh khaneh is now blocked. For footage from an old promotional DVD that shows this now-blocked opening, see Eisazadeh, "Tak-Negari," 129.

19. For a broader discussion of light and viewing context of devotional objects and spaces, see Pentcheva, "Moving Eyes," 225–27; Pentcheva, *The Sensational Icon*, 1–16, 121–22, 128–38.

20. For a discussion of olfactory traditions in mosques and mausolea, see Ergin, "The Fragrance of the Divine," 70–97; Bursi, "Scents of Space," 200–34.

21. Bashir, *Sufi Bodies*, 58.

22. On the use of drugs and other intoxicants among Sufis, see Mihrabi Kermani, *Mazarat-i Kerman*, 124–27; Ergin, "Rock Faces, Opium and Wine," 71–72; Matthee, *The Pursuit of Pleasure*, 98–110; Karamustafa, *God's Unruly Friends*, 46.

23. Schimmel, *Mystical Dimensions of Islam*, 167.

24. Aubin, *Matériaux*, 302.

25. Ibid., 302. On the Naqshbandi "four-beat" dhikr, see Bashir, *Sufi Bodies*, 73.

26. Aubin, *Matériaux*, 303.

27. See minutes 22:50–24:50 and 32:50–34:12 of the film *Voyage au pays des dervish sufi: l'ultime pèlerinage*, Harvard Fine Art Library (FLS2270), accessed August 25, 2020, http://archnet.org/media_contents/132.

28. This seating arrangement can be seen in the footage discussed above, although the location within the shrine is not clear.

29. Ekhtiar and Parikh, "Power and Piety," 428.

30. On repetition in dhikr, see Gruber, "'Go Wherever You Wish," 26.

31. Schimmel, *Mystical Dimensions of Islam*, 161.

32. Ibid., 173; Bashir, *Sufi Bodies*, 68.

33. On paintings of Sufi saints as meditation aids in the Mughal context, see: Mumtaz, "Contemplating the Face of the Master," 106–28.

34. On visual and verbal repetitions in dhikr, see Leoni, "Sacred Words, Sacred Power," in Leoni, *Power and Protection*, 65. On objects and architectural elements joining in samaᶜ with Shaykh Safi al-din Ardabili, see Ardabili, *Safvat al-Safa*, 643; also discussed in Bashir, *Sufi Bodies*, 75. On the Kaᶜba joining in the circumambulation ritual of Sufis, see O'Meara, *The Kaᶜba Orientations*, 91–93.

35. On the relationship between cryptic and legible inscriptions, see Gruber, "From Prayer to Protection," in Leoni, *Power and Protection*, 34; Ettinghausen, "Arabic Epigraphy," 297–317.

36. Some examples include Bush, *Reframing the Alhambra*, 85; Johns, "Arabic Inscriptions in the Cappella Palatina," 124–47.

37. Yürekli, "Dhu'l-faqar and the Ottomans," 163, 172; Alexander, "Dhu'l-faqar," 157–63.

38. Yürekli, "Dhu'l-faqar and the Ottomans," 163–67.

39. Porter, Saif, and Savage-Smith, "Medieval Islamic Amulets," 546.

40. Yürekli, "Dhu'l-faqar and the Ottomans," 167–68; Felek, "Fears, Hopes, and Dreams," 665–66; Leoni, "Sacred Words, Sacred Power," in 58. On the transformation of talismanic seals into graphic signs, see Gruber, "Go Wherever You Wish," 25.

41. Alexander, "Dhu'l-faqar," 166.

42. Felek, "Fears, Hopes, and Dreams," 647–72; Porter, Saif, and Savage-Smith, "Medieval Islamic Amulets," 548–49. See also Al-Saleh, "'Licit Magic,'" 151–66; Munroe, "Wrapped Up," 6. On abstract flowers and medallions, see Leoni, *Power and Protection*, 84; Muravchick, "God Is the Best Guardian," 251.

43. Leoni, "Sacred Words, Sacred Power," 65; Berlekamp, "Symmetry, Sympathy, and Sensation," 59–109, esp. 82.

44. On talismans and military ambition, see Porter, Saif, and Savage-Smith, "Medieval Islamic Amulets," 522. On talismanic motifs on arms and armor, see Ekhtiar and Parikh, "Power and Piety," 421–22, 427–39. On talismans affixed to walls, see Gruber, "From Prayer to Protection," 38.

45. On architectural talismans, see Berlekamp, "Symmetry, Sympathy, and Sensation," 59–109; Gruber, "Go Wherever You Wish," 26; Gruber, "Power and Protection," 2–6; Porter, Saif, and Savage-Smith, "Medieval Islamic Amulets," 534–35; Flood, "Image against Nature," 150–151; Flood, *Objects of Translation*, 168–69. For the talismanic use of architectural representations and diagrams of holy sites, see Göloğlu, "Depicting the Islamic Holy Sites," 324; Chekhab-Abudaya and Bresc, *Hajj*, 130. On accessibility of talismanic shirts, see Felek, "Fears, Hopes, and Dreams," 650; Gruber, "From Prayer to Protection," 33–34.

46. Porter, Saif, and Savage-Smith, "Medieval Islamic Amulets," 533.

47. Leoni, "Sacred Words, Sacred Power," 58.

48. On Sufis as makers of talismans, see Felek, "Fears, Hopes, and Dreams," 653.

49. Mufid, *Jamiᶜ-i Mufidi*, 3:55–56.

50. Bashir, "The Origins," 364–65, 367–68.

51. On militant Sufis, see Melvin-Koushki, "Early Modern Islamicate Empire," 364; Babayan, *Mystics, Monarchs, and Messiahs*, 297–301; Babayan, "The Cosmological Order," 246–55.

52. On Zu'lfiqar and the return of Mahdi, see Alexander, "Dhu'l-faqar," 166–68.

53. See Felek's similar approach to the study of Ottoman talismanic shirts in Felek, "Fears, Hopes, and Dreams," especially page 649. On talismans as devices against particular royal figures, see Berlekamp, "Symmetry, Sympathy, and Sensation," 79–81.

54. For examples of inscribed swords, see Alexander, *The Arts of War*, 196–97; Ekhtiar and Parikh, "Power and Piety," 436.

55. On the relationship between prosopopoeia and the beholder, see Bush, *Reframing the Alhambra*, 101.

56. Savage-Smith, "Magic and Islam," 106, 116–17; Flood, "Bodies and Becoming," 478; Gruber, "The Rose of the Prophet," 237–38; Gruber, "From Prayer to Protection," 33–57; Gruber, "In Defense and Devotion," 109–12; Göloğlu, "Depicting the Islamic Holy Sites," 324; Mumtaz, "Contemplating the Face of the Master," 120–21. For similar examples from the Western Christian context, see Bynum, *Christian Materiality*, 65.

57. On first-person pronouns in inscriptions, see Anderson and Rosser-Owen, "Great Ladies and Noble Daughters," 37–38.
58. For an example of the sword's genealogy reflected in a late fifteenth-century source, see Waʿiz Kashifi, *Futuwwatnama-yi Sultani*, 350.
59. On questions of legitimacy and the Zu'lfiqar, see Alexander, "Dhu'l-faqar," 157–60, 162–63.
60. On talismans as intermediaries between the visible and invisible worlds, see Gruber, "From Prayer to Protection," 33; Alexander, "Dhu'l-faqar," 162–63.
61. For a comparative example, see Bashir, *Sufi Bodies*, 5.
62. For nineteenth-century paintings depicting the Neʿmatullahi taj, see Ekhtiar, "Ahl al-Bayt Imagery Revisited," 80–93.
63. Aubin, *Matériaux*, 316. See also chapter 2, section I, "The Iconography of Encounter: Sufis in the Sacred Landscape of the Bahmanid Deccan."
64. Astarabadi, *Tarikh-i Fereshteh*, 382–83.
65. Vali, *Divan*, Garrett no. 1469Y, ff. 384b–385a.
66. On associating a strict Shiʿa affiliation with the Bahmanids in relation to the Neʿmatullahis, see Merklinger, "The *Madrasa* of Maḥmūd Gāwān," 155.
67. On the *Qizilbash* twelve-gored cap, see, for instance, Rizvi, *The Safavid Dynastic Shrine*, 27; Munroe, *Sufi Lovers*, 126.
68. Firouzeh, "Between the Spiritual and Material," 141–44.
69. Kashifi, *Futuwwatnama*, 194.
70. Ibid., 168.
71. Saberi, *Majmaʿ al-rasaʾil*, 1193–94.
72. Bashir, "The World as a Hat," in Mir-Kasimov, *Unity in Diversity*, 359–60. For a nineteenth-century treatise, see Gruber, "The Rose of the Prophet," 246–49.
73. Ahmad, "The Sufi and Sultan," 143–44. On the gored headdress of the Mughal ruler Humayun, see Moin, *The Millennial Sovereign*, 123–24.
74. Curry, *The Transformation of Muslim Mystical Thought*, 178.
75. Bashir, "The World as a Hat," 343–65.
76. Ibid., 345, 352–53.
77. Ibid., 356; Saberi, *Majmaʿ al-rasaʾil*, 1193–94.
78. Bashir, "The World as a Hat," 355.
79. Ibid., 346, 354.
80. Saberi, *Majmaʿ al-rasaʾil*, 1193.
81. Bashir, "The World as a Hat," 345, 350–51, 355.
82. Ibid., 348, 357.
83. For similar arguments based on the *Tariq al-irshad*, see ibid., 355.
84. Saberi, *Majmaʿ al-rasaʾil*, 1193.
85. See Bashir, "The World as a Hat," 360; Elias, "Mevlevi Sufis," in Rizvi, *Affect, Emotion, and Subjectivity*, 189; İşli, *Ottoman Headgears*.
86. Saberi, *Majmaʿ al-rasaʾil*, 1194.
87. Munroe, *Sufi Lovers*, 128–33.
88. On the relationship between the work of art and the body of the beloved considering the poetic genre of *shahrashub* (city disturber), see Losensky, "The Palace of Praise," 23–24.
89. Nagel and Wood, *Anachronic Renaissance*, see especially chapter 6 on "Architectural Models."
90. Porter, Saif, and Savage-Smith, "Medieval Islamic Amulets," 545; Porter, *Arabic and Persian Seals*, 161; Gruber, "From Prayer to Protection," 44–46; Stanley, "From Text to Art Form," 559–70.

91. Gruber, "The Rose of the Prophet," 227.

92. Mumtaz, "Contemplating the Face of the Master," 116–24; Schimmel, *Mystical Dimensions of Islam*, 170.

93. On the "readable body," see Bashir, *Sufi Bodies*, 45.

94. Ibid., 195.

95. Saberi, *Majmaʿal-rasaʾil*, 550. See appendix 8.5.c.

96. On Sufi bodies as thresholds, "as a critical doorway between the interior and exterior realms," see Bashir, *Sufi Bodies*, 27–28, 37.

Epilogue

The Fragility of Transregionality

And some Sufis believe in the superiority of Satan . . . like this vicious rejected yogi (*chuki, juki*), Maʿsum Ali-yi Hindi, the [fake] Hindu Sayyid.

Behbahani, *Risala-yi Khayratiyeh*, 16.

In 1770, a Neʿmatullahi disciple known as Maʿsum ʿAli Shah (d. 1795) arrived in Shiraz, having followed the land and sea routes that many Neʿmatullahi followers had traveled in prior centuries from the Deccan to southern Iran. His journey was prompted by requests from Neʿmatullahi Sufis in Iran to the then qutb of Neʿmatullahiyya in Hyderabad, Reza ʿAli Shah Dakkani (d. 1796), for a teacher to revive and reorganize the Neʿmatullahis in Iran.[1]

The epigraph of this epilogue contains words written about Maʿsum ʿAli Shah by Aqa Muhammad ʿAli Behbahani (d. 1801), a leading *mujtahid* (jurist) in the eighteenth century. Behbahani's remarks should be understood in the context of bitter animosities between Sufis and ʿulamas and the vigorous suppression of Sufism by mujtahids since the late Safavid period.[2] Such persecutions led to the murder of Maʿsum ʿAli Shah in 1795 and earned Behbahani the title *Sufi kush* (Sufi killer).[3] At its heart, Behbahani's attack on Sufis generally, and on Maʿsum ʿAli Shah specifically, is a response to the threats of what Leonard Lewisohn dubbed the "revival" of Sufism in the late eighteenth and early nineteenth centuries in Iran, pinpointing the advent of Maʿsum ʿAli Shah as the beginning of this process.[4]

As in earlier periods in the history of the Neʿmatullahis, their reception by the court was never a simple, straightforward affair. While Neʿmatullahi leaders were banned from the court of Karim Khan Zand (r. 1749–79) and the Qajar ruler Fath ʿAli Shah (r. 1797–1834) sided with Behbahani against Neʿmatullahi leaders, his successor, Muhammad Shah Qajar (r. 1834–48), supported the Neᶜmatullahis. During Muhammad Shah's reign, stipends were granted to Neᶜmatullahi leaders, and the shrine at Mahan—which, thanks to its relative isolation from the Qajar-Zand conflicts, had become a haven for the Neᶜmatullahi disciples in the eighteenth century—was greatly expanded with the construction of the Sahn-i Muhammad Shahi (also known as the Husayniya) and a grand portal (fig. 1.7).[5] The scale of Muhammad Shah's patronage, however, was an exception rather than the rule at the time.[6]

Despite the challenges posed by the campaigns led against institutional Sufism, myriad anti-Sufi treatises composed in this period, and the assassination of several of the network's leaders, the Neᶜmatullahis did achieve remarkable success in gathering followers in major cities like Shiraz, Isfahan, Tehran, Mashhad, Herat, Kabul, Najaf, and Karbala.[7] It was such popularity that prompted Behbahani's words.

What is most revealing, and most relevant to the subject of this book, is the theological foundation on which Behbahani's criticism is constructed. Behbahani specifically and repeatedly targets the Indianness of dhikr and meditation as well as Sufi narratives and stories, which he identifies as practices originating among *jungiyan-i hunud* (Indian Yogis).[8] As Oliver Scharbrodt has pointed out, Behbahani's critique of Sufism builds on the work of scholars before him who retraced the Christian and Indian sources that allegedly played a role in the formation of Sufism and its rituals:[9] "The Sufis of Islam derive the foundation of their doctrine (*mazhab*) from the book of Christians, and Christians took theirs from the book of Indian yogis (Juk-i Hinduvan)."[10]

Maᶜsum ᶜAli Shah, who was held captive and poisoned by Behbahani, was an easy target for the criticism of such mixing of non-Islamic traits into Sufism, having been born in India and having practiced the teaching of Neᶜmatullahi tariqa there. While Behbahani's treatise shifts between its attack on Sufism at large and vilifying Maᶜsum ᶜAli Shah and his disciples, he is unmistakably clear about his condemnation of the latter. Writing in the same year as the author's imprisonment of Maᶜsum ᶜAli Shah, he rallied numerous religious scholars across the region against the Sufi and included in his treatise their responses to his petition in support of Maᶜsum ᶜAli Shah's murder.[11] Behbahani also went after the Sufi masters in the Neᶜmatullahi's chain of initiation one by one and accompanied his portrayal of Maᶜsum ᶜAli Shah as an Indian Sufi, a Yogi, and a nonbeliever, with theological rulings on the prohibition of magic alongside stories about the futility of Yogic magic in influencing Muslim communities.[12] In essence, Behbahani's words point to the risks and liabilities of Maᶜsum ᶜAli Shah's geographical mobilities as a target. They encapsulate the extreme fragility of transregional networks.

Behbahani's critique is reminiscent of the tensions around the constant mobility of the Neᶜmatullahi family in the fifteenth century and their implications for the maintenance of the network's shrines as they traveled between Iran and India. What was likely an underlying and unspoken current in the fifteenth-century tensions is articulated all too explicitly by Behbahani. The problem at hand is the tendency to interpret hybridity as impurity. Like much nineteenth-century Islamic art that is characterized, among other things, by its engagement with European artistic practices, the hybridity of the Neʿmatullahi network made it vulnerable to criticism and negative evaluation. As Barry Flood has argued, depending on the time period and sources of inspiration, hybridity in the arts of the Islamic world has been received as either innovative and vibrant or impure and worthy of exclusion from the canon of art history.[13] The transregional network of the Neʿmatullahi shrines, too, has posed both opportunities and constraints for its members, shifting in conjunction with changing sociopolitical and economic circumstances.

Transregionality involves networks of people and material culture that assume "unstable social identities" and, as a result, earn an ambiguous place both in their respective communities and in broader art historical canons.[14] Muslim and Hindu, Iranian and Indian—neither here nor there. Just as their seafaring made it difficult to locate the Neʿmatullahis in historical sources and letters written by family members—for contemporaries and modern historians alike—their fluctuation between such binaries complicates the task of placing them and their material culture in any definitive fashion. The generative force of the shrine networks considered in this book lies precisely at the convergence of this *placeless-ness* and the drive toward place-making.

Notes

1. Lewisohn, "An Introduction to the History of Modern Persian Sufism," 440–41; Scharbrodt, "Anti-Sufism in Early Qajar Iran," in Tabandeh and Lewisohn, *Sufis and Their Opponents*, 329.
2. Lewisohn, "An Introduction to the History of Modern Persian Sufism," 439–40; Scharbrodt, "Anti-Sufism in Early Qajar Iran," 331–63.
3. Lewisohn, "An Introduction to the History of Modern Persian Sufism," 441–42.
4. Ibid., 440; Tabandeh, "Majdhub ʿAli Shah," in Tabandeh and Lewisohn, *Sufis and Their Opponents*, 369; Rahbari, "A Review on the Life," in Tabandeh and Lewisohn, *Sufis and Their Opponents*, 419.
5. Lewisohn, "An Introduction to the History of Modern Persian Sufism," 444, 448; Scharbrodt, "Anti-Sufism in Early Qajar Iran," 330.
6. Scharbrodt, "Anti-Sufism in Early Qajar Iran," 328.
7. Lewisohn, "An Introduction to the History of Modern Persian Sufism," 441–44; Nurbakhsh, *Masters of the Path*, 81–92.
8. Scharbrodt, "Anti-Sufism in Early Qajar Iran," 346
9. Ibid., 345–46.
10. Behbahani, *Risala-yi khayratiyah*, 41.
11. Ibid., 76–127.
12. Ibid., 47–48, 64–69.
13. Flood, "From the Prophet to Postmodernism?," 35–38.
14. Ibid., 40.

APPENDIXES

Appendix 0.1: Ne^cmatullahi family trees and intermarriages

Building on Connell's work, the four family trees included here are the result of comparisons between references to the members of the family and their intermarriages with the Bahmanids, Qara Qoyunlus, and Safavids in primary sources.[1] Combining the biographies of the family with other sources such as the *Munsha'at* of Sharaf al-din ʿAli Yazdi and the family's endowment documents sheds light on the identity of a few previously unknown members of the family. Secondary names and lesser-known titles of family members are included in parentheses. Letters in front of each name indicate the main primary source that discusses the individuals.

M = *Munshaʾat*
W = Waʿizi's biography
B = *Burhan-i maʾasir*
F = *Tarikh-i Fereshteh*
KH = Waqfnama of Khanish Begum
R = *Rawzat al-Safaviyya*
S = Sunʿullah's biography

Notes:
(a) It is possible that the two Shah Zahir al-din ʿAlis (son of Habib al-din Muhibbullah and son of Ziaʾ al-din Nurullah)—marked with a star in the first two tables—are the same person.
(b) The Safavid line of the family starts with an Amir Habibullah, but there is a disconnect between him and the members of the family in the fifteenth century. It is possible that he was the son of Shah Safi Allah.[2]

Chart 0.1. The Neʿmatullahis active in the fifteenth century

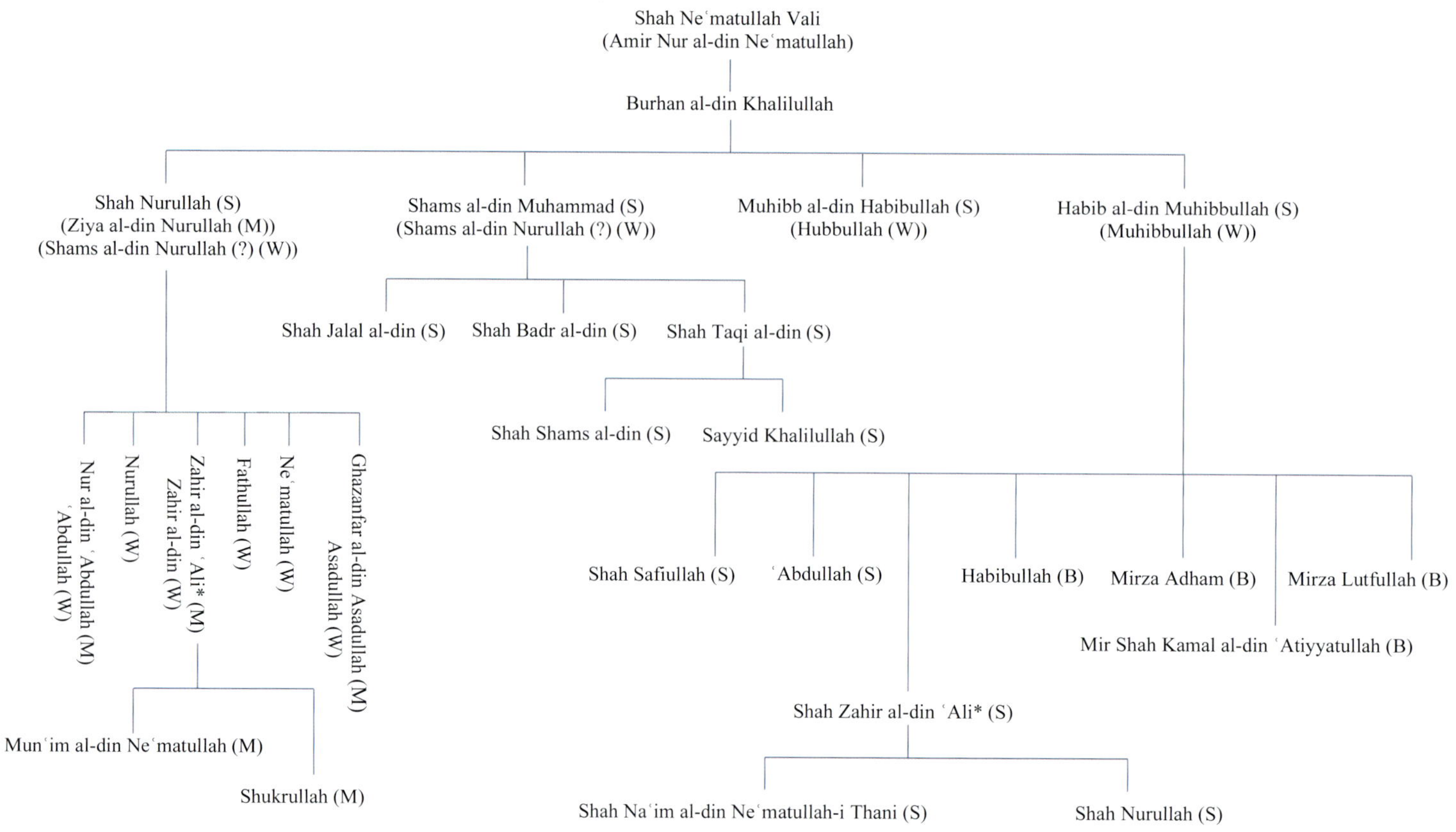

Shah Neʿmatullah Vali
(Amir Nur al-din Neʿmatullah)

Burhan al-din Khalilullah

Shah Nurullah (S)
(Ziya al-din Nurullah (M))
(Shams al-din Nurullah (?) (W))

Shams al-din Muhammad (S)
(Shams al-din Nurullah (?) (W))

Muhibb al-din Habibullah (S)
(Hubbullah (W))

Habib al-din Muhibbullah (S)
(Muhibbullah (W))

Shah Jalal al-din (S)

Shah Badr al-din (S)

Shah Taqi al-din (S)

Shah Shams al-din (S)

Sayyid Khalilullah (S)

Nur al-din ʿAbdullah (M)
ʿAbdullah (W)

Nurullah (W)

Zahir al-din ʿAli* (M)
Zahir al-din (W)

Fathullah (W)

Neʿmatullah (W)

Ghazanfar al-din Asadullah (M)
Asadullah (W)

Munʿim al-din Neʿmatullah (M)

Shukrullah (M)

Shah Safiullah (S)

ʿAbdullah (S)

Habibullah (B)

Mirza Adham (B)

Mirza Lutfullah (B)

Mir Shah Kamal al-din ʿAtiyyatullah (B)

Shah Zahir al-din ʿAli* (S)

Shah Naʿim al-din Neʿmatullah-i Thani (S)

Shah Nurullah (S)

Chart 0.2. Neʿmatullahi intermarriages in the fifteenth century

Shah Neʿmatullah Vali
(Amir Nur al-din Neʿmatullah)

Burhan al-din Khalilullah

Shah Nurullah (S)
(Ziya al-din Nurullah (M))
= daughter of Ahmad Shah I (F)

Shams al-din Muhammad (S)
(Shams al-din Nurullah (?) (W))

Muhibb al-din Habibullah (S)
(Hubbullah (W))
= daughter of Ahmad Shah I (B; F)

Habib al-din Muhibbullah (S)
(Muhibbullah (W))
= Khanza Humayra
daughter of Ahmad Shah II (B)

Shah Jalal al-din (S)

Shah Badr al-din (S)

Shah Taqi al-din (S)

Shah Shams al-din (S)

Sayyid Khalilullah (S)

Nur al-din ʿAbdullah (M)
ʿAbdullah (W)

Nurullah (W)

Zahir al-din ʿAli* (M)
Zahir al-din (W)

Fathullah (W)

Neʿmatullah (W)

Ghazanfar al-din Asadullah (M)
Asadullah (W)

Munʿim al-din Neʿmatullah (M)

Shukrullah (M)

Habibullah (B)
= Fatima, daughter of Sultan Muhammad
Bahmani (B)

ʿAbdullah (S)

Shah Saffiullah (S)

Mirza Adham (B)
= sister of Mahmud Shah
Bahmani (B)

Kamal al-din ʿAtiyyatullah (B)

Mirza Lutfullah (B)

Shah Zahir al-din ʿAli* (S)

Shah Naʿim al-din Neʿmatullah-i Thani (S)
= Khanum
daughter of Jahanshah Qara Qoyunlu (S)

Shah Nurullah (S)

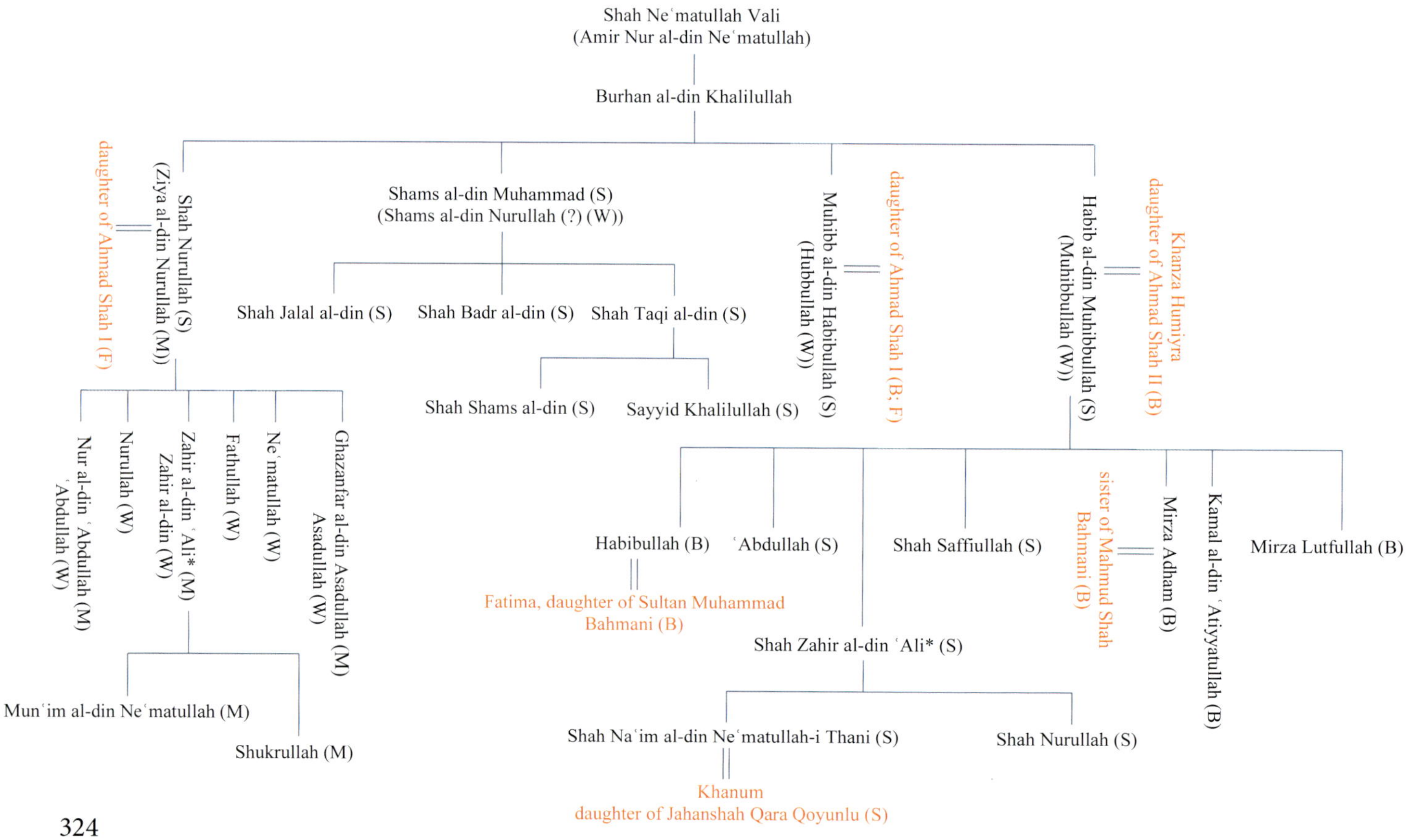

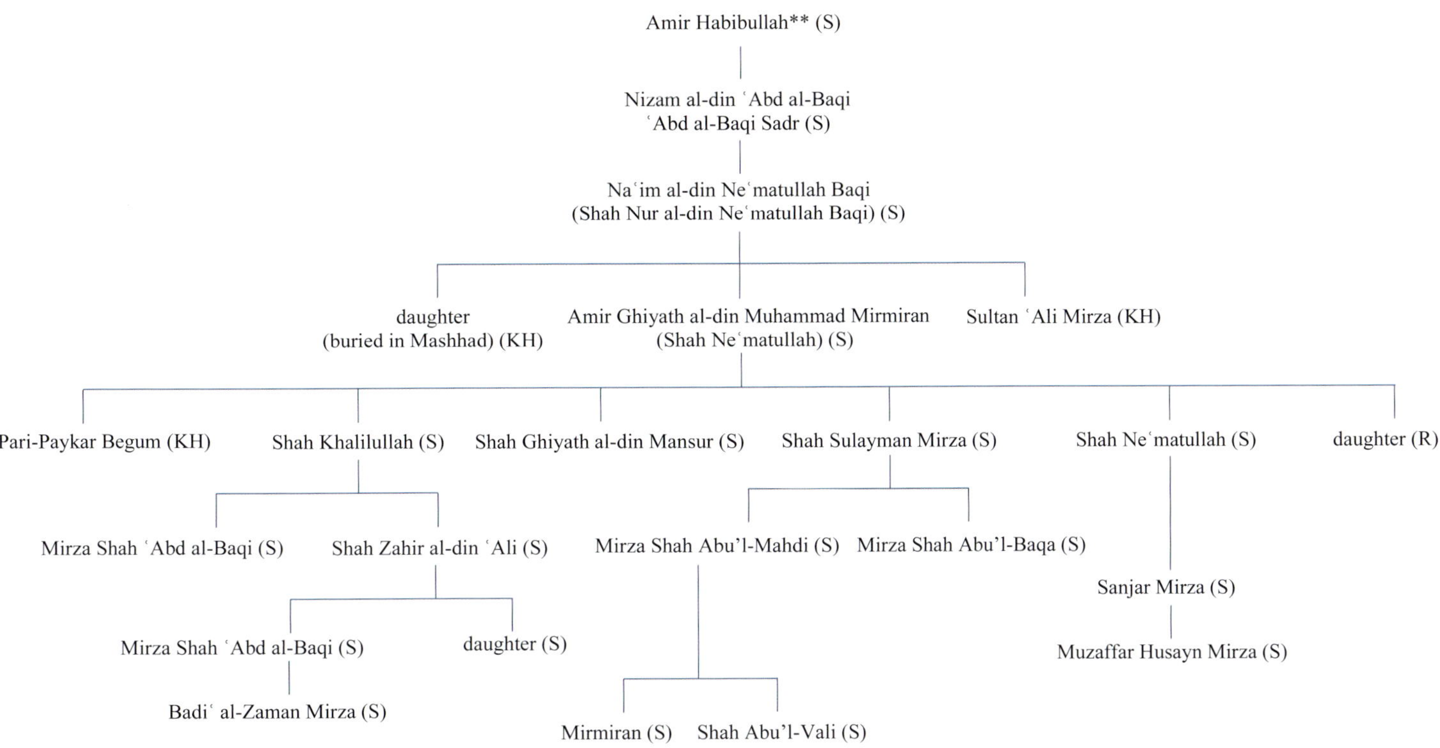

Chart 0.3. The Neʿmatullahis active during the Safavid era

Chart 0.4. Neʿmatullahi intermarriages during the Safavid era

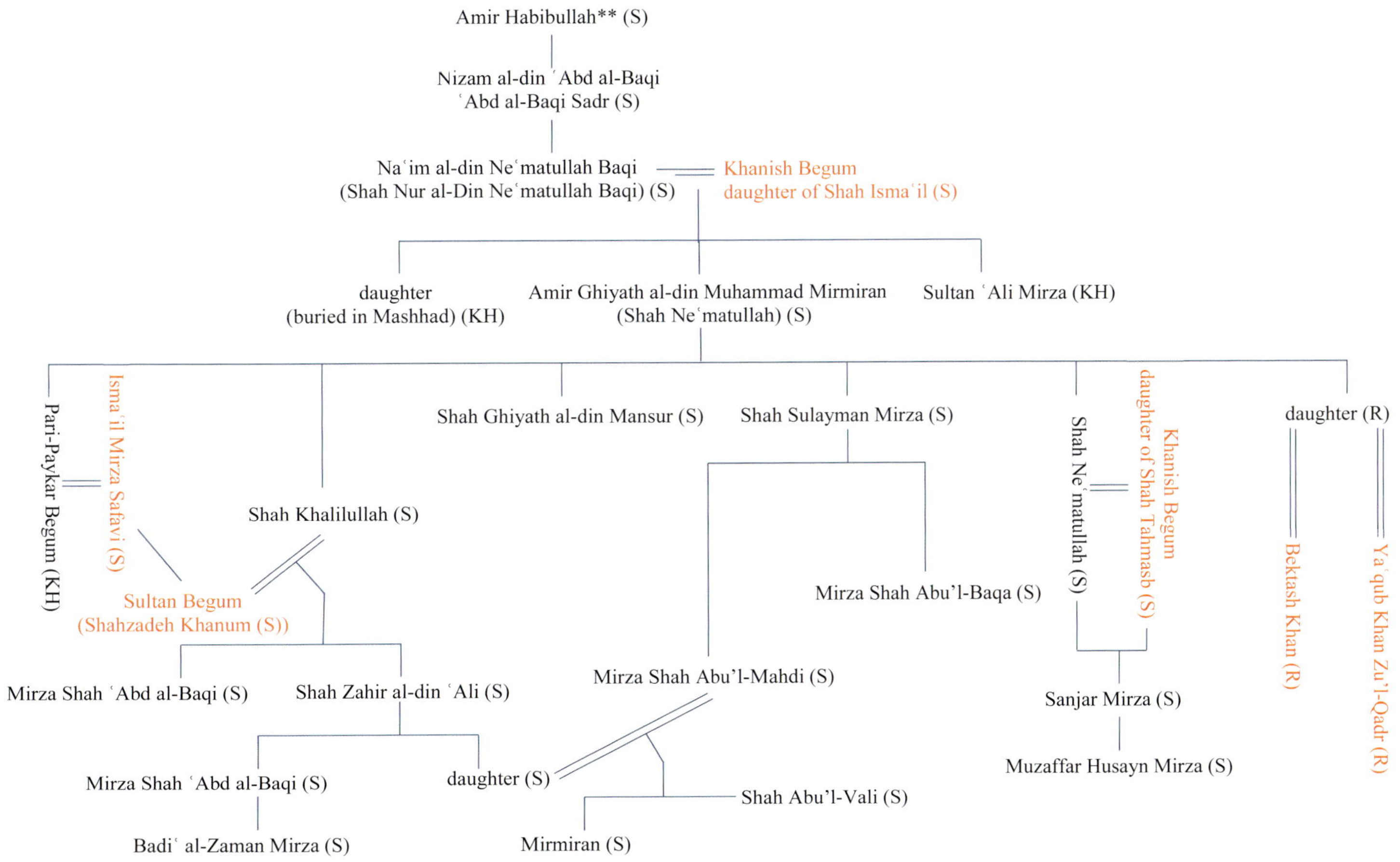

Amir Habibullah** (S)

Nizam al-din ʿAbd al-Baqi
ʿAbd al-Baqi Sadr (S)

Naʿim al-din Neʿmatullah Baqi
(Shah Nur al-Din Neʿmatullah Baqi) (S)

Khanish Begum
daughter of Shah Ismaʿil (S)

daughter
(buried in Mashhad) (KH)

Amir Ghiyath al-din Muhammad Mirmiran
(Shah Neʿmatullah) (S)

Sultan ʿAli Mirza (KH)

Pari-Paykar Begum (KH)

Ismaʿil Mirza Safavi (S)

Shah Khalilullah (S)

Sultan Begum
(Shahzadeh Khanum (S))

Shah Ghiyath al-din Mansur (S)

Shah Sulayman Mirza (S)

Shah Neʿmatullah (S)

Khanish Begum
daughter of Shah Tahmasb (S)

daughter (R)

Bektash Khan (R)

Yaʿqub Khan Zu'l-Qadr (R)

Mirza Shah Abu'l-Baqa (S)

Mirza Shah ʿAbd al-Baqi (S)

Shah Zahir al-din ʿAli (S)

Mirza Shah Abu'l-Mahdi (S)

Sanjar Mirza (S)

Mirza Shah ʿAbd al-Baqi (S)

daughter (S)

Shah Abu'l-Vali (S)

Muzaffar Husayn Mirza (S)

Badiʿ al-Zaman Mirza (S)

Mirmiran (S)

Appendix 1.1: Poetic inscription bands around the doors of the Mahan mausoleum

Appendix 1.1.a. Western entrance (fig. 0.2):

(1) سلطان سراپرده‌ی میخانه کجا شد — از مجلس رندان خرابات چرا شد
(2) معنیش همین جاست اگر صورت او رفت — پنهان ز نظر گشت نگویی که فنا شد
(3) ما جام و حبابیم که پر از آب حیاتیم — سیراب شود هر که چو ما همدم ما شد
(4) سلطان سراپرده‌ی میخانه عالم — از ذوق گدایان خرابات گدا شد
(5) صوفی به صفا دردی دردش چو بنوشید — این درد بود صافی و آن درد دوا شد
(6) یاری که چو ما بندگی سید ما کرد — هر چند گدا بود شه هر دو سرا شد

(1) Where has the sultan of the veiled quarters of [our] tavern gone? Why did he leave the assembly of the drunken [Sufis]?
(2) His essence is here, [even] with his appearance gone; he has not passed into annihilation, he is [just] hidden from sight.
(3) We are the goblet, and [we are] the bubble filled with the water of life; whoever, like us, opts for our company will have their thirst quenched.
(4) [It is] out of his penchant for the beggars of the tavern that the sultan of the veiled quarters of the winehouse, that is, this world, turned a beggar.
(5) When, out of purity, the Sufi drank the dregs of his pain, the dregs became the filter, and the pain medicine.
(6) The companion who, like us, served our Sayyid became the king of the two worlds, even if a beggar.

Appendix 1.1.b. Northern entrance (figs. 1.31 and 1.32):

(1) ما را بغیر او نبود التفات هیچ — زیرا که نیست جز کرم او نجات هیچ
(2) خضر و هوای چشمه و آب حیات و ما — نبود به جز زلال وصالش حیات هیچ
(3) هیچ است این جهان و تو دل را در او مپیچ — وین بند پیچ پیچ مپیچان به پای هیچ
(4) در حضرتی گریز که روحانیان قدس — جز حضرتش دگر نکند التفات هیچ
(5) در عرصه ممالک او هر دو کون پست — با ملک کبریایی اوکاینات هیچ
(6) سید تو جان بباز به عشقش که غیر او — شایسته نیست در دو جهان خونبهات هیچ

(1) Our reverence is only toward him, for there is no salvation except through his mercy.
(2) Without the water of his union, the Prophet Khizr, the desire for the fountain [of immortality], and the water of life all amount to nothing.
(3) This world is nothing, and you should not entangle your heart with it! Do not tie this twisted chain around your feet!
(4) Take refuge with the holiness toward whom all sacred spirits direct their reverence, and nowhere else.
(5) To the realm of his dominions, both worlds are inferior; in comparison to his holy dominion, the universe amounts to nothing.
(6) O sayyid! Sacrifice your life for his love, for he is the only one deserving of your blood in the two worlds.

Appendix 1.2: Foundation inscription at the western portal of the Mahan mausoleum

Appendix 1.2.a. Late sixteenth-century segment added to the beginning of the panel (fig. 1.26):

حضرت سلطنت پناه حشمت معدلت دستگاه و نصفت عظمت و رفعت انتباه

His majesty, the refuge of the kingdom and his servants, the place where justice is exercised, the magnitude of justice and the exalted awakened one.

Appendix 1.2.b. Fifteenth-century section (fig. 0.2):

شهاب الملک و الدنیا و الدین احمد شاه ابوالمغازی به انشاء این گنبد حصین الرکان و بناء این عمارت گردون رفعت عالی بنیان امر فرمود و در زمان دولت فرزند دلبند آنحضرت مغفرت پناه سلطان علاالدوله و الدنیا و الدین احمد شاه اتمام یافت تحریر فی ایام محرم الحرام السنة الاربعین و ثمانمایه

The flame of the kingdom and the world and religion, Ahmad Shah, the father of conquests, ordered the construction of this stable dome and lofty well-founded structure, which was finished during the reign of the beloved son of his majesty, the refuge of forgiveness, Sultan ʿAla al-dawla wa al-din wa al-dunya Ahmad Shah. Written in the month of Muharram of the year 840.

Appendix 1.2.c. Late sixteenth-century segment added to the end of the panel (fig. 1.27):

الهجریة النبویة الهلالیة المصطفویة النبویة المحمد.

[Of the] lunar prophetic hijra of the chosen Prophet Muhammad.

Appendix 1.3: Safavid-era foundation inscription in the dar al-huffaz in Mahan

Appendix 1.3.a. Safavid-era section (figs. 1.16 and 6.12):

در زمان خلافت نواب کامیاب سپهر رکاب شاه جمجاه سلیمان بارگاه سپاه ملایك ابوالظفرعباس پادشاه خلد الله ملکه و سلطانه بولی امر ؟ امارت حضرت پناه دستگاه حکومت و معالی رفعت انتباه بکتاش خان از امارت حضرت پناه اقبال آثار ولی خان افشار باتمام این دار الحفاظ توفیق یافت تحریرا فی شهر شوال سنه ثمان و تسع و تسعمایه.

During the reign of his prosperous highness whose [imperial] stirrups reach the sky, the imperial king, the Solomon of the court of the army of angels, the father of victories, ʿAbbas Padshah, may his dominion and kingdom last for eternity, the executer of the commands of his sovereignty, the refuge of the excellence of his dominion and the highest of the exalted awakened, Bektash Khan, the authority of his highness, vestiges of his relics, Vali Khan Afshar, succeeded at completing this dar al-huffaz. Written in the month of Shawwal of the year 998.

Appendix 1.3.b. Verses in the middle of the Qajar-era segments at the two ends of the panel (fig. 1.28):

بعهد ناصر دین شه ز فیض شاه ولایت   مزار گشت چه جنت بسعی سید هدایت ۱۳۰۰

During the reign of Nasir al-din Shah, from the bounty of the king of the dominion, the shrine turned into a paradise from the efforts of Sayyid Hedayat. [The year] 1300.

Appendix 1.4: Inscribed roundels under the ceiling of the dar al-huffaz in Mahan

Appendix 1.4.a. Middle vaults (figs. 1.17 and 8.1):

عمل بنده درگاه شاهی
کمال الدین بن حسین نعمت اللهی

Work of the servant of the shrine of the Shah,
Kamal al-din b. Hysayn-i Neʿmatullahi

Appendix 1.4.b. Far north:

عمل استاد عبدالسلام کاشی تراش

Work of master ʿAbd al-Salam, the tile-maker

Appendix 1.5: Roundels above the western portal in the shrine at Mahan

Appendix 1.5.a. Fifteenth-century roundel (fig. 1.18):

Top and bottom verses

الله و محمد و علی یاور باد   حفظ ازلی حق نگهدار تو باد

May God, Muhammad, and ʿAli be your companion! May God's eternal protection save you!

Middle verses

در زمان دولت یعقوب سلطان این مزار   نوبت ثانی عمارت یافت بادا برقرار

During the time of Yaʿqub Sultan, this grave was constructed for a second time, may it last.

Appendix 1.5.b. Sixteenth-century roundel (fig. 1.18):

به نهصد ونود و هشت بعد هجرت شد   که باز روضه سید ز نو عمارت شد

[It was] nine hundred and ninety-eight [years] after hijra that the rawza of Sayyid was constructed anew.

Appendix 1.6: Signatures on the western portal of the Mahan mausoleum

Appendix 1.6.a. Middle panels to the left and right of the door (fig. 0.2):

عمل غلام باخلاص شاه ولی
عبد السلام حسن بن علی الهروی

Work of the sincere servant of Shah Vali,
ʿAbd al-Salam Hasan b. ʿAli al-Herawi

Appendix 1.6.b. Side panels from right to left (figs. 1.26 and 1.27):

غلام محبت خاندان آل صفدر شاه نقدی ابن حیدر

Servant of the affection of the family of ʿAli, Shah Naqdi b. Haydar

نذر غلام باخلاص شاه ولي علي ابواغلي

Endowed by the sincere servant of Shah Vali, ʿAli Abu Ughli

Appendix 1.6.c. Corners of narrow band of poetry around the door from right to left (figs. 1.30 and 0.2):

نذر بنده درگاه علي ابواغلي
نمقه قطب الدين محمد ابن حافظ

Endowed by the servant of the shrine, ʿAli Abu Ughli
Written by Qutb al-din Muhammad b. Hafiz

Appendix 3.1: Poetry by Shah Neʿmatullah Vali inscribed in the Taft khanaqah and quoted in his hagiography

(1) نعمة الله را اگر خواهی که مهمانی کنی　　سفره ای گرد جهان سر تا به سر باید کشید
(2) ور به قدر همتش سازی سرای مختصر　　چاردیواری به هفت اقلیم در باید کشید

(1) If you should wish to host Neʿmatullah, the tablecloth must stretch all the way around the sphere of the world.
(2) And if you should build a small palace to match his magnanimity, the four walls must enclose the seven climes.

Appendix 4.1: Chronogram inscriptions on the tombstone of Khalilullah Thani in Taft

Top and bottom lines on one side of the tombstone (fig. 4.2):

(1) شاه برهان دین خلیل الله	کرد از خاکدان چو قطع حیات
(2) سال تاریخ موت او جستم	از دل خویشتن به وقت وفات
(3) گفت چون در هرات گشت شهید	سال فوتش بود شهید هرات

(1) When Shah Burhan al-din Khalilullah's life was disconnected from this world,
(2) at the time of his death I asked my heart after the year of his passing,
(3) [my heart] responded: because he was martyred in Herat, his death year [chronogram] is "the martyr of Herat."

Appendix 4.2: Inscription panel in the dome chamber of the khanaqah at Taft

Line 1 (hadiths) (fig. 4.3):

قال رسول الله صلی الله علیه و آله و سلم احبو الله لما یغذوکم من نعمة فاحبونی لحب لله و احبوا اهل بیتی لحبی قال علیه . . . إن مثل اهل بیتی مثل سفینة نوح من رکبها نجا و من تخلف عنها هلک قال علیه الصلوة و السلم انّ تارک فیکم ما إن تمسکتم

Said the messenger of God, peace be upon him and his family: Love God for what He nourishes you with from His Blessings, love me for the love of God, and love the people of my house for the love of me. Said [the messenger of God] . . . my family is like the Ark of Noah; to ride it is to gain deliverance, to oppose it is to drown in destruction. Said [the messenger of God] peace be upon him and his family: I am leaving among you, as long as you hold on to them.

Lines 2 and 3 (Persian poetry):

(1) ما مظهر نور مصطفائیم	ما منبع سر مرتضائیم
(2) ما فاتحة الکتاب عشقیم	ما آیة کرسی خداییم
(3) ما سر خلیفهٔ زمینیم	ما نور صحیفهٔ سمائیم
(4) ما کاشف معنی کلامیم	ما واصف صورت شمائیم

(1) We are the manifestation of the light of Mustafa; we are the source of the secrets of Murtaza;
(2) We are the opening chapter of love; we are the Throne Verse of God;
(3) We are the secret of the caliph of the earth; we are the light of the celestial book;
(4) We unlock the meaning of the word; we are the praiser of your outward form.

Appendix 5.1: Inscriptions on the loose tablet of Nurullah in Khalilullah's complex near Bidar

(1) سال تاریخش از خرد جستم   گفت هاتف که جنت الفردوس

(2) مقبره شا[ه] نور الله حسینی تیار بود در زمان بریدیان شکستند* بعده اسدالله خان نبیره شاه مذکور از سر نو در عمل محمد شاه بادشاه در سنه ۱۱۵۷ باتمام رسانید[3]

(1) I asked reason after his chronogram, Hatef responded: "jannat al-firdaws."

(2) The mausoleum of Shah Nurullah was standing. They broke it during the reign of Baridian. After that, Asadullah Khan, the descendant of the aforementioned Shah, completed the building from scratch under the name of Muhammad Shah Padshah, in the year 1157.

Appendix 5.2: Inscriptions on the stepwell in Khalilullah's complex near Bidar (fig. 5.26):

(1) بحمدالله که این بائین موزون   مرتب شد بوقت سعد و میمون

(2) ز هجرت بود هیصد سال و پنجه   نهم تاریخ ماه ربّ بیچون

(3) بعهد بادشاه بو المظفر   علا الدین شاه ربع مسکون

(4) شهنشه احمد ابن شاه احمد   که هست از نسل بهمن واز فریدون

(5) بنایش کرد مجموع ممالک   که قدرش برترست از اوج گردون

(6) نصیر ابن علا خانشه که دارد   فضایل بی‌حد و خیرات افزون

(7) قبول حق باد این خیر جاری   بقا بانیش با خلد مقرون

(1) Praise be to God, this delightful baʾin was built in an auspicious and happy time,

(2) the *hijri* year was 850 and it was the 9th of the month of Rajab,

(3) during the reign of the victorious king, ʿAla al-din, the sovereign of the inhabited [quarter of the] world,

(4) the emperor Ahmad, son of King Ahmad, who is the descendant of Bahman and Faridun,

(5) who built whole kingdoms, higher than the Heaven.

(6) Nasir, son of ʿAla Khanshah, who possesses innumerable virtues and whose charity is increasing,

(7) may God accept this flowing (jari) charity and may its builder enter Heaven.

Appendix 5.3: Inscriptions on tile panel from Taft at the National Museum of Iran (fig. 5.33):

قال الله تعالى ان تتوبآ الى الله فقد صغت قلوبكما و إن تظاهرا عليه فإنّ الله هو مولئه و جبريل و
صالح و المومنين و الملئكة بعد ذلك ظهير و قال تعالى واذكر فى الكتاب ادريس انه كان صدّيقا نبيّا
و رفعنه مكاناًعليّاً و قال تعالى جلت آلاؤه و عظمت نعماؤه قوام (؟) اذكروا نعمة الله عليكم اذ جعل
فيكم انبيآء و جعلكم مّلوكا و ءاتيكم مّا لم يؤت احداً مّن قوم العلمين يا قوم ادخلوا الارض المقدّسة الّتى
كتب [الله] لكم صدق الله العظيم قال نبي صلى عليه و آله و سلم إذا تحيرتم في الأمور(؟) فاستعينوا
أهل القبور كتبه محمود فى ٨٧٦

Said God the Almighty: It will be better if you wives both turn to Allah in repentance, for your hearts have certainly faltered. But if you continue to collaborate against him, then know that God himself is his guardian. And Gabriel, the righteous believers, and the angels are all his supporters as well. And said God the Almighty: And mention in the Book, O Prophet, the story of Enoch. He was surely a man of truth and a prophet. And we elevated him to an honorable status. And said God the Almighty: His favors are great and his blessings are innumerable. Remember God's favors upon you when He raised prophets from among you, made you sovereign, and gave you what He had never given anyone in the world. O my people! Enter the Holy Land that God has destined for you to enter. God Almighty has spoken the truth. Said the Prophet peace be upon him and his family: when there is difficulty in your affairs, seek help from the people of the tombs. Written by Mahmud in 876.

Appendix 5.4: Inscriptions on the Mahan carpet fragment with three surviving cartouches (fig. 5.39):

(1) فرش حرم شاه ولی از اعزاز — بنمود تمام مهدی از روی نیاز
(2) گردید رقم ز کلک غیب این تاریخ — . . .

(1) The carpet of Shah Vali's tomb was completed by Mahdi out of supplication and respect.
(2) This chronogram was written by the hidden pen . . .

Appendix 5.5: Inscriptions on the Mahan carpet fragment with four surviving cartouches (fig. 5.38):

(1) در روضه شه ملک صف آرائی کرد — فانوس بجلوه مشق بینایی کرد
(2) . . . . . . تاریخ بیان کرد غنی — قالی بمزار شه جبین سایی کرد

(1) Angels lined up at the shrine of Shah [Neʿmatullah], the lantern learned a lesson in visibility from the splendor [of the shrine]
(2) . . . . . . Ghani stated the date [i.e., chronogram]: the carpet rubbed its forehead to the tomb of the Shah.

Appendix 5.6: Inscriptions on largest fragment of Mahan carpets with ten cartouches (fig. 5.34):

(1) زهی ساحت روضه پاک پر نور   که فرشش سزد پرده دیده خور
(2) گل باغ احسان سلیمان دوران   کزو تازه شد گلشن میرمیران
(3) ابو المهدی آن گوهر بحر تحقیق   باتمام این فرش چون یافت توفیق
(4) بدین روضه انداخت این فرش عالی   چو تاریخ جستم باتمام قالی
(5) ندا امد از غیب تاریخ مرغوب   جناح ملک کن بان فرش جاروب
(6) سنه ۱۰۶۷

(1) How excellent is the pure illuminated threshold of this tomb, its carpet worthy of the sun's pupil.
(2) The flower of the garden of benevolence, Sulayman of [our] time, from whom the flower garden of Mirmiran was freshened,
(3) Abu'l Mahdi, that gem of the sea of truth, having the fortune of finishing this carpet,
(4) spread this excellent carpet in the tomb. When I asked after the date of the carpet's completion,
(5) the coveted date came [through] a voice from the invisible world: The angel's wing is to serve the carpet as a broom.
(6) Year 1067.

Appendix 6.1: Tent band inscription at the tomb of Ahmad Shah I outside Bidar

Appendix 6.1.a. Portions of the tent band on the south wall (fig. 6.10):

(1) غیر معشوقم نیاید در نظر   عاشقان را گر چه خیلی دیده ام
(2) تا محیط دیده بر زد موج عشق   هفت دریا را چو سیلی دیده ام

(1) No one except for the beloved is in my sight; even though I have seen the armies of lovers.
(2) When the wave of love broke into my eye, I saw the seven seas like a flood.

Appendix 6.1.b. Portions of the tent band on the east wall (continued) (fig. 6.5):

(1) نعمت الله یافتم در هر وجود   با همه عشقی و میلی دیده ام[4]
(2) نعمت الله در همه عالم یکیست   لا تجد مثلی و مثلی لا تجد[5]

(1) I found the bounty of God (Neʿmat Allah) in every form of existence, for I have seen love and desire in them all.
(2) Neʿmat Allah is a singular being in the whole universe; you will not find anyone like me, no one like me will be found.

Appendix 6.2: Shah Neʿmatullah's silsilas under the dome of Ahmad Shah's tomb outside Bidar

Appendix 6.2.a. Outer silsila (written as a continuous inscription within the circular band) (fig. 6.11):

نعمة الله الحسینی، عبدالله الیافعی، صالح البربری، کمال الدین الکوفی، ابو فتوح سعیدی، ابو مداین المغربی، ابو سعید الاندلسی، ابو البرکات، ابوالفضل البغدادی، احمد غزالی، ابوبکر نساج، الشیخ ابو القاسم، ابو عثمان المغربی، ابو علی الکاتب، ابو علی رودباری، جنید البغدادی، سری السقطی، معروف الکرخی، داوود الطائی، حبیب العجمی، حسن البصری، علی المرتضی، محمد رسوالله[6]

Neʿmatullah al-Husayni, ʿAbdullah al-Yafiʿi, Salih al-Barbari, Kamal al-din Kufi, Abu Futuh Saʿidi, Abu Madayin al-Maghribi, Abu Saʿid al-Andalusi, Abu'l-Barakat, Abu'l-fazl al-Baghdadi, Ahmad Ghazzali, Abu Bakr Nassaj, al-Shaykh Abu'l-Qasim, Abu ʿUsman al-Maghribi, Abu ʿAli Katib, Abu ʿAli Rudbari, Junayd al-Baghdadi, Sarri al-Saqati, Maʿruf al-Karkhi, Dawud al-Taʾyi, Habib al-ʿAjami, Hasan al-Basri, ʿAli al-Murtaza, Muhammad Messenger of God.

Appendix 6.2.b. Inner silsila (written in arch-shaped cartouches):

نعمة الله الولی، عبدالله الیافعی، ابراهیم المکی، . . . ، احمد الواسطی، محي الدین العربی، یونس الهاشمی، عبدالقادر جیلانی، ابوسعید المخرمی، علی الهکاری، ابوالفرج . . . ، ابوالفضل التمیمی، الشبلی، جنید البغدادی، سری السقطی، معروف الکرخی، داوود الطائی، حبیب العجمی، حسن البصری، علی المرتضی، محمد المصطفی[7]

Neʿmatullah al-Vali, ʿAbdullah al-Yafiʿi, Ibrahim al-Makki, . . . , Ahmad al-Wasiti, Muhiyy al-din al-ʿArabi, Yunis al-Hashimi, ʿAbd al-Qadir Jilani, Abu Saʿid al-Mukhrami, ʿAli al-Hakkari, Abu'l Faraj . . . , Abu'l-Fazl al-Tamimi, Al-Shibli, Junayd al-Baghdadi, Sarri al-Saqati, Maʿruf al-Karkhi, Dawud al-Taʾyi, Habib al-ʿAjami, Hasan al-Basri, ʿAli al-Murtaza, Muhammad al-Mustafa.

Appendix 6.3: Inscriptions on Bektash Khan's tomb in the shrine at Mahan (fig. 6.14):

وفات سلطنت و حکومت پناه جنت مکان فردوس آشیان سعید شهید مغفور الواصل الی بحار رحمه الله الملک الغفار ابن ولی بکتاش خان افشار فی ۱۴ شهر ربیع الاول سنه ۹۹۸[8]

The death of the refuge of dominion and sovereignty, the one whose dwelling is in heaven, the blessed martyr, the one whose sins are forgiven, the one united with the seas of mercy of God, the forgiver of sins, Ibn Vali Bektash Khan Afshar on the 14th of the month Rabiʿ I of the year 998.

Appendix 6.4: Inscriptions on the mihrab stone at the Shah Vali Mosque in Taft (fig. 6.21):

الله اکبر لا اله الا الله محمد رسول الله علی ولی الله قال الله و تبارک وتعالی و تقدس اقم الصلوة لدلوک الشمس إلی غسق الیل و قرءان الفجر انّ قرءان الفجر کان مشهودا و من الیل فتهجّد به نافلة لّک عسی أن یبعثک ربّک مقاماً محموداً صدق الله العظیم قال النبی علیه السلم المصلی یناجي ربّه فی ربیع الثانی سنة ثلاث و سبعین و ثمانمایه

God is great. There is no God but God, Muhammad is His messenger, and ʿAli is the vali of God. Said God, the blessed, the exalted, the sanctified: observe the prayer from the decline of the sun until the darkness of the night and the dawn prayer, for certainly the dawn prayer is witnessed by angels. And rise at the last part of the night, offering additional prayers, so your Lord may raise you to a station of praise. God Almighty has spoken the truth. Said the Prophet peace be upon him: the prayer communes with his Lord. In [the month of] Rabiʿ II of the year 873.

Appendix 6.5: Inscriptions around the wooden door of the Shah Vali Mosque in Taft (fig. 6.23):

اللهم ّصل علی محمد المصطفی و علیّ المرتضی و الحسن الرضی و الحسین الشهید بکربلا و علی زین العابدین و محمد الباقر و جعفر الصادق و موسی الکاظم و علیّ بن موسی الرضا و محمد الجواد و علیّ الهادی و الحسن العسگری و الحجة القایم محمد المهدی صلوات الله و سلامه علیهم و علی اجمعین الهم اللهم وال من والاهم و عاد من عاداهم و انصر من نصرهم و اخذل من خذلهم و ؟ ؟ مقتدر فی شهر شهبان المعظم نوشت این کتابه کمال شهاب به تسع و ثمانین و ثمانمایة

O Allah! Peace be upon Prophet Muhammad, and ʿAli al-Murtaza, and Hasan al-Raza, and Husayn the martyr of Karbala, and ʿAli Zayn al-ʿAbidin, and Muhammad al-Baqir, and Jaʿfar al-Sadiq, and Musa al-Kazim, and ʿAli b. Musa al-Riza, and Muhammad al-Javad, and ʿAli al-Hadi, and al-Hasan al-ʿAsgari, and the hidden Imam Muhammad al-Mahdi, may peace be upon him, and upon them all. O Allah! Befriend who befriends them and be the enemy of who is their enemy, assist who assists them, and disgrace whoever disgraces them. . . . In the greatest of months, Shaʿban, Kamal Shahab wrote this inscription in 889.

Appendix 6.6: Inscriptions on the zilu at the Museum of Anthropology in Taft (fig. 6.24):

وقف مسجد جامع خانقاه علیه نوریه قریه تفت تحریرا فی شهر رمضان المبارک سنة ۹۶۳ عمل شمس قطب الدین میبدی

Endowed to the Jamiʿ mosque of the sublime enlightened khanaqah of the village of Taft. Written in the blessed month of Ramadan of the year 963. Work of Shams Qutb al-din Meybodi.

Appendix 7.1: Inscriptions on the ivans of Nizamuddin Awliya's tomb (figs. 7.5 and 7.6):

در عهد اعلیحضرت صاحبقران ثانی احقر العباد خلیل الله خان ابن میرمیران الحسینی نعمت اللهی
که حاکم شاه جهان آباد بود این ایوان را بر دور روضه متبرکه مرتب نمود
فی سنة ۱۰۶۳

During the reign of his majesty, the second lord of auspicious conjunction, his lowest of servants, Khalilullah Khan b. Mirmiran al-Husayni Neʿmatullahi, who was the governor of Shahjahanabad, constructed this ivan around the blessed tomb in the year 1063.

Appendix 8.1: Signature under muqarnas carvings at the entrance of the recitation hall from the western courtyard in the shrine at Mahan (fig. 8.2):

عمل كمال الدين بن حسين طيان نعمت اللهى

Work of the plaster mason, Kamal al-din b. Husayn-i Neʿmatullahi.

Appendix 8.2: Inscriptions at the entrance of the chelleh khaneh in Mahan

Appendix 8.2.a. Inscriptions inside the large medallion on the right (fig. 8.6):

(1) درگاه الهست درگاه علی درگاه علیست درگه لم یزلی
(2) حق باز کند در رفیع الدرجات از درگه شاه نعمت الله ولی

(1) The dargah of ʿAli is the dargah of God, the eternal dargah is the dargah of ʿAli.
(2) God opens the door to the highest of levels, through the dargah of Shah Neʿmatullah Vali.

Appendix 8.2.b. Signature of the disciple in a roundel to the left of the entrance (fig. 8.7):

عبدالوفای طالبی نعمت اللهی از طالبان حضرت شاه ولی

ʿAbd al-Vafa-yi Talibi-yi Neʿmatullahi, one of the disciples of his majesty Shah Vali.

Appendix 8.3: Inscriptions on the north wall of the chelleh khaneh in Mahan

Appendix 8.3.a. Diagonal inscriptions on the body of the sword (fig. 8.16):

. . .

(1) ذوالفقار علیست تیغ شاه والا — تیغ شاه والا ذوالفقار علیست

(2) ذوالفقار علیست صفدر اندر غزا — صفدر اندر غزا ذوالفقار علیست

. . .

(1) The Zu'lfiqar of ʿAli is the sword of the sublime shah [i.e., Shah Vali], the sword of the sublime shah is the Zu'lfiqar of ʿAli.

(2) The Zu'lfiqar of ʿAli is the most courageous warrior on the battlefield; the most courageous warrior on the battlefield is the Zu'lfiqar of ʿAli.

Appendix 8.3.b. Band of oval cartouches above the largest inscription band (fig. 8.16):

(1) الهی یا الهی یا الهی — کریما یا رحیما یا الهی

(2) کریمی و کرم داری کرم کن — رحیما یا کریما یا الهی

. . .

(3) تو بخشاینده بخشا به بنده — تویی بخشنده بخشا یا الهی

(1) Allah, O' Allah, O' Allah, O' the Merciful, O' the Compassionate, O' Allah.

(2) You are merciful, you have mercy, have mercy on us, O' the Compassionate, O' the Merciful, O' Allah.

. . .

(3) You are bountiful, give bounty to your servants, you are forgiving, forgive O' Allah!

Appendix 8.3.c. Inscriptions around the sword's hilt:

داریم بدست قبضه شاه — این قبضه بکف نگاه داریم

We hold the sword (qabza) of the Shah in our hand; we will hold this hilt (qabza) in the palm of our hand.

Appendix 8.4: Inscriptions on the west wall of the chelleh khaneh in Mahan

Appendix 8.4.a. Underneath the hilt of the sword (fig. 8.19):

(1) این قوت شصت من ز شصت علیست . . .
(2) هستی که مرا هست ز هست علیست   این قبضه بدست من ز دست علیست

(1) This power in my thumb is from the thumb of ʿAli . . .
(2) The existence that I have is from the existence of ʿAli, this sword in my hand is from the hand of ʿAli.

Appendix 8.4.b. Verses on the hilt (fig. 8.19):

با قبضه ذوالفقار همدستانم   با دشمن مرتضی عداوت دارم

I am a companion (ham-dastan) of the hilt of the Zu'lfiqar; I am hostile to the enemy of ʿAli.

Appendix 8.4.c. Verses above the hilt:

همدست بدستم شده شمشیر دوسر   سیف آمده دست یارم از دست علی

The double-headed sword has become the companion (ham-dast) of my hand, this sword (sayf) from the hand of ʿAli has become my helper (dast-yar).

Appendix 8.5: Relevant verses from the *Taj-nama (Book of the Crown)*

Appendix 8.5.a.

تاج سر عارفان آگاه   فرزند رسول نعمت الله

[He is] the crown of the wise gnostics; [He is] the Neʿmat Allah [lit. bounty of God], the offspring of the Prophet.

Appendix 8.5.b.

هر که نهد تاج سر ما بر سر   فارغ شود از دردسر هر دو سرا

Whoever places our crown over their head will be liberated from the troubles of the two worlds.

Appendix 8.5.c.

روح از آن رو که جوهریت و تجرد اوست و از عالم ارواح مجرده است، مغایر بدن است . . . و محتاج نبود به بدن در بقا و قوام، اما از آن وجه که بدن صورت اوست، و مظهر کمالاتش در عالم شهادت:

محتاج بود به صورت خویش خواه شاه است و خواه درویش

Since ruh [i.e., soul] is its [the body's] essence, and is from the realm of the immaterial, it is contrary to the body . . . and does not need the body for its survival and strength. But, since the body is its [outward] form (surat) and the manifestation of its virtues in the realm of visibility (shahadat):
Whether a king or a dervish, one is in need of their [outward] form.

Notes

1. Connell, "The Nimatullahi Sayyids of Taft," 117, 120. For the descendants' family tree under the Mughals see: Connell, "The Nimatullahi Sayyids of Taft," 262.
2. Mufid, *Jamiᶜ-i Mufidi*, III:28–29.
3. With a minor difference in the text, marked by the star, and a different reading of the date as 1195, this inscription is published in Yazdani, *Epigraphia Indica*, 19.
4. This verse and the ones on the south wall are consecutive lines from a ghazal in the *divan* of Shah Neᶜmatullah: Neᶜmatullah Vali, *Divan*, 326–27.
5. This line is from a qitᶜa in: Neᶜmatullah Vali, *Divan*, 604.
6. Except for the name of Salih al-Barbari, my reading is the same as Yazdani's: Yazdani, *Bidar*, 115.
7. Except for the names of Yunis al-Hashimi and Abu Saᶜid al-Khurrami, Yazdani's reading of this silsila is correct: ibid., 115.
8 This inscription is also published in Waziri, *Tarikh-i Kerman*, 609, fn.29; Eisazadeh, "Tak-Negari," 125.

BIBLIOGRAPHY

Abisaab, Rula Jurdi. *Converting Persia: Religion and Power in the Safavid Empire.* London: I. B. Tauris, 2004.

Abouʾi Mehrizi, Muhammadreza. "Muʿarrifi-yi Guldasteh-yi Andisheh: taʾlif-i Maulana Muhammad Amin Vaqari Tabasi Yazdi." *Aʾina-yi Miras* 29, no. 2 (1384 [2005]): 256–62.

———. *Sadat-i Neʿmatullahi Yazd dar ʿasr-i Safavi.* Yazd: Reyhanat al-rasul-i Yazd, 1383 [2004–5].

Abuali, Eyad. "Words Clothed in Light: *Dhikr* (Recollection), Colour and Synaesthesia in Early Kubrawi Sufism." *Iran* 58, no. 2 (2020): 279–92.

ʿAfif, Shams Siraj. *Tarikh-i Firuz Shahi.* Edited by Vilayat Husain. Calcutta: Asiatic Society, 1891.

Afshar, Iraj, ed. *ʿAlam ara-yi Shah Tahmasp.* Tehran: Dunya-yi kitab, 1370 [1991–92].

———. *Yadgarha-yi Yazd: Muʿarrifi-yi abniyi-yi tarikhi wa asar-i bastani.* 2 Vols. Tehran: Anjuman-i asar-i milli, 1969.

———. "Zilū." *Iranian Studies* 25, no. 1–2 (1992): 31–36.

Afushta-yi Natanzi, Mahmud b. Hedayatullah. *Naqawat al-athar fi zikr al-akhyaar dar tarikh-i Safaviyya.* Tehran: ʿilmi wa farhangi, 1994.

Ahmad, Aziz. "The Sufi and Sultan in Pre-Mughal Muslim India." *Der Islam* 38 (1962): 142–53.

Alexander, David. *The Arts of War: Arms and Armour of the 7th to 19th Centuries.* London: Nasser D. Khalili Collection of Islamic Art, 1992.

———. "Dhu'l-faqar and the Legacy of the Prophet: Mirath Rasul Allah." *Gladius* 19 (1999): 157–88.

Alfieri, Bianca Maria. *Islamic Architecture of the Indian Subcontinent.* London: Laurence King, 2000.

Algar, Hamid. "Horufism." *Encyclopaedia Iranica.* Accessed June 3, 2020. https://iranicaonline.org/articles/horufism.

———. "Nakṣẖband." *Encyclopaedia of Islam* (Brill Online). Accessed July 16, 2015. http://referenceworks.brillonline.com/entries/encyclopaedia-of-islam-2/nakshband-SIM_5781.

———. "The Naqshbandī Order: A Preliminary Survey of Its History and Significance." *Studia Islamica* 44 (1976): 123–52.

Algar, Hamid, and J. Burton-Page. "Niʿmat-Allāhiyya." In *Encyclopaedia of Islam*, 2nd ed., edited by P. Bearman, Th. Bianquis, C. E. Bosworth, E. van Donzel, and W. P. Heinrichs. Accessed August 4, 2020. http://dx.doi.org/10.1163/1573-3912_islam_COM_0865.

Allan, James. *The Art and Architecture of Twelver Shi^cism: Iraq, Iran, and the Indian Sub-continent*. London: Azimuth Editions, 2012.

Allen, Terry. *A Catalogue of the Toponyms and Monuments of Timurid Herat*. Cambridge, MA: Aga Khan Program for Islamic Architecture at Harvard University and the Massachusetts Institute of Technology, 1981.

Al-Qushayri, Abu'l-Qasim. *Al-Risala al-Qushayriyah*. Translated by Badiᶜ al-Zaman Furuzanfar. Tehran: Bungah-i Tarjumih wa nashr-i kitab, 1345 [1966].

Al-saleh, Yasmine F. "'Licit Magic': The Touch and Sight of Islamic Talismanic Scrolls." PhD diss., Harvard University, 2015.

Al-Samᶜani, Abu Saᶜd. *Al-ansab*. Vol. 8. Edited by ᶜAbd al-Rahman b. Yahya Muᶜallimi al-Yamani. Hyderabad: Majlis al-daʾirat al-maᶜarif al-Usmaniyya, 1962.

Anderson, Glaire D., and Mariam Rosser-Owen. "Great Ladies and Noble Daughters: Ivories and Women in the Umayyad Court at Córdoba." In *Pearls on a String: Artists, Patrons, and Poets at the Great Islamic Courts*, edited by Amy S. Landau, 28–51. Baltimore: Walters Art Museum and University of Washington Press, 2015.

Anooshahr, Ali. "Shirazi Scholars and the Political Culture of the Sixteenth-Century Indo-Persian World." *Indian Economic and Social History Review* 51, no. 3 (2014): 331–52.

———. *Turkestan and the Rise of Eurasian Empires: A Study of Politics and Invented Traditions*. New York: Oxford University Press, 2018.

Ardabili, Ibn Bazzaz. *Safvat al-Safa*. Edited by Ghulamreza Tabatabaie Majd. Tabriz: Musahhih, 1994.

Ardalan, Nader, and Laleh Bakhtiar. *The Sense of Unity: The Sufi Tradition in Persian Architecture*. 2nd ed. Chicago: ABC International Group, 1999.

Arjomand, Said Amir. *The Shadow of God and the Hidden Imam: Religion, Political Order, and the Societal Change in Shiᶜite Iran from the Beginning to 1890*. Chicago: University of Chicago Press, 1984.

Asher, Catherine. *The New Cambridge History of India: Architecture of Mughal India*. Cambridge: Cambridge University Press, 1992.

Astarabadi (Fereshteh), Muhammad Qasim Hendu Shah. *Tarikh-i Fereshteh*. Vol. 2. Edited by Muhammadreza Nasiri. Tehran: Anjuman-i athar wa mafakhir-i farhangi, 2009.

Aube, Sandra. "In Search of 'Kamāl': Five Monumental Inscriptions From Yazd (Second Half of the Fifteenth Century)." *Eurasian Studies* 13 (2015): 69–91.

Aube, Sandra, Thomas Lorain, and Julio Bendezu-Sarmiento. "The Complex of Gawhar Shad in Herat: New Findings about Its Architecture and Ceramic Tile Decorations." *Iran* 58, no.1 (2020): 62–83.

Aubin, Jean. "De Kūhbanān a Bidar: la famille Niᶜmatullahī." *Studia Iranica* 20, no. 2 (1991): 233–61.

———. *Deux Sayyids de Bam au XVe siècle: contribution a l'histoire de l'Iran Timouride*. Wiesbaden: Akademie der Wissenschaften und der Literatur in Mainz in Kommission bei F. Steiner, 1956.

———. "Le royaume d'Ormuz au debut du XVIe siecle." *Mare Luso-indicum* 2 (1973): 77–179.

———. *Matériaux pour la biographie de Shah Niᶜmatullah Walī Kermani: textes persans*. Tehran: Département d'iranologie de l'Institut franco-iranien, 1956.

Auer, Blain H. *Symbols of Authority in Medieval Islam: History, Religion and Muslim Legitimacy in the Delhi Sultanate*. London: I. B. Tauris, 2012.

Awrangabadi, Shahnavaz Khan. *The Maāṯhir-ul-umarā: Being Biographies of the Muhammadan and Hindu Officers of the Timurid Sovereigns of India from 1500 to about 1780 A.D.* Vol. 1. Translated by Henry Beveridge. Patna: Janaki Prakashan, 1979.

Babaie, Sussan. *Isfahan and Its Palaces: Statecraft, Shiʿism and the Architecture of Conviviality in Early Modern Iran*. Edinburgh: Edinburgh University Press, 2008.

———. "Qavam Al-Din Shirazi." In *The Great Builders*, edited by Kenneth Powell, 29–33. London: Thames and Hudson, 2011.

———. "Sacred Sites of Kingship: The *Maydan* and Mapping the Spatial-Spiritual Vision of the Empire in Safavid Iran." In *Persian Kingship and Architecture: Strategies of Power in Iran from the Achaemenids to the Pahlavis*, edited by Susan Babaie and Talinn Grigor, 174–217. London: I. B. Tauris, 2015.

Babaie, Sussan, Kathryn Babayan, Ina Baghdiantz-McCabe, and Massumeh Farhad. *Slaves of the Shah: New Elites of Safavid Iran*. London: I. B. Tauris, 2004.

Babayan, Kathryn. "The Cosmological Order of Things in Early Modern Safavid Iran." In *Falnama: The Book of Omens*, edited by Massumeh Farhad and Serpil Bagci, 245–54. Washington, DC: Freer Gallery of Art and the Arthur M. Sackler Gallery, 2009.

———. "The Isfahani Era of Absolutism: 1590 to 1666." In *Mystics, Monarchs and Messiahs: Cultural Landscapes of Early Modern Iran*, edited by Kathryn Babayan, 349–402. Cambridge, MA: Harvard University Center for Middle Eastern Studies, 2003.

———. *Mystics, Monarchs, and Messiahs: Cultural Landscapes of Early Modern Iran*. Cambridge, MA: Harvard University Press, 2002.

Baker, Patricia L. "Safavid Carpets and Nineteenth-Century European Notions." In *Safavid Art and Architecture*, edited by Sheila R. Canby, 77–82. London: Trustees of the British Museum, 2002.

Baloch, N. A. "Kalmati Tombs in Sindh and Balochistan." *Pakistan Archaeology* 26 (1991): 243–56.

Bashir, Shahzad. *Messianic Hopes and Mystical Visions: The Nūrbakhshīya between Medieval and Modern Islam*. Columbia: University of South Carolina Press, 2003.

———. "The Origins and Rhetorical Evolution of the Term Qizilbāsh in Persianate Literature." *Journal of the Economic and Social History of the Orient* 57, no. 3 (2014): 364–91.

———. *Sufi Bodies: Religion and Society in Medieval Islam*. New York: Columbia University Press, 2011.

Beattie, May. *Carpets of Central Persia, with Special Reference to Rugs of Kirman*. London: World of Islam Festival, 1976.

Behbahani, Muhammad Ali. *Risala-yi khayratiyah: dar ibtal-i tariqa-yi sufiya*. Vol. 1. Qum: Ansariyab, 1991.

Berlekamp, Persis. "Symmetry, Sympathy, and Sensation: Talismanic Efficacy and Slippery Iconographies in Early Thirteenth-Century Iraq, Syria, and Anatolia." *Representations* 133 (2016): 59–109.

Bier, Carol, ed. *Woven from the Soul, Spun from the Heart: Textile Arts of Safavid and Qajar Iran, 16th–19th Centuries*. Washington, DC: Textile Museum, 1987.

Binbaş, İlker Evrim. "The Anatomy of a Regicide Attempt: Shāhrukh, the Ḥurūfīs, and the Timurid Intellectuals in 830/1426–27." *Journal of the Royal Asiatic Society* 23, no. 3 (2013): 391–428.

———. *Intellectual Networks in Timurid Iran: Sharaf al-Dīn ʿAlī Yazdī and the Islamicate Republic of Letters*. Cambridge: Cambridge University Press, 2016.

———. "Sharaf al-Dīn ʿAlī Yazdī (ca. 770s–858/ca. 1370s–1454): Prophecy, Politics, and Historiography in Late Medieval Islamic History." PhD diss., University of Chicago, 2009.

Blair, Sheila. "The Ardabil Carpets in Context." In *Society and Culture in the Early Modern Middle East, Studies on Iran in the Safavid Period*, edited by Andrew Newman, 125–43. Boston: Brill, 2003.

———. "Epigraphy iii. Arabic Inscriptions in Persia." *Encyclopaedia Iranica*. Accessed January 17, 2021. https://iranicaonline.org/articles/epigraphy-iii.

———. *The Ilkhanid Shrine Complex at Natanz, Iran*. Cambridge, MA: Center for Middle Eastern Studies, Harvard University, 1986.

———. *Islamic Calligraphy*. Edinburgh: Edinburgh University Press, 2008.

———. *Text and Image in Medieval Persian Art*. Edinburgh: Edinburgh University Press, 2014.

———. "Texts, Inscriptions, and the Ardabil Carpets." In *Iran and Iranian Studies: Essays in Honor of Iraj Afshar*, edited by Kambiz Eslami, 137–47. Princeton, NJ: Zagros, 1998.

Blair, Sheila, and Jonathan Bloom. *The Art and Architecture of Islam: 1250–1800*. New Haven, CT: Yale University Press, 1995.

Blake, Stephen. *Time in Early Modern Islam: Calendar, Ceremony, and Chronology in the Safavid, Mughal and Ottoman Empires*. Cambridge: Cambridge University Press, 2013.

Blochet, Edgar. *Catalogue des manuscrits persans de la bibliothèque nationale*. Vol. 2. Paris: E. Leroux, 1912.

Böwering, Gerhard, and Matthew Melvin-Koushki. "K̲ĀNAQĀH." *Encyclopaedia Iranica*. Accessed on January 2, 2022. https://www.iranicaonline.org/articles/kanaqah.

Bursi, Adam. "Scents of Space: Early Islamic Pilgrimage, Perfume, and Paradise." *Arabica* 67 (2020): 200–34.

Bush, Olga. *Reframing the Alhambra: Architecture, Poetry, Textiles and Court Ceremonial*. Edinburgh: Edinburgh University Press, 2018.

Bynum, Caroline Walker. *Christian Materiality: An Essay on Religion in Late Medieval Europe*. New York: Zone, 2015.

Carey, Moya. *Persian Art: Collecting the Arts of Iran for the V&A*. London: V&A, 2018.

Chardin, Sir John. *Voyages du chevalier Chardin en Perse, et autres lieux d'orient*. Vol. 7. Edited by L. Langlès. Paris: Le Normant, 1811.

Chattopadhyay, Swati. "Architectural History or a Geography of Small Spaces." *Journal of the Society of Architectural Historians* 81, no. 1 (2022): 5–20.

Chekhab-Abudaya, Mounia, and Cécile Bresc. *Hajj—The Journey through Art*. Doha: Museum of Islamic Art, 2013.

Collins, Jeffrey, Elizabeth Fraser, Elizabeth Mansfield, Amelia Rauser, Kristel Smentek, Wendy Bellion, Paris Spies-Gans, Nancy Um, and Amy Freund. "Reflections on HECAA at 25: A Roundtable Discussion." *Journal18* 9 (Spring 2020). https://www.journal18.org/4933.

Connell, Michael Paul. "The Nimatullahi Sayyids of Taft: A Study of the Evolution of a Late Medieval Iranian Sufi Tariqah." PhD diss., Harvard University, 2004.

Curry, John W. *The Transformation of Muslim Mystical Thought in the Ottoman Empire: The Rise of the Halveti Order, 1350–1650*. Edinburgh: Edinburgh University Press, 2010.

Dadlani, Chanchal. *From Stone to Paper: Architecture as History in the Later Mughal Empire*. New Haven, CT: Yale University Press, 2018.
Daneshvari, Abbas. *Medieval Tomb Towers of Iran: An Iconographic Study*. Lexington, KY: Mazda, 1986.
Dekkiche, Malika. "New Source, New Debate: Re-evaluation of the Mamluk-Timurid Struggle for Religious Supremacy in the Hijaz (Paris, BnF MS ar. 4440)." *Mamlūk Studies Review* XVIII (2015): 247–71.
Dervišević, Haris. "Sarajevska kermanska halija (tepih) iz Mahana." *Prilozi za orijentalnu filologiju* 65 (2015): 275–93.
Desai, Ziauddin. "Sahm-i hunarmandan-i Irani dar khattati-yi Islami-yi Hend." Translated by Mohsen Shujaʿ Khani. *Kitab-i mah-i Hunar* (2004): 130–39.
DeWeese, Devin. "The Eclipse of the Kubraviyah in Central Asia." *Iranian Studies* 21, no. 1–2 (1988): 45–83.
———. "Yasavī Šayhs in the Timurid Era: Notes on the Social and Political Role of Communal Sufi Affiliations in the 14th and 15th Centuries." *Oriente Moderno* 15 (76), no. 2 (January 1, 1996): 173–88.
Diamond, Debra. *Yoga: The Art of Transformation*. Washington, DC: Arthur M. Sackler Gallery, Smithsonian Institution, 2013.
Digby, Simon. "The Sufi Shaykh and the Sultan: A Conflict of Claims to Authority in Medieval India." *Iran* 28 (1990): 71–81.
Dunlop, Anne, ed. *The Mongol Empire in Global History and Art History*. Cambridge, MA: Harvard University Press, 2023.
Eaton, Richard. "From Bidar to Timbuktu: Views from the Edge of the 15th Century Muslim World." *Medieval History Journal* 14, no.1 (2011–14): 1–20.
———. *A Social History of the Deccan, 1300–1761: Eight Indian Lives*. Cambridge: Cambridge University Press, 2008.
Eaton, Richard Maxwell, and Phillip B. Wagoner. *Power, Memory, Architecture: Contested Sites on India's Deccan Plateau, 1300–1600*. New Delhi: Oxford University Press, 2014.
Eisazadeh, Negin. "Tak-negari-yi majmuʿih Shah Neʿmatullah-i Vali dar Mahan." MA diss., Shahid Beheshti University, 2010.
Ekhtiar, Maryam. "Ahl al-Bayt Imagery Revisited: A Drawing by Ismaʿil Jalayir at the Metropolitan Museum of Art." In *Revealing the Unseen: New Perspectives on Qajar Art*, edited by Gwenaëlle Fellinger, 80–93. London: Gingko, 2021.
———. "Exploring Ahl al-Bayt Imagery in Qajar Iran (1785–1925)." In *People of the Prophet's House: Artistic and Ritual Expressions of Shiʿi Islam*, edited by Fahmida Suleman, 146–54. London: Azimuth Editions, 2015.
Ekhtiar, Maryam, and Rachel Parikh. "Power and Piety: Islamic Talismans on the Battlefield." In *Islamicate Occult Sciences in Theory and Practice*, edited by Liana Saif, Francesca Leoni, Matthew Melvin-Koushki, and Farouk Yahya, 420–53. Boston: Brill, 2021.
Elias, Jamal. "Throne of God." In *Encyclopedia of the Qurʾān*, edited by Jane Dammen McAuliffe. Washington, DC: Georgetown University.
Emami, Farshid. *Isfahan: Architecture and Urban Experience in Early Modern Iran*. University Park: Pennsylvania State University Press, 2024.
———. "Royal Assemblies and Imperial Libraries: Polygonal Pavilions and Their Functions in Mughal and Safavid Architecture." *South Asian Studies* 35, no. 1 (2019): 63–81.
Erdmann, Kurt. *Seven Hundred Years of Oriental Carpets*. Berkeley: University of California Press, 1970.

Ergin, Nina. "The Fragrance of the Divine: Ottoman Incense Burners and Their Context." *Art Bulletin* 96, no.1 (2014): 70–97.

———. "Rock Faces, Opium and Wine: Speculations on the Original Viewing Context of Persianate Manuscripts." *Der Islam* 90 (2013): 65–105.

Ernst, Carl. *Eternal Garden: Mysticism, History and Politics at a South Asian Sufi Center.* Albany: State University of New York Press, 1992.

———. "Khuldabad: Dargahs of Shaykh Burhanuddin Gharib and Shaykh Zaynuddin Shirazi." In *Dargahs: Abodes of the Saints*, edited by Mumtaz Currim and George Michell, 104–19. Bombay: Marg, 2004.

———. "Situating Sufism and Yoga." *Journal of the Royal Asiatic Society* 15, no. 1 (2005): 15–43.

———. "The Spirit of Islamic Calligraphy: Bābā Shāh Iṣfahānī's Ādāb al-mashq." *Journal of the American Oriental Society* 112, no. 2 (1992): 279–86.

———. "Sufism and the Aesthetics of Penmanship in Sirāj Al-Shīrāzī's 'Tuḥfat Al-Muḥibbīn' (1454)." *Journal of the American Oriental Society* 129, no. 3 (2009): 431–42.

Ettinghausen, Richard. "Arabic Epigraphy: Communication or Symbolic Affirmation." In *Near Eastern Numismatics, Iconography, Epigraphy & History: Studies in Honor of George C. Miles*, edited by Dickran Kouymjian, 297–317. Beirut: American University of Beirut, 1974.

Farhad, Massumeh, and Simon Rettig. *The Art of the Qur'an: Treasures from the Museum of Turkish and Islamic Arts.* Washington, DC: Arthur M. Sackler Gallery, Smithsonian Institution, 2016.

Farhat, May. "Islamic Piety and Dynastic Legitimacy: The Case of the Shrine of Ali Al-Rida in Mashhad (10th–17th Century)." PhD diss., Harvard University, 2002.

Felek, Özgen. "Fears, Hopes, and Dreams: The Talismanic Shirts of Murād III." *Arabica* 64 (2017): 647–72.

Firouzeh, Peyvand. "Architecture, Sanctity, and Power: Neʿmatullahi Shrines and Khanaqahs in Fifteenth-Century Iran and India." PhD diss., University of Cambridge, 2016.

———. "Between the Spiritual and Material: The Niʿmat Allāhī Order's Institutionalisation and Architectural Patronage in the 9th/15th Century." In *Shiʿi Islam and Sufism: Classical Views and Modern Perspectives*, edited by Denis Hermann and Mathieu Terrier, 123–56. London: Bloomsbury, 2019.

———. "Ritual Personification, Performative Allusion: The Mahan Carpet Fragments between Architecture and the Body." In *Meaning in Islamic Art: Studies in Honour of Bernard O'Kane*, edited by Heba Mostafa. Edinburgh: Edinburgh University Press, forthcoming.

———. "Sacred Kingship in the Garden of Poetry: Aḥmad Shāh Bahmanī's Tomb in Bidar (India)." In *Divine Intervention: The Role of Religion and Ritual in South Asian Visual Culture*, special volume of *South Asian Studies*, edited by Rachel Parikh and Imma Ramos, 187–214. London: Taylor and Francis, 2015.

Flatt, Emma J. *The Courts of the Deccan Sultanates: Living Well in the Persian Cosmopolis.* Cambridge: Cambridge University Press, 2019.

Flood, Finbarr Barry. "Bodies and Becoming: Mimesis, Mediation and the Ingestion of the Sacred in Christianity and Islam." In *Sensational Religion: Sensory Cultures in Material Practice*, edited by Sally M. Promey, 459–94. New Haven, CT: Yale University Press, 2014.

———. "Bodies, Books, and Buildings: Economies of Ornament in Juridical Islam." In *Clothing Sacred Scriptures: Book Art and Book Religion in Christian, Islamic, and Jewish Culture*, edited by David Ganz and Barbara Schellewald, 49–68. Berlin: De Gruyter, 2019.

———. "From the Prophet to Postmodernism? New World Orders and the End of Islamic Art." In *Making Art History: A Changing Discipline and Its Institutions*, edited by Elizabeth Mansfield, 31–53. London: Routledge, 2007.

———. "Image against Nature: Spolia as Apotropaia in Byzantium and the Dar al-Islam." *Medieval History Journal* 9, no. 1 (2006): 143–66.

———. "The Ka'ba Orientations: Readings in Islam's Ancient House, by Simon O'Meara; Islam and the Devotional Object: Seeing Religion in Egypt and Syria, by Richard J. A. McGregor; and Hajj and the Arts of Pilgrimage, by Qaisra M. Khan." *Art Bulletin* 105, no. 2 (2023): 143–53.

———. *Objects of Translation: Material Culture and Medieval "Hindu-Muslim" Encounter.* Princeton, NJ: Princeton University Press, 2009.

———. *Technologies de dévotion dans les arts de L'islam: Pèlerins, Reliques, Copies.* Paris: Hazan, 2019.

Gavan, Khvajah ʿImad al-din Mahmud. *Riyaz al-Insha'*. Edited by Chand ibn Husain. Haidarbad: Dar al-Tibb'i Sarkar-i Ali, 1948.

Ghelichkhani, Hamidreza. *Daramadi bar khushnivisi-yi Irani.* Tehran: Farhang-i muʿasir, 2013.

Göloğlu, Sabiha. "Depicting the Islamic Holy Sites: Mecca, Medina, and Jerusalem in Late Ottoman Illustrated Prayer Books." In *Proceedings of* the *15th International Congress of Turkish Art*, edited by Michele Bernardini, Alessandro Taddei, and Michael Douglas Sheridan, 323–38. Ankara: Republic of Turkey Ministry of Culture and Tourism, 2018.

Golombek, Lisa. "The Chronology of Turbat-i Shaikh Jām." *Iran* 9 (1971): 27–44.

———. "The 'Citadel, Town, Suburbs' Model and Medieval Kirman." In *City in the Islamic World*, edited by Salma Khadra Jayyusi, Renata Holod, Antillio Petruccioli, and André Raymond, 445–63. Leiden: Brill, 2008.

———. "Discourses of an Imaginary Arts Council in Fifteenth-Century Iran." In *Timurid Art and Culture: Iran and Central Asia in the Fifteenth Century*, edited by Lisa Golombek and Maria Subtelny, 1–17. Leiden: Brill, 1992.

———. "The Draped Universe of Islam." In *Content and Context of Visual Arts in the Islamic World*, edited by Priscilla Soucek, 25–49. University Park: Pennsylvania State University Press, 1988.

Golombek, Lisa, and Donald Wilber. *The Timurid Architecture of Iran and Turan.* Princeton, NJ: Princeton University Press, 1988.

Graham, Terry. "The Niʿmatullāhī Order under Safavid Suppression and in Indian Exile." In *The Legacy of Mediæval Persian Sufism; Late Classical Persianate Sufism (1501–1750)*, edited by Leonard Lewisohn and David Morgan, vol. 3, 165–200. Oxford: Oneworld, 1999.

Green, Nile. "Auspicious Foundations: The Patronage of Sufi Institutions in the Late Mughal and Early Asaf Jah Deccan." *South Asian Studies* 20, no. 1 (2004): 71–98.

———. *Making Space: Sufis and Settlers in Early Modern India.* Oxford: Oxford University Press, 2012.

———. "Migrant Sufis and Sacred Space in South Asian Islam." *Contemporary South Asia* 12, no. 4 (2003): 493–509.

———. *Sufism: A Global History.* Malden, MA: Wiley-Blackwell, 2012.

Gross, Jo-Ann. "The Economic Status of a Timurid Sufi Shaykh: A Matter of Conflict or Perception?" *Iranian Studies* 21, no. 1/2 (1988): 84–104.

Gruber, Christiane. "'Go Wherever You Wish, for Verily You Are Well Protected': Seal Designs in Late Ottoman Amulet Scrolls and Prayer Books." In *Visions of Enchantment: Occultism, Magic and Visual Culture*, edited by Daniel Zamani and Judith Noble, 23–35. Lopen: Fulgur, 2019.

———. "Power and Protection: Late Ottoman Seal Designs." *Hadeeth al-Dar* 38 (2012): 2–6.

———. *The Praiseworthy One: The Prophet Muhammad in Islamic Texts and Images*. Bloomington: Indiana University Press, 2018.

———. "The Rose of the Prophet: Floral Metaphors in Late Ottoman Devotional Art." In *Envisioning Islamic Art and Architecture: Essays in Honor of Renata Holod*, edited by David Roxburgh, 223–49. Leiden: Brill, 2014.

Günther, Sebastian. "The Poetics of Islamic Eschatology: Narrative, Personification, and Colors in Muslim Discourse." In *Roads to Paradise: Eschatology and Concepts of the Hereafter in Islam*, edited by Sebastian Günther and Todd Lawson, 181–217. Leiden: Brill, 2017.

Gupta, Vivek. "Interpreting the Eye (ʿain): Poetry and Painting in the Shrine of Aḥmad Shāh al-Walī al-Bahmanī (r. 1422–1436)." *Archives of Asian Art* 67, no. 2 (2017): 189–208.

Habibi, ʿAbd al-Hayy. *Hunar-i ʿahd-i Teymuriyan va mutifarriʿat-i an*. Tehran: Bunyad-i Farhang-i Iran, 1976.

Haidar, Navina Najat, and Marika Sardar, eds. *Sultans of Deccan India, 1500–1700: Opulence and Fantasy*. New York: Metropolitan Museum of Art, 2015.

———.*Sultans of the South: Arts of India's Deccan Courts, 1323–1687*. New York: Metropolitan Museum of Art; Yale University Press, 2011.

Haneda, Masashi. "Emigration of Iranian Elites to India during the 16–18th Centuries." *Cahiers d'Asie central* 3/4 (1997): 129–43.

Hasan, Maulvi Zafar. *A Guide to Nizamu-d Din*. Calcutta: Superintendent Government Printing, 1922.

Hasheminezhad, ʿAlireza. "Muʿarrifi-yi yiki az qadimitarin katibeh-ha bi khatt-i nastaʿliq." *Mutaleaʿt-i Irani* 7 (2005): 245–58.

Hillenbrand, Robert. *Islamic Architecture*. Edinburgh: Edinburgh University Press, 2000.

———. *Studies in Medieval Islamic Architecture*. 2 Vols. London: Pindar, 2006.

Hofer, Nathan. "On the Material and Social Conditions of Khalwa in Medieval Sufism." *MAVCOR* 6, no. 2 (2022). https://doi.org/10.22332/mav.ess.2022.2.

Holod-Tretiak, Renata. "The Monuments of Yazd, 1300–1450: Architecture, Patronage and Setting." PhD diss., Harvard University, 1973.

Housego, Jenny. "Kirman: A Contemporary View—with Notes on the Nematollah Shrine at Mahan." In *Carpets of Central Persia, with Special Reference to Rugs of Kirman: Proceedings of the Colloquium Held in Conjunction with the Exhibition, 9th–11th April 1976*, edited by May Beattie, 13–17. Sheffield: Sheffield City Art Galleries, 1978.

Husayni Naʾini, Muhammad Jaʿfar b. Muhammad. *Jamiʿ Jaʿfari*. Edited by Iraj Afshar. Tehran: Anjuman-i athar-i melli, 1353 [1974–75].

Hutton, Deborah. *Art of the Court of Bijapur*. Bloomington: Indiana University Press, 2006.

İşli, Necdet. *Ottoman Headgears*. Istanbul: Ebru, 2009.

ʿIsami, ʿAbd Al-Malik. *Futuh al-Salatin*. Edited by Mahdi Husain. London: Asia, 1967.

Jacobsen, Knut. "Pilgrimage Space, Hinduization of Space, Hindutva Politics of Space, and the Case of Ayodhyā as a Religious and Religiopolitical Hotspot." *Numen* 70, no. 1 (2023): 95–112.

Jaʿfari, Jaʿfar b. Muhammad b. Hasan. *Tarikh-i Yazd*. Edited by Iraj Afshar. Tehran: Bungah-i tarjumih va nashr-i kitab, 1338 [1959].

Jahangir. *The Tuzuk-i-Jahangiri: or, Memoirs of Jahangir.* Vol. 1. Edited by Henry Beveridge and translated by Alexander Roger. Project Gutenberg, 2016.

Johns, Jeremy. "Arabic Inscriptions in the Cappella Palatina: Performativity, Audience, Legibility, and Illegibility." In *Viewing Inscriptions in the Late Antique and Medieval World*, edited by Antony Eastmond, 124–47. Cambridge: Cambridge University Press, 2019.

Jowzjani, Abu ʿUmar Minhajj al-din ʿUsman b. Siraj al-din. *Tabaqat-i Nasiri.* Edited by Mawlawi Khadim Hosain, Mawlawi Abd al-Hayy, and W. Nassau Lees. Calcutta: College Press, 1864.

Junabadi, Mirza Beg b. Hasan. *Rawzat al-Safaviyya*. Edited by Ghulamreza Majd Tabatabayi. Tehran: Bunyad-i mawqufat-i Mahmud Afshar, 1999.

Juneja, Monica. *Can Art History Be Made Global?: Meditations from the Periphery.* Berlin: De Gruyter, 2023.

Karamustafa, Ahmet. *God's Unruly Friends: Dervish Groups in the Islamic Later Middle Period, 1200–1550*. Oxford: Oneworld, 2012.

Katib, Ahmad b. Husayn. *Tarikh-i jadid-i Yazd*. Tehran: Bahman, 1978.

Keshani, Hussein. "Building Nizamuddin: A Delhi Sultanate Dargah and Its Surrounding Buildings." MA diss., University of Manitoba, 1992.

Khalidi, Omar. "Sacred Spaces and Objects of Popular Muslim Devotion, Practices and Festivals." In *The Visual World of Muslim India: The Art, Culture and Society of the Deccan in the Early Modern Era*, edited by Laura Emilia Parodi, 319–36. London: I. B. Tauris, 2012.

Khan, ʿInayat. *Shah Jahannamah*. Edited and translated by W. E. Begley and Z. A. Desi. Delhi: Oxford University Press, 1990.

Khan, Sayyid Ahmad, and R Nath. *Monuments of Delhi: Architectural & Historical.* Calcutta: A. Mukherjee, 1948.

Khan, Yusuf Husain. *Faramin wa Asnad-i Salatin-i Deccan*. Hyderabad: State Archives, Government of Andhra Pradesh, 1963.

Khaziʿin, Muhammad-Taqi. "Waqfnama-yi Khanish Begum." In *Yadnama-yi ustad Karim-i Pirniya*, edited by Akbar Qalamsiyah, 498–508. Yazd: Bunyad-i marhum Pirniya, 1997.

Khwandamir, Ghiyath al-din. *Tarikh-i habib al-siyar.* Vol. 4. Edited by Jalal al-din Humaʾi. Tehran: Kitabkhanah-yi Khayam 1333 [1954].

Kinberg, Leah. "Paradise." In *Encyclopaedia of the Qurʾān*, edited by Jane Dammen McAuliffe. Washington DC: Georgetown University.

Knobloch, Edgar. *The Architecture and Archaeology of Afghanistan*. Charleston, SC: Tempus, 2002.

Koch, Ebba. "Shah Jahan's Visits to Delhi Prior to 1648: New Evidence of Ritual Movement in Urban Mughal India." *Environmental Design: Journal of the Islamic Environmental Design Research Centre* 1, no. 2 (1991): 18–29.

Krautheimer, Richard. "Introduction to an 'Iconography of Mediaeval Architecture.'" *Journal of the Warburg and Courtauld Institutes* 5 (1942): 1–33.

Kugle, Scott Alan. *Sufis & Saints' Bodies: Mysticism, Corporeality & Sacred Power in Islam*. Chapel Hill: University of North Carolina Press, 2007.

Lambton, Ann K. "The Office of Kalantar under the Safawids and Afshars." In *Mélanges d'orientalisme offerts à Henri Massé*, 206–18. Tehran: University of Tehran, 1963.

Leisten, Thomas. "Between Orthodoxy and Exegesis: Some Aspects of Attitudes in the Shariᶜa toward Funerary Architecture." *Muqarnas* 7 (1990): 12–22.

Lentz, Thomas W. "Dynastic Imagery in Early Timurid Wall Painting." *Muqarnas* 10 (1993): 253–65.

Leoni, Francesca, ed. *Power and Protection: Islamic Art and the Supernatural.* Oxford: Ashmolean Museum, 2016.

Lewisohn, Leonard. "An Introduction to the History of Modern Persian Sufism, Part I: The Niᶜmatullāhī Order: Persecution, Revival and Schism." *Bulletin of the School of Oriental and African Studies* 61, no. 3 (1998): 437–64.

Lifchez, Raymond. "The Lodges of Istanbul." In *The Dervish Lodge: Architecture, Art, and Sufism in Ottoman Turkey*, edited by Raymond Lifchez, 209–53. Berkeley: University of California Press, 1992.

Losensky, Paul. "The Palace of Praise and the Melons of Time: Descriptive Patterns in Abdi Bayk Shirazi's Garden of Eden." *Eurasian Studies* 2, no. 1 (2003): 1–29.

———. "Qitᶜa." In *The Princeton Encyclopedia of Poetry and Poetics*, edited by Roland Greene, Stephen Cushman, Clare Cavanagh, Jahan Ramazani, and Paul Rouzer, 1136–37. Princeton, NJ: Princeton University Press, 2012.

Loth, Otto. *A Catalogue of the Arabic Manuscripts in the Library of the India Office*. Vol. 1. London: Print, by order of the Secretary of State for India in Council, 1877.

Lowe, Lisa. *The Intimacies of Four Continents*. Durham, NC: Duke University Press, 2015.

Mahendrarajah, Shivan. "A Revised History of Mongol, Kart, and Timurid Patronage of the Shrine of Shaykh Al-Islam Ahmad-i Jam." *Iran* 54, no. 2 (2016): 107–28.

Mancini-Lander, Derek. "Memory on the Boundaries of Empire: Narrating Place in the Early Modern Local Historiography of Yazd." PhD diss., University of Michigan, 2012.

———. "Tales Bent Backward: Early Modern Local History in Persianate Transregional Contexts." *Journal of the Royal Asiatic Society* 28, no. 1 (2018): 23–54.

Manz, Beatrice Forbes. *Power, Politics and Religion in Timurid Iran*. Cambridge: Cambridge University Press, 2007.

Mardomi, Karim, and Mohsen Dehghani Tafti. "Baztab-i sayr-i muwajiha ba tasawwuf-i Neᶜmatullahi dar miᶜmari-yi majmuᶜi-yi khanaqahi-ziyaratgahi-yi Shah Vali-yi Taft." *Pajuhish-ha-yi miᶜmari-yi Islami* 1, no. 1 (1392 [2014]): 139–58.

Mardomi, K., M. Noghsanmohammadi, and M. Dehghani Tafti. "An Inquiry in Historical Evolution and Retrieval of the Process of Formation and Transformation of Shah Wali Complex, Taft, Iran." *International Journal of Architectural Engineering and Urban Planning* 23, no. 2 (2013): 92–102.

Mashizi, Mir Muhammad Saᶜid. *Tazkira-yi Safaviyya-yi Kerman*. Edited by Muhammad Bastani Parizi. Tehran: ᶜIlm, 1990.

Matthee, Rudi. "Loyalty, Betrayal and Retribution: Biktash Khan, Yaᶜqub Khan and Shah ᶜAbbas I's Strategy in Establishing Control over Kirman, Yazd and Fars." In *Ferdowsi, the Mongols and the History of Iran: Art, Literature and Culture from Early Islam to Qajar Persia: Studies in the Honour of Charles Melville*, edited by Robert Hillenbrand, Andrew Peacock, and Firuza Abdullaeva, 184–200. London: I. B. Tauris, 2013.

———. *The Pursuit of Pleasure: Drugs and Stimulants in Iranian History, 1500–1900.* Princeton, NJ: Princeton University Press, 2011.
McChesney, Robert. *Central Asia: Foundations of Change*. Princeton, NJ: Darwin, 1996.
———. *Waqf in Central Asia: Four Hundred Years in the History of a Muslim Shrine, 1480–1889*. Princeton, NJ: Princeton University Press, 1991.
Melville, Charles. "From Qars to Qandahar: The Itineraries of Shah ʿAbbas I (995–1038/1587–1629)." In *Études Safavides*, edited by Jean Calmard, 195–224. Tehran: IFRI, 1993.
———. "History and Myth: The Persianisation of Ghazan Khan." In *Irano-Turkic Cultural Contacts in the 11th–17th Centuries*, edited by Éva M Jeremiás, 133–60. Piliscaba: Avicenna Institute of Middle Eastern Studies, 2003.
———. "Shah ʿAbbas's Patronage of the Dynastic Shrine at Ardabil." *Muqarnas* 37, no. 1 (2020): 111–38.
Melvin-Koushki, Matthew. "Early Modern Islamicate Empire: New Forms of Religiopolitical Legitimacy." In *The Wiley Blackwell History of Islam*, edited by Armando Salvatore, Roberto Tottoli, and Babak Rahimi, 351–75. Hoboken, NJ: Wiley, 2018.
———. "In Defense of Geomancy: Šaraf al-Dīn Yazdī Rebuts Ibn H̱aldūn's Critique of the Occult Sciences." *Arabica* 64, no. 3–4 (2017–19): 346–403.
———. "Powers of One: The Mathematicalization of the Occult Sciences in the High Persianate Tradition." *Intellectual History of the Islamicate World* 5, no. 1–2 (2017): 127–99.
Merklinger, Elizabeth. *Indian Islamic Architecture: The Deccan 1347–1686*. Warminster: Aris & Phillips, 1981.
———. "The *Madrasa* of Maḥmūd Gāwān in Bīdar." *Kunst Des Orients* 11, no. 1/2 (1976/1977): 145–57.
———. "Seven Tombs at Holkonda: A Preliminary Survey." *Kunst Des Orients* 10, no. 1/2 (1975): 187–97.
Michell, George, and Helen Philon. *Islamic Architecture of Deccan India*. Woodbridge: ACC Art Books, 2018.
Michell, George, and Mark Zebrowski. *Architecture and Art of the Deccan Sultanates*. Cambridge: Cambridge University Press, 1999.
Mihrabi Kermani, Saʿid. *Tadhkirat al-awliyi-yi Mihrabi-yi Kermani ya mazarat-i Kerman*. Edited by Muhammad Hashemi Kermani. Tehran: Majles, 1951.
Minorsky, Vladimir. "The Qara-qoyunlu and the Qutb-shāhs." *Bulletin of the School of Oriental and African Studies* 17, no. 1 (1955): 50–73.
Mir-Kasimov, Orkhan, ed. *Unity in Diversity: Mysticism, Messianism and the Construction of Religious Authority in Islam*. Leiden: Brill, 2014.
Mir Khwand. *The rowzat al-safa*. Vol. 8. Edited by Edward Rehatsek and F. F Arbuthnot. London: Royal Asiatic Society, 1891.
Mitchel, Colin. *The Practice of Politics in Safavid Iran: Power, Religion and Rhetoric*. London: I. B. Tauris, 2009.
Modarres, Ali. *Modernizing Yazd: Selective Historical Memory and the Fate of Vernacular Architecture*. Costa Mesa, CA: Mazda, 2006.
Moin, Azfar. *The Millennial Sovereign: Sacred Kingship and Sainthood in Islam*. New York: Columbia University Press, 2015.
Mondini, Sara. "Architectural Heritage and Modern Rituals: The Ahmad Shah Bahmani Mausoleum between Old Political Concerns and New Religious Perceptions." In *Object of Worship in South Asian Religions: Forms, Practices and*

Meanings, edited by K. A. Jacobsen, M. Aktor, and K. Myrvold, 129–42. London: Routledge, 2015.
———. "Vague Traits: Strategy and Ambiguities in the Decorative Program of the Aḥmad Šāh I Bahmanī Mausoleum." In *Borders: Itineraries on the Edges of Iran, Eurasiatica Quaderni di studi su Balcani, Anatolia, Iran, Caucaso e Asia Centrale* 5, edited by Stefano Pellò, 155–80. Venice: Venezia Università Ca' Foscari, 2016.
Morimoto, Kazuo. "An Enigmatic Genealogical Chart of the Timurids: A Testimony to the Dynasty's Claim to Yasavi-ʿAlid Legitimacy?" *Oriens* 44 (2016): 145–78.
Morton, Alexander H. "The Ardabil Shrine in the Reign of Shāh Ṭahmāsp I." *Iran* 12 (1974): 31–64.
Mufid Mustawfi Yazdi, Muhammad. *Jamiʿ-i Mufidi*. Vol. 3. Edited by Iraj Afshar. Tehran: Asadi, 1961.
Mulder, Stephennie. *The Shrines of the ʿAlids in Medieval Syria: Sunnis, Shiʿis and the Architecture of Coexistence*. Edinburgh: Edinburgh University Press, 2014.
Mumtaz, Murad Khan. "Contemplating the Face of the Master: Portraits of Sufi Saints as Aids to Meditation in Seventeenth-Century Mughal India." *Ars Orientalis* 50 (2020): 106–28.
———. *Faces of God: Images of Devotion in Indo-Muslim Painting, 1500–1800*. Leiden: Brill, 2023.
Munroe, Nazanin Hedayat. *Sufi Lovers, Safavid Silks and Early Modern Identity*. Amsterdam: Amsterdam University Press, 2022.
———. "Wrapped Up: Talismanic Garments in Early Modern Islamic Culture." *Journal of Textile Design, Research and Practice* 7, no. 1 (2019): 4–24.
Munshi, Iskandar Beg. *Tarikh-i ʿalam-ara-yi ʿAbbasi*. Vol. 1. Edited by Iraj Afshar. Tehran: Chapkhana-yi Musavi, 1955–56.
Munshi, Iskandar Beyg Turkman, and Muhammad Yusuf Muvarrikh. *Zayl-i tarikh-i ʿalam-ara-yi ʿAbbasi*. Edited by Suhayli Khwansari. Tehran: Chapkhaneh-yi Islamiya, 1317 [1938–39].
Munshi-yi Qumi, Qadi Ahmad. *Calligraphers and Painters: A Treatise by Qādī Ahmad, Son of Mīr Munshī (circa A.H. 1015/A.D. 1606)*. Translated by Minorsky. Washington, DC: Freer Gallery of Art, 1959.
———. *Gulistan-i hunar*. Edited by Ahmad Suhayli Khwansari. Tehran: Bonyad-i Farhang-i Iran, 1973–74.
Muravchick, Rose Evelyn. "God Is the Best Guardian: Islamic Talismanic Shirts from the Gunpowder Empires." PhD diss., University of Pennsylvania, 2014.
Muʿtamid Khan, Mirza Muhammad. *Tarikh-i Muhammadi*. Vol. 2. Edited by Imtiaz ʿAli ʿArshi. Rampur: Sayyid Nur al-Hasan, 1960.
Nafisi, Saʿid, ed. "Maqamat-i Tahir al-din Muhammad wa Shams al-din Ibrahim." *Farhang-i Iran-zamin* 2 (1954): 93–232.
Nagel, Alexander, and Christopher Wood. *Anachronic Renaissance*. Brooklyn, NY: Zone Books, 2010.
Nasiri Jami, Hasan. "Du shah dar yik iqlim: nigah-i bi muravidat va qirabat-i Shah Neʿmatullah-i Vali va Shah Qasim-i Anvar." *Fasl-nama takhassosi zaban va adabiyat-i farsi danishgah-i azad-i islami Mashhad* 30 (2011): 79–91.
Navayi, ʿAbdulhusayn. *Asnad wa mukatibat-i tarikhi-yi Iran; az Timur ta Shah Ismaʿil*. Tehran: ʿilmi wa farhangi, 1991.
Nayeem, M. A., ed. *Studies in History of the Deccan: Medieval and Modern: Professor A. R. Kulkarni Felicitation Volume*. Delhi: Pragati, 2002.

Neʿmatullah Vali, Nur al-din. *Divan . . . [etc.]*, dated 1518–19. Princeton, NJ: Princeton University Library Special Collections, Islamic Manuscripts, Garrett no. 1469Y.
———. *Divan*. Edited by Saʿid Nafisi. Tehran: Negah, 2008.
Newman, Andrew J. *Safavid Iran: Rebirth of a Persian Empire*. London: I. B. Tauris, 2006.
Noghsanmuhammadi, Mohammadreza, and Mohsen Dehghani Tafti. "Majmuʿih Shah Vali: yadgar-i mandigar-i shahr-i Taft." *Soffeh* 55 (1390 [2012]): 141–54.
Nurbakhsh, Javad. *Masters of the Path: A History of the Masters of the Nimatullahi*. London: Khaniqahi Nimatullahi, 1980.
Nurbakhsh Kermani, Javad. *Zendegi va athar-i qutb al-muwahhidin jinab-i Shah Neʿmatullah-i Vali va farzandan-i u*. Tehran: Khanqah-i Neʿmatullahi, 1959.
O'Kane, Bernard. *The Appearance of Persian on Islamic Art*. New York: Persian Heritage Foundation, 2009.
———. *Timurid Architecture in Khurasan*. Costa Mesa, CA: Mazda, 1987.
O'Meara, Simon. *The Kaʿba Orientations: Readings in Islam's Ancient House*. Edinburgh: Edinburgh University Press, 2020.
Overton, Keelan. "Book Culture, Royal Libraries and Persianate Paradigms in Bijapur, ca. 1580–1630." *Muqarnas* 33 (2016): 91–154.
———, ed. *Iran and the Deccan: Persianate Art, Culture, and Talent in Circulation, c. 1400–1700*. Bloomington: Indiana University Press, 2020.
Overton, Keelan, and Jake Benson. "Deccani Seals and Scribal Notations: Sources for the Study of Indo-Persian Book Arts and Collecting (C. 1400–1680)." In *Empires of the Near East and India: Source Studies of the Safavid, Ottoman, and Mughal Societies*, edited by Hani Khafipour, 554–96. New York: Columbia University Press, 2019.
Palmer, Edward Henry. *Oriental Mysticism: A Treatise on Sufiistic and Unitarian Theosophy of the Persians*. London: Octagon, 1974.
Parizi, Muhammad Bastani. *Rahnama-yi asar-i tarikhi-yi Kerman*. Kerman: Farhang-i ustan-i hashtum, 1956–57.
Paul, Jürgen. "Forming a Faction: The Himayat System of Khwaja Ahrar." *International Journal of Middle East Studies* 23, no. 4 (1991): 533–48.
———. "Hagiographische Texte als historische Quelle." *Saeculum*, 41 (1990): 17–43.
———. "Scheiche Und Herrscher Im Khanat Čaġatay." *Der Islam* 67, no. 2 (1990): 278–321.
Pazuki, Shahram. *Majmuʿih maqalat darbarih-yi Shah Neʿmatullah Vali*. Tehran: Haqiqat, 2004.
Peacock, Andrew. "ʿIyani, A Shirazi Poet and Historian in the Bahmani Deccan." *Iran* 59, no. 2 (2021): 169–86.
———. "Sufis and the Seljuk Court in Mongol Anatolia: Politics and Patronage in the Works of Jalāl Al-din Rūmī and Sulṭān Walad." In *The Seljuks of Anatolia: Court and Society in the Medieval Middle East*, edited by Sara Nur Yildiz and Andrew Peacock, 206–26. London: I. B. Tauris, 2013.
Pentcheva, Bissera. "Moving Eyes: Surface and Shadow in the Byzantine Mixed-Media Relief Icon." *RES. Anthropology and Aesthetics* 53 (2009): 223–34.
———. *The Sensational Icon: Space, Ritual, and the Senses in Byzantium*. University Park: Pennsylvania State University Press, 2010.
Perry, John R. "Toward a Theory of Iranian Urban Moieties: The Ḥaydariyyah and Ni'matiyyah Revisited." *Iranian Studies* 32, no. 1 (1999): 51–70.
Philon, Helen. "The Chaukhandi at Ashtur, Outside Bidar: A Bahmani Period Saintly Funerary Complex." In *Studies in Medieval Deccan History (14th–17th*

Century): Dr. M. A. Nayeem Festschrift, edited by Seyed Ayub Ali, 51–56. Warangal: Deccan History Society, 2015.

———. *Gulbarga, Bidar, Bijapur.* Mumbai: Jaico, 2014.

———. "The Murals in the Tomb of Ahmad Shah Near Bidar." *Apollo* 152, no. 465 (2000): 3–10.

———. "New Considerations on the City of Bidar, Integration and Conflict." In *Forts of the Deccan 1200–1800*, edited by Nicolas Faucherre and Nicolas Morelle, 106–17. New Delhi: Aryan, 2019.

Pope, Arthur Upham. "The National Museum in Teheran." *Bulletin of the Iranian Institute* 6, no. 1–4 (1946): 78–102.

Pope, Arthur Upham, ed., and Phyllis Ackerman, Assistant ed. *A Survey of Persian Art from Prehistoric Times to the Present.* 6 vols. London: Oxford University Press, 1938–58.

Popović, Cvetko Đ. "Fragmenti persiskih ćilima iz XVII veka." *Glasnik zemaljskog muzeja u Sarajevu* 10 (1955): 31–50.

Porter, Venetia. *Arabic and Persian Seals at the British Museum.* London: British Museum, 2011.

Porter, Venetia, Liana Saif, and Emilie Savage-Smith. "Medieval Islamic Amulets, Talismans, and Magic." In *A Companion to Islamic Art and Architecture*, edited by Finbarr Barry Flood and Gulru Necipoğlu, vol. 1, 521–57. Hoboken, NJ: Wiley Blackwell, 2017.

Porter, Yves. *The Glory of the Sultans: Islamic Architecture in India.* Paris: Flammarion, 2009.

Potter, Lawrence. "Sufis and Sultans in Post-Mongol Iran." *Iranian Studies* 27, no. 1–4 (1994): 77–102.

Pourjavady, Nasrollah. "Khalil Allāh Shāh." *Encyclopaedia Iranica*, Online edition, December 15, 2010. Accessed January 1, 2015. http://www.iranicaonline.org/articles/kalil-allah-sah-15th-century-nematullahi-sufi.

Prown, Jules David. "Mind in Matter: An Introduction to Material Culture Theory." *Winterthur Portfolio* 17, no. 1 (1982): 1–19.

Pugachenkova, G. A. "ʿIshrat-Khāneh and Ak-Saray, Two Timurid Mausoleums in Samarkand." *Ars Orientalis* 5 (1963): 177–89.

Qalamsiyah, Akbar. *Tarikh-i salshumari-yi Yazd.* Tehran: Farhang-i Iran Zamin, 1370 [1991].

Qaraʾizadeh, Muhammad. *Report on Majmuʿi-yi Imam (Shah Vali).* Province of Yazd: Cultural Heritage Foundation, 1999.

Qayyumi Bidhendi, Mehrdad. "Patronage and the Hidden Aspects of the History of Iranian Art." *Golestan-e Honar* 4, no. 3 (2008): 5–7.

Qazvini, Keyvan. *Sharh-i hal-i Abu Saʿid Abu'l-Khayr wa wazʿiyat-i sahn-i Shah Neʿmatullah.* Tehran: Fathi, 1992.

Quinn, Sholeh. *Historical Writing during the Reign of Shah ʿAbbas: Ideology, Imitation, and Legitimacy in Safavid Chronicles.* Salt Lake City: University of Utah Press, 2000.

———. *Persian Historiography across Empires: The Ottomans, Safavids, and Mughals.* Cambridge: Cambridge University Press, 2020.

———. "Rewriting Niʿmatu'llāhī History in Safavid Chronicles." In *The Heritage of Sufism: Late Classical Persianate Sufism*, edited by Leonard Lewisohn and David Morgan, vol. 3, 201–22. Oxford: Oneworld, 1999.

Quiring-Zoche, Rosemarie. "Aq Qoyunlu." *Encyclopaedia Iranica.* Accessed January 18, 2021. https://iranicaonline.org/articles/aq-qoyunlu-confederation.

Quraishi, Fatima. "'This Is Makkah for Me!' Devotion in Architecture at the Makli Necropolis." In *Saintly Spheres and Islamic Landscapes: Emplacements of Spiritual Power across Time and Place*, edited by Daphna Ephrat, Ethel Sara Wolper, and Paulo G. Pinto, 270–300. Leiden: Brill, 2021.

Ram, Kewal. *Tazkirat al-umara*. Translated by S. M. Azizuddin Husain. New Delhi: Munshiram Manoharlal, 1985.

Reza'i, Omid. *Fihrist-i asnad-i mawqufat-i Iran: ustan-i Kerman*. Vol. 2. Tehran: Osveh, 2003.

Richard, Francis. "Nasr al-Soltāni, Nasir al-Din Mozahheb et la bibliothèque d'Ebrāhim soltān à Širāz." *Studia Iranica* 30, no. 1 (2001): 87–104.

Rizvi, Kishwar, ed. *Affect, Emotion, and Subjectivity in Early Modern Muslim Empires: New Studies in Ottoman, Safavid, and Mughal Art and Culture*. Leiden: Brill, 2017.

———. "Its Mortar Mixed with the Sweetness of Life: Architecture and Ceremonial at the Shrine of Shaykh Safi al-Din Ishaq Ardabili during the Reign of Shah Tahmasb I." *Muslim World* 90, 3/4 (2000): 323–51.

———. *The Safavid Dynastic Shrine: Architecture, Religion and Power in Early Modern Iran*. London: I. B. Tauris, 2011.

Roxburgh, David J. *The Persian Album 1400–1600: From Dispersal to Collection*. New Haven, CT: Yale University Press, 2005.

Rubin, Patricia. "Signposts of Invention, Artists' Signatures in Italian Renaissance." *Art History* 29, no. 4 (2006): 563–99.

Ruggles, D. Fairchild. *Women, Patronage and Self-Representation in Islamic Societies*. Albany: State University of New York Press, 2000.

Saberi, Ali Muhammad, ed. *Majmaʿ al-rasa'il-i Shah Neʿmatullah-i Vali*. Tehran: Nashr-i ʿilm, 2013.

Safavi, Sam Mirza. *Tazkari-yi tuhfa-yi Sami*. Edited by Rukn al-din Humayunfarrukh. Tehran: Asatir, 1384 [2005–6].

Safi, Omid. "Bargaining with Baraka: Persian Sufism, 'Mysticism,' and Pre-Modern Politics." *Muslim World* 90, no. 3–4 (2000): 259–88.

———. *Religion and Politics in Saljuq Iran: Negotiating Ideology and Religious Inquiry*. Karachi: Oxford University Press, 2007.

Samarqandi, ʿAbd al-Razzaq Kamal al-din b. Ishaq. *Matlaʿ-i saʿdayn wa majmaʿ-i bahrayn*. Vol. 2. Edited by ʿAbd al-Husayn Navayi. Tehran: Pazhuhishgah-i Ulum-i Insani va Mutaliʿat-i farhangi, 2004.

Samarqandi, Dowlatshah. *Tazkirat al-shuʿara*. Edited by Muhammad ʿAbbasi. Tehran: Barani, 1958.

Samarqandi, Muhammad b. Burhan al-din. *Silsilat al-ʿarifīn va tazkirat al-siddiqin*. Edited by Ihsanullah Shukrullahi. Tehran: Kitabkhani-yi Muzeh va Markaz-i Asnad-i Majlis-i Shura-yi Milli, 2009.

Sardar, Marika. "Golconda through Time: A Mirror of the Evolving Deccan." PhD diss., New York University, 2007.

Savage-Smith, Emilie. "Magic and Islam." In *Science, Tools and Magic*, 2 vols, edited by Francis Maddison and Emilie Savage-Smith, 59–71. London: Nour Foundation: Azimuth Editions: Oxford University Press, 1997.

Sayadi, Nader. "Prophets and Caterpillars: The Story of Job and the Social Mobility of Silk Workers and Weavers in the Early Modern Islamic World." In *Skilled Immigrants in the Textile and Fashion Industries: Stories from a Globe-Spanning History*, edited by Nazanin Hedayat Munroe. London: Bloomsbury, 2024.

Schimmel, Annemarie. *Islam in the Indian Subcontinent*. Leiden: Brill, 1980.

———. *Mystical Dimensions of Islam*. Chapel Hill: University of North Carolina Press, 1975.

Shalem, Avinoam. "The Four Faces of the Kaʿba in Mecca." In *Synergies in Visual Culture / Bildkulturen im Dialog*, edited by Nicola Suthor, Annette Hoffmann, Manuela De Giorgi, and Laura Veneskey, 139–53. Leiden: Brill, 2013.

———. "Made for the Show: The Medieval Treasury of the Kaʾba in Mecca." In *The Iconography of Islamic Art: Festschrift in Honour of Professor Robert Hillenbrand*, edited by Bernard O'Kane, 269–84. Edinburgh: Edinburgh University Press, 2005.

Shayesteh Far, Mahnaz. *Shîʾah Artistic Elements in the Tîmûrid and the Early Safavid Periods: Book Illustrations and Inscriptions*. London: London BookExtra, 1999.

Sherwani, Haroon Khan. *Mahmud Gawan: The Great Bahmani Wazir*. Allahabad: Kitabistan, 1941.

Shirazi, ʿAbdi Beyg. *Rawzat al-safat*. Edited by Abu'l-Fazil Hashimughli Rahimuf. Moscow: Danish, 1974.

Shirazi, Yaʿqub ibn Hasan. *Tuhfat al-muhibbin dar aʾin-i khushnivisi wa latayif-i maʿnavi-yi an*. Edited by Muhammad Taqi Daneshpazhuh, Karamat Husayni, and Iraj Afshar. Tehran: Nuqteh, 1997.

Shukri, Yadullah, ed. *ʿAlam ara-yi Safavi*. Tehran: Intisharat-i Ittilaʿat, 1363 [1984].

Siddiqi, Suleiman. "The Pro-alien Policy of Ahmad Shah and the Role of the Nimatullahis of Bidar." In *Sufi Cults and the Evolution of Medieval Indian Culture*, edited by Anup Taneja, 179–203. Delhi: Indian Council of Historical Research, 2003.

Sikand, Yoginder. "Shared Hindu-Muslim Shrines in Karnataka: Challenges to Liminality." In *Lived Islam in South Asia: Adaptation, Accommodation and Conflict*, edited by Imtiaz Ahmad and Helmut Reifield, 166–86. Delhi: Social Science Press, 2004.

Sims, Eleanor. "Ibrahim-Sultan's Illustrated Zafarnama of 1436 and Its Impact in the Muslim East." In *Timurid Art and Culture: Iran and Central Asia in the Fifteenth Century*, edited by Lisa Golombek and Maria Subtelny, 132–43. Leiden: Brill, 1992.

———. "The Illustrated Manuscripts of Firdausī's 'Shāhnāma' Commissioned by Princes of the House of Tīmūr." *Ars Orientalis* 22 (1992): 43–68.

Sivasundaram, Sujit. "The Indian Ocean." In *Oceanic Histories*, edited by David Armitage, Alison Bashford, and Sujit Sivasundaram, 31–61. Cambridge: Cambridge University Press, 2017.

Soucek, Priscilla. "The Manuscripts of Iskandar Sultan: Structure and Content." In *Timurid Art and Culture: Iran and Central Asia in the Fifteenth Century*, edited by Lisa Golombek and Maria Subtelny, 116–31. Leiden: Brill, 1992.

Speziale, Fabrizio. "A Propos Du Renouveau Niʿmatullāhī: Le Centre de Hyderabad Au Cours de La Première Modernité." *Studia Iranica* 42, no. 1 (2013): 91–118.

Stanley, Tim. "From Text to Art Form in the Ottoman Hilye." In *Filiz Çağman'a Armağan*, edited by Lale Uluc, 559–70. Istanbul: Lale Yayincilik, 2018.

Subrahmanyam, Sanjay. "Connected Histories: Notes towards a Reconfiguration of Early Modern Eurasia." *Modern Asian Studies* 2, no. 3 (1997): 735–62.

———. "Global Intellectual History beyond Hegel and Marx." *History and Theory* 54 (2015): 126–37.

———. "Iranians Abroad: Intra-Asian Elite Migration and Early Modern State Formation." *Journal of Asian Studies* 51, no. 2 (1992): 340–63.

Subtelny, Maria. *Timurids in Transition: Turko-Persian Politics and Acculturation in Medieval Iran*. Leiden: Brill, 2007.
Subtelny, Maria, and Anas B. Khalidov. "The Curriculum of Islamic Higher Learning in Timurid Iran in the Light of the Sunni Revival under Shāh-Rukh." *Journal of the American Oriental Society* 115, no. 2 (1995): 210–36.
Sykes, Ella. *Through Persia on a Side Saddle*. London: A. D. Innes, 1898.
Sykes, Percy M. *Ten Thousand Miles in Persia or Eight Years in Iran*. London: John Murray, 1902.
Szántó, Iván. "Persian Art for the Balkans in Austro-Hungarian Cultural Policies." In *The Shaping of Persian Art: Collections and Interpretations of the Art of Islamic Iran and Central Asia*, edited by Iván Szántó and Yuka Kadoi, 130–59. Newcastle: Cambridge Scholars, 2013.
Szuppe, Maria. "The 'Jewels of Wonder.'" In *Women in the Medieval Islamic World: Power, Patronage, and Piety*, edited by Gavin Hambly, 325–48. New York: St. Martin's, 1998.
———. "Status, Knowledge, and Politics: Women in Sixteenth-Century Safavid Iran." In *Women in Iran from the Rise of Islam to 1800*, edited by Guity Nashat and Lois Beck, 140–69. Champaign: University of Illinois Press, 2003.
Tabandeh, Reza. *The Rise of the Niʿmatullāhī Order: Shiʿite Sufi Masters against Islamic Fundamentalism in 19th-Century Persia*. Leiden: Leiden University Press, 2021.
Tabandeh, Reza, and Leonard Lewisohn, eds. *Sufis and Their Opponents in the Persianate World*. Irvine, CA: UCI Jordan Center for Persian Studies, 2020.
Tabasi, Muhammad b. ʿAlishah. *Athar-i Darwish Muhammad-i Tabasi*. Edited by Iraj Afshar and Muhammad Taqi Daneshpajuh. Tehran: Khanqah-i Neʿmatullahi, 1972.
Tabataba, ʿAli ʿAziz Allah. *Burhan-i maʾasir*. Delhi: Matbaʿ-i Jamiʿa-yi Delhi, 1936.
Tasdiqi, Muhammadreza. "Wagf-nama-yi Khanish Begum dukhtar-i Shah Ismaʿil-i Safavi." In *Yadgar-i mandigar: majmuʿi-yi mawqufat-i Yazd*, edited by Muhammadreza Tasdiqi, 452–63. Yazd: Sitayish, 2001.
Tottoli, Roberto. "Ahl al-Ṣuffa." In *Encyclopaedia of Islam, THREE*. Edited by Kate Fleet, Gudrun Krämer, Denis Matringe, John Nawas, and Everett Rowson. Accessed March 2, 2022. https://referenceworks.brill.com/display/entries/EIEO/SIM-0385.xml.
Trivellato, Francesca. "Microstoria/Microhistoire/Microhistory." *French Politics, Culture & Society* 33, no. 1 (2015): 122–34.
Ullens de Schooten, Marie-Thérèse. "*Voyage au pays des dervish sufi: l'ultime pèlerinage*." Harvard Fine Art Library (FLS2270). Accessed August 25, 2020. http://archnet.org/media_contents/132.
Um, Nancy. "Chairs, Writing Tables, and Chests: Indian Ocean Furniture and the Postures of Commercial Documentation in Yemen, 1700–1750." In *Objects in Motion in the Early Modern World*. Edited by Daniela Bleichmar and Meredith Martin. Special issue, *Art History* 38, no. 4 (2015): 718–31.
ʿUqabi, Muhammad Mehdi, ed. *Dayirat al-maʿarif-i banaha-yi tarikhi-yi Iran dar daureh Islami: banaha-yi aramgahi*. Tehran: Pazhuhishgah-i farhang wa hunar-i Islami, 1997.
Wagoner, Phillip B., and John Henry Rice. "From Delhi to the Deccan: Newly Discovered Tughluq Monuments at Warangal-Sulṭānpur and the Beginnings of Indo-Islamic Architecture in Southern India." *Artibus Asiae* 61, no. 1 (2001): 77–117.

Waᶜiz Kashifi, Husayn. *Futuwwatnama-yi Sultani*. Edited by Muhammad Jaᶜfar Mahjub. Tehran: Bunyad-i Farhang-i Iran, 1970.

Waziri, Ahmad ᶜAli Khan. *Tarikh-i Kerman: Salariya*. Edited by Muhammad Bastani Parizi. Tehran: Ibn Sina, 1352 [1961].

Weaver, Martin E. "The Ardabil Puzzle." *Textile Museum Journal* 23 (1984): 43–51.

Welch, Anthony. "The Emperor's Grief: Two Mughal Tombs." *Muqarnas* 25 (2008): 255–74.

Wilber, Donald. *The Architecture of Islamic Iran: The Il-Khanid Period*. New York: Greenwood, 1955.

———. *The Masjid-i ᶜAtiq of Shiraz*. Shiraz: Pahlavi University, 1972.

Wolper, Ethel Sara. *Cities and Saints: Sufism and Transformation of Urban Space in Medieval Anatolia*. University Park: Pennsylvania State University Press, 2003.

Woods, John E. *The Aqquyunlu: Clan, Confederation, Empire*. Salt Lake City: University of Utah Press, 1999.

Wright, Elaine. *The Look of the Book: Manuscript Production in Shiraz, 1303–1452*. Washington, DC: Freer Gallery of Art and Arthur M. Sackler Gallery, 2013.

Yazdani, Ghulam. *Bidar, Its History and Monuments*. London: Oxford University Press, 1947.

———. *Epigraphia Indica*. New Delhi: Archaeological Survey of India, 1927.

Yazdi, Sharaf al-din ᶜAli. *Manzumat*. Edited by Iraj Afshar. Tehran: Thurayya, 2007.

———. *Munshaʾat*. Edited by Iraj Afshar and Muhammad Reza Abouʾi Mehrizi. Tehran: Farhang-i Iran Zamin, 2010.

———. *Zafarnama*. Vol. 1. Edited by Saᶜid Mir Muhammad Sadiq and ᶜAbdulhusayn Navayi. Tehran: Majles, 2008.

Yürekli, Zeynep. *Architecture and Hagiography in the Ottoman Empire: The Politics of Bektashi Shrines in the Classical Age*. London: Ashgate, 2012.

———. "Dhu'l-faqar and the Ottomans." In *People of the Prophet's House: Artistic and ritual expressions of Shiᶜi Islam*, edited by Fahmida Suleman, 163–72. London: Azimuth Editions, 2015.

Zajadacz-Hastenrath, Salome. *Chaukhandi Tombs: Funerary Art in Sind and Balochistan*. Translated by Michael Robertson. Karachi: Oxford University Press, 2003.

Zarcone, Thierry. "Pilgrimage to the 'Second Meccas' and 'Kaᶜbas' of Central Asia." In *Central Asian Pilgrims: Hajj Routes and Pious Visits between Central Asia and the Hijaz*, edited by Alexandre Papas, Thierry Zarcone, and Thomas Welsford, 251–77. Berlin: De Gruyter, 2020.

Žutić, Fatima. "Safavid Number Games in Sarajevo." *Hali* 197 (2018):74–79.

———. "Tri safavidska tepiha iz turbeta šaha Niᶜmatullāha Valīja u Mahanu iz zbirke Zemaljskog muzeja BiH." *Prilozi za orijentalnu filologiju* 67 (2019): 299–326.

INDEX

Page numbers in *italic* indicate figures and tables.

Peyvand Firouzeh

(PhD, University of Cambridge) is Senior Lecturer in Islamic Art at the University of Sydney, Australia. She specializes in the art, architecture, and material cultures of the early modern Islamic world, particularly the material cultures of Sufism and artistic connections between Iran and India and in the broader Indian Ocean world.

For Indiana University Press

Tony Brewer *Artist and Book Designer*
Anna Garnai *Production Coordinator*
Sophia Hebert *Assistant Acquisitions Editor*
Katie Huggins *Production Manager*
Alyssa Lucas *Marketing and Publicity Manager*
Darja Malcolm-Clarke *Project Manager/Editor*
Bethany Mowry *Acquisitions Editor*
Dan Pyle *Online Publishing Manager*
Michael Regoli *Director of Publishing Operations*
Pamela Rude *Senior Artist and Book Designer*